The Future of Africa

"Cilliers refuses to adopt a fatalistic attitude . . . or to get stuck in simplistic models that equate GDP growth with genuine development . . . His very practical recommendations, largely focusing on issues of governance and policy efficiency, are based on solid empirical evidence and sound argument. This book can make a difference and will contribute to improving the human condition on our continent."
—Professor Maxi Schoeman, *Professor Emeritus, Department of Political Sciences, University of Pretoria*

"*Africa First!* suggests that the future lies in Africa's ability to seize the significant opportunities opened up by its youthful population, new technologies and infrastructural innovations. Jakkie Cilliers builds on his long experience as a keen analyst of Africa . . . essential reading for those interested in Africa's development."
—Gilbert Khadiagala, *Jan Smuts Professor of International Relations, University of the Witwatersrand*

Jakkie Cilliers

The Future of Africa

Challenges and Opportunities

Jakkie Cilliers
Head of African Futures & Innovation
Institute for Security Studies
Pretoria, South Africa

ISBN 978-3-030-46589-6   ISBN 978-3-030-46590-2 (eBook)
https://doi.org/10.1007/978-3-030-46590-2

© The Editor(s) (if applicable) and The Author(s) 2021. This book is an open access publication.
Open Access This book is licensed under the terms of the Creative Commons Attribution 4.0 International License (http://creativecommons.org/licenses/by/4.0/), which permits use, sharing, adaptation, distribution and reproduction in any medium or format, as long as you give appropriate credit to the original author(s) and the source, provide a link to the Creative Commons license and indicate if changes were made.
The images or other third party material in this book are included in the book's Creative Commons license, unless indicated otherwise in a credit line to the material. If material is not included in the book's Creative Commons license and your intended use is not permitted by statutory regulation or exceeds the permitted use, you will need to obtain permission directly from the copyright holder.
The use of general descriptive names, registered names, trademarks, service marks, etc. in this publication does not imply, even in the absence of a specific statement, that such names are exempt from the relevant protective laws and regulations and therefore free for general use.
The publisher, the authors and the editors are safe to assume that the advice and information in this book are believed to be true and accurate at the date of publication. Neither the publisher nor the authors or the editors give a warranty, expressed or implied, with respect to the material contained herein or for any errors or omissions that may have been made. The publisher remains neutral with regard to jurisdictional claims in published maps and institutional affiliations.

Cover illustration: shutterstock 1438769294, Jozsef Bagota

This Palgrave Macmillan imprint is published by the registered company Springer Nature Switzerland AG
The registered company address is: Gewerbestrasse 11, 6330 Cham, Switzerland

Preface and Acknowledgments

This book draws on a decade of work on Africa's prospects at the African Futures and Innovation (AFI) programme at the Pretoria office of the Institute for Security Studies (ISS). I founded the Institute in 1990 and today the ISS is Africa's largest independent strategic studies institute with offices in each of Africa's five regions.

The bulk of the work done at the Institute is on traditional human security issues, trying to understand radicalisation, crime, advice on peacekeeping and suchlike. The AFI programme that I established after stepping down as executive director in 2015 takes a broader, interdisciplinary and longer-term perspective. I previously worked on peace and security issues but became increasingly frustrated by the extent to which that focus seemed akin to bandaid and did not address the origins of Africa's low levels of development.

I am indebted to the ISS for allowing me to draw on previous work that I authored at the Institute. These are Chapters 4 (demographic dividend), 8 (manufacturing), 12 (violence) and 13 (governance). In addition, Chapter 14 on external support draws on an ISS report that I published on the future of aid. These publications were reviewed by academics and colleagues that are listed in the original studies.

At AFI we have also published a number of country-level forecasts on the long-term prospects that include Ethiopia, Kenya, Mozambique, Namibia, South Africa, Zimbabwe, Angola, Algeria and Tunisia, in addition to regional forecasts on Central Africa and the G5 Sahel countries. The results of our previous studies are freely available on the ISS website at www.issafrica.org as well as on my website at www.jakkiecilliers.org.

Zachary Donnenfeld, Marlene Barnard, Annie Olivier, Zachel van Aswegen and Julia Bello-Schünneman have all worked extensively on the manuscript and I owe them all immense thanks. In addition Alanna Markle, Lily Welborn and Stellah Kwasi each reviewed specific chapters. The result is a book that I hope is comprehensive, logically structured and easily readable. That would not have been the case without their hard work and dedicated support.

An earlier but quite different version of this book was published in South Africa by Jonathan Ball with the title *Africa First! Unleashing a Growth Revolution*. This textbook uses a more recent version of the International Futures forecasting platform (version 7.45) with updated data and some modelling improvements, among various other changes. The structure of the book has also been rearranged to more logically first deal with health, then demographics, agriculture, education, etc.

Institutionally the support for our work on the future of Africa has come from the Hanns Seidel of Germany and the Swedish International Development Cooperation Agency (SIDA). Both have allowed AFI freedom in pursuit of our priorities, offering ongoing support and encouragement along the way.

Finally, my long-standing friends at the Frederick S. Pardee Center for International Futures at the University of Denver, professors Jonathan Moyer and Barry Hughes, were gracious in again allowing me to use their forecasting platform, International Futures, extensively in this book. Barry Hughes, as always, provided detailed and meticulous commentary on an earlier version of the book and Jonathan reviewed the scenarios. Technical details on the interventions used with the International Futures forecasting system for this book is available at www.jakkiecilliers.org.

Although I include reference to the COVID-19 pandemic that is currently sweeping across the world it is still too early to include its long-term impact in the modelling that follows, in part because it is later coming to Africa than elsewhere. Like the situation that followed the 2008/2009 global financial crisis, it may take some time before its impact is sufficiently well understood to include in long-term forecasts.

Eventually the views and analysis presented in these pages do not reflect the views of the ISS, any of its donors or from the Pardee Center, but are my own.

Pretoria, South Africa   Jakkie Cilliers
April 2020

Contents

1	**The Growing Gap**	1
	The Growing Income Divergence	3
	South Korea and Ghana	6
	The Importance of Labour and Demographics	8
	Productivity and Economic Structure	11
	The Global Context	13
	Dealing with Africa's Diversity—Using Country Income Groups	16
	Previous Studies and the International Futures Forecasting Platform	19
	Structure of the Book	22
	Further Reading	22
2	**Africa's Current Path**	23
	From Brundtland to the Sustainable Development Goals (SDGs)	25
	The Impact of the Structural Adjustment Programmes	26
	Africa's Growing Dependence on Commodities	30
	The Challenges of Commodities-Dependent Growth	32
	Rising Debt Levels	35
	The Third Wave of Democratisation in Africa	37
	Africa's Slow Pace of Urbanisation	41
	The Current Path Scenario	43

3	**Health**	49
	The Impact of HIV and AIDS	53
	Africa's Approaching Health Transition	56
	Urbanisation and Health Services	58
	Current Path: Access to Basic Infrastructure	60
	Modelling the Impact of Better Health and WASH Infrastructure: The Improved Health Scenario	63
	Impact on Disability Adjusted Life Years	66
	Conclusion: Planning Comprehensively and Long-Term	68
	Further Reading	69
4	**Getting to Africa's Demographic Dividend**	71
	What History Reveals	75
	The Impact of the Demographic Dividend	76
	Comparing Niger, Egypt, Japan and Sweden	78
	Africa's Slow Demographic Transition	80
	The Peak and Length of the Demographic Dividend	83
	The Potential Benefits of Reducing Fertility Rates	85
	The Components of the Demographic Dividend Scenario	87
	Scenario Impact on Global Population	88
	Impact of the Demographic Dividend on Africa	89
	Conclusion: Reducing Fertility Rates and Working Towards Africa's Demographic Dividend	93
	Further Reading	95
5	**Wanted: A Revolution in Agriculture**	97
	After Independence	100
	Agriculture Today	101
	Obstacles to a Revolution in Agriculture	104
	Achieving Food Security	106
	The Challenge for the Future	109
	Lessons from Elsewhere	110
	Modelling a Coordinated Push on Africa's Agricultural Sector: The African Agriculture Revolution Scenario	112
	The Contributions from Technology and Innovation	116
	Conclusion: Aiming at Food Security and Growth	119
	Further Reading	121
6	**Boosting Education**	123
	Recent Education Trends in Africa	127
	Comparing Education in Africa with Other Regions	131

	The Low Quality of Education in Africa	132
	Rates of Gender Exclusion	134
	Africa's Future Education Requirements	135
	Modelling the Impact of Improved Quality, Quantity and Nature of Education Across Gender: The Boosting Education Scenario	138
	From Basics to Technology	141
	Conclusion: Prioritising Education Outcomes	143
	Further Reading	145
7	**Poverty, Inequality and Growth**	147
	Globalisation and the Sense of Relative Deprivation	149
	The Interplay Between Inequality and Growth	152
	The SDGs and Measuring Extreme Poverty	154
	The Impact of the Additional Poverty Lines	156
	The Current Situation in Africa	158
	The Potential of Social Grants to Reduce Poverty	159
	The Promise of an African Welfare State?	163
	Modelling the Impact of Using Tax Revenues for Social Grants: The Social Grants for Africa Scenario	165
	Conclusion: Reducing Poverty Through Rapid and Inclusive Economic Growth	167
	Further Reading	168
8	**Changing Productive Structures**	169
	The Contribution of Services to Growth	174
	The Impact of the Diffusion of Knowledge	175
	Manufacturing in Africa	178
	Composition of African Economies	180
	Industrialisation and Growth in Africa	183
	Modelling the Impact of Industrialisation: The Made in Africa Scenario	188
	Costs and Benefits of a Manufacturing Pathway	190
	Conclusion: Promoting and Intensifying Local Production and Trade	192
	Further Reading	193
9	**The Future of Work in Africa**	195
	Trends in Employment	200
	Automation and the Threat to Work	206
	The Impact of Digitisation in Ghana	211

	The Promise of Greater Economic Formalisation in Ghana	214
	Conclusion: Thinking Differently About the Future	216
	Further Reading	218
10	**Technological Innovation and the Power of Leapfrogging**	221
	The Shale and Tight Oil Revolution in the USA	225
	The Potential of Renewable Energy in Africa	226
	The Challenge of Energy Storage (Power-to-X)	232
	Mobile Phones and Access to the Internet—A Big Leap for Africa	234
	M-Pesa and Innovation in Mobile Banking	237
	Mobile Phones and Social Change	238
	Formalising the Informal Sector	239
	Modelling the Impact of Improved Electricity Access, ICT and Digitisation: The Leapfrogging Scenario	241
	Conclusion: Harnessing Technology for the Future	243
	Further Reading	246
11	**Trade and Growth**	249
	From GATT to the Decline of Multilateralism	251
	The Impact of Preferential Access: Everything But Arms and AGOA	253
	Africa's Shifting Trade Relations with the Rest of the World	256
	Intra-African Trade and Efforts at Advancing Regional Integration	260
	The Need for Connecting Infrastructure—And the Challenge of Non-Tariff Barriers	264
	Perspectives on the Promise of the African Continental Free Trade Area (AfCFTA)	268
	The Potential Impact of AfCFTA?	270
	Modelling the Impact of Regional Economic Integration: The Africa Free Trade Area Scenario	272
	Conclusion: Advancing Africa's Trade	274
	Further Reading	276
12	**Prospects for Greater Peace**	279
	Trends in Conflict	281
	Africa's Leadership in Conflict Prevention and Management	287
	Changing Characteristics of Organised Violence	288
	More Riots	290
	Structural Drivers of Violence	293

	Regime Capacity, Type and Regime Dissonance	295
	Youth and Unemployment	297
	Poor Governance and High Levels of Inequality	300
	Modelling the Prospects for Greater Peace: The Silencing the Guns Scenario	302
	Conclusion: Focusing on Conflict Prevention	303
	Further Reading	305
13	**Good Governance, Democracy and Development**	307
	The State of Democracy in Africa	312
	Is Democracy Making a Difference to Development Prospects in Africa?	316
	The Realities of Neopatrimonialism in Africa	321
	The Role of Leadership in Development	324
	Modelling the Impact of More Democracy: The Fourth Wave of Democracy Scenario	326
	Conclusion: Promoting Democracy, State Capacity and Human Development	328
	Further Reading	330
14	**Aid, Remittances and Foreign Direct Investment**	331
	The Shifting Global Aid Landscape	334
	Leveraging Foreign Direct Investment for Africa	338
	China's Growing Footprint in Africa	342
	Remittance Flows to Africa	347
	Modelling Increased FDI, Aid and Remittances: The External Support Scenario	348
	The Impact of the Combined External Support Scenario	349
	Conclusion: Unlocking Foreign Assistance	350
	Further Reading	353
15	**Climate Change**	355
	Africa as a Climate Change Taker	357
	The Global Energy Transition	362
	Carbon Emissions and Energy in Africa	365
	The Impact of Climate Change	367
	Comparing Carbon Emissions in Different Scenarios	371
	Responding to Climate Change	373
	Development as a Coping and Planning Mechanism	376

	Conclusion: Finding an Environmentally Sustainable Pathway	377
	Further Reading	378
16	**Closing the Gap**	**381**
	Prospects in the Close the Gap Scenario	383
	GDP Per Capita in the Close the Gap Scenario	384
	Size of Economies in the Close the Gap Scenario	386
	Extreme Poverty in the Close the Gap Scenario	387
	Carbon Emissions in the Close the Gap Scenario	389
	Structural Change of Economies in the Close the Gap Scenario	390
	Comparing the Impact of Individual Scenarios Over Time	392
	Scenario Comparison Using Income Per Person as Key Indicator	392
	Scenario Comparison Using Progress with the Human Development Index, Inequality and Extreme Poverty	395
	What Is Possible? A Comparison with China	398
	A Passion for Knowledge and Development	399
	In Conclusion	403
	Further Reading	406
Index		**407**

List of Figures

Fig. 1.1	GDP per capita in purchasing power parity: from 1960 with a forecast to 2040	4
Fig. 1.2	Ghana vs South Korea: income per person vs demographic dividend: 1960 to 2015	6
Fig. 1.3	Composition of the global population: 1980–2040 for Africa, China, India, EU27, USA and the Rest of the World (RoW)	15
Fig. 1.4	Comparing economies: 1980–2040	16
Fig. 1.5	Economic size and population size for low, lower-middle and upper-middle-income Africa in 2018	17
Fig. 1.6	Regions in Africa	18
Fig. 2.1	Africa's population 1980 to 2040 with top five by 2040	44
Fig. 2.2	Country composition of the African economy in 2018 and 2040 (in bn US$)	45
Fig. 3.1	Population and deaths from communicable disease in 2018	58
Fig. 3.2	The difference between government consumption on health and infrastructure in Africa between the Improved Health scenario and the Current Path	65
Fig. 4.1	Population pyramid for the Africa, World except Africa, North Africa, sub-Saharan Africa and EU27 in 2018	73
Fig. 4.2	Population pyramid for the Africa, World except Africa, North Africa, sub-Saharan Africa and EU27 in 2040	74
Fig. 4.3	Percent of persons aged 15–64 in Niger, Egypt, Sweden and Japan in 2018 and 2040	80

Fig. 4.4	Demographic dividend of Nigeria, China and India: 1960–2100	84
Fig. 4.5	Peak World population in 2018 and 2100 under different scenarios	88
Fig. 4.6	Ratio of working age to dependants: Africa vs World except Africa: 1980 to 2100	90
Fig. 4.7	Population education distribution for sub-Saharan Africa in 2063 in Current Path vs Demographic Dividend scenario	93
Fig. 5.1	Yields per hectare (pre-loss): 1980 and 2000, and Current Path forecast for 2020 and 2040	102
Fig. 5.2	Agricultural imports dependence: Current Path vs Revolution in Agriculture	114
Fig. 5.3	Difference in size of agricultural sector in 2040: Revolution in Agriculture vs Current Path	115
Fig. 6.1	Current Path forecast of mean years of education (25+ age group)	130
Fig. 6.2	Mean years of education for 20–29 year age cohort: 2018 and 2040 for Current Path and Boosting Education scenario	139
Fig. 7.1	Extreme poverty in Africa and the World except Africa: 2015 to 2040 using US1.90	156
Fig. 7.2	Change in millions of extremely poor people in Africa: Social Grants for Africa scenario compared to Current Path in 2030 and 2040	166
Fig. 8.1	Sectoral composition of larger African economies by value added to GDP, ranked by relative size of industry (2017)	182
Fig. 8.2	Percentage point shift in sectoral contribution to African economy 2020 to 2040: Made in Africa compared to Current Path	189
Fig. 8.3	Comparing GDP: Current Path vs Made in Africa (2018 to 2040)	189
Fig. 9.1	2018 size of the informal sector in Africa by contribution to GDP and portion of labour	198
Fig. 9.2	2018 employment by sector for low, lower-middle and upper-middle-income Africa	201
Fig. 9.3	2018 contribution of economic sectors to low, lower-middle and upper-middle-income Africa	202
Fig. 10.1	Difference in GDP per capita in 2040 between the Leapfrogging Scenario and the Current Path	243
Fig. 10.2	Percentage point difference in size of economy when comparing Leapfrogging Scenario and Current Path in 2040	244
Fig. 11.1	African export and import share with main partners, 2018	258
Fig. 11.2	Current Path growth rate vs AfCFTA	273

List of Figures

Fig. 12.1	Total fatalities from all events, Africa, 1990–2018	283
Fig. 12.2	Ratio of youth (15–29) to adults (+15), selected regions in 2018 and 2040	299
Fig. 13.1	Average levels of electoral and liberal democracy in the world and in Africa according to V-Dem: 1960–2018	309
Fig. 13.2	Fourth Wave of electoral democracy scenario using Polity IV data	327
Fig. 14.1	Contribution of remittances, aid and FDI in 2020, 2030 and 2040: Current Path vs External Support scenario	349
Fig. 15.1	History and Current Path forecast of carbon emissions from Africa and the world: 1960 to 2100	360
Fig. 15.2	Carbon Emissions by countries or region as a percent of the total (2018)	363
Fig. 15.3	Current Path forecast of world energy production by type: 1980 to 2050	364
Fig. 15.4	Current Path carbon emissions: African countries that release more than 10 million tonnes in 2018 and 2040 vs Rest of Africa	366
Fig. 15.5	Current Path forecast of Africa's energy production by type: 1980 to 2050	367
Fig. 15.6	Africa's carbon emissions under different scenarios: 2020–2050	372
Fig. 16.1	GDP per capita: Africa vs World except Africa	384
Fig. 16.2	GDP per capita in Current Path and Close the Gap in 2018 and 2040	385
Fig. 16.3	Size of the regional economy in MER in Current Path vs Close the Gap scenario compared to population size	386
Fig. 16.4	Extremely poor people: 2020 to 2040 using US$1.90 and other extreme poverty lines	387
Fig. 16.5	Changes in value added to the economy in percent of GDP: Close the Gap vs Current Path for lower-middle-income Africa: 2019 to 2040	390
Fig. 16.6	Africa: value added by sector in billion US$: 2020 vs 2040 for Current Path and Close the Gap scenario	391
Fig. 16.7	Comparing the results of selected scenarios for lower-income Africa: percentage point reduction in people living below US$1.90 per person per day	396

List of Tables

Table 4.1	Impact of demographic dividend: selected countries and indicators of impact	92
Table 6.1	Progress through the education funnel (gross percentages) (2018)	129
Table 7.1	Current Path of population and extreme poverty in Africa	157
Table 7.2	African countries with 50% or more of their populations in extreme poverty using US$1.90, US$3.20 and US$5.50	158
Table 12.1	Most fatalities versus highest fatality rate	284
Table 16.1	Impact on selected countries: millions fewer extremely poor people in 2040: difference between Current Path and Close the Gap scenarios	388

1

The Growing Gap

Abstract In this chapter Cilliers introduces the growing divergence in income and other indices of well-being between Africa and the Rest of the World. He touches on various aspects such as extreme poverty and Africa's marginal role in the global economy and illustrates the challenge by comparing the divergent experiences of South Korea and Ghana in demographics and income, before moving to introduce matters relating to productivity, digitisation, agriculture and manufacturing. The chapter presents key characteristics of Africa compared to other countries and regions to 2040, defines some of the terms, introduces the International Futures forecasting platform that is used for the forecasts, and the structure of the book.

Keywords Africa · Forecasts · Scenarios · Africa · Ghana · South Korea · Economic size · Population · Agriculture · Manufactures · Demographics · Poverty · Growth

I founded the Institute for Security Studies in 1991 as an effort to contribute to policy development in post-apartheid South Africa. Reflected in our name we focussed our efforts on policies and measures to research and recommend improvements domestically, in the region and eventually to contribute to stability and security in Africa. From about 1994 I worked intimately with the secretariat of the Organization of African Unity, today the Commission of the African Union, sometimes spending week on week in Addis Ababa, attending an incalculable number of planning and strategy sessions there and elsewhere.

The end of the Cold War was a heady time in Africa, offering the prospect for an end to the proxy wars that had been fought across the length and breadth of the continent for decades. But over time my sense of disillusionment increased at the lack of focus on the underlying drivers of insecurity.

We helped the OAU/AU develop numerous policies and plans on peacekeeping, combatting terrorism, organised crime, security sector reform and the establishment of various systems such as those related to early warning. My sense of frustration increased with each effort. It's not that things were not improving. Africa is, today, significantly more stable than the years leading up to the end of the Cold War when large-scale armed conflict was the order of the day. It's just that we forever seemed to be dealing with the symptom of the problem. Like a band-aid plaster we were trying to stop the bleeding but did little to help the patient recover and avoid a relapse. And everything was a crisis with little time spent on reviewing the strategic choices being made and even less on monitoring implementation.

After stepping down as head of the Institute in 2015 I was able to devote my full attention to the study of causality and trends, something I had by then been dabbling in for several years. Following a Fulbright fellowship in the USA, my second career at the Institute, now as chair of the ISS board of trustees and as head of the programme on African Futures & Innovation, has allowed me to indulge in trend analysis, looking much more broadly at the drivers and the solutions to Africa's slow progress and the measures required to accelerate broad progress in governance and development.

For successive decades I've paid regular visits to many countries across the continent, travelling from our head office in Pretoria. I can confirm the good news story of a vibrant and dynamically developing continent, particularly in its cities. Gleaming new airports, bustling streets, traffic jams and youthful vigour and life can be found from Addis Ababa and Lusaka to Nairobi and Lagos. A far cry from the stereotype generally conveyed in most Western media.

Africa is undoubtedly experiencing a broad-based improvement in human well-being, which is reflected in a number of health indicators such as declining rates of infant mortality, improvements in life expectancy and others. In this regard, Africa is catching up with global averages.

However, looking at the bigger picture, one can argue that this is largely because rapid improvements at lower levels of development are easier to achieve while continued improvements in rich countries are more difficult at their much higher levels. On most other indicators of well-being the gap between Africa and the rest of the world is actually *increasing*. In the words of colleague Julia Bello-Schünemann 'things are getting better, but not everywhere and not for everybody'.[1]

If Africa could have talked itself into development it would be doing very well. But only rarely do the many plans and visions translate into reality. These plans and visions include the 1980 Lagos Plan of Action for the Economic Development of Africa, the New Partnership for Africa's Development (NEPAD) and recently Agenda 2063, the long-term development vision of the African Union.

The Growing Income Divergence

This book has its origin in the growing gap in average gross domestic product (GDP) per capita in Africa and the rest of the world. GDP per capita is a key indicator of progress since it reflects economic productivity and the relative standard of living. It is a relatively crude measure as it does not take the quality of life into account or the distribution of the economic output among the population. It is calculated by simply dividing the total economic output of a country (GDP) in a year by the total population. Because of this simplicity it remains the most popular measure of national economic productivity that allows easy comparisons between different countries.

In 1960, generally considered the start of the postcolonial era, GDP per capita in Africa was about half of the average in the rest of the world and the gap has been growing larger ever since. It fell to below 40% in 1986 and below 30% in 2011. In fact, average GDP per capita actually declined by more than US$600 from 1980 to 1995. Then, from 1995 to the global financial crisis in 2008/2009, Africa experienced its most sustained period of growth since 1960. But, in 2018, the standard year of reference used in this book, GDP per capita in Africa is still only 27% of the average in the rest of the world. By 2040, GDP per capita in Africa is projected to be less than one-quarter of the average for the rest of the world.[2]

Figure 1.1 presents this information in a line graph that compares the average GDP per capita in Africa with that in the rest of the world from 1960 to 2040. Up until 2018 the underlying data originates with the World Bank and thereafter it is a forecast.

---

[1] Cilliers, J., Bello-Schünemann, J., Donnenfeld, Z., Aucoin, C., and Porter, A. 2017. *Institute for Security Studies*. [Online] Available at: https://issafrica.org/research/policy-brief/african-futures-key-trends-to-2035.
[2] Using purchasing power parity.

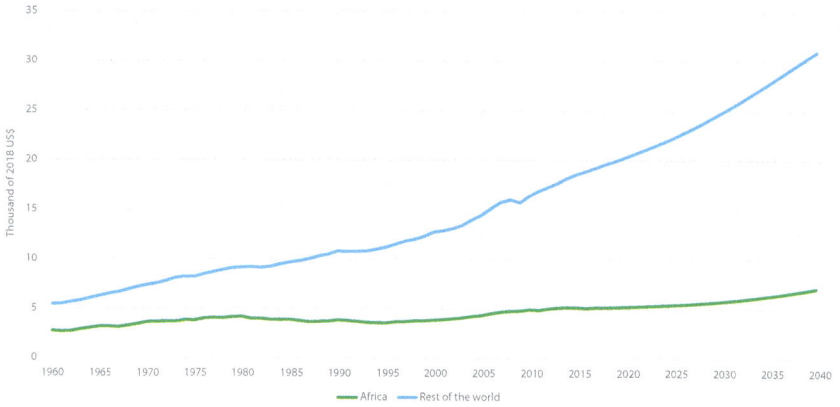

Fig. 1.1 GDP per capita in purchasing power parity: from 1960 with a forecast to 2040 (*Source* IFs version 7.45 initialised from World Bank, World Development Indicators, 2018)

Like the jaws of a yawning crocodile, it paints a picture of increasing divergence. At the ISS I use this graph at the start of most of my presentations on African futures to illustrate the progress made and the challenges that lie ahead.

The increasing divergence between the trend in GDP per capita in Africa versus the average for the rest of the world correlates with many other indices of human development or well-being, such as average levels of education and various measures of health. Since this book is finalised in mid-2020 the graph does not yet capture the impact of the COVID-19 pandemic, sure to eventually represent a global and African kink similar to that evident from the 2008/2009 financial crisis or worse.

We therefore find ourselves in a situation where Africa is progressing slower even than other developing regions such as South America and South Asia. The future is always clouded by uncertainty. However, based on our understanding of where Africa is today and the correlation between variables across different development systems, we have a good sense of where Africa is currently heading.

For long-term forecasting, I use a general time horizon to 2040, which is well beyond the time horizon of the 2030 Agenda for Sustainable Development but significantly shorter than Agenda 2063. While I will consistently benchmark progress to 2040, in certain areas, such as climate change, demographics and projected waves of democracy and/or autocracy, the presentation of trends extend over longer time horizons, in some instances to the end of the century.

So why does Africa continue to slip further and further behind global averages of well-being and what could be done about it?

My goal with this book is to present a cohesive story about human and economic development in Africa revolving around three essential questions: (1) Where does Africa find itself today in relation to the situation elsewhere in the world and generally, what explains this state of affairs? (2) Given historical trends and what we know about the world, where do we think Africa will be in 2040? Is this future really inevitable? And ultimately, (3) What can be done to improve this trajectory and create a better tomorrow for the continent?

Clearly something drastic is needed. Doing more of the same is not going to lead to tangible progress. The momentum from a burgeoning population, the continued growth of China, India and others, the swift pace of technological change, the impact of climate change and other disruptive events such as pandemics, presents a complex picture. On the one hand there are huge opportunities in electricity generation and access, expansion of mobile broadband networks and better access to financial services. On the other, it is evident that Africa will suffer immensely from the impact of changes in the global climate. What is clear is that on its current trajectory, Africa could be left further behind as development accelerates elsewhere particularly if crises, such as the COVID-19 pandemic hammer the developing world more seriously than the developed world.

In essence this book describes and models the impact of a series of fundamental transitions in health, demographics, agriculture, education, manufacturing, technology, trade integration, stability and governance that is needed if Africa is to narrow and start closing the gap in development between itself and the rest of the world.

Governments need to intervene in many areas. They are supposed to improve education, spend on health, build infrastructure and provide security. But since resources are limited the most important policy question is what to prioritise? What gives the best return on investment? And what is the role of the private sector and external agencies?

These choices imply that some degree of trade-off is inevitable—some short-term pain will accompany long-term gain. This is an issue to which I return in the concluding chapter.

South Korea and Ghana

A comparison between the reasons for the divergent development trajectories of Ghana and South Korea—one that is often used in academic literature—emphasises the difference in outcomes and the role that demographics, policy choices and leadership played. The difference is presented in Fig. 1.2 and illustrates the extent to which the demographic dividend and average incomes in these two countries coincide. When Ghana and South Korea gained independence, South Korea was actually poorer than Ghana, but today its average income levels is nine times that of Ghana as measured using GDP per capita in purchasing power parity.

With a focus on food self-sufficiency, basic education, family planning and the provision of basic health care, South Korea managed to rapidly reduce its rates of fertility and, as a result, experienced a steady increase in the number of working age persons to dependents. Thanks to this demographic dividend, the ratio of working age persons to dependents went from 1.2 in the

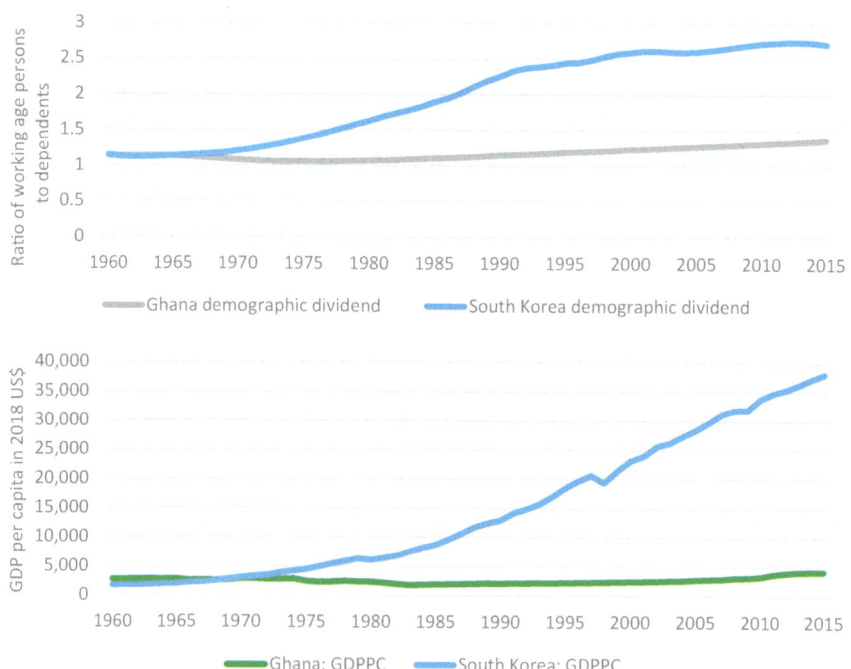

Fig. 1.2 Ghana vs South Korea: income per person vs demographic dividend: 1960 to 2015 (*Source* IFs 7.45 initialising from World Bank, World Development Indicators, 2018 and UN Population Division, World Population Prospects: The 2017 Revision)

late 1950s to a recent peak of almost 2.8—an extraordinary high ratio only achieved by China and the Asian Tiger economies in modern history.

Ghana has always had a very low ratio of working age persons. Even in 2018 it is less than 1.4, although it is improving. In retrospect it is perhaps not that surprising that Korea developed so quickly from around 1980, but the foundation for this growth was already laid in the late 1950s and 1960s. Not everything went smoothly, however, and the impact of the 1997–1998 Korean financial crisis on incomes is plain to see as the graph briefly dips in its otherwise smooth upward trajectory.

South Korea's *Saemaul Undong*, the New Village Movement, played an important role in its spectacular growth. This was a community-driven self-help movement facilitated by the government. It is not an approach where the government sought to pursue prestige projects meant to leapfrog Korea into an industrial age (as was tried in Ghana in the 1960s). Rather, it was an initiative that first, and primarily, sought to change the mindset at community level towards self-help and self-reliance.

Once Korea had achieved food self-sufficiency and started making steady agricultural and educational progress, it embarked on an export-led manufacturing pathway, starting at a very basic level.[3]

South Korea had another advantage. It had no oil, gas or other large-scale natural resource. All it had was its people. By comparison Ghana, originally called the Gold Coast as a British colony until independence in 1957, has always had the potential of benefiting from its much more significant natural resources. Except that it did not.

It is now well-established that enclave economics such as those that develop around the oil and gas industry in particular, does not work. The largesse of oil and natural gas have had a particularly deleterious impact on countries like Nigeria, Angola, Equatorial Guinea, and shortly Mozambique. This resource curse occurs when the main driver of the economy creates small, highly developed bubbles with no forward or backward linkages to the domestic economy but serve to prop up the exchange rate and effectively makes it impossible to produce local goods at competitive rates. The only people that benefit are foreign investors, local frontmen and -women, and corrupt government officials.

Saemaul Undong was instituted by an authoritarian government and it is seldom mentioned in mainstream analysis of South Korea's escape from underdevelopment. Generally, economic development was the first priority of the South Koreans. This stands in stark contrast to the famous slogan

---

[3] See Park, J.-D., 2019. *Re-Inventing Africa's Development Linking Africa to the Korean Development Model.* Basingstoke: Palgrave Macmillan.

of Ghana's independence leader, Kwame Nkrumah, to first seek 'the political kingdom and all things shall be added unto you'.[4] When comparing the general human development indicators of Ghana and South Korea today, the different results are demonstrable.

Ghana and South Korea were, for much of their independent history, autocratic countries and suffered under colonialism with the latter additionally suffered a debilitating war from 1950 to 1953. Both became hugely corrupt after independence, but whereas South Korea had a leadership that prioritised development and self-help, Ghana did not. Democracy played no role in Korea's development but is, today, highly valued in much of Africa because the alternative, autocracy, has had disastrous results on the continent.

This points to the unique challenges that Africa faces when compared to developing Asia where industrialisation occurred under autocratic but generally developmentally oriented regimes. Here leaders could discount the popular discontent associated with the disruptive changes required for productivity improvements. The ruling elite can introduce tariff protection to support a particular sector or industry and more easily phase it out once that goal has been achieved than in a democracy.

The world of the mid-twentieth century is, however, very different to the twenty-first century. It is not possible to roll back democracy in Africa, even if it were desirable from a narrow economic mindset. Africans simply would not stand for it—given centuries of external intervention and oppression they place a high premium on political freedom.

Although Korea also received substantial conditional development aid, it worked hard to wean itself off it. The contrast with much of Africa cannot be more stark. Instead of becoming economically independent in the 1960s, African countries have willingly subjected themselves to a relationship of dependency, often appearing to look to others rather than themselves for their development—initially to Europe, today towards China.

The Importance of Labour and Demographics

Economies grow as a result of increases in the contribution of labour, capital and multifactor productivity to the economy. The latter is generally calculated as the residual or the remaining improvement in the expansion of the economy after accounting for labour and capital and is sometimes also termed the contribution from technology or total factor productivity.

---

[4]Biney, A., 2011. *The Political and Social Thought of Kwame Nkrumah.* New York: Palgrave Macmillan, see Chapter 1

At low levels of development the contribution of labour to economic growth is most important. For the purposes of this book three components of labour are important namely the absence of widespread ill-health, disease, hunger and malnutrition, a sufficient number of working age persons to dependents (to enable a demographic dividend), and education or improvements in knowledge. Once countries achieve middle-income status the contribution of capital gains in importance which can come from various sources, although generally foreign direct investment would follow domestic investment. Remittances also play an important role in Africa's ability to receive sufficient capital to speed up growth. In high-income economies technology generally drives improvements in productivity, although the exact contribution and calculation of each of these three components is complicated, country-specific and contested.

Many studies have tried to explain why Africa has remained so much poorer than other regions over successive centuries. The continent is richly endowed with commodities, including large land for agriculture and is, after all, the birthplace of our species. But it is exactly for this reason—humanity's origins in Africa—that development here progressed at a slower pace than elsewhere even in recent centuries. Humans only started to multiply once they escaped the high disease risk on the continent where Homo sapiens and nature had coexisted for thousands of years. I explain my understanding of the associated dynamics in Chapter 3 (on health).

In retrospect it is clear that the rapidly increasing size of the labour force in relation to dependents such as that in South Korea, but also in the other Asian Tiger economies, Japan and China was key to their rapid economic growth and development, although other factors certainly also played a role.[5] Today, several decades later, they all face the opposite problem of a slowdown in growth since a shrinking workforce (as a portion of the total population) has to look after a growing ageing population.

Only since around 1987 has the ratio of working age persons to dependents in Africa started to improve, albeit very slowly. Before that it was declining. As that ratio increases, growth generally accelerates at low levels of development because of the additional contribution that more working age persons make to economic growth. This is discussed in Chapter 4.

Today, the vast majority of African countries are net food importers, despite the continent having millions of hectares of arable land, with huge untapped agricultural potential. Africa imported US$170 billion food in

---

[5] Japan bottomed out at a dependency ratio of 0.43 in 1992, China and the Asian Tigers bottomed out at 0.36 in 2010 and 2013, respectively. All experienced their periods of most rapid economic growth in the years during which their dependency ratios were declining.

2018 and exported only US$67 billion, implying a food trade deficit bill of more than US$100 billion. That is expected to increase more than sixfold by 2040.[6] Exports are dwarfed by the value of imports although a large portion of the increase in imports is due to changed diets as Africans become more wealthy and change their eating habits, reflected in the rise of obesity and non-communicable diseases such as heart conditions hitherto more common in the developed West.

Whereas agriculture is generally considered the mainstay of Africa's economy, yields per hectare are the lowest globally and improving more slowly than in other regions. Since food is cheaper on the international market than domestically and because palates change with income, Africa is becoming more, not less, dependent on food imports.

Furthermore, the impact of climate change is such that it will impact very negatively on the Sahel and West Africa with more variable impacts elsewhere. With very low levels of basic infrastructure such as access to safe water and sanitation, Africa's population is more vulnerable to the impact of climate change than people living in other world regions.

Clearly there is much that can be done to improve agriculture even as it inevitably declines as a share of national economies. Take South Africa for example. Although primary agriculture only contributes about 2.5% to GDP, South Africa is one of the few African countries that provides food security on the back of a highly productive private agricultural sector, meaning that food imports are dwarfed by exports with sufficient calories available per person.

Looking to the future, the impact of climate change on agricultural yields in Africa is a big uncertainty. Recently, while conducting a long-term forecast on the future of five of the Sahel countries, Mali, Niger, Burkina Faso, Chad and Mauritania, colleagues and I were struck by the impact climate change has already had and will continue to have in this region. The Intergovernmental Panel on Climate Change (IPCC) soberly notes that the Sahel, where agriculture accounts for more than 75% of total employment, has 'experienced the most substantial and sustained decline in rainfall recorded anywhere in the world within the period of instrumental measurements'.[7]

The impact of climate change will, of course, vary across Africa in terms of changes in temperature and rainfall and the increased variability of weather with many more extreme events such as floods, tornadoes and droughts. That said there is huge potential for technology to increase agricultural production—not through the traditional route of expanding land under cultivation,

---

[6]Calculated by deducting total value of food exports from food imports within IFs 7.45.
[7]IPCC, 2018. *Working Group II Impacts, Adaptation and Vulnerability.* [Online] Available at: https://www.ipcc.ch/working-group/wg2/?idp=403.

but through the use of more precise farming and more sustainable farming methods. Eventually solar-powered cold storage, accurate weather forecasts, monitoring of soil conditions and access to market information can all play an important role, as could greater efficiencies to reduce food waste. However, this will require current practices to change. I explore agriculture in Chapter 5 and the possible impact of climate change in Chapter 15.

Productivity and Economic Structure

One of the great economic mysteries of our time is why, with all the hype around the impact of artificial intelligence, digitisation, information and communication technologies, labour productivity is not increasing at a greater rate? In the aftermath of the 2008/2009 financial crisis, labour productivity growth has actually slowed in many economies, dropping to an average of 0.5% in 2010–2014 from 2.4% a decade earlier in the USA and major European economies. By 2016 the output per hour of work had actually been declining for more than a decade, argues well-known author and investment fund manager Ruchir Sharma.[8]

In theory the potential for improvements in productivity as part of digitisation and automation is large. But, with a shrinking labour force as a portion of the total population in most middle- and high-income countries, artificial intelligence and automation first need to offset the reduction in productivity from that smaller labour force as a portion of total population before these countries will experience general improvements in productivity. With its growing working age population Africa is potentially in a positive position but is coming off a very low base.

A second reason for low productivity to date is the ongoing shift in the structure of the global economy towards services at the expense of manufacturing. Currently the services sector (lending, recreation, tourism, transport, food) constitutes the largest economic sector by value and is significantly larger than any other sector in Africa, including agriculture and manufacturing. COVID-19 will accelerate this transition as persons working in offices were forced to work from home, using Zoom, Teams and Skype for Business, among others, to communicate, and dedicated conference-goers (like myself) moved to video-conferencing.

Unlike the manufacturing sector, the services sector has not been fully disrupted by technology. Since the service sector is more labour-intensive,

---

[8]Sharma, R., 2016. *The Rise and Fall of Nations—Ten Rules of Change in the Post-crisis World.* New York: Penguin Random House.

the shift to services reduced overall productivity, but that is now rapidly changing although more slowly in Africa given the nature of much of the low-end services, often provided in informal settings.

Many believe that artificial intelligence and automation have the potential to reverse the recent declines in global productivity that have followed the decline in the working age portion of the total population. According to the McKinsey Institute, productivity growth could potentially reach 2% annually over the next decade, with 60% of this increase due to digital opportunities.[9] New 'digital ecosystems' are emerging that combine goods and services in a highly customer-centric manner, shifting the border between these sectors.[10] Many of these issues are discussed in Chapters 8 and 10 that unpack manufacturing and the potential for Africa to leapfrog.

Being the least developed region in the world, Africa has significant potential for fast improvements in labour productivity through the use of modern technology and practices. Some degree of catching up or even leapfrogging is possible but to date, labour productivity in Africa has been improving much slower than elsewhere and, together with others, I tend towards the belief that an important explanation for the generally slow economic growth of the continent is the fact that the contribution of Africa's already small manufacturing sector has been declining, giving credence to the view that what Africa is experiencing is so-called 'premature deindustrialisation' although there are signs of some recent improvements.

In fact, from already low levels Africa is deindustrialising and becoming even more dependent on low value commodity exports for its foreign exchange earnings. It is the only region globally where the number of commodity-dependent countries (in terms of value of export earnings) increases year on year.[11]

A vibrant manufacturing sector plays a unique role in boosting productivity throughout the economy, thanks to its forward and backward linkages that fuel the development of other sectors such as agriculture and services. 'Manufacturing contributes disproportionately to exports, innovation and growth', writes James Manyika and other authors in a comprehensive 2012

---

[9] Manyika, J., and Sneader, K., 2018. *McKinsey Global Institute*. [Online] Available at: https://www.mckinsey.com/featured-insights/future-of-work/ai-automation-and-the-future-of-work-ten-things-to-solve-for.

[10] In a recent article McKinsey Analytics, set out the extent to which the ongoing digital revolution is reducing frictional transaction costs within and across sectors. Atluri, V., Dietz, M., and Henke, N., 2017. *McKinsey Quarterly*. [Online] Available at: https://www.mckinsey.com/business-functions/mckinsey-analytics/our-insights/competing-in-a-world-of-sectors-without-borders.

[11] United Nations Conference on Trade and Development (UNCTAD), 2019. State of Commodity Dependence 2019, Geneva. [Online] Available at https://unctad.org/en/pages/PublicationWebflyer.aspx?publicationid=2439.

report for the McKinsey Global Institute.[12] The big question is if African leadership and African workers are prepared for the associated labour practices that accompany this growth path?

Going forward, Africa needs to seize the opportunity offered by renewable energy and the promise of the fourth industrial revolution to rapidly improve productivity growth and to provide many more jobs. But how can that be achieved in a global economic environment where Africa is becoming more, not less, dependent on the export of commodities and where the contribution of its small but growing labour force (as a portion of the total population) is likely of declining value? And all of this while growth of the manufacturing sector is constrained by the fact that Southeast Asia has become the world's factory.

Whereas manufacturing is often referred to as the automatic escalator that lifts countries to higher levels of productivity, Africa appears to be embarking on a low-productivity services and commodity escalator. Africa's services escalator does go upward, but only slowly while the manufacturing window is closing. In addition, it has become much harder to establish export manufacturers as the entire sector is shrinking worldwide and competition is fierce.

Africa's structural transformation from low-productivity, often subsistence agriculture to low-productivity, urban-based retail services in the informal sector has therefore been growth reducing rather than productivity improving. This is largely because the share of workers employed in higher-productivity sectors such as manufacturing is declining, resulting in a drop of the average growth output per worker.[13]

The Global Context

The challenge of the growing divergence between Africa and the rest of the world is reflected in Africa's marginal role in the global economy. In 1960, Africa accounted for 3% of the global economy. Sixty years later that share has increased to 4% despite the fact that Africa's share of the global population

---

[12]Manyika, J., Sinclair, J., Dobbs, R., Strube, G., Rassey, L., Mischke, J., Remes, J., Roxburgh, C., George, K., O'Halloran, D., and Ramaswamy, S., 2012. *McKinsey Global Institute*. [Online] Available at: https://www.mckinsey.com/business-functions/operations/our-insights/the-future-of-manufacturing.
[13]UNU-WIDER Studies in Development Economics, 2016. Manufacturing Transformation: Comparative Studies of Industrial Development in Africa and Emerging Asia. In: C. Newman, et al. eds. Helsinki: Oxford University Press, p. 5. See also Bhorat, H., Kanbur, R., Rooney, C., and Steenkamp, F., 2017. *Sub-Saharan Africa's Manufacturing Sector: Building Complexity, Working Paper Series N° 256*. Abidjan: African Development Bank.

almost doubled from 9 to 17%. Compare this to East Asia and the Pacific, a region that increased its share of global economic output from about 11% in 1960 to more than 30% today. East Asia's share of the global population, on the other hand, has shrunk from 34 to 30% during this period pointing to its much more productive economies.

On current trends it would be safe to refer, by mid-century, to a global economic system that is likely to consist of four centres of power, China, the USA, the EU and a rising India. These countries already account for almost 60% of global GDP and their share is slowly increasing. By 2040 the Chinese economy should be about 70% larger than the US economy, which will, in turn, be a bit larger than the EU group of 27 countries (now excluding the United Kingdom). India would then still be about 25 years away from having an economy that is comparable in size to that of the USA although it would have doubled its slice of the global economy to around 7% and would be growing quickly.

China could constitute one-quarter of the global economy by 2040. This is roughly equivalent to the position the USA occupied around 10 years ago while the USA would see its portion of the global economy decline from the current 21–15% by then.

But it is unlikely that the world of 2040 will resemble our current obsession with national economies. The future is likely greater regionalisation, particularly in Asia which may increasingly look inward for growth and development rather than to the rest of the world. Already intra-Asia trade surpassed Asian trade with the rest of the world in 2004 and partly protected the region from the impact of the global financial crisis that followed a few years later.

And Asia, in particular, is likely to be much more dynamic than Europe or North America. In this future an economically interdependent and integrated Asia will become more important.

Asia is, of course, hugely diverse including a group of advanced economies such as Japan, and South Korea, the two giants (China and India), a group of large countries such as Indonesia and Bangladesh and a group of poorer countries that includes Afghanistan, Bhutan and Papua New Guinea.[14]

On the Current Path forecast Africa is likely to remain a peripheral player in this world, although its share of the world's population will increase very quickly. By 2040 Africa's population will have crossed the two billion mark and be significantly larger than the population of India or China. In fact, Nigeria alone would have a population of 360 million by 2040, making it

---

[14] According to Economy Watch, 2019. *Developing Asia (Emerging and Developing Asia) Economic Statistics and Indicators*. [Online] Available at: http://www.economywatch.com/economic-statistics/country/Developing-Asia/.

the fourth most populous country globally after India, China and the USA. But because of poor growth prospects, Nigeria will account for less than 1% of the global economy and is unlikely to emerge even as a global middle power.

Figure 1.3 presents the total populations of key countries and groupings namely Africa, China, India, the EU27, USA and the rest of the world at twenty-year intervals from 1980 to 2040. Africa's population size is set to rapidly increase over the time horizon set out in this book.

Although Africa's population is set to increase from its current 17% of the global population to 23% by 2040, the continent will then only represent 4% of the global economy. And Asia, knitted together by China's Belt and Road Initiative, an infrastructure superhighway, will have more than double the population of Africa.

Figure 1.4 presents the same countries and groupings as in Fig. 1.2, also with 20 year time intervals, this time presenting the size of each economy in market exchange rates.

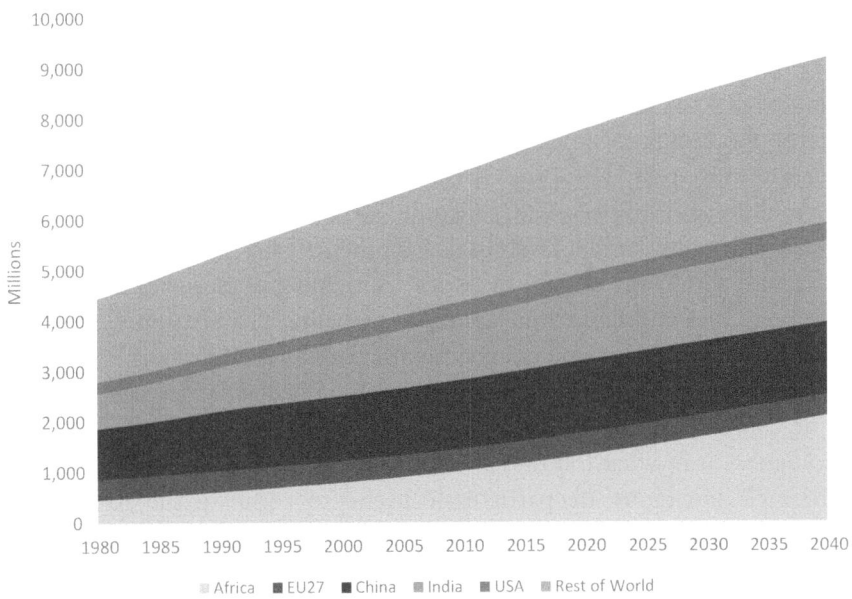

Fig. 1.3 Composition of the global population: 1980–2040 for Africa, China, India, EU27, USA and the Rest of the World (RoW) (*Source* Historical data from United Nations Population Division, forecast in IFs 7.45)

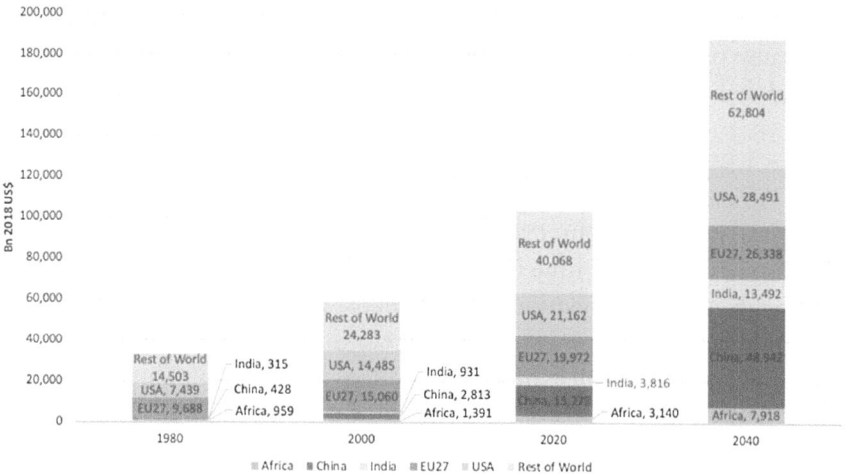

Fig. 1.4 Comparing economies: 1980–2040 (*Source* Historical data from IMF World Economic Outlook, forecast in IFs 7.45)

Dealing with Africa's Diversity—Using Country Income Groups

A book of this nature can hardly do justice to the rich diversity of Africa, its 55 states, thousands of languages and many different cultures.

For the most part, I use the 2019/2020 World Bank groupings of low, lower-middle and upper-middle-income groups to explore trends across countries at roughly similar levels of development.[15] Of 31 low-income countries around the world, 24 are in Africa. And African countries account for 21 of the 47 low-middle-income countries globally. Africa has only eight (out of 60) upper-middle-income countries namely Algeria, Botswana, Equatorial Guinea, Gabon, Libya, Mauritius, Namibia and South Africa. Of 80 high-income countries, only one is in Africa, the island state of Seychelles and I largely ignore it in what follows.

These classifications are particularly useful to compare the structure of economies, levels of income, education and access to infrastructure between countries at roughly the same levels of economic development. Where appropriate, I benchmark Africa to the rest of the world within these categories such as comparing averages in low-middle-income Africa with that for the average for low-income countries globally or for low-middle-income countries in the rest of the world (Fig. 1.5).

---

[15] For its 2020 fiscal year. See World Bank Country and Lending Groups. Available at https://datahelpdesk.worldbank.org/knowledgebase/articles/906519-world-bank-country-and-lending-groups.

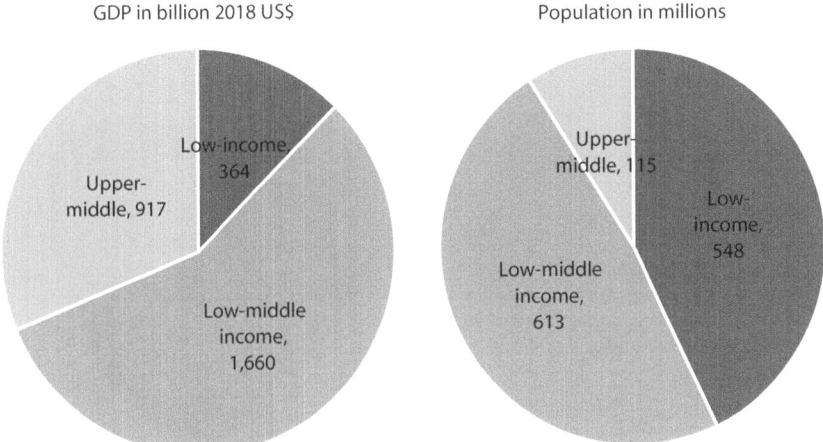

Fig. 1.5 Economic size and population size for low, lower-middle and upper-middle-income Africa in 2018 (*Source* UN Population Division and IMF World Economic Outlook data in IFs 7.45)

Generally low-income countries grow more rapidly, so the average economic growth forecast from 2020 to 2040 for Africa's 24 low-income countries is 6.7%, 5.1% for the 21 low-middle-income countries and 2.6% for Africa eight upper-middle-income countries.

Occasionally, I look at Regional Economic Communities (RECs) such as the East African Community (EAC), the Southern African Development Community (SADC) or the Economic Community of West African States (ECOWAS). Since many of these communities have overlapping membership I define Africa's five geographic regions as follows (see Fig. 1.6):

- North Africa: Algeria, Egypt, Libya, Mauritania, Morocco and Tunisia.
- West Africa: Benin, Burkina Faso, Cape Verde, Côte d'Ivoire, The Gambia, Ghana, Guinea, Guinea-Bissau, Liberia, Mali, Niger, Nigeria, Senegal, Sierra Leone and Togo.
- East/Horn of Africa: Burundi, Comoros, Djibouti, Eritrea, Ethiopia, Kenya, Madagascar, Mauritius, Rwanda, Seychelles, Somalia, Sudan, South Sudan, Tanzania and Uganda.
- Central Africa: Cameroon, CAR, Chad, DRC, Republic of Congo, Equatorial Guinea, Gabon and São Tomé and Príncipe.
- Southern Africa: Angola, Botswana, Lesotho, Malawi, Mozambique, Namibia, South Africa, eSwatini (Swaziland), Zambia and Zimbabwe.

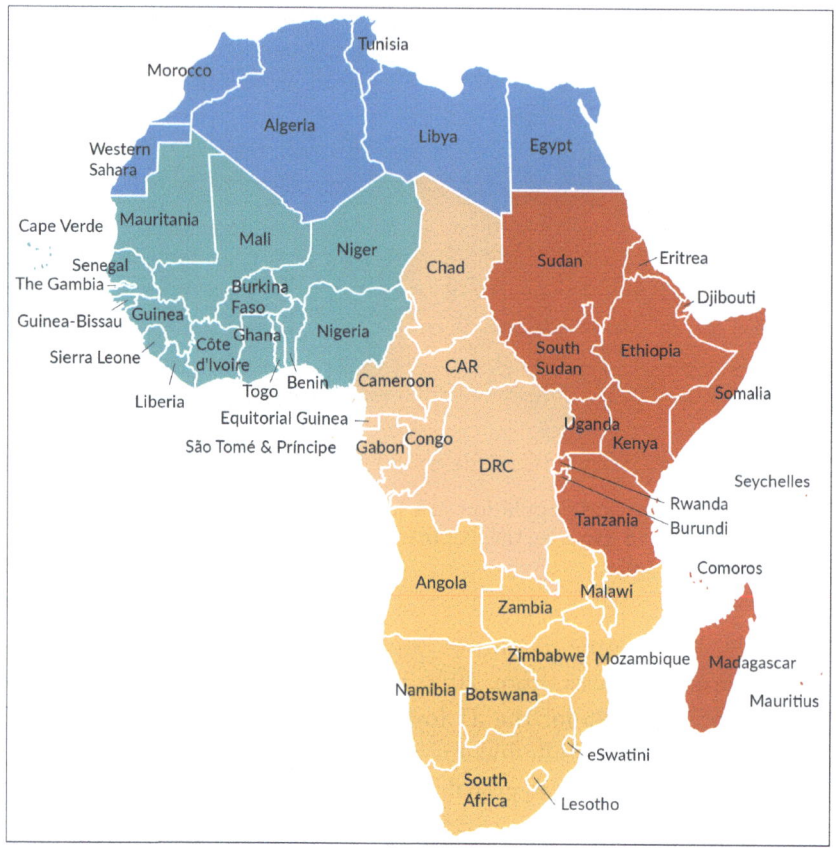

Fig. 1.6 Regions in Africa

These categories are exclusive in that no country belongs to more than one geographical region.

Looking at the average rates of economic growth for these five regions, East/Horn of Africa is set to experience the most rapid economic growth from 2020 to 2040, at 6.3%, followed by West Africa at 5.5%. Northern and Southern Africa will grow at 3.7 and 3.8%, respectively, and Central Africa at 4.7%. Over this period the population of Central Africa is expected to increase by 75%, however, meaning that average GDP per capita in purchasing power parity in this region will only increase by US$840 from 2020 to 2040. The population in West Africa will increase by 68% and, by 2040, West Africa will have a GDP per capita that is US$2270 larger than in 2020. The number for East/Horn is a 60% population growth and an increase in GDP per capita of US$1890. The population of Southern Africa will increase by 50% and, by 2040, it will have a GDP per capita that is

US$2035 bigger than in 2020. The population of North Africa will increase by only 25% and, because it includes a number of upper-middle-income countries, therefore coming off a higher base, by 2040 it will have a GDP per capita that is US$4020 larger than in 2020.

In summary, this is a picture of Central Africa that, with each passing year, falls further and further behind the rest of the continent. Average income growth will be highest in North Africa followed, at some distance by West and Southern Africa with East/Horn of Africa trailing slightly behind.

There is, of course, a limit to the utility of these regional comparisons since each region includes countries at very different levels of development and with unique population and income characteristics, such as the very high levels of inequality in Southern Africa compared to the rest of Africa (and the lowest average levels of inequality in North Africa compared to other regions in Africa).

In the interest of standardisation, all US dollar figures taken from the International Futures forecasting system (see below) and used in this book (such as those on GDP per capita in the previous paragraphs) have been converted to 2018 values. Unless indicated otherwise, figures and data presented in the various chapters are estimates taken from IFs for 2018 is used as a general reference year throughout, also when using material from other sources.[16]

Finally, I sometimes compare Africa with two other developing regions, namely South America and South Asia,[17] that align most closely on a host of development indicators except in agricultural yields where South America is close to a global leader.

Previous Studies and the International Futures Forecasting Platform

Long-term trends are affected by deep drivers that are slow-moving but powerful, like demographics, education or commodity super cycles, which also unfold over decades. These deep drivers are increasingly well understood

---

[16]The rate of conversion from the 2011 US$ values in IFs to 2018 prices is 1.1163. Where no data is available for 2018, I use the forecasts from the International Futures forecasting platform (IFs, which initialises from 2015 values) but make no distinction in the use of the term data or forecast. Since the IFs forecasts generally demonstrate a high level of continuity with historical trends, the forecasts are a close representation of reality and likely paint a more accurate picture than 'most recent data', which can often be several years old.

[17]Within IFs South America consists of Argentina, Bolivia, Brazil, Chile, Columbia, Ecuador, Guyana, Paraguay, Peru, Suriname, Uruguay and Venezuela. South Asia includes Afghanistan, Bangladesh, India, Iran, Maldives, Nepal, Pakistan and Sri Lanka.

in forecasting literature, even though the exact contribution and sometimes the direction of causality remains a subject of intense academic debate. Some prospects, such as demographics, are easier to forecast than others, like the potential impact of technology or how changes in governance may evolve, but none are impossible.

When all is said and done, it is much more useful to spend time and effort on systematically exploring plausible futures than relying on speculation or gut-feel. Which brings me to another important characteristic of the type of forecasting that follows, namely that each chapter is based on realistic expectations of what could be possible (benchmarked against historical precedent) instead of a desired future. This is not a blue-skies book on where I would like to see Africa, but on what could realistically be possible given the right policy choices, clear leadership and determined implementation.

The forecasts in this book rely on the International Futures (IFs) modelling platform that is developed and housed at the Frederick S Pardee Center for International Futures at the Josef Korbel School of International Studies at the University of Denver. The model is open source and is available for download at the Pardee Center website at https://pardee.du.edu/access-ifs.

Each of the following chapters compare the IFs Current Path forecast with a set of interventions grouped as a coherent scenario. The Current Path is an integrated forecast (or scenario) of the likely future development trajectory. In other disciplines it is also known as the Base Case or Business as Usual forecast. It does not assume any major paradigm shifts, seismic policy changes, or transformative events such as global war, pandemic (such as COVID-10) or cataclysmic climate change tipping point. In other words, it is not a forecast that anticipates very low probability but high impact events, although one can create scenarios within IFs that emulate anything from global war to drought, or swift technological progress. Rather, the Current Path represents a reliable expectation of how major development systems are likely to unfold, and is a useful starting point from which to design alternative future scenarios.

The details of the modelling and the specific levers pulled within IFs can be found at www.jakkiecilliers.org that also details the benchmarking of each intervention, as well as the adjustments that have been made in the IFs Current Path forecast for the purposes of this book.

The forecasts presented in this book are sure to be wrong in many respects. Beyond our limited ability to understand the evolution of human, environmental and other systems, data from many African countries are poor or even absent. Fortunately, the quality of international data gathering is improving as the efforts to improve statistical service agencies bear fruit. Governments also more regularly recalculate the overall price structure of their economies. To that end the African Union and various partners have embarked on a *Strategy for the Harmonization of Statistics in Africa (SHaSA)*, now in its second strategic period with a time horizon from 2017 to 2026.[18]

In 2014 alone, Kenya, Nigeria, Tanzania,[19] Uganda and Zambia all completed economic rebasing exercises, which led to significant revaluations of their GDPs. Nigeria's (2013) GDP nearly doubled and the country overtook South Africa as the largest economy in Africa when measured in market exchange rates. The increase of about 90% in the size of the Nigerian economy was attributed to the inclusion of new sectors of the economy such as telecommunications, the burgeoning local film industry (known as Nollywood), the retail and informal sectors.

The calculations also revised the size of Kenya and Zambia upward by a quarter and the World Bank categorised Kenya from a low-income to a lower-middle-income country. Ghana found that its economy increased by 60% when the previous rebase was announced in 2010—and by another 25% when the latest rebase was announced in 2018. When Zimbabwe rebased its economy in 2018 it also concluded with a 40% increase in the size of its economy, much of which was now sadly part of the informal rather than the formal sector. Country classifications also go the other way. In contrast to Kenya, Zimbabwe was downgraded from lower-middle to low-income in 1991, but was again reclassified as lower-middle in mid-2019.[20]

Finally, since data for Africa is often incomplete, the IFs system has a preprocessor—a sophisticated series of algorithms—that estimates and fills data gaps. In this manner the model is able to provide a solid foundation for each of the 500 or so variables that are forecast for each country.

In all instances where data is provided without a reference in the form of an endnote, the reader should assume that the data comes from IFs.

---

[18]African Union Commission; African Development Bank; United Nations Economic Commission for Africa; African Capacity Building Foundation, 2017. *Strategy for the Harmonization of Statistics in Africa 2017–2026 (SHaSA 2)*. [Online] Available at: https://www.tralac.org/documents/resources/african-union/2031-strategy-for-the-harmonization-of-statistics-in-africa-shasa-2017-2026/file.htm.

[19]The 2019 rebase of Tanzania to 2015 found that its economy had increased by 3.8%. Reuters Africa, 2019. *Tanzania Rebases Economy, 2015 GDP Now 3.8 pct Larger—Stats Office*. [Online] Available at: https://af.reuters.com/article/investingNews/idAFKCN1Q91G0-OZABS.

[20]Sy, A., 2015. *Brookings*. [Online] Available at: https://www.brookings.edu/blog/africa-in-focus/2015/03/03/are-african-countries-rebasing-gdp-in-2014-finding-evidence-of-structural-transformation/; Benghan, B., and Noshie, A., 2018. *AllAfrica*. [Online] Available at: https://allafrica.com/stories/201810010595.html; Musarurwa, T., 2018. *The Herald*. [Online] Available at: https://www.herald.co.zw/economy-rebasing-to-grow-zim-revenue/.

Structure of the Book

In addition to some characteristics already presented in this chapter, Chapter 2 presents the Current Path forecast for Africa to 2040 and serves as a broad overview for the eleven scenarios, each in a separate chapter, on health, demographics, agriculture, education, poverty, manufacturing, leapfrogging, trade, security, governance and external support. Chapters 9 and 15 do not have separate scenarios, but compares the impact of key scenarios on the future of jobs and the impact of climate change. Chapter 16 concludes and includes the impact of a combined scenario ("Closing the Gap"). It shows what could be possible by 2040 and compares those outcomes with the Current Path trajectory.

The book adopts a structured approach to Africa and the analysis builds from one chapter to the next, although some chapters can be read in a different sequence. But what Africa needs is the combined impact of all of the interventions across the different sectors and hence there is no shortcut to either a better future or to this book but to read it all.

Further Reading

www.jakkiecilliers.org.
www.issafrica.org.
www.pardee.du.edu.

Open Access This chapter is licensed under the terms of the Creative Commons Attribution 4.0 International License (http://creativecommons.org/licenses/by/4.0/), which permits use, sharing, adaptation, distribution and reproduction in any medium or format, as long as you give appropriate credit to the original author(s) and the source, provide a link to the Creative Commons license and indicate if changes were made.

The images or other third party material in this chapter are included in the chapter's Creative Commons license, unless indicated otherwise in a credit line to the material. If material is not included in the chapter's Creative Commons license and your intended use is not permitted by statutory regulation or exceeds the permitted use, you will need to obtain permission directly from the copyright holder.

2

Africa's Current Path

Abstract Cilliers provides a summary and analysis of Africa's development history since the 1980s including the impact of the Brundtland Commission report that culminated in the Millennium Development Goals and, in 2015, the Sustainable Development Goals. Other key matters covered in the chapter are the impact of the various structural adjustment programmes, Africa's growing dependence upon commodities, the continents rapid democratisation and slow pace of urbanisation. The chapter concludes with a summary of key characteristics of Africa's likely future—the Current Path forecast to 2040—that includes a forecast of economic size, demographics, income and poverty levels. The chapter serves as essential backdrop to the struggle for development that is examined across different sectors in subsequent chapters.

Keywords Africa · Development · Growth · Population · Economy · Forecast · Brundtland · Aid · MDGs · SDGs · Commodities · Democratisation · Urbanisation · Washington consensus · Structural adjustment programmes

Learning Objectives

– Understand and be able to explain the considerations that culminated in the 2030 Sustainable Development Goals
– The impact of commodity-dependent growth
– Democratisation in Africa in a comparative perspective
– To provide an overview of Africa's likely development trajectory to 2040.

Between 1980 and 1990 Africa lost considerable ground—in development terms it was actually moving backwards. Average income per person decreased by about 12% and declined by a further two percent in the early 1990s.

Then, from 1994 until 2008 (when the financial crisis hit), Africa experienced its most sustained period of growth since independence in the 1960s—an average of 4.6% per annum. During this period the average per capita income increased by 35%.[1] However, the share of Africans living in extreme poverty decreased by only about five percentage points, in part due to the high levels of inequality on the continent and rapid population growth.

Africa's low levels of integration into the global economy provided it with a degree of protection from the global financial crisis but its impact was nevertheless significant. In its aftermath global and African growth was significantly slower. From 2010 to 2019 Africa experienced average growth of only 3.1%. Yet, even shortly after the financial crisis, in 2010, the United Nations Development Programme (UNDP) could report that 'the past 20 years have seen substantial progress in many aspects of human development. Most people today are healthier, live longer, are more educated and have more access to goods and services'.[2] Almost all countries in the world have benefited from this progress, except three African countries, namely the Democratic Republic of the Congo, Zambia and Zimbabwe, which have a lower Human Development Index score today than in 1970.[3] This positive story, the UNDP report notes, 'paints a far more optimistic picture than a perspective limited to trends in income, where divergence has continued'.[4]

Four factors likely explain the post 2008/2009 lower growth. The first is that North African countries and the Sahel region have been caught up in the turmoil that followed the Arab Spring. A decade later Libya is still trapped in a debilitating civil war and the region is awash with weapons spreading across the Sahel to West Africa. The second is that oil exporters have been affected by the sharp decline in oil prices that has accompanied the shale revolution in the USA and the general decline in commodity prices that follows the restructuring of China's economy. The third is that, outside of Africa, the size of the working age population relative to dependents had started to decline, meaning that labour was no longer contributing positively to improvements in productivity. These developments are all discussed in subsequent chapters.

---

[1] From US$3 482 to US$4 685 in constant 2017 US$ at PPP.
[2] United Nations Development Programme (UNDP), 2010. *Human Development Report 2010.* New York: Palgrave Macmillan.
[3] Ibid., p. 3.
[4] Ibid.

Then, in 2020, the Sars-CoV-2 virus spread to humans in China's Wuhan province and the subsequent COVID-19 pandemic brought the global economy to a shuddering halt. Recovery is dependent on the development, manufacture and global delivery of an effective vaccine that is, at the time of writing, still unsure but unlikely to materialise before 2021.

Against that background, this chapter discusses the key events and trends that currently shape Africa's development trajectory. It concludes with a summary of characteristics of Africa's likely future—the Current Path forecast to 2040—that includes economic size, demographics, income and poverty levels. It provides an essential backdrop to the struggle for development that is examined across different sectors in the chapters that follow.

From Brundtland to the Sustainable Development Goals (SDGs)

In 1983 concern about growing poverty in low-income countries and the extent to which the world had embarked on an unsustainable growth path saw United Nations Secretary-General Javier Pérez de Cuéllar appoint the World Commission on Environment and Development. It came at a time of deep pessimism about the environment and about Africa's development prospects in particular.

The purpose of the commission, that was named after its chairwoman, Gro Harlem Brundtland, was to chart and agree on a common sustainable development pathway.[5] The Brundtland Commission report was released in October 1987 under the title *Our Common Future*. It popularised the notion of 'sustainable development' by establishing a clear relationship between economic growth, the environment and social equality. The commission presented its results just as the Cold War came to its messy conclusion with the collapse of the Berlin Wall in 1989.

The Brundtland Report called for an international meeting to map out goals and programmes to pursue sustainable development. It led to the Earth Summit in Rio de Janeiro in Brazil that was held five years later, in 1992. As an aside, the impact of the report and the Summit continues to resonate several decades later, first with the eight Millennium Development Goals that were adopted at the United Nations Millennium Summit in 2000 and more recently with the Sustainable Development Goals 2030 (SDGs), adopted by the UN General Assembly in 2015. To that end, the Brundtland

---

[5] Gro Harlem Brundtland is the former prime minister of Norway served; 1981, 1986–1989 and 1990–1996.

Report served as an important impetus to the developmental vision of the twenty-first century.

An important tool to assist in achieving this vision of sustainable development was international cooperation and solidarity, including the provision of overseas development assistance (aid) which will be examined in greater detail in Chapter 14. However, instead of increasing in constant dollar terms, aid levels declined steadily from their peak in 1990 to the Millennium Summit in New York a decade later. Kenya, Somalia, Sudan and the former Zaïre (now the Democratic Republic of Congo) experienced some of the largest declines.

One of the reasons for this was that a prolonged recession began in 1991 in Japan, a major aid provider. A second reason was the resource pull exerted by transition economies in South Asia that was steadily diverting attention away from Africa. But the most important reason was that the dissolution of the Soviet Union freed Western countries from the need to prop up African dictators who supported the West during the Cold War. With the collapse of the Berlin Wall, Africa lost much of its previous geostrategic relevance and hence the external motivation to assist.

Aid only started to regain momentum with the 2000 UN Millennium Summit in New York. It was substantially bolstered by the support of international celebrities such as Bono and Bob Geldof who campaigned for greater awareness about poverty and the AIDS crisis and also helped to raise funds for relief programmes in Africa.

In addition, the post-2000 momentum was marked by various initiatives such as the Report of the Commission for Africa, spearheaded by UK Prime Minister Tony Blair and the European Consensus on Development. The 2005 World Summit in New York also called for increased aid transfers in order to reach the Millennium Development Goals of halving poverty and hunger by 2015.

The Impact of the Structural Adjustment Programmes

The Brundtland Report and the broader context within which the debates around poverty occurred, also had a wider impact. Among others, it led to deep introspection by the World Bank and the International Monetary Fund (IMF)—the two global financial institutions mandated to respond to underdevelopment—about the effectiveness of their structural adjustment programmes.

The oil and debt crises during the late 1970s created numerous economic problems in sub-Saharan Africa. During the 1980s the World Bank and the IMF responded by creating loan packages for highly indebted poor countries that required them to reduce spending on health and education in favour of debt repayment and the liberalisation of the economy through privatisation and other means.

These measures were not new. The World Bank and the IMF had been attaching conditionalities to their loans since the early 1950s and their policy prescriptions inevitably closely aligned with the free-market economics dominant in the USA, where their secretariats are located and who is the largest contributor to both.

In return for budget and balance of payments support, the Bank and the Fund required African governments to adhere to an agreed set of policy reforms geared towards achieving macroeconomic stability. Perhaps the most significant impact of these structural adjustment programmes was the devaluation of Africa's overvalued currencies to more reasonable levels.

But the negative impact on health, education, poverty and agriculture that followed would resonate for many years and earn both institutions the enduring enmity of many Africans in what has been described as an effective 'race to the bottom'.[6] These painful reforms impacted very negatively on large populations in the recipient countries and offered African leaders and activist academics a ready target.

The conditionalities, generally known as the Washington consensus, put an effective end to national industrial policies that countries as diverse as Ethiopia, Ghana, Kenya, Mauritius, Mozambique, Nigeria, Senegal and Tanzania had tried to implement, albeit with very limited success. Consequently, industrialisation as a development option for Africa was replaced by trade liberalisation, deregulation, the free market and a small state.

The development framework had shifted away from the state as the main engine and instigator of growth to a reliance on markets and the private sector for resource allocation. Henceforth, the role of the state would be limited to policymaking and regulatory functions. This was based on many African states' inability, in the view of the Bank and the Fund, to effectively deliver public goods and limit the abuse of funds.

Whereas development elsewhere had been facilitated through an active role for the state, the corruption and mismanagement by African governments now presented the continent with an impossible situation. It had to develop without the guiding hand of government.

---

[6] See for example, Shah, A., 2013. *Global Issues*. [Online] Available at: http://www.globalissues.org/article/3/structural-adjustment-a-major-cause-of-poverty.

Unable to rapidly improve productivity and with a fast-growing and youthful population, per capita average income levels in Africa peaked in 1980 and declined to 1994 as trade shocks and economic crises took their toll. The percentage of people living in poverty in Africa followed suit and steadily increased.

From 1989 onwards, development assistance from the West—which a number of African states had become addicted to—also shifted ground. The focus shifted to the importance of democracy, good governance and anti-corruption as part of the efforts to correct some of the egregious misuse of public money and abuse of power by a number of African leaders that followed decolonisation and the end of the Cold War.

Africa's Western development partners subsequently invested in civil service reform and efforts to improve public financial management, and helped to set up anti-corruption watchdogs and public audit bodies. Multi-party elections, decentralisation and other methods to encourage greater citizen participation were equally popular. In the process, democracy became associated with liberal economic policies that envisioned a small state and a dominant role for the private sector in development. The problem is that poor countries need an activist, developmental government if they are to engineer an escape from poverty.

By 1999, the IMF had replaced its structural adjustments programme with the Poverty Reduction Growth Facility and placed poverty alleviation at the heart of its efforts. The following year the World Bank admitted that the poor are better off without structural adjustment.[7] Writing for the African Development Bank, John Page notes, 'Structural adjustment had taken place without producing structural change'.[8]

But in the interim it was alleviating Africa's large debt burden that focussed the minds of many in the international development community. Africa's debt peaked twice during these years, first at 79% of gross domestic product (GDP) in 1988 and then slightly lower at 77% in 1995. Whereas a general debt-to-GDP ratio of 60% is generally seen as a responsible ceiling that should not be exceeded, the suggested long-term debt-to-GDP ratio for developing and emerging countries is sometimes set at 40% although there is also evidence that it is the debt trajectory and rate of economic growth rather than the debt level that is more important. Perhaps even more important is

---

[7] Easterly, W., 2001. The Effect of International Monetary Fund and World Bank Programs on Poverty. *Open Knowledge Repository*, Working Paper (No 2517).

[8] African Development Bank Group, 2017. Introductory Remarks: Promoting Sustainable Industrial Policies. In: *Industrialize Africa: Strategies, Policies, Institutions, and Financing*. Côte d'Ivoire: African Development Bank Group, p. 74.

the very high interest rates that African countries generally pay on commercial loans that may go up to five or sixteen percent interest on a ten-year bond.⁹

In response to the alarming levels of debt in many poor countries, the IMF, the World Bank and other creditors began the Heavily Indebted Poor Country (HIPC) Initiative in 1996 that was reviewed and comprehensively expanded in 1999. From 2005 HIPC was complemented by the Multilateral Debt Relief Initiative, a debt relief proposal initially advanced by the G-8 in June 2005.¹⁰

Public debt among low-income countries declined from close to 100% in the early 2000s to a median debt ratio of just over 30% in 2013. By 2018 30 African countries had been assisted (out of the global total of 36 countries that were relieved of US$99 billion in debt). As the HIPC programme matured, the international community has focused on strengthening the links between debt relief and progress in implementing Poverty Reduction Strategies and macroeconomic and structural reform programmes.¹¹

The debate about the role of the state in Africa's development trajectory evolved markedly during this period. The mantra of 'good governance'—defined as 'the manner in which power is exercised in the management of a country's economic and social resources for development'¹²—steadily replaced the need to downsize the state. For donors like the IMF and the World Bank the focus on good governance was a way to respond to the inefficiencies, corruption and predation that had become a defining characteristic of many African governments.

Later the debate would again shift, now to the need to attract and enable foreign direct investment from the private sector as the best means to facilitate growth. In its most recent incarnation the focus is on the importance of domestic resource mobilisation, effectively completing a circle where the role of capable African governments is again being recognised as key to the continent's future.

---

⁹Pescatori, A., Sandri, D., and Simon, J., 2014 Debt and Growth: Is There a Magic Threshold? IMF Working Paper (WP/14/34). [Online] Available at: https://docs.google.com/viewer?url=https%3A%2F%2Fwww.imf.org%2Fexternal%2Fpubs%2Fft%2Fwp%2F2014%2Fwp1434.pdf; Mutize, M., 2020. African Countries Aren't Borrowing Too Much—They're Paying Too Much for Debt. *Quartz Africa*. [Online] 22 February 2020. https://qz.com/africa/1806793/imf-world-bank-are-wrong-africa-is-piling-on-too-much-debt/.

¹⁰World Bank, January 2019. *Debt in Low-Income Countries: A Rising Vulnerability.* [Online] Available at: https://blogs.worldbank.org/developmenttalk/debt-low-income-countries-rising-vulnerability.

¹¹World Bank, 2018. *Heavily Indebted Poor Country (HIPC) Initiative.* [Online] Available at: http://www.worldbank.org/en/topic/debt/brief/hipc.

¹²World Bank, 1992. *Governance and Development.* Washington, DC: The World Bank.

While aid as a portion of government revenues have steadily declined, remittances and private capital flows have both increased significantly in the intervening years. In current dollars, by 2015, personal remittances (US$43 billion) and net foreign direct investment (US$45 billion) to sub-Saharan Africa were approximate to aid flows (US$46 billion).[13]

The general trend suggests a steady decline in aid dependency in the region. For example, in 2015, 22 out of 54 African countries received more foreign direct investment than aid.[14] Since their economies are growing quite rapidly, middle-income countries are experiencing the sharpest declines in aid as a share of total inward flows, despite the fact that the portion of aid that goes to lower-middle-income countries (compared to low-income countries) has remained relatively constant.

The debate about the potential contribution of the Washington consensus to Africa's recent growth rates remains mired in controversy but it is undeniable that the lack of policy certainty and high transaction costs attracted little private investment to Africa outside of the resources sector.[15] And when looking to the future along Africa's current development pathway, commodities will likely continue to drive growth with all its attendant risks and opportunities. This is a concerning trend.

Africa's Growing Dependence on Commodities

Much of Africa's recent growth was enabled by the commodities supercycle that started in 1996 and peaked in 2011. The demand behind the supercycle came from the higher primary export volumes that were required to feed Asia's manufacturing and construction boom. Its recent decline is largely a function of the economic restructuring and lower growth in China. The Arab spring caused a brief spike in oil prices, but the ongoing shale oil and gas revolution in the USA and the economic contraction associated with the COVID-19 crisis will ensure a continued downswing until such time

---

[13]World Bank, n.d. *World Development Indicators*. [Online] Available at: https://datacatalog.worldbank.org/dataset/world-development-indicators.

[14]Angola, Botswana, Cameroon, Republic of Congo, Djibouti, Egypt, Equatorial Guinea, Gabon, Ghana, Lesotho, Mauritania, Mauritius, Morocco, Mozambique, Namibia, Nigeria, Seychelles, South Africa, Sudan, Tunisia, Zambia and Togo. See World Bank, n.d. *World Development Indicators*. [Online] Available at: https://datacatalog.worldbank.org/dataset/world-development-indicators.

[15]See for example; African Development Bank Group, 2017. Introductory Remarks: Promoting Sustainable Industrial Policies. In: *Industrialize Africa: Strategies, Policies, Institutions, and Financing*. Côte d'Ivoire: African Development Bank Group.

as growth in India, globally likely to be the next growth point, reignites the demand for commodities.

Supercycles are not smooth and consequently the upward and downward cycles can vary greatly. Furthermore, each commodity class also has its own pendulum, so that shifts in the price of base metals do not generally correspond with that of livestock, agricultural products or oil, which has evidenced most volatility as the Organization of Petroleum Exporting Countries (OPEC) tries to govern oil prices. For example, despite the 2007/2008 depression that depressed prices for a year thereafter, commodity prices subsequently recovered until the impact of sharp deterioration of the global economic outlook as a result of COVID-19 saw a sharp drop in most commodity prices.

Particularly significant is that during the most recent supercycle the prices for oil, base metals and agricultural produce, all started to increase at roughly the same time. It was therefore generally a stronger and more uniform up and downward cycle than with previous supercycles, lifting economic growth across all regions in the world, including in Africa, hence the more rapid growth prior to the 2008/2009 financial crisis.

When the United Nations Conference on Trade and Development (UNCTAD) released its 2019 report on *The State of Commodity Dependence*, it noted that an increased number of countries, 102 out of 189, were dependent on commodity exports. Nine out of ten sub-Saharan African countries are commodity dependent.[16] Only 82 countries were considered commodity dependent in 2009–2010.[17]

While the number of commodity-dependent countries in Africa has increased markedly in the intervening years, it generally remained static in other global regions, contributing to the relative decline in Africa's competitiveness. Actually, the extent to which African countries are dependent on commodities when measured by value of exports has increased, most of it exported to Europe and increasingly China.

It is unclear exactly when the downturn that started after the 2011 peak will bottom out.[18] Based on the duration of previous cycles it can

---

[16] United Nations, 2019. *The State of Commodity Dependence*. New York: UNCTAD, p. 3.

[17] Ibid. UNCTAD defines a country as dependent on commodities when its commodity exports account for more than 60% of its total merchandise exports in value terms and "strongly commodity export dependent" when this share exceeds 80%.

[18] According to research done by the Bank of Canada, the previous four commodity super cycles have peaked in 1904, 1947 and 1978 and lasted for 33, 29 and 34 years respectively from trough to trough. Commodity prices subsequently declined to 1995. The most recent supercycle peaked in 2011.
Bahattin Büyükşahin, B., Mo, K., and Zmitrowicz, K., 2016. Commodity Price Supercycles: What Are They and What Lies Ahead? In: *Bank of Canada Review*. Ottawa: Bank of Canada, p. 37.

take anywhere from five to 17 years before a general improvement in commodity prices occurs again. On average, full trough-to-trough supercycles take 32 years—but no two supercycles are the same and the length and intensity of each down and upswing varies considerably from cycle to cycle. That said, on the 32-year average we should reach the trough around 2027 and the cycle would then peak at around 2043. It is still too early for any confident forecast as to the impact of COVID-19 on these broad cycles of commodity prices over the medium to long term.

In addition to favourable demographics, the next commodities supercycle will lift African growth rates, but likely to a lesser extent than before the 2008/09 global financial crisis and it may also take several years for demand for commodities to recover from the impact of the COVID-19 pandemic. But the world will still require commodities, even though the resource intensity of growth is declining and that the previous Chinese demand for base commodities is shifting from iron ore, copper and coal to consumer-related commodities such as meat, dairy and apparel. Just how rapid China is growing (in spite of moderating rates in recent months) is difficult to grasp. For example, in the four years from 2014 to 2018, China added the size of the entire economy of Africa to its GDP in market exchange rates. The Chinese economy is already larger than the US economy in purchasing power parity and is expected to overtake the size of the US economy in market exchange rates around 2028.

In addition, a next supercycle (i.e. from around 2030 onward) would be driven by the expected demand for commodities from a rising India that is experiencing a steady improvement in growth rates. Although the world appears to have entered a lower growth trajectory due to having passed the peak relationship between working age and dependents discussed in Chapter 5, the larger global economy will continue to drive a steady demand for commodities. Global GDP will expand by more than 40% by 2030 (from 2018) and by 2040 the world economy would have almost doubled in size (all figures in market exchange rates).

The Challenges of Commodities-Dependent Growth

There is ample evidence that commodity dependence leads to slow and poor quality growth over long time horizons.

Extreme commodity dependence is also closely associated with poor governance and supporters of the 'resource curse' hypothesis argue that a too heavy dependence on energy resources such as oil or gas impedes rather than accelerates economic growth and investment. It may also hinder the broadening of the economic base by impeding value-add in agriculture and manufacturing, while impeding the development of the various institutions of good government.[19]

Some of the severe risks that single-commodity exporters face include the inevitable exposure to price volatility of that commodity (that occurred, for example, in 2014 and again early in 2020 with the collapse of the oil price), the decline in the contribution from other economic sectors (the so-called Dutch disease), an increased likelihood of undemocratic government (since governance is dominated by competition for control over the income stream from its single commodity and not by other considerations such as service delivery), the prevalence of a rentier state (where the state is not accountable to citizens but to special interest groups aligned to the commodity income), pressures to spend within a short-term horizon to maintain support (also to align with surge in commodity incomes) and a greater likelihood of low-quality institutions (the sum impact of all of the above). A recent article by Larry Diamond and Jack Mosbacher summarises it as follows:

> The surge of easy money fuels inflation, fans waste and massive corruption, distorts exchange rates, undermines the competitiveness of traditional export sectors such as agriculture, and preempts the growth of manufacturing … Rather than fostering an entrepreneurial middle class, oil wealth, when controlled by the government, stifles the emergence of an independent business class and swells the power of the state vis-á-vis civil society.[20]

The result is an 'observable correlation between resource abundance and political corruption'.[21]

To date Botswana is the only African country that has successfully developed its resources sector (diamonds) to the general benefit of its populace, yet it too struggles to spread its commodity-led growth beyond a small, privileged elite in a country that has the third highest level of inequality globally.

The result is that resource poor economies generally outperform resource rich countries with South Korea, Japan and Taiwan often cited as the best examples of the former and Nigeria, Angola and Equatorial Guinea as examples of the latter. South Korea, contrasted with Ghana in the previous chapter,

---

[19] Gylfason, T., and Zoega, G., 2006. Natural Resources and Economic Growth: The Role of Investment. *The World Economy*, 29(8), pp. 1091–1115.
[20] Diamond, L., and Mosbacher, J., 2013. Petroleum to the People: Africa's coming Resource Curse—And How to Avoid It. *Foreign Affairs*, September/October, pp. 87–88.
[21] Ibid.

has virtually no natural resources of any value. In 1962 the country exported mostly raw materials like fish, rice, iron ore and unprocessed silk while today it boasts a well-diversified export portfolio that includes electronics, cars, ships and other high-end machinery.

By contrast, Nigeria's main exports in 1962 were assorted agricultural products—mostly groundnuts, soybeans and cocoa beans—and crude petroleum. In 2014, crude petroleum and liquefied petroleum gases accounted for about 85% of Nigeria's total exports. In 1962 GDP per capita in South Korea was about half that of Nigeria, in 2018 it is about sixfold larger.

To a degree the CFA franc that is practically still used in fourteen west and central African states has the same negative impact as a high level of commodity export dependence.

The original meaning of CFA in 1945, when it was established, was Colonies Francaises d'Afrique (French Colonies in Africa), accurately reflecting its intent. In this arrangement participating states had their currency pegged to the French franc and, as from 1999, to the euro. Participant states needed to keep half their foreign reserves in France, on which the French treasury paid 0.75% interest and agreed to a French representative on the currency union's board. The arrangement provided monetary stability, controlled inflation and supported trade with Europe but made it very difficult for other sectors in the economy to establish themselves since it kept the exchange rates artificially high, in spite of a once-off 1994 devaluation intended to boost exports from the region. Since a number of these countries are also petro-states, heavily dependent upon oil experts, they are unable to go up the value-added curve.

A December 2019 announcement by eight Francophone members of the West African Economic and Monetary Union (generally known by the French acronym UEMOA) to rename the CFA to the Eco changed some of the details. As from 2020 Eco members would no longer keep half of their reserves in the French Treasury and there would no longer be a French representative on the board, but the Eco will still be linked to the Euro. Without a much more flexible currency arrangement that reflects the relative economic conditions in West and Central Africa, the Eco is unlikely to differ from the CFA in its impact.

In much of low-income Africa people are moving from subsistence agriculture in rural areas to informal jobs in the urban services sector. Investment and jobs are often limited to capital-intensive commodity enclaves such as in northern Mozambique's gas fields with little or no forward or backward linkages into the surrounding economy. And the few jobs that are created through these megaprojects do little to provide employment or create local value chains. They provide jobs for a small number of expatriates and generate large streams of revenue for governments, but generally enclave economics don't benefit national economies. Yet commodity-based enclave development is often the norm.

Rising Debt Levels

Debt has also resurfaced as a serious challenge. In a wide-ranging study on the relationship between debt and growth Carmen Reinhart and Kenneth Rogoff concluded: 'When external debt reaches 60 percent of GDP, annual growth declines by about two percent'.[22] On average, Africa's low and low-middle-income countries consistently had debt levels in excess of 60% of GDP from the mid-1980s for almost two subsequent decades, levels that clearly contributed to slow growth.

After 2011, when commodity prices declined, commodity exporters such as Angola, Chad, Republic of Congo, Niger, Nigeria and Zambia were the first to be particularly badly affected. Rising debt had also been driven by a number of other factors such as internal conflict (Burundi), the impact of epidemics such as Ebola (in Liberia and Sierra Leone) and fraud/corruption (Mozambique and The Gambia). Finally, a larger liquidity crunch, delays in the start of natural resource production, and weaknesses in revenue administration contributed to large increases in debt in Benin, Cameroon, Djibouti, Ethiopia, Ghana, Kenya, Senegal, São Tomé and Princìpe, Rwanda, Togo, Uganda and Zimbabwe.[23]

In its 2018 Regional Economic Outlook for Sub-Saharan Africa, the IMF noted that public debt rose above 50% of GDP in 22 countries at the end of 2016, up from ten countries in 2013. 'Debt servicing costs are becoming a burden, especially in oil-producing countries, and Angola, Gabon and Nigeria are expected to absorb more than 60% of government revenues in 2017', the IMF said.[24]

It was against this background that the announcements of additional large loans from China (such as on the margins of the Forum on China–Africa Cooperation meeting held in September 2018 in Beijing) elicited concern

---

[22] Reinhart, C. M., and Rogoff, K. S., 2010. Growth in a Time of Debt. *American Economic Review: Papers & Proceedings 100*, pp. 573–578.
[23] International Monetary Fund, 2018. *Macroeconomic Developments and Prospects in Low-Income Developing Countries*. Washington, DC: IMF, pp. 39–40.
[24] International Monetary Fund, 2018. *Regional Economic Outlook. Sub-Saharan Africa: Capital Flows and the Future of Work*. Washington, DC: World Economic and Financial Surveys, p. 6.

that debt levels in sub-Saharan Africa were rapidly becoming unsustainable. Exact information is hard to decipher since China does not release comprehensive data, but it seems that interest-bearing loans from the Chinese government, banks and contractors have gone from almost nothing in 2000 to US$143 billion in 2017.[25] To some analysts it appeared that Africans had to borrow money from the IMF to repay China but others argued that it was only in Zambia, Djibouti and the Republic of the Congo where Chinese loans were a significant contributor to high risk of debt distress.[26] Actually, Chinese lending appears to have resulted in an increase of nearly four percent of debt-to-GDP of low-income countries in recent years while that of multilateral institutions like the World Bank had seen an equal decline.

Recently, a systematic comparison of Chinese and World Bank lending terms found that Chinese lending to developing countries is 'generally offered on less concessional terms than those offered by Western and multilateral creditors, although more favourable than the market would offer'.[27] Always careful about the associated tide of criticism, in 2019 Beijing announced that it would establish an analysis framework on debt sustainability for Belt and Road Initiative projects and improve transparency.[28] The shift in debt away from the concessional (i.e. below market) rates offered by the World Bank and IMF towards China has also seen other effects such as higher interest rates, shorter maturities and shorter grace periods.[29]

All of this has been dramatically accentuated by COVID-19.

---

[25] John Hopkins School of Advanced International Studies, Data: Chinese Loans to Africa. [Online] Available at: http://www.sais-cari.org/data-chinese-loans-to-africa.

[26] Moore, W. G, 17 September 2018, The Language of "Debt-Trap Diplomacy" Reflects Western Anxieties, Not African Realities. Quartz. [Online] Available at: https://qz.com/1391770/the-anxious-chorus-around-chinese-debt-trap-diplomacy-doesnt-reflect-african-realities/. Also see *The Economist*, 2018. *Reckless in Lusaka: Zambia's Looming Debt Crisis Is a Warning for the Rest of Africa.* [Online] Available at: https://www.economist.com/leaders/2018/09/15/zambias-looming-debt-crisis-is-a-warning-for-the-rest-of-africa?frsc=dg%7Ce; Neuweg, I., 2018. What Types of Energy Does China Finance with Its Development Aid? [Online] Available at: http://www.lse.ac.uk/GranthamInstitute/news/china-energy-development-aid/. Also see Brautigam, D., 2019. Is China the World's Loan Shark? [Online] Available at: www.nytimes.com/2019/04/26/opinion/china-belt-road-initiative.html.

[27] Morris, S., Parks, B., and Gardner, A., 2020 Chinese and World Bank Lending Terms: A Systematic Comparison Across 157 Countries and 15 Years, 2 April 2020, Center for Global Development Paper 170. [Online] Available at: https://www.cgdev.org/publication/chinese-and-world-bank-lending-terms-systematic-comparison.

[28] Yao, K. China in Bid to Allay Fears of Debt Risk in Its Belt and Road Initiative Business Day, 25 April 2019. [Online] Available at: https://www.businesslive.co.za/bd/world/asia/2019-04-25-china-in-bid-to-allay-fears-of-debt-risk-in-its-belt-and-road-initiative/.

[29] Morris, S., Parks B., and Gardner, A., 2020. In Global COVID-19 Response, New CGD Research Shows China Should Lead on Poor Country Debt Relief, Center for Global Development, 2 April 2020. [Online] Available at: https://www.cgdev.org/blog/global-covid-19-response-new-cgd-research-shows-china-should-lead-poor-country-debt-relief.

In April 2020, the IMF released its first post-COVID-19 growth forecasts, now indicating a sharper global growth contraction than even during the 2008/2009 financial crisis, although, perhaps optimistically, expecting a sharp recovery in 2021. Global growth for 2020 was revised downward by 6.4 percentage points (its forecast is now for −3% growth in 2020) with a bounce to global growth at 5.8% in 2021.[30]

As the impact of COVID-19 has become more evident, the Group of 20 countries agreed, in April 2020, to suspend debt service payments for 76 low-income countries, including 40 in sub-Saharan Africa, eligible for the World Bank's most concessional lending via the International Development Association. In related news, the IMF approved six months of debt service relief for 25 low-income countries, including 19 in Africa, and approved additional funding support for several.[31] Slow growth will transform Africa's debt challenge into a full-blown crisis.

The Third Wave of Democratisation in Africa

Contrary to the general trend elsewhere, Africa's recent cycle of commodities-led growth was accompanied by unprecedented democratisation. The world experienced various surges in democracy in the previous two centuries, with the third wave of democracy cresting between 1989 and 1993 with the collapse of the former Soviet Union and its immediate aftermath.

Prior to that there was little to distinguish independent Africa from colonial Africa in terms of the quality of governance. The events in the Soviet Union changed things as pro-democracy movements and reforms washed across the continent.

According to the *Freedom in the World* annual index published by Freedom House, levels of democracy in Africa increased by 12 percentage points from 1988 to 1994 with 25 out of 54 countries classified as free or partly free.[32] The West had triumphed, or so it appeared, and with the subsequent

---

[30] IMF, 2020, World Economic Outlook, April 2020: Chapter 1. [Online] Available at https://www.imf.org/en/Publications/WEO/Issues/2020/04/14/weo-april-2020.

[31] Gandi, D., Golubski, C. 2020. International Community Looks to Support Africa with Debt Relief, Health Aid, Brookings Institution, 18 April 2020. [Online] Available at: https://www.brookings.edu/blog/africa-in-focus/2020/04/18/africa-in-the-news-african-governments-and-multilaterals-address-covid-19-emergency-debt-relief/.

[32] In 1988 only 17 out of the 50 African countries included in the Freedom in the World survey could be classified as 'free' or 'partly free'. Shortly after the collapse of the Berlin Wall, in 1994, the organisation estimated that 25 out of 54 countries were now 'free' or 'partly free'. Freedom House, 2018. *Freedom in the World.* [Online] Available at: https://freedomhouse.org/report/freedom-world/freedom-world-2018.

concerns for elections, human rights and accountability (rather than ideological orientation), came the closely associated belief in liberal capitalism.

However, history has shown that democracy is generally more resilient above certain minimum levels of income and education, when a solid web of institutions and the rule of law are able to constrain the misuse and abuse of state institutions.[33] In countries with low levels of income, democracy is often fragile, largely because the formal institutions, rules and norms upon which it rests and depends for effective functioning are absent or insufficiently developed.[34]

When comparing the average levels of democracy in low- and upper-middle-income countries on the continent to that of other countries with similar levels of education and income elsewhere in the world, Africa is more democratic than one would expect.[35] In fact, improvements in the levels of democracy have outpaced improvements in levels of income and education in Africa. Hence, democracy here rests on somewhat fragile foundations.[36]

The fact that levels of democracy are somewhat out of sync with levels of income and education could be attributed to a number of factors. The conditional engagement by Western donors over several decades created space for civil society, a free press and competitive elections that otherwise would not have emerged or at least not as rapidly. Moreover, a series of national democratisation conferences in French-speaking Africa (Benin, Gabon, Congo, Mali, Togo, Niger and the Democratic Republic of Congo)

---

[33] The American social scientist Barrington Moore popularised the notion of 'no bourgeois, no democracy', denoting the fact that minimum levels of economic development were required for democracy. See Moore, B., 1966. *Social Origins of Dictatorship and Democracy: Lord and Peasant in the Making of the Modern World*. Boston: Beacon Press. For more recent work see Przeworski, A., and Limongi, F., 1993. Political Regimes and Economic Growth. *Journal of Economic Perspectives*, 7(3), pp. 51–69.

[34] Glaeser, E. L., Ponzetto, G., and Shleifer, A., 2006. Why Does Democracy Need Education? *NBER Working Paper*, Issue No. 12128, pp. 3–4.

[35] Varieties of Democracy (V-Dem) distinguishes between five high-level indices of democracy ideals: electoral, liberal, participatory, deliberative and egalitarian, and collects data to measure these and numerous component indices and indicators. It is a large collaborative project, with headquarters at the V-Dem Institute at the Department of Political Science at the University of Gothenburg, Sweden. In version 8 of its data release (June 2018) the project now covers 201 political units with historical data from 1789 to 2017.

[36] Various large datasets track and measure comparative levels of democracy globally including the Varieties of Democracy or V-Dem (Gothenburg University) and Polity datasets (Center for Systemic Peace) with their results now going back more than a century. Others, such as from the Economist Intelligence Unit are more recent and less compelling.

served to confront the economic and political crisis that had enveloped these countries and ignited a thirst for pro-democracy reforms.[37]

But the most important reason for the relative high levels of democracy in Africa is simply the lived experience of decades of brutal authoritarianism. Numerous opinion surveys, such as those conducted by Afrobarometer in more than 35 African countries, point to the strong and growing support for democracy in Africa.[38]

For decades the military dominated politics and often yesterday's liberation heroes became today's autocrats.

Muammar Gaddafi in Libya and Omar Bongo Ondimba of Gabon were Africa's longest modern rules. Teodoro Obiang Nguema Mbasogo of Equatorial Guinea has been in power since 1979, i.e. for 40 years, a number only equalled by Haile Selassie of Ethiopia. Paul Biya has presided over Cameroon since 1982 and King Mswati lll of eSwatini and Yoweri Museveni of Uganda since 1986. José Eduardo dos Santos of Angola was president for 36 years and Robert Mugabe of Zimbabwe for 35 years. When he was toppled by his military in April 2019, Sudan's Omar Al-Bashir had been in power for 30 years.

Long-term incumbency often leads to looting of the state and almost inevitably culminates in a violent uprising and turbulent transition. Mobutu Sese Seko of the former Zaïre, now the Democratic Republic of the Congo, allegedly stole at least US$4 billion while serving as president.[39] More recently, Teodoro Nguema Obiang—vice president of Equatorial Guinea and son of the current president—was accused of embezzling more than US$100 million. Human Rights Watch describes the situation in that country as one where the state foregoes investment in health and education in favour of grandiose infrastructure projects that really function as 'conduits for enriching the ruling elite'.[40]

The problem is that, with few exceptions, Africans don't yet benefit from substantive democracy. In many countries, Africans go through the motions

---

[37] Robinson, P.T., July 1994. The National Conference Phenomenon in Francophone Africa. *Comparative Studies in Society and History,* 36(3), pp. 575–610. Cambridge University Press. [Online] Available at: https://www.cambridge.org/core/journals/comparative-studies-in-society-and-history/article/national-conference-phenomenon-in-francophone-africa/F20505B66CA65C8D71ACBB7919ADE1D0; also see Banzet, A., 2017. #CAFDO2017: The First Francophone African Conference on Open Data and Open Government. [Online] Available at: https://www.opengovpartnership.org/stories/cafdo2017-the-first-francophone-african-conference-on-open-data-and-open-government/.
[38] Afrobarometer, n.d. [Online] Available at: http://afrobarometer.org.
[39] Transparency International, n.d. *Seize Mobutu's Wealth or Lose Your Own Money, Western Governments Told.* [Online] Available at: https://www.transparency.org/news/pressrelease/seize_mobutus_wealth_or_lose_your_own_money_western_governments_told.
[40] Saadoun, S., 2017. *Human Rights Watch.* [Online] Available at: https://www.hrw.org/news/2017/07/10/trial-one-africas-most-corrupt-politicians-shows-fighting-graft-global.

of regular elections but incumbent leaders have become adept at interfering in the electoral process, as recently seen in countries as diverse as Zambia, Cameroon and Uganda.[41]

Incumbents will even change the constitution to retain the presidency if that is what it takes.[42] In January 2019 in the Democratic Republic of the Congo, outgoing president Laurent Kabila blatantly rigged the presidential and national assembly election held on 30 December 2018 to instal himself as the power behind newly elected president Félix Tshisekedi.[43] The rest of the continent remained silent, thankful that the transfer of power (if that is what it could be called) occurred peacefully.

Leaders in these countries invest significant resources in ensuring a favourable electoral outcome by constraining the democratic space. This is done by rigging the registration process, running interference (for instance, by tying opposition candidates down in spurious legal cases or barring public gatherings), misusing state resources to dispense patronage, controlling the diet of information (particularly through the abuse of public media in favour of the ruling party) and, if all else fails, directly manipulating the results or frustrating any subsequent legal challenge.

The situation is further complicated by the fact that competitive politics in a multi-ethnic context generally rely on the mobilisation of ethno-linguistic groupings for political support.

For decades African leaders have primarily taken their cue from the West in pursuit of their governance and social model. Today autocratic China is increasingly calling the shots. Since 2000, China has embarked on a vigorous process of courting African states with its offers to build infrastructure financed by Chinese banks as it sought a new role for its excess capacity, sometimes as part of its Belt and Road Initiative. However, while their leaders increasingly look East, Africa's citizens generally continue to look to the West.

---

[41] In Gabon the incumbent, Ali Bongo Ondimba, son of the previous ruler of some 41 years, 'won' with 49.8% of the vote, while the presidential candidate of the Démocratie Nouvelle party, Jean Ping, received 48.23%. This followed the delivery of implausible results that boosted the national voter turnout from 59.46 to 99.93% in Haut-Ogooué, where Bongo won 95.5% of the votes cast. In Zambia numerous malpractices and irregularities were reported. President Edgar Lungu of the Patriotic Front was eventually declared the winner with 50.35% of the vote, with a lead of 100 530 over rival Hakainde Hichilema of the United Party for National Development.

[42] Paul Biya of Cameroon, serving as the prime minister, has been in power since 1975, but has only technically been president since 1982. If one includes his time as prime minister he comes in at 43 years.

[43] Wolters, S., 2019. *Will This Election Change the DRC?* [Online] Available at: https://issafrica.org/iss-today/will-this-election-change-the-drc.

Democratisation and economic growth is buoyed by Africa's unfolding urban transition. The question now is what kind of urbanisation is taking place on the continent and how does it impact on the political situation?

Africa's Slow Pace of Urbanisation

Historically, urbanisation has gone hand in hand with growth and development. A 2010 analysis by the McKinsey Global Institute found that the shift from rural to urban employment could account for 20–50% of productivity growth in Africa.[44]

Yet, by historical standards urbanisation is taking place very late in Africa. At the time of independence in 1960 less than one-fifth of Africans could likely be classified as urban. By 1980 that number had increased to around 27%, by 2000 to 34% and should, by 2037 or thereabout, cross the halfway mark. The rest of the world crossed that point shortly after the turn of the century. Africa is likely to only get to the two-thirds mark around 2070 compared to 2040 for the rest of the world. The impact of climate change may, of course, accelerate this process.

East/Horn of Africa is the most rural part of the continent by a long stretch, and likely to stay that way with levels of urbanisation currently almost 30 percentage points below North Africa, the most urban region. West Africa is experiencing the most rapid rates of urbanisation (average rates are currently roughly on par with Central Africa) and will, beyond mid-century, approach rates of urbanisation in North or Southern Africa. Currently Gabon, Djibouti and Libya are the most urbanised countries and Malawi, Rwanda, Niger and Burundi the least urbanized, with less than 20% of their populations considered urban.

However, contrary to the historical experience in much of the rest of the world, Africans currently don't move to urban areas in response to existing job opportunities in the manufacturing sector (that would increase productivity), but rather to escape the destitution and poverty of rural existence. Consequently, poverty is urbanizing and urban slums and informal settlements are expanding.[45] Sharp income inequalities in many African cities also mean that

---

[44] Roxburgh, C., Dörr, N., Leke, A., Tazi-Riffi, A., van Wamelen, A., Lund, S., Chironga, M., Alatovik, T., Atkins, C., Terfous, N., and Zeino-Mahmalat, 2010. *Lions on the Move: The Progress and Potential of African Economies*. Brussels: McKinsey Global Institute, p. 19.

[45] Ravallion, M., Chen, S., and Sangraula, P., 2007. The Urbanization of Global Poverty. *World Bank Research Digest*, 1(4).

the contribution of economic growth to poverty reduction is limited. As a result, Africa has more urban poor than any other region.

The result of the foregoing is that Africa's urban population growth is the fastest globally although from a low base. Each year urban Africa grows by an estimated 20 million people and, by 2040, that number will be more than 30 million every year. By 2030 Africa will host six of the world's 41 megacities. Cairo, Lagos, Kinshasa, Johannesburg, Luanda and Dar es Salaam will have more than 10 million inhabitants each and 17 African cities will have a population of more than five million each.[46] The African Economic Outlook 2016 predicted that Africa could see its slum population triple by 2050 as population growth and urbanisation without industrialisation proceeds apace.[47]

The move from rural subsistence farming to urban informal employment in low-end services is positive in that it is moderately growth enhancing. However, the nature and delay in Africa's urbanisation is a significant drag on economic transformation.

It is also much easier and less expensive to provide bulk services such as clean water, sanitation and electricity to people in denser settlements than to a population spread out across large rural areas. Writing for the International Growth Centre in 2016, Paul Collier succinctly summarised the challenge and the opportunity as follows:

> At its best, urbanisation can be the essential motor of economic development, rapidly lifting societies out of mass poverty. At its worst, it results in concentrations of squalor and disaffection which ferment political fragility. To date, African urbanisation has been dysfunctional, the key indication being that cities have not generated enough productive jobs.[48]

Unless leaders are able to reap the benefits of the greater economies of scale that is offered within an urban setting, Africa's accelerating urbanisation will come with considerable risks. The management of its urban areas will present African leadership with immense challenges.

Urbanisation has powerful socio-political implications and it has become an important consideration in explaining the rise of populism in the West

---

[46] Leke, A., Chironga, M., and Desvaux, G., 2018. *Africa's Overlooked Business Revolution*. [Online] Available at: https://www.mckinsey.com/featured-insights/middle-east-and-africa/africas-overlooked-business-revolution?cid=other-eml-alt-mkq-mck-oth-1811&hlkid=d07ce11e35584866845b18ad9b7c7578&hctky=9322113&hdpid=9fc500fa-86ef-4249-87f0-d873aea796b9.

[47] AFDB., OECD DEV., UNDP, 2016. *African Economic Outlook 2016. Special Theme: Sustainable Cities and Structural Transformation*. Abidjan: African Development Bank Group.

[48] Collier, P., 2016. *African Urbanisation: An Analytic Policy Guide*. London: International Growth Centre.

and, in Africa, urban areas are first to turn away from support of the governing party evident in cities as diverse as Algiers, Addis Ababa, Harare and Johannesburg. Like elsewhere in the world, Africa urbanites also tend to be much more politically engaged than ruralites. Inevitably, it is in the capital city that support first goes to opposition parties. In Zimbabwe, the ruling Zanu(PF) party has therefore run an extraordinarily violent campaign over several decades to keep the country's population dominantly rural and under its firm control.

Whereas urban populations are more cosmopolitan and often younger, rural populations are generally older and politically more conservative.[49] Consequently, there is usually a marked difference in attitude between rural and urban people. 'The young, regardless of where they live, tend to associate more with urban outlooks',[50] Auerswald and Joon write.

The Current Path Scenario

In this section, I briefly summarise some of additional characteristics to that in Chapter 1 of Africa to 2040 along the Current Path forecast within the International Futures forecasting platform (IFs), namely demographics, the composition of the African economy and GDP, as well as rates of poverty, and compare it to the global trends.

The IFs Current Path forecast is that Africa's total population will increase from 1276 million in 2018 to 2115 million by 2040. At that point the global population will number 9210 million people of which 23% will be African compared to 17% in 2018.

Figure 2.1 presents the total population in Africa from 1980 (477 million), and breaks out the five countries that, by 2040, would have the largest population in the continent. Nigeria's large population historically constitutes around 15% of Africa's population and will, by 2040, constitute about 17%. With the exception of Nigeria and Egypt, consistently the top two, the top population rankings have shifted over time. In 2004 Ethiopia's burgeoning population surpassed that of Egypt, for example. And while, in 2018, South Africa was still at number five it will be overtaken by Tanzania in 2020.

Figure 2.2 presents the size of the total African economy at market exchange rate in 2018 (US$2.9 trillion) and 2040 (US$7.2 trillion) and breaks out the economies that, by 2040, would be the ten largest. Nigeria, the

---

[49] Philip, A., and Joon, Y., 2018. *The New York Times*. [Online] Available at: https://www.nytimes.com/2018/05/22/opinion/populist-populism-fertility-rates.html.
[50] Ibid.

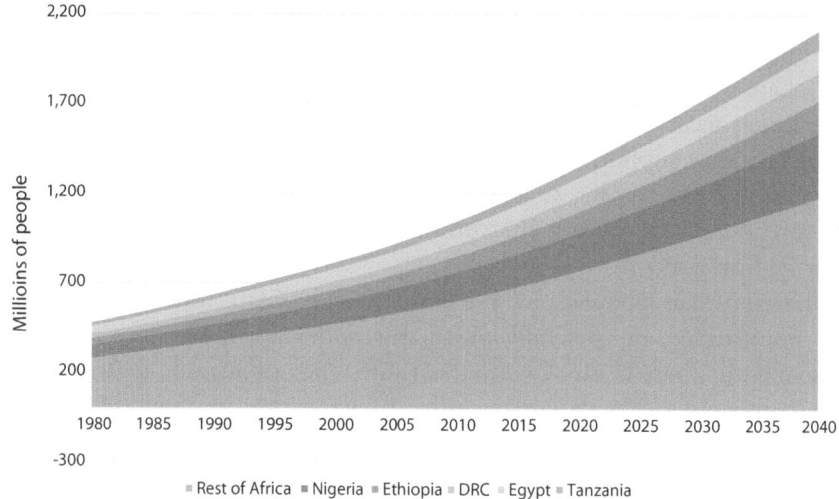

Fig. 2.1 Africa's population 1980 to 2040 with top five by 2040 (*Source* Historical data from United Nations Population Division 2019 medium term forecast, forecast in IFs 7.45)

continent's largest economy, constituted around 0.6% of the global economy in 2018 and, by 2040, it should constitute around 0.8% of the global economy.

Of all the indications of progress, levels of extreme poverty is perhaps the most meaningful in Africa. Poverty has many dimensions ranging from health and education levels to income and how disempowered people feel. Since poverty also has a subjective side, i.e. how it makes people feel about important aspects of their lives, the different dimensions to poverty and how it can be measured is part of an ongoing debate.[51]

In recent years, broader measures of poverty have gained increased support, such as the Multidimensional Poverty Index that focuses on a set of tangible goods and services without which people might be defined as poor.[52] Different regions also use different measures to more accurately reflect poverty in their member states. For example, the European Union typically uses a relative poverty line that is set at 50 or 60% of national median income.

---

[51] Carolina, R., and Monica, J., 2018. *United Nations Development Programme: Human Development Reports*. [Online] Available at: http://hdr.undp.org/en/content/measuring-multidimensional-poverty-leaving-no-one-behind.

[52] See Oxford Poverty and Human Development Initiative, Global Multidimensional Poverty Index. [Online] https://ophi.org.uk/multidimensional-poverty-index/.

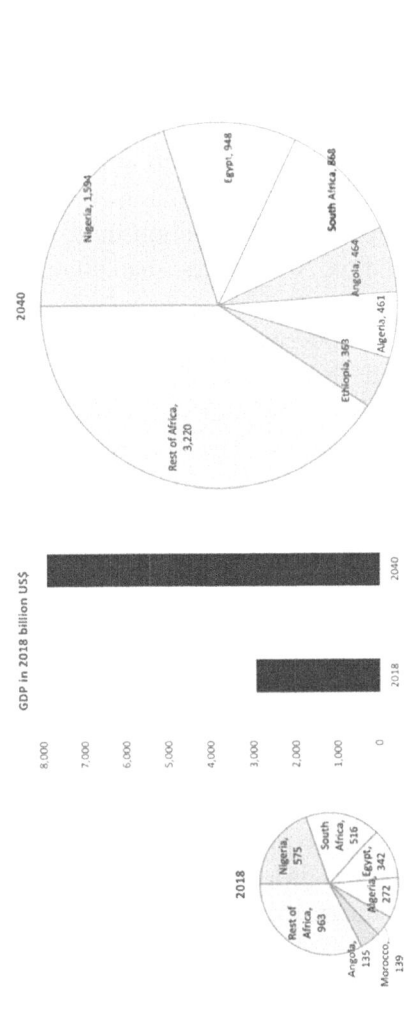

Fig. 2.2 Country composition of the African economy in 2018 and 2040 (in bn US$) (Source IFs 7.45 initialising from International Monetary Fund World Economic Outlook 2017)

For many years the international community used a single income-based definition of extreme poverty for the purposes of cross-country comparisons. It was first set at US$1.00, then US$1.25 and more recently US$1.90 per person per day. Each was successively set in purchasing power parity, the latest in 2011 constant dollars. That value was, in turn, anchored in the poverty thresholds used by some of the world's poorest countries since national poverty lines inevitably increase as national incomes rise. Using the US$1.90 threshold, 36% of Africa's total population is considered extremely poor, a ratio that will decline to 33% by 2030 and 24% by 2040, with the continent experiencing an average GDP growth rate of 4.7% to 2040. Due to rapid population growth, by 2040, 513 million Africans would therefore live in extreme poverty compared to 458 million in 2018. Extreme poverty in the rest of the world would, in 2040, be less than 90 million people, down from 320 million in 2018.

In addition to the US$1.90 international poverty line, in October 2017, the World Bank announced that it will also be reporting poverty rates using three new international poverty lines, namely a lower-middle-income threshold set at US$3.20 per person per day, an upper-middle-income line set at US$5.50 per person per day and US$22.70 for high-income countries.[53]

Although Western and Eastern Africa have Africa's largest regional populations of people living in extreme poverty, the use of country income categories is an important step in understanding a growing consensus that poverty was relative—it differed between rich and poor countries and that it is different to be poor in the DRC as opposed to Algeria, never mind the difference between poverty in Kinshasa and Algiers.

Previously, using US$1.90, North Africa was the only region in Africa that would achieve the goal of eliminating extreme poverty as set out in the 2030 Agenda for Sustainable Development headline goal. In fact as a group it has already done so (except for Mauritania) with the portion of its extremely poor population at below three percent. Since the countries in North Africa have all graduated to either low-middle or upper-middle-income status, extreme poverty has now suddenly 'increased' when applying the two additional poverty lines relevant to Africa (US$3.20 and US$5.50). The Bank has, however, made it clear that for the purposes of achieving the headline goal on eliminating extreme poverty by 2030 it will continue to apply only the US$1.90 line since shifting the goalposts in this dramatic manner several years into the SDG process would not make practical sense.

---

[53]Ferreira, F., and Sánchez-Páramo, C., *2017*. A Richer Array of International Poverty Lines. *Worldbank Blogs*, 13 October 2017. [Online] Available at: http://blogs.worldbank.org/developmenttalk/richer-array-international-poverty-lines.

Looking at this Current Path forecast on poverty, the impact of Africa's very rapid population growth should be clear. African economies need to grow at an exceptionally high rate to reduce poverty under these circumstances. In fact, while it was impossible for Africa to reach the 2030 target to eliminate extreme poverty when using the single US$1.90 poverty line, the goalposts are now very distant indeed.

More than any other single indicator, the Current Path forecast of the expected increase in poverty for the next three decades underpins the reason for understanding what else needs to be done to change Africa's development prospects. In the next chapter, I turn to the first requirement for this change namely the importance of health.

Open Access This chapter is licensed under the terms of the Creative Commons Attribution 4.0 International License (http://creativecommons.org/licenses/by/4.0/), which permits use, sharing, adaptation, distribution and reproduction in any medium or format, as long as you give appropriate credit to the original author(s) and the source, provide a link to the Creative Commons license and indicate if changes were made.

The images or other third party material in this chapter are included in the chapter's Creative Commons license, unless indicated otherwise in a credit line to the material. If material is not included in the chapter's Creative Commons license and your intended use is not permitted by statutory regulation or exceeds the permitted use, you will need to obtain permission directly from the copyright holder.

3

Health

Abstract In this chapter Cilliers covers Africa's unique epidemiological history from the early migration of homo sapiens to the devastation of HIV/AIDS and, more recently, the unfolding impact of COVID-19. It explains how humans' proximity to nature, slow urbanisation and Africa's distinct climatic conditions have led to an unusually high burden of communicable diseases, particularly the HIV/AIDS pandemic. The chapter also explains the double-burden of communicable and non-communicable disease evident in Africa. The chapter highlights the central role that infrastructural improvements and urban planning play in supporting better health outcomes and impact that poor basic infrastructure and lack of urban planning has in much of Africa. The chapter places a particular emphasis on the central role of potable water and water-borne sanitation in preventing the spread of disease. Finally, scenario analysis is used to demonstrate the relationship between health and economics.

Keywords Disease · Infectious diseases · Non-communicable diseases · HIV/AIDS · Homo sapiens · Safe water · Sanitation · Urbanisation · Infrastructure · Human development

Learning Objectives

– Understand Africa's unique health challenges in a historical context
– Have a better awareness of origins, spread and impact of the HIV/AIDS epidemic

- Know the difference between communicable and non-communicable disease
- Be able to define the double-burden of disease
- Understand the relationship between urbanisation, infrastructure and health.

Homo sapiens evolved in Africa around 300,000 years ago and, although there is evidence of previous waves of migration, only successfully migrated from Africa some 70,000 years ago. Human DNA and archaeologists confirm that all humans who have ancestors outside of Africa today come from a single small group of migrants and not from earlier waves. About 50,000 years ago, they spread along the southern coast of Asia to Oceania, and eventually to Europe—a process that occurred over several thousand years. In the process Homo sapiens eventually displaced Neanderthals and eventually emerged as the dominant species globally. This was not a linear process and there is ample evidence that Homo sapiens, Neanderthals and others interbred and even cohabited.[1]

Early humans gained an initial health reprieve that lasted for several thousand years when they moved out of Africa for cooler regions with fewer insect-borne diseases and 'the many parasites and disease organisms that had evolved in parallel with the human species'.[2] As a result they multiplied rapidly in these new areas.

The development of agriculture and farming was key to humanity's rapid increase in numbers as it increased food production and allowed much higher population densities although density in turn bred new diseases. Larger population concentrations caused competition and sometimes conflict between people over grazing, land, food and status that required political organisation and further role differentiation. Competition spurred innovation and technological advancement.[3]

In contrast to the situation that developed elsewhere, large parts of ancient Africa's interior appears to have been characterised by very low population densities very likely as a result of the scourge of sleeping sickness and

---

[1] Research findings are constantly being updated. For the most recent findings see Harvati, K., Röding, C., Bosman, A. M., Karakostis, F. A., Grün, R., Stringer, C., Karkanas, P., Thompson, N. C., Koutoulidis, V., Moulopoulos, L. A., Gorgoulis, V. G., and Kouloukoussa, M. Article 2019 Apidima Cave Fossils Provide Earliest Evidence of Homo Sapiens in Eurasia. *Nature*, 10 July 2019, https://www.nature.com/articles/s41586-019-1376-z.
[2] Reader, J., 1998. *Africa: A Biography of the Continent.* New York: Penguin Books, p. 234.
[3] Diamond, J., 2015. *Guns, Germs and Steel: The Fates of Human Societies.* New York City: W. W. Norton & Company, p. 386.

other vector-borne diseases, such as malaria. Geography, and hence climate, therefore limited population growth in Africa compared to other regions.

Vector-borne diseases are illnesses caused by parasites, viruses and bacteria that are transmitted to humans by insects such as mosquitoes, ticks and tsetse flies that are commonly found in tropical and subtropical regions such as in Central Africa and places where access to safe drinking water and sanitation is limited. In temperate zones, such as much of Europe, parts of Asia and North Africa, the annual seasonal fluctuations serves as a natural constraint on the breeding cycle of insects.[4] In Central, West and East Africa where Homo sapiens originated, this cycle is not similarly disrupted, with the result that sub-Saharan Africa has a constant high burden of vector-borne diseases, come summer, autumn, winter or spring.

Malaria, the most deadly vector-borne disease, is particularly prevalent in Africa. The continent also accounts for 34 of the 47 countries prone to yellow fever outbreak and about 40% of the global burden of lymphatic filariasis (elephantiasis).[5] Today, Africa is still home to 16 of the 30 countries listed by the World Health Organisation (WHO) as having a high burden of tuberculosis, though none are under the top five.[6] Diseases including yellow fever and sleeping sickness were endemic, and insect-borne diseases also prevented the use of the horse, ox or camel, thereby limiting opportunities for more rapid progress.[7]

The belt of open Savannah south of the Sahara and north of the tropical rain forests in central and western Africa eventually became an exception to the high burden of vector-borne diseases. Higher population densities allowed these regions to experience a modest agricultural revolution, although not on the same magnitude as seen elsewhere in the world.[8]

Nature eventually reasserted itself into humanity's new habitats outside of Africa. In fact, most of today's most prominent infectious diseases only emerged in the last 11,000 years, following the rise of agriculture. Larger

---

[4] Wolfe, N. D., Dunavan, C. P., and Diamond, J., 2012. Origins of Major Human Infectious Diseases. In: *Institute of Medicine. Improving Food Safety Through a One Health Approach: Workshop Summary.* Washington: National Academies Press. Also Reader, J., 1998. *Africa: A Biography of the Continent.* New York: Penguin Books, p. 242.
[5] World Health Organization, 2018. *Lymphatic Filariasis.* [Online] Available at: https://www.who.int/news-room/fact-sheets/detail/lymphatic-filariasis; World Health Organization, 2018. Yellow Fever. [Online] Available at: https://www.who.int/news-room/fact-sheets/detail/yellow-fever.
[6] World Health Organization, 2018. *Global Tuberculosis Report 2018.* Geneva: World Health Organization.
[7] Aydon, C., 2009. *A Brief History of Mankind: An Introduction to 150,000 Years of Human History.* Philadelphia: Running Press, p. 125.
[8] John Reader argues that this relates to the poor and hard soils on great parts of the continent that would not have allowed ploughing. Reader, J., 1998. *Africa: A Biography of the Continent.* New York: Penguin Books, p. 99.

settlements in the form of permanent villages and towns swept away the spatial limitation on the spread of disease. In particular the introduction of domesticated animals such as dogs, pigs, cattle, horses and cats increased human exposure to infectious diseases mostly spread by rats and fleas, very much like it did at the end of 2019 when the SARS-CoV-2 virus spread from Wuhan city, Hubei province in China, to become a global pandemic within a matter of months.[9]

Large populations (estimated at around 20 million people each at around 1000 years BC) eventually appear to have grouped in five regions globally: in China, the Indian subcontinent, Egypt, the Fertile Crescent[10] and Iran, and in Europe.[11] Perhaps half of Africa's much smaller population was by then concentrated in a single area along the fertile Nile Valley.

Largely because of its low population densities and hence ability to continue with hunter-gatherer lifestyles, the technological developments that had accompanied the Bronze and the Iron Ages essentially bypassed much of sub-Saharan Africa. Because of its relative isolation from global trade and conquest, Africa was also less affected by the great plagues that affected the rest of the world such as the Plague of Justinian that reduced Eurasian populations by a quarter from 541 to 542 AD.[12]

During the bubonic plague or Black Death that swept through Asia, Europe in the fourteenth century, anything between a quarter and two-thirds of the European population died. However, such was the momentum provided by agriculture, that population numbers recovered and soon again started to increase.[13]

For a while, it seemed that the African civilizations that had in the meanwhile developed in modern-day Ethiopia (Aksum) and in the west along the Niger River and that these could come to rival those elsewhere. South of the Sahara, the Bantu people had domesticated cattle and were growing sorghum

---

[9]Wolfe, N. D., Dunavan, C. P., and Diamond, J., 2007. Origins of Major Human Infectious Diseases. *Nature*, 447, pp. 279–283. At the time of writing the origins of COVID-19 is still not fully clear, but apparently it is a recombination of two different viruses, likely from bats and pangolins, that had simultaneously infected the same organism and from there, infected and spread among humans. Hassanin, A., 2020. Coronavirus Origins: Genome Analysis Suggests Two Viruses May Have Combined. World Economic Forum. [Online] Available at www.weforum.org/agenda/2020/03/coronavirus-origins-genome-analysis-covid19-data-science-bats-pangolins/.

[10]Iraq, Israel/Palestine, Syria, Lebanon, Egypt and Jordan as well as the southeastern fringe of Turkey and the western fringes of Iran.

[11]Aydon, C., 2007. *The Story of Man*. Philadelphia: Running Press, p. 71.

[12]Regions isolated from Eurasian plagues such as Japan, the Central and South America and parts of sub-Saharan Africa did not suffer the same fate.

[13]Austin Alchon, Suzanne, 2003. *A Pest in the Land: New World Epidemics in a Global Perspective*. University of New Mexico Press. p. 21. ISBN 978-0-8263-2871-7. The third, much more recent plague in the late nineteenth and early twentieth century, was largely confined to Asia.

and millet. They had also discovered iron but they and other groups were not technologically advanced enough to resist external intrusion. During the centuries of African slavery that followed from around 1500, first Muslim slave traders, and later the Atlantic slave trade denuded the continent of much of its ability to pursue farming since, without sufficient labour and the ability to store foodstuffs, it was not possible to identify and cultivate crops and domesticate animals—both prerequisites of farming.

The growth of large cities that agriculture had enabled had required authorities to give attention to water-borne sewage and other measures to combat communicable diseases. But by the time that Africa started to become more urbanized towards the end of the nineteenth century, its higher population densities was partially enabled by imported modern medicine (vaccines and later the discovery of penicillin) that allowed for the prevention and treatment of these diseases. Larger communities of people were now able to live in larger settlements not because of city planning, housing laws, adequate municipal water and sewerage as was required elsewhere to contain disease and plague, but because modern medicines served as an effective alternative to keep infectious diseases under control.[14]

Because of its climate and the much longer time period during which humanity and its predecessors coexisted, Africa has therefore had a significantly larger disease burden than other regions, which partly explains why it is here that human immunodeficiency virus (HIV) and the acquired immunodeficiency syndrome (AIDS) originated.

The Impact of HIV and AIDS

HIV's ancestor is simian immunodeficiency virus (SIV), an infection of African monkeys that has also spread to chimpanzees. SIV is several thousand years old, and may even have been around millions of years ago.[15] That SIV spread to humans is no surprise, for several major human infectious diseases such as the plague, sleeping sickness, yellow fever, various forms of influenza, Creutzfeldt-Jakob's disease and, most recently, ebola, have all done so. Once transmitted to humans, SIV evolved to HIV. Like many other diseases, its origin in Africa is essentially a function of the fact that humanity and its

---

[14]Bollyky, T. J., 2018. *Plagues and the Paradox of Progress Why the World Is Getting Healthier in Worrisome Ways.* Cambridge: MIT Press.
[15]Dolgin, E., 2010. *Nature.* [Online] Available at: https://www.nature.com/news/2010/100521/full/news.2010.259.html.

primate predecessors have had a longer and closer relationship here than anywhere else.

Scientists believe that the HIV virus originated in the western equatorial region of Africa (today known as Cameroon and the Democratic Republic of Congo) in the first half of the previous century. During the subsequent decades, subgroups of the virus were carried away from the epicentre to infect eastern, southern and western Africa. As a result, by the time that the epidemic was discovered, it had already silently spread across large areas. Its slow-acting, asymptomatic incubation period and the eventual appearance of diverse opportunistic infections defied prompt action until such time as it had reached momentous proportions.[16] By the mid-1970s, HIV/AIDS was a true pandemic.

HIV/AIDS remained silent and unrecognised for so long because it affected the immune system, meaning that people were apparently dying from a variety of opportunistic infections that take advantage of a weak immune system and not from a single disease. It remained undetected because of Africa's poor health systems, bad infrastructure and limited medical research capacity and silently spread across the continent. Africa has consistently shouldered between 75 and 85% of the global AIDS burden, which peaked in 2004–2005. In each of these years, more than 1.5 million Africans died from AIDS, although the actual number of people who passed away in the 1960s, 1970s and 1980s will likely never be known.[17] AIDS is, of course, not the first modern pandemic. The Spanish influenza killed 40–50 million people in 1918. Asian flu killed two million people in 1957 and Hong Kong influenza killed one million people in 1968.

The AIDS pandemic had a dramatic impact on Africa's ability to improve health outcomes relative to other developing regions, with a serious knock-on effect on economic productivity and disastrous impacts on families and communities. For example, between 1980 and 2000, life expectancy in sub-Saharan Africa improved by only about 2.5 years, compared to an increase of about 5.5 years globally and close to nine years in South Asia.

The first known case of HIV was eventually traced to a man who died in 1959 in the Democratic Republic of the Congo. Initially global attention focussed on young homosexual men but, by 1982, it was understood that the 'slim disease', a condition previously considered to be a wasting disorder linked to malnutrition, was in fact HIV/AIDS.

---

[16]Iliffe, J. 2006. *The African AIDS Epidemic: A History*. Oxford: James Currey, pp. 4–5, 158–159.
[17]For a helpful timeline see Pickrell, J., 2006. *NewsScientist*. [Online] Available at: https://www.newscientist.com/article/dn9949-timeline-hiv-and-aids/.

Once it was identified, lack of government capacity and the denialism of influential leaders such as President Thabo Mbeki of South Africa led to the unnecessary loss of hundreds of thousands of lives. Mbeki's stance, in the country with the largest AIDS death rates globally at the time, would eventually contribute to his ouster as president in 2008 in favour of a flawed replacement, Jacob Zuma.

While life expectancy in Africa has recovered to a certain extent in the last decade, it has still not caught up with the rest of the world. In 2018, the gap in life expectancy between Africa and the global average was about eight years—in spite of the fact that the ready availability of medicines for most communicable diseases should allow Africa to make much more rapid progress. By 2040 the gap in life expectancy between Africa and the global average should be slightly below five years.

In contrast, South Asia more than halved the gap in life expectancy between itself and the rest of the world—from 11 years in 1960 to less than four years today.

HIV/AIDS dealt sub-Saharan Africa a devastating blow. It came at a time when the continent had shown signs of a turnaround from the declining economic growth prospects in the 1980s and 1990s that were discussed in Chapter 2. This change in fortune was the result of various factors, including a determined effort by some in the international community to place poverty alleviation at the core of global concerns—an occurrence that was facilitated by the end of the Cold War.

It remains to be seen what the medium and long-term impact of the COVID-19 virus will be in Africa. At the time of writing it is still too early to responsibly model the interplay between competing variables including Africa's much younger population (the virus affects elderly people more seriously resulting in much higher levels of morbidity), low levels of urbanisation (providing rural people with a degree of initial protection meaning it could spread more slowly here), the challenge of comorbidity (given the continents high communicable disease burden such as from HIV/AIDS and tuberculosis) and a host of other factors including low levels of testing, the very limited public health capacity, and low levels of access to potable water and water-borne sewage. And then there are the climatic and seasonal impacts that are all still speculative.

The damage that COVID-19 will inflict in the short term cannot, however, be disputed. Millions more Africans will be condemned to extreme poverty, incomes will decline and many will succumb to lack of food as the efforts to constrain infection rates reduce economic activity, jobs and impact upon livelihoods. The unfolding global recession will hit Africa very hard particularly given the commodity dependence of many of its economies. The result will be to constrain growth and economic improvements—but eventually the deep drivers of economic growth in Africa will reassert themselves.

Africa's Approaching Health Transition

Looking back over time, it is clear that Africa's high communicable disease burden partly explains its unique development trajectory. More concerning, because Africa has such low levels of safe water and poor sanitation, it is potentially more susceptible to the impact of new viruses such as COVID-19 although the virus generally affects younger populations less severely.

To an extent the HIV/AIDS pandemic occurred as part of a long-term characteristic of Africa's high burden of communicable diseases compared to other regions that have first experienced a declining burden of communicable diseases and only later an increased incidence of non-communicable diseases. Sub-Saharan Africa has a much younger population than other regions in the world. With a median age below 19 years it naturally suffers from a much higher communicable (or infectious) than non-communicable disease burden because children are especially susceptible to the former. The median age in Asia is 27 and in Europe it is 43 years. Poor living conditions including unsafe water, poor housing and inadequate sanitation also create an environment for pathogens to propagate.

Infants and children often die of infectious diseases while elderly people generally die of chronic diseases or die from communicable diseases after living for a while with non-communicables. As incomes rise, people live longer, eat more processed foodstuffs and more readily develop heart disease, high blood pressure, diabetes and cancer.

The so-called epidemiological transition takes place when improved food security and innovations in public health and medicine result in infectious diseases, such as influenza, being replaced as the dominant cause of death by chronic diseases, such as cancer. This transition is generally associated with age and income as it relates to lifestyle, and is often used as an indicator of the transition from developing to developed nation.

In Europe and North America the transition from communicable to non-communicable diseases as the main cause of death occurred more than a century ago. In Latin America and the Caribbean the transition happened around 1970 and in North Africa around 1980. In South Asia it occurred around 2000 but is only set to occur around 2030 in sub-Saharan Africa.

The nature of the epidemiological transition is, however, changing. Modern medicine means that people in sub-Saharan Africa are now living long enough to succumb to non-communicable afflictions, with the result that many people in poor countries are contracting the 'diseases of affluence' at younger ages. So in sub-Saharan Africa the transition is happening at lower levels of income and urbanisation than elsewhere. At the same time, the burden of communicable diseases remains high, resulting in the so-called double-burden of disease. This will present health systems with very large cost implications as they navigate increasingly complex public health landscapes. The high costs associated with non-communicable diseases will pose a major problem for many African countries as their comparatively low average incomes translate into limited state budgets and capacity to provide the necessary health care. Providing a US$2 mosquito nets to every vulnerable person in Africa every two years is one thing, but ensuring that every African has reliable access to insulin (annual cost more than US$300 per person[18]), cancer screenings and dialysis is quite another.

The result of the approaching double-burden of disease will be more sick adults, leading poor countries to have to devote more resources to preventing and treating costlier non-communicable diseases. Pollution and tobacco are also proving to be a huge challenge, as tobacco companies are now actively targeting the next generation of smokers, all of whom are in the developing world.

Still, communicable diseases continue to have a disproportionate and devastating impact on Africa, by any standard. In 2018, about 90% of malaria deaths worldwide occurred in Africa—for HIV/AIDS the figure was about 80%. The continent accounts for nearly 50% of all communicable disease deaths worldwide, despite making up only 16% of the global population, as shown in Fig. 3.1. In other words, people in Africa are about four and a half times more likely to die from a communicable disease than people elsewhere.

This trend is forecast to continue beyond 2040 in the Current Path. By then, Africa is projected to account for about 95% of global malaria deaths, 80% of global AIDS deaths and almost half of total communicable disease deaths worldwide. It is partly because of this disease burden that the average life expectancy at birth in 2018 in Africa (at 66 years) is so much lower than that in the rest of the world (at 75 years) and is also forecast to remain significantly below global averages beyond the 2040 time horizon.

Addressing Africa's disproportionate communicable disease burden is obviously a high priority, but any progress in this regard will inevitably mean

---

[18] Ewen, M., Joossem H.-J., Beran, D., and Laing, R., 2019. Insulin Prices, Availability and Affordability in 13 Low-income and Middle-income Countries. *BMJ Global Health*, 4, p. e001410.

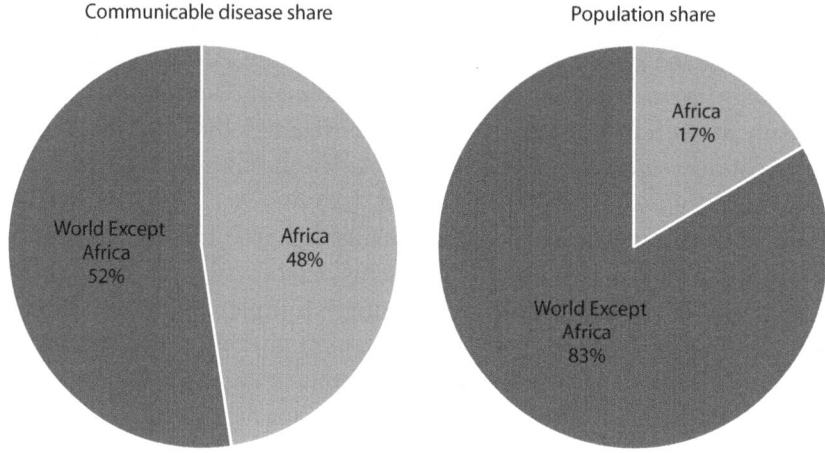

Fig. 3.1 Population and deaths from communicable disease in 2018 (*Source* IFs v 7.45 using United Population Division and Institute for Health Metrics and Evaluation data)

a greater prevalence in non-communicable causes of morbidity. Africa's epidemiological transition will hence occur at a point when incomes are still quite low compared to other parts of the world that have already gone through the transition.

Non-communicable diseases are more difficult and expensive to diagnose, treat and manage than communicable diseases, and many health systems will likely struggle to respond effectively. In fact, almost one-third of all deaths in sub-Saharan Africa are already categorised as non-communicable, a share which is forecast to rise to more than 50% by 2040, even in the absence of additional interventions.[19]

Urbanisation and Health Services

Whereas the transition in Western Europe and North America was largely as a result of infrastructure investments, such as closed sewage systems and clean water supply by public utilities in the nineteenth century, and later by vaccines and the discovery of penicillin, in Africa different dynamics are at play since poor people are generally moving to cities without the prospect of a job or an improved lifestyle, but to escape the destitution in rural areas. The

---

[19] IFs use three main ICD categories—communicable, non-communicable and injuries. The calculations were done as a portion of the total of all three.

result is massive increases in large, sprawling slum cities, some of which are already evident in places such as Lagos, Dar es Salaam and Nairobi.

Chapter 2 noted that Africa is urbanising much later compared to other regions, and that urbanisation is accompanied by the rapid growth of slum cities that do not have the required basic infrastructure such as safe water and water-borne sewage to cope with the influx and natural population growth. Earlier sections in this chapter noted that it is access to modern medicine that is helping to keep urban epidemics ill health at bay.

According to the Current Path forecast, Africa only becomes predominantly urban at around 2038 and sub-Saharan Africa several years later. This means that Africa remains the most rural continent in the world, although the absolute increase in growth of the urban population is large.

The continent's urban population is forecast to more than double by 2050, adding more than 800 million people to Africa's cities. The UN Population Division (UNPD) anticipates that, between 2018 and 2035, all ten of the world's fastest growing cities will be in Africa—and 21 of the top 30.[20] Twelve of these 30 cities are in West Africa, four of which are in Nigeria. The four Nigerian cities alone are projected to add about 200 million people to urban areas in Africa by 2050.

Since most African governments don't have the means to invest in the vast and dense network of transport systems required for such sprawling cities, poorly constructed and poorly maintained roads are crowded with cars and other means of private transport. The result is that the city sprawls out further and further, lowering urban density and increasing the potential cost of providing the required additional infrastructure. Consequently, instead of increasing productivity and access to services—one of the main advantages of urbanisation—it actually starts to decrease.[21]

African cities from Nairobi to Cape Town are already known for their slums. Slums and informal townships present a number of problems, largely because they develop in the absence of planning. Housing units are almost exclusively self-constructed and neighbourhoods are organised independently of the central governing authority.

Some governments even go out of their way to avoid acknowledging that these places exist. Until 2009 the Kibera, one of the largest slums in Africa, was officially designated by the Government of Kenya as a lake next to the

---

[20] United Nations Department of Economic and Social Affairs, 2018. *United Nations Population Division*. [Online] Available at: https://population.un.org/wup/.
[21] Collier, P., 2016. *African Urbanisation: An Analytic Policy Guide.* London: International Growth Centre, p. 23.

Nairobi Dam—an illustration of the chasm between the demand for basic services and the ability of the government to provide them.

Current Path: Access to Basic Infrastructure

Previous sections have noted that Africa appears to be approaching its epidemiological transition despite a serious lack in basic services such as clean water. Even so, poor access to safe water and sanitation present a major crisis. In actual fact, WASH access serves as a useful proxy for a government's ability to fulfil the basic needs of its people and for this reason, unlike other forms of infrastructure like electricity, reliable access to safe water is a basic human right—as proclaimed by the UN General Assembly in 2010.[22]

Hypothetically speaking, the centralization of service delivery points for water, sanitation and health in urban areas should make service delivery easier compared to the challenge of, for instance, rolling out health care or sanitation in sparsely populated rural areas. However, as discussed, most of Africa's cities are poorly designed, congested and growing rapidly.

It is therefore not surprising that Africa's urban citizens have some of the lowest levels of access to basic services worldwide. In 2018, only about 40% of the continent had access to an improved sanitation facility, while the global average was approximately 70%. For clean water, the rates are only slightly improved, with about 77% of people in Africa having access, while in the rest of the world that figure was more than 97%. In comparison, about 53% of people in South Asia had access to an improved sanitation facility in 2018, and about 94% of the region had access to potable water.

The picture is similar for nearly any other measure of access to infrastructure or services. For instance, in 2018 about 95% of global populations outside of Africa had access to electricity. In Africa, the figure was approximately half of that, at 53% (44% in sub-Saharan Africa). The use of solid fuels for cooking and heating instead of electricity is also a large source of indoor air pollution. This lack of access to physical infrastructure and basic services constrains Africa's ability to fully develop its human potential and thus to capitalise on its future demographic dividend.

Partly as a result of these differences, people in South Asia can expect to live on average about six years longer at birth and receive more than a full year of additional education relative to their counterparts in sub-Saharan Africa.

---

[22]General Assembly resolution 64/292, The human right to water and sanitation, A/64/L.63/Rev.1 and Add.1 (28 July 2010). [Online] Available at: https://www.un.org/en/ga/search/view_doc.asp?symbol=A/RES/64/292.

Infant mortality is about 50% higher in sub-Saharan Africa than in South Asia, and the rate at which African children under the age of five die is nearly twice as high.

WASH infrastructure supports the development of broader human potential through its strong forward linkages to other important aspects of the SDGs such as poverty, education and gender equality. In other words, improvements in WASH infrastructure generally translates into sizable gains in the overall development of a country since it improves the human capital contribution.

For example, children that do not have adequate access to WASH facilities have difficulty absorbing nutrients and are more vulnerable to the negative consequences of undernutrition. Malnourished children are highly susceptible to communicable diseases with diarrheal diseases being among the most frequent and severe examples. UNICEF estimates that, of the roughly 1600 children that die from diarrheal disease each day globally, about half are attributable to a lack of WASH access.[23] In recognition of this, in 2015 the World Health Organization (WHO) and UNICEF's Joint Monitoring Project recognised access to WASH facilities as 'fundamental to good health, dignity and quality of life'.[24]

Children who don't succumb to diarrheal disease may suffer other lifelong effects, like stunting, generally recognised as low height for age.[25] Although stunting is commonly described in physiological terms, it also significantly impairs the development of the human brain. According to the WHO, stunted individuals suffer from 'poor cognition and educational performance, low adult wages, lost productivity and, when accompanied by excessive weight gain later in childhood, an increased risk of nutrition-related chronic diseases in adult life'.[26] Put bluntly, stunting is an irreversible condition that inhibits the potential of the affected individual or community for life and the rate in Africa is at a quarter of its population and for a very modest decline to 2040.

---

[23] UNICEF, 2015. *How WASH Relates to Health, Education and Development.* [Online] Available at: https://www.unicef.org/wash/index_healthandeducation.html.

[24] WHO/UNICEF Joint Monitoring Programme for Water Supply, Sanitation and Hygiene (JMP), 2012. *WASH Post-2015: Proposed Targets and Indicators for Households, Schools and Health Centres.* Washington: JMP.

[25] Stunting is a medical condition that is reached when a child's height-for-age ratio is more than two standard deviations below the World Health Organization's (WHO) Child Growth Standards median. WHO, 2006. *WHO Child Growth Standards Length/Height-for-Age, Weight-for-Age, Weight-for-Length, Weight-for-Height and Body Mass Index-for-Age: Methods and Development.* Geneva: WHO Press.

[26] WHO, 2015. *Stunting in a Nutshell.* [Online] Available at: https://www.who.int/nutrition/healthygrowthproj_stunted_videos/en/.

Insufficient WASH access leaves all children vulnerable, but as they mature, the negative impacts begin to stack up disproportionately against women and girls. Poorly maintained or non-existent WASH facilities are one of the main causes of high school dropout rates among teenage girls who lack menstrual hygiene services, for example.[27] This in turn could lead to a large disparity among educational attainment between men and women and significantly diminish the economic opportunities for the latter, translating to lower growth for society as a whole.

However, there are immense challenges to advancing access to WASH infrastructure in sub-Saharan Africa.[28] Even upper-middle-income countries in Africa are struggling to expand access to WASH infrastructure fast enough, in particular sanitation facilities. Of Africa's eight upper-middle-income countries only Mauritius, Libya and Algeria register access rates above the global average for countries in this category (about 80%).[29]

In the five remaining upper-middle-income African countries with below-average access levels—South Africa, Namibia, Botswana, Equatorial Guinea and Gabon—about 19 million people were still living without access to an improved sanitation facility in 2018. It is likely no coincidence that four of these five countries, namely South Africa, Namibia, Botswana and Equatorial Guinea, rank among the twelve most unequal countries in the world according to the Gini index. In South Africa alone, nearly 15 million people live with increased vulnerability to water-borne illness and other negative health consequences due to lack of access to an improved sanitation facility.

Unfortunately, looking to the future, the picture is not likely to improve much. On the Current Path forecast, only half of Africa's population is projected to have access to an improved sanitation facility and just over 80%

---

[27] A study from Malawi, for instance, found that only 46% of girls who reached menarche before age 14 completed primary school, compared to 70% who reached it after 16 years of age due to a lack of appropriate menstrual hygiene management resources. Sommer, M., 2013. Menarche: A Missing Indicator in Population Health from Low-Income Countries. *The National Center for Biotechnology*, 128(5), pp. 399–401. In many instances, women and girls also face an increased risk of sexual assault when using these facilities at night, in part due to the absence of decent lighting. In fact, a 2015 study in Khayelitsha conducted by Yale University found that simply increasing the number of toilets could lead to a reduction in sexual violence against women and girls. When the 'social cost' of sexual violence, including tangible costs like medical expenses, legal adjudication and correctional time, but also intangible costs like trauma and risk of homicide, is taken into account, erecting more toilets could actually save costs, too. Gonsalves, G. S., Kaplan, E. H., and Paltiel, A. D., 2015. Reducing Sexual Violence by Increasing the Supply of Toilets in Khayelitsha, South Africa: A Mathematical Model. [Online] Available at: https://journals.plos.org/plosone/article?id=10.1371/journal.pone.0122244.

[28] Markle, A., and Donnenfeld, Z., 2016. Refreshing Africa's Future: Prospects for Achieving Universal WASH Access by 2030. *African Futures Paper*, June 2016.

[29] This average is calculated using a bivariate regression with GDP per capita as the independent variable, fit to a log distribution to obtain an expected value for a given level of income.

is forecast to have reliable access to clean drinking water in 2030. In 2018, 297 million people in the DRC, Ethiopia and Nigeria alone, were living without access to improved sanitation facilities. This number is projected to increase to about 350 million by the time the SDGs are meant to be achieved in 2030.

Modelling the Impact of Better Health and WASH Infrastructure: The Improved Health Scenario

Although a coordinated cross-sectoral approach is necessary to overcome the negative impact that poor health outcomes have on development in Africa, a push on the most immediate health and infrastructure priorities would have significant and visible effects on the health situation on the continent. It will also improve productivity and economic growth prospects.

Given how far behind Africa is on these various indicators compared to other regions, the interventions in the Improved Health scenario that follow are not calibrated to represent Africa achieving the SDG goals by 2030 (Goals 3 and 6 are dedicated to health and WASH infrastructure, respectively). Those ambitions appear to be out of reach. Rather they reflect a determined and ambitious push against what was historically achieved in South America and South Asia, the two regions most comparable to Africa.

The Improved Health scenario simulates a combination of three sets of improvements. The first is the more rapid provision of basic infrastructure (clean water and improved sanitation) that particularly push on the drivers of Africa's very high communicable disease burden as well as indirectly improving productivity given a generally healthier workforce. The second is large reductions in the incidence of HIV/AIDS and malaria on the back of expectations regarding rapid progress in prevention and treatment. The third is modest reductions in the incidence of non-communicable diseases such as diabetes based on ongoing improvements in medical technology.[30] In all instances the interventions accelerate the expectation in the Current Path forecast that things will steadily improve in all these dimensions.

Access to clean water is improved by 9% points above the 2030 Current Path forecast and by 15% points in the case of improved sanitation. The associated additional burden on government consumption required by these improvements in basic infrastructure is steep and comes to US$6.5 billion in 2030 alone.

---

[30]Includes malignant neoplasm, cardiovascular, digestive, respiratory, other non communicable diseases, diabetes and mental health.

On their own, i.e. without the additional push from the other two sets of interventions, more clean water and better sanitation reduce rates of infant mortality to 23 deaths per thousand by 2040 instead of 25. The result, among others, is that births start declining from around 2025 as society reacts to the fact that more infants are surviving. By 2040, Africa would cumulatively have 6.5 million less births, meaning that the total population of the continent will decline by about a million people. Average life expectancy also increases by a few months by 2040. From an economic productivity point of view Africa will experience an increase in its average growth rate of 0.1% from 2020 to 2040 with the result that the African economy will be US$164 billion larger in 2040 than in the Current Path. The benefits from the other two sets of interventions, on HIV/AIDS and malaria, and reductions on non-communicable diseases amplify these already impressive results.

The interventions on the incidence of malaria and HIV/AIDS are aggressive. In 2040, the Improved Health scenario is that 304,000 fewer Africans will die from malaria and 266,000 less from AIDS, roughly 70% less than the Current Path forecast for 2040 in both instances. Cumulatively 4.7 and 4.5 million less people will succumb to malaria and AIDS from 2020 to 2040. Already in 2019, some 360,000 children a year in Malawi, Ghana and Kenya are to receive a powerful new anti-malaria drug, Mosquirix, as part of a pilot project that will last for several years.[31] Due to HIV's ability to mutate rapidly, a preventive vaccine doesn't exist yet, in spite of many scientific advances but it surely is only a question of time while treatment has improved immensely.[32]

The improvements in infrastructure, also result in a 17% reduction in the broad category of "other communicable diseases" by 2030.[33]

The third set of improvements modestly reduces Africa's non-communicable disease burden. The result is that the number of Africans that die from this broad category is reduced by around 470,000 in 2030 and moderates to 450,000 by 2040. Since non-communicable diseases are more prevalent with age, the impact is to increase Africa's average life expectancy

---

[31] The vaccine triggers the immune system to defend against the first stages of malaria shortly after the parasite enters the bloodstream after a mosquito bite. Deutsche Welle, 2019. *Africa Begins World's Biggest Anti-Malaria Vaccine Campaign.* [Online] Available at: https://www.dw.com/en/africa-begins-worlds-biggest-anti-malaria-vaccine-campaign/a-48436460?utm_source=Media+Review+for+April+23%2C+2019&utm_campaign=Media+Review+for+April+23%2C+2019&utm_medium=email.

[32] Pavlakis, G. N., and Felber, B. K., 2018. A New Step Towards an HIV/AIDS Vaccine. *The Lancet*, 21 July, 392(10143), pp. 192–194.

[33] The category 'other communicable diseases' excludes diarrheal diseases, HIV/AIDS, malaria and respiratory infections.

to almost 74 years by 2040, i.e. an increase of two years above the Current Path forecast.

The Improved Health Scenario illustrates the impact that improvements in one area—basic infrastructure—can have on another sector—health. In interpreting the results it is, however, important to recognise that some of the interventions to improve health outcomes, such as rapid reductions in malaria and HIV/AIDS are modelled to follow medical breakthrough and progress and hence require limited additional funding since the interventions push on the result (less deaths) rather than on the cause, such as rolling out HIV/AIDS treatment, better management and improved treatment facilities.

The implication of the Improved Health scenario is on the one hand to increase government consumption on basic infrastructure (by US$8.8 billion in 2030) and to reduce government consumption on health (by US$3.7 billion in 2030). That said, the degree to which the latter offsets the increase in infrastructure related expenditure only increases to 2030. From around 2035 the scenario requires increased expenditure in both categories when compared to the Current Path forecast of African government consumption on infrastructure and health. These results are presented in Fig. 3.2.

Technological advances will undoubtedly help the drive for improved basic infrastructure at lower cost. For example, since 2011, the Bill and Melinda Gates Foundation has invested more than US$200 million in the Reinvent the Toilet challenge. Although there has yet to be a technical breakthrough, the level of investment and talent that the challenge is attracting

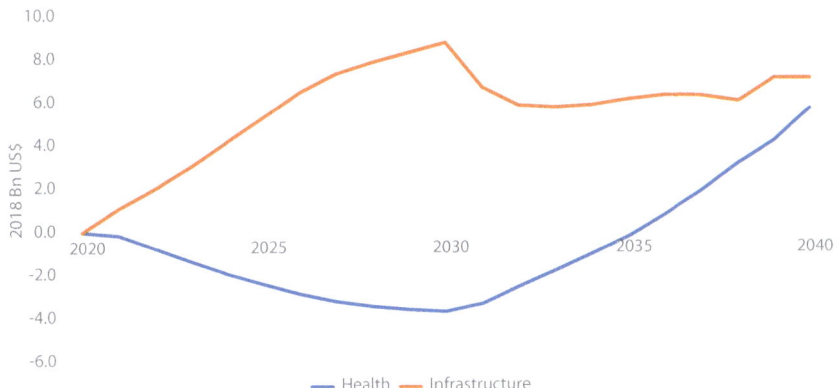

Fig. 3.2 The difference between government consumption on health and infrastructure in Africa between the Improved Health scenario and the Current Path (*Source* IFs 7.45 initialising from WHO and Africa Country Infrastructure Diagnostic)

is promising.[34] Bill Gates estimates that the market for this new toilet technology could be as big as US$6 billion a year by 2030, more than the current GDP of 16 African countries.

The result of the Improved Health scenario is that there are 1.3 million fewer births on the continent in 2040 (cumulatively 12.1 million over the period 2020–2040) and eleven million fewer Africans in 2040 than would otherwise be the case.

In the Improved Health scenario, about 5 million more Africans receive piped water by 2040 and 78 instead of 68% of the continents people have access to improved sanitation. Even with the significant push on WASH infrastructure in this scenario Africa does not provide reliable access to clean water and approximately 607 million live without access to an improved sanitation facility by the end of the SDGs in 2030.

This scenario also reduces the number of fatalities from AIDS by about 266,000 in 2040 and forecast almost 600,000 fewer instances of fatalities due to malaria compared to the Current Path forecast.

Although this scenario doesn't get the continent quite to the finish line in time for the SDGs, a push to combat communicable diseases and improve WASH infrastructure would still have significant benefits for human and economic development.

Using US$1.90 the Improved Health scenario decreases extreme poverty by around 18 million people by 2040.

Impact on Disability Adjusted Life Years

One way of measuring the impact of the Improved Health scenario is to use a standard metric for capturing a country or region's disease burden, called disability adjusted life years (DALYs). DALYs are a commonly used, if imperfect, measure of the burden of disease in a society, and are generally used to compare the relative disease and mortality burden across countries and regions. It offers a way of accounting for the difference between a current situation and an ideal situation where everyone lives up to the life expectancy in Japan (the country with the longest life expectancy globally), free of disease and disability.[35] Early death would provide years of life lost while sickness

---

[34]Katrina, Y., 2018. *Goats and Soda: Stories of Life in a Changing World.* [Online] Available at: https://www.npr.org/sections/goatsandsoda/2018/11/09/666150842/why-did-bill-gates-give-a-talk-with-a-jar-of-human-poop-by-his-side.

[35]Murray, C. J., and Lopez, A. D., 1997. Global Mortality, Disability, and the Contribution of Risk Factors: Global Burden of Disease Study. *The National Center for Biotechnology Information*, 17 May, pp. 1436–42.

would translate into years lost due to disability. The two are added together to provide the DALY—a combined measure of mortality (or death) and morbidity (poor health).

Using Japan as a benchmark, the World Health Organization (WHO) currently defines standard life expectancy as 81 years for men and 87 years for women. So a man who dies at 70 would add 11 years to a country's DALY count, while a woman who died at 70 would account for 17 years. Illness is measured on a scale where 0 represents perfect health, and 1 represents a condition equivalent to death.[36]

Even relative to other developing regions, Africa stands out in rates of DALYs. In per capita terms, DALYs are about 75% higher in sub-Saharan Africa than in South Asia, and more than twice as high as in Latin America and the Caribbean or in East Asia and the Pacific.

In the Improved Health scenario, Africa suffers from almost 30% fewer DALYs caused by communicable disease by 2040, and 9% fewer DALYs from non-communicable diseases. With a reduced disease burden on top of significant investments in basic infrastructure, the Improved Health scenario increases Africa's economic growth rate by an average of almost 0.3% from 2020 to 2040 which translates into an increased GDP—measured at market exchange rates—to US$8.36 trillion instead of US$7.92 trillion in 2040. Furthermore, the scenario drives a US$230 increase in GDP per capita to US$7370 by 2040—measured at purchasing power parity.

The infant mortality rate also declines by almost five deaths per thousand live births (to 18.9) by 2040 compared to the Current Path forecast of 24.8.

In the intervening years, the gap between Africa and the average male life expectancy in the rest of the world would have decreased from 8.1 to 3.4 years. That of women would have decreased from almost 10 to 5.2 years.

So in terms of life expectancy, Africa is slowly reducing the gap with global averages and the rate of catch up increases with the Improved Health scenario. However, one must bear in mind that it is of course much easier to make rapid progress at lower levels of life expectancy.

---

[36]The measure is actually designed in reverse, where 1 represents a state of perfect health and 0 represents a state equivalent to death, which makes more sense logically, but it is inverted for the purposes of accounting. Murray, C. J., and Lopez, A. D., 1997. Global Mortality, Disability, and the Contribution of Risk Factors: Global Burden of Disease Study. *The National Center for Biotechnology Information*, 17 May, pp. 1436–1442.

Conclusion: Planning Comprehensively and Long-Term

This chapter started by briefly explaining the impact of the extended period of time during which humans have interacted with nature in Africa on the continent's ongoing high disease burden. It included an analysis of the impact of the most serious epidemic, HIV/AIDS, on Africa, and examined the positive impacts of modern medicines (that partly obviate the requirements for functioning basic infrastructure), under resourced and poorly designed health systems.

It is quite likely that we underestimate the relationship between health and economic growth, and in Chapter 16, I compare the fiscal and economic impact of the Improved Health scenario with other scenarios. The analysis reflects findings in other studies, such as one that found a one-year increase in life expectancy could be associated with a 4% increase in GDP.[37] Another by the UN Economic Commission for Africa found that the impact of the Ebola epidemic reduced the GDP of Guinea, Liberia and Sierra Leone by between 2 and 5% compared to the Current Path.[38]

Moreover, the inclusion of infrastructure in the Health scenario underscores the imperative to design health programmes that extend well beyond the health sector itself. In Africa, providing basic infrastructure like WASH facilities and electricity reduces the impact of diarrheal and vector-borne diseases, as well as the respiratory harm caused by indoor use of traditional fuels like dung and charcoal. There is also a role for the international community. Installing taps and toilets has historically not been as attractive to donors (and sometimes governments) as say, eliminating river blindness, but it would have a tremendous impact on livelihoods on the continent.

Demographic growth and technological change can work in Africa's favour, but deferred action will be extremely costly. Delays in urban planning will only result in larger and more dangerous unplanned urban spaces. In addition to provision for roads, railways and ports, urban planning in Africa must emphasise the provision of basic infrastructure like clean water, improved sanitation facilities and electricity, as well as increasing access to, and the general quality of, health and education services.

Africa's health systems are desperately trying to battle the world's worst communicable disease burden with rising rates of non-communicable

---

[37] Bloom, C. E., Canning, D., and Sevilla, J., 2004. The Effect of Health on Economic Growth: A Production Function Approach. *World Development*, 32(1), pp. 1–13.

[38] United Nations Economic Commission for Africa, 2014. *Socio-economic Impacts of Ebola on Africa*. Addis Ababa: Economic Commission for Africa.

diseases. This is a complex challenge with many moving parts, but a better understanding of the trade-offs in health policy versus investments like providing basic WASH infrastructure should lead to better outcomes.

Against this background, getting more rapidly to Africa's demographic dividend and improvements in education—the subject of the next two chapters—may be among the most important drivers of better health in much of Africa, among its various other obvious benefits. Awareness and information programmes can contribute greatly to communicating the benefits of good hygiene and preventing the spread of communicable diseases like HIV/AIDS. They can also instil healthy, lifelong habits around the importance of exercise and healthy diets, which could help to prevent or at least delay the onset of expensive lifestyle diseases like type-2 diabetes and heart disease.

Spending more money on WASH and health requires more rapid progress in moving Africa through its demographic transition, which is discussed next.

Further Reading

Yuval Noah Harari, 2015. *Sapiens: A Brief History of Humankind*. New York: Harper.

Pepin, J., 2011. *The Origin of AIDS*. Cambridge: Cambridge University Press.

Progress on household drinking water, sanitation and hygiene 2000–2017: Special Focus on Inequalities, 2019. New York: United Nations Children's Fund (UNICEF) and World Health Organization (WHO). [Online] Available at https://washdata.org/sites/default/files/documents/reports/2019-07/jmp-2019-wash-households.pdf.

Open Access This chapter is licensed under the terms of the Creative Commons Attribution 4.0 International License (http://creativecommons.org/licenses/by/4.0/), which permits use, sharing, adaptation, distribution and reproduction in any medium or format, as long as you give appropriate credit to the original author(s) and the source, provide a link to the Creative Commons license and indicate if changes were made.

The images or other third party material in this chapter are included in the chapter's Creative Commons license, unless indicated otherwise in a credit line to the material. If material is not included in the chapter's Creative Commons license and your intended use is not permitted by statutory regulation or exceeds the permitted use, you will need to obtain permission directly from the copyright holder.

4

Getting to Africa's Demographic Dividend

Abstract In this chapter, Cilliers defines the demographic dividend and explains its relationship to economic growth, with a focus on the African continent. It first covers the fundamentals of the relationship between population and economics, then offers an in-depth discussion of two key concepts, the demographic transition and demographic dividend. The chapter demonstrates that sub-Saharan Africa's high fertility rates are a drag on development rather than an advantage, as the region can only expect to enjoy a demographic dividend after mid-century. It then uses scenario analysis to demonstrate that, given the right policy conditions, Africa can accelerate population-driven economic growth by reducing its fertility rate through interventions in education, infrastructure, human capital and, most importantly, women's empowerment.

Keywords Population · Demography · Economic growth · Fertility · Mortality · Dependency ratio · Migration · Demographic transition · Youth · Labour

Learning Objectives

– Understand the demographic transition and why it has not yet occurred in Africa
– Explain the relationship between population and economic growth
– Define the demographic dividend and recognise the multiple means of measuring it
– Interpret demographic data visualisations such as a population pyramid.

The African Union's annual theme for 2017 was *Harnessing the demographic dividend through investments in youth*. In preparation, the AU Commission in Addis Ababa spent considerable resources to review progress with the 2006 African Youth Charter[1] and its 2009–2018 Plan of Action,[2] that included a roadmap[3] aimed at unlocking the potential of the continent's youth.

The basic premise was that Africa's youthful population would ensure fast economic growth and that, as a general notion, rapid population growth was positive for development. If this is indeed the case, the analysis begs the obvious question why Africa, with its youthful populations, does not see commensurate improvements in income?

When, in October 2018, I presented our research on demographics and economic growth to staff from the African Union in Addis Ababa. I argued that the Charter, Plan of Action and roadmap skirted around the need for a more rigorous analysis of the demographic dividend and that it basically missed the point. In fact, Africa's very high fertility rates were actually a serious constraint on development and until such time as the continent significantly lowered fertility rates, it would not be able to economically grow quickly enough to reduce poverty and improve livelihoods. Although trends were going in the right direction, much more urgent action was required to speed up Africa's demographic transition.

It was for some as if I had let the air out of a very large balloon. Actually nothing I presented was particularly new or innovative and has been reflected in mainstream demographic analysis for several decades. As I had expected, the one diplomat after the other, including from a country like Uganda with its young population and elderly president for life, objected strongly to this attempt at stigmatising motherhood and apparently, children, and muttered darkly that I obviously did not understand the benefits of high fertility rates.

In my presentation, I first made the standard distinction between children (aged 0–15) and the elderly (above 64)—the two components of the dependent portion of the population. Forty-three million Africans are born every year, a number that will increase to 53 million annually by 2040.

I then pointed to the well-known youthful structure of the African population with a median age just shy of twenty years, meaning that half the African

---

[1]The African Union Commission, 2006. *African Youth Charter*. [Online] Available at: https://www.un.org/en/africa/osaa/pdf/au/african_youth_charter_2006.pdf.
[2]African Union, 2011. *African Youth Decade 2009–2018 Plan of Action*. [Online] Available at: https://www.un.org/en/africa/osaa/pdf/au/african_youth_decade_2009-2018.pdf.
[3]The African Union Commission, 2017. *AU Roadmap on Harnessing the Demographic Dividend Through Investment in Youth*. Addis Ababa: African Union.

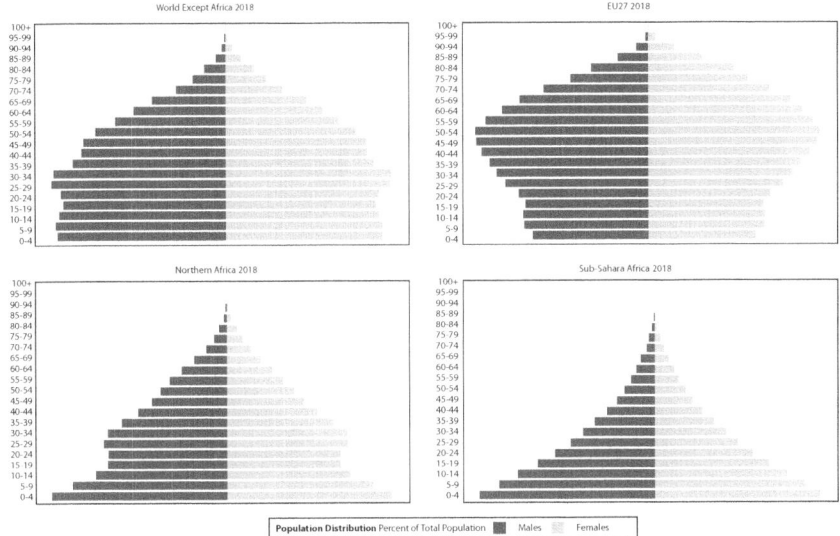

Fig. 4.1 Population pyramid for the Africa, World except Africa, North Africa, sub-Saharan Africa and EU27 in 2018 (*Source* UN Population Division medium term forecast, 2017 revision in IFs v 7.45)

population is younger than twenty and a half are older. The result is a population pyramid that has a very broad base and quickly narrows with each age group. The contrast is presented in Fig. 4.1 that compares the population pyramid for 2018 for the World without Africa, the EU27 group of countries, North Africa and sub-Saharan Africa. The working-age portion of the population aged 15–64 is shaded.

The large cohort of children below 15 years of age means that African countries generally require huge and ongoing investments in education, health and infrastructure that detract from other required improvements.

A next figure, Fig. 4.2, advances the population pyramid for each of these groups to 2040 to illustrate the ongoing youthful character of the population of sub-Saharan Africa.

A large body of research done over several decades by the World Bank and others have found that it is the increase in the size of the working age population (15–64) *relative* to the dependants that contributes most to economic growth at low- and even middle-income levels of development. In other words, it is the ratio of working age persons to dependents that is important, and whether that ratio is changing.

According to the World Bank, in East Asia one-third of the increase in economic growth during its economic miracle can be attributed to a growing labour force. A substantial portion of the remainder is achieved by

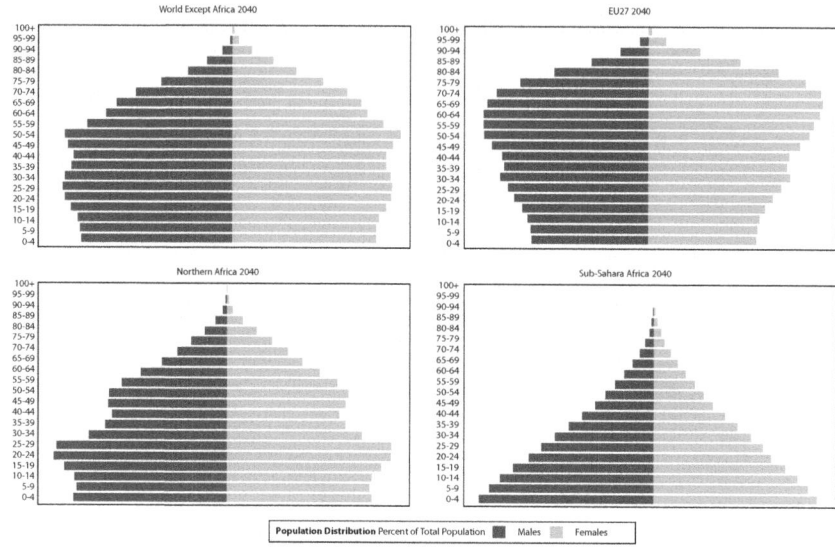

Fig. 4.2 Population pyramid for the Africa, World except Africa, North Africa, sub-Saharan Africa and EU27 in 2040 (*Source* UN Population Division medium term forecast, 2017 revision in IFs v 7.45)

the determined pursuit of export-oriented policies that provided productive employment for its rapidly expanding population.[4] Others estimate that the contribution that an increase in the size of the working age population makes to economic growth is even higher.[5] Literacy and quality basic education is an obvious additional requirement.

At the moment 56% of Africa's population fall within this working age bracket, implying that there are 1.3 persons of working age for every dependent. The ratio in the rest of the world is at 67% of the total population being of working age or two persons of working age to every one dependent. The difference of 0.7 is extraordinarily significant given the large numbers involved.

The underlying logic is quite simple. Economic growth is determined by the contribution from labour, capital and technology. At low levels of development, labour makes the biggest contribution to economic growth and at high levels of development it is technology. So the larger the labour pool in developing regions such as Africa, the quicker it can grow.

---

[4] Canning, D., Sangeeta R., and Abdo Y. S., eds. 2015. *Africa's Demographic Transition: Dividend or Disaster?* Africa Development Forum series. Washington, pp. 6–7.

[5] Sharma, R., 2016. *The Rise and Fall of Nations: Ten Rules of Change in the Post-crisis World*. London: Penguin Random House, pp. 6–7, 19.

The size of the labour force does not necessarily correspond exactly with the number of people in the age bracket 15–64 since many would still be getting an education, or would not have a job, but the essential relationship holds even after accounting for these differences.

What History Reveals

Several centuries ago, up until around the middle of the seventeenth century, the countries with the largest populations and the most fertile farming land boasted the largest economies. The size of the labour force and the suitability of the land to agriculture were the main engines of growth, even if they seldom made a difference to average incomes and by modern standards the vast majority of citizens were destitute.

The industrial revolution in the West upended this state of affairs. The technological breakthroughs of the eighteenth and nineteenth centuries transformed the economic structures of the previous centuries by shifting some elements of production from manual labour to machines. Productivity was no longer determined by the fertility of the land or the size of the workforce alone, but also by the unprecedented output of inventions like the steam engine and the cotton gin.

Workers could now produce more output than before, although their actual living conditions only changed very slowly. Productivity soared in Europe and North America, although it generally remained stagnant in the rest of the world. Burdened by colonialism the industrial revolution bypassed much of Africa. This was the start of the 'great divide' that saw Europe, and eventually North America, overtake countries like China, previously one of the largest economies, and come to dominate the world—a global order that has held until very recently.[6]

With industrialisation, population structures changed. People moved to cities to work in factories and birth rates declined, eventually increasing the number of persons or working age compared to dependents. These developments largely also bypassed Africa for a host of reasons mentioned in other chapters, including geography, the continent's high disease burden, the impact of slavery, then colonialism and other factors.

Population growth and age structure remain critical components of economic growth, particularly at lower levels of development. Even in the

---

[6] Roser, M., 2019. Economic Growth. [Online] Available at: https://ourworldindata.org/economic-growth.

twenty-first century, economies generally do not grow unless their populations also do. Today, countries like Japan, Italy and Germany are experiencing slower economic growth as their populations age. Their population pyramids no longer rest on a wide base, but take the form of an inverted pyramid as the elderly section of the population grows ever larger.[7] Once populations start to decline in size, economies also struggle to grow in size but can continue to experience steady improvements in income per capita since the golden rule is that economic growth must simply be more rapid than population growth.

All in all population structure is very important for economic growth. The relationship between economic growth and population structure is most often operationalised with reference to the demographic dividend or the dependency relationship, of which the latter is the inverse of the former.

The Impact of the Demographic Dividend

There are a number of ways in which to define the demographic dividend such as median age and rates of fertility. In this book, and in the presentation to the AU and others, I prefer to use the ratio of the working age population (aged 15–64 years) to the dependent population, i.e. children below 15 years of age and those older than 64.[8]

A country's income generally rises when this ratio improves. The quicker the rate of improvement and the higher the rate achieved, the more rapid economic growth will be.[9] This is particularly true for poor, developing countries.

---

[7] Pearson, C. S., 2015. *On the Cusp: From Population Boom to Bust.* Oxford: Oxford University Press.

[8] A second definition is that a favourable 'demographic window' opens when children (i.e. below 15) make up less than 30% of the population and those 64 or older make up less than 15%. Cincotta, R., 2017. *Opening the Demographic Window: Age Structure in Sub-Saharan Africa.* [Online] Available at: https://www.newsecuritybeat.org/2017/10/opening-demographic-window-age-structure-sub-saharan-africa/. Alternatively (the third definition) is that the window opens when the median age is above 25.5 years and below 36–41 years. The median age is the age that divides a population into two equal groups, half younger and half older. The maximum median age for the demographic dividend differs because of variations in life expectancy. For example, in 2074, when Africa's demographic dividend ratio peaks at 2:1, the median age is expected to only be 36.5 years. In developed countries with longer life expectancy the top end of the demographic dividend is at 41 years median age. In Africa it is currently 19.8 years. In 1987 it was 17.5 years and by mid-century it should be at roughly 25.5 years. Finally (the fourth definition), a demographic dividend occurs when the total fertility rate is between 2.8 and 2.1 children per woman. In 1987 Africa's total fertility rate was 6.2 children per woman and in 2074 it should be at around 2.1 children. The number 2.1 children per woman is generally considered replacement fertility rate for below that populations start to decline and economic growth generally follows. Exactly when that occurs is affected by changes in life expectancy which, in Africa, is significantly below the global mean.

[9] This is also known as the first dividend since there is also a second and third dividend that is the result of savings and investments, and improvements in productivity.

The ratio of working age persons to dependents in Africa started to slowly improve from the late 1980s from only 1.1 persons of working age for everyone dependent to its current ratio of 1.3. In other words, whereas there were 10 dependents for every 11 people of working age in 1987, today there are 13 persons of working age for every dependent. When the continent gets to a ratio of 1.7 persons of working age to dependants as from the mid-2050s, it will enter a window of particularly rapid income growth through the contribution that is made by labour to growth (as opposed to capital and technology) that will last for about two decades on the Current Path forecast. Eventually Africa experienced a peak ratio of around two persons of working age to every dependent shortly after 2070. Thereafter the relationship starts to decline and, if labour is then still as important as it is today, rates of economic growth will decline.

Once the demographic dividend has peaked, economic growth is very likely to taper off unless an economy has managed to shift gears so that capital and technology are able to compensate for the decline in the relative size of the labour pool and hence for the declining portion of working age persons to dependents.

China and the Asian Tigers peaked at an extraordinarily high ratio of 2.8 working age persons to every one dependent in 2010 and 2013, respectively, and are now in this exact situation. However, Africa is unlikely to be able to experience the high rates of economic growth achieved by China and the Asian Tigers, since the ratio of working age population to dependants will peak at a relatively low level of two working age persons to every one dependent compared to their ratio of 2.8. And then it seems quite certain that the fourth industrial revolution will change the labour-capital-technology relationship in favour of the latter.

Unsurprisingly, the ratio of working age persons to dependents has played an important role in the improvements in prosperity in Japan, China and the Asian Tigers since the 1960s, as well as in the USA and the Nordic countries, albeit over longer time horizons. In the case of the USA and the Nordic countries, the ratio of working age persons to dependents did not swiftly peak at the levels of China and the Asian Tigers and then decline, but slowly increased and then remained in positive territory for an extended period of time.

The benefit of a constantly growing pool of working age persons played an important role in the steady rates of economic growth and improvements in productivity in the USA and the Nordic countries as these countries eventually graduated to high income status.

Fast growth in the working age population relative to the number of dependents does not automatically translate into rapid economic growth, since other facilitators like food sufficiency, literacy and basic education, an export orientation and a governing elite committed to growth also need to be present, but it still has some interesting benefits. Smaller families mean fewer additional schools are needed and the ratio of teachers to pupils can be improved more readily. As a result, parents and the state can invest more resources in those fewer children. Eventually governments need to provide fewer additional houses and water and electricity connection, and can invest in higher technology, in research and other measures that are necessary to maintain improvements in productivity, even as the size of the working age population later starts to decline as the size of the elderly population increases to displace child dependents.

In summary, an increasing working age population to dependents boosts economic growth since more working age persons contribute to economic activity although that, in itself, is insufficient.

Comparing Niger, Egypt, Japan and Sweden

In 2018 half of Niger's population was estimated to be younger than 15 years and it only gets to a 16-year median age by 2026. The country has the lowest median age in the world and the life expectancy is 62 years.[10] Niger has fewer than one person of working age to its dependants and this very low relationship means that Niger cannot grow per capita income, except in the unlikely scenario that it is able to grow its economy at sustained rates of around 10% per year or more for successive decades. The disproportionate size of the cohort of children makes it difficult to build enough schools, train enough teachers and roll out an education (or health) system able to cope with the massive influx of pupils and simultaneously improve average levels and quality of education for those children already within the system.

Egypt, on the other hand, with a median age of 25 years and a life expectancy of 72 years, is on the cusp of achieving an age structure favourable for rapid economic growth with a ratio of 1.6 working age persons to every dependant—a ratio that is increasing. Given the right policies and leadership, Egypt should be able to grow improvements in income levels rapidly. The challenge is that Egypt's closed political system mirrors its statist and

---

[10]Chad has the lowest life expectancy in Africa at 52 years in 2018.

closed economy and means that it could squander this once in a century opportunity.

Sweden, on the other hand, is about to exit the demographic sweet spot (median age of 41 and life expectancy of 83), having been in the demographic sweet spot for most of the twentieth century. It also has a ratio of 1.7 working age persons to dependants but in contrast to Egypt, Sweden's ratio is deteriorating rather than accelerating. With its advanced technology and longevity, Sweden is, however, largely able to compensate for its changing demographics as its people are generally more productive into old age.

Japan has the highest median age in the world at 47 years (with a life expectancy of 84 years). The ratio of working age to dependants is 1.5 and declining with the result that the disproportionate size of the elderly cohort is a large burden on the state. The fact that Japan still manages to grow the size of its economy in spite of its declining population speaks volumes about the high productivity of its economy, particularly its use of technology.

In Sweden and Japan average incomes are still growing, although slowly, but these countries have raised income levels to extraordinary high levels in previous years and the current slow improvements are therefore from a very high base. In these countries, longer life expectancy means that people can extend their working lives beyond 64, thereby expanding the size of the working age population. A higher retirement age can compensate for the high median age to a degree, particularly by adopting practices related to healthy ageing. But because of the prevalence of non-communicable diseases such as cancer in an elderly population, health expenditure is much higher and, in many rich countries, there is considerable resistance to raising the retirement age, perhaps most famous for the repeated efforts to do so in France.

The evolution of the demographic dividend is compared in Fig. 4.2 that presents the percent of the population aged with a forecast to 2050 for Sweden, Egypt, Japan and Niger is presented in Fig. 4.3 with the caveat that the historical data for Egypt and Niger are, for the most part, likely estimations from the UN Population Division.

A demographic dividend provides a structural foundation that can enable rapid economic growth. Since it is the size of a well-educated labour force rather than the amount of capital or technology that makes the largest contribution to economic growth at low levels of development, harnessing the demographic dividend is very important for Africa.

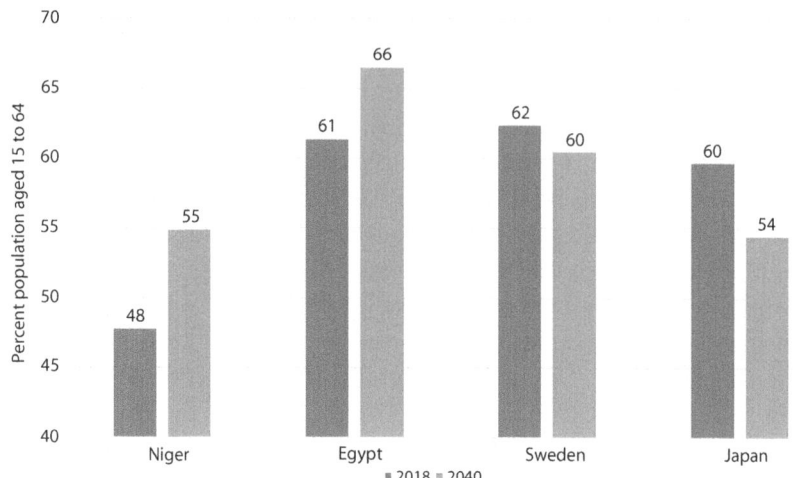

Fig. 4.3 Percent of persons aged 15–64 in Niger, Egypt, Sweden and Japan in 2018 and 2040 (*Source* Historical data from UNPD, forecast in IFs v 7.45)

Africa's Slow Demographic Transition

Globally, the size of the working age population relative to dependents peaked at around 2010. As a result, the world has entered a structural period of slower growth from which it can only emerge through advances in technology, including capitalising on the digital economy and the fourth industrial revolution, factors that I explore further in Chapter 10.

Africa's youthful population stands out against this global backdrop of ageing populations. Only in Africa is the size of the working age population as a portion of the total population still increasing. This development is positive, but it is happening slowly and from a very low ratio of the working age population to dependants.

The result is that Africa is only likely to experience a real demographic dividend from the middle of this century onward. Consequently, for the next three decades Africa's dependent youth population will remain a drag on economic growth, although to a lesser extent with every passing year.

Today, most of Africa still finds itself in the early stages of the demographic transition. In other words, the shift from high death and birth rates to low death and birth rates has started but it is progressing gradually and much slower than it historically did in other regions.

Generally countries (and regions) that have been unable to rapidly progress through the demographic transition and therefore not reach the demographic dividend ratio of 1.7 are characterised by severe poverty and large disease burdens, as well as high birth and death rates that structurally constrain their ability to reduce poverty and improve livelihoods. The rapid increase in the number of children offsets the increases in income from economic growth and prevents the accumulation of savings resulting in low capitalisation in the economy.

There are many reasons for Africa's comparably slow demographic transition. Historically, low population density—a function of Africa's high disease burden—translated into low levels of urbanisation and lower rates of income growth. Some of these aspects are explored in Chapter 3 on health.

In more recent generations, the continent has also not been able to raise education quality and attainment, roll out the use of modern contraceptives quickly enough or transition to economies where child labour is no longer required.[11] Nor has Africa been able to produce sufficient job opportunities to provide meaningful work for its growing population.

Most African countries are experiencing slow income growth because their populations are very young, although the picture is heterogeneous. A few African countries, including Mauritius, Libya, Tunisia, Seychelles, Cape Verde, South Africa and Morocco are much further along in their demographic transition.

Fertility rates across Africa vary significantly. In 2018 they ranged from 7 (in Niger) to 1.4 (in Mauritius). In addition to Mauritius, the countries with the lowest fertility rates are Seychelles, North African countries such as Tunisia, Morocco, Libya and Algeria, and South Africa and Botswana in Southern Africa. The fertility rate for sub-Saharan Africa as a whole is currently estimated at 4.8 children per woman.[12]

In countries such as Tunisia, fertility rates are approaching the level at which population size first stagnates and then starts to decline (understood to be just above two children per woman of childbearing age) unless there is a significant young, net inward migration and/or changes in fertility rates.[13] Many other countries like Mozambique appear to be stalling in their transition by maintaining very high levels of fertility, while a third group (including Ethiopia) is achieving a rapid reduction from previously very high fertility rates. Ethiopia will therefore achieve the 1.7 ratio of working age persons to

---

[11] According to the World Report on Child Labour, one in four children (aged 5–17) in least-developed countries are involved in child labour. International Labour Organization, 2015. International Labour Organization, 2018. *Women and Men in the Informal Economy: A Statistical Picture.* Geneva: International Labour Office. And also: *World Report on Child Labour 2015: Paving the Way to Decent Work for Young People.* Geneva: International Labour Office.

[12] Africa reaches 2.8 two years earlier, since Northern Africa has a more mature population structure.

[13] 2.1 children per woman is generally accepted as the replacement fertility rate. Without inward migration, below that rate populations start to decline.

dependents in 2040, more than a decade before other low-income countries in Africa.¹⁴

Countries with high child mortality rates also tend to have high fertility rates, and a reduction in infant and child mortality supports a virtuous cycle that is key to reducing fertility rates. As children's health and survival improve, family demand for more children slowly declines. Smaller family size improves maternal and child education in a positive reinforcing manner. As female education improves, and as child mortality declines, women have fewer children which in turn allows for healthier and better-educated children. Female education at the secondary level has a particularly strong impact on reducing the average number of births per woman.

The result is that fertility rates are closely associated with education and income levels, as well as with urbanisation. In Ethiopia, for instance, the fertility rate based on 2016 data was 6.4 children for poor women and 2.6 for the wealthy. The corresponding numbers in Tanzania for the same year were 7.5 and 3.1.¹⁵ Geographically speaking, fertility rates in capital cities such as Accra and Addis Ababa are close to replacement levels, while those in rural parts of the Democratic Republic of the Congo are close to seven children per woman.¹⁶

Life expectancy in many African countries is also low. Whereas life expectancy in North Africa was estimated at almost 74 years in 2018, roughly a year longer than the global average, in sub-Saharan Africa it is 64 years—nine years below the global average. In 2018, 28 African countries, ranging from Chad (life expectancy estimated at 52.2 years) to Liberia (life expectancy estimated at 62.9 years), had a life expectancy below 64 years—the final year at which people are typically assumed to still be of working age.

Lower child mortality rates, higher incomes, the education of women, and the availability of contraception all reduce fertility rates.¹⁷ These socio-economic changes are a result of modernisation. Globally better health care, structural changes to the economy, and a rise in women's status and opportunities have all contributed to a reduction in total fertility rates and hence in slowing population growth.

---

¹⁴See Eloundou-Enyegue, P., Giroux, S., and Tenikue, M., 2017. African Transitions and Fertility Inequality: A Demographic Kuznets Hypothesis. *Population and Development Review*, 43(S1), pp. 59–83.

¹⁵The averages are for the top and bottom quintile. Institute for Health Metrics and Evaluation, 2019. Global Health Data Exchange. [Online] Available at: http://ghdx.healthdata.org/series/demogr aphic-and-health-survey-dhs.

¹⁶Canning, D., Sangeeta, R., and Abdo, Y. S, eds. 2015. Africa's Demographic Transition: Dividend or Disaster? Africa Development Forum series. Washington, p. 18.

¹⁷Roser, M., 2017. Fertility Rate. [Online] Available at: https://ourworldindata.org/fertility-rate.

The Peak and Length of the Demographic Dividend

An important explanation for the dynamism and growth of the US economy over an extended period of time is that it entered its demographic dividend shortly before 1930 and will only exit it around 2036, after having been in this favourable position for more than a century. Like Sweden, the demographic dividend explains much of the high levels of income that the USA has been able to attain during this lengthy period.

China, on the other hand, will spend around 50 years in this fortunate window, less than half that of the USA. This explains why China is unlikely to ever approximate income levels of the USA, reflected in the oft-repeated mantra that China will grow old before it gets rich.

Development takes time. Eventually India will spend around 60 years in the demographic high growth range, having only recently attained a ratio of 1.7 working age persons to dependents. However, while China experienced a peak ratio of 2.8 working age persons to dependents, India's likely peak ratio will be at around 2.2 and achieve that shortly before 2040. By this metric, India could experience a modest degree of income catch up with China, but only in the second half of the twenty-first century.

Nigeria only progresses to the 1.7 ratio at roughly 2060 in the Current Path forecast. Less than thirty years later it then peaks at two and will exit the 1.7 ratio early in the next century. Given this long-term horizon, it is virtually impossible to speculate responsibly on Nigeria's long-term future growth prospects, also because the region is expected to suffer significant impacts from climate change at a time of huge technological advances. But what is sure is that current demographic forecasts condemns Nigeria to moderate income growth and even then, only over extended time horizons.

In this context it is important to remind oneself that the impact of technology on productivity is increasing every year. While labour is an important component in productivity at lower levels of development, capital and technology are becoming ever more important, which would reduce Nigeria's growth advantage—indeed that of much of sub-Saharan Africa.

The point is that the level at which countries achieve their peak demographic dividend—and how long they stay there—significantly impacts on economic growth. The longer a country is within this demographic window, the better—although it is again important to emphasise that the contribution that labour makes to growth is declining over time due to the impact of labour-saving technology.

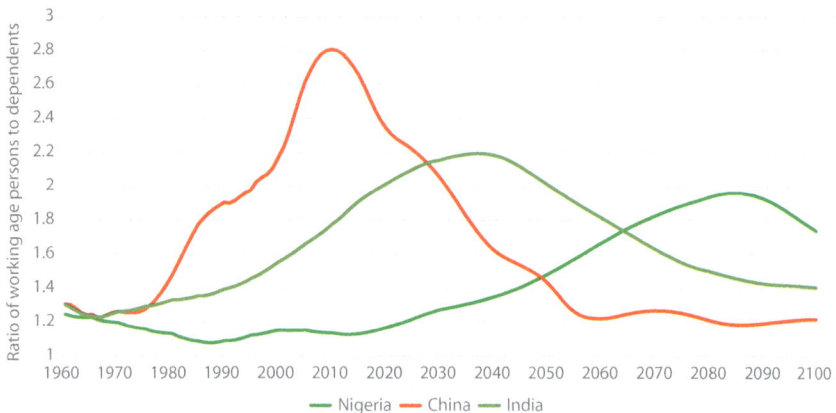

Fig. 4.4 Demographic dividend of Nigeria, China and India: 1960–2100 (*Source* Historical data from UNPD, forecast in IFs v 7.45)

A peak of 2.8 working age persons to dependants (China in 2010) delivers much more rapid economic growth than a peak of 2.2 (India in 2035) or a peak of 2.0 (Nigeria in 2084). This is because the size of the potential labour force relative to dependants is larger.[18] That peak of 2.8 contributed significantly to China's almost 11% rate economic growth in 2010. According to the IFs Current Path forecast, India is projected to grow at 6.2% in the decade from 2030 to 2040 and Nigeria at less than half that in the 2090s, which is partly explained by its low peak of 2.0 (Fig. 4.4).[19]

Looking to the end of this century, the ratio of working age persons to dependents is set to contract in all regions except in sub-Saharan Africa, where it will only peak at a ratio slightly below 2.1 at around 2075. At that point, Africa will have a population of 3.3 billion people (of which 3 billion will be living in sub-Saharan Africa).

A different way to express this metric is that 67% of the population of sub-Saharan Africa will be of working age while the global average at that point is expected to be 62%. In this context, a 5 percentage point difference would indicate that sub-Saharan Africa will grow at a greater rate than global

---

[18] The dependency ratio is the inverse of the demographic dividend. If the labour force increases in size relative to dependents, it causes the dependency ratio to decrease (or the demographic dividend to increase), in which case economic growth is very likely to follow. So, a dependency ratio of one to one means that every worker has to support one dependent. In a country like South Korea, which had a dependency ratio of 0.39 in 2018, each person of working age only has to support one-third of a dependent.

[19] Growth rates for the USA would be around 1.5% in 2050 and around 1% for the EU27. Europe, globally the oldest region, is well on its way to emulating Japan—having too large an elderly population compared to its working age population.

averages, but not by much. Also, because Africa will achieve a relatively low worker to dependant ratio, it will very likely grow at quite modest rates along the Current Path forecast. None of this is good news for a continent that aspires to catch up with global income averages.

Whereas Europe and Japan are experiencing slow economic growth partly because of their large elderly population, sub-Saharan Africa is now the only region in the world where a high child dependency burden is a main cause of slow growth in low income levels.

Only Tunisia, Morocco, Libya and Algeria, the small island states Mauritius and Seychelles, Botswana, South Africa and Djibouti currently have a ratio of 1.7 and higher.

Africa also has a larger youth bulge (people between 15 and 29) as a portion of the total adult population (i.e. those aged above 15) than any other global region. It is typical of many poor countries to have a large share of young people relative to the total adult population and this is also associated with increased risk of conflict and high rates of criminal violence. This is compounded when young people lack opportunities in terms of education, training and employment and feel they have no voice and are excluded from the economy and politics. Whereas the youth bulge in the rest of the world peaked in around 1980 at around 42% of the adult population, Africa only gets to the 42% rate at around 2040.

The Potential Benefits of Reducing Fertility Rates

Generally, a decline in fertility follows a decline in child mortality with a time lag of several years, as parents come to no longer expect to lose as many children.[20] The provision of basic infrastructure for water and sanitation, as well as advances in primary healthcare, reduce infant mortality and eventually lead to lower fertility rates.

The need to have many children is not only based on the expectation that some children could die before reaching adulthood, but also because in economies dominated by employment in the agricultural sector (a characteristic of many poor and developing countries), families need children as labour. Child labour was widespread in most agrarian societies, even during industrialisation.

---

[20]Roser, M., 2017. Fertility Rate. [Online] Available at: https://ourworldindata.org/fertility-rate.

Although many factors impact fertility rates, levels of female education is perhaps the most important driver. In addition, women's increased participation in the labour force, which is closely linked to improved female education and steady improvements in gender parity, also reduces total fertility rates.[21]

For example, women who are better educated have more employment opportunities and are likely to want fewer children. Educated women (and men) are also more likely to be better informed about modern contraceptives and the benefits that lower fertility offers in terms of better education for a smaller number of children. Alternatively, where women have a lower social status, lower levels of decision-making opportunities and fewer opportunities outside the household, fertility rates tend to be higher.

While the Middle East and North Africa is generally not considered a progressive region in terms of gender parity (with the limited exception of Tunisia), in 2015 girls in the region were about 5 percentage points more likely to enrol in primary school than girls in sub-Saharan Africa. From an economic productivity perspective, the investment in female education in North Africa is, however, largely wasted, with the female share of the total labour force being roughly half that of sub-Saharan Africa (24% versus 43%). Whereas the labour force participation rate for females is only 23% in North Africa, it is 64% in sub-Saharan Africa.[22]

The use of modern contraceptives is a more immediate driver of total fertility rates than education, although poor access to education among women constrains uptake. Research suggests that the average gap between actual and desired fertility could be as high as two children per woman in sub-Saharan Africa,[23] pointing to a large pent-up demand for the provision of modern contraceptives.

Data from the UN Population Division forecasts that the unmet demand for modern contraceptives in low-income Africa will be 28% in 2018 and 25% in lower-middle-income African countries, with large country to country variations. Estimates for the unmet need for family planning in Africa for women of reproductive age (15–49 years) who are married or in-union for 2017 range from 12% in Zimbabwe to 41% in the Democratic Republic of the Congo.[24]

---

[21] Ibid.

[22] International Labour Organization, 2018. *World Employment and Social Outlook: Trends 2018*. Geneva: International Labour Office, pp. 11–12.

[23] Canning, D., Sangeeta, R., and Abdo, Y. S, eds. 2015. Africa's Demographic Transition: Dividend or Disaster? Africa Development Forum series. Washington, p. 19.

[24] United Nations Department of Economic and Social Affairs, 2018. Estimates and Projections of Family Planning Indicators 2018. [Online] Available at: https://www.un.org/en/development/desa/population/theme/family-planning/cp_model.asp.

The potential for a rapid uptake of contraceptives with a large impact on fertility and the potential to improve Africa's demographic dividend is therefore large.[25]

The Components of the Demographic Dividend Scenario

In this section, I explore a scenario called the Demographic Dividend that could set the continent on a demographic trajectory quite different to the Current Path. In designing and exploring this scenario, I do not ask how these policies are motivated or assess the inevitable socio-political challenges that would accompany them. Rather, I only look at the potential impact of successful implementation.

Owing to the slow-moving nature of demographic dynamics, I also take a longer view than in most of the other chapters in the book. As with other chapters the interventions in the IFs system are detailed at www.jakkiecillie rs.org and benchmarked against the historical and expected progress in South America and South Asia as two comparable regions.

The first, and most impactful, intervention is the ambitious roll-out of modern contraceptives in sub-Saharan Africa (since total fertility rates in North Africa are already very low) which should be possible given the unmet demand mentioned previously. Whereas, in 2020, only 31% of fertile women in sub-Saharan Africa use modern contraceptives, the intervention pushes that rate up to 68% by 2040—21 percentage points above the Current Path forecast for that year.

A second intervention is a modest reduction in child and adult female mortality rates from communicable diseases. This intervention imitates a health system better equipped for family planning. A high under-five mortality rate is an important driver of high levels of desired fertility since high child mortality rates translate into families having more children. Maternal mortality is already forecast to decrease on the Current Path from 402 deaths per 100,000 live births in 2020 to 190 in 2040. The intervention

---

[25] For example, three low-income countries (Rwanda, Ethiopia and Malawi) achieved a 13–19% increase in contraceptive use over 15 years (2000–2015) and 22–27% over 30 years (1985–2015). Three lower-middle-income countries (eSwatini, Lesotho and Zambia) achieved an 11–12% increase in contraceptive use over 15 years (2000–2015) and 22–23% over 30 years (1985–2015).

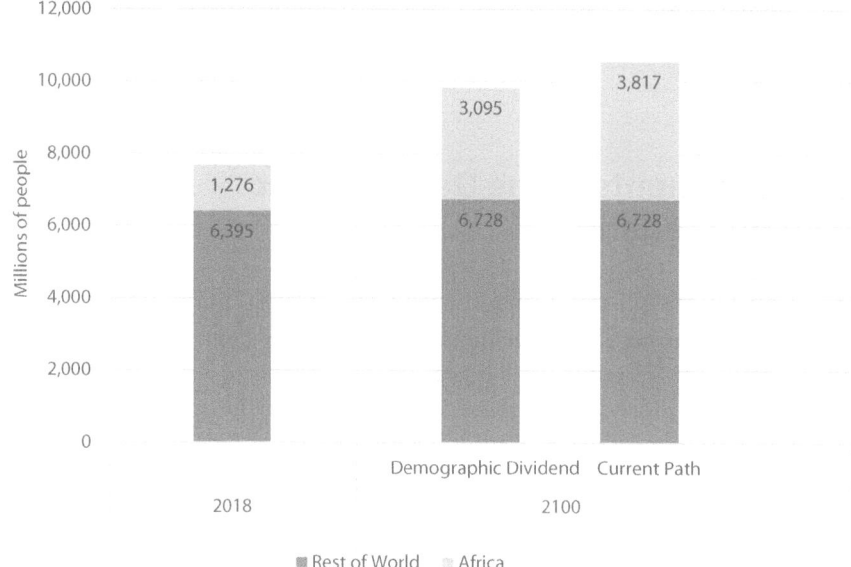

Fig. 4.5 Peak World population in 2018 and 2100 under different scenarios (*Source* IFs v 7.45 initialising from UN Population Division World Population Prospects, 2017 revision)

reduces the 2040 number to 90, which is still significantly above the 2040 number of 29 in South America and 39 in South Asia.[26]

A final intervention is a 20% improvement on a general index that measures female empowerment.[27] Although generally considered the fundamental or deep driver of changes in the number of children that women decide to have, women's empowerment is also the intervention with the least direct impact on demographics. This is because changes in social norms normally take longer to impact on fertility than other measures.

Scenario Impact on Global Population

Given the momentum behind Africa's youthful population, the impact of the Demographic Dividend scenario on the size of the world's population would be substantial. These forecasts are presented in Fig. 4.5 that presents

---

[26] Eastern and Southern Africa have seen the most improvement since 2000 United Nations Children's Fund, September 2019. Maternal Mortality Declined by 38 Percent Between 2000 and 2017. [Online] Available at: https://data.unicef.org/topic/maternal-health/maternal-mortality/.

[27] IFs still uses the Gender Empowerment Measure (GEM) for its history and forecasts. GEM has now been discontinued and replaced by the Gender Inequality Index (GII).

the forecast of peak world population in the Current Path and Demographic Dividend scenario. In the Demographic Dividend scenario peak world population should occur just before 2080 at roughly 10 billion people with enormous positive implications for global sustainability. In the Current Path forecast peak global population would occur a decade or so later, at 10.5 billion people. Whereas Africa would constitute 29% of the global population at the time of the Demographic Dividend peak in 2077, it would constitute 35% of the global population in 2089 along the Current Path.

By the end of the century, Africa's population would grow to 3.1 billion people in the Demographic Dividend scenario (constituting 32% of global population) and be close to its peak population (as opposed to peak World population discussed in the previous paragraph), while on the Current Path it is expected to be more than 3.8 billion people (constituting 36% of global population) and still be several decades away from a Current Path population peak for the continent.

These forecasts over extended time horizons are, I need to emphasise, very uncertain. Forecasting to 2040 is already stretching our understanding of how human and natural systems interact. Things will certainly be very different by 2100. For example, while the UNPD medium variant population forecast to 2100 is for a global population at 10.88 billion people (compared to the IFs Current Path forecast of 10.5 billion). Its low variant projection is only 7.32 billion and its high variant for a much larger number of 15.60 billion people.[28] Many things could impact this forecast of which the impact of climate change, discussed in Chapter 15, could be the most important.

Impact of the Demographic Dividend on Africa

The impact of the Demographic Dividend on sub-Saharan Africa compared to the Current Path forecast is presented in Fig. 4.6. I include only the Current Path ratio of working age persons to dependents for North Africa since this region is much further along in the demographic transition and benefits little from the Demographic Dividend scenario. Figure 4.6 also includes a line graph on the ratio of working age persons to dependents for the World except Africa, that peaked in 2012. I include this to show that, outside of Africa, the size of the working age population relative to dependents is now declining, although it differs from region to region, implying

---

[28] United Nations, Department of Economic and Social Affairs, World Population Prospects 2019, https://population.un.org/wpp/Download/Standard/Population/. Accessed on 31 December 2019.

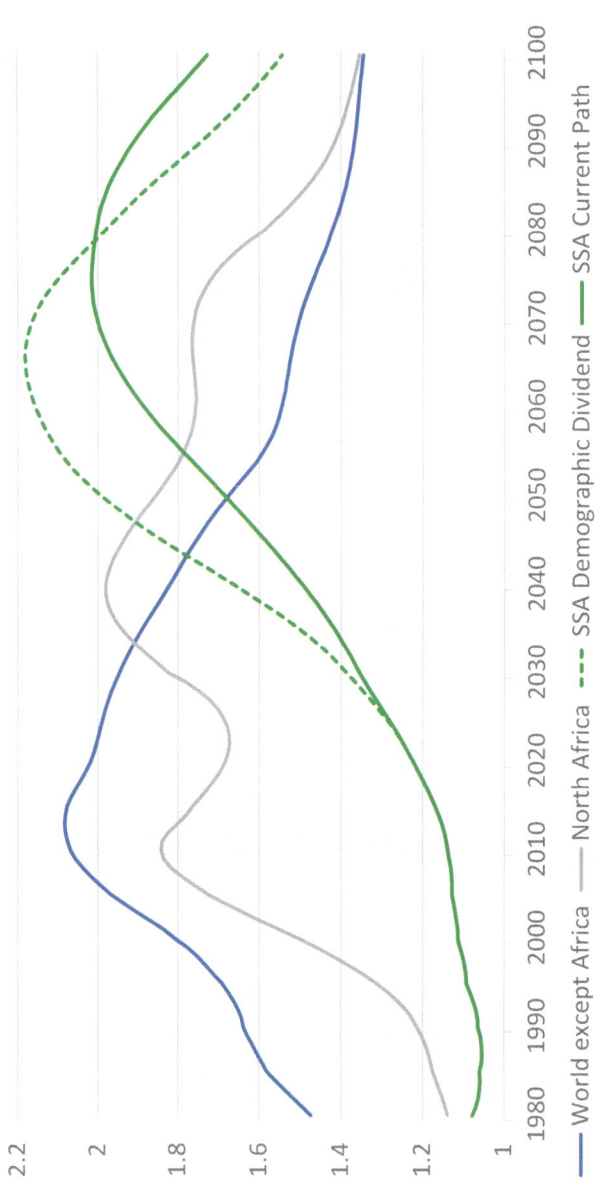

Fig. 4.6 Ratio of working age to dependants: Africa vs World except Africa: 1980 to 2100 (Source Historical data from United Nations Population Division World Population Prospects, the 2017 revision. Forecast in IFs v 7.45)

that these regions have to first compensate for that decline with more capital and technology to maintain current levels of productivity.

The Demographic Dividend scenario advances the onset of sub-Saharan Africa's peak demographic dividend by 8 years (from 2074 to 2066), and increases the peak ratio of persons of working age to dependents from 2.0 to 2.2, resulting in a larger portion of persons of working age to dependants than would otherwise be the case. In the Demographic Dividend scenario sub-Saharan Africa gets to the 1.7 ratio in 2042 and exits in 2093, more than half a century later, about the same period as it spends in this favourable window in the Current Path. But because the peak ratio is higher, economic growth and incomes grow more rapidly in the Demographic Dividend scenario. For that reason the total size of the economy of sub-Saharan Africa is smaller, as one would expect with a smaller population, but only by about US$61 billion in 2040. Much more important is what happens to GDP per person for sub-Saharan Africa which is more than US$220 higher by 2040 at US$6055 than on the Current Path—and this would be for a population of 1.785 billion people! All these indicators gain momentum over time and their true impact only becomes evident a decade or so later.

With more persons of working age and fewer children to educate, less basic infrastructure to build and slowing population growth, the improvements cascade across various indices of human well-being. For example, the number of people living below the US$1.90 extreme poverty line in sub-Saharan Africa would be 9 million people fewer in 2030 and 50 million people fewer in 2040.

Table 4.1 presents the impact of the Demographic Dividend scenario on the five countries in Africa that, by 2040, would have the largest population.

Inevitably the impact of the Demographic Dividend scenario accelerates over time. Whereas, by 2040, the population of sub-Saharan Africa would be about 80 million fewer, by 2063 (the end year of the African Union's Agenda 2063 vision) sub-Saharan Africa would have a population that is about 340 million people less, a slightly smaller total economy, but because of more rapid growth, average GDP per capita (in purchasing power parity or PPP) that is US$830 more.

The difference between the Current Path and the Demographic Dividend scenarios on population structure and education by 2063 is presented in Fig. 4.7, using a common scale for each pyramid. In the Demographic Dividend scenario, Africa has a much more mature population structure with a distinctive bulge along the midriff, compared to the more youthful structure of its population that is evident in the Current Path forecast.

Table 4.1 Impact of demographic dividend: selected countries and indicators of impact

	Population: Demographic Dividend compared to Current Path	Economy: Demographic Dividend compared to Current Path	Reduction in people without access to safe water	GDP per capita	Reduction in people in extreme poverty (US$1.90)
Nigeria	353 instead of 361 million	US$15.5 billion smaller	1.9 million	US$185 increase to US$8330	6.5 million
Ethiopia	166 instead of 178 million	US$0.2 billion smaller	541,000	US$205 increase to US$4840	2 million
DRC	155 instead of 161 million	US$0.7 billion smaller	1.2 million	US$50 increase to US$1520	6.8 million
Tanzania	95 instead of 101 million	US$4 billion smaller	1.7 million	US$320 increase to US$5810	3.8 million
Uganda	83 instead of 89 million	US$3.5 billion smaller	61,5000	US$234 increase to US$4070	4.2 million

Source IFs v7.45

The red grouping at the heart of each population pyramid indicates no education or incomplete primary education. The blue ribs on the outer edge of the pyramid indicate completed tertiary education. In the Demographic Dividend scenario the median years of adult education in Africa would have increased by two months (to 8.8 years), with a concomitant impact on labour productivity.

In the Demographic Dividend scenario, Africa also reduces the gap in average education levels for adults between itself and the rest of the world.

While Zimbabwe, Malawi, Zambia São Tomé & Príncipe, Kenya and Rwanda would experience the largest increase in percentage point terms of their working age persons by 2040, Morocco, Seychelles, Libya and Mauritius would actually have a marginally smaller working age population than in the Current Path forecast.

The effects of the interventions in the Demographic Dividend scenario are also significant in various other indices of well-being. The infant mortality rate in Africa would fall to approximately 18 deaths per live births by 2040,

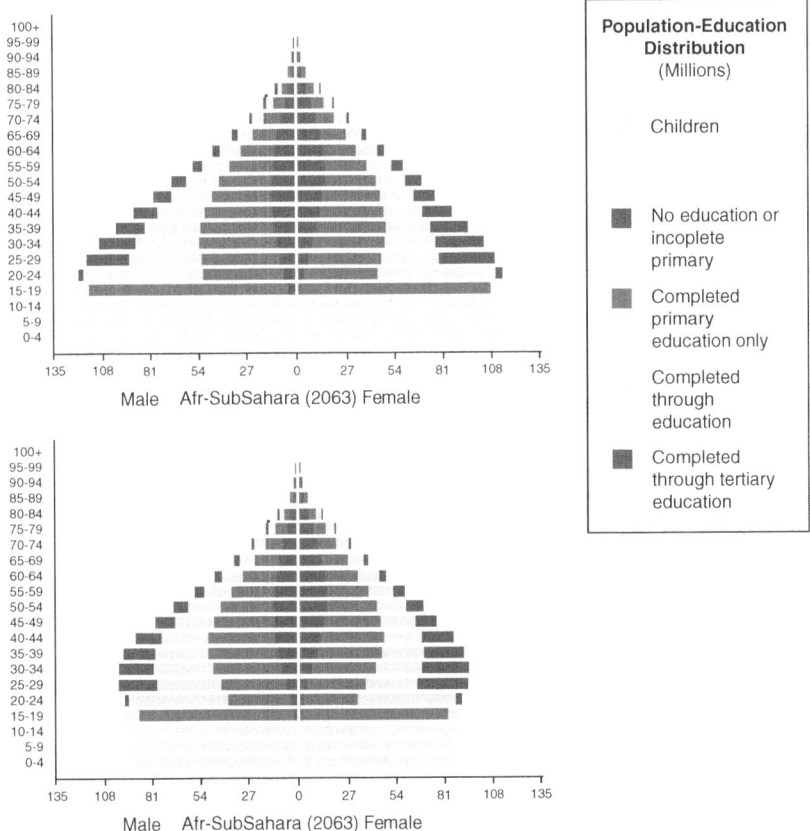

Fig. 4.7 Population education distribution for sub-Saharan Africa in 2063 in Current Path vs Demographic Dividend scenario (*Source* IFs 7.36 initialising from United Nations Population Division medium term forecast and Barro-Lee educational attainment dataset)

compared to 25 deaths on the Current Path. Meanwhile, the average fertility rate would drop to 2.6 children per woman by 2040 and to two children before 2060. On the Current Path, this average is expected to drop to 3.3 children by 2040, and 2.3 children by 2060.

Conclusion: Reducing Fertility Rates and Working Towards Africa's Demographic Dividend

This chapter has explained how very high fertility rates in much of Africa currently are a drag on development. Although Africa's demographic profile started to change for the better from the late 1980s, the ratio of working age persons to dependants has only slowly improved. Under current expectations sub-Saharan Africa will only achieve a demographic dividend in the second half of the twenty-first century at which point the value of the contribution of a larger labour force to economic growth is likely to have reduced.

The empowerment of women lies at the root of fertility rates. As the World Bank noted in an extensive study on African demographics. '[T]he number of children that a couple have depends directly on a woman's position in the household and her bargaining power relative to that of her husband'.[29]

There is a large body of literature supporting the idea that greater inclusion of women can improve overall development outcomes and potentially economic growth.[30] A study from the McKinsey Global Institute concludes, maybe somewhat hyperbolically, that advancing women's equality to a 'best in region' benchmark, could add US$12 trillion to the global economy by 2025, while a 'full potential' scenario could add US$28 trillion.[31]

A demographic dividend can be enhanced and intensified through the accelerated roll-out of modern contraceptives and the improved health of women and children by investing in basic infrastructure such as the provision of clean water and improved sanitation that was discussed in Chapter 3. In addition, access to quality education and adequate nutrition are other key enablers that improve human capital. These are all discussed in separate chapters.

Finally, in order to fully realise the potential of the demographic dividend people need job opportunities which is probably Africa's biggest challenge. This matter will be examined further in Chapter 9.

All these interventions to unlock Africa's human capital will require governments, especially those in low- and lower-middle-income countries, to make family planning a high priority on their developmental agenda. This applies most pertinently to Niger, Somalia, the Democratic Republic of the Congo, Mali, Chad, Angola, Burundi, Nigeria, Uganda, The Gambia, Burkina Faso and Mozambique. In all these countries the total fertility rate currently exceeds five children per woman. In an additional 23 countries, the average fertility rate exceeds four children per woman. That rural fertility

---

[29] Canning, D., Sangeeta, R., and Abdo, Y. S, eds. 2015. Africa's Demographic Transition: Dividend or Disaster? Africa Development Forum series. Washington, p. 17.

[30] Barro, R. J., 1996. Determinants of Economic Growth: A Cross-Country Empirical Study. NBER Working Paper No. 5698, August. And also: Rothman, D. S., Irfan, M. T., Margolese-Malin, E., Hughes, B. B., and Moyer, J. D., 2014. *Building Global Infrastructure: Forecasting the Next 50 Years. Patterns of Potential Human Progress*. Boulder: Paradigm Publishers, Volume 4.

[31] Woetzel, J., Madgavkar A., Ellingrud, K., Labaye, E., Devillard, S., Kutcher, E., Manyika, J., Dobbs, R., and Krishnan, M. 2015. McKinsey Global Institute. [Online] Available at: https://www.mckinsey.com/featured-insights/employment-and-growth/how-advancing-womens-equality-can-add-12-trillion-to-global-growth.

rates are significantly higher than those in urban areas and differ according to income complicates these dynamics.

From a societal point of view, this means that Africans need to engage candidly and robustly in public discussions and scholarly analysis on the economic and developmental implications of the continent's large youthful population. Changes in fertility reflect shifts in social and cultural norms that may take time, but while the fertility transition is slow to get started it can rapidly pick up momentum.

Political leadership in discussing gender inequality, fertility and family size is vital, as are public media campaigns that demonstrate the health and economic benefits of smaller families.

Subsequent chapters will touch on the additional benefits of advancing Africa's demographic dividend, including the prospect for less political turbulence with a declining youth bulge, the lower chance of experiencing a violent political transition (Chapter 12), and the increased chance of being a liberal democracy as median age increases (Chapter 13).

Although the impact of the Demographic Dividend scenario is significant, it is insufficient to reverse the Current Path forecast of growing divergence in average incomes between Africa and the rest of the world. To improve its human capital endowment, the continent requires a consort of structural transitions, including an agricultural revolution, that is the subject of the next chapter.

Further Reading

Lee, R., and Mason, A., 2006. *Back to Basics: What Is the Demographic Dividend?* [Online] Available at: https://www.imf.org/external/pubs/ft/fandd/2006/09/basics.htm.

Preston, S., Heuveline, P., and Michel Guillot, 2001. *Demography: Measuring and Modeling Population Processes.* Oxford: Blackwell Publishers Ltd.

United Nations Department of Economic and Social Affairs (Population Division), 2019. World Population Prospects 2019: Highlights. [Online] Available at https://population.un.org/wpp/Publications/Files/WPP2019_Highlights.pdf.

Open Access This chapter is licensed under the terms of the Creative Commons Attribution 4.0 International License (http://creativecommons.org/licenses/by/4.0/), which permits use, sharing, adaptation, distribution and reproduction in any medium or format, as long as you give appropriate credit to the original author(s) and the source, provide a link to the Creative Commons license and indicate if changes were made.

The images or other third party material in this chapter are included in the chapter's Creative Commons license, unless indicated otherwise in a credit line to the material. If material is not included in the chapter's Creative Commons license and your intended use is not permitted by statutory regulation or exceeds the permitted use, you will need to obtain permission directly from the copyright holder.

5

Wanted: A Revolution in Agriculture

Abstract Agriculture is the backbone of many African economies. Cilliers explores the history and role of agriculture in development, and the likely future trajectory of agriculture in Africa along the Current Path, drawing lessons from other regions. Improvements in this sector, particularly access to finance and use of modern technology can unlock the significant potential to achieve food security, improve health and nutrition outcomes, create agribusiness ventures that influence employment, earn foreign exchange through exports and promote economic prosperity. The chapter concludes with a scenario that emulates the impact of a revolution in agriculture on food security and growth.

Keywords Yields · Productivity · Calories · Food security · Agricultural efficiency · Intensive-farming · Poverty · Agriculture

Learning objectives

- Agriculture as foundational to human development and industrialisation
- Constraints on agricultural development in Africa
- Importance of food self-sufficiency for sustainable development.

Agriculture is the bedrock of human development—in many ways, farming is the organising principle of civilisation. The clustering of societies alongside the great rivers of the world from the Nile and the Euphrates to the Yangtze would not have been possible without the domestication of animals and the cultivation of crops that allowed for denser concentrations

© The Author(s) 2021
J. Cilliers, *The Future of Africa*,
https://doi.org/10.1007/978-3-030-46590-2_5

of people. This historical occurrence, the Neolithic revolution, started more than 12,000 years ago when the pressure of rising numbers and changing climates forced humans to adapt from their nomadic hunter-gatherer lifestyle and slowly turned to farming to meet the needs of their growing populations.

The Neolithic revolution led to food being stored in granaries and the domestication of animals for slaughter, transport and work. It also brought new infectious diseases, such as tuberculosis, smallpox and measles due to the concentration of people in permanent settlements. While this greater concentration of people did little to improve the quality of life for many, it was key to development.

Previously hunter-gatherer societies were constantly on the move in search of food. Farmers, on the other hand, needed to remain close to their fields and could store food surpluses for winter or to feed more animals. They generally had more children, in part as a source of labour but also because many died. With the transition to farming, humanity became sedentary in settled villages and towns with specialised food-crop cultivation, irrigation and close to cleared areas for tilling and planting. They made pots to preserve foods and developed ways of storing knowledge (writing). Soon a division of labour followed and communities started a barter system of trade, developed rules of property ownership and learnt how to use metal.

With the noteworthy exceptions of the Nile river, modern-day Ethiopia and some parts of West Africa and the Sahel, the agricultural development pathway in Africa followed a somewhat unique trajectory. The low population density was partly a function of Africa's high disease burden (examined in Chapter 3). Because much of Africa is located in the tropics with relatively high and stable temperatures and little seasonal change there is little relief from the activities of harmful bacteria or disease-bearing insects and mammals such as mosquitoes and bats. The subsequent high disease burden kept population levels down in large parts of the continent even as humanity expanded rapidly elsewhere.

In addition poor soil quality also seems to have played a role in constraining agricultural development in Africa. The overall availability of nutrients in soil is initially determined by the nature of the geological parent material, which in the continent's more ancient soils are poor. The most significant exception is along great rivers such as the Nile and along the length of the Great Rift Valley in East and Central Africa.[1]

---

[1] Reader, J., 1998. *Africa: A Biography of the Continent.* New York: Penguin Books, p. 99. Also see Diamond, J., 2015. *Guns, Germs and Steel: The Fates of Human Societies.* New York City: W. W. Norton. Also Tignor, R., Adelman, J., Brown, P., Elman, B., Liu, X., Pittman, H., and Shaw., B., 2010. *Worlds Together, Worlds Apart: A History of the World: Beginnings Through the Fifteenth Century.* 3rd Edition ed. New York: W. W. Norton. A 1997 study by the US Department of Agriculture

For these and other reasons, farming seems to have emerged in sub-Saharan Africa much later than elsewhere, although our evidence on exactly how and why this happened continues to evolve. Another reason could relate to the relative short lifespan of Africa's numerous empires, which all collapsed or were forcibly dismantled by outsiders before organised agriculture could establish itself and spread.[2]

In more recent history, slavery, particularly the Arab slave trade in North and East Africa in the mid-seventh century and the European slave trade from late fifteenth century, disrupted agricultural development. From the sixteenth to the nineteenth-century slave trade in North and East Africa overlapped with the Transatlantic slave trade. Collectively the two had a devastating impact on the African continent. While the ten centuries of the Arab slave trade was more of a steady trickle rather than a deluge, the size of the Arab slave trade was at least equal to if not larger than the 10–12 million Africans that were forcibly captured and shipped to the Americas.[3] Slavery meant that African societies remained more dispersed and mobile than others.

In a situation of lawlessness and violence where large populations were constantly on the move to avoid capture, farming was challenging. Once potential slaves had been captured it was often the young, elderly or disabled who were left behind. In the process large parts of Africa were denuded of its productive labour force. Farming and herding could therefore not develop in a systematic manner and neither could social, political and economic systems mature to allow for technological and productivity improvements to track development in other regions of the world.[4]

With the demise of slave trade at the beginning of the nineteenth century following abolishment in Britain in 1807 and the USA in 1865, the continuous drain of labour ended. However, it was soon replaced by other forced labour schemes under the guise of imperialism and colonialism.

During the Berlin conference in 1884 Africa was divided between various European states. In the decades that followed the continent became an increasingly important source of raw materials such as cotton to feed the factories in Great Britain, Germany, Belgium, France, Italy, Portugal and

---

calculates that 'Fifty five percent of the land in Africa is unsuitable for any kind of agriculture except nomadic grazing.' Eswaran, H., Almaraz, R., Reich, P., and Zdruli, P., 1997. Soil Quality and Soil Productivity in Africa. *Journal of Sustainable Agriculture*, 10(4).

[2] Aydon, C., 2009. *A Brief History of Mankind: An Introduction to 150,000 Years of Human History.* Philadelphia: Running Press; Diamond, J., 2015. *Guns, Germs and Steel: The fates of human societies.* New York City: W.W. Norton; Reader, J., 1998. *Africa: A Biography of the Continent.* New York: Penguin Books.

[3] Shahadah, A., 2017. *Arab Slave Trade.* [Online] Available at: http://www.arabslavetrade.com/.

[4] Lewis, T., 2018. *Transatlantic Slave Trade.* [Online] Available at: https://www.britannica.com/topic/transatlantic-slave-trade.

Spain, linking and shaping Africa's agricultural exports to the demands of its colonisers. Exports had to be supplied at the lowest possible price and since labour costs were the most important cost consideration, it comes as no surprise that Africans generally received poverty wages at the sprawling colonial farms on which they worked.

Elsewhere the introduction of crops such as peanuts and sesame replaced dietary staples such as millet and sorghum. The result was declining food reserves, chronic malnutrition and famine in spite of the development of a sizable commercial cash crop system that was, in turn, dominated by settler farmers.

With a firm focus on exports to feed and industrialise its colonial masters, Africa's infrastructure of road and rail was orientated towards the coast from where its produce could be shipped to Europe. Consequently, the rural and domestic agricultural sector and regional trade were either destroyed or remained economically marginal. In this way slavery, imperialism and colonialism fundamentally altered the development of agriculture on the continent. It effectively destroyed Africa's burgeoning trade in food and displaced a host of indigenous crops with foodstuffs and commodities that were useful for the industrialising economies in Europe but that undermined food security at home.

Effectively, Africa was forced to export more commodities whose values were declining as the terms of trade, i.e. the ratio between export prices versus import prices for non-oil primary commodities, steadily declined over the long term. According to one estimate Africa's terms of trade in 1940 had reverted to the levels it experienced in 1800 as the continent became poorer compared to all other regions.[5]

After Independence

Independence brought many benefits, but few accrued to agriculture for, with limited exceptions, Africa's post-independent leaders placed rural and agricultural development at the very end of the line in terms of resource and budgetary allocation. Locked into an inequitable supply chain that effectively penalised efforts towards food self-sufficiency and disincentivised improvement of domestic value-add to its agricultural commodities, Africa's agricultural productivity continued to lag further and further behind other regions.

---

[5]Frankema, E., 2015. *How Africa's Colonial History Affects Its Development.* [Online] Available at: https://www.weforum.org/agenda/2015/07/how-africas-colonial-history-affects-its-development/.

In September 1973 World Bank president Robert McNamara, in an oft-cited speech delivered to his Board of Governors in Nairobi, clearly identified the root of Africa's major problem of rural poverty as the lack of smallholder agricultural development.[6]

McNamara's speech came at a time of relative growth in Africa although more than 200 million Africans lived in absolute poverty (with many more in Asia). He pointed out that official development assistance was 'acutely inadequate' to respond to this situation while government debt was increasing in the most affected countries.

Under his leadership, the Bank aggressively pursued a strategy for rural development with an emphasis on productivity of smallholder agriculture. By the time that McNamara stepped down in 1981 the World Bank had significantly extended its efforts at agricultural development.[7] However, the Bank's efforts were scaled down and dismantled after he left.

McNamara's resignation in 1981 after 13 years as president of the Bank coincided with a decline in Africa's fortunes as successive oil and other shocks took their toll. From 1980 to 1994 income per capita declined and only returned to its 1980 levels in 2004—although things were improving, Africa was falling further behind.[8]

Agriculture Today

According to the most recent (2017) UN Food and Agriculture Organization (FAO) data, 14 of the 20 countries with the lowest average cereal yields per hectare globally, were in Africa.[9] At the same time Africa is home to only one of the top 10 most productive agricultural sectors in terms of cereal yields. That country is Egypt, which obviously benefits from having one of the most productive agricultural deltas in the world in the form of the Nile river.

---

[6] McNamara, R., 1973. *Address to the Board of Governors by Robert S. McNamara Presidential speech.* Washington, DC: World Bank.
[7] See Jochen Kraske with Becker, William H., Diamond, William, and Galambos, Louis, 1996. *Bankers with a Mission: The Presidents of the World Bank, 1946–91.* Oxford University Press, pp. 159–211.
[8] Rowen, H., 1980. *McNamara to Step Down At World Bank Next Year.* [Online] Available at: https://www.washingtonpost.com/archive/politics/1980/06/10/mcnamara-to-step-down-at-world-bank-next-year/a7f20b6b-f3cb-4661-9e10-a22a55eedc6a/?noredirect=on&utm_term=.846cd4f3f97c.
[9] The data is taken from the World Bank, cereal yield (kg per hectare) https://data.worldbank.org/indicator/AG.YLD.CREL.KG?most_recent_value_desc=false&view=chart. The African countries, in ascending order of productivity, are Cape Verde, Botswana, Niger, Algeria, Burkina Faso, Eswatini, Togo, Guinea, Senegal, Rwanda, Liberia, Comoros, Maurania and Burundi. The geographical spread of African countries highlights the scope of the problem.

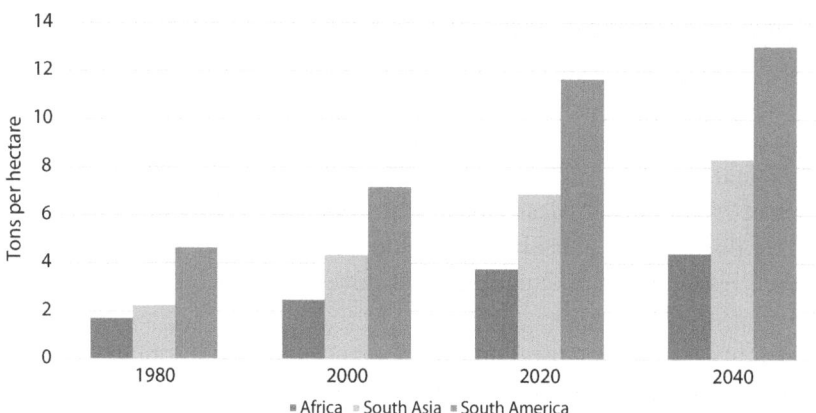

Fig. 5.1 Yields per hectare (pre-loss): 1980 and 2000, and Current Path forecast for 2020 and 2040 (*Source* Historical data from the Food and Agriculture Organization and forecast in IFs 7.45)

After Egypt, one has to scroll past 15 countries to find the next African state, South Africa, where agriculture contributes less than three percent to GDP.

Despite a few recent success stories like Ethiopia, Madagascar, Mauritania and Sierra Leone which doubled cereal yields between 2000 and 2016 the agricultural sector in sub-Saharan Africa is significantly less productive than in other regions. In 1980 agricultural yields in Africa were roughly similar to those in South Asia. But with crop yields at below four tons per hectare today, average agricultural yields in Africa are one-third of the average for South America (agriculturally one of the most productive regions globally) and three tons per hectare below that in South Asia. Figure 5.1 presents a snapshot of the growing gap in average yields between these three regions with historical data for 1980 and 2000 and the Current Path forecast for 2020 and 2040.

Furthermore, in Africa very little of the land under cultivation is irrigated. Globally, irrigated agriculture represents 21% of the total cultivated land, but contributes 40% to the total amount of food produced. Sub-Saharan Africa has the lowest portion of cultivated land under irrigation at just over three percent.[10] This means that the vast majority of cropland is dependent on good rainfall which is increasingly irregular due to the impact of climate change.

---

[10]Food and Agriculture Organization, 2014. *Aquastat Facts and Figures About.* [Online] Available at: http://www.fao.org/nr/water/aquastat/didyouknow/index3.stm.

Even though the agricultural yields per hectare on the continent is improving, it reflects a growing gap when compared to averages in the rest of the world, evident in Fig. 5.1. The pedestrian improvement in agriculture productivity in Africa amidst rapid population growth contributes to the slow rate of poverty reduction among other factors such as relatively high levels of inequality. Food security is declining as African countries import larger quantities of food with each passing year.[11]

In recent years Africa's annual agricultural trade deficit (the difference between the value of imports minus exports) stood at roughly US$100 billion per annum and is expected to increase to more than US$330 billion by 2030. Along the Current Path forecast Africa could be importing more than a third of its agricultural requirements by 2040, which leaves the continent extremely vulnerable to fluctuations in food and other commodity prices.

This import dependence is largely a result of low agricultural yields in much of Africa and large post-production losses, i.e. the loss and waste that occurs from production on the farm to consumption. Whereas the average loss and waste of agricultural produce in the rest of the world is roughly 14%, in Africa it is calculated at 25%. In West Africa it accumulates to more than 30%. Unlike in Europe and North America where food reaches the consumer but is then discarded or wasted, most of the food loss in Africa happens in the production stage meaning that almost a third of the food being produced does not even reach the consumer. Better storage and infrastructure would help reduce losses, but more detailed data on the supply chain would also help—and here modern technology can play a large role.

The contribution of agriculture as a portion of an economy generally declines as countries graduate from low to middle and eventually to high-income status. For instance, in Africa's 24 low-income countries agriculture contributes an average of about 32% to GDP, about 22% in the 21 low-middle-income countries and about 8% in Africa's eight upper-middle-income countries. By 2040 these portions will have declined to 12, 9 and 6%, respectively. Currently the agricultural sector in Western Africa is the largest (at US$198 billion) and is expected to experience the most rapid growth since this is also the region where economies will expand most rapidly across the forecast horizon. By 2040 the size of West Africa's agricultural sector will have increased to US$238 billion (or by 120%). The agricultural sector in Central Africa is the smallest (currently at US$33 billion) and although it too will grow (by 70%) will only amount to US$46 billion by 2040.

---

[11] Veras, O., 2017. *Agriculture in Africa: Potential Versus Reality.* [Online] Available at: https://www.howwemadeitinafrica.com/agriculture-africa-potential-versus-reality/57635/.

Obstacles to a Revolution in Agriculture

According to the World Bank agricultural markets regularly fail African farmers. It notes in one of its reports that the 'pattern of market failures is general and structural, and not related to the head-of-household's gender, or to geographic characteristics such as distance to roads or to large population centers'.[12] In other words, African farms are less productive because farmers are chronically unable to access the finances (or credit) that would allow them to purchase critical inputs that could improve yields such as fertiliser and seed.

Take for example the matter of fertilisers. Generally the soil on the continent is poor in nutrients[13] and since African farmers use significantly less fertiliser than their counterparts in other regions of the world, soil fertility depletion generally continues unabated. The reason for low fertiliser use is that prices in Africa are between two and six times the average world price because the continent generally imports fertiliser instead of manufacturing it.[14] Then there is the issue of limited irrigation, low levels of mechanisation (since labour is cheap and farmers lack capital), lack of consensus and investment in genetically modified seeds that are more resilient to disease, slow progress with organic farming and the low use of indigenous crops that are better suited to the continent but that were largely phased out during colonialism.

African farmers have traditionally followed a practice of land rotation using slash and burn practices—they would clear new lands and leave the old field fallow for a year or two to recover. But as population numbers have increased, shortages of arable land have forced farmers to cultivate the same fields season after season. A lot of agricultural land is located in peri-urban areas (for instance in Kenya and Ethiopia) where urban sprawl is driving up land prices and swallowing up some of Africa's best farmland. These are often also the only areas with sufficient roads to allow the transport of produce to the market.

Elsewhere, where prime agricultural land is located far away from major population centres, the lack of paved roads and other infrastructure means

---

[12]World Bank, n.d. *Agriculture in Africa: Telling Facts from Myths*. [Online] Available at: http://www.worldbank.org/en/programs/africa-myths-and-facts.

[13]Hengl, T. Leenaars, J. G. B., Shepherd, K. D., Walsh, M. G., Heuvelink, G. B. M., Mamo. T., Tilahun, H., Berkhout, E., Cooper, M., Fegraus, E., Wheeler, I., and Kwabena, N. A., 2017. Soil Nutrient Maps of Sub-Saharan Africa: Assessment of Soil Nutrient Content at 250 m Spatial Resolution Using Machine Learning. *Nutrient Cycling in Agroecosystems*, 109(1), pp. 77–102.

[14]See, for example, Doukkali, M. R., and Guèdègbé, T. 2018, Fertilizer Use in Africa: A Price Issue, Policy Brief 18, OCP Policy Center, 29 August 2018, accessed on 23 December 2019. https://www.policycenter.ma/sites/default/files/OCPPC-PB1827-ENG.pdf.

that arable land is effectively not used for large-scale production. The Democratic Republic of Congo and Angola are excellent examples of two countries with significant agricultural potential that have been wracked by conflict and the destruction of their limited infrastructure, hence constraining their ability to expand production.

Angola is one of Africa's largest and most fertile countries and was, before independence in 1975, self-sufficient in all main food crops except wheat. In fact it was the fourth largest coffee producer globally, but the subsequent war that lasted until 2002 destroyed much of its infrastructure.[15] Most of its population fled to urban areas, generally to the capital Luanda. Today nearly seven out of ten Angolans reside in urban areas and it has a total road network that is in the region of 76,000 kilometres—only marginally better than the 72,300 kilometres that it had when it gained independence.[16] And even these modest improvements followed a concerted recent effort by the government to invest in connecting infrastructure. Available data suggest that the extent of paved roads as a portion of total roads now stands at around 24% (it was around 10% before independence).[17] As a result, in 2018, Angola ranked a poor 159th of 167 countries globally on the World Bank's Logistics Performance Index. Neighbouring Democratic Republic of Congo, host to the largest peacekeeping mission in the world and still wracked by instability in the east and elsewhere, is ranked at number 120.[18]

Unsustainable cultivation practices in high-density areas are leading to serious soil degradation.[19] What's more, as average farm sizes shrink, the pressure to get more food from less land in order to feed one's family tends to lead to unsustainable farming practices, which further decreases soil fertility. To this end the Alliance for a Green Revolution in Africa (AGRA) calls for a

---

[15] Food and Agriculture Organization, Angola Country Programming Framework, 2013–2017. www.fao.org/3/a-bp627e.pdf, p. 12; Nathan Associated Inc., 2006. Angola: Diagnostic Trade Integration Study. World Bank, p. 2.

[16] African Economic Outlook: Angola Country Note. African Development Bank, p. 9. www.afdb.org/fileadmin/uploads/afdb/Documents/Generic-Documents/country_notes/Angola_country_note.pdf. See "Notes on road data" in the annexure for the sources of data.

[17] African Economic Outlook: Angola Country Note. African Development Bank, p. 9. www.afdb.org/fileadmin/uploads/afdb/Documents/Generic-Documents/country_notes/Angola_country_note.pdf. See "Notes on road data" in the annexure for the sources of data.

[18] https://openknowledge.worldbank.org/bitstream/handle/10986/29971/LPI2018.pdf, p. 12.

[19] Fleshman, M., n.d. *Boosting African Farm Yields*. [Online] Available at: https://www.un.org/africarenewal/magazine/special-edition-agriculture-2014/boosting-african-farm-yields. And AGRA, 2016. *Africa Agriculture Status Report 2016: Progress Towards Agriculture Transformation in Sub-Saharan Africa*. Nairobi: Africa Fertilizer and Agribusiness Partnership.

holistic land management strategy that includes raising organic matter, moisture retention and other forms of soil rehabilitation in addition to greater inorganic fertiliser.[20]

Two findings from the literature on agriculture in Africa highlight its risks and dormant potential. Firstly, the World Bank notes that 'price risk is the most commonly reported covariate shock, much more so than weather shocks'.[21] Price shocks can come in the form of increases in the cost of inputs like fertiliser and seeds, a collapse in output prices caused by a change in trade policy or just changes to the prices of other staple goods that influence people's ability to survive.

Secondly, farmers' inability to access credit and technology, combined with ineffective labour and input markets complicates matters.[22] Very few farmers are able to purchase additional inputs credit and inevitably spend most of it on fertiliser. The result is that the vast majority of farmers count on bumper harvests to tide them over lean years to the next bumper harvest. These are few and far between and may become increasingly so as the impact of climate change is felt.

The result is that Africa is the most food insecure region globally. According to a joint communique issued by the World Bank, the Food and Agriculture Organization of the UN (FAO), the African Development Bank and the International Fund for Agricultural Development (IFAD) about 256 million Africans faced undernutrition in 2018.[23] The situation is getting worse in many parts of the continent, the organisations stated, because of the negative effects of climate change on agricultural productivity, natural resource degradation, rapid population growth, increasing fragility and insecurity and economic stagnation.

Achieving Food Security

Traditionally, many countries in Africa have had large agricultural sectors but merely exported raw products without adding much, if any, value. For

---

[20]Jayne, T., and Ameyaw, D. S., 2016. Africa's Emerging Agricultural Transformation: Evidence, Opportunities and Challenges. In: *Africa Agriculture Status Report 2016: Progress Towards Agriculture Transformation in Sub-Saharan Africa.* India: AGRA.
[21]World Bank, n.d. *Droughts Dominate Africa's Risk Environment.* [Online] Available at: http://www.worldbank.org/en/programs/africa-myths-and-facts/publication/droughts-dominate-africas-risk-environment.
[22]Alliance for a Green Revolution in Africa (AGRA), 2017. To Ensure Food Security, Keep Soils Healthy. https://agra.org/news/to-ensure-food-security-keep-soils-healthy/.
[23]Communique: Africa Food Security Leadership Dialogue, 5 August 2019. [Online] Available at: https://allafrica.com/view/resource/main/main/id/00121601.html.

example, Africa produces 70% of the world's cocoa, the main ingredient in a chocolate industry that is worth more than US$100 billion globally. Between the two of them Ghana and Côte d'Ivoire produce nearly two-thirds of the global supply of cocoa but Ghana only earns about US$2 billion a year from its colonial-style arrangement with the world's chocolate manufacturers. In fact, Africa accounts for less than one percent of chocolate exports. Europe, which grows no cocoa of its own, exported US$19.2 billion worth of chocolate in 2016.[24]

After years of ineffective efforts at responding to the symptoms of this unequal relationship, such as well-meaning efforts to reduce widespread child labour, things have started to change. Through the Africa Cocoa Initiative, Côte d'Ivoire has overtaken the Netherlands as the world's largest processor of cocoa during the 2014–15 season as it moves up the chocolate value chain. And Ghana is now processing more than a third of its own cocoa.[25] In an effort to increase the farm-gate prices to levels high enough to allow small cocoa producers to escape extreme poverty Ghana and Côte d'Ivoire unilaterally announced that, as from October 2020, they will be charging a fixed premium of US$400 a ton over the benchmark futures price.[26] The problem with such an approach, of course, is that it is likely to increase production and drive down the price, leaving the government to foot the difference. The policy is therefore unlikely to succeed without simultaneous management and control of domestic cocoa production.

But agricultural import dependence is not simply a balance of payments issue. It is also about calories. Hunger, malnutrition and low levels of educational attainment are all well-established causes and symptoms of Africa's underdevelopment and represent significant bottlenecks in the effort to build human capacity and bring about structural economic transformation.[27]

---

[24] Adegoke, Y., 2018. *Why Europe Dominates the Global Chocolate Market While Africa Produces All the Cocoa*. [Online] Available at: https://qz.com/africa/1320998/where-does-chocolate-come-from-eur ope-and-africas-roles-in-the-valuable-market/; Philling, D., 2019. The African Farmers Taking on Big Chocolate. *The Financial Mail*, 16 December 2019.

[25] Fofack, H., 2019. *Overcoming the Colonial Development Model of Resource Extraction for Sustainable Development in Africa*. [Online] Available at: https://www.brookings.edu/blog/africa-in-focus/2019/01/31/overcoming-the-colonial-development-model-of-resource-extraction-for-sustainable-development-in-africa/.

[26] Philling, D., 2019. The African Farmers Taking on Big Chocolate. *The Financial Mail*, 16 December 2019.

[27] Stunting in particular reduces cognitive development and can negatively impact the productivity levels of those that are affected by it for their entire lives. Stunted children grow into stunted adults and if roughly 20% of a population suffers from this condition, as is currently the case in Africa, then it is going to be difficult—if not impossible—to promote the development of industries that require a healthy and reliable workforce.

Between 1970 and 1990, Kenya was mostly a net exporter of food, exporting about one percent of total demand each year. But from 1997 to 2013 the country imported about five percent of total demand per year. The growing reliance on imported food in Kenya has coincided with a decrease in the number of available calories. In 1980, the average Kenyan had access to about 2300 calories per day, which is about equal to the recommended daily average.[28] By 2000, though, the average Kenyan could only expect to access about 2050 calories per day, about 11% less than the recommended allowance.

Insufficient access to calories is a driver of undernutrition and stunting and, together with a lack of access to improved WASH facilities, can lead to a variety of health problems leading to psychosocial and learning challenges (discussed in Chapter 3).[29]

To transition economies towards higher value-added activities, a *healthy*, well-educated population is a prerequisite. A lack of access to safe and affordable food can disrupt education and negatively affect other programmes aimed at improving long-run economic productivity.

In order to capitalise on the benefits of having an educated and healthy population there needs to be an unwavering emphasis on first achieving self-sufficiency, for research conducted by the World Bank finds 'little evidence of a relationship between increased commercialization and improved nutritional status'.[30]

It is particularly imperative for low and low-middle-income African countries to first produce agricultural products for domestic consumption and only then to pursue cash crops for the export market. For example, Africa produces about 45% of the world's cashew nuts, with 90% of that crop being exported for processing overseas but with little obvious benefit to the 2.5 million farmers involved in the industry. The Africa Cashew Alliance estimates that a 25% increase in raw cashew nut processing in Africa would generate more than US$100m household incomes in the sector. As it is, a recent report noted that Tanzania's farmers 'get rock bottom prices and the country imports its own nuts back after processing to meet buoyant domestic

---

[28] The recommended daily caloric intake will vary by individual but the British National Health Service recommends about 2500 calories a day for men and about 2000 for women. NHS, n.d. *What Should My Daily Intake of Calories Be?* [Online] Available at: https://www.nhs.uk/common-health-questions/food-and-diet/what-should-my-daily-intake-of-calories-be/.
[29] Hughes, B. B., et al., 2011. *Improving Global Health: Forecasting the Next 50 Years Is Third in the Patterns of Potential Human Progress.* Volume 3 ed. Denver. Oxford: Paradigm.
[30] World Bank, n.d. *Agriculture in Africa: Telling Facts from Myths.* [Online] Available at: http://www.worldbank.org/en/programs/africa-myths-and-facts.

demand'.³¹ Then, like with cocoa, efforts to increase prices for raw nuts could actually increase production resulting in reduced prices for both raw and processed nuts, hence defeating the purpose.

The Challenge for the Future

Talking about the importance of agriculture in Africa has been a serious business for several decades but actually *doing* something about it is taken much less seriously. The New Partnership for Africa's Development (NEPAD—now the African Union Development Agency-NEPAD) published its Comprehensive Africa Agriculture Development Programme (CAADP) in 2003 with ambitious goals:

> … to allocate at least 10% of national budgets to agriculture, to reach rural growth rates of 6% annually by 2015, integrate and invigorate regional and national agricultural markets, significantly increase agricultural exports, transform Africa into a "strategic player" in global agricultural science and technology, practice sound environmental and land management techniques, and reduce rural poverty.³²

The commitment to devote at least 10% of national budgets to agriculture and rural development was included in the 2003 Maputo Declaration by African heads of state and government and reiterated in the 2014 Malabo Declaration on Accelerated Agricultural Growth and Transformation in Africa. But according to the Food and Agriculture Organization (FAO), only Malawi has achieved the 10% goal, and the average investment is around 2.5% of GDP and declining.³³

Talk is cheap and many African governments, NGOs and citizens generally prefer to blame Europe for lack of access to its agricultural market instead of looking to the need to focus comprehensively on the production of staple foodstuffs for domestic consumption, advancing regional rather than international trade in agriculture, investing in agriculture research, advancing rural

---

³¹IPPMedia, 2019. *Value Add in Africa: First Steps in a Long Journey.* [Online] Available at: https://www.ippmedia.com/en/business/value-add-africa-first-steps-long-journey Also see website of African Cashew Alliance. https://www.africancashewalliance.com/en/about-us.

³²Fleshman, M., 2014. *Boosting African Farm Yields.* [Online] Available at: https://www.un.org/africarenewal/magazine/special-edition-agriculture-2014/boosting-african-farm-yields. NEPAD has subsequently been renamed to African Development Agency (ADA).

³³Tignor, R., Adelman, J., Brown, P., Elman, B., Liu, X., Pittman, H., and Shaw, B., 2010. *Worlds Together, Worlds Apart: A History of the World: Beginnings Through the Fifteenth Century.* 3rd Edition. New York: W. W. Norton.

property rights, in schooling for agriculture and generally focusing attention on rural poverty rather than on urban elites.[34] If African countries prioritise growing staple foods while actively encouraging intensive smallholder farming and sustainable practices, it will increase rural incomes and reduce poverty and eventually open up the potential of agribusiness. This will lead to the much needed revolution in agriculture that will reduce Africa's agricultural import dependence and improve food security.

The potential advantages of agriculture are well known. Boosting the income of farmers' helps stimulate general demand for goods and services in rural areas, which result in new enterprises being established and the economy diversifying. This in turn contributes to the broader process of structural economic transformation.[35] Improving agricultural productivity and boosting local demand 'leads to the development of both upstream and downstream activities, the consolidation of value chains and the expansion of agro-industries, which are significant sources of employment and present real opportunities for economic diversification', notes the International Labour Organization.[36] That will remain true, even if most of the continent's intense agriculture often occurs in the periphery of urban centres, i.e. closer to the market, thanks to the denser network of roads and access to markets here, compared to low rural road density in Africa. The implication is that agricultural development is unlikely to detract from urban slum growth and may even exacerbate it. However, as Africa moves up the agricultural value chain, growth in this sector will expand employment opportunities further along that chain.

Lessons from Elsewhere

Africa is complex and its 55 countries are very different from one another and from other regions, but lessons can be learnt from elsewhere. Contrast, for example, the way in which Deng Xiaoping in China transformed the domestic agricultural sector into a much more productive market-oriented structure in the 1970s and 1980s through the household responsibility system. Land formerly farmed by a collective was henceforth contracted to individual households and, with this new responsibility and various other

---

[34]Food and Agriculture Organization, 2019. *Government Expenditure on Agriculture.* [Online] Available at: http://www.fao.org/economic/ess/investment/expenditure/en/.
[35]Losch, B., 2016. *Structural Transformation to Boost Youth Labour Demand in Sub-Saharan Africa: The Role of Agriculture, Rural Areas and Territorial Development.* Geneva: Employment Working Paper: No. 204. ILO.
[36]Ibid., p. 2.

market-related reforms came productivity improvements to the order of 20% above collective era output. The basis for China's agricultural revolution, the first twenty years, was to focus first on improving productivity on smallholder farms through institutional incentivisation, improving access to better seeds and better farming practices.[37]

China subsequently experienced three consecutive decades of steady improvements in agricultural yields. Average yields nearly tripled between 1970 and 2013 and was an important catalyst in the economic growth enjoyed by the country during those decades. The number of available calories per person increased by nearly 70% and there were more than 20 million fewer undernourished children in 2017 than there were in 1987.

The African experience where small patches of land are owned or farmed by different families relying on unproductive, often traditional practices is quite similar to the situation in China several decades previously. By working from the individual farmer upward, by focusing on techniques and practices that improve smallholder productivity, China was able to transform its agricultural sector and feed its rapidly growing population. Today modern technology plays an important role in China (today copied in Rwanda) through numerous electronic land use transfer systems where farmers can lease their land out to others, creating larger and potentially more productive farms.[38]

China is not the only large and geographically diverse country to transform its agricultural sector in recent decades and from which Africa can learn. Brazil enjoyed rapid improvements in agricultural production in the decade between 2000 and 2010, and while it has traditionally been a net food exporter, the country has improved that position by nearly seven percentage points over that time period. Between 1981 and 2016 Brazil more than doubled average cereal yields despite the size of the land under cultivation only increasing by about 6%.

Not only has Brazil's agricultural sector grown in absolute terms, it has also become very diverse, but like China only achieved that progress once it had graduated to an upper-middle-income country. Today Brazil is the world's largest exporter of both sugar and coffee, second only to the USA

---

[37] In contrast to the tripling in growth cited earlier, this was an improvement across the entire country, so is understandably much smaller. Lin, J. Y., 1988. The Household Responsibility System in China's Agricultural Reform: A Theoretical and Empirical Study. *Economic Development and Cultural Change*, 36(S3).

[38] The China-Africa project podcast no 437: Chinese and African Agriculture, Interview with Xinqing Lu, associate program officer for Alliance for a Green Revolution in Africa, 3 December 2019. https://chinaafricaproject.com/podcasts/chinese-and-african-agriculture-have-a-lot-more-in-common-than-most-people-think/, accessed on 25 December 2019.

in soybean exports and third to the USA and Argentina in maize (corn) exports.[39] The genetic tailoring of seeds and plants played an important role in these changes.

Brazil is now at a stage in development where it can afford to move beyond agricultural production for food security. The country exported approximately 12% more food than it consumed in 2018 and has begun to embrace a 'forest, agriculture and livestock integration' approach to farming that is widely acknowledged to have benefits for both agricultural production and environmental sustainability.[40]

At the other end of the spectrum is Zimbabwe—a country now with little food security. In 2005 former Zimbabwean President Robert Mugabe famously marked the occasion of Zimbabwe's 25th year of independence by saying 'we have turned East, where the sun rises and turn our back to the West, where the sun sets'.[41] Like many of his speeches it was in defence of his disastrous land redistribution programme that eventually destroyed its most productive sector. Later his party would embark upon centralised 'command agriculture', which dealt a further blow to Zimbabwe's agricultural sector, once the breadbasket of Southern Africa.[42]

Between 1960 and 1990 Zimbabwe exported about ten percent more food than it consumed. By 2018 it was importing close to 26% of total demand.

Modelling a Coordinated Push on Africa's Agricultural Sector: The African Agriculture Revolution Scenario

A coordinated push on Africa's agricultural sector can unlock profound changes. This scenario, the African Agriculture Revolution, improves average yields in Africa from about 3.7 metric tons per hectare in 2018 to about 5.8

---

[39] Simoes A. J. G., and Hidalgo, C. A., 2011. The Economic Complexity Observatory: An Analytical Tool for Understanding the Dynamics of Economic Development. Workshops at the Twenty-Fifth AAAI Conference on Artificial Intelligence.

[40] Galford, G. L., Soares-Filho, B., and Cerri, C. E. P., 2013. Prospects for Land-Use Sustainability on the Agricultural Frontier of the Brazilian Amazon. *Philosophical Transactions of the Royal Society B*, 5 June.

[41] Meldrum, A., 2005. *Mugabe Turns Back on West and Looks East*. [Online] Available at: https://www.theguardian.com/world/2005/apr/19/zimbabwe.andrewmeldrum.

[42] It occurred as part of the 2016 Targeted Command Agriculture Programme, formally known as the Special Maize Import Substitution Programme. See Mazwi, F., Chemura, A., Mudimu, G. T., and Chambati, W., 2019. Political Economy of Command Agriculture in Zimbabwe: A State-led Contract Farming Model. *Agrarian South: Journal of Political Economy*, 8(1–2), pp. 232–257. https://doi.org/10.1177/2277976019856742.

tons per hectare in 2030 and 6.5 tons by 2040. That would represent a 2040 increase of 180% compared to a mere 75% improvement expected along the Current Path. Latin America and the Caribbean achieved a much more rapid increase between 2000 and 2010, moving from roughly 6.9 tons per hectare to about 9.6 tons.

In addition to a direct increase in yields per hectare, the interventions within the IFs forecasting system that contribute to these impressive improvements consist of an increase in the area size of land used for crops (eventually by 17% above the Current Path in 2040) as well as a six percent increase in the portion of land under irrigation (above the 2040 Current Path forecast), and a reduction of seven percent in the loss and waste rate as expressed as a share of agricultural production by 2040.

In addition the scenario increases the land area equipped for irrigation in Africa by almost a million hectares by 2040 (or by around seven percentage points).

The scenario also includes an increase in the number of available calories per person per day from about 2600 in 2018 to around 3100 in 2040, compared to a 2040 Current Path forecast of 2800 calories per person. This intervention is done to ensure that the increase in agricultural production does not only benefit exports, but improves domestic calorie consumption.

The impact of the African Agriculture Revolution scenario is impressive. By 2040, Africa will produce a total of 630 million tons of additional food (crop, meat and fish), i.e. above the Current Path forecast for 2040 of 1390 million metric tons of total agricultural production. With more domestic food being produced, the agricultural import bill is US$285 billion lower in 2040 than it would otherwise have been the case. The increase in calories helps to reduce the number of children suffering from malnourishment by more than four million in 2040—a cumulative total, from 2020 to 2040, of almost eighty million less children suffering from malnourishment—and achieve a minor reduction in stunting. Finally, it reduces infant mortality by almost two children per 1000 live births under one year of age. In considering this, bear in mind that more than 43 million births occurred in Africa in 2018 and that the Current Path forecast is for almost 54 million to occur in 2040!

Figure 5.2 presents a picture of Africa's growing food dependence over time, including demand for crops, meat and fish. In 2018, Africa already imports 13% of its agricultural demand, much of that consisting of staple foods such as rice and maize that is cheaper on the international market than can currently be produced domestically. Along the Current Path forecast that number will reach an alarming 35% by 2040. The Revolution in Agriculture

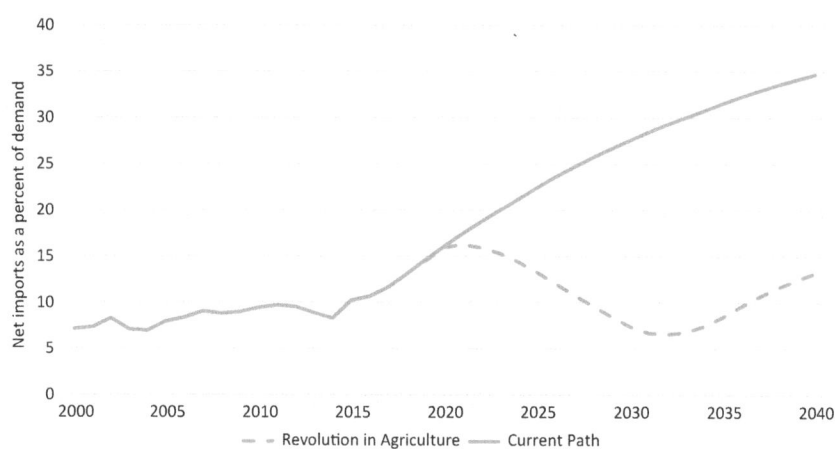

Fig. 5.2 Agricultural imports dependence: Current Path vs Revolution in Agriculture (*Source* Historical data from the Food and Agriculture Organization and forecast within IFs version 7.45)

reduces the continent's food insecurity dramatically to a situation, in 2040, where Africa will have reduced its forecast of import dependence to a much less alarming 13%.

These averages conceal huge differences between countries and regions. Those countries that achieve the most spectacular increases in production volumes; Nigeria, Egypt, Ethiopia, the Democratic Republic of Congo and Tanzania, are well known for their agricultural potential while arid and small island states gain the least.

The African Agriculture Revolution scenario also has major economic impacts. It reduces the number of extremely poor Africans living below US$1.90 by almost 130 million people in 2040. Gross domestic product (GDP) per person is in excess of US$310 more in 2040. By 2040, Africa's total economy is almost US$460 billion larger than it would otherwise be.[43]

Figure 5.3 presents the 2040 difference in the size of the agricultural sector between the Current Path and the Revolution in Agricultural scenario for each of the five regions used in this book. The difference in Central Africa is US$21 billion, in Southern Africa it is US$32 billion, in North Africa and East/Horn of Africa it is US$74 billion each and in West Africa it is US$109 billion. Currently the agricultural sector is the largest, as a percent of GDP in East/Horn of Africa (at 32% of GDP) compared to only seven percent in Southern Africa.

---

[43]Numbers in MER except for GDP per capita, which is in PPP.

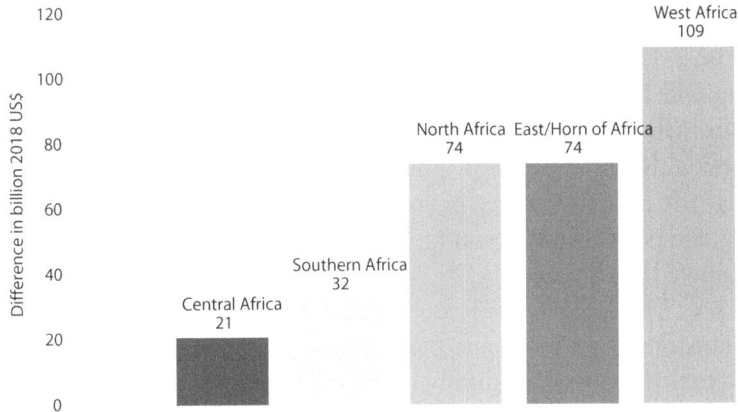

Fig. 5.3 Difference in size of agricultural sector in 2040: Revolution in Agriculture vs Current Path (*Source* Historical data from the Food and Agriculture Organization and forecast in IFs 7.45)

A different expression of the same metric is that instead of agriculture representing 22% of the economy in Central Africa, as it does in 2018, by 2040 it would have reduced to only 15% in the Revolution in Agriculture scenario compared to a more rapid decline to 11% in the Current Path. On top of that the economy of Central Africa will be significantly larger than in the Current Path. Although the agricultural sector in Southern Africa shows the second least impressive growth in absolute size, the sector is already significantly smaller as a percent contribution to the total economy (at only seven percent in 2018), declining to six percent in the Revolution in Agriculture scenario instead of four percent in the Current Path. So instead of an agricultural sector that is valued at US$71 billion in 2040 (the Current Path forecast) it would be US$103 billion in size in the Revolution in Agriculture scenario.

These improvements are not given, however. Factors that could impact on the achievement of these changes include the utilisation of the water endowment available for irrigation, the effect of carbon fertilisation due to climate change on crop growth, as well as the possibility of new cultivars and genetically modified plants that are more temperature tolerant.[44]

The Agricultural Revolution could also—at least temporarily—reverse the long-term declining employment share in the agricultural sector. This would not only because farm labour will expand (since a larger sector is likely to

---

[44]Some of these constraints can be overcome through technology, such as the use of precision irrigation and application of precise amounts of fertiliser exactly where it is required. Then there is the potential of vertical farming that could produce 180 m tons of food globally, according to some.

employ more people, even if that will be less workers per ton of output as productivity improves), but also because employment in up- and downstream from farming will increase as the size and sophistication of the agricultural sector expands. More than half of Africa's labour force is engaged in the agricultural sector with some estimates putting that portion much higher. But like in China, the agricultural sector in Africa is steadily losing its productive, working age population as young men and women migrate to cities in search of improved livelihoods.

A report on *The Future of Work in Africa* by the African Center for Economic Transformation in Ghana finds that boosting agricultural productivity may actually reduce the number of jobs in agriculture.[45] However, they conclude that by lowering the costs of raw materials, jobs will be created downstream in the much larger agro-processing sector. Productivity improvements could come by upgrading value chain activities such as logistics, input services, storage and other off-farm activities—all of which will require improved connectivity and basic infrastructure.[46]

The Contributions from Technology and Innovation

When thinking about the future of agriculture (and the improvements modelled in the African Agricultural Revolution scenario) it is important to recognise the rapid improvements occurring in this sector and the extent to which agriculture is changing all over the world.

Countries such as Australia, the USA and some European nations, where large-scale industrial agriculture is well established, are experimenting with robotics to remove weeds and harvest crops. A fleet of small robots has even been tested to achieve tasks that were once the domain of large tractors, sprayers and planters. On high-intensity commercial farms remote-controlled spraying helicopters are already quite common.

Rather than replacing farm workers, of which there is an abundant supply on the African continent, agricultural technologies will likely help farmers to reduce inputs such as herbicides, pesticides and fertilisers through greater

---

[45] World Economic Forum, 2017. *The Future of Jobs and Skills in Africa Preparing the Region for the Fourth Industrial Revolution.* Geneva: World Economic Forum.
[46] Ibid., p. 4.

precision in their use and application. And high technology devices like drones could help to inspect fields and monitor herd animals.[47]

While there is a general consensus that inefficient markets and lack of access to credit plague Africa's agricultural sector, the particular ways in which it affects farmers vary greatly. Even the World Bank recommends that 'researchers must locate the sources and causes of factor market failures more precisely'.[48] For one, mobile technology can alleviate the bottlenecks in Africa's smallholder agricultural credit system and enable farmers to access farming inputs. Much of the reforms that could drive improved productivity are actually to be found in the way in which agricultural markets are structured at local level, but inputs are also important.

In Kenya, for example, the company FarmDrive[49] uses mobile phones, alternative data and machine learning to unlock access to credit for smallholder farmers. FarmDrive does so firstly by collecting and aggregating various datasets, for instance from individual phone use, social media, agronomic, environmental, economic and satellite data, to produce a credit score for smallholder farmers.

The process involves many incremental steps such as first determining the exact location of the smallholder farm.[50] Once the location is known on Google maps, it allows the system to access geospatial information that determines soil quality, weather conditions and market accessibility and then, using an algorithm, to determine a credit score. The best time, they found, to engage with farmers, is at 10 am (when cows are out grazing) and when they have their morning tea, switching their phones on for a short while.[51]

Secondly, FarmDrive offers a decision-making tool that enables financial institutions to develop small-scale agriculture loan products. In this way the company facilitates a process for smallholder farmers to access capital to purchase critical farming inputs such as seed, fertiliser and implements that could increase yields and revenues.

---

[47] Abboud, L., 2018. *The Robot Revolution Down on the Farm*. [Online] Available at: https://www.ft.com/content/5854088a-ddda-11e8-b173-ebef6ab1374a.

[48] The World Bank, n.d. *Agriculture in Africa: Telling Facts from Myths*. [Online] Available at: http://www.worldbank.org/en/programs/africa-myths-and-facts.

[49] Kimani, R., and Bosire, P., 2019. *FarmDrive*. [Online] Available at: https://farmdrive.co.ke/.

[50] In most of rural Africa this is objectively unknown. FarmDrive resolves this challenge by determining location with reference to a known landmark. In rural Kenya, for example, the location of primary schools is objectively known, so the location of a farm is determined via a series of SMS questions such as time to walk to different primary schools. The more schools a farmer is familiar with in their area, the easier it is to hone into their specific location.

[51] Edwards, R., n.d. *Finding Our Farmers; or, Shamba Iko Wapi?* [Online] Available at: https://farmdrive.co.ke/insights/3.

In this manner, modern technology is opening up opportunities for smallholder farmers that would have been impossible a few years ago. The services provided by FarmDrive in Kenya benefits women in particular as they constitute the majority of smallholder farmers. FarmDrive has won a number of awards and gained substantial recognition as it rolls out its solution, one of many that are emerging in Africa for the continent's estimated 50 million smallholder farmers. It is part of an emerging trend across the continent to change a straightforward farming mindset to a modern, agribusiness mindset.

In Ghana, Kenya and Uganda more than 20,000 farms have access to simple and affordable smart insurance contracts (such as against crop failure or the loss of expensive breeding stock) via their smartphone, using blockchain technology. The system uses high-resolution satellite images to detect rainfall and plant growth data.[52] Using digital platforms it is possible to connect smallholders directly to research and large packaging and distribution centres, to provide advice on what, when and where to plant, as well as weather forecasts. Companies such as AgroCenta in Ghana and Zenvus in Nigeria are all making a difference in this regard.[53]

The World Food Programme Rural Resilience Initiative (R4) is also helping to implement innovations in finance and insurance to reduce the risk of farming. Their efforts reached more than 57,000 farmers in Ethiopia, Senegal, Malawi, Zambia and Kenya in 2018. This has increased food and income security by managing climate-related risks.[54] Remote sensing from drones can monitor soil moisture content and help to make irrigation systems more efficient. In addition, over the last decade the Alliance for a Green Revolution in Africa (AGRA) has invested hundreds of millions of dollars in improved seeds and has doubled maize yields in the 18 countries where they work.[55]

According to the Food and Agriculture Organization currently one-third of the world's food, approximately 1.3 billion tons worth US$1.2 trillion a year is wasted. In sub-Saharan Africa this mostly occurs in the distribution process

---

[52] Bird, J., 2018. *'Smart' Insurance Helps Poor Farmers to Cut Risk*. [Online] Available at: https://www.ft.com/content/3a8c7746-d886-11e8-aa22-36538487e3d0.

[53] AgroCenta. [Online] Available at: https://agrocenta.com/ and Zenvus. [Online] Available at: https://www.zenvus.com/.

[54] World Food Programme & Oxfam America, 2011. *The R4 Rural Resilience Initiative*. [Online] Available at: https://www1.wfp.org/r4-rural-resilience-initiative.

[55] Gebre, S., 2016. *AGRA Plans to Invest $500 Million in African Seed Companies*. [Online] Available at: https://www.bloomberg.com/news/articles/2016-09-07/agra-plans-to-invest-500-million-in-african-seed-companies.

from production to retailing. In rich countries food is generally thrown away by the consumer.[56]

By using modern technology it is now possible to reduce losses significantly by tracking inventory and reducing food waste along the distribution chain from farm-gate to the domestic retailer or the export market. One example is InspiraFarms that produces affordable, energy-efficient cold storage and processing equipment for on or off-grid use.[57]

Low internet penetration rates and electricity access in rural areas in Africa are the biggest obstacles to applying modern technology in agriculture. Both challenges can be overcome by using renewables and the various innovations discussed in Chapter 10.

Conclusion: Aiming at Food Security and Growth

Without food security, developing countries cannot escape from hunger, poverty and the variances of nature. Without food security meaningful advancement is difficult, if not impossible, to sustain and it is increasingly evident that the effects of climate change are likely to hold significant negative consequences for agriculture in much of Africa (see Chapter 15).

Because of the way in which colonialism shaped and then locked Africa's agricultural sector into the global economy, and subsequent insufficient, poorly designed and inefficient government support for agriculture, Africa has not been able to benefit from this key sector. Yet the continent has a huge potential and it is agriculture upon which the largest portion of Africans depend for survival. Subsistence and smallholder agriculture that largely caters for household consumption needs targeted and coordinated support from government which is quite different from the private-sector-led growth model of medium and large-scale commercial farming, although that too has its place. Actually clumsy interventions by African governments to set minimum prices for commodities such as cocoa, coffee and cashew nuts without much wider consideration of the impact often have unintended consequences. For example it could encourage an increase in production by many more poor farmers, causing the price of the commodity to fall. The result is to trap more poor people in subsistence farming from which they are unable to escape. In fact low and even most lower-middle-income African

---

[56] Food and Agriculture Organization, n.d. *Key Facts on Food Loss and Waste You Should Know!* [Online] Available at: http://www.fao.org/save-food/resources/keyfindings/en/.
[57] InspiraFarms. [Online] Available at: http://www.inspirafarms.com/about-us/?lang=za.

countries should probably place an emphasis on food self-sufficiency rather than exports.

There have been some progress but World Bank president Robert McNamara's prognosis in Nairobi in 1973 that 'there can be no long-term solution to the food problem'[58] without rapid progress in smallholder agriculture remains valid today in much of Africa.

For a successful agricultural transition and to expand local agricultural markets it is especially important to focus on indigenous crops, such as cassava, cowpea, soybean and yam, as well as indigenous practices before looking elsewhere.[59] Once that is achieved, steady progress up the agro-processing value chain will unlock improvements elsewhere rather than efforts to enter the global food export market without sufficient domestic reform.

Much is changing in Africa. The Indorama Eleme public–private fertiliser plant that was completed in 2016 and that will shortly double its capacity helped to turn Nigeria from a large fertiliser importer to a self-sufficient producer and now to a net exporter.[60] In addition, Morocco's OCP Group, which holds 75% of the world's phosphate reserves (a key ingredient for phosphate-based fertilisers), has announced its own plans for a US$1 billion industrial investment in fertiliser plants in Nigeria while construction of its massive plant in Dire Dawa in Eastern Ethiopia (at a cost of US$3.7 billion) has started.[61] Across Africa, from Angola to Kenya, governments and the private sector are investing in the key enablers of agricultural growth. But much more is required, particularly in incorporating resilience and adaptation to climate change into Africa's Revolution in Agriculture.

Prosperity requires that a country move up the agricultural value chain and avoid being suckered by corporate social responsibility programmes that promise to tinker with the worst effects of colonial-style production, but that does not structurally intervene to promote food self-sufficiency and shifting value addition to Africa. The attraction often sold to Africans is to use its

---

[58] McNamara, R., 1973. *Address to the Board of Governors by Robert S. McNamara Presidential speech.* Washington, DC: World Bank.

[59] The International Institute of Tropical Agriculture (IITA). [Online] Available at: https://www.iita.org/ does particularly impressive work in this regard.

[60] African Development Bank Group, 2019. Nigeria: Fertilizer Project Raises Yields by Over 50%, Showcases Successful PPPS, 21 January 2019. https://www.afdb.org/en/news-and-events/nigeria-fertilizer-project-raises-yields-by-over-50-showcases-successful-ppps-18933.

[61] Bazza, T. 2019. Morocco's OCP to Build 2 Fertilizer Plants in Nigeria. Morocco World News, 17 January 2019. https://www.moroccoworldnews.com/2019/01/263594/morocco-ocp-fertilizer-plants-nigeria/; 2m Editor, 2019. Ethiopia's New Fertilizer Plant to Help Fulfill Local Demands: Ministry of Agriculture, 8 July 2019. 2Merkato.com. https://www.2merkato.com/news/alerts/5736-ethiopia-s-new-fertilizer-plant-to-help-fulfill-local-demands-ministry-of-agriculture.

leverage in products such as cocoa and coffee to improve their share of value-add in these massive markets. But in the absence of effective agricultural management and producer associations with the muscle to manage the sector it is probably more important to diversify the agricultural products in countries such as Ghana and Côte d'Ivoire than trying to develop a cocoa cartel. And then there is the challenge that for much of Africa's young population the idea of turning to agriculture as a source of livelihood is a strong association with poverty. Changing that mindset will be difficult since the sector suffers from poor infrastructure, insecure property rights, lack of access to credit, no or limited provision of electricity and lack of access to modern technologies. All of these hurdles can be overcome but it requires a host of interventions including challenging current practices of tenure insecurity, unlocking access to credit, using high-yielding seed varieties and modern inputs such as fertilisers, pesticides and eventually introducing agricultural machinery to emulate some of the positive aspects of the so-called Green Revolution in South Asia and South America during the 1950s and 1960s.

An African Agricultural Revolution could potentially have a major impact, ranging from reduced stunting among children and undernourishment among adults to increased incomes and a reduction in poverty. Most importantly, the continent would become less dependent on food imports with huge attendant advantages. Food self-sufficiency can play an important role to reduce poverty, which is the subject of the next chapter.

Further Reading

AGRA. 2018. Africa Agriculture Status Report: Catalyzing Government Capacity to Drive Agricultural Transformation (Issue 6). Nairobi, Kenya: Alliance for a Green Revolution in Africa (AGRA).

FAO, The role of agriculture and rural development in achieving SDG 1.1 February 22, 2019, Paper for presentation at the United Nations Expert Group Meeting on Eradicating Rural Poverty to Implement the 2030 Agenda for Sustainable Development, 27 February to 1 March 2019, UNECACC-AA, available at https://www.un.org/development/desa/dspd/wp-content/uploads/sites/22/2019/03/FAO-ending-extreme-rural-poverty-1.pdf. Accessed on 25 December 2019.

Jane Nelson No Smallholder Farmer Left Behind, chapter 4 in Homi Kharas, John W. McArthur, and Izumi Ohno (eds.). 2019, October 29. *Leave No One Behind: Time for Specifics on the Sustainable Development Goals*. Brookings.

Open Access This chapter is licensed under the terms of the Creative Commons Attribution 4.0 International License (http://creativecommons.org/licenses/by/4.0/), which permits use, sharing, adaptation, distribution and reproduction in any medium or format, as long as you give appropriate credit to the original author(s) and the source, provide a link to the Creative Commons license and indicate if changes were made.

The images or other third party material in this chapter are included in the chapter's Creative Commons license, unless indicated otherwise in a credit line to the material. If material is not included in the chapter's Creative Commons license and your intended use is not permitted by statutory regulation or exceeds the permitted use, you will need to obtain permission directly from the copyright holder.

6

Boosting Education

Abstract In this chapter Cilliers provides an overview of trends in education in Africa and compares that with progress in other regions. In addition to a review of common educational outcomes such as measuring years of schooling, he places attention on the poor quality of education and roles of gender exclusion. That is followed by a summary of future education requirements and a scenario, Boosting Education, that explores the impact of improvements in the quality and quantity of education in Africa while taking advantage of technology to promote learning outcomes and human development.

Keywords Education · Education systems · Literacy · Skills · Future of work · Education policy · Education technology · Gender parity · Basic education · Vocational training

Learning Objectives

- Explain the reasons for poor educational outcomes in Africa
- Recognise and explain the key metrics for measuring education outcomes (e.g. enrolment and completion rates, gender parity)
- Understand why a focus on basic education and the use of technology in education are central to improving education outcomes in Africa

Education lies at the foundation of human development and self-attainment. It enables us to lead a self-determined existence, to increase professional performance and to improve our health. It is the reason successful modern societies are called knowledge societies. Governments, world leaders and NGOs across the world, literally all of humanity with the exception of terror and extremist organisations such as the Islamic State, Al-Qaeda and Boko Haram are all in favour of more, better and broad-based education for men and women.

Education and prosperity go hand in hand. Whereas the average years of adult education in low-income countries is just below five years, in lower-middle-income countries it is more than seven years, in upper-middle-income countries it is almost nine years, and in high-income countries it is twelve years.

The accepted economic wisdom is that investments in education increase the talent in the labour pool, raise productivity and boost economic growth and incomes. Let's refer to this as a supply-side model, where parents, governments and others invest in education in the belief that it will improve the chances of well-paying jobs for their children (and themselves) and generally a better quality of life.

A study from Eric A. Hanushek and Ludger Woessmann found that each year of additional school is associated with a nearly 0.6% increase in long-term gross domestic product (GDP) growth rates.[1] And many studies have linked the economic boom that followed in the United Kingdom and the USA after the Second World War to the advent of mass public education before the First World War.[2]

But could it not be equally plausible that a growing economy requires and therefore incentivises education? In other words, is it demand that drives improved education outcomes? According to this line of reasoning, the potential for better employment drives educational improvements above a certain basic level.

China, for instance, only introduced the Law on Nine-Year Compulsory Education in 1986 at which point the Chinese economy was already averaging more than 10% growth per annum. At that point, compulsory education could build on adult literacy rates that were at roughly 72%.[3]

---

[1] Hanushek, E. A., and Wößmann, L., 2010. Education and Economic Growth. In: P. Peterson, E. Baker, and B. McGaw, eds. *International Encyclopedia of Education. volume 2.* Oxford: Elsevier, pp. 245–252.

[2] Morris, P., 1996. Asia's Four Little Tigers: A Comparison of the Role of Education in Their Development. *Comparative Education,* 32(1), pp. 95–109.

[3] Education in China has evolved so rapidly that today it is the second most popular destination for African students studying abroad, after France. Mo Ibrahim Foundation, Africa's Youth: Jobs of Migration?, Mo Ibrahim Foundation, 2019. *Africa's Youth: Jobs or Migration?* London: Mo Ibrahim Foundation.

So, beyond basic literacy and primary education (the two generally go together), do subsequent improvements in levels of education precede or follow economic development? And, exactly what type and level of education will Africans require for a future characterised by digitisation and the fourth industrial revolution? What needs to be done, and what is practically possible to improve education?

History tells both supply and demand stories. Generally, literacy and high-levels of primary school education attainment is a requirement for countries to graduate from low to middle-income status. However, whereas in Europe and the US rising levels of education foreshadowed development, in Asia improvements in education beyond primary school levels generally accompanied more rapid economic growth.[4] In the two decades between 1960 and 1980, the East Asia and Pacific region increased the number of average years of education in its adult population by about 80%, and growth in gross domestic product (GDP) per capita tracked closely at about 85%.

However, in the following two decades (from 1980 to 2000) GDP per capita more than doubled from about US$3500 per person in 1980 to about US$7700 per person. Over the same time period, the number of average years of education in the adult population increased by just one-third. Of course, when coming off a higher base it is not as easy to maintain the previous momentum of improved education as levels approach saturation (or 100%). But could it not also be the case that educational requirements for the region had largely been met in the first phase of growth, and that the education being provided may not have been well suited to the requirements for further growth?

In practice, the demand model of education therefore reinforces the supply-side model but the latter is clearly the more important of the two. In the supply model, educationalists, governments and parents invest in core knowledge and competencies (traditionally termed reading, writing and arithmetic) and complement that core knowledge by trying to anticipate where more specific opportunities lie. What is in demand today could, of course, change completely by the time students graduate given the inevitable time that it takes to roll out a particular curriculum. And in the twenty-first-century demand is changing with each passing decade.

The complexity and level of sophistication of the economy certainly play a particular demand-side role. In general, all economies require a better skilled and more highly educated workforce over time, although countries that specialise in the production and export of unprocessed commodities perhaps

---

[4]See, for example, Roser, M., and Ortiz-Ospina, E., 2018. *Literacy*. [Online] Available at: https://ourworldindata.org/literacy.

less so. Going up the technology ladder towards greater productivity requires constant improvements in knowledge levels. Hence the global trend for a decrease in the demand for unskilled labour and an increase in semi-skilled and skilled labour.[5]

Furthermore, skilled labour and capital also tend to flow from poorer to richer countries rather than the other way around.[6] This is part of the story of the African brain drain, where well-educated Africans such as nurses, doctors and engineers often seek employment in higher-income countries. In fact, recent data from AfroBarometer confirms that sub-Saharan African nations account for eight out of the ten fastest growing international migrant populations since 2010.[7] This steady exodus means that the education system in origin countries needs to work twice as hard.[8]

There is little doubt that advancing the average number of years of education in the adult population can give a substantial boost to GDP over the long-run, but improving the general level of education takes time and the economic returns take even longer to materialise. A study by the Education Policy and Data Center[9] found that it could take as many as 150 years, or seven generations, to move from 10% adult primary school completion to 90% secondary school completion. The average length of the transition for the countries in the group was nearly 90 years.

At the same time, the example of South Korea demonstrates that rapid progress is possible. Following a devastating war that split the country into two, the 'Miracle on the Han River' (the nickname for the period of rapid economic growth in South Korea after the Korean War) saw mean years of education triple from four years in 1960 to more than 12 years in 2015. At this point, South Korea had caught up with established Western democracies like the United Kingdom and surpassed others such as Sweden. It also achieved 42 consecutive years of exceptional primary enrolment rates, affirming the importance of getting the foundation right as part of an investment in the future.

---

[5]Reinert, E.S., 2010. *How Rich Countries Got Rich and Why Poor Countries Stay Poor*. London: Constable, p. 113.
[6]Ibid., p. 191.
[7]Sanny, J.A.-N., Logan, C., and Gyimah-Boadi, E., 2019. *In Search of Opportunity: Young and Educated Africans Most Likely to Consider Moving Abroad*. Accra: Afrobarometer Dispatches no 288.
[8]This is the view advanced by Swedish economist and Nobel Laureate Gunnar Myrdal. His work preempted that of John Maynard Keynes.
[9]Carrol, B., Barrow, K., and Wils, A., 2005. *Educating the World's Children: Patterns of Growth and Inequality*. Washington, DC: Education Policy and Data Center. Available at https://www.epdc.org/education-data-research/educating-worlds-children-patterns-growth-and-inequality.

As countries graduate to middle-income status, the educational system needs to provide additional skills and knowledge that respond, in part, to the anticipated future demand. Therefore the evidence suggests that demand becomes more relevant only after countries have mastered the basics.

Recent Education Trends in Africa

The negative consequences of Africa's lost decades during the 1980s and 1990s are difficult to overestimate. Rather than simply sluggish growth, Africa experienced an actual decline in gross domestic income per capita of about 12% between 1980 and 1990 and another two percent during the 1990s before rebounding by about 30% in the first decade of the 2000s.

During this period, the continent also suffered stagnation or, in some instances, a relative decline in average years of adult education compared to other regions. During the 1960s and 1970s adults in sub-Saharan Africa were on average better educated than people in South Asia, by a margin of nearly half a year of schooling. By 1995 South Asia had closed the education gap and by 2018 it had surpassed sub-Saharan Africa by almost a year and a half. In 2018 adults in South Asia could expect to receive about seven years of education compared to just 5.6 years in sub-Saharan Africa.[10] Again, while things are improving in Africa it is at a slower rate than elsewhere.

The divergence in education between Africa and the rest of the world is driven by a number of factors that relate to rates of economic growth, policy and government expenditure on education, among others. For the purposes of this chapter, three considerations are particularly relevant. The first is the massive annual influx of more and more children into educational systems that are already struggling to deal with overcrowding and often inefficient use of resources. This challenge underlines the importance for Africa to accelerate its demographic transition, as discussed in Chapter 4.

The second consideration is the inability of many African countries to retain students within the education system, i.e. to enable them to progress from one grade to the next and not leave school. The third is about the quality of education, which is discussed separately below.

To understand the challenge of retaining children in school, the second challenge mentioned above, the education system can be viewed as a long funnel, with various cracks and fissures along the way. Children enter the

---

[10]The numbers in this paragraph relate to the age group above 15 years.

system at the wider end and graduate with a tertiary or equivalent education at the other end, having lost many of its original entrants along the way.

The inevitable goal of educational systems is to increase the pass rates or number of graduates along the length of the funnel. Once the funnel has changed to become a straight pipeline with no 'leaks', we would have a perfect system where, ideally, the full complement of potential students enter at one end and progress through to achieving relevant higher education at the other end. In Finland, generally considered the country with the best education system globally, the gross intake ratio to the last grade of primary school is basically 100%. For lower secondary education it is 99%, and for upper secondary education is at almost 90%. What this means is that all Finns complete at least lower secondary education and that 10 percentage points of those that enter upper secondary school don't complete it.[11] Only when one gets to tertiary education is there a substantial drop off in these numbers.

To this end, policymakers should generally focus on steadily widening the width of the funnel from its origin in order to maximise the number of entrants that enter and successfully complete primary education, measured in primary enrolment and completion rates. Put differently, as many pupils as possible should first progress through primary, then on to lower and then to upper secondary levels. This will expand the pool of students at each successive level and is generally the most cost-effective way to proceed since it raises general levels of education throughout society and hence improve skills and potential as part of a comprehensive development strategy.

Africa needs to attack all aspects of the educational funnel to ensure that it retains as many students at every level and enables as many as possible to progress from one level to the next. In a number of countries that we have studied, too much funds and attention is often spent on improving say upper secondary education without also looking at the extent to which the preceding primary and lower secondary school sections of the pipeline constrain progress at upper secondary level.

As shown in Table 6.1, the situation in sub-Saharan Africa is very different compared even to East and Southeast Asia, the Middle East and North Africa (MENA), Latin America and the Carribean and South Asia. Poor outcomes in each column at either enrolment or completion are coded orange and red depending upon the severity compared to the situation in other regions. While not included in the table, the situation at tertiary level is especially problematic.

---

[11] http://data.uis.unesco.org/.

Table 6.1 Progress through the education funnel (gross percentages) (2018)

	Primary		Lower Secondary		Upper Secondary	
	Enrolment	Completion	Enrolment	Completion	Enrolment	Completion
Sub-Saharan Africa	102	75	57	43	37	29
East and South East Asia	105	103	99	94	87	73
MENA (Middle East and North Africa)	105	101	96	82	76	64
Latin America & Caribbean	106	105	105	83	81	63
South Asia	108	97	86	61	61	41

Source IFs 7.45 initializing from Barro-Lee

The percentages used in Table 6.1 are gross numbers, and can be quite misleading if not placed into context. Gross rates include all students in a grade irrespective of whether or not they are at the appropriate age. Students who are over-age, including students who are repeating the grade, would therefore also be included in the gross rate. The result is that percentages are sometimes above 100%.

The completion rate is the percentage of students aged 3–5 years above the intended age of the last grade of each level of education who have completed that grade.[12]

Had I used the net figure, it would only include students at the appropriate age. For example, the gross enrolment rate for primary school in sub-Saharan Africa in Table 6.1 is 102% but the net primary enrolment rate (not shown in the table) is only 69% indicating that a large number of children that are supposed to be in school are not, and that many classes are crowded by older children. Crowded classrooms have a variety of negative consequences that range from a higher pupil to teacher ratio to insufficient desks, books and equipment.

Table 6.1 shows the acute drop from 75% primary completion to a mere 29% upper secondary completion rate in sub-Saharan Africa. It is

---

[12] UNESCO, Institute for Statistics, http://uis.unesco.org/en/glossary-term/completion-rate.

therefore clear that the educational funnel contracts very rapidly in sub-Saharan Africa—quite different to the situation in North Africa where upper secondary completion rates are at 65%. North Africa is part of the MENA region which is 64%.

Furthermore, educationalists generally distinguish between official enrolment and school attendance rates and numbers. Table 6.1 uses the former. Attendance rates are sourced by asking households directly as opposed to using information pulled from official registration data. In the majority of poor countries enrolment rates are significantly higher than attendance rates as many children who are officially enrolled do not regularly attend school.

Another set of statistics that is used to measure the general level of education in a country is to look at the mean level of education of adults. Figure 6.1 presents the mean years of education for sub-Saharan Africa, North Africa and the mean in the World except Africa in 2018 with the Current Path forecast for 2040. The comparison is done for the age grouping 25 years and older and would look slightly better if one looks at say the cohort of young adults aged 15–24 years of age, or 15–29 years, given the generation gap in education levels evident in much of Africa.

Currently, Eastern/Horn of Africa has the lowest level of educational attainment among the five regions in Africa, but it overtakes Central Africa by 2040, with Seychelles, Mauritius and Kenya doing particularly well. Southern Africa presently has the highest levels of adult education but will be overtaken by North Africa by 2040.

The main reason for Southern Africa's slow rate of improvement is that the level of adult education in South Africa is forecasted to remain stagnant

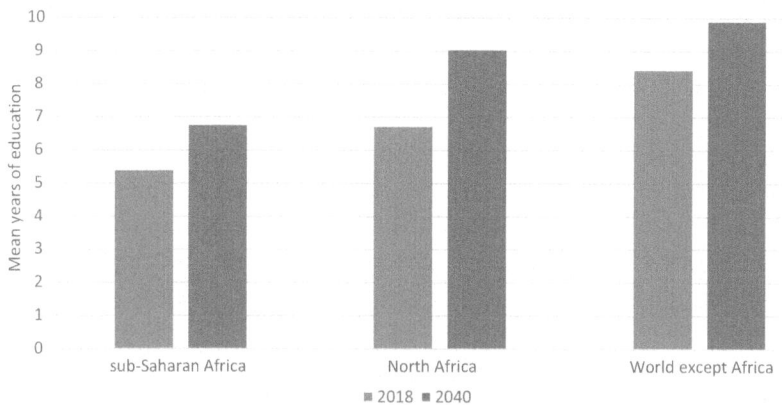

Fig. 6.1 Current Path forecast of mean years of education (25+ age group) (*Source* IFs 7.45 initializing from United Nations Population Division medium term forecast and Barro-Lee educational attainment dataset)

while those in Angola could even deteriorate slightly. This is an alarming forecast for South Africa, the economic giant in the region, as it finds itself in a demographic sweet spot for growth with a ratio of 1.9 working age persons to dependents (discussed in Chapter 4).

South Africa is often used as an example of how to get education wrong. For two decades after Nelson Mandela was elected president in 1994 the country served as a guinea pig for educational experimentation. For example, the early dismantling of the country's separate teacher colleges in favour of standard university teaching dealt teacher education a blow from which it is only now starting to recover. In addition, extensive unionisation of the teaching profession resulted in a situation where union leadership practically ran schools with reports of positions, such as the head of a department or school principal being sold. Effective systems such as independent inspections have been dismantled in favour of self (i.e. union)-regulation. There are recent signs of progress, but that is of little consolation for a population that was expecting more.

Bad policies, poor management and corruption in the governing African National Congress have prevented South Africa from benefiting from its remarkable transition from apartheid. Instead of focusing on getting the basics right, the rush to apply imported educational models with limited regard for the local context has meant that education has improved at a rate significantly lower than its potential.[13] South Africa is also forecast to grow slowly, and slow growth translates into limited revenues to invest in education, implying that future options are limited.

Comparing Education in Africa with Other Regions

At this point in time, no region in Africa is on par with average levels of education in the second-lowest region for attainment globally, South America. Only Northern Africa will probably surpass South America's 2018 level by 2040. This is not a pretty picture.

The contrast with average levels of adult education in North America, which is already at above 12 years in 2018, is even more stark. Whereas the average adult in North America has completed upper secondary school, the average adult in Central, East and West Africa does not have the equivalent of primary schooling.

---

[13] The best example is the experiment with so-called Outcomes Based Education.

There is progress to the extent that the level of education in Africa among young people aged 20–29 years is often much higher than that of their parents. Africa therefore also has a large intergenerational gap. The literacy and education rates for the youngest population group in poor countries can be up to three times higher than it is for the oldest population group.[14]

These large differences in outlook and expectations inevitably translate into discontent and even violence. A prime example is the Arab Spring in North Africa, where the protests were generally led by younger, well-educated groupings, many of whom were unable to find formal sector jobs in economies stifled by state bureaucracy and corruption.

The gap in adult educational attainment between Africa and other developing regions is forecast to widen in the Current Path forecast. By 2030, IFs forecasts that people in South Asia can expect to receive about 8 full years of education while people in sub-Saharan Africa will only achieve about 6.2 years.

This trajectory means that it is highly unlikely that Africa will be able to meet the primary school education target of the Sustainable Development Goals (SDGs). Target 4.1 intends that all girls and boys have access to 'free, equitable and quality primary and secondary education', as measured by a minimum proficiency in mathematics and reading.[15] In fact, in the Current Path forecast only about two-thirds of African adults will have completed primary school in 2030 while just half of the continent's population will have completed lower secondary school.

The Low Quality of Education in Africa

According to research published by Erik Hanushek and Ludger Wössmann for the World Bank in 2007,[16] there is a stronger correlation between educational *quality* and economic growth than between educational *quantity* and growth. This makes intuitive sense, as attending class does not automatically guarantee that one will learn something!

It's therefore not as much the quantity of schooling, as measured by mean years of education at various age levels, that is important, but more the quality of education that is being provided. According to the authors, 'expanding

---

[14] Roser, M., and Ortiz-Ospina, E., 2018. *Literacy*. [Online] Available at: https://ourworldindata.org/literacy.
[15] United Nations, 2018. *Sustainable Development Goal 4*. [Online] Available at: https://sustainabledevelopment.un.org/sdg4.
[16] Hanushek, E. A., and Wössmann, L., 2007. *Education Quality and Economic Growth*. Washington, DC: The World Bank.

school attainment, at the center of most development strategies, has not guaranteed better economic conditions. What's been missing', they write, 'is … ensuring that students actually learn'.[17] Fortunately, a number of international standardised tests that have been developed in recent years help to systematically measure learning outcomes at the primary and secondary school levels across countries.[18]

We know that learning starts slowly in low-income countries, where pre-schooling is mostly non-existent, and even students who make it to the end of primary school often do not master basic competencies. Research has found that the average primary school student from a low-income country, would be singled out for remedial attention on the basis of being below standard should he/she attend primary school in a high-income country![19]

In sub-Saharan Africa, less than half of students meet the minimum proficiency threshold that is used in the standardised testing, whereas the mean for developed countries is at 86%.[20] To put that in comparative context—when it comes to learning outcomes 'the top-performing country in sub-Saharan Africa has a lower average score than the lowest-performing country in Western Europe'.[21] It is, therefore, not surprising that the World Bank in 2017 warned of a 'learning crisis in global education'.[22] The report presented an analysis of reading, mathematics and science outcomes and the results for sub-Saharan Africa making for disheartening reading.

Although school attendance is generally good in the region, many children suffer from illness, malnutrition and/or income deprivation. Since teachers are often not particularly well educated themselves, the quality of teaching is poor, while absenteeism among teachers is rife. Many pitch up at school, but then don't attend the class they are supposed to teach. Some even engage in a second (or third) job to support themselves and their families. Since schools

---

[17] Ibid., p 1.

[18] A recent dataset has created a common measurement system for 163 countries including 30 in sub-Saharan Africa. Altinok, N., Angrist, N., and Patrinos, H. A., 2018. Global Data Set on Education Quality (1965–2015). *World Bank Group Policy Research Working Paper 8314*, January.

[19] Ibid., p. 5. The findings from Altinok and colleagues are that: 'learning outcomes in developing countries is generally clustered at the bottom of the global scale and even the top developing country performers still often perform worse than the bottom performers in developed countries'.

[20] Ibid., p. 23.

[21] Ortiz-Ospina, E., 2018. *Global Education Quality in 4 Charts, Our World in Data*. [Online] Available at: https://ourworldindata.org/edu-quality-key-facts.

[22] The World Bank, 2018. *World Development Report 2018: Learning to Realize Education's Promise*. Washington, DC: The World Bank Group.

are short-staffed, those teachers who do attend to their duties are inundated with administrative tasks.[23]

For the World Bank, the immediate causes of the crisis are fourfold: children arrive unprepared to learn (generally children from poor households learn much less); teachers often lack the skills or motivation to teach effectively; inputs like books and teaching material often fail to reach classrooms or to affect learning and poor management and governance often undermine schooling quality.[24]

Rates of Gender Exclusion

Changing gender parity in education—the number of female students participating in a given level of education relative to the number of male students at the same level—is another important milestone on the road to improved education.

In sub-Saharan Africa, gender parity in education has improved over time but still trails behind regions such as the Middle East and North Africa (MENA) that often have a bad reputation when it comes to the rights of girls and women. In sub-Saharan Africa the average woman aged 25 years and above has received about 4.6 years of education compared to 5.8 years for every male. The gap is slightly smaller when extending the cohort to women and men aged 15 years and above where the mean is at 5.2 years versus 6.1 years, again indicating the extent to which younger Africans are better educated than their parents. In the MENA region female adults aged 25 and above have more than seven years of education and those aged 15 and above almost eight.

Improving levels of educational attainment is a slow process. Leaving quality aside it took sub-Saharan Africa 14 years, from 2001 to 2015, to increase the average number of years of education of women by one year. The global mean for years of adult female education stands at 7.9 years—a goal sub-Saharan Africa will only achieve after mid-century on the Current Path, at which point the global average will likely have increased to about 10 years. On the Current Path there is no indication of Africa closing this gap under current conditions.

---

[23] Sow, M., 2018. *Figures of the Week: Africa, Education, and the 2018 World Development Report.* [Online] Available at: https://www.brookings.edu/blog/africa-in-focus/2017/10/06/figures-of-the-week-africa-education-world-development-report-2018/.

[24] The World Bank, 2018. *World Development Report 2018: Learning to Realize Education's Promise.* Washington, DC: The World Bank Group, pp. 9–11.

In 2015 in sub-Saharan Africa, 95 girls attended primary school for every 100 boys, a ratio that worsens significantly at secondary school level (only 90 girls for every 100 boys) and decreases to 73 women for every 100 men that enrol in tertiary education. In four countries (Liberia, the Democratic Republic of the Congo, Mozambique and Niger), adult women have less than half the mean years of education compared to males.

Compare that to the situation in South America where the average woman aged 25 and older will have received about the same number of years of education as their male counterparts, while in East Asia, Central Asia and Europe the gap between the mean for male and female levels of education vary between about 0.9 and 0.97 years. So in these regions women still get less education compared to men, but are rapidly approaching equality. Of the regions explored in this book, only women in South Asia (with a gap of 2.6 years between the mean for men and women) face higher barriers to educational attainment than in Africa. Given the link between female education and fertility, this large difference to a great degree explains Africa's very high fertility rates as discussed in Chapter 4.

Africa's Future Education Requirements

Before proceeding to the development of an improved education scenario and an analysis of its associated impact, we must first ask ourselves what future Africa's students need to be prepared for.

A recent study from the African Development Bank found that three main factors constrain more rapid job creation in Africa. First, job creation has not kept pace with the number of graduates from secondary and tertiary institutions. Second, those who finish school are not equipped with the skills required in the available jobs. Finally, young people generally lack the soft skills, social networks and professional experience to compete with older job applicants.[25]

In its study on the future of work in Africa, the Ghana-based African Center for Economic Transformation is more specific:

> There is far too little emphasis on relevant training in science, technology, engineering, and math; on technical and vocational education and training; and on higher-order cognitive and analytical skills. Hence, the considerable skills

---

[25] African Development Bank, Asian Development Bank, European Development Bank for Reconstruction, Inter-American Development Bank, 2018. *The Future of Work: Regional Perspectives.* Washington, DC: Co-publishers.

mismatch, with most job seekers lacking the skills that employers require. They may have good paper qualifications but not 4IR [Fourth Industrial Revolution] skill sets.[26]

We know that education in Africa needs to respond to the demand to expand smallholder farming and agribusinesses (Chapter 5), which will allow African countries to enter low-end manufacturing (Chapter 9), and prepare for the rapid expanded use of modern systems and technologies (Chapter 11) as digitisation and the Fourth Industrial Revolution present new opportunities and risks for the future. The trend is away from a demand for low-skilled (and even semi-skilled) labour and towards skilled labour.

Future job requirements differ from country to country and defy easy generalisation. At a broad level, education must equip students with the skills to lead healthy, productive and meaningful lives. As the authors of the 2018 World Bank report on education explain, this means students should for instance know 'how to interpret many types of written passages - from medication labels to job offers, from bank statements to great literature'.[27]

The modern trend appears to be towards broader sectoral training, which includes a set of generic business and life skills rather than preparing an individual for a specific job such as being an accountant, welder, carpenter or chef. This allows the individual to more readily move from an entry-level job to a longer-term career. The most recent report from the Commission on the Future of Work refers to 'a universal entitlement to lifelong learning that enables people to acquire skills and to reskill and upskill'. Since the world of work 'begins at home' the authors also emphasise the importance of strengthening women's voice and leadership in addressing gender equality and the rural economy 'where the future of many of the world's workers lies'.[28]

African educators should also balance the need for academic education with vocational training. For example, the 2018 World Development Report devotes considerable attention to the need to replicate successful job skills training programmes and to the well-established extent to which most Africans aspire to academic versus technical training. In addition to advocating for Technical and Vocational Training (TVET) as a parallel education stream from secondary school onward, the World Bank advocates for

---

[26] African Center for Economic Transformation, The Future of Work in Africa—the impact of the fourth industrial revolution on job creation and skill development in Africa, 2018, p. 2.
[27] The World Bank, 2018. *World Development Report 2018: Learning to Realize Education's Promise.* Washington, DC: The World Bank Group, p. 4.
[28] Global Commission on the Future of Work, 2019. *Work for a Brighter Future.* Geneva: International Labour Organization, p. 13.

workplace training and short-term job training programmes.[29] It finds that informal apprenticeships are most common in sub-Saharan Africa and offers examples from Benin, Cameroon, Côte d'Ivoire and Senegal where they account for almost 90% of the training that prepares workers for crafts jobs, as well as employment in some trades.[30]

Modern Germany offers a few valuable examples of technical teaching innovation, although in an entirely different setting, of course. One of the most widely acclaimed German practices is its vocational training system at secondary level schooling and the partnership that has been established, in law, between small and medium-sized companies, on the one hand, and publicly funded vocational schools on the other. The system culminates in providing a student with a certificate issued by a competent body, i.e. a chamber of industry and commerce or a chamber of crafts and trades in around 330 occupations requiring formal training in Germany in a win–win partnership between employers, unions and government.[31]

However, what works in highly formalised and developed Germany will not work in most of Africa, where the largest part of the economy is informal. In addition to many other challenges, the low quality of education in most sub-Saharan countries means that students may not have fully mastered the foundational skills of reading, writing, numeracy, critical thinking and problem-solving that are required before entering the vocational training stream. The World Bank refers to this as 'not just a lack of trained workers; it is a lack of readily trainable workers'.[32] Regardless of the continent's preparedness, digitisation and the Fourth Industrial Revolution will require a large cadre of technical skills, and the poor quality of general schooling in Africa implies that great care must be taken to ensure that students who do choose this vocational line of education have sufficient grounding.

---

[29] The World Bank, 2018. *World Development Report 2018: Learning to Realize Education's Promise.* Washington, DC: The World Bank Group, p. 154.
[30] Ibid., p. 155.
[31] Federal Ministry of Education and Research, n.d., *The German Vocational Training System.* [Online] Available at: https://www.bmbf.de/en/the-german-vocational-training-system-2129.html.
[32] The World Bank, 2018. *World Development Report 2018: Learning to Realize Education's Promise.* Washington, DC: The World Bank Group, p. 9 and 157.

Modelling the Impact of Improved Quality, Quantity and Nature of Education Across Gender: The Boosting Education Scenario

This section briefly sets out the interventions within the IFs modelling platform that represent ambitious but reasonable improvements in the quantity, quality and nature of education across gender in Africa. I then measure the impact of the Boosting Education scenario on the Current Path on various indices of human well-being, including on growth rates, size of economies, average incomes and inequality. In line with the reasoning that was set out in the preceding pages, the interventions simultaneously attack all aspects of poor education in Africa.

A first set of interventions improves throughput along the entire education funnel. It increases intake (or enrolment), survival and graduation rates at primary, lower secondary, upper secondary and tertiary levels, as well as the transition rates between these various levels of schooling. The impact is that Africa rockets from 82% primary school completion in 2020 to 100% primary school attendance by 2030 instead of after mid-century. This is, for sure, an extremely aggressive intervention but without a huge effort to improve this foundational aspect of Africa's development, subsequent progress on most other dimensions is virtually impossible. In the process, Africa catches up on primary school completion rates with comparable regions such as South America and South Asia within the next ten years. The interventions on lower secondary are such that the average percent of age children that complete this next level converges with the average for South Asia and South America by 2040. The increase is steep—at 24 percentage points above the Current Path in 2040 and completion rates climb from a current 51% of age-appropriate children to 85% by 2040. Improvements for upper secondary education are of a similar aggressive nature although Africa will, by 2040, remain slightly below the 2040 rate in South Asia and South America. Whereas the Current Path forecast is for upper secondary completion rates to improve from 37 to 48%, the interventions take Africa to 66%. Coming from a very low base of 7% graduation rate in 2020, the Boosting Education scenario raises the rate to 18% by 2040, some four percentage points above the Current Path forecast for that year.

Next I improve gender parity in education at primary, secondary and tertiary levels to achieve rates close to that in East Asia and the Pacific by 2050.

A third set of interventions improves the quality of education at the primary and secondary levels by about seven and six percentage points above the Current Path by 2040, respectively. That is enough, at primary school level, to improve quality to the level of South America by 2040. In the process African averages improve significantly above the levels approximating that for South Asia. At secondary level, where the gap between averages for South America, South Asia and Africa are smaller than with primary education, the intervention pushes African averages marginally above that for both these other two regions by 2040.

The final set of interventions is designed with an eye on the skills requirements for the future. This is achieved by strongly boosting the ratio of vocational to academic students in secondary school as well as the share of science and engineering students at tertiary level.

There are many different ways in which to measure the impact of the Boosting Education scenario. Figure 6.2 compares the mean years of education for adults aged 20–29 years of age for the five subregions in Africa that were defined in Chapter 1. By using a youthful age cohort (20–29 years), the findings best illustrate the very rapid improvements modelled in the Boosting Education scenario. Had I used an older population cohort, such as the average educational attainment of persons older than 25 (as done in Fig. 6.1) the improvements in Africa would be less impressive when compared to the World except Africa.

Figure 6.2 compares the mean years of education for the age group 20–29 years in 2018 with the Current Path forecast for 2040 and the forecast from the Boosting Education scenario for each subregion. These are

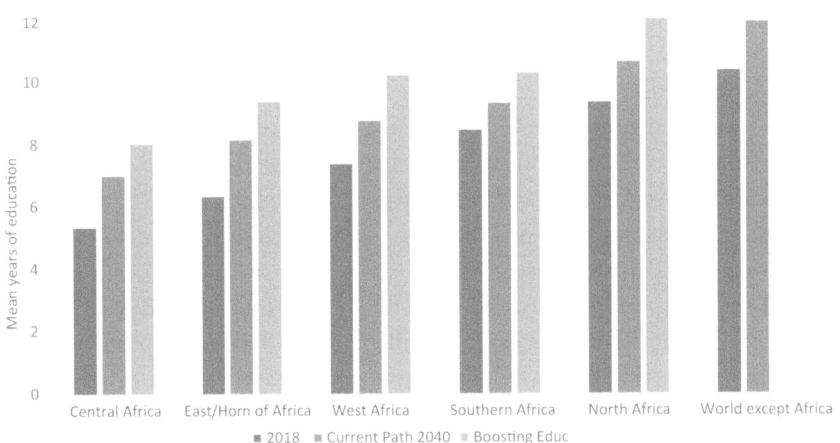

Fig. 6.2 Mean years of education for 20–29 year age cohort: 2018 and 2040 for Current Path and Boosting Education scenario (*Source* IFs 7.45 initializing from United Nations Population Division medium term forecast and Barro-Lee educational attainment dataset)

compared to the Current Path forecast for the World except Africa in 2018 and 2040.

In the Boosting Education scenario and when using this young age cohort as a lens to measure progress, all five regions start closing the gap with the World except Africa but even so, Southern Africa only gets to the 2018 mean for the World except Africa by 2040! Coming off a much higher base, North Africa could actually surpass the mean in the World except Africa by 2040. East/Horn of Africa does the best in terms of increasing mean years of education from 6.3 years in 2018 to 9.4 years in 2040. Central Africa, generally a laggard in improvements also closes the gap although to a lesser degree than others.

Had I used the older population cohort (25 years and above, used in Fig. 6.1), North Africa will not fully catch up with the mean for the World Except Africa by 2040, although narrowing the difference substantially across the forecast horizon, as does West and East/Horn of Africa. The gap between Southern Africa and the World Except Africa actually modestly increases while it remains constant for Central Africa from 2018 to 2040. Just to stand still, Central Africa has to run very hard indeed.

The impact of the Boosting Education scenario is to increase expenditure on education in Africa by an average of 0.3 percentage points of GDP by 2040, requiring US$41 billion of additional investment in education in that year alone. Cumulatively, Africa would spend an additional US$264 billion from 2020 to 2040 on education. That's a lot of money but these additional costs are, in time, offset by improvements in Africa's human capital endowment. As the level of skills improves, Africa's economies start to grow more rapidly and this increase in economic growth accelerates over time.

By 2040 the difference in the GDP growth rate is between the Boosting Education and Current Path 0.5 percentage points, leading to an African economy that is US$266 billion larger in that year compared to the 2040 Current Path forecast. By 2050 the growth difference is 0.75 percentage points and an African economy that is US$1.4 trillion larger in that year than the Current Path forecast.[33]

Therefore, by spending an additional US$264 billion on education from 2020 to 2040, the African economy will by 2040 have increased by about the same amount. But since the investment increases the stock of education, improvements accelerate over time and, inevitably, benefits accrue to more developed countries. Average levels of GDP per capita (in PPP) will increase

---

[33]These numbers are all at market exchange rates.

by US$90 per person in low-income Africa by 2040, by US$245 for low-middle-income Africa and by US$393 in upper-middle-income countries.

Just imagine the impact if Africa could simultaneously reduce the size of the annual influx of primary school children by appropriate family planning interventions as set out in Chapter 4? Reductions in the number of children entering primary school will soon cascade through the entire education system meaning more funds could be spent on the smaller cohort of children as they progress from primary to secondary, and eventually tertiary levels. In this manner the Demographic Dividend and Boosting Education scenarios could reinforce one another in a very powerful way.

Improved levels and quality of education also have a small positive effect in reducing inequality (using the Gini index) and would reduce extreme poverty by about 28 million people in 2040 (using the US$1.90 per person extreme poverty threshold) and 64 million by 2050.

The Boosting Education scenario could have a massive impact. But the results will not be achieved without great effort and new ways of thinking. On the one hand Africa needs to get the basics right. On the other hand the sheer magnitude of the challenge requires a very rapid uptake of modern technology to help compensate for deficits in teacher quality and numbers. I briefly discuss each of these points below.

From Basics to Technology

Models of education do not change rapidly. Because of colonialism most African countries still adhere to the Prussian model of rote education that was introduced in the eighteenth and nineteenth century and thereafter copied by most other countries. It has often, and rightly so, been criticised for being overly rigid and inflexible. But at its core we find the commitment to first teach students how to learn.

In Africa large classrooms staffed by poorly educated teachers and containing only the minimum of educational facilities are the norm. Moreover, many are attended by poor, often hungry children, many of whom have to walk several kilometres every day to school. Looking at the rather dismal state of education in Africa, the continent could clearly do with much greater order and a sense of educational purpose, particularly when it comes to improving levels of reading, writing and arithmetic and teacher attendance, and in finding ways to manage the large classes that are typical in so many schools. We desperately need to find a way to raise the bar, particularly in poorer schools.

Certainly, each African country faces different challenges, but more parent involvement, upskilling teachers and designing teaching and learning methods that are sensitive to local conditions are central to creating functioning education systems in Africa. Not all of this requires sophisticated technology. Already a number of schooling projects require teachers to post a daily selfie by 8 am every day to prove they are in class and teaching showing how much greater use of technology can help Africa to catch up in terms of education.

Against that background, technology in the form of 5G and augmented reality could be the key ingredient to enable the progress modelled in the Boosting Education scenario.

In just a few years cell phones, tablets and even computers may all allow three-dimensional holograms as augmented reality becomes a reality. Billions of dollars are being spent on research and development by companies such as Microsoft and startups like Mojo Vision to make all of that practicable. In 2017 spending on education technology investments surpassed US$9.5 billion, up 30% from the year before.[34]

The application of new technologies could replace a teacher in front of a whiteboard (or chalkboard) with apps, gameplay and entirely new ways of teaching. For example, each student could have an artificial intelligence (AI) teaching companion in the cloud that delivers information at the optimal speed for him or her if the promise of 5G speeds and connectivity examined in Chapter 10 comes to Africa. In this brave new world, students will be able to consume lectures at their own pace with time in class used for discussing problems or collaborative work.

Instead of students huddling around a teacher in front of an oven to learn how to bake or around an electric motor to assemble, disassemble and repair it, each student will have his own virtual oven or motor. Using an augmented reality headset they will be able to experiment with different ingredients or take the motor apart, study each part and put it back together. Meanwhile, students studying biology will be able to dissect virtual animals and view their organs. Medical students will be able to do the same with the human body, while trainee nurses will be able to track blood flow, the digestive system and see how muscles work.

Augmented reality will make learning more immersive, exciting and effective. It could enable learners in the most isolated and disadvantaged rural areas to see and do things that they would otherwise never have the opportunity to. It is a powerful way to provide individual and flexible learning,

---

[34] Diamandis, P. H., 2018. *A Model for the Future of Education.* [Online] Available at: https://singularityhub.com/2018/09/12/a-model-for-the-future-of-education-and-the-tech-shaping-it/.

connecting theory with the real world. Want to get a child to learn a foreign language or to understand computer coding? Get them to play a game in that language or to experiment with coding. In tomorrow's world, understanding technology and coding will be crucial, and augmented reality and AI can help understand computation, sensors, networks, artificial intelligence, digital printing, genetic engineering and robotics, to name a few. New technology will also help with basic literacy.[35]

Conclusion: Prioritising Education Outcomes

The previous chapters on health (Chapter 3), demographics (Chapter 4) and agriculture (Chapter 5) reference the extent to which geography, slavery, colonialism and, after independence, the path dependency created by these histories played an important role in Africa's poor development outcomes. Determined African leadership could have changed this, but did not.

Effective education requires students who are sufficiently nourished, stimulated and cared for, capable teaching, skilled management and a government and education system that pull all of this together. Many countries in sub-Saharan Africa do not have these four key ingredients, and face a crisis in education which the World Bank describes as a low-learning trap.[36]

It is possible to escape this trap, as is demonstrated by the advances made in South Korea, China and Vietnam, but it will require a tremendous effort, political leadership, whole-of-society engagement and the use of modern technology.[37]

The chapter presented a supply- and demand-side view of looking at the provision of education and found that beyond basic levels of (primary) education and literacy an education system must evolve to supply many requirements while also being able to respond to changing education demands to help prepare students for the future's job requirements. The world of work requires more skilled and fewer semi- and unskilled workers.

---

[35] For example, winners of the 2019 XPRIZE (aimed at eliminating adult illiteracy in the USA, retooling tomorrow's workforce and encouraging lifelong learning) included Learning Upgrade, which has developed an app that helps students learn English and mathematics through video, songs and gamification from kindergarten to adult education; and PeopleForWords, which offers an immersive virtual environment and gamification to improve vocabulary and comprehension.
[36] The World Bank, 2018. *World Development Report 2018: Learning to Realize Education's Promise.* Washington, DC: The World Bank Group.
[37] Ibid., p. 16.

There is clearly a very powerful relationship between citizens' level of education and the prosperity of nations, but it's also quite complicated. Duke University educationalist Ricardo Hausmann[38] provides an apt example:

> In 1998, Ghana's workforce had an average of about seven years of education and its per capita income was about $1000. When Mexico's workforce first achieved an average of seven years of education – in 1993 – its income was over $10,000, while France's per capita income when its workforce first got to an average of seven years of education (in 1985), was over $20,000. These figures tell us that rich countries are rich not just because of education, and, conversely, that investing in education alone won't make you rich.

Hausmann attributes the ability to translate education and technology into growth to 'collective know-how'—the ability to *apply* knowledge. That, he argues, comes through imitation and repetition of tasks—learning by doing. For a country to develop and grow, it needs to provide the opportunity for learning while doing. What he does not examine, however, is the matter of the quality of the education provided in Ghana, Mexico and France, pointing to the need to dig deep when considering key relationships.

A review of the widening gap between education levels and quality when comparing Africa to the rest of the world makes it clear that much more strategic planning, innovation, investment and, most of all, leadership is required to address the continent's education backlog. The picture that emerged during this chapter's review of the general African situation and likely prospects along the Current Path forecast is depressing when compared to the progress being achieved in other regions. If the continent fails in this dimension it will fail in all others.

Education systems are notoriously slow-moving and those in most African countries are particularly so. Clearly new teaching technologies and methods must be exploited to help meet the challenges of the future. African countries will not close the gap in average levels of education compared to the rest of the world by using current systems and practices. Technology can fundamentally change the nature of education and enable the move away from brick and mortar campuses to electronic or virtual campuses that will facilitate much broader access for both students and teachers. Much of that is already possible in so-called point learning where the curious African can Google how to make, disassemble, repair, cook or understand almost anything by watching a YouTube video. I don't need to be an accredited Apple dealer with years of

---

[38]Hausmann, R., 2017. Centre for Development and Enterprise. [Online] Available at: https://cde.org.za/wp-content/uploads/2018/06/CDE-Insight-Professor-Ricardo-Hausmann-Is-South-Africa-about-to-make-a-historic-mistake.pdf.

formal training to understand how to replace and repair a smartphone. You just need the internet and a set of very small screwdrivers.

Moreover, it is imperative to find ways to channel many more students towards vocational training programmes that benefit from broader integration into the educational system and, that enable informal, virtual self-empowerment.

Further Reading

Habyarimana, James and Sabarwal, Shwetlena. 2018. Re-Kindling Learning: eReaders in Lagos. Policy Research Working Paper No. 8665. World Bank, Washington, DC. © World Bank. https://openknowledge.worldbank.org/handle/10986/30987. License: CC BY 3.0 IGO.

Launay, Robert (ed.). 2016. *Islamic Education in Africa: Writing Boards and Blackboards*. Indiana University Press. JSTOR. www.jstor.org/stable/j.ctt1zxz0gv.

UNESCO. Director-General, 2009–2017 (Bokova, I.G.). 2017. Writer of Foreword. Cracking the Code: Girls' and Women's Education in Science, Technology, Engineering and Mathematics (STEM). UNESDOC Digital Library. https://unesdoc.unesco.org/ark:/48223/pf0000253479.locale=en. ISBN: 978-92-3-100233-5.

Open Access This chapter is licensed under the terms of the Creative Commons Attribution 4.0 International License (http://creativecommons.org/licenses/by/4.0/), which permits use, sharing, adaptation, distribution and reproduction in any medium or format, as long as you give appropriate credit to the original author(s) and the source, provide a link to the Creative Commons license and indicate if changes were made.

The images or other third party material in this chapter are included in the chapter's Creative Commons license, unless indicated otherwise in a credit line to the material. If material is not included in the chapter's Creative Commons license and your intended use is not permitted by statutory regulation or exceeds the permitted use, you will need to obtain permission directly from the copyright holder.

7

Poverty, Inequality and Growth

Abstract Cilliers first explores the progress that has been made globally in poverty reduction in a historical context and then the relationship between inequality and growth. He concludes that Africa will miss goal 1 of the Sustainable Development Goals on the elimination of extreme poverty by 2030 by a substantial margin. The chapter uses three income measures of extreme poverty for low, lower-middle and upper-middle countries to frame the current situation in Africa and then discusses and forecasts the impact of social grants on poverty alleviation. A final section presents the results of a scenario, Social Grants for Africa, and compares the results with the poverty forecast in the Current Path.

Keywords Poverty · Inequality · Economic growth · Inclusivity · Multidimensional poverty · Redistributive policies · Social grants · Conditional and unconditional grants · Welfare state · ID system

Learning objectives

– Income inequality is the outcome of complex and multidimensional determinants
– Despite recent improvements, the slow rates of growth in Africa among other issues are barriers to eliminating poverty
– Social protection mechanisms can play an important role in the short to medium term to alleviate poverty and inequality.

Over the last two centuries the world witnessed a transition to levels of peace and prosperity that are almost unimaginable by historical standards. We often don't realise exactly how recent this progress is.

In 1651 English philosopher Thomas Hobbes wrote in his book, Leviathan, that in the absence of a strong central authority the inevitable inclination of nations is towards civil war 'where every man is enemy to every man ... and the life of man, solitary, poor, nasty, brutish, and short'.[1] Hobbes was describing the situation for most of humanity for, until the industrial revolution that began in Britain in the eighteenth century, poverty was widespread and pervasive. Only a very small elite enjoyed decent living conditions.

The improvement in well-being that followed the industrial revolution came off a very low base. Everyone was basically dirt poor, but the situation improved rapidly thereafter. The result was also inevitably to increase inequality between and within countries, a trend that decelerated somewhat between the two World Wars and only stabilised after 1950 when growth in Europe and the USA slowed, coinciding with more rapid economic growth in Japan, East Asia and eventually China. Even at that point, 1950, three-quarters of the world's population still lived in what we today would term extreme poverty.[2]

During the first half of the previous century *rates* of poverty came down even as global populations continued to increase. Then, from around 1970, the decrease in poverty rates became so rapid that we saw the *absolute number* of people living in extreme poverty also starting to fall in spite of the huge increase in global population. That progress was largely delivered by capitalism and the expansion of trade—developments that we often consider synonymous with globalisation and a neoliberal phase of economic development, discussed in Chapter 11 on trade.

Until the early 1990s, numbers of extremely poor people hovered at above two billion people but, from around 1994, it declined precipitously, much of it due to rapid progress in China. In the eleven years from 2006 to 2017 the number of people living in extreme poverty actually *halved* to less than 800 million people despite the fact that the world's population *increased* by almost one billion people during this period.[3]

---

[1] Hobbes, T., 1909. Being the First Part of Leviathan. In: C. W. Eliot, ed. *Of Man*. New York: Bartleby.

[2] Bourguignon, F., and Christian Morrisson, C., 2002. Inequality Among World Citizens: 1820–1992. *The American Economic Review*, 92(4, September), pp. 727–728. http://links.jstor.org/sici?sici=0002-8282%28200209%2992%3A4%3C727%3AIAWC1%3E2.0.CO%3B2-S.

[3] Roser, M., and Ortiz-Ospina, E., 2018. *Literacy*. [Online] Available at: https://ourworldindata.org/literacy.

The improvements have been so fast that in 2005 the international community was emboldened to adopt a target to halve extreme poverty by 2015 as part of the Millennium Development Goals. When that was met, an even more ambitious goal, to *end* extreme poverty by 2030, was adopted as part of the Sustainable Development Goals (SDGs). It is captured in Goal 1, which refers to 'ending poverty in all its forms everywhere'. Technically this means that less than three percent of the population of every country in the world should be living in extreme poverty using US$1.90 per person average income.

Because of Africa's rapid population growth, modest rates of economic growth and relatively high levels of inequality, the absolute number of extremely poor people in Africa has steadily increased since 1960 and is likely to continue to do so until around 2032 before slowly starting to decline. However, since the early nineties, the *percentage* of people living in extreme poverty in Africa has started to decline. The reason is that even though economic growth in the continent is now slower than before the 2007/2008 financial crisis, was, until COVID-19, robust enough to reduce the portion of Africans living in extreme poverty but not enough to reduce the absolute number along the Current Path forecast for at least the next decade.[4]

Sadly, Africa will miss the SDG goal of eliminating extreme poverty by 2030 by a very large margin. In this, the widening gap between Africa and the rest of the world again becomes clear. Things are improving in Africa but much slower than in other regions and, in the wake of the COVID-19 pandemic, progress is bound to be even more modest than before.

Globalisation and the Sense of Relative Deprivation

For much of our recent history, certainly from the end of the nineteenth century onward, globalisation drove economic growth and played a positive role in the remarkable improvements in human prosperity that virtually exploded in the twentieth century in spite of two world wars. Today, though, the impact is less visible, particularly in high-income countries like the USA, Japan and Germany. Because Africa suffered under the yoke of colonialism and its economic legacies, it has generally not been part of the accompanying expansion in trade and value as examined in Chapter 11.

---

[4] This analysis uses US$1.90 as extreme poverty line.

The last four decades have witnessed dramatic reductions in income inequality between countries. In 1975, world income distribution was akin to the two-humped shape of a camel's back with one hump (the developing world, particularly Asia and the Pacific as well as Africa) below the international poverty line. The second hump (the developed world) was at considerably higher average incomes. In the subsequent four decades the poorer countries, particularly in Southeast Asia, have caught up as the incomes of the world's most poor increased rapidly, although not sub-Saharan Africa. Today there is only one hump as global prosperity has generally improved and incomes have increased.[5] But not in sub-Saharan Africa, where, in comparison with the rest of the world, the camel still has two humps.

Globally the pre-2007/2008 period of globalisation appears to have seen a convergence among a group of rich states, the stagnation of middle-income countries and a convergence among poor countries. It is as if hyper-globalisation reached a tipping point with the 2007/2008 global financial crisis, which temporarily turbocharged income inequality within and between countries.[6] As I mentioned previously, it is still too early to speculate responsibly on the impact of the COVID-19 virus on inequality and poverty, although the short- and medium-term trends are inevitably going to be negative. Exactly how negative remains to be seen, however.

While the numbers and percentages may tell one story as regards the situation when comparing incomes between countries, our interconnected world and access to information seem to have intensified a sense of relative deprivation among large swathes of the global populace, from India and China to the American Midwest and Afghanistan. It is particularly evident in Africa.

Initially, the 2007/2008 financial crisis led to anti-establishment protests such as the 'Occupy Wall Street' movement although with important regional variations. Financial benefits seem to be flowing to small urban elites, financial institutions and a handful of large corporations while little changed for the middle class. In almost all countries with data on income distribution, income is increasingly concentrated among top earners—the poor (and often

---

[5] Roser, M., 2016. *Global Economic Inequality.* [Online] Available at: https://ourworldindata.org/global-economic-inequality.

[6] Ruchir Sharma, investment strategist and author of *The Rise and Fall of Nations: Forces of Change in a Post-Crisis World* refers to before and after the 2007/2008 crisis. In the region with the highest average income, Europe, the national income share of the top 10% is only at 37%. It is highest in the Middle East at 61%. The average for sub-Saharan Africa is 54%, marginally below the average for Brazil and India at 55% each Sharma, R., 2016. *The Rise and Fall of Nations—Ten Rules of Change in the Post-crisis World.* New York: Penguin Random House, p. 5.

the middle class) are not doing very well while the rich are clearly getting richer.[7]

This sense of absolute and relative deprivation, that actual improvements in living standards are vastly out of kilter with expectations, is clearly on the rise. In fact, although people in high-income countries have never enjoyed a better living standard, they seem to feel particularly insecure, scared that they will not be able to maintain their standard of living and that migrants from poor countries will somehow overwhelm them. The result is a rise in developed world identity politics in the midst of the most peaceful and prosperous era known to humankind. Ironically, these improvements have largely been created by the exact political and market liberalisation ideals promoted by the west that are now blamed for driving the increase in inequality.[8] All reflect a view, for different reasons, that the current political system is not managing to hold the fort against special interests.

The recent debate was arguably started by a 2013 door stopper of a book by French economic historian Thomas Piketty with the title *Capital in the Twenty-First Century*. Other books, both more serious and popular, include the 2018 *The Future of Capitalism: Facing the New Anxieties* by Paul Collier and the *Edge of Chaos: Why Democracy is Failing to Delivery Economic Growth and How to Fix It* by Dambisa Moyo. All seek either to reform capitalism or democracy or both, even as dedicated pro-business magazines such as *The Economist* flail around in their efforts to question the data and associated research findings[9] while a steady drumbeat of reports from the UN and advocacy organisations such as Oxfam and others underline the extent to which increases in wealth today largely accrue to the rich.[10]

---

[7] See for example, UNDESA, Income Inequality Trends: The Choice of Indicators Matter, Social Development Brief #8, December 2019. [Online] Available at: https://www.un.org/development/desa/dspd/wp-content/uploads/sites/22/2019/12/SDB_8_Income_inequality_trends_2.pdf. Accessed 5 January 2020.

[8] Kozul-Wright, R., 2017. *The Trade and Development Report 2017. Beyond Austerity: Towards a Global New Deal*. New York and Geneva: United Nations Conference on Trade and Development.

[9] *The Economist*, Inequality: Measuring the 1%, 30 November 2019.

[10] See for example: UNDESA. 2019. Income Inequality Trends: The Choice of Indicators Matter, Social Development Brief #8, December 2019. [Online] Available at: https://www.un.org/development/desa/dspd/wp-content/uploads/sites/22/2019/12/SDB 8 Income_inequality_trends_2.pdf. Accessed 5 January 2020, and Oxfam. 2018. The Commitment to Reducing Inequality Index 2018. October 2018 [Online] Available at: https://oxfamilibrary.openrepository.com/bitstream/handle/10546/620553/rr-commitment-reducing-inequality-index-2018-091018-en.pdf.

The Interplay Between Inequality and Growth

Economic growth and income distribution are the two key variables when forecasting rates of poverty at national level. In general, higher rates of economic growth are strongly associated with higher rates of poverty reduction but high levels of inequality limit the extent to which that can occur. A growing economy must, in particular, increase the number of formal sector jobs and the amount of money in circulation to provide more revenues to the government to invest in infrastructure, health and education (and hence improve the quality of its human capital), as well as for use in more direct measure of poverty alleviation such as social grant programmes.

The global achievements towards halving poverty in 2015 was largely achieved on the back of the remarkable progress in China since 1978 that transformed a rural, centrally planned economy, into the most dynamic and largest in the world, now generally referred to as a socialist market economy that has come to challenge Western, neoliberal, orthodoxy. Then classified as a low-income country, the vast majority of its population lived in extreme poverty. By 2018, the number of Chinese living below US$1.90 per day was less than 2 million representing less than 1% of its 1.4 billion people.[11] In the intervening years, China has experienced almost unprecedented growth rates for such a large country. The extraordinary ability of the Communist Party to accelerate industrialisation and urbanisation, and hence shift surplus agricultural labour from the countryside into more productive urban employment in low-end manufacturing, to affect more equitable distribution of cultivated agricultural land and to institute universal compulsory education up to grade 9, roll out basic health care and minimum living allowance schemes that contributed to the remarkable improvements in income growth.[12] Poverty reduction in India has also accelerated in recent years but at significantly lower rates than it did in China in spite of the fact that China measures higher on the Gini index than India, pointing to the importance of additional factors to translate growth into poverty reduction.[13]

---

[11] Ravallion, M., and Chen, S., 2007. China's (Uneven) Progress Against Poverty. *Journal of Development Economics*, 82(1), pp. 1–32. Also World Bank, The World Bank in China, 2019. [Online] Available at: https://www.worldbank.org/en/country/china/overview.

[12] Wu, G., 2016. Ending Poverty in China: What Explains Great Poverty Reduction and a Simultaneous Increase in Inequality in Rural Areas? World Bank Blogs, 19 October 2016. [Online] Available at: http://blogs.worldbank.org/eastasiapacific/ending-poverty-in-china-what-explains-great-poverty-reduction-and-a-simultaneous-increase-in-inequality-in-rural-areas. Accessed on 4 January 2020.

[13] Express News Service, 2018. *UNDP Report Lauds India's Strides in Reducing Poverty in Past Decade*. [Online] Available at: https://indianexpress.com/article/india/undp-report-lauds-indias-strides-in-reducing-poverty-in-past-decade/. Still, 650 million people (49%) on the Indian subcontinent

Gini is the most widely used measure to express income distribution. Its index ranges from zero, corresponding to complete equality, i.e. everyone earns the same income, and one that represents complete inequality where all the income accrues to only one person in society. Being a summary measure of income distribution, Gini does not identify whether a change in inequality is triggered by shifts at the bottom, middle or top of the income distribution. When comparing regions according to the Gini Index, Southern Africa, where I live, is the most unequal region globally, even worse than Latin America and the Carribean that is often mentioned as the most unequal region globally. In Africa, Northern Africa is significantly more equal than any other subregion on the continent. Central, West and the Horn/Eastern Africa are somewhere between Southern and North Africa.[14] There are additional problems with Gini which, as a summary measure of inequality, is based on survey data that is often not well suited to capture very high or very low incomes. The challenge is particularly acute for many developing countries that do not have much information on income distribution such as that earned by the bottom ten or top one percent.

That inequality is complex and not well captured using Gini is well illustrated by understanding the relative lower levels of inequality in North Africa, since it begs the question why the Arab spring would occur in this region and not elsewhere? The reasons, which are explored in greater detail in Chapter 12, come down to the fact that this region has relatively high levels of education compared to the rest of Africa but very limited economic, social and political opportunity. Consequently, frustration boiled over.

These concerns and caveats aside, generally countries with low levels of inequality, such as Ethiopia, that grow rapidly, can translate that growth into extraordinary rapid reductions in poverty but much more is required than simply economic growth.[15]

For example, since the early 1960s Botswana has consistently grown its economy much more rapidly than Ghana and did so until very recently. The average growth rate for Botswana from 1961 to 1999 was 10.1% while for Ghana it was only 2.5%. But because Ghana is significantly more equal

---

continue to live in debilitating conditions (using the US$3.20 poverty line for low-middle-income countries).

[14]The IFs forecast on poverty levels uses the average levels of income and a lognormal distribution as indicated by the Gini index. Since the internal calculation using those variables will, however, almost inevitably produce a rate of poverty at odds with those provided by national surveys, the system computes an adjustment in the first year for the subsequent forecast years.

[15]Edward, P., and Sumner, A., 2013. The Future of Global Poverty in a Multi-Speed World: New Estimates of Scale and Location, 2010–2030. *Center for Global Development*, Volume Working Paper 327.

than Botswana, poverty reduction in the two countries does not differ as much as one would expect.[16] From 1970 to 1996 poverty in Botswana had come down by 25 percentage points and by 14 percentage points in Ghana (using the US$1.90 poverty line).[17] Clearly growth matters, but so does levels of inequality and considerations such as the effectiveness and quality of government. Whereas Botswana is generally an island of stability and good governance in its region, Ghana has suffered from coups and significant instability for much of its independent history.

The SDGs and Measuring Extreme Poverty

The various goals and targets of the Sustainable Development Goals (SDGs) are described as being 'integrated and indivisible'. Many of them refer to the relationships between economic growth, inequality (using various different indices and measure) and decent employment, three of the key factors that determine poverty rates.

SDG Target 8.1, for example, aims for sustained per capita economic growth of 'at least 7 percent gross domestic product growth per annum in the least developed countries', 33 of which are in Africa. Target 8.5 is about 'full and productive employment and decent work for all women and men'. Target 10.1 commits countries to 'progressively achieve and sustain income growth of the bottom 40% of the population at a rate higher than the national average' and 'to reduce at least by half the proportion of men, women and children of all ages living in poverty in all its dimensions according to national definitions by 2030'.

The SDG goals and targets have led to a global effort to develop the data and associated tools with which the international community can more accurately measure progress. But definitions of poverty differ from country to country, among academics and between agencies. Poverty is closely related to the imbalances in people's opportunities in education, health, level of empowerment and access to technology. It is about much more than just a lack of sufficient income. Nonetheless, GDP per capita in purchasing power parity remains the most widely used comparative measure of average standards of living and is often used to make comparisons between countries. It does not

---

[16] By about 19 percentage points.
[17] In 1970 Botswana still had an average GDP per capita that was US$1.246 below that of Ghana. Within four years average income levels in Botswana surpassed Ghana's and, by 1999 GDP per capita in Botswana was four times higher (or US$7.167) than in Ghana.

take the quality of life into consideration, since it's simply a measure of the value of goods and services produced divided by the total population.

In using GDP per capita (and Gini) one must therefore be fully cognisant of the associated restrictions and distortions, such as the fact that poverty in the eastern DRC is quite different from that experienced in Mali or South Africa, for example. Poverty in rural Uganda is also quite different from that in the capital city of Kampala. These imbalances often reflect unequal opportunities. Poverty under men and women also differ sharply, firstly from each other, as well as from the poverty experienced by children.

Since women tend to be disproportionately responsible for household chores and caregiving, poverty restricts the time that girls can commit to staying in school. It also determines whether families can afford school fees, purchase supplies or guarantee that their children can attend school when their help is needed at home, either to help generate income or to take care of household tasks.

Since income is quite a blunt instrument through which to view poverty, there have been numerous efforts to flesh out new approaches and definitions, such as the Multidimensional Poverty Index (MPI)[18] developed by the Oxford Poverty and Human Development Initiative and subsequently adopted by the United Nations Development Programme.[19] The most recent edition of the Human Development Report[20] is entirely devoted to exploring the different dimensions of inequality and poverty and carries the subtitle 'Inequalities in human development in the 21st century'.

When the negotiations on the SDGs were finalised, extreme poverty was defined as living below a daily income of US$1.90 per person in 2011 prices. It is the most recent incarnation of an international poverty line, originally defined as a dollar a day and has often been criticised for its focus on income and that it does not reflect the lived experience of extreme poverty.

These caveats aside, Fig. 7.1 presents extreme poverty in Africa and the World Except Africa from 2015 with a forecast to 2040 using the US$1.90 extreme poverty income level. Whereas, in 2018, 36% of Africans (or 458 million) lived in extreme poverty that portion would decline to 33% by 2030 and 24% (equivalent to 513 million) by 2040. Almost all of the extremely poor people in Africa, and indeed globally, will be in sub-Saharan Africa.

---

[18]The MPI measures multiple deprivations in the same households in education, health and living standards across ten indicators ranging from nutrition and child mortality to assets.
[19]In 2010 the UNDP also launched its Inequality Adjusted Human Development Index (IHDI) and Gender Inequality Index (GII).
[20]United Nations Development Programme, 2019. *Human Development Report 2019 Beyond Income, Beyond Averages, Beyond Today: Inequalities in Human Development in the Twenty-first Century*. New York.

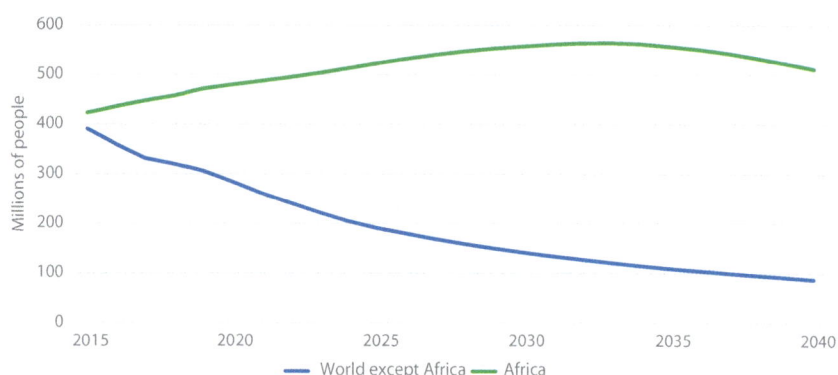

Fig. 7.1 Extreme poverty in Africa and the World except Africa: 2015 to 2040 using US1.90 (*Source* IFs 7.45 initializing from United Nations Population Division World Population Prospects medium variant life expectancy)

To compensate for the fact that extreme poverty in richer countries occurs at higher levels of income than in poor countries, the World Bank in October 2018 announced an important addition to the way in which it would measure poverty. While progress to the SDG headline goal of eliminating extreme poverty would still be measured using US$1.90 as well as for the 31 countries that the Bank classifies as low income, It now introduced three additional poverty lines for lower-middle (47 countries globally) and upper-middle-income countries (60 countries globally) at US$3.20 and US$5.50, respectively. Extreme poverty in high-income countries will be measured using US$22.70 (applicable to 80 countries).

The Bank also intends to moving away from the household to individuals as the primary unit of analysis (as was the practice before) since there is considerable evidence that there are poor women and children living in non-poor households. So, while the main breadwinner in a household may technically not be classified as extremely poor, others in the same household may be living on much lower levels of income.[21]

The Impact of the Additional Poverty Lines

The three additional poverty lines compensate for one crucial imbalance in that the amount of income that a person needs to escape the burden

---

[21]Sharma, D., 2018. *Why the World Bank Is Taking a Wide-Angle View of Poverty*. [Online] Available at: https://www.brookings.edu/blog/future-development/2018/11/14/why-the-world-bank-is-taking-a-wide-angle-view-of-poverty/.

of extreme poverty in low-income Mozambique is quite different from the income that a person in upper-middle-income neighbour South Africa would need.

Applied in Africa the impact of the differentiated poverty rates is to sharply *increase* the number of Africans deemed to live in extreme poverty and to sharply *reduce* the number of African countries likely to achieve the target of eliminating extreme poverty by 2030 should the observer use the relevant income threshold for each country income group rather than US$1.90 for all countries instead of just for low-income countries.

Using the three poverty lines, each applied to the relevant income group, the Current Path forecast is that the extreme poverty rate in Africa will, by 2040, have declined from 50% in 2018 (634 million out of a total of 1.28 billion people) to 35% (or 735 million out of 2.1 billion people).

The associated forecast for low, lower-middle and upper-income countries is set out in Table 7.1.

Currently, roughly 50% of Africans would be classified as living in extreme poverty, that is after combining the averages for the three country income groups. This rate will decline to 38% by 2040. The number of extremely poor Africans will, however, have increased from 638 million to 796 million on the back of rapid population growth.

Only the island state of Seychelles (with less than a million people) is considered to be a high-income country and is disregarded in the numbers and rates used in this chapter.

Other regions and countries are similarly affected. Whereas China met the US$1.90 goal of eliminating extreme poverty some years ago, using the US$5.50 extreme poverty line for upper-middle-income countries, China had around 234 million extremely poor people in 2018. Even then, with an average GDP growth rate of 6% from 2020 to 2040, China will eliminate extreme poverty as measured using US$5.50 by 2030, illustrating the

Table 7.1 Current Path of population and extreme poverty in Africa

Year	Low-income Africa		Low-middle Africa		Upper-middle Africa	
	Population	Of which below US$1.90	Population	Of which below US$3.20	Population	Of which below US$5.50
2018	548m	268m	613m	311m	11m	56m
2030	765m	331m	813m	379m	133m	66m
2040	973m	307m	999m	375m	143m	55m

Source IFs 7.45 initializing from United Nations Population Division World Population Prospects medium variant life expectancy and World Development Indicators data

Table 7.2 African countries with 50% or more of their populations in extreme poverty using US$1.90, US$3.20 and US$5.50

	2018	2040
Low-income countries with poverty above 50% using US$1.90	Madagascar (76%); Burundi (74%); DRC (73%); CAR (68%), Malawi (68%), Guinea-Bissau (65%), South Sudan (62%), Mozambique (62%), Somalia (57%)	Burundi (79%); Liberia (74%); CAR (69%); Madagascar (67%); Malawi (61%); Sierra Leone (60%); Somalia (54%)
Low-middle-income countries with poverty above 50% using US$3.20	Zambia (76%); Nigeria (76%); Lesotho (76%); Sao Tome & Principe (68%); Senegal (63%); Rep of Congo (63%); Swaziland (61%); Angola (61%); Kenya (52%)	Lesotho (73%); Swaziland (60%); Zambia (70%); Nigeria (62%); Rep of Congo (54%)
Upper-middle-income countries with poverty above 50% using US$5.50	Namibia (63%), South Africa (53%), Algeria (51%)	None

Source IFs 7.45 initializing from United Nations Population Division World Population Prospects medium variant life expectancy and World Development Indicators data

remarkable impact that high growth and effective government can have on poverty levels.[22]

The Current Situation in Africa

Table 7.2 presents a summary of those countries with more than 50% of their population below the extreme poverty line in 2018 and 2040 along the Current Path forecast.

African countries also vary widely with regard to the depth of extreme poverty, meaning that many extremely poor people live far below the US$1.90, US$3.20 and US$5.50 income levels per person per day. They are chronically poor and it will take a long time for extremely poor people in these countries to improve their prospects and to reach even the extreme poverty income levels discussed here.

---

[22] Ravallion, M., and Chen, S., 2007. China's (Uneven) Progress Against Poverty. *Journal of Development Economics*, 82(1), pp. 1–32. Also World Bank, The World Bank in China, 2019. [Online] Available at: https://www.worldbank.org/en/country/china/overview.

Whereas, using US$1.90, Africa got close to eliminating extreme poverty by 2070, some forty years after the SDG 2030 goal, the newly established additional poverty lines moved the goalposts even further to the right.

Although some countries such as Botswana have experienced very rapid rates of growth, few have been able to translate this growth into rapid reductions in rates of poverty. This is not the case for all countries, though. Cameroon, Egypt, Ghana, Kenya, Mali, Mauritania, Senegal, eSwatini, Tunisia and Uganda have all been relatively efficient in transmitting income growth into poverty reduction, generally because of relatively lower levels of inequality and the implementation of various additional poverty reduction measures.[23]

The Potential of Social Grants to Reduce Poverty

The extent of poverty in Africa, and the various factors that reinforce it, makes it clear that there are no quick fixes to reduce extreme poverty. Beyond policies that accelerate economic growth and redistribution, African governments can reduce poverty by investing in education, job creation and the provision of basic services, as discussed in previous chapters.

Discussed in Chapter 6, improvement in education is generally perceived as the great leveller that can eventually allow for more complex, productive and hence better-paid work. But improvements in education take a very long time to impact upon inequality and poverty.

Second, large increases in employment in the formal sector can push up low-end wages and reduce inequality. Being part of the formal sector locks workers into annual wage negotiations, allowing them to qualify for sick leave and other benefits and to be part of pension schemes. This is discussed in more detail in Chapter 9, where I look at the very large component of employment in the informal sector and the challenges that need to be overcome to create jobs for Africa's rapidly growing population.

Social grants have proven to be an effective short-term solution to assist the poor and alleviate extreme inequality. This is demonstrated by the impact of grant programmes in countries as diverse as Brazil, South Africa and India. In its original conceptions, income grants were conditional. Poor people were provided with food stamps or other means to subsidise food, education and transport if they fell below a certain income threshold. The latter had to be monitored through regular means testing, i.e. is the beneficiary still alive, does

---

[23] Cillier, J., Hughes, B., and Turner, S., 2015. *Reasonable Goals for Reducing Poverty in Africa: Targets for the Post-MDGs and Agenda 2063*. Pretoria: Institute for Security Studies.

he/she still qualify for the income grant, etc.—a process which is cumbersome and costly.

Recent years have also witnessed a steady move towards universal, non-means tested grants in other countries, including South Africa where the ruling party has placed particular emphasis on redistributive policies rather than on growth. Whereas in 1994 four million South Africans received social grants, that figure has expanded to more than 17 million and is set to increase further. Today, social grants in some form or another are paid to 46% of South Africans.[24]

But as we saw when examining poverty levels in different African countries, even with this hugely expensive and expansive grant system, more than half of South Africans still live in extreme poverty (using US$5.50). With only 7.28 million taxpayers out of a total population of 58 million, the South African system is eventually unsustainable without much more rapid economic growth.[25] Without significantly higher economic growth, extreme poverty in South Africa is unlikely to decrease as it squeezes out productive government spending in favour of spending on consumption.[26]

Another positive example of where social grants were used as part of a poverty reduction strategy is India with a government heavily committed to a campaign to ensure that every Indian has a bank account, is linked to the internet and can be biometrically identified.

The Aadhaar (meaning foundation) project started off as a voluntary programme to help tackle corruption and fraud. Today Aadhaar offers the first national database of the Indian population. It has enrolled more than 1.1 billion Indians on its biometric, digital and physical identity system. Linking bank accounts to biometric identification and cell phones creates a system that can overcome the pervasive corruption that is often part of social grant systems where large amounts of cash are doled out to sometimes illiterate beneficiaries by poorly paid officials who are themselves often destitute.

Aadhaar requires that each person goes through an enrolment process, during which a facial photograph, ten fingerprints and scans of both irises are recorded along with the citizen's demographic information (name, address,

---

[24] South African Social Security Agency, Fact Sheet: Issue No. 14–February 2018 A Statistical Summary of Social Grants In South Africa. [Online] Available at: https://www.sassa.gov.za/Statistics/Documents/Fact%20Sheet%20-%20Issue%20No.14%20%E2%80%93%20February%202018.pdf. Accessed on 5 January 2020.

[25] BusinessTech, 2017. *This Is Who Is Paying South Africa's Tax.* [Online] Available at: https://businesstech.co.za/news/finance/207631/this-is-who-is-paying-south-africas-tax/.

[26] StatsSA, 2015. *A Statistical Summary of Social Grants in South Africa.* Pretoria: Strategic Monitoring Branch: Strategy and Business Development. See also Zembe-Mkabile, W., 2017. *Social Grants: More Than Just Money at Stake.* [Online] Available at: https://www.news24.com/Columnists/GuestColumn/social-grants-theres-more-than-just-money-at-stake-20170314.

gender and date of birth). Once the enrolment is completed and the biometric data verified, he/she is issued with a 12-digit unique identification number.

The advantages are clear—service providers can verify the identity of a person with the Unique Identification Authority of India. Registration on the system is required to open a bank account, file a tax return or to get a sim card. Using mobile phone systems, funds (including social grants) can now be transferred directly to individuals doing away with physical cash payments. There are, of course, risks with such systems, particularly in autocratic countries such as China where government control of such systems readily translates into political and population control measures.

Many African countries are doing the same, but in some, such as Kenya where corruption is truly endemic, repeated efforts to collect the biometric data of its population and establish a national ID system is treated with deep suspicion as yet another means by which politicians can manipulate situations to their advantage.[27]

A second, more radical concept than social grants is the idea of a Universal Basic Share. A Universal Basic Share would be an equal payment to all citizens, without any conditions or a means test. While this concept is also under consideration in some rich countries, the attraction of a Universal Basic Share lies in its simplicity. Instead of having to determine if an individual falls below a certain income level and hence meets the means test, the payment is simply made to everyone above a certain minimum age.

The problem with a Universal Basic Share payment may actually not be the availability of money but the tax policies of African governments. Tax rates in Africa are notoriously low, largely because African governments 'forgo revenues worth almost a third of those they actually collect'[28] through a bewildering array of tax breaks to donors, special economic zones and by offering tax holidays to big investors, often mining houses. Thus 'tax collection in Africa resembles an exasperating fishing expedition, in which the big fish wriggle into tax havens and the tiddlers hide in the informal sector'.[29]

In addition to low rates, inefficiencies in revenue collection mean that African governments forgo large amounts of tax revenue.

---

[27] Sounds BBC, 2019. Kenya's Controversial Biometric Project. [Sound Recording] (World Service).
[28] *The Economist*, 2018. African Governments Let Too Many Taxpayers Off the Hook. [Online] Available at: https://www.economist.com/finance-and-economics/2018/08/18/african-governments-let-too-many-taxpayers-off-the-hook. Also see Coulibaly, S. B., and Gandhi, D. 2018 *Mobilization of Tax Revenues in Africa State of Play and Policy Option*. Brookings. [Online] Available at: https://www.brookings.edu/research/mobilization-of-tax-revenues-in-africa/.
[29] Ibid.

Today the debate around poverty alleviation includes the question whether various subsidies, particularly on fuel, shouldn't be replaced with direct cash transfers. Would it not be more effective to simply give farmers cash instead of trying to subsidise inputs such as seed or fertiliser?[30] However, this could create another problem, as direct cash transfers over extended periods of time can lead to dependency and reduce the incentive to undertake or seek employment. Why would a farmer try and improve productivity if he/she could live off a government grant? I return to this matter in Chapter 9 where I look at the future of employment in Africa.

The experiences of different countries illustrate the complexities involved in cash grants. While modern technology can solve most of the issues around corruption, the essential challenge of dependency on state grants must also be addressed. The challenge therefore goes beyond reducing poverty in the short term. The actual question is how African economies can be transformed to ensure sustained income growth in the long term. How to get people off social grants and into paid employment with taxable incomes?

To this end social protection policies are best employed in tandem with other economic reform efforts that focus on changing the productive structures. In Egypt, for example, the Takaful and Karama (Solidarity and Dignity) conditional and unconditional cash transfer programme was launched in 2015 and covers 2.26 million households—approximately 10% of Egypt's population.

Takaful and Karama were introduced to cushion the impact of Egypt's ambitious 2014 economic reform programme that included the removal of energy subsidies, the adoption of a flexible exchange rate and the introduction of new value-added tax. The government has also scaled up its social protection programmes. The Takaful (solidarity) part of the programme provides modest unconditional monthly pensions to elderly and disabled citizens while Karama (dignity) provides conditional family income support aimed at increasing food consumption, reducing poverty and encourages families to keep children in school while providing them with health care.[31]

In the meantime, modern technology now makes a social grant system feasible in which much of the inefficiency and corruption of past programmes can be avoided.

The political and practical challenges for many of the measures set out in this chapter should, however, not be underestimated. In Ethiopia, one

---

[30] For example in India the fertiliser subsidy alone is about 0.8% of GDP and is hugely distortionary.
[31] The World Bank, 2018. The Story of Takaful and Karama Cash Transfer Program. [Online] Available at: https://www.worldbank.org/en/news/feature/2018/11/15/the-story-of-takaful-and-karama-cash-transfer-program.

of Africa's top performers, efforts launched in 2006 to expand the tax base initially made steady progress but then stalled for several years after the death of Prime Minister Meles Zenawi in August 2012. Zenawi had championed the reforms and insulated it from political interference. When he died, tax reform, modernisation and increased revenue collection ground to a halt, although there were signs in 2018 of a renewed push under Prime Minister Abiy Ahmed. Total taxes collected nearly tripled from US$1.3 billion in 2007 to US$3.8 billion in 2013 and by 2017 it reached US$7.8 billion. As a share of total government revenue, the contribution from tax grew from 48% in 2007 to 82% in 2016. Therefore, the growth in revenue collection failed to keep up with an economy that, on average, was growing at more than 10% per annum since 2000.[32]

The Promise of an African Welfare State?

In the past, today's developed countries responded to the problem of inequality and large-scale unemployment with the creation of a welfare state. In such a system the state plays a key role in the protection and promotion of the economic and social well-being of its citizens.

This was possible because these (mostly Western) states were strong, having evolved through external war and competition, including the extraction of resources from colonies into a system of governance that was underpinned by a social contract between the elected government and its citizens. In return for compliance and taxes, governments provided services and protection.

At the heart of the welfare model are various mechanisms through which the state provides key services such as education and healthcare and redistributes income from richer to poorer people through a progressive tax system. Modern welfare states include Germany and France but it is most developed in the social democratic system in the Nordic countries. This system, which has created the most advanced, egalitarian and competitive societies in modern history is rooted in the bitter experience of centuries of war and poverty.

The Nordics are all small, open economies that export a large portion of GDP into a highly competitive world. Wage inequality is among the lowest globally yet they have higher sustained economic growth than most, which is largely a function of the fact that as a group these countries have loitered in

---

[32] Schreiber, L., 2018. *Funding Development: Ethiopia Tries to Strengthen its Tax System, 2007–2018, Innovations for Successful Societies.* Princeton University.

the demographic sweet spot for economic growth with ratios of 1.7 working age persons to dependents for successive decades (see Chapter 4).

A number of highly developed countries that are very exposed to international competition have therefore managed to simultaneously invest in greater social inclusion and in building globally competitive economies. Admittedly, this social consensus is under considerable political pressure today, even in a country like Sweden, but that may be due to the successes achieved in the past and the political impact of migration, rather than to other factors.

The kind of welfare societies found in the Nordic countries with their low inequality and a degree of economic security provided by the state are good for growth. Since the 1930s, economic growth per capita in Sweden and Norway (even if one excludes oil income in Norway) has been higher than in the USA over the same time period.

In the long run, a more inclusive and less unequal society eventually also becomes a higher growth economy. Contrary to the history of the USA (a classic immigration country), these countries evidence strong labour unions and strong worker associations that have resulted in wage moderation and assisted in modernisation. The social contract is strong. And as a result, high-end wages in these countries are lower than they otherwise would have been. The wage differential between the least and most productive enterprises are also much lower than in more unequal countries such as the USA.

Social institutions have therefore been crucial in creating the high productivity economies of the Nordic countries. They serve as equalising institutions that constrain the growth of inequality by lifting low-end wages and pushing down on high-end wages.

There are, of course, also many variations on the welfare state and permutations that range from conservative to liberal. As people have become more wealthy, their desire for autonomy, to be free from the helping hand of the state, tends to increase. And then, with the ageing population structure in many Western and some Asian countries, caring for older people suffering from costly non-communicable diseases has become a big burden. The welfare state is therefore increasingly under pressure, even in the Nordic countries, but this is only after these countries had become extraordinarily productive and wealthy.

In some countries like South Africa, in Latin America and in some parts of Asia, the notion of a welfare state has followed a completely different pathway, largely moving towards the introduction of conditional and lately unconditional cash grants.

To reiterate—there are obviously huge differences between the classic welfare state tied benefits to economic activity evident in developed countries and the situation in much of Africa where formal sector jobs are scarce. The essential question is, however, if there is going to be sufficient jobs in the formal sector, and since improved average levels of education are going to take a very long time to achieve, what are the options for a continent facing such high levels of inequality and poverty?

In addition to the policies discussed and presented in other chapters, for instance around education, the structural transformation of economies and how to provide many more jobs, Africa will also have to accelerate efforts to roll out social grants to alleviate extreme poverty. In the next section, I model the potential impact of such efforts and present its impact on poverty and inequality.

Modelling the Impact of Using Tax Revenues for Social Grants: The Social Grants for Africa Scenario

To forecast the impact of social grants on poverty reduction in Africa, the first step is to raise additional funds through increased taxes on skilled households and firms, and then to transfer those funds as social grants to poor households. The exact interventions used for the scenario is at www.jakkieciliers.org.

By 2040 African governments would raise US$298 billion in additional taxes in this scenario. This is large, but the size of the African economy, in market exchange rates in 2040, is forecast to be US$7.2 trillion. On average, the government to household welfare and pension transfers in Africa increase by 3 percentage points of GDP as from 2030, equating to US$150 billion and US$245 billion above the Current Path forecast by 2030 and 2040.

In terms of progress towards the SDG headline goal of eliminating extreme poverty by 2030 using the US$1.90 income measure, the Social Grants for Africa scenario will reduce extreme poverty in Africa by 25 million people, or by about 1.2 percentage points by 2030. Using the total from the three extreme poverty measures at US$1.90, US$3.20 and US$5.50 for the respective country income groups the results are 25 million fewer persons in extreme poverty by 2030 and 34 million fewer by 2040.

The results are presented in Fig. 7.2 that shows the difference in millions of extremely poor people in the Social Grants for Africa scenario compared

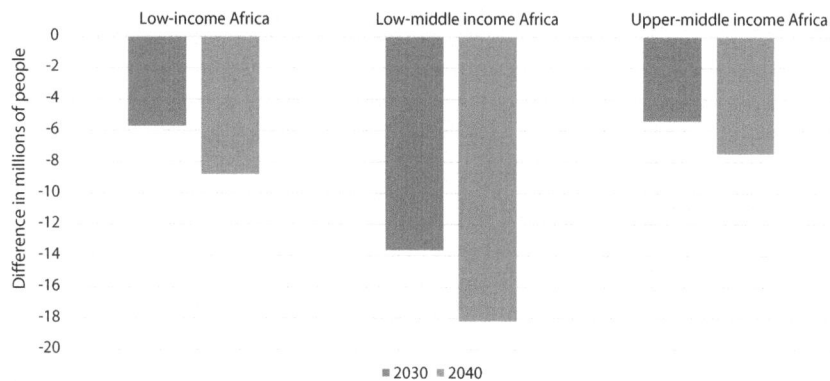

Fig. 7.2 Change in millions of extremely poor people in Africa: Social Grants for Africa scenario compared to Current Path in 2030 and 2040 (*Source* IFs 7.45 initializing from United Nations Population Division World Population Prospects medium variant life expectancy and World Development Indicators data)

to the Current Path forecast for low, lower-middle and upper-middle group of countries.

Inequality comes down in all three country income groups, although the impact is most significant in upper-middle-income countries coming off a higher base.

This represents solid but unspectacular improvements in the livelihoods of a large portion of the African population. Safety nets help to reduce chronic poverty and to limit the impact of shocks on poor and vulnerable households but clearly much more is needed.

It is evident that the Social Grants for Africa scenario does not change the rather dismal extreme poverty forecast that was explored in this chapter and that it should not be viewed in isolation from the other scenarios that are set out in this book such as on agriculture and manufacturing. Rather, it should be seen as a measure to reduce absolute deprivation for poor people who otherwise would continue to suffer since they have limited opportunities to improve their dire situation through better education or job opportunities. It is an important policy that can cushion the impact on the poor and vulnerable of other reforms such as the removal of fuel subsidies and tax reforms that generally benefit the middle and upper classes.

Conclusion: Reducing Poverty Through Rapid and Inclusive Economic Growth

Generally, poverty reduction requires rapid economic growth, redistributive policies such as progressive taxes, investments in health and basic infrastructure, improved levels of education, as well as investments in agriculture.

With a declining agriculture and manufacturing sector and an increase in the relative contribution of the services sector along the Current Path, Africa is likely to experience only slow reductions in poverty.

Agriculture is usually the sector with the biggest potential impact on poverty reduction. This applies particularly to low-income economies. And indeed, the scenario on Revolution in Agriculture in Chapter 5 achieves more than four times the reduction in the number of Africans living in extreme poverty in 2040 than the scenario on Social Grants for Africa.

The IFs Current Path forecast suggests that most African countries will make only slow progress to reduce extreme poverty, with the bulk of extremely poor people increasingly concentrated in countries like Nigeria, the Democratic Republic of Congo and Madagascar. However, with the right policies and a dedicated effort more rapid progress is possible.

African governments need to make a greater effort to introduce large-scale social assistance schemes, something along the lines of Universal Basic Share mentioned earlier. In other words, to reduce poverty, temper rising inequality, and to alleviate suffering, African governments should establish or expand cash grants, giving poor people small amounts of money that they can spend on their most important needs such as education for their children, transport, food, etc. Such measures are much better than fuel or other subsidies that tend to lock governments into expenditure that may fluctuate wildly and create an obligation that is difficult to scale down later or remove. In effect, social protection is an important tool that can be used to cushion the impact of policies that focus on economic growth. It is possible to be pro-growth and inclusive at the same time.

However, none of this is possible without a huge push to provide Africans with secure identity systems and the establishment of a national population register in each country. Even the SDGs recognise that some form of official proof of identity is a prerequisite to participate in a modern economy and to access basic rights and services. The advances in digital technology, with biometrics and its incorporation into ID systems, means this can be made available much more rapidly and cheaply than before—an issue I turn to in Chapter 10.

So if the time has come to give consideration to an African welfare state, the question is how can the inescapable need to reduce poverty and combat inequality be reconciled with the need for greater productivity in African economies? Efforts at a welfare society will offset the symptoms of underdevelopment but will not deal with the underlying causes.

To develop, Africa needs to transform its economies to become more productive and enable more rapid income growth. Traditionally that has been achieved through industrialisation, which is the topic of the next chapter.

Further Reading

United Nations Development Programme, Income Inequality Trends in Sub-Saharan Africa: Divergence Determinants and Consequences. www.africa.undp.org/.

World Bank, Poverty and Shared Prosperity 2018: Piecing Together the Poverty Puzzle. openknowledge.worldbank.org/.

World Poverty Clock by World Data Lab. https://worldpoverty.io/.

Open Access This chapter is licensed under the terms of the Creative Commons Attribution 4.0 International License (http://creativecommons.org/licenses/by/4.0/), which permits use, sharing, adaptation, distribution and reproduction in any medium or format, as long as you give appropriate credit to the original author(s) and the source, provide a link to the Creative Commons license and indicate if changes were made.

The images or other third party material in this chapter are included in the chapter's Creative Commons license, unless indicated otherwise in a credit line to the material. If material is not included in the chapter's Creative Commons license and your intended use is not permitted by statutory regulation or exceeds the permitted use, you will need to obtain permission directly from the copyright holder.

8

Changing Productive Structures

Abstract In this chapter, Cilliers offers various explanations for Africa's lack of sustained, structural economic transformation from low-value economic activities towards high-value services and manufacturing, and explores the challenges associated with the continent failing to industrialise. He offers historical context for how this situation emerged, drawing from global datasets such as trade data from the UN Conference on Trade and Development. The chapter then proceeds to look to the future of industrialisation in Africa in the context of technology-driven changes to the manufacturing sector globally via the fourth industrial revolution, which could offer the continent opportunities to gain a foothold in global value chains. The latter portion of the chapter models key interventions in a Made in Africa scenario, and examines its economic impact to 2040.

Keywords Industrialisation · Trade · Deindustrialisation · Economic sophistication · Fourth industrial revolution · Digitisation · Services · Research and development · Productivity · China in Africa

Learning Objectives

- Explain the main characteristics of Africa's current economic profile in terms of the agricultural, services, manufacturing and energy sectors
- Understand why the ongoing dominance of low-end services sector could be problematic for Africa's economic future

- Explain how global knowledge and technology diffusion is changing manufacturing
- Understand the role that China now plays in Africa's industrial development
- Recognise the main inputs, strategies and policy conditions needed to spur industrialisation in Africa.

With its fast-growing population, rapid economic growth is a prerequisite to reduce poverty and improve livelihoods in Africa. To rapidly grow, an economy needs to improve productivity in agriculture, industry and services. It also has to move labour and capital from a low-productivity sector like agriculture to a higher-productivity sector like manufacturing, as well as from the informal to the formal sector. Employment in the formal sector is particularly important for it improves stability, reduces inequality, and most importantly, contributes tax revenues that enable governments to invest in better health, more education and appropriate infrastructure.

The problem is that on current trends, much of sub-Saharan Africa's economic future is likely to consist of a large subsistence agricultural sector in rural areas and low-end, informal services in urban areas that generally consist of wholesale and retail trade.[1]

There is no silver bullet to improving productive structures (although digitisation can help). African countries are also very different from one another. But the common prerequisite is for an activist government that expands the country's human capital endowment, encourages labour-intensive (even gardening-style) small-scale agriculture; places an unrelenting focus on expanding its value-added exports (largely manufacturing) and orients economic policy, including the financial sector, towards improving productive capacity.

According to the World Bank,[2] the services sector constituted more than half of economic activity in sub-Saharan Africa by value in 2018, while industry (including manufacturing at 10%) constituted 25%. Agriculture constituted 16%.[3] The forecast within IFs is for a very steep increase in the

---

[1] Bhorat, H., Kanbur, R., Rooney, C., and Steenkamp, F., 2017. Sub-Saharan Africa's Manufacturing Sector: Building Complexity. *African Development Bank Group, Working Paper Series No. 256*, May. see also Newman, C., Page, J., Rand, J., Shimeles, A., Söderbom, M., Tarp, F., 2016. The Pursuit of Industry: Policies and Outcomes. In: *Manufacturing Transformation: Comparative Studies of Industrial Development in Africa and Emerging Asia.* Oxford University Press. See also Fox, L., Thomas, A. H., and Haines, C., 2017. *Structural Transformation in Employment and Productivity: What Can Africa Hope For?* Washington: International Monetary Fund.

[2] World Bank Open Data at https://data.worldbank.org/.

[3] Industry includes manufacturing, mining, electricity, water and gas. Agriculture includes livestock and crop production, forestry, hunting and fishing.

size of the services sector to 2040, with manufacturing as a portion of gross domestic product (GDP) remaining stagnant and agriculture declining. That forecast, if accurate, is for a slow-growth Africa where the increase in the size of the population inevitably translates into a larger economy, but only slow improvements in average incomes since the growth of low-end services evident in much of Africa, does not really improve productive structure.

Low-end services—which is particularly dominant in urban Africa—were by 2010 only twice as productive as agriculture.[4] Due to its marginally better levels of productivity, the growth in low-end services in Africa has done little to improve per capita incomes.[5]

Estimates as to the levels of productivity in different economic sectors in Africa differ. Carol Newman and colleagues find that the manufacturing sector in Africa is six times more productive than agriculture. In his best-selling book *Kicking away the ladder* the South Korean author and academic Ha-Joon Chang described the view that developing countries can largely skip industrialisation and enter the post-industrial phase where services increasingly drive employment and productivity growth as 'a fantasy'. This is because the manufacturing sector has 'an inherently faster productivity growth than the services sector',[6] he argues.

Beyond the various schools of economic theory, authors as diverse as Arthur Lewis, Erik Reinert, Calestous Juma and recently Dani Rodrik have written extensively on the importance of early industrialisation—and the significant role of governments/ruling elites in charting this course. A 2016 report prepared by the United Nations University World Institute for Development Economics Research (UNU-WIDER) explains the importance of industrialisation as follows:

> Between 1950 and 2006, about half of the catch-up by developing countries to advanced economy levels of output per worker was explained by rising productivity within industry combined with structural transformation out of agriculture. Industry is the pre-eminent destination sector at early stages of

---

[4] Newman, C., Page, J., Rand, J., Shimeles, A., Söderbom, M., Tarp, F. 2016. The Pursuit of Industry: Policies and Outcomes. In: *Manufacturing Transformation: Comparative Studies of Industrial Development in Africa and Emerging Asia*. Oxford University Press, p. 5.

[5] The challenge, notes Carol Newham and her co-authors, is that 'the marginal productivity of new services workers is low and possibly negative'. Ibid.; see also Bhorat, H., Kanbur, R., Rooney, C., and Steenkamp, F., 2017. Sub-Saharan Africa's Manufacturing Sector: Building Complexity. *African Development Bank Group, Working Paper Series No 256*, May, p. 5.

[6] Chang, H.-J., 2003. *Kicking Away the Ladder: Development Strategy in Historical Perspective*. London: Anthem Press, p. 43.

development because it is a high productivity sector capable of absorbing large numbers of moderately skilled workers.[7]

The problem is that, in much of Africa, manufacturing is declining while the contribution from services is growing. The IFs Current Path forecast expects the services sector to contribute around 60% of GDP for low, lower-middle and upper-middle-income African countries by 2040. That trend mimics trends globally with transport, financial, health and recreation growing more rapidly than any other in terms of their contribution to global GDP across all country income groups, but services are set to grow particularly rapidly in Africa.

I have explained, in Chapter 2, that with a few exceptions, Africa tends to export unprocessed commodities such as coffee, cocoa and suchlike, and to import processed products and finished goods from the European Union, China and elsewhere. This trend is likely to continue, reflecting the limited value addition that is characteristic of most African economies.

The law of diminishing returns is that countries that specialise in supplying raw materials, unprocessed agricultural products or low-end services yield a progressively smaller return for every unit of capital or labour compared to the provision of value-added goods. For example, a recent study by the UN Conference on Trade and Development (UNCTAD) entitled Identifying and Promoting Regional Value Chains in Leather and Leather Products in Africa laments the fact that Africa is the largest source of hides and skins in the world but that these exports come with very little value addition.[8] Like coffee (from Ethiopia of Kenya), 'Italian' handbags or shoes (often made from African leather) demand high prices but are not produced in Africa.

The growth that is based on increasing commodity exports, as opposed to exports of value-added products, cannot induce structural economic transformation. Instead it has led to high technology 'bubbles' or economic enclaves with very few linkages into the rest of the economy. Examples include the oil-producing parts of Angola off the coast of Cabinda, parts of oil-producing Nigeria (in the Niger delta), sections of Equatorial Guinea and soon areas in northern Mozambique with its rich natural gas endowment.

Compare this with the experience of rapidly developing Asian countries such as Japan, the Asian Tigers and Vietnam, where activist governments

---

[7]Newman, C., Page, J., Rand, J., Shimeles, A., Söderbom, M., Tarp, F., 2016. The Pursuit of Industry: Policies and Outcomes. In: *Manufacturing Transformation: Comparative Studies of Industrial Development in Africa and Emerging Asia.* Oxford University Press, p. 5.
[8]Banga,. R., Kumar, D., and Cobbina, P., 2018. *Identifying and Promoting Regional Value Chains in Leather and Leather Products in Africa.* Geneva: United Nations Conference on Trade and Development.

encouraged growth in the manufacturing sector and their entry into global value chains that served to steadily improve the quality and productivity of the associated goods. In this manner, these countries steadily upgraded their technical capabilities to meet global standards, often by inviting and partnering with multinational companies for the transfer of technology, skills and knowledge.[9]

Today global value chains are again evolving rapidly and offer opportunities for Africa, which is generally only peripherally part of these chains. First, modern technology offers significant opportunities for industrial latecomers to skip over the brick and mortar institutions of yesterday into a world where banking and sourcing of inputs are done remotely, while benefiting from a decline in the financial investment that is required to embark upon manufacturing. Second, there are signs of increased manufacturing nationalism (leading to the so-called reshoring of manufacturing back to the 'home' country) that has accompanied concerns in the USA and elsewhere that the rise of Asia has decimated their industrial power base. Finally, new technologies enable much greater flexibility and customerisation, with production shifting closer to the consumer. The result is that the complex global value chains that emerged prior to the 2007/2008 global financial crisis are now contracting and moving closer to end markets.

With its large and growing population, these developments are to Africa's potential advantage.

In Chapter 5, I recounted how the transformation of the agricultural sector assisted many countries in Asia in alleviating poverty and improving general well-being. Agriculture has served as a stepping stone for many poor countries. Once economies gained some momentum and basic education and literacy had shown sufficient progress, these countries pursued a manufacturing transition that was facilitated by favourable demographics and determined leadership. This eventually led to unprecedented rates of economic growth and improved incomes.

This is the history of the Japanese economic miracle that took place between 1950 and 1990, which was repeated in South Korea, Hong Kong, Macau, Singapore, Brunei, Taiwan and recently China. Countries such as Brazil, Indonesia, Malaysia, Mexico, Philippines, South Africa and Turkey

---

[9]Lund, S., Manyika, J., Woetzel, J., Bughin, J., Krishnan, M., Seong, J., and Muir, M. McKinsey&Company ed., 2019. Executive Summary. In: *Globalization in Transition: The Future of Trade and Value Chains*. New York: McKinsey Global Institute. And also Dollar, D., 2019. Executive Summary. In: *Technological Innovation, Supply Chain Trade, and Workers in a Globalized World*. Geneva: World Trade Organization.

also experienced substantive growth for several years as a result of industrialisation, but generally not at the rates and not for the extended period seen in Asia.

In Africa, Rwanda and Ethiopia have embarked upon a similar pathway and the results are visible for all to see—these countries have the most rapid improvements in indices of well-being on the continent.

The Contribution of Services to Growth

The focus that I place on an activist government, going up the agriculture value chain, export-oriented manufacturing and investments in human capital should not be misconstrued. The contribution from services is expanding at all levels of income, and most rapidly in low-income countries. This has become known as the servicification of the global economy, and reflects the extent to which services have become an integral requirement of agriculture, manufacturing and other sectors. And at high levels of development, financial services, computer and software services, as well as transport and distribution services have become a very dynamic requirement for continued growth. But high-value services constitute a very small segment of the large and growing services sector in Africa, much of which is in the informal retailing sector.[10]

At low levels of development, predominantly service-based economies have less ability to export or trade. Lower export earnings mean a weaker ability to buy advanced technology from abroad, which in turn leads to slower growth. According to Célestine Monga, writing for the African Development Bank in 2017, the problem is that at low levels of development, 'most services are low-productivity, subsistence, and even informal activities that may help households escape poverty, but are not sustainable sources of growth'.[11]

India is often considered an example of a country that, until recently, pursued a services-led growth strategy. The contribution of the services sector to GDP overtook that of agriculture in 1975 but the contribution of manufacturing to GDP only overtook agriculture three decades later. India's developmental model has been unique among major economies in the manner in which it has shifted from low-end agriculture to low-end

---

[10]Szirmai, A., 2009. *Is Manufacturing Still the Main Engine of Growth in Developing Countries?* [Online] Available at: https://www.wider.unu.edu/publication/manufacturing-still-main-engine-growth-developing-countries.

[11]Monga, C., 2017. Industrialization: A Primer. In: *Industrialized Africa—Strategies, Policies, Institutions, and Financing*. Abidjan: African Development Bank Group.

services without major industrial expansion. On its Current Path, Africa is following in India's low-growth footsteps. India's inward-looking economic model has relied on domestic markets more than exports, on consumption more than investment, on services more than industry and on high-tech more than low-skilled manufacturing.[12]

The early growth in services and the fact that India only recently entered a favourable demographic window—a period discussed in Chapter 4 in which there is a large working age population relative to the dependent population—are two important reasons for India's lower-than-expected growth over a number of decades (derogatorily referred to as its 'Hindu levels of growth'). Since 1991, economic liberalisation has partly unshackled an economy stifled by over-regulation, corruption and lack of competition. Furthermore, education levels are improving but India is still not living up to its potential although a convergence of factors, including improvement in the ratio of working age persons to dependents, prioritisation of investment in infrastructure and greater emphasis being placed on expanding the manufacturing sector offers prospects for improvement.

The Impact of the Diffusion of Knowledge

In a widely acclaimed book on the impact of information technology on globalisation, aptly titled *The Great Convergence*,[13] Richard Baldwin argues that knowledge flows that consist of data, information searches, communications, transactions and video, dominate new globalisation instead of physical goods and finance flows across borders.[14] For example, in 2016 cross-border flows in data were 45 times bigger than a decade before.[15]

Global flows of knowledge contribute to economic growth and present an opportunity for lagging countries to catch up through investment in information and communications technology (ICT). In theory, individuals can directly participate in globalisation by using digital platforms to study, find

---

[12]Freemantle, S., and Stevens, J., 2010. Lessons for Africa Inherent in India's Meteoric Economic Ascent, Economics: BRIC and Africa, Standard Bank, 9 June, p. 5.
[13]Baldwin, R., 2016. *The Great Convergence: Information Technology and the New Globalization*. Cambridge: Harvard University Press.
[14]McKinsey Global Institute, 2016. *Digital Globalization: The New Era of Global Flows*. New York: McKinsey&Company.
[15]McKinsey Global Institute, 2017. *What's Now and Next in Analytics, AI, and Automation*. [Online] Available at: https://www.mckinsey.com/featured-insights/digital-disruption/whats-now-and-next-in-analytics-ai-and-automation.

jobs, showcase their talent and build networks. In practice, this opportunity is limited to those who are connected to the internet and who have the inclination, knowledge and interest to pursue it.

This caveat aside, ICT-led globalisation and associated knowledge flows are undermining the previous competitive advantage that industrialised countries had, and is changing the outlook for global value chains. The reason for this is that an increased number of jobs in the developed world are now in direct competition with jobs in emerging economies. The cross-border flow of data and knowledge has broken the monopoly that workers in wealthy nations had on the use of advanced industrial-manufacturing intellectual property.

While globalisation has had a disruptive impact in much of North America and Europe, where it has fuelled populist politics, the phenomenon has had a cohesive impact on emerging Asia, where the middle class has flourished and millions of people have been lifted out of poverty.

In an interconnected and globalised world knowledge flows inevitably undermine the concept of country comparative advantage—even in those countries that are part of integrated trade blocs, such as the United States–Mexico–Canada Agreement (USMCA), the European Union (EU) and the numerous bi- and plurilateral trade agreements in East and Southeast Asia, where regional value chains have been well established.[16] Financial flows are already generally deregulated, knowledge is also now flowing more freely across boundaries—only labour mobility remains restricted.

In response to the impact of this 'new globalisation', industrialised countries have embraced policies to protect their knowledge—excessive use of patent protection being an important example—as well as requirements for minimum labour standards and the like. Conversely, emerging factory economies have embraced policies that foster knowledge sharing and creation. It is for this reason that China champions globalisation (despite having significant domestic barriers to foreign companies), while the previous advocate of free trade, the USA, now seeks to protect its domestic manufacturing sector from foreign competition. It does so by withdrawing or renegotiating trade agreements that now include a much higher domestic and labour content requirements, thereby raising the bar for less developed countries.

The problem for the US and other high-income economies is that digital communication, the internet and the ICT revolution has broken

---

[16] Stiglitz, J. E., 2017. Introductory Remarks: Promoting Sustainable Industrial Policies. In: *Industrialize Africa: Strategies, Policies, Institutions, and Financing*. Abidjan: African Development Bank Group. Ethiopia, Kenya, Morocco, the Seychelles, South Africa, and Tanzania have managed to make strides into GVCs. Manufacturing leads the integration into GVCs, ahead of agriculture and business services.

the monopoly industrialised nations had on knowledge and even on copyright. The result of these changes is that barriers faced by manufacturers and specific industries and services in emerging countries, including in Africa, are constantly being lowered, often quite dramatically.

Trends in robotics, automation, computerised manufacturing and artificial intelligence all appear to reduce the advantage of low labour cost locations, but not necessarily to the detriment of Africa. Originally corporations sought to locate manufacturers in those countries with the cheapest labour. Today rapid growth in multinationals and consumers occurs within emerging rather than developed economies, hence in Vietnam, Malaysia, India and eventually also in Africa. According to one estimate, by 2025 almost half of the world's largest companies will have headquarters in emerging markets and closer to consumer growth.[17] These trends will first benefit Asia but are also beginning to be felt in Africa.

A variety of digital technologies (particularly in the media), new materials (such as bio or nano-based materials) and new processes (such as 3D printing, not to mention artificial intelligence, and robotics) threaten to disrupt existing manufacturing patterns. Collectively these new trends have caused widespread concern about the nature and availability of jobs in the future (discussed in Chapter 9) and our understanding of economic growth theory. But at the moment it seems as if the future should see the evolution of a more distributed global economy where manufacturing and services are closely linked and value chains are shorter and closer to the future markets. All offer opportunities to Africa. Generally, new technology decreases the required input costs of manufacturing and it will become cheaper to manufacture, particularly for smaller production runs. Technologies such as 3D printing may in due course put an end to the smokestack factory model of production and perhaps the world could even see the evolution of something akin to a cottage industry model.[18]

Production is therefore experiencing a shift towards customisation for millions of niche markets by consisting of smaller production runs closer to the end markets and greater flexibility.[19] The local manufacturer of says a spare part for a car or a replacement gear in a machine will be able to purchase the plan from the cloud and print locally. That means no more

---

[17] Ibid., pp. 16 and 20.
[18] African Center for Economic Transformation, The Future of Work in Africa—the impact of the fourth industrial revolution on job creation and skill development in Africa, 2018.
[19] De Backer, K., and Flaig, D., 2017. *The Future of Global Value Chains: Business as Usual or "a New Normal"?* Paris: OECD Publishing, p. 21.

international shipping, tracking or customs is required. Instant gratification, at a lower environmental cost.

Ghanaian entrepreneur and president of mPedigree, Bright Simons[20] refers to this as the rise of 'Alibaba industrialisation'. He writes eloquently about the 'unsung industrial revolution underway in places like Ghana, Uganda, Senegal and Côte d'Ivoire' that is powered by 'a worldwide revolution in modular design, multi-purpose machinery, efficient small-batch production, global SME-SME [small and medium enterprises] engagement, new forex transfer practices, and the growing strategic transformation of China's late-phase industrial players'. This is a world where small- and medium-sized Chinese suppliers provide large chunks of the industrial jigsaw and 'African hustlers and unconventional industrialists act as shuttle-brokers of the various factors of production between China and Africa'. The fourth industrial revolution and digitisation therefore make it easier for African states to become part of value chains from which they were previously excluded.

One of the unforeseen results of lower barriers to entry is that it allows companies to venture into new areas outside their traditional area of specialisation. Startups can quickly go up the productivity curve to threaten established businesses. It is even evident in something as established as the manufacturing of cars where companies such as BYD in China threaten to outflank traditional car manufacturers in Germany, the USA, Japan and South Korea by investing heavily in future electric vehicle technologies.

Instead of an ownership economy, digital platforms also allow and facilitate the development of a sharing economy—this is where individuals rent or borrow goods and services for a specific time or task rather than to buy and own them.

Manufacturing in Africa

In their 2016 multi-year study of industrial development, Carol Newman and her co-authors[21] compared eight African countries with Cambodia and Vietnam and offer a number of reasons that, taken collectively, explain Africa's lack of industry.

---

[20]Simons, B., 2019. *Africa's Unsung "Industrial Revolution"*. [Online] Available at: https://www.cgdev.org/blog/africas-unsung-industrial-revolution?utm_source=190326&utm_medium=cgd_email&utm_campaign=cgd_weekly.

[21]Newman, C., Page, J., Rand, J., Shimeles, A., Söderbom, M., Tarp, F., 2016. The Pursuit of Industry: Policies and Outcomes. In: *Manufacturing Transformation: Comparative Studies of Industrial Development in Africa and Emerging Asia*. Oxford University Press.

Firstly, is the widely held belief that the initial conditions for industrial development did not exist in Africa, including core infrastructure such as roads and rail, and human capital—basically an educated, healthy workforce. Furthermore, there were barriers to entry and the financial sector is not large or sophisticated enough, with small banks and underdeveloped financial markets being the norm. Without greater financial depth, many African countries have long struggled to attract larger investments.

However, at the time of their industrialisation, these conditions also did not exist in Japan, the so-called Asian Tigers (Hong Kong, Singapore, South Korea and Taiwan) or China. Greater financial depth, core infrastructure and a better-educated workforce developed in response to incentives, policies and effort. Governments are responsible for creating the right incentives to allow physical, human, social and knowledge capital to develop. That, in turn, requires a governing elite committed to economic growth and sufficient government capacity to formulate and implement policy.

Secondly, few African countries (Mauritius is a rare exception), set out and implemented a concerted package of public investments, appropriate policy and institutional reforms to increase the share of industrial exports in GDP. In the majority of African countries, little or no consistent effort was made to boost non-traditional exports, which still mostly consist of commodities.

Thirdly, contrary to successes achieved elsewhere, most African governments have paid little or no attention to making special economic zones (SEZs) work. SEZs have played a large part in the successful industrialisation in Asia. It allowed export-oriented industrial agglomerations to benefit from the advantages of being in close proximity to knowledge-intensive institutions including foreign and domestic companies that are more productive, research institutes and universities, which in turn led to information and knowledge spillovers.

The provision of improved social services and infrastructure in a limited physical area attracts foreign companies and high-quality staff.[22] In low-income countries, the domestic industry generally benefits from positive knowledge spillovers from foreign-owned firms, especially if it's part of the same value chain. Since African governments did not pursue the establishment of local value chains, African firms did not benefit.[23] Instead, manufacturing firms have been dispersed across urban areas (instead of located in close proximity to one another) with limited requirements or incentives to source locally, train locals and establish local value chains.[24]

---

[22] Ibid., p. 18.
[23] Ibid., p. 19.
[24] Ibid.

African governments also did not invest in high-quality infrastructure in SEZs, did not promote these zones or bring in professional management. African SEZs are generally not connected to domestic value chains, since the practice (if not policy) of governments was to treat them as stand-alone enclaves.[25]

Fourthly, even though African governments created agencies and boards that advocated for foreign direct investment, this was done without real commitment and implementation support, which explains why these efforts achieved very little.[26] For this reason most African countries linger at the bottom of various indices concerning the ease of doing business and attraction to foreign investment.

Finally, a large number of African countries such as Ghana, Kenya, Mozambique, Nigeria, Senegal and Tanzania have embarked on investment reforms in an effort to improve the physical, institutional and regulatory environments in which firms operate. However, active efforts to improve the competitiveness of domestic industries or practical measures to reduce trade friction costs resulting from poor trade logistics have not accompanied these reforms.[27]

Bad luck has also played a role in Africa's inability to industrialise. When African economies again spluttered into life at the end of the twentieth century, they not only had to compete with the industrial North but now also with a number of countries in East Asia, including China.

Composition of African Economies

Current levels and potential for expansion of manufacturing differ greatly between countries and regions. At roughly 20% of manufacturing value added to GDP, North Africa is the most industrialised region on the continent and West and East Africa the least industrialised (both at below 12%).

On average, the contribution of manufacturing to African economies has steadily declined since independence, and never reached the manufacturing peak share of 20–35% of GDP that was achieved in Europe and North America. After that peak in manufacturing employment and output in the

---

[25] Newman, C., Rand, J., Page, J., Shimeles, A., Söderbom, M., Tarp, F., 2016. Can Africa Industrialize? In: *Manufacturing Transformation: Comparative Studies of Industrial Development in Africa and Emerging Asia*. Oxford University Press. Also see Mills, G., 2019. A Tale of Two Free Zones: Learning from Africa's Success. *The Brenthurst Foundation Discussion Paper 01/2019*, February.
[26] Ibid., pp. 17–20.
[27] Ibid., p. 12.

West, wages increased and employment and output in the manufacturing sector declined and, with some exceptions, services became an even more important source of growth at high levels of income. Consumers had more money to spend on services while the requirement for services in all sectors grew, and growth in this sector therefore accelerated.[28]

Figure 8.1 presents the sectoral composition of larger African economies as reflected in the World Bank open data portal, with countries ranked according to the contribution of manufacturing to GDP. According to the Bank data there is no statistically significant manufacturing in Mali, Sudan and Chad.

With a few exceptions, Africa's economies are dominated by large, low-productivity services sectors. Generally the contribution from agriculture is lowest among upper-middle-income countries and highest among low-income countries. The contribution from energy (not shown separately) and manufacturing is the opposite from agriculture, with low-income countries having the smallest energy and manufacturing sectors.

Sierra Leone has the largest contribution from agriculture to GDP at 60% and South Africa is among the smallest at slightly more than 2%. Yet, South Africa, which has an efficient commercial farming sector, is one of the few African countries that is largely self-sufficient in terms of foodstuffs. Countries like Liberia, Mali, Niger, Chad and Guinea-Bissau all have very large agricultural sectors as a portion of their economy but are all net food importers—and import dependency is set to expand significantly.

The energy sector (not shown separately) makes the smallest contribution to GDP in Togo, whereas in South Sudan and Equatorial Guinea it constitutes almost one-third of the economy. Other countries where energy this sector makes up a large portion of the national economy are the Republic of Congo, Angola, Libya and Algeria.

Lesotho, Djibouti and the Seychelles, have the smallest economic contribution from the raw materials sector. The two countries with the largest contribution from raw materials are Guinea (gold and aluminium ore), Zambia (copper) and Mauritania (mostly iron ore and phosphate).

The countries with the smallest services sector are Togo, Sierra Leone, Guinea-Bissau, Chad and the Democratic Republic of Congo at 38–34%. The services sector constitutes more than 60% of GDP in South Africa, Cape Verde, Mauritius, Seychelles, São Tomé and Príncipe and Djibouti.

Over the last two decades, the information and communication sector (ICT) has overtaken agriculture as the third largest contributor to GDP by

---

[28] Mckinsey & Company, 2012. *Manufacturing the Future: The Next Era of Global Growth and Innovation.* New York: Mckinsey Global Institute.

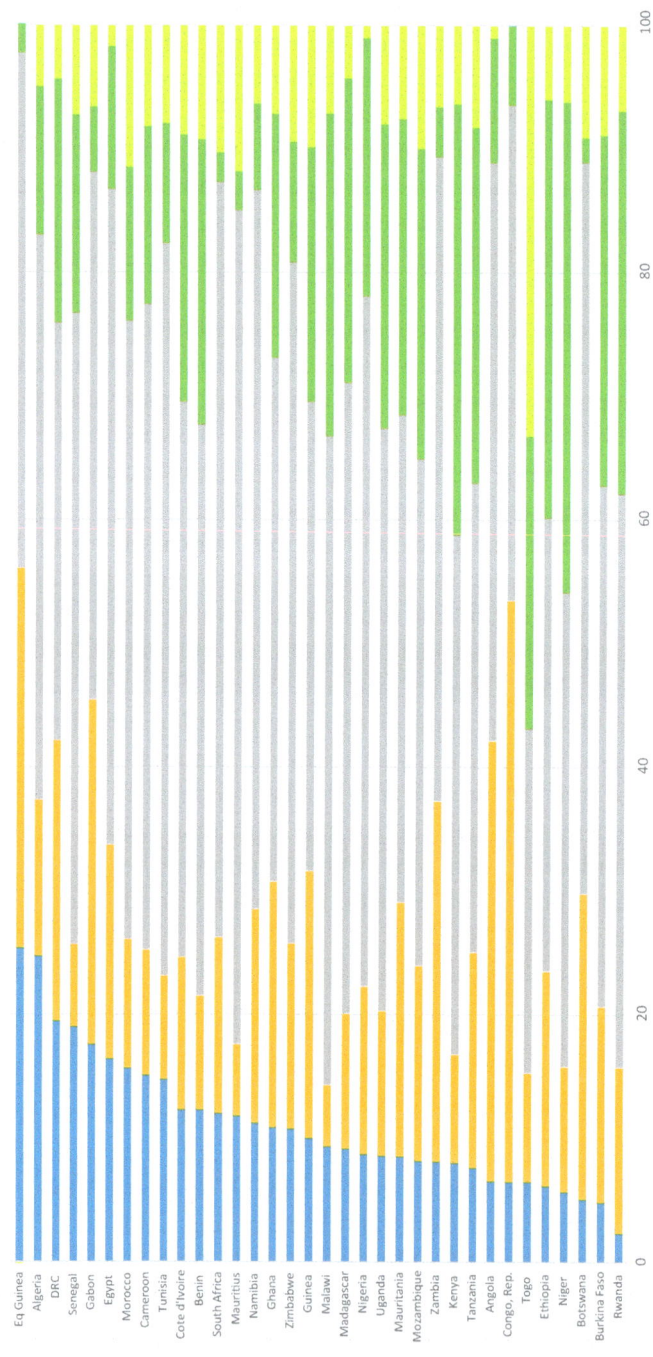

Fig. 8.1 Sectoral composition of larger African economies by value added to GDP, ranked by relative size of industry (2017) (*Source* World Bank Open Data)

value globally (at around six percent of GDP), and it has become particularly important in high-income economies. Whereas the ICT sector is responsible for only one percent of the value-add to GDP in low-income countries, it contributes almost eight percent to GDP in high-income countries. Despite its relatively small contribution to added value, in many instances ICT is a growth multiplier as countries go up the GDP per capita ladder because it facilitates knowledge exchanges, including the effective functioning of regional and multinational value chains that include goods and services.

However, Africa's upper-middle-income economies trail behind those in the rest of the world in terms of the contribution made by ICT to the economy by an average of two percentage points. Only in Mauritius does ICT contribute more than five percent of GDP. In addition to the focus on manufacturing, a focus on ICT can also increase growth in Africa particularly as a means to deliver more effective education and improve service delivery such as the roll-out of identification systems and grants discussed in the previous chapter. The contribution of ICT to GDP for upper-middle-income countries in Africa is only half the global average for that group.

Industrialisation and Growth in Africa

From the preceding analysis, two points become apparent. The first is simply the low levels of manufacturing and ICT in Africa relative to comparable regions such as South America and South Asia. From 1999 to 2018, the manufacturing value added to GDP in lower-middle and upper-middle-income Africa is, respectively, around 9 and 11 percentage points below the global average for these two country groupings. Thus, on a comparative basis, Africa is significantly under-industrialised.

In a 2017 working paper for the African Development Bank, Bhorat et al., describe a sub-Saharan African productive structure that is 'inherently characterised by lower levels of economic complexity, which informed the notion of limited productive capabilities … the African manufacturing sector is marginal in nature and points to limited employment opportunities'.[29]

The second is the trend towards deindustrialisation in key upper-middle-income economies, particularly in South Africa and Mauritius, and until recently also in Algeria. Among others, this decline reflects the extent to

---

[29] Bhorat, H., Kanbur, R., Rooney, C., & Steenkamp, F., 2017. Sub-Saharan Africa's Manufacturing Sector: Building Complexity. *African Development Bank Group, Working Paper Series No. 256*, May. In this, understanding consists of the diversity of firms and productive capabilities described as non-tradable networks of collective know-how, such as logistics, finance, supply and knowledge networks.

which Asian and other exporters have successfully penetrated markets in the region.[30]

The percentage of GDP consisting of services has steadily increased since the 1980s to an estimated 57, 52 and 47% average for Africa's upper-middle, lower-middle and low-income country groupings, respectively. By 2040 these numbers would all be close to 60%. Whereas manufacturing and high-end services have grown in other regions such as in East, Southeast and South Asia, this has not occurred in Africa.

Africa produces about US$500 billion of manufactured goods per annum. In a recent book, Acha Leke, Mutsa Chironga and Georges Desvaux argue that this could be doubled if two-thirds were designated for local consumption.[31]

In this context, China's increased role in manufacturing in Africa in recent years (as opposed to exporting to Africa) presents an interesting paradox.[32] For example, the largest ceramic tile factory in Africa was recently built by China in Ethiopia. Nearly a third of the more than 10 000 Chinese companies that McKinsey[33] estimates are active in Africa and are involved in manufacturing. Together they are responsible for more than 12% of Africa's industrial production. Most of them are small and privately owned companies, not state-owned behemoths and their focus is on serving the needs of Africa's fast-growing domestic and regional market rather than on exports, with some exceptions such as Ethiopia.

The dominance of Chinese firms is even more pronounced in infrastructure where they claim nearly 50% of Africa's internationally contracted construction market. That observation raises the obvious question why, when the Chinese are constrained by the same lack of infrastructure, a poorly educated workforce and other conditions as locals, have such a large number of privately owned small Chinese companies been able to penetrate the African manufacturing market in a way that local and Western companies have not?

In fact, they appear to 'represent a long-term commitment to Africa rather than trading or contracting activities'.[34] The McKinsey report goes on to argue that

---

[30] Bhorat, H., Kanbur, R., Rooney, C., and Steenkamp, F., 2017. Sub-Saharan Africa's Manufacturing Sector: Building Complexity. *African Development Bank Group, Working Paper Series No 256*, May, pp. 9–10.
[31] Ibid.
[32] Jayaram, K., Kassiri, O., and Sun, I. Y., 2017. *The Closest Look Yet at Chinese Economic Engagement in Africa*. New York: McKinsey&Company.
[33] Ibid.
[34] Ibid.

... 89 percent of employees were African... this suggests that Chinese-owned business employ several million Africans. Moreover, nearly two-thirds of Chinese employers provided some kind of skills training ... Half of Chinese firms had introduced a new product or service to the local market, and one-third had introduced a new technology. In some cases, Chinese firms had lowered prices for existing products and services by as much as 40 percent through improved technology and efficiencies of scale. African government officials overseeing infrastructure development for their countries cited Chinese firms' efficient cost structures and speedy delivery as major value adds.

In short, if Chinese entrepreneurs and companies can enter and grow the manufacturing sector in Africa, why can't Africans?

Some self-defeating policies are self-evident. South Africa, for example, which has a large domestic vehicle manufacturing industry, could stipulate that the government will only procure locally produced vehicles for official use and in that manner support local industry, but it does not. An excessive regulatory burden including requirements for black economic empowerment ensure that South Africa's ability to compete against Chinese imports is steadily eroding.

On the other hand, there have been successful state efforts to support localised manufacturing development. Several years ago, Nigeria established a domestic cement industry by offering a four-year licence to import cement on the condition that the licence holder would invest in a domestic cement production plant. Today Nigeria is a net exporter of cement and the deal has created the richest African (Aliko Dangote).[35]

But the biggest opportunity to grow domestic manufacturing is with intra-African trade (see Chapter 11).

Close to 60% of African imports consist of manufactured goods by value, while the dominant export segment is in energy exports such as oil, coal and gas. Many of the imported goods can be manufactured locally and boost the value of intra-African trade. There is great potential to increase intra-African trade in a host of foodstuffs, beverages and cigarettes, rubber and plastics, electronics and non-metallic mineral products.[36]

Replacing imported manufactured goods with goods made in Africa will not be easy since global value chains have improved efficiencies and reduced prices, making it difficult for new entrants to compete. Still, it remains

---

[35] Dangote Cement has three plants in Nigeria with operations in ten African countries. It produces around 44 million metric tons of cement every year and plans to increase output by a third in the next two years. See Dangote Cement at www.dangotecement.com.
[36] Oosthuizen, M., Linde, E., Durrant, K.-L., and Gopaldas, R., 2018. *The Future of Energy and Power Utilities in Africa*. Johannesburg: Gordon Institute of Business Science, p. 65.

a crucial step in the transformation of African economies and previous sections have indicated that global value chains are evolving with potential opportunities for Africa.[37]

Growth in Africa's manufacturing sector requires a stable and facilitating policy framework, government support and incentives.

The entry point for manufacturing traditionally involved labour-intensive segments of regional manufacturing value chains, meaning that labour costs needed to be competitive. Given that Africa suffers from various disadvantages, such as poor physical infrastructure,[38] a high disease burden and poor rule of law, low regulatory and policy quality and a lack of policy certainty among others, the general view is that African labour costs need to be cheap enough to compensate for these deficits.[39]

However, a 2017 study on Africa's manufacturing labour costs by Alan Gelb and others[40] concluded that poor African countries have higher labour costs than their average income levels would suggest. The study compared 12 African countries to 17 non-African countries. Only Ethiopia compared favourably. In all other African countries included in the study, labour costs were higher than those of their non-African peers. In this regard South Africa stands out as a middle-income country with particularly high labour costs and a very capital-intensive industrial sector—partly explaining its extraordinarily large burden of unemployed.

Manufacturing labour costs in low- and lower-middle-income countries Kenya, Tanzania and Senegal—three relatively stable coastal countries with strong business sectors—are higher than in Bangladesh, a country with a comparable World Economic Forum (WEF) competitiveness rating and income levels.

However, one of the effects of the fourth industrial revolution is the declining importance of labour costs in the location of industry while the trend to locate manufacturing closer to end markets has also been discussed.

For these and other reasons, Carol Newham and her co-authors believe that industrialisation in Africa remains possible, although its shape and form

---

[37] Bhorat, H., Kanbur, R., Rooney, C., and Steenkamp, F., 2017. Sub-Saharan Africa's Manufacturing Sector: Building Complexity. *African Development Bank Group, Working Paper Series No 256*, May, p. 92.

[38] Page, J. 2017. Industrial Policy in Africa: From State Leadership to the Investment Climate. In: *Industrialize Africa: Strategies, Policies, Institutions, and Financing*. Abidjan: African Development Bank Group, p. 81.

[39] Newman, C., Page, J., Rand, J., Shimeles, A., Söderbom, M., Tarp, F., 2016. The Pursuit of Industry: Policies and Outcomes. In: *Manufacturing Transformation: Comparative Studies of Industrial Development in Africa and Emerging Asia*. Oxford University Press, p. 5.

[40] African Development Bank. 2017. Industrialize Africa—Strategies, Policies, Institutions, and Financing. African Development Bank Group, p. 46.

will differ from that previously experienced elsewhere. Writing in 2016 they offer three considerations:

> First, economic changes are taking place in Asia that create a window of opportunity for late industrializers elsewhere to gain a toehold in global markets. Second, the nature of manufactured exports themselves is changing. A growing share of global trade in industry is made up of stages of vertical value chains – or tasks – rather than finished products. Trade in tasks offers late industrializers an opportunity to enter global markets in areas suited to their factor costs and endowments of skills and capabilities. Third, trade in services and agro-industry is growing faster than trade in manufacturers. These 'industries without smokestacks' broaden the range of products in which Africa can compete, and a number of them are intensive in locations specific factors abundant in Africa.[41]

And eventually, because Africa is growing so much slower than other regions, wages in Africa will become competitive and offset the productivity advantage of incumbent industrial producers, including those in East Asia.

Even so, according to a 2017 analysis by Alan Gelb and others at the Center for Global Development,[42] most African countries (with the exception of Ethiopia) are still some way from this point. China and other countries in East Asia are, however, restructuring their economies to meet growing domestic demand, which will create space for Africa to compete with countries such as Bangladesh as the low-end manufacturing location of choice for the future.[43]

---

[41] Newman, C., Rand, J., Page, J., Shimeles, A., Söderbom, M., Tarp, F., 2016. Can Africa Industrialize? In: *Manufacturing Transformation: Comparative Studies of Industrial Development in Africa and Emerging Asia*. Oxford University Press, p. 258.

[42] Gelb, A., Meyer, C., Ramachandran, V., and Wadhwa, D., 2017. Can Africa Be a Manufacturing Destination? Labor Costs in Comparative Perspective. *Center for Global Development Working Paper 466*, 15 October, p. 8.

[43] Newman, C., Rand, J., Page, J., Shimeles, A., Söderbom, M., and Tarp, F., 2016. Can Africa Industrialize? In: *Manufacturing Transformation: Comparative Studies of Industrial Development in Africa and Emerging Asia*. Oxford University Press, p. 259. Gelb question some of these conclusions: 'for any given level of GDP, labor is more costly for firms that are located in Sub-Saharan Africa. However, we also find that there are a few countries in Africa that, on a labor cost basis, may be potential candidates for manufacturing – Ethiopia in particular stands out'. Gelb, A., Meyer, C., Ramachandran, V., and Wadhwa, D., 2017. Can Africa Be a Manufacturing Destination? Labor Costs in Comparative Perspective. *Center for Global Development Working Paper 466*, 15 October.

Modelling the Impact of Industrialisation: The Made in Africa Scenario

This section briefly presents a set of intervention clusters modelled within IFs to emulate industrialisation in Africa with a time horizon to 2040, and compares its impact to the Current Path.

Clear industrial policy and determined government leadership and action are critical if African economies are to grow more rapidly. For this reason, a first cluster of interventions increases investment in the economy. It reflects the determined efforts by forward-looking African governments to industrialize.

A second cluster of interventions aggressively increases government expenditure in research and development to twice the expected level in 2040 on the Current Path (from the current African average of 0.12% of GDP to 0.23% by 2030 and 0.26% by 2040), provides export support to the manufacturing and ICT sectors, and modestly raises prices on manufacturing and ICT imports. An increase in expenditure on research and development is a particularly powerful driver of improvements in multifactor productivity.

A final intervention is to improve economic freedom as a proxy for lowering the barriers to entry for foreign companies and ease of doing business for small businesses.[44]

At this point I need to remind the reader that the exploratory interventions modelled for this chapter (and the book as a whole) were all done at a continental or country-income level and were neither tailored to improve the use of labour, capital or multifactor productivity at the national level nor to primarily focus on industrialisation in middle as opposed to low-income economies. At best, the efforts presented here emulate a continent that commits to actively pursue greater industrialisation and serves to illustrate potential, rather than map out the specific associated benefits.

With that caveat in mind, Fig. 8.2 presents the shift in the sectoral composition that would occur at the continental level as a result of the Made in Africa scenario. The manufacturing sector is, by 2040, 2.1 percentage points larger than it otherwise would have been (a difference of roughly US$355 billion) and the ICT sector about 0.2 percentage points larger (US$45 billion difference). Agriculture declines more rapidly than in the Current Path and the services sector is almost one percentage point (or US$425 billion) smaller. But because the African economy grows more rapidly, all sectors are actually

---

[44] IFs used the economic freedom index from the Fraser Institute as a proxy for the level of economic freedom and the intervention means that Africa converges to the level of economic freedom of South Asia by 2030.

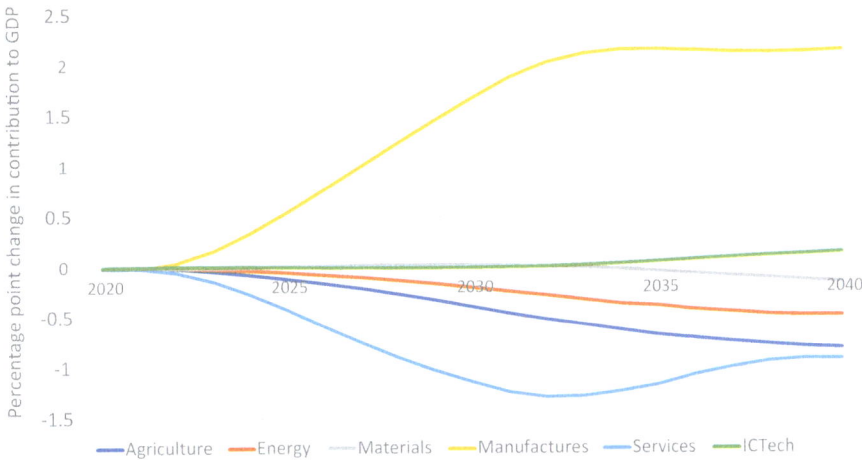

Fig. 8.2 Percentage point shift in sectoral contribution to African economy 2020 to 2040: Made in Africa compared to Current Path (*Source* IFs v7.45 initializing from IMF World Economic Outlook 2017)

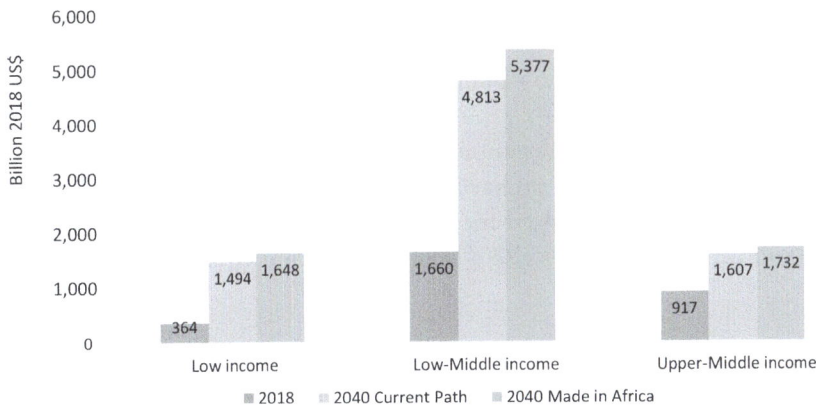

Fig. 8.3 Comparing GDP: Current Path vs Made in Africa (2018 to 2040) (*Source* IFs v. 7.45 initializing from International Monetary Fund World Economic Outlook 2017)

larger by 2040 than in the Current Path forecast. Services grow rapidly under all scenarios, constituting almost 60% of the total African economy by 2040.

Figure 8.3 presents the size of the African economy in 2018 and 2040 under the Current Path and Made in Africa scenario. Whereas, in 2018, the GDP of Africa is estimated at US$2.9 trillion, it should, under the Current Path forecast, increase to US$7.9 trillion at an average growth rate of 4.7% per annum to 2040. In the Made in Africa scenario, the 2040 African economy is substantially larger, at US$8.8 trillion. Instead of the

4.7% average growth rate, in the Made in Africa scenario, Africa is now forecast to experience an average growth rate of 5.2%.

The initial impact is limited but compound growth is incredibly powerful. Although the average difference between the Current Path and Made in Africa rate of growth is only 0.5 percentage points from 2020 to 2040, the result is, by 2040, and African economy that is a full ten percent (or almost US$850 billion) larger in the Made in Africa scenario than in the Current Path forecast. The rates of growth also accelerate over the forecast horizon and since it alters the composition of Africa's economy, it sets the continent on a more positive growth trajectory.

The Made in Africa scenario is significantly more modest than the wildly optimistic forecast published by McKinsey in their 2017 report *Lions on the move II: Realizing the potential of Africa's economies*. According to this report, Africa could double its manufacturing output by 2025 'provided countries take decisive action to create an improved environment for manufacturers'.[45]

In the Made in Africa scenario, low-income African economies are forecast to be roughly 10% larger in 2040 than it would be in the Current Path forecast (equivalent to US$154 billion) and increases rapidly thereafter. The economies of low-middle-income and upper-middle-income countries would be, respectively, 12% (US$565 billion) and seven percent (US$125 billion) bigger.

Income levels increase substantially in the Made in Africa scenario. By 2040 the average African would have an income that is US$514 more than in the Current Path with the largest increases in upper-middle-income countries at US$890 (in PPP). There is also a small decline in inequality using the gini index.

Costs and Benefits of a Manufacturing Pathway

A manufacturing pathway comes with short to medium-term costs relating to poverty and employment since it diverts expenditure towards higher-value activities against the promise of more rapid and sustainable growth. In addition, there are political constraints in Africa that are quite different to those of South East Asia. Countries like Bangladesh, Vietnam and others built their manufacturing success on the back of extreme labour exploitation in the thousands of factories and sweatshops that eventually made this region

---

[45] Bughin, J., Chironga, M., Desvaux, G., Ermias, T., Jacobson, P., Kassiri, O., Leke, A., Lund, S., van Wamelen, A., and Zouaoui, Y., 2016. *Lions on the Move II: Realizing the Potential of Africa's Economies*. New York: Mckinsey & Company.

the global manufacturing hub. It is debatable if this pathway is open in the twenty-first century on a continent where democracy is at significantly higher levels and where the voice of the people readily translates into street protests and even violence.

That constraint aside, the analysis on poverty in Chapter 7 showed that extreme poverty was at 50% of the total African population in 2018 and that it would decline to 35% by 2040, using the three income levels of extreme poverty now used by the World Bank.

In the Made in Africa scenario poverty levels marginally *increase* for a decade above the Current Path before the more rapid economic growth makes up for this initial increase. For example, at its peak in 2030, 25 million *more* Africans will be living in extreme poverty in low-income Africa than would be the case in the Current Path, But by 2040, 8 million *less* Africans will be living in extreme poverty. Thereafter the positive impact accelerates dramatically.

It is unclear if a manufacturing pathway will create more jobs in the short term, but it is certain to increase employment in the medium and long term as rates of economic growth accelerate. Quite likely the Made in Africa scenario will initially *increase* unemployment slightly before the economy starts growing more rapidly. In contrast, the blue-skies forecast by the McKinsey group is that an expanded and more productive manufacturing sector could already create six to 14 million stable jobs by 2025.[46]

These results point to two important conclusions. The first is the importance of additional measures to reduce extreme poverty, including efforts to directly support extremely poor families through social programmes like cash grants. The second is that the largest increase in poverty during the initial period of industrialisation will take place in low-income countries, which is why industrialisation should probably be pursued after countries have graduated to low-middle-income status.

None of these costs should, however, detract from the fact that eventually a growing manufacturing sector has important spillover effects on other sectors beyond more rapid growth. It generally leads to improved productivity in the agricultural sector and incentivises the development of higher-value services.

---

[46]Ibid., p. 14.

Conclusion: Promoting and Intensifying Local Production and Trade

Since the 1970s, African economies have experienced a limited—as well as limiting—form of structural transformation from low-productivity agriculture to low-end services. Manufacturing and industrial development have never taken off in Africa. In fact, the continent appears to be deindustrialising from already low levels.

By comparison, countries in East Asia grew rapidly and over sustained periods of time after they had achieved food security because of the rapid productivity gains that followed determined efforts by an activist government to move labour from low to higher-productivity sectors of the economy and to invest in the same. Labour typically moved from subsistence agriculture to low-end manufacturing and then to increasingly complex manufacturing products.

Starting from a low base, where the majority of workers engage either in subsistence farming or informal services, Africa has more to gain from structural transformation than other developing regions, but to date it has not managed to achieve this. The primary reason why it is so crucial to grow Africa's manufacturing and high-end services sector is not only because of the potential that manufacturing has to create more formal sector jobs, but because it would change the productive structures of African economies and unlock more rapid growth. In fact, James Manyika and colleagues remind us that the contribution of manufacturing to an economy shifts as a nation matures and that in advanced economies, 'manufacturing promotes innovation, productivity, and trade more than growth and employment'.[47] Eventually more rapid growth also translates into more employment.

Digital production—particularly through the impact of artificial intelligence, automation and robotics—will also play a role. Meanwhile, the continent needs to invest in lowering transport and infrastructure costs, ensure policy certainty and a low regulatory burden to compensate for Africa's relatively high labour costs. It also must ensure the success of trade integration to provide larger markets and rapid digitisation. Collectively this will attract and grow manufacturing.

In a future where more goods will be produced and consumed in regional rather than global markets and possibly in a much more distributed manner, Africa has considerable opportunities for industrialisation as well as regional trade (see Chapter 11). However, this will only happen if leaders in key

---

[47] Mckinsey & Company, 2012. *Manufacturing the Future: The Next Era of Global Growth and Innovation*. New York: Mckinsey Global Institute.

growth-locomotive countries embark on a deliberate effort to go up the manufacturing curve and establish and support SEZs, set clear industrial policies, provide relevant education and invest in the necessary digital backbone.

On this journey, ICT could play an important role in improving productivity in various sectors.

Without much greater emphasis on actively pursuing structural transformation of the economy towards more highly productive sectors, Africa will not be able to add value to its agricultural sector or develop higher-end services. African economies must be infused with technology, otherwise Africa will remain poor.

The transition from low to higher productivity requires active governments that set up, nurture and support dynamic local industries and services, changing the dominant mode of production—in effect, changing society as a whole. These measures will need very careful, if not surgical, engagement by a competent and modern bureaucracy.

Taking a ten year or longer forecast horizon the Made in Africa scenario will create many more jobs than the Current Path forecast as economic growth accelerates, but in the shorter term too sharp a focus on manufacturing would limit job growth pointing to the need to complement the Made in Africa efforts with others. And generally the employment intensity of the manufacturing sector is declining globally when compared to the period when Asia experienced its most rapid manufacturing growth.[48]

It is against this backdrop that the next chapter looks at jobs and the changing nature of work in Africa.

Further Reading

Dani Rodrik. 2016. Premature Deindustrialization. *Journal of Economic Growth*, 21(1), pp. 1–33. https://www.nber.org/papers/w20935.

Farole, Thomas, and Deborah Winkler, eds. 2014. *Making Foreign Direct Investment Work for Sub-Saharan Africa: Local Spillovers and Competitiveness in Global Value Chains.* Directions in Development. Washington, DC: World Bank. https://doi.org/10.1596/978-1-4648-0126-6. ISBN: 978-1-4648-0126-6. License: Creative Commons Attribution CC BY 3.0.

---

[48] Levels of peak manufacturing employment have declined with each wave of industrialisation from around 30% of employment with the first wave of smokestack industries in Europe two centuries ago to levels roughly half that of today. Bhorat, H., Kanbur, R., Rooney, C., and Steenkamp, F., 2017. Sub-Saharan Africa's Manufacturing Sector: Building Complexity. *African Development Bank Group, Working Paper Series No. 256*, May.

World Manufacturing Forum. 2019. The 2019 World Manufacturing Forum Report: Skills for the Future of Manufacturing. Accessed 17 December 2019: https://www.worldmanufacturingforum.org/report-2019.

Open Access This chapter is licensed under the terms of the Creative Commons Attribution 4.0 International License (http://creativecommons.org/licenses/by/4.0/), which permits use, sharing, adaptation, distribution and reproduction in any medium or format, as long as you give appropriate credit to the original author(s) and the source, provide a link to the Creative Commons license and indicate if changes were made.

The images or other third party material in this chapter are included in the chapter's Creative Commons license, unless indicated otherwise in a credit line to the material. If material is not included in the chapter's Creative Commons license and your intended use is not permitted by statutory regulation or exceeds the permitted use, you will need to obtain permission directly from the copyright holder.

9

The Future of Work in Africa

Abstract In this chapter, Cilliers addresses the challenge of widespread unemployment in Africa, and how trends collectively labelled as the 'future of work' could unfold on the continent. It describes the differences between the ways in which Africa will likely experience the effects of automation and digitisation on the labour market, and argues that the fourth industrial revolution is less a threat to jobs in Africa than in developed economies. Nevertheless, clear action is needed. Using Ghana as an example, the chapter explores innovative approaches to expanding inclusion in the formal sector, including enabling policies for financial inclusion and increased revenue collection. In addition, it speaks to Africa's readiness to benefit from the emergent 'gig economy', and other forms of labour flexibilisation.

Keywords Unemployment · Gig economy · Flexible labour · Future of work · Automation · Digitisation

Learning Objectives

- Explain whether the formal or informal sector is dominant in Africa and why
- Explain the degree to which automation poses a challenge to employment in Africa
- Recognise examples of policy interventions from the Ghana case study that could support more formalised work futures for Africa
- Define the 'gig economy' and explain why its prospects are different in Africa than Europe and other high-income regions.

The International Labour Organization (ILO) estimates the 2018 unemployment rate for adults (aged 15 and older) in Southern Africa at 26% making it the region with the highest unemployment rate globally. Unemployment in Northern Africa is at 12.5% and it is less than half that in Western, Central and Eastern Africa. Females struggle for employment in North Africa, however. Whereas the gap between males and females is below four percentage points in West, East, Central and Southern Africa, female unemployment in North Africa is significantly higher than for males.[1] The reason for the large difference in male/female unemployment ratios relate to levels of education and the barriers placed in many, but not all, Muslim-dominated countries on female advancement.

The ILO finds that low-income Africa generally has the lowest levels of unemployment and upper-middle income the highest.

The reason for these somewhat counterintuitive findings is that the ILOs definition of employment includes employment in the informal sector in its estimations of work.[2] Employment data therefore would include an executive of a company who may be earning a million dollars a year and a teacher in the Democratic Republic of the Congo who earns US$100 per month. It also includes a street vendor who sells packets of peanuts by the side of the road who may be earning 20 or 30 cents per day.

Previous chapters have already pointed to the dominance of the informal sector in Africa. On much of the continent the actual meaning of employment—a situation of having paid work or earning an income—therefore means earning something, anything, but seldom a living wage. Hence the ILO finds that almost 250 million persons in employment survive in extreme or moderate poverty—a number that is expected to rise annually by 4 million as the working age population increases.[3]

Many people in the informal sector live below or just above rates of extreme poverty. In the absence of a social net, employment in the informal sector is better than no employment. Informal workers lack benefits such as health insurance, unemployment insurance and paid leave. Most informal workers, many of which are self-employed, need to work every day to earn

---

[1] Data from ILOSTAT.

[2] According to the International Labour Organization (ILO), a person is unemployed if he/she is not in employment, is actively seeking work, and is available to take up work. International Labour Organization, 2013. *Resolution I Adopted at the 19th International Conference of Labour Statisticians*. Geneva, ILO, 2018. Also ILO, *Women and Men in the Informal Economy: A Statistical Picture*, 3rd Edition. Geneva: International Labour Office, p. 49.

[3] International Labour Organization, 2018. *World Employment and Social Outlook: Trends 2018*. Geneva: International Labour Office, pp. 11–13. Moderate and extreme poverty would include the share of workers living in households with income or consumption per capita below US$3.10 per day.

their living and pay for their basic household necessities. Their lives are precarious and their ability to survive shocks such as lock-down strategies to prevent the spread of COVID-19 is therefore very limited.

While the informal sector provides employment for unskilled and under-educated individuals, employment in this context is clearly not 'decent work', which the ILO defines as including 'a fair income, security in the workplace and social protection for families'.[4]

Estimates and even data from the field that purport to reflect the size of the informal sector and the contribution it makes to African economies differ widely. According to the International Monetary Fund (IMF) the informal sector is responsible for only around 16% of the gross domestic product (GDP) of the 35 member Organization of Economic Development (OECD) countries, all of which are high income, and around 38% in sub-Saharan Africa.[5] According to the ILO, in 2016, 86% of employment in Africa was in the informal sector (72% excluding agriculture), the highest globally. Informal employment outside the agricultural sector ranges from 34% in South Africa to 90.6% in Benin.[6]

Within the IFs forecasting system, which models its estimates differently from either the IMF, OECD or the ILO, the informal sector contributes about 36% of the economy of low-income countries in Africa, 30% of lower-middle-income countries and 15% of upper-middle-income countries. IFs also models the contribution of the informal sector to GDP in Africa which is at around 36% for low income, 30% to low-middle income and 15% for upper-middle-income countries in 2018. See Fig. 9.1.

Whichever the most accurate, the various estimates reflect the fact that a larger portion of the economies of poor countries are informal compared to rich countries and many more people are employed in the informal sector in poorer countries than in wealthier countries. At low levels of development the informal sector provides an important means of survival for poor people. To this end, goal 8 of the Sustainable Development Goals (SDGs) explicitly refers to the formalisation of micro, small and medium-sized enterprises.

---

[4] International Labour Organization, 2019. *Decent Work.* [Online] Available at: https://www.ilo.org/global/topics/decent-work/lang--en/index.htm.
[5] International Monetary Fund, 2017. *Chart of the Week: The Potential for Growth and Africa's Informal Economy.* [Online] Available at: https://blogs.imf.org/2017/08/08/chart-of-the-week-the-potential-for-growth-and-africas-informal-economy/.
[6] International Labour Organization, 2018. *Women and Men in the Informal Economy: A Statistical Picture,* 3rd Edition. Geneva: International Labour Office, p. 3. International Labour Organization, 2018. *World Employment and Social Outlook: Trends 2018.* Geneva: International Labour Office, p. 14. The gender gap in informal employment in some parts of sub-Saharan Africa is more than 20% (the rate at which women are more unemployed than men) and increases amongst youth.

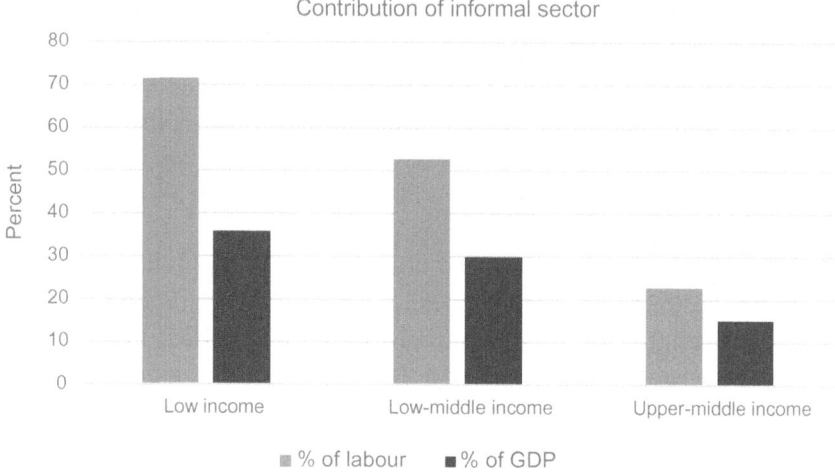

Fig. 9.1 2018 size of the informal sector in Africa by contribution to GDP and portion of labour (*Source* IFs v 7.45 initialising from ILO and IMF data)

While it is possible to imagine a growing informal economy alongside a growing formal sector, disproportionate growth in the informal sector hinders long-term inclusive growth. As a result, the reverse is more likely, and has also been observed historically, namely that the size of the informal sector generally declines as economies develop and grow.

It follows that generally, at low levels of development, the informal sector is generally significantly less productive than the formal sector. But typically the productivity gap between the informal and formal sector reduces as countries move up the income ladder and that, at higher levels of development, a large informal sector may often reflect a determined effort to avoid regulation. Generally, while informality is survivalist orientated at low levels of development, it is often more nefarious at higher levels of income. At higher levels of income, productivity in the informal sector could, in select instances, be comparable to that in the formal sector since the primary orientation here is often not survival but regulatory avoidance. Therefore, productivity in the informal sector in a high-income country such as Italy or Greece where the shadow or illicit economy is large, is not likely to differ much from that in the formal sector in these countries.

Irrespective of the level of development, generally, the existence of a large informal sector is costly for society and constrains sustainable development. People active in the informal sector do not contribute to direct taxes (since they are not registered to pay personal or company tax) but the informal sector still has to be served by police and requires infrastructure such as roads, water, sewerage, electricity and suchlike. The result is that a large informal sector places an additional burden on service delivery and congests public infrastructure while not contributing to either, except through unavoidable indirect taxes such as value-added and service taxes. This well-known negative drag that a large informal sector has is, however, balanced by the extent to which it soaks up people that would otherwise have no employment or opportunity.

Southern Africa has the smallest informal sector on the continent, with 40% in informal employment when the agricultural sector is included.[7] The portion in the rest of the continent is much larger. In this subregion the informal sector therefore serves as less of a cushion to unemployment than elsewhere, reflected in the data from the ILO quoted at the start of this chapter that indicated its high levels of unemployment. With low levels of employment, inequality is generally high. There is probably a historical reason for this, since Southern Africa achieved independence most recently and the ruling parties (most of which were previously liberation parties heavily infused with ideological models that predate the collapse of the Berlin Wall) all stick to an ideology of economic centralism that offers little room for innovation and self-help. As a result, the economic emancipation of its majority peoples has not yet taken place. Government's promise to provide for their citizens but rarely do. Furthermore, in South Africa, the most recent country in the region to transition to majority rule, the previous system of mining, education and business was historically premised on the extraction of maximum profits and burdened the country with huge inequalities. With low levels of entrepreneurship and education, employment is particularly low and inequality is exceptionally high.

The ILO data on unemployment in Africa quoted at the start of this chapter is therefore actually quite misleading without appropriate context. Africa obviously has a huge unemployment challenge whichever way one looks at the matter, with the vast majority of its peoples forced to eke out a living in the informal sector. Estimates vary. For example the African Development Bank[8] estimates that ten to twelve million youths, many of them educated, enter the African workforce annually, yet only three million formal

---

[7] And 36.1% when employment in agriculture is excluded. International Labour Organization, 2018. *Women and Men in The Informal Economy: A Statistical Picture*, 3rd Edition. Geneva: International Labour Office, p. 29. https://www.ilo.org/global/publications/books/WCMS_626831/lang--en/index.htm.

[8] African Development Bank, 2017. *Growth and Job Creation: Policy Options for Pro-Employment Growth*. Abidjan: AFDB.

jobs are created each year. The International Monetary Fund (IMF)[9] calculates that sub-Saharan Africa has to create 20 million formal jobs per year for the next two decades compared to an average of 9 million jobs added annually since 2000. The Africa Growth Initiative at the Brookings Institution[10] believes that Africa needs to create 12–15 million jobs annually to absorb youth entering the labour market.

The job prospects along the Current Path forecast for Africa are not good. Between 2000 and 2014 formal employment in Africa expanded by less than 1.8% annually,[11] but the labour force expanded by 2.6% per annum. Even at the robust 4.8% per annum average economic growth rate evident during these years, Africa's economy was not growing rapidly enough to create enough formal sector jobs.

Trends in Employment

Across all country income groups, the share of employment in services (the largest sector in most countries) is growing, and the share of employment in both agriculture and manufacturing employment is declining. This applies as much to Africa as to the rest of the world. Historically, technology-driven shifts in employment—for example, following the introduction of the personal computer—have created more jobs than they have destroyed.[12] In this future the demand for skilled and semi-skilled workers is steadily increasing and that for unskilled labour (of which Africa has a large supply) decreases. As explained in Chapter 8, workers in much of Africa are moving out of subsistence agriculture in rural areas into low-end services in the informal sector in urban areas. Working conditions are generally worse in the services sector than in the manufacturing sector and only marginally better than in the subsistence agriculture sector.

---

[9] Abdychev, A., Alonso, C., Alper, E., Desruelle, D., Kothari, S., Liu, Y., Perinet, M., Rehman, S., Schimmelpfennig, A., and Sharma, P., 2018. *The Future of Work in Sub-Saharan Africa.* Washington: International Monetary Fund.

[10] Coulibaly, B. S, Gandi, D., and Mbaye, A. A., 2019. Job Creation for Youth in Africa: Assessing the Employment Intensity of Industries Without Smokestacks, 16 December 2019. [Online] Available at: https://www.brookings.edu/blog/africa-in-focus/2019/12/16/job-creation-for-youth-in-africa-assessing-the-employment-intensity-of-industries-without-smokestacks/.

[11] International Labour Organization, 2018. *World Employment and Social Outlook: Trends 2018.* Geneva: International Labour Office.

[12] Magwenthshu, Nomfanelo, Rajagopaul, Agesan, Chui, Michael, and Singh Alok, 2019. *The Future of Work in South Africa—Digitisation, Productivity and Job Creation.* McKinsey & Company, September.

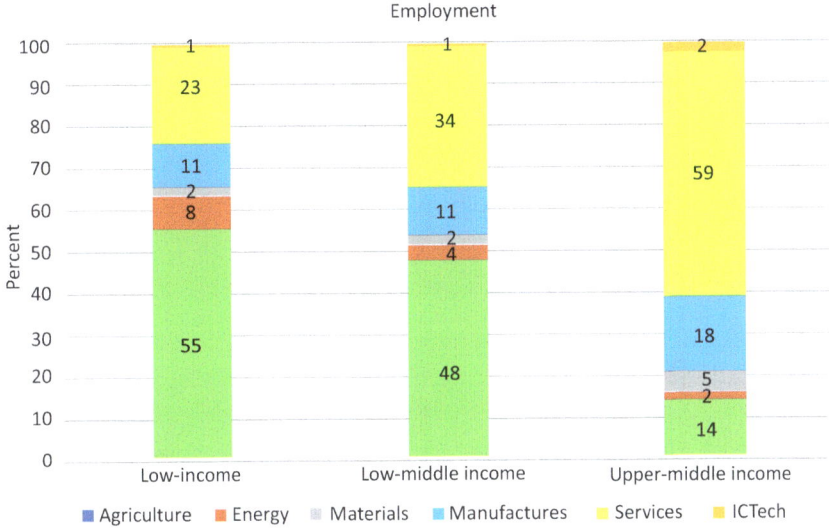

Fig. 9.2 2018 employment by sector for low, lower-middle and upper-middle-income Africa (*Source* IFs v 7.45 initializing from ILO and IMF data)

Currently most Africans are employed in the agricultural sector, which has roughly double the size of the labour force employed in the services sector, although, as noted in Chapter 8, the contribution of the services sector to GDP is substantially larger than the agricultural sector. Services, in turn, employ more than double the number of Africans that are employed in the manufacturing sector. Other sectors such as energy, materials and information technology employ significantly fewer people. Given the low levels of productivity in Africa's agricultural and large services sector, it comes as no surprise that Africa grows slowly.

Figure 9.2 presents the percent of employment for each of the six sectors within the IFs forecasting system for low, lower-middle and upper-middle Africa. Figure 9.3 presents the composition of low, lower-middle and upper-middle-income Africa as the contribution of each of these six sectors to GDP. The data in both is an estimation from the IFs forecasting system for 2018.

At a first glance the employment contribution to a sector (Fig. 9.2), when read against the contribution of that sector to the economy (Fig. 9.3) would give an indication of productivity in each sector, but the relationship is complicated. For example, due to the large surplus of labour on the continent, economic growth in Africa is actually more employment intensive than it would otherwise be.[13] It's often cheaper to employ more labour than to invest

---

[13] Kapsos, S., 2005. *The Employment Intensity of Growth: Trends and Macroeconomic Determinants.* Geneva: International Labour Office.

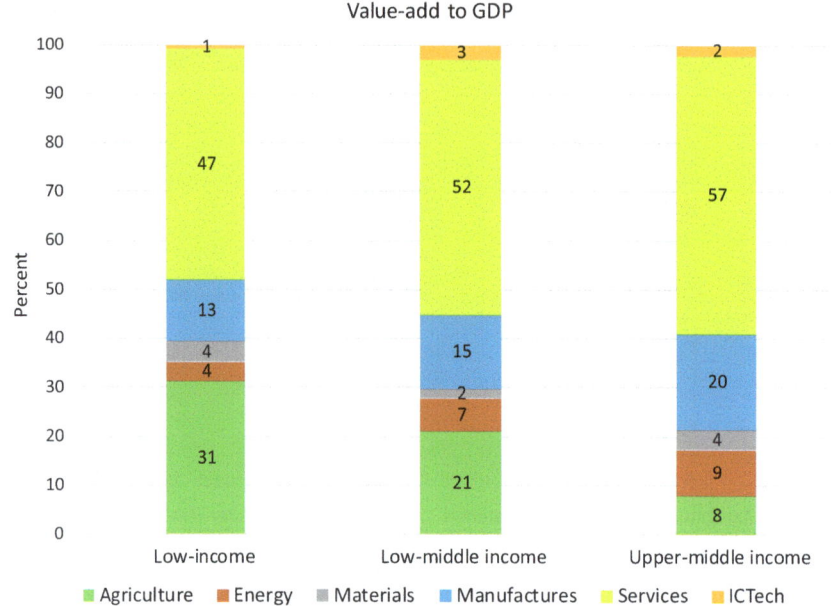

Fig. 9.3 2018 contribution of economic sectors to low, lower-middle and upper-middle-income Africa (*Source* IFs v 7.45 initializing from ILO and IMF data)

in better systems or technology. Labour productivity is quite low due to the skills gap on the continent since investments in human capital, particularly in health (Chapter 3) and education (Chapter 6), are meagre.

The World Bank runs a Human Capital index that measures the lost productivity of the next generation of workers as a consequence of under-investments in health and education. Sub-Saharan Africa can be found at the bottom of this index's global ranking.[14]

There is an unavoidable tension between employment-intensive growth as opposed to productivity-intensive growth. If an economy does not grow, the pressure for more output per worker will contribute to the steady decline in employment or a reduction in average remuneration. Typically that would happen through the process of automation. To grow employment Africans need to pay particular attention to measures that can unlock more rapid economic growth. This matter has already been discussed in previous chapters, pointing to the rather obvious fact that over long time horizons more rapid economic growth generally performs better in increasing employment than redistributive policies. Both are, of course, required. The often unspoken

---

[14]The World Bank, 2019. *Human Capital Project*. [Online] Available at: http://www.worldbank.org/en/publication/human-capital.

challenge is if it is politically possible for Africa to pursue the exploitative manufacturing labour practices through which other countries such as China and the Asian Tiger economies initially developed. I discuss this in Chapter 13 when dealing with governance, only to note that it is inherently more difficult for low-income democracies (of which Africa has a steadily increasing number) to institute the measures required for rapid economic growth than for authoritarian states. But then the latter is seldom focussed on implementing pro-growth policies in any case.

In Chapter 8 I briefly examined the phenomenon of premature deindustrialisation (from already low levels) in Africa, and argued that it appears unlikely that Africa will be able to rapidly grow employment based on growth in manufacturing. The analysis presented there is that middle-income countries are experiencing declining shares of industry as a contribution to GDP and hence declining shares of industrial employment. This is occurring at an earlier stage of development compared to the history of today's developed countries. But because manufacturing is important in changing the productive structures within the entire economy, i.e. also within the agriculture and services sector, I also argued that African countries need to aggressively pursue industrialisation where this is possible.[15]

This trend of premature deindustrialisation complicates the potential impact of structural transformation towards more formal and less vulnerable employment in many African countries. In effect, the opportunity for industrialisation in Africa as a pathway to provide employment and productivity improvements seems to be slipping away. And since manufacturing is the single most important vehicle through which economies transition to higher productivity, the long-term impact of premature deindustrialisation could be debilitating. The conclusion, presented by many, is that African countries need to look elsewhere for growth, primarily towards tourism, agriculture, natural resource extracts and information technology services.[16]

The problem is that few of these sectors offer particularly exciting employment or productivity prospects. Africa is already overly dependent upon

---

[15] International Labour Organization, 2018. *World Employment and Social Outlook: Trends 2018.* Geneva: International Labour Office, p. 2.

[16] See, for example, the paper and presentation delivered by Joseph Stiglitz at the UNU-WIDER Development Conference in Helsinki, 13–15 September 2018. Beyond manufacturing export-led growth. [Online] Available at: https://www.wider.unu.edu/plenary-session/beyond-manufacturing-export-led-growth. Also the Brookings Institution and UNU-WIDER work on Industries without Smokestacks: Industrialization in Africa Reconsidered. Page, J., Newfarmer, Richard S., Page, John, and Tarp, Finn, eds. 2018. *Industries Without Smokestacks: Industrialization in Africa Reconsidered*. Oxford University Press. https://www.wider.unu.edu/publication/industries-without-smokestacks-2. Also Page, J. How Industries Without Smokestacks Can Address Africa's Youth Unemployment Crisis. [Online] Available at: https://www.brookings.edu/wp-content/uploads/2019/01/BLS18234_BRO_book_007_CH3.pdf.

natural resource extraction and very vulnerable to the associated swings in commodity prices. Commodity dependence is linked to political dysfunction and traps a country at the low end of the value chain. Tourism is employment intensive but not all countries have the offerings to be able to provide attractive packages or destinations. Nor does tourism offer the kind of learning-driven productivity improvements generally common to manufacturing. And then agriculture, where Africa has significant potential, automates even faster than industry.[17]

The African Agricultural Revolution scenario modelled in Chapter 5 is about the transformation of current traditional agriculture from subsistence to smallholder and eventually to be part of value chains that link smallholding farmers to retailers using ICT technology and a host of applications which becomes the glue holding this complex system together. In this manner, agriculture moves into manufacturing through agro processing with significantly higher levels of productivity.

In the short to medium term the African Agricultural Revolution scenario also has the potential to have a positive impact on creating employment, if not on the farm then certainly in the associated supply and distribution chain. The analysis in Chapter 8 illustrates that, over a time horizon of a decade and longer, a manufacturing growth path unlocks more rapid economic growth and eventually also provides more jobs than agriculture—although not initially. On top of this, improvements in productivity in agriculture are bound to reduce employment intensity as it introduces modern technology into the sector—although a growing agricultural sector would increase the number of jobs even as employment intensity declines. In other words, there is probably a limit on the potential of agriculture to provide the jobs that Africa so desperately needs, although it certainly would play an important role.

Chapter 8 therefore emphasised the importance of growing Africa's manufacturing sector. It does so not because of the (limited) potential of manufacturing to create jobs in the twenty-first century, but because of its importance in changing the productive structures of African economies and unlocking faster growth. Also important, although less explicit in that chapter, is the limits that Africa's higher-than-expected levels of democratisation play on a manufacturing led growth path. Whereas semi-democracies such as Ethiopia and Uganda can pursue the exploitative manufacturing labour practices that enable them to compete on cost with emerging Asia, it is doubtful if that

---

[17] Smith, N., 2019. Africa Could Become the New China If It Plays to Its Industrial Strengths. ThePrint. [Online] Available at: https://theprint.in/opinion/africa-could-become-the-new-china-if-it-plays-to-its-industrial-strengths/245303/.

is replicable in countries where democratic accountability is more deeply entrenched. More on this in Chapter 13.

The evidence is that a larger manufacturing sector has important enabling spillover effects. For example, it incentivises high-end services such as financial intermediation which is crucial for the development of the private sector and also encourages a more productive agricultural sector and consequently the transition into agro processing and agribusiness. These changes eventually produce higher growth rates and a more rapidly growing economy that in turn creates more jobs, though only in the medium to longer term.

The African Center for Economic Transformation in Ghana (ACET) is one of many institutions that advocates that both agriculture and light manufacturing are key requirements for the future. In its *African Transformation Report 2017* it argues in favour of 'a dual-track to industrialisation. The one track should leverage their relative labor-abundance for labor-intensive and export-oriented light manufacturing, while the other should leverage their advantages in agriculture for globally competitive agriculturally based manufacturing'.[18] While an agricultural growth path is appropriate for low-income countries, once these countries achieve middle-income status, a manufacturing growth path generally becomes more important.

However, as a contribution to GDP, or portion of the total economy, the services sector already dominates. In the Current Path forecast, the contribution from the services sector to Africa's economy steadily increases from its current 53% to almost 60% by 2040 while that of agriculture almost halves to 9%. This is in line with a global trend towards more service-oriented economies, with job growth particularly in non-routine work such as personal care services. Given the dominance of the services sector, most future employment growth on the African continent is set to come from here, which includes trade, transportation, finance and other commercial services.

These trends are confirmed by Louise Fox, Alun Thomas and Cleary Haines who write for the IMF that, 'Sub-Saharan Africa will not be able to transform through manufacturing as East Asia did over the past two decades'.[19] According to them, the African growth experience over the last 35 years can, in general, be characterised as:

> growth in capital-intensive resource- and energy-based industries – which in turn have not generated a sufficient number of jobs. Africa's manufacturing

---

[18] The African Center for Economic Transformation, 2017. *African Transformation Report 2017: Agriculture Powering Africa's Economic Transformation.* Ghana, p. 1. [Online] Available at: http://acetforafrica.org/publications/african-transformation-report-2017/african-transformation-report-2017/.

[19] Fox, L., Thomas, A. H., and Haines, C., 2017. *Structural Transformation in Employment and Productivity: What Can Africa Hope For?* Washington: International Monetary Fund, p. viii.

sector has stagnated in output and employment terms. The latter happened in an environment of an unproductive agriculture sector and an employment intensive, urban-based informal retail sector.[20]

The authors then caveat their conclusion by pointing out that most of the new jobs, 'were created in sectors with low-productivity levels, such as subsistence agriculture and low value-added services. Self-employment has continued to be predominant'.[21]

Given the size of the informal sector and the nature of work in Africa, the key question when looking to the future of work is if digitisation will help to more rapidly formalise African economies and accelerate employment growth, with all the associated benefits listed above?

Automation and the Threat to Work

Estimates about the impact of the fourth industrial revolution, robots, the digital economy and automation differ hugely and include alarmist forecasts about the destruction of up to 30% of all jobs globally by 2030. This is highly unlikely. In fact, the rich world, Europe and North America in particular, is enjoying an unprecedented bonanza of jobs, facilitated, of course, by their shrinking labour force as a portion of the total population. And, instead of the exploitation of low-end workers, workers are being upskilled and wages are generally rising.[22]

With each successive industrial revolution, technology has created many more jobs than it has destroyed. Despite the hype around artificial intelligence, robotics and automation, it is doubtful that the fourth industrial revolution will change this broad trend. The question we need to answer, though, is where these jobs will be created—in the developed or developing world, in Africa or in Asia? Remember that the capital and labour intensity of manufacturing is declining, i.e. less capital and less labour is required to produce the same value of goods and that technology (or knowledge) is globalising. Although knowledge does not translate into know-how (that requires practice and repetition), in theory someone with a fast enough internet connection in the Central Africa Republic has access to many of the

---

[20] Bhorat, H., Kanbur, R., Rooney, C., and Steenkamp, F., 2017. *Sub-Saharan Africa's Manufacturing Sector: Building Complexity, Working Paper Series N° 256*. Abidjan: African Development Bank.

[21] Abdychev, A., Alonso, C., Alper, E., Desruelle, D., Kothari, S., Liu, Y., Perinet, M., Rehman, S., Schimmelpfennig, A., and Sharma, P. 2018. *The Future of Work in Sub-Saharan Africa*. Washington: International Monetary Fund, p 1.

[22] *The Economist*, 2019. The Feature Is Entitled the Great Jobs Boom, 25 May.

same knowledge resources as a consultant in Brussels. And the tools available through YouTube and other sites enable someone building a house in Lagos to teach himself to do the entire electrical wiring and installation, if perhaps not entirely safely.

Artificial intelligence, robotics and automation will have very different impacts in the developing world compared to the developed world, largely because robotics present a huge threat to higher-paid routine labour in the more mature countries. Although, as with every previous industrial revolution, new jobs will emerge that will replace the jobs lost to robots and automation. These developments will occur at every level and would, in some instances, appear to threaten large communities. For example, as China transitions to electric vehicles and the rest of the world follows, millions of established jobs associated with the internal combustion engine will eventually become redundant, to be replaced by skill requirements related to electric engines, battery storage and energy management systems. The question is only if the current crop of workers will be able to reskill or not. Similarly, as countries transition from coal to renewables as the dominant source of energy, thousands of coal miners in places such as Mpumalanga in South Africa will lose their jobs. But thousands of more new jobs will be created across the country as distributed wind, solar and biomass energy sources come online. Work, the saying goes, fills the time available.[23]

The largest potential for robot-based automation is in those states with large and well-paying manufacturing sectors like Germany, Japan, South Korea, the USA and increasingly China. The automation of low-wage and light manufacturing jobs, such as those generally found in Africa, seems much less likely in the foreseeable future. According to the African Development Bank:

> So far, robotization has had only a small effect on most developing countries, where mechanization continues to be the predominant form of automation. Despite the hype surrounding the potential of robot-based automation, today the use of industrial robots globally remains quite small and amounts to less than two million units. Industrial robots are concentrated in the automotive, electrical and electronics industries, and in a small number of countries.[24]

According to UNCTAD:

---

[23] Sharma, R., 2016. *The Rise and Fall of Nations—Ten Rules of Change in the Post-crisis World.* New York: Penguin Random House, p. 56.
[24] Monga, C., 2017. Industrialization: A Primer. In: *Industrialized Africa—Strategies, Policies, Institutions, and Financing.* Abidjan: African Development Bank Group, p. 10.

job displacement by robots is economically more feasible in relatively skill-intensive and well-paying manufacturing, such as the automotive and electronics sectors, than in relatively labour-intensive and low-paying sectors, such as apparel production.... Indeed, the countries currently most exposed to automation through industrial robots are those with a large manufacturing sector that is dominated by industries which offer relatively well-paying jobs, such as automotives and electronics. By contrast, robotisation has had a relatively small direct effect in most developing countries so far, and this is unlikely to change in the foreseeable future, given their lack of diversification and technological upgrading[25]

According to mainstream analysis, the demand for jobs that cannot easily be replaced by robots, especially those that require non-routine cognitive and socio-behaviour skills, will increase; such as managing teams, nursing and cleaning. However, the demand for routine, job-specific skills, such as those required for processing payroll, bookkeeping or assembling goods, will fall. And jobs that combine different skill sets will increase. As a result, global value chains are becoming more knowledge-intensive and low-skilled labour is becoming less important as a factor of contribution compared to capital and technology.[26] The demand for labour is increasingly away from low-skilled to semi-skilled and skilled labour and it is for this reason that more and better education is so important for Africa.

A 2017 report by McKinsey estimates that less than 5% of occupations are candidates for full automation and that the 'correct' lens through which automation should be viewed is that of tasks, not occupations or jobs.[27] Even so, care work that requires empathy and judgement (such as nurses and elderly care), are harder to automate and are likely to increase as populations around the world age. So people will have to transition from one set of skills that may be replaced by automation to another, where that threat is not as acute. This is clearly less of a challenge in Africa, where employment is less formal and structured than elsewhere.

Technology by technology and job by job, there will be continued progress—and it will differ hugely between countries at different levels

---

[25] United Nations Conference on Trade and Development, 2017. *Trade and Development, Beyond Austerity: Towards a Global New Deal.* New York and Geneva: United Nations Conference on Trade and Development, p. ix.

[26] Lund, S., Manyika, J., Woetzel, J., Bughin, J., Krishnan, M., Seong, J., and Mac Muir. 2019. *Globalization in Transition: The Future of Trade and Value Chains.* New York: McKinsey Global Institute, p. 2.

[27] Manyika, J., Chui, M., Miremadi, M., Bughin, J., George, K., Willmott, P., and Dewhurst, M. 2017. *Harnessing Automation for a Future That Works.* [Online] Available at: https://www.mckinsey.com/featured-insights/digital-disruption/harnessing-automation-for-a-future-that-works.

of development. In Japan and Germany that have highly paid and scarce workers, many of whom work in the automotive industry, a higher percentage of additional work could be automated. However, in many parts of Africa new jobs could be created at much lower start-up costs due to the reductions in the capital costs and lower barriers to entry referred to previously.[28]

In view of these considerations, and contrary to the trepidation with which the fourth industrial revolution is viewed in Europe and North America, the view from Africa is positive since progress, coming from a low base, offers prospects for a degree of catch up and because of the expectation that it would create more jobs in the formal sector.

A recent study by ACET that included extensive field work in eleven African countries found that less than a fifth of survey respondents thought the fourth industrial revolution would have a negative impact on jobs. In fact, the vast majority were excited about its positive impact.

> The sectors seen as most positively affected by 4IR [fourth industrial revolution] technologies are software development, information and communication technology (ICT), and infrastructure – not surprising since 4IR will create demand for jobs in these sectors. But agriculture, finance, manufacturing, retailing, and tourism are also seen as benefiting from 4IR; the informal sector is seen as deriving the least benefit from 4IR.[29]

In this vein, a report entitled *The Future of Work* prepared for the European Commission concluded as follows:

> The world of work is part-and-parcel of the changing economy, heavily influenced by globalisation, international value and supply chains, more division of labour, and digital disruption. Work is no longer a static concept but an umbrella term for roles performed in a different manner and under different legal arrangements.[30]

---

[28] McKinsey estimates that across 46 countries (mixture of developing and developed economies) it looks as if by 2030 a range with a midpoint of 16% of occupations will have been automated and dislocated by automation. That number has a very large range and can go from very little to 30% since it depends on the rate of adoption, nature of the country and wage dynamics in the various sectors in that country. One can expect that in advanced economies it would be higher, say 20%, whereas for developing countries the midpoint will be much lower since wages are lower. McKinsey podcast What is the future of work?, 1 December 2017.

[29] The African Center for Economic Transformation, 2017. *African Transformation Report 2017: Agriculture Powering Africa's Economic Transformation*. Ghana, p. 2.

[30] European Commission, 2016. The Future of Work Skills and Resilience for a World of Change. *EPSC Strategic Notes*, Issue 13, p. 11.

Instead of workers being replaced completely by machines, the more likely future is where people work next to highly productive machines with the one augmenting the other. This is already evident in the way in which ICT is penetrating modern life through the use of smartphone applications to augment or ease the completion of everyday tasks.

Therefore the impact of the digital economy in OECD countries where we see the reshoring of the provision of goods and top-end services will include a trend towards short-term contracts and part-time work, although the vast majority of workers in the EU, for example, are still on full-time contacts. In addition, the Commission believes that automation will reduce routine job opportunities, such as those on a typical assembly line, in the formal sector.[31]

Yet, in a certain sense Africans might find this an easier transition, since Africans in the formal and informal sector often already juggle a number of part-time jobs. According to The Future of Work report:

> work' is increasingly becoming an umbrella concept for tasks performed under different legal, functional and geographic frameworks. Jobs are being broken down into projects that may either be outsourced to independent professionals and experts, or be reconfigured into assignments that assemble physical or virtual teams, across borders and time-zones'[32]

The trend towards the so-called gig economy or internet employment, which is characterised by freelance, on-demand work, is the latest manifestation of this greater fragmentation of work. The impact of COVID-19 is that many countries adopted lock-down strategies, forcing many employees to work remotely, providing a huge boost to the gig and off-site work. In the gig economy independent workers are hired for short-term tasks, often via online work platforms which pays them for each transaction or 'gig' they complete. At high levels of complexity and value, the gig economy is about digital technologies enabling geographically dispersed teams, who often come from different countries, to be assembled around a given project.[33] Although still quite small in much of Africa (at less than 0.3% of the active labour force) it is burgeoning especially in on-demand services ranging from the delivery

---

[31] Ibid., p. 4.
[32] Ibid., p. 2.
[33] Africans in the informal sector do not have much job security and global developments such as the gig economy appear to now also shift the risk of employment steadily to the employee in an environment where there are little or no social safety nets such as unemployment benefits and where unions are weak meaning that employees have less bargaining power, opening up the potential for job insecurity and greater wage differentials. European Commission, 2016. The Future of Work Skills and Resilience for a World of Change. *EPSC Strategic Notes*, Issue 13, p. 2.

of fast food to more sophisticated tasks such as accounting and editing.[34] But even in the USA, the gig economy accounts for only around one percent of jobs.[35]

The interesting thing about the notion of the gig economy is that it is already a much wider reality in Africa, although in a different form. Many entrepreneurial Africans in countries like Kenya already hustle to keep bread on the table by doing any number of jobs, tasks and functions in a seamless and often informally structured work environment. What will surely follow would be innovations that will provide safety nets such as unemployment insurance, health care and the means to cover various risks. The fourth industrial revolution is unlocking opportunities for millions of self-employed that did not previously exist.

It is therefore unlikely that we will witness widespread automation in sub-Saharan Africa. The region's large-scale informal economy and lack of the necessary digital infrastructure currently precludes such a development since low pay levels mean that labour will remain cheap.

The Impact of Digitisation in Ghana

Repeat visits to Accra in Ghana over the past two decades has made me a witness to the amazing political and developmental revolution that is taking place there, which is reflective of many other African states, and to consider its potential for job creation and progress.

By African standards, Ghana has a small population of around 30 million people. It is more urbanised than most African countries (close to 60%), allowing for a more rapid transition to digital services, and also making it easier to provide water, sanitation and other services. By 2040 almost 70% of its citizens will live in urban areas—a huge advantage that will allow for rapid economic growth. This could eventually allow Ghana to graduate from its current low middle to upper-middle-income status.

Partly because of higher-than-average rates of urbanisation, the total fertility rate (currently at four children per woman) is declining rapidly and Ghana will enter its demographic sweet spot earlier than most West African countries, in around 2035. Thereafter the positive ratio of working-age persons to dependents should ensure even more rapid growth rates—provided

---
[34] Mo Ibrahim Foundation, 2019. *Africa's Youth: Jobs or Migration?* London: Mo Ibrahim Foundation, p. 46.
[35] The Great Jobs Boom, in *The Economist*, 25 May 2019.

that Ghana manages to sustain the progress it has demonstrated towards inclusive, democratic governance over the last decade.

On a recent trip to the country in December 2018, I was invited to speak at a conference on the future of work in sub-Saharan Africa that was hosted by the IMF. Terminal 3 at Kotoka International Airport is gleaming and brand new, a far cry from the colonial-era building that had served as a sorry excuse for an international airport for so many years.

Officials are smart, courteous and clearly proud of the new facility. The construction was done by the Turkish construction company, Mapa Construction MNG Holding, cost US$400 million and is unpretentious, solid and well maintained—in contrast to many of the Chinese constructions elsewhere.

At the opening session of the IMF conference in a swanky Accra hotel, Ghana's vice president Mahamudu Bawumia set out the country's plans to leapfrog its development by using information and digital systems. In 2012 Ghana introduced Biometric Voter Registration and since May 2018 a smart national ID system (dubbed Ghana Card) that uses biometrics is being rolled out (free of charge to all Ghanaians). This is being done region by region and before the end of 2019, it will provide each Ghanaian with a unique personal identification number or PIN.

Hereafter a smart national ID will be a requirement to open a bank account, apply for a passport or driver's licence, to register a SIM card, buy property, register a business or even to enroll children in school (children are linked to the ID of their parents). Globally nearly a billion people lack any type of legally recognised form of identification, without which it is impossible to access banking, government benefits, education and many other critical services.[36]

Exports or imports are directly linked to the PIN to eliminate fraud and theft in the shipping and clearing of goods at ports and harbours. Already the number of agencies required to inspect a container has been reduced from 16 to just three, which cuts a lot of red tape.

Furthermore, the PIN will be used to verify a person's identity during job searches and applications, for e-tickets at airports, at border crossings, police checkpoints and the like. It will eventually become mandatory for the validation of payments, particularly electronic payments.

Most importantly, an ID number allows large portions of the informal sector to be brought into the formal economy. This is a huge leap forward

---

[36]The World Bank, 2019. *Identification For Development (ID4D) Global Dataset*. [Online] Available at: https://datacatalog.worldbank.org/dataset/identification-development-global-dataset.

in a country like Ghana that has, until recently, had no comprehensive identity system. It is also occurring at a pace that would astound bureaucrats in China and Western countries, where such systems were originally rolled out manually and with great effort over several decades.

In addition, the GhanaPostGPS will provide a unique digital address for each 5 × 5 meters of land area in a country that previously had no formal system of finding a specific location without local knowledge. Armed with a digital address, small and informal businesses can now register for a bank account and access credit. It basically means that anyone with a phone technically has a bank account.

The GhanaPostGPS app comes with other functions as well, such as panic buttons for emergency communication to the police, fire and ambulance services.[37] A unique digital address will allow door-to-door delivery of literally everything. For example, the country will shortly start with the delivery of emergency medical and other supplies by drone. Here Ghana is copying the example of Rwanda where this has been done for some time (they used corporate social responsibility funds for the initiative).

Besides many other benefits, these innovations will improve tax collection since both informal and formal businesses will steadily be forced to use electronic payment systems that are all part of the formal economy, increasing government revenues. This will again enable the state to deliver other services such as education, roads, water and sanitation.

Soon Ghana will also have a fully digital platform for the payment for all government services, including smart driver's licences and digital car registration. Moreover, Ghana is busy with the digitisation of land ownership. By the time that this book is published it should have a new base map survey (the first since 1974) that uses blockchain technology to secure and verify the ownership of all land. Furthermore, with the support of the World Bank the Ghanaian Ministry of Education is adopting modern technology by delivering its lessons through the use of e-learning technology.[38]

Modern technology also allows for better policing of something like mining licenses, for example. In many African countries, including in South Africa and the Democratic Republic of the Congo, illegal mining is rife, where it is often done by foreigners who mine at night in extremely dangerous

---

[37] See unique, digital addresses for all locations across Ghana at: GhanaPostGPS, 2019. *My Digital Address*. [Online] Available at: https://www.ghanapostgps.com/.

[38] The intelligence Box (iBox) is a home-grown proprietary technology for the delivery of premium, curricular-specific, educational content for Senior High School (SHS), Junior High School (JHS), and non-formal and skills training: B&FTonline, 2018. *Out of the Box*. [Online] Available at: https://thebftonline.com/2018/opinions/investing-in-human-capital-innovation-and-knowledge-with-the-ibox/.

conditions. Already 150 drone pilots have been trained to monitor illegal mining across Ghana.

In recognition of these efforts Google opened its first African Artificial Intelligence (AI) research centre in Accra, bringing together top machine learning researchers and engineers dedicated to AI research and its applications. The centre will work with local universities and jointly with a small number of other centres in Paris, Zurich, Tokyo, Beijing, Montreal, Toronto, Seattle, Cambridge / Boston, Tel Aviv / Haifa, New York, and the Google headquarters in Mountain View, San Francisco.[39]

This is an example of what is possible in a future Africa where the demand for new services are met and job opportunities for young people in urban areas are unlocked.

The Promise of Greater Economic Formalisation in Ghana

Using the IFs forecasting platform, I find that the size of Ghana's economy increases by roughly US$0.7 billion dollars (in PPP) over the first ten-year period for every one percent decrease in the size of the informal sector as a portion of GDP. And the benefits just keep on growing. In other words, if Ghana could use digitisation to draw people into the formal sector and hence reduce the size of the informal economy as a portion of GDP by five percentage points from 2020 to 2030, it would gain US$4.6 billion in the size of its economy by 2030 and US$14 billion by 2040.

A larger economy translates into higher average incomes and the result is an increase of US$140 average annual income per person above the Current Path forecast by 2030 for each of Ghana's 38 million citizens, and US$340 by 2040, at which point Ghana would have 45 million people. That is an enormous improvement. Other livelihood improvements that follow are decreases in poverty and inequality.

The 2019 report on Africa by the United Nations Commission for Africa (UNECA) finds that in the long-term government revenue on the continent can be increased by 12–20% of GDP through the rigorous pursuit of tax and non-tax income collection, which is possible through digitisation. Leveraging digital systems to increase revenue collection through e-taxation increased revenue collection in Rwanda by six percent of GDP. South Africa

---

[39]Adeoye, A., 2019. Google Has Opened Its First Africa Artificial Intelligence Lab in Ghana. CNN. [Online] Available at: https://edition.cnn.com/2019/04/14/africa/google-ai-center-accra-intl/index.html.

used online tax payments to reduce compliance costs and the time to comply with the value-added tax by 22%.[40]

Technology also enables the documentation of vital events in a person's life (live births, adoptions, legitimations and recognitions, deaths, marriages, divorces, separations and annulments) that are fundamental to having a legal identity and guaranteeing human rights and access to public services. It can provide access to finance, information about health, and offers a way to educate and connect people.[41]

The analysis on the potential positive impact of a more rapid formalisation of Ghana's economy corresponds broadly with the gist of an article by Amolo Ng'weno and David Porteus in a contribution for the Center for Global Development.[42] The authors argue that the explosion in digital platforms is slowly changing the nature of what it means to be in the informal or formal sector. The result is the incremental formalisation of the latter through a process of digital business progression where each small step is low cost and low risk. Instead of being casual labour, many workers who are active in the informal economy already live in the gig economy.

> In the short-term, it looks like technology is going to create a set of new opportunities in the gig economy: shared-ride drivers, homestay hosts, e-commerce logistics, e-commerce sellers, and small-scale e-commerce producers. These will be supplemented by an army of 'digital translators'. ... As an economy digitizes, more people are needed to help the customer and the citizen transition into the digital economy. Most of these translators work on commission and set their own hours.[43]

On the future nature of work, they write that 'it's time we recognized the truth about the future of work in Africa ... it isn't in the growth of full-time formal sector jobs. The future of work will be people working multiple gigs with "somewhat formal" entities'.[44]

---

[40] United Nations Economic Commission for Africa, 2019. *Fiscal Policy for Financing Sustainable Development in Africa*. Addis Ababa: UNECA, p. 113.
[41] Ibid, p. xiii.
[42] Ng'weno, A., and Porteous, D., 2018. *Let's Be Real: The Informal Sector and the Gig Economy are the Future, and the Present, of Work in Africa*. [Online] Available at: https://www.cgdev.org/publication/lets-be-real-informal-sector-and-gig-economy-are-future-and-present-work-africa.
[43] Ibid.
[44] Ibid.

Eventually, 'in Africa, as elsewhere, the future of work will depend on the battle between automation and innovation', argues the Mo Ibrahim Foundation. 'While automation leads to a decline in employment in old sectors, innovation makes new sectors or tasks possible'.[45]

Of course the gig economy doesn't only have positive effects. Generally the impact of digitisation is to lower barriers to entry and increase competition. In Africa this could however further force down wages and increase the number of people engaged in informal and unregulated work. The gig economy is therefore likely to result in precarious or insecure work with lower job and income security, poorer working conditions and lower social protection coverage when compared to employees in standard employment relations. But even that is not a given. Business innovation and government intervention is sure to fill this gap.

Then again digital technologies could make a huge contribution to help formalise African economies. I will explore this point further in Chapter 10 as part of a discussion on the continent's ability to benefit from digitisation and to leapfrog into the future thanks to the fourth industrial revolution.

Conclusion: Thinking Differently About the Future

On the current trajectory, the growth in the African labour force will far outstrip the supply of jobs, leaving many of the continent's citizens destitute, frustrated and dependent on the informal sector to survive. This will make some of them eager to migrate elsewhere in search of opportunities including to neighbouring Europe which seems particularly fixated on this challenge above all others. These conclusions re-emphasise the importance of an agricultural and manufacturing revolution that would increase growth and employment.

Only if one views employment in Africa through the lens of self-employment (much of which occurs within the informal sector), digitisation and the fourth industrial revolution does it become possible to think differently about the future of work in Africa. With large numbers of youth entering the labour market, the demand for formal sector jobs in Africa is huge and steadily increasing. However, previous chapters have also indicated that Africa's labour force generally lacks many of the purported enablers

---

[45] Mo Ibrahim Foundation, 2019. *Africa's Youth: Jobs or Migration?* London: Mo Ibrahim Foundation, p. 44.

for rapid job creation, such as adequate health and appropriate basic infrastructure (Chapter 3), and minimal levels of education and the right skills (Chapter 6).

A large cohort of young people with improving levels of education that are either unemployed or eaking out a survival in the informal sector could be a destabilising force both in Africa and in the neighbourhood. Young Africans are increasingly connected with one another and the rest of the world through the internet and social media and will not stop seeking out the opportunities and lifestyles their peers have in the developed parts of the world.

Chapter 12 deals with the structural drivers of instability, including the combination of youth and unemployment. In a different context this group coincides with the NEETS—the large group of Africans Not in Education, Employment or Training. Clearly the orientation of education opportunities towards the actual opportunities or needs within the economy, vocational training in particular, could assist in lowering the political temperature. In addition, there is the potential for job creation in agriculture, light manufacturing, modern services, tourism and creative industries.

Since much of Africa's growth is going to come from commodity exports it is equally incumbent upon governments to raise incomes through commodity value addition and to find ways of extending the value chains of the capital-intensive projects such as the gas projects in northern Mozambique into the domestic economy. Furthermore, governments have to find ways of enhancing productivity and improving working conditions and regulations to reduce workers' vulnerability.

There will also be an important role for the public sector in creating jobs for social development and through public works programmes, both to improve livelihoods and enhance skills.

Most concerning is that the vast number of Africans that survive in the informal sector appear unable to overcome the hurdles created by the fourth industrial revolution. This underlines the importance of using digitisation to open up new opportunities for this group, such as access to finance and bringing the informal sector into the mainstream. Every effort should be made to overcome the segregation between the formal and informal sectors through productive linkages and by reforming laws and regulations.

In this chapter I used the example of Ghana to illustrate how modern technology could potentially formalise its economy more rapidly. I provided an indication of the results using economic growth, poverty and GDP per capita. By following this example, African governments can harness the potential of digitisation to formalise and empower portions of the informal economy and empower ordinary citizens with access to finance, education and opportunity. Digitisation can help with the modernisation of agriculture and lift smallholder farmers out of poverty, but only if governments and leaders are aware of the opportunities it offers and develop effective digital strategies that support local innovation firms to compete and invest in ICT. Many Africans will still be working on subsistence farms or struggling through various forms of informal employment. The future of employment for those people will be just as impacted by climate change as it will be robots. For them it will be very similar to how work looks today, with some improvements and changes.

To provide sufficient meaningful work the continent needs a shift in mindset that would allow a speedier escape from poverty compared to the slow progress envisioned under the Current Path forecast. This change in mindset can be captured as a change from consumption to production and towards innovation, community self-sufficiency and independence.

Only if African governments are able to create a culture of entrepreneurship will the continent be able to reduce unemployment. Attitudes need to change from 'getting education to get a job', to 'getting education to create jobs and opportunities'. Even then, such entrepreneurship and self-employment will make only a small contribution to employment rather than solving the unemployment challenge.

The next chapter builds on these findings to explore the potential of technology to allow Africa to leapfrog towards a better future.

Further Reading

African Development Bank. 2020. African Economic Outlook 2020: Developing Africa's Workforce for the Future, 30 January 2020. https://www.afdb.org/en/documents/african-economic-outlook-2020.

Global Commission for the Future of Work. January 2019. *Work for a Brighter Future*. International Labour Organisation. https://www.ilo.org/infostories/en-GB/Campaigns/future-work/global-commission#intro.

Graham, M., Hjorth, I., and Lehdonvirta, V. 2017. Digital Labour and Development: Impacts of Global Digital Labour Platforms and the Gig Economy on Worker Livelihoods. *Transfer: European Review of Labour and Research*, 23(2), pp. 135–162. https://doi.org/10.1177/1024258916687250.

International Labour Organisation. Abidjan Declaration on the Future of Work in Africa, December 2019. https://www.ilo.org/wcmsp5/groups/public/—ed_norm/—relconf/documents/meetingdocument/wcms_731646.pdf.

Open Access This chapter is licensed under the terms of the Creative Commons Attribution 4.0 International License (http://creativecommons.org/licenses/by/4.0/), which permits use, sharing, adaptation, distribution and reproduction in any medium or format, as long as you give appropriate credit to the original author(s) and the source, provide a link to the Creative Commons license and indicate if changes were made.

The images or other third party material in this chapter are included in the chapter's Creative Commons license, unless indicated otherwise in a credit line to the material. If material is not included in the chapter's Creative Commons license and your intended use is not permitted by statutory regulation or exceeds the permitted use, you will need to obtain permission directly from the copyright holder.

10

Technological Innovation and the Power of Leapfrogging

Abstract Technological innovation and the notion of leapfrogging are imperative to Africa's future and will shape development on the continent in ways that are difficult to anticipate. However, the impact of the shale and tight oil revolution in the USA demonstrates the potential of new technologies to leapfrog aspects of traditional development. This is most likely in the renewable energy space provided the challenges associated with energy storage can be overcome. Already the uptake of mobile phones and the internet have brought financial services to millions and mobile telephony is at the forefront of social change in Africa. Building on the example of what is happening in Ghana that was explored in Chapter 9, this chapter models the impact of a Leapfrogging scenario.

Keywords Leapfrogging · Innovation · Digitisation · ICT · Mobile technology · Fourth industrial revolution · Renewable energy · Education · Investment

Learning objectives

- Understand the innovative opportunities outside the traditional development paradigm available for rapid progress in Africa.
- Quality and up to date education is a key pillar if Africa is to leap into the future.
- Technology and digitisation can promote better governance in Africa

The term leapfrogging has become almost as popular as the fourth industrial revolution and digitisation. They are, of course, intimately related.

Leapfrogging occurs when we use technology to solve a particular problem or to radically improve an existing process, such as generating energy, or even something as mundane as the ability to more efficiently find, hire and electronically pay for transport using mobile phone applications instead of standing on a street to hail a passing taxi. It makes previous systems and processes redundant, such as generating electricity from ocean currents instead of by burning coal. It is inherently disruptive as it either destroys the value of 'old stuff' and/or presents ways of doing things where it was not previously possible.

What distinguishes the twenty-first century from previous periods is the exponential rate at which scientific knowledge is advancing and our ability to more rapidly translate that knowledge into practical application, in other words, the rate at which we are leapfrogging. Each new generation of technology stands on the shoulders of its predecessors but today the rate of progress from version to version is driving advancement at rates of change that are sometimes breathtaking. Leapfrogging is the story of innovation, disruption and rapid development. At sufficient scale, technology can have a transformative effect on nations and on the relations between nations. Although it is always important to remember that what is technologically possible is not always commercially feasible.

Chapter 3 dealt with health and provided an overview of the extent to which Africa trails on basic infrastructure such as for water and sanitation. The story is, of course, much broader. We trail, globally, on every dimension of infrastructure, with the largest deficits being the lack of reliable electricity, transport, particularly roads, rail and suchlike. In fact the International Monetary Fund (IMF) estimates that Africa's deficit in physical infrastructure reduces growth by 2 percentage points a year.[1] The drag that poor infrastructure has on economic growth is particularly evident in Africa's low and lower-middle-income countries. It is less severe for upper-middle-income countries since graduation to upper-middle-income status is generally accompanied by improved infrastructure.[2] Of course when we speak of infrastructure today it's much more than roads and railway, it's increasingly about digital infrastructure—the ability to transact and act globally through the access that is provided by the internet.

---

[1] International Monetary Fund, 2014. Is It Time for an Infrastructure Push? The Macroeconomic Effects of Public Investment. In: *World Economic Outlook (WEO) Legacies, Clouds, Uncertainties.* Washington: ILO, pp. 75–114.

[2] Within IFs, multifactor productivity is composed of physical, social, human and knowledge capital.

An IMF study of infrastructure spending in several countries from 1985 to 2014, found that an unanticipated one percent increase in public infrastructure boosted gross domestic product (GDP) by 0.4% the following year, but by 1.5% four years later.[3] The Economic Policy Institute agrees, noting in a 2014 report that 'our analysis confirms with a large and growing body of literature persuasively arguing that infrastructure investments can boost even private sector productivity growth'.[4]

It is very likely, however, that we underestimate the potential for leapfrogging in infrastructure and that we are locked into a particular vision of how things should be done.[5]

For, once a country has invested and built an elaborate network of pipes, wires, roads, bridges, buildings and other expensive physical infrastructure, which is characteristic of today's developed countries, it becomes very difficult to imagine or to take the risk of investing in a different way of doing things. Every piece of existing infrastructure creates vested interests that are subsequently difficult to uproot. The result is a tendency towards 'path dependency' where governments and the private sector do things in a particular manner because that seems to be the way things should be done and because it is difficult to get the public to change their ways. Furthermore, since other countries have done things in one way for so long, Africans tend to believe that it should follow the same infrastructure and development pathway that is presented by their former colonial masters in Europe, or as was illustrated through the cultural pop culture of the USA and today, the rapid improvements in livelihoods and global power in China.

Can we really imagine the impact of wireless power, automated bulk delivery systems via thousands of heavy-lift drones, individual air transport instead of cars and mass transportation systems that don't require asphalt roads to replace buses or trains? What would happen if there was a widespread adoption of atmospheric water generators that are capable of extracting water from the air during the day and produced electricity at night (wind speed allowing)?[6] Once we find ways of fully developing a circular economy, where waste is used as biomass the household becomes steadily more independent

---

[3] International Monetary Fund, 2014. Is It Time for an Infrastructure Push? The Macroeconomic Effects of Public Investment. In: *World Economic Outlook (WEO) Legacies, Clouds, Uncertainties.* Washington: ILO, pp. 75–114.

[4] Bivens, J., 2014. *The Short- and Long-Term Impact of Infrastructure Investments on Employment and Economic Activity in the U.S. Economy.* Washington: Economic Policy Institute.

[5] Frey, T., n.d. *The Curse of Infrastructure.* [Online] Available at: http://foresightfordevelopment.org/featured/infrastructure-v?ct=t(FFD_Aug_2018_Future_of_Infrastructure.

[6] Originally by Eole Water.

from the need for delivery of bulk services such as water, electricity and waterborne sewage. This is the long-term impact of modern technology, one of greater independence and choice.

In 2019 the eThekwini municipality in South Africa's KwaZulu-Natal province completed a pre-feasibility study that found that the powerful Agulhas current that runs from North to South along its steep continental shelf in the Indian Ocean has the potential to generate 50.4 GW of power. That is roughly equivalent to South Africa's *total* domestic electricity generation capacity.[7] And South Africa is, by a substantial margin, Africa's largest electricity producer. Instead of importing power from dirty coalfields further inland, the province could generate all of its electricity needs offshore from a renewable source with hardly any environmental impact.

Can we even begin to imagine the impact of the wide adoption of contour crafting—a layered fabrication system similar to 3D printing that can be used to rapidly construct buildings and other large pieces of infrastructure using local materials and not requiring the construction company to truck in bricks, cement, conduiting, roof trusses and other bulk items?[8]

These are all examples of technological innovations that will bring about major changes. That change is well underway since it inevitably starts modestly but it creeps upon us. It is only one day when we look back that we realise the journey that has been travelled. That's what happened with mobile phones which have literally transformed the way we socialise, work and play. The distance that we travel from the crest of one transformative technological wave to the next is steadily decreasing.

Perhaps the best recent example of technology's potential to literally shift the ground beneath our feet is the way in which the US shale and oil gas revolution has reshaped the global energy market and global politics—another example of the extent with which technology is empowering ever greater domestic independence at the expense of an interconnected, globalised, world.

---

[7]ZLM Project Engineering, The Case for Offshore Energy in KwaZulu-Natal, 26 April 2019, 2018 Draft IRP Released by the South African Department of Energy.
[8]Sculpteo, 2018. *3D Printing for Construction: What Is Contour Crafting?* [Online] Available at: https://www.sculpteo.com/blog/2018/06/27/3d-printing-for-construction-what-is-contour-crafting/. Saunders, S., 2018. *Contour Crafting Will Develop Concrete 3D Printer for Disaster Relief, Thanks to DoD Contract*. [Online] Available at: https://3dprint.com/222125/contour-crafting-dod-contract/.

The Shale and Tight Oil Revolution in the USA

By 2005 US domestic oil production had declined for 35 years after its 1970 peak at 9.6 million barrels per day. The USA was importing almost half of its total petroleum consumption. The future appeared to consist of growing imports of oil and gas from unstable countries such as Venezuela and dictatorships like Saudi Arabia. To the chagrin of the Americans, Russia was also rapidly emerging as an energy superpower. The situation with natural gas was only marginally better.[9]

Then came the fracking revolution.

Fracking has been around for several decades and has been used extensively to increase production rates from conventional oil and gas wells. It involves the high-pressure injection of water, chemicals and sand into shale deposits to release more of the gas and oil trapped within the rock. The original mode of fracking entailed drilling vertically through a deposit, but today, horizontal drilling and other improvements in technology are commonly used. Once in the permeable layer of rock where the gas or oil is locked up, the drill is turned horizontal to access a greater portion of the deposit. In this manner fracking is able to harvest large stores of gas and oil that could not previously be commercially extracted.

Gas suppliers were the first to benefit. From 2005 US natural gas production increased year on year for ten straight years and by 2015 the USA was the world's largest gas producer. From 2008 oil production followed. By 2018 domestic US crude production was running at about 11.6 million barrels per day, a little ahead of Russia, the world's second largest producer.

In just a few years the shale oil and gas revolution in the USA has changed geopolitics. It reduced the price of energy and thus broke the stranglehold that the Organization of Petroleum Exporting Countries (OPEC) had on energy production. It also led to a severe slump in the prospects of many oil exporting countries such as those in the Middle East, Venezuela, Angola and Nigeria.[10] By 2025, US oil production could equal the combined output

---

[9]Rapier, R., 2017. *How The Shale Boom Turned The World Upside Down*. [Online] Available at: https://www.forbes.com/sites/rrapier/2017/04/21/how-the-shale-boom-turned-the-world-upside-down/#13052ef77d24.

[10]Ibid., and Crooks, E., 2018. *Opec Strikes a Deal, CO2 Emissions Rise But Shell Targets Cuts, Historic US Oil Exports and the Positives of Electric Scooters*. [Online] Available at: https://www.ft.com/content/cde85f22-fa97-11e8-8b7c-6fa24bd5409c.

of Saudi Arabia and Russia and, according to the head of the International Energy Agency (IEA), 'completely change the balance of oil markets'.[11]

In the process the Middle East and Africa lost much of its strategic relevance to the USA. But it has not fully achieved energy independence as the law of unintended consequences took its toll. Low energy prices have pushed up domestic demand as consumers flock to gasoline-guzzling sports utility vehicles and consumption of liquid fuels may soon be back to the 2005 peak at 20.8 million barrels of oil a day.[12]

The Potential of Renewable Energy in Africa

Whereas the shale gas revolution in the USA is based on a large oil and gas industrial ecosystem that is still difficult to replicate elsewhere, many other rapid advances in technology such as those linked to renewable sources of energy require a much smaller technology footprint. They could have a significant impact on Africa.

Hydropower, geothermal, solar and wind have the potential to revolutionise electricity access in Africa in a way not dissimilar to fracking in the USA, but with the same result of empowering the local versus those further away. It is coming to Africa in three forms. The first is through distributed local systems using renewables, mostly solar, wind and geothermal. The second is through the improvement and distributed installation of electricity storage systems such as new types of batteries. The third is through new technologies such as harnessing the energy in ocean currents and waste-to-biomass conversion.

In addition to its large hydro schemes, Ethiopia alone has the potential to generate up to 10 gigawatt (GW) of power from its geothermal resources. And then Power Africa, the initiative started under former US president Barack Obama, already supports 15 geothermal projects with 1 GW potential generation capacity. Different to the fluctuating energy supply from wind and solar, ocean currents and geothermal can probably provide near-stable baseload electricity generation comparable to that provided by hydro, coal, oil, gas and nuclear.[13]

---

[11]Sertin, C., 2018. *IEA: US Oil Production Will Equal Saudi Arabia and Russia's Combined Output by 2025*. [Online] Available at: https://www.oilandgasmiddleeast.com/drilling-production/33221-iea-us-oil-production-will-equal-saudi-arabia-and-russias-combined-output-by-2025.

[12]Crooks, E., 2018. *US Energy Independence Is Not the Shining Prize It Seems*. [Online] Available at: https://www.ft.com/content/74a79f22-0442-11e9-99df-6183d3002ee1.

[13]USAID, 2018. *Power Africa 2018: Annual Report*. [Online] Available at: https://www.usaid.gov/sites/default/files/documents/1860/2018-Annual_Report1015_508.pdf. ZLM Project Engineering, The

Data on the share of renewables in global energy supply vary between sources. According to *Global Trends in Renewable Energy Investment*, in 2017, 12% of electricity globally came from clean sources since it does not include large hydroelectric dams.[14] Other estimates are that renewable electricity transmission is around 22% globally, of which 17% is hydropower, about five or six percent is wind, and one or two percent is solar. The share of fossil energy in the global energy mix (oil, coal and gas) has remained at about 80% for the last two decades.[15]

The IFs Current Path forecast points to a plateauing of fossil fuel use in the 2030s followed by a steady decline after 2040, with non-fossil fuel sources overtaking fossil fuels around mid-century and constituting more than 80% of all supply by 2100. Leaving the huge challenge of the environment and climate change aside for the moment (see Chapter 15), this will be a world where electricity for households will likely be provided by individual supply or decentralised micro or mini-grids that are powered by renewables, not from large-scale coal, nuclear or other plants. According to a recent report,[16] at least 19,000 mini-grids installed in 134 countries already provide electricity to about 47 million people, most of whom are in rural areas. It will be a world of potential energy abundance at a time when the lack of electricity is generally considered one of the largest constraints on Africa's development.

In a region with more than 600 million extremely poor people (see Chapter 7 for the associated definitions), electricity is often an unaffordable luxury even where connections exist. The average price for electricity in Africa is about US$0.14 per kilowatt hour (kWh), compared to US$0.04 in South Asia and US$0.07 in East Asia. Some in the industry cite the actual cost of electricity in Africa closer to US$0.20 per kWh, largely due to the high cost of running a backup generator during regular power shortages.[17]

High electricity prices and intermittent supply means that many households in Africa do not even try to access electricity from a central system.

Case for Offshore Energy in KwaZulu-Natal, 26 April 2019, 2018 Draft IRP released by the South African Department of Energy.

[14] Including wind, solar, biomass and waste-to-energy, geothermal, marine and small hydro. Frankfurt School of Finance & Management, 2018. *Global Trends in Renewable Energy Investment 2018*. Frankfurt: Frankfurt School, UNEP Centre & BNEF, p. 11.

[15] Coony, J., Jaffe, A. M., & Lewis, J. I., 2018. *Event: The Future of Renewable Energy*. [Online] Available at: https://www.cfr.org/event/future-renewable-energy.

[16] Solar Power Europe. 2019. Digitalisation & Solar in Emerging Markets, Task Force Report. Available at: https://storage.pardot.com/339321/93833/SolarPower_Europe_Digitalisation_solar_in_emerging_markets.pdf.

[17] Patel, S., 2018. *Power in Africa: Prospects for an Economic Foothold*. [Online] November 2019. Available at: https://www.powermag.com/power-in-africa-prospects-for-an-economic-foothold/, p. 11.

Those homes that have an electricity connection often find the supply inconsistent and cost extremely high. Lack of electricity also acts as a strong disincentive to private investment especially in sectors where a dependable supply is crucial such as cold storage in the distribution of food from farm to consumer to minerals beneficiation and manufacturing.[18] Consider that, in 2018 only about 53% of Africa's population had access to electricity in contrast to about 85% in South Asia and well over 90% in the World except Africa. The rapid electrification of the African continent would improve both human development and economic prospects. Among its obvious many economic benefits, affordable, reliable electricity eliminates the need to use traditional fuels inside the home for cooking and heating—thereby reducing the potential for respiratory ailments—and also allows children to study longer at night.

Currently Africa generates very little electricity. The continent had about 168 GW of installed capacity in 2018, but more than half of this is concentrated in three countries (South Africa, Egypt and Algeria). Together these countries account for only about 15% of the continent's total population. China has about 1770 GW of installed capacity—seven times that of Africa—of which 150 GW is solar with plans to add another 23 GW per year until 2023.[19] At current rates of growth China's installed *solar* capacity will shortly equal Africa's *total* installed capacity.

However, a number of large hydroelectric schemes are currently being built in Africa. For example, Ethiopia is completing the construction of the US$5 billion Grand Ethiopian Renaissance Dam (GERD) on the upper reaches of the Blue Nile close to its border with Sudan. Once completed it will be the third largest hydroelectric facility in the world in terms of installed capacity, capable of generating almost 6.5 GW in peak operating conditions, but threatens livelihoods further downstream in Egypt whose entire population, virtually its survival, is dependent on the waters of the Nile.[20]

---

[18] African Development Bank Group, 2013. *The High Cost of Electricity Generation in Africa*. [Online] Available at: https://www.afdb.org/en/blogs/afdb-championing-inclusive-growth-across-africa/post/the-high-cost-of-electricity-generation-in-africa-11496/.

[19] Hill, J. S., 2018. *China Installs 24.3 Gigawatts of Solar In First Half Of 2018*. [Online] Available at: https://cleantechnica.com/2018/08/06/china-installs-24-3-gigawatts-in-first-half-of-2018/ and Anon., 2018. *China's Installed Capacity Grew by 7.6% in 2017 to Nearly 1800 GW*. [Online] Available at: https://www.enerdata.net/publications/daily-energy-news/chinas-installed-capacity-grew-76-2017-nearly-1800-gw.html.

[20] Ethiopia capitalised on the chaos following the Arab Spring to start construction, and intends to start filling the 74 billion cubic meters reservoir shortly, equivalent to roughly a year-and-a-half's flow of the Blue Nile.

Ethiopia's ambitions are to alleviate its own electricity shortages and to eventually emerge at the hub of a regional distribution network to sell electricity in the larger Horn of Africa.

The potential for hydroelectric power on the Congo River in the Democratic Republic of Congo (DRC) is similarly impressive, equivalent to nearly a quarter of the entire installed capacity of Africa. The DRC has long been promising to start construction on Inga 3, the third of a series of hydroelectric dams connected to the Inga Falls at a cost up to US$18 billion. Inga 3 could produce about 11 GW at full capacity and the full series of dams could eventually yield up to 50 GW at full operating capacity, according to the World Bank.[21]

Inga Falls is the world's largest waterfall by volume, and it is also unique in that the Congo River drops an astonishing 96 meters in less than 15 kilometres along the proposed site of the Grand Inga project. Since the drop is close to the mouth of the river at the Atlantic Ocean, the water volumes are very large. This translates into an incredible power generating capacity compared to most other rivers where such a steep drop is often located much further upstream where water volumes are much lower.

Central Africa's mining sector is particularly interested in the potential of hydroelectric power given the potential to beneficiate its copper and other minerals. But unlike GERD in Ethiopia that has moved very rapidly from planning to construction, the Grand Inga project has been perpetually held back by uncertainty, poor planning, delays, inefficiencies and corruption. And, despite being a priority for several pan-African organisations, like the African Union Development Agency-New Partnership for Africa's Development (AUDA-NEPAD), the Southern African Development Community (SADC) and the East African Power Pool, there has been little tangible progress on the project in a country wracked by chronic instability and poor governance.

It's not as if the need is not there. The DRC is one of the most resource rich countries on earth. It is the leading producer of copper in Africa and contains much of the world's cobalt. In addition to that it has sizeable gold, diamond and other mineral deposits, including the so-called 3TG's—cassiterite (tin), wolfram (tungsten) and coltan (tantalum)—that are infamous for being so-called 'conflict minerals' since they are generally mined in conflict-affected

---

[21] International Rivers, n.d. *Grand Inga Hydroelectric Project: An Overview*. [Online] Available at: https://www.internationalrivers.org/resources/grand-inga-hydroelectric-project-an-overview-3356.

poor countries. Other resource rich countries such as Zambia also suffer from a debilitating electricity shortage.[22]

Wind and solar generation are already having a transformative effect on wellbeing in parts of the continent. Kenya recently finished construction of the Lake Turkana Wind Project, the largest wind project in Africa that is capable of delivering 310 MW (or 17% of Kenya's installed capacity) to the grid. This is small by international standards, but still is more than the installed capacity of several African countries, including Chad and Liberia.[23]

At the same time, Lake Turkana is emblematic of the governance failures that hamper technological adaptation and economic growth on the continent. The wind farm was completed in 2017, but only connected to the grid the following year since the connecting infrastructure, which was the responsibility of the Kenyan government, was not in place in time. In the interim the Kenyan government had to pay royalties in lieu of electricity sales to the investors.[24]

Already global investments in solar capacity outstrip the combined investments in coal, gas and nuclear plants as renewable energy costs plummet. China's impact on global solar markets has been well documented. In 2018 the country accounted for about half of total solar capacity globally but uptake has also been rapid elsewhere, including in developing countries. This growth, fuelled by rapidly falling prices has enabled countries like India, Mexico and Chile to offer electricity from photovoltaic solar (US$0.03 per kWh) at a fraction of the cost of electricity in Africa.

We are only at the start of the solar energy revolution. According to the UN, the greater Sahara, which is one of the most uninhabitable places on the planet, has solar potential equivalent to approximately 13.9 billion kWh/year. In 2016 global electricity consumption was 0.02 billion kWh/year.[25] Only a revolution in electricity storage would be able to unlock some of this potential, but the geostrategic incentives are substantial, such as diluting Europe's increased energy dependence on imported gas from Russia and its

---

[22]Clowes, W., 2018. *Congo to Start $13.9 Billion Hydropower Project This Year*. [Online] Available at: https://www.bloomberg.com/news/articles/2018-06-13/congo-plans-to-start-13-9-billion-hydropower-project-this-year.

[23]Bill, B., & Kimuge, S., 2018. *Lake Turkana Wind Power Project Set to Come on Line by September*. [Online] Available at: https://www.nation.co.ke/business/Lake-Turkana-wind-power-project-set-to-come-/996-4593956-x16b1fz/index.html. Installed capacity in Chad is 130 MW and Liberia 126 MW, according to USAID's Power Africa. USAID, 2018. *Chad Power Africa Fact Sheet*. [Online] Available at: https://www.usaid.gov/powerafrica/chad.

[24]Ibid.

[25]United Nations, 2018. *UN Support Plan for the Sahel: Working Together for a Prosperous and Peaceful Sahel*, New York: s.n.

own limited solar capacity during its winters. Beyond the need for technological innovation the most important impediment is the lack of stability in North Africa.

Solar energy prices have dropped to less than US$0.05 per kWh in some regions, and levelised costs that can now compete with those of electricity generated by burning fossil fuels. In Africa, solar energy could significantly change the overall picture of electricity supply although, without a breakthrough in storage capacity, off-grid renewables do not provide enough thermal energy for cooking and space heating or cooling. Electrifying rural areas would make many other development goals easier to achieve: access to clean water, independent economic activity, the use of electric appliances in general, or access to information via communication technologies.

Once the storage problem has been resolved renewable energy could also fundamentally change the political landscape in many countries, leading to a redistribution of political and economic power as cities become less dependent on central governments. Biomass, biogas and gas from waste from municipal and city dumping sites have large potential in complementing other energy sources.

Off-grid solutions could reach consumers in rural areas without the hefty expense of large coal, oil or gas powered power plants that are linked to the hinterland through massive transmission lines and complex distribution systems. In sub-Saharan Africa roughly 60% of the population live in rural areas. At about 25% the region has by far the lowest rural electrification rate worldwide.

In this context, mini-grids powered by sun and wind that are independent of the larger national grid could provide many opportunities. These technologies can also be deployed much more rapidly than traditional methods of electrification. In fact, in a recent study on the long-term future of Kenya[26] we saw clear evidence of the impact leapfrogging is having on dramatic increases in electricity access when taking renewables into account.

Globally, Bangladesh and Laos are two countries widely cited as having expanded electricity access particularly rapidly. Bangladesh increased access by about 50 percentage points in roughly 20 years, while Laos increased it by approximately 60 percentage points in 25 years. Kenya has moved from about 20% access in 2010 to about 70% in 2018. In other words, Kenya

---

[26]Cilliers, J., Donnenfeld, Z., Kwasi, S., Shah, S. SR., & Welborn, L. 2018. *Shaping the Future: Strategies for Sustainable Development in Kenya*. Pretoria: Institute for Security Studies. [Online] Available at: https://issafrica.org/research/east-africa-report/shaping-the-future-strategies-for-sustainable-development-in-kenya.

achieved similar rate increases to Bangladesh and Laos in about a third of the time.

Remotely deployed renewables are already bringing about major shifts in how Africa will provide electricity to its people. What could really prove to be transformative, allowing cooking, space heating and energy-intensive economic activity is a breakthrough in energy storage technology since the sun does not shine every day or for 24 hours and neither does the wind blow constantly. Consequently, electricity grids that include a large component of renewables have to allow for large redundancies (surplus capacity) to be able to meet demand on a guaranteed basis.

The Challenge of Energy Storage (Power-to-X)

Apart from our dependence on carbon sources of energy, a key challenge remains our inability to store excess energy supply at large scale during periods of relatively high production and low demand so that we can access it during periods of lower energy production and higher demand, or to be able to save up energy for specific energy-intensive applications such as cooking or heating.

There are some systems that do this, for example, the various water storage schemes that use surplus electricity to pump water into an upstream dam when electricity demand is low, so that it can be released to generate surge electricity when demand increases. South Africa, Africa's largest electricity producer and consumer by a substantial margin, has two pumped-storage hydroelectricity schemes, one is at Palmiet near Grabouw in the Western Cape and a second is the Drakensberg Pumped Storage Scheme in KwaZulu-Natal.

Other energy storage technologies include compressed air, efforts to conserve energy for instance by using kinetic rotational energy (using flywheels), thermal storage (such as molten salt) and various types of rechargeable batteries. At the industrial, large-scale level there is a lot of innovation in this field, generally known as 'power-to-X', the ability to convert and store energy and then reconvert it through decoupling of power from the electricity sector for use in other sectors (such as transport or chemicals), possibly using power that has been provided by additional investments in generation. Examples include power-to-chemicals, power-to-fuel, power-to-gas, power-to-heat, power-to-hydrogen, power-to-liquid, power-to-methane, power-to-mobility and power-to-food.

In Africa the leapfrogging potential for energy storage lies in the widespread application of these technologies in a decentralised and dispersed manner. The potential is for individual households, buildings and businesses to manage their own energy production and consumption. In the era of intelligent energy management energy efficiencies are designed into buildings and production processes and rural dwellers will be able to produce their own electricity through renewable systems as part of thousands of mini-grids.

The transition to renewable energy will accelerate dramatically once the challenge of affordable energy storage has been resolved. Huge resources are being poured into this challenge, particularly by vehicle manufacturers such as BYD in China, Volkswagen, Tesla and General Motors. In 2016 Bill Gates also launched the Breakthrough Energy Ventures, a US$1 billion fund for new energy technologies that prioritised investments in energy storage companies, as well as in nuclear fusion power and geothermal systems.[27] It's just a matter of time…

The costs of lithium-ion batteries, which is currently the leading battery technology in large-scale production, have been falling rapidly as the one large production facility after the other comes online and economies of scale come into play.[28]

Battery costs are expected to achieve parity with petrol engines by 2023.[29] Tesla recently announced a new modular energy storage system (the Megapack) and, together with Pacific Gas & Electricity will build an energy storage park in California that will consist of 268 Megapack modular units with a total capacity of 730 MWh. Each Megapack unit can now store 12 times more power than its predecessor, the Powerpack 2, that was launched just two years before, illustrating the rapid progress in battery storage capacity.[30]

Meanwhile, China will soon complete a virtual power plant with a 720 MWh storage capacity that could store unused electricity for four hours.[31]

---

[27] Crooks, E., 2018. *The Year in Energy*. [Online] Available at: https://www.ft.com/content/2b420a2a-06c2-11e9-9fe8-acdb36967cfc.

[28] Bloomberg NEF estimates that the capital costs of a utility-scale lithium-ion storage system will fall by 52% by 2030.

[29] Sanderson, H., 2019. *Hydrogen Power: China Backs Fuel Cell Technology*. [Online] Available at: https://www.ft.com/content/27ccfc90-fa49-11e8-af46-2022a0b02a6c.

[30] Rosane, O., 2020. Tesla, PG&E to Help Build World's Largest Energy Storage Facility in California. Echowatch. 28 February 2020, [Online]. Available at https://www.ecowatch.com/tesla-megapack-2645326345.html?rebelltitem=2#rebelltitem2.

[31] Robitzski, D., 2018. *China Is Building Its First Huge Battery Storage Facility*. [Online] Available at: https://futurism.com/the-byte/china-battery-storage-facility?utm_source=Digest&utm_campaign=c665396d3f-EMAIL_CAMPAIGN_2018_12_27_08_50&utm_medium=email&utm_term=0_03cd0a26cd-c665396d3f-247991121&mc_cid=c665396d3f&mc_eid=09aee6b307.

Progress with smart metering, intelligent management of use and mini-grid solutions are also all powering ahead.[32]

And then there are the massive investments being made in fuel cell technology using hydrogen gas that could emerge as an alternative to batteries. Fuel cell technology has a number of advantages above lithium-ion batteries. The latter require a host of scarce metals such as cobalt, lithium and nickel whereas most fuel cells only require platinum of which there is abundant supply, especially in southern Africa.

China alone spent US$12.4 billion on supporting fuel cell powered vehicles in 2017 and will continue with its massive subsidies until at least 2025 although its subsidies for battery electric vehicles are expected to be phased out five years earlier.

An advantage of fuel cell technology is that surplus electricity can be used during off-peak times to split water through electrolysis to produce hydrogen which can be stored to generate electricity during peak demand or used in off-grid energy applications. This is a particularly useful application of surplus electricity in a country such as China where an estimated 150 GW of renewable energy generating capacity is lost every year because it cannot be integrated into the grid.[33]

Among other things, distributed energy from renewables will facilitate the rapid expansion of communications and the internet.

Mobile Phones and Access to the Internet—A Big Leap for Africa

To date the most ubiquitous example of leapfrogging in many parts of Africa is the use of cellular telephones in areas that don't have fixed telephone lines. This obviates the expense and complication of connecting every telephone to a copper wire connection.

Cellular phones are portable and provide much greater flexibility and productivity than fixed telephones. Cellular phone technology has allowed users to leap over fixed-line technology and opens up all the opportunities of internet access to smartphone users.

When the price of mobile technology fell through the floor—prices dropped by about 40% globally and nearly 60% in Africa in the last five years

---

[32]Crooks, E., 2018. *The Year in Energy*. [Online] Available at: https://www.ft.com/content/2b420a2a-06c2-11e9-9fe8-acdb36967cfc.

[33]Sanderson, H., 2019. *Hydrogen Power: China Backs Fuel Cell Technology*. [Online] Available at: https://www.ft.com/content/27ccfc90-fa49-11e8-af46-2022a0b02a6c.

of the twentieth century alone—so did the demand for costly fixed telephone lines. This led to rapid improvements in the proportion of the population with access to a cell phone without much additional cost to the consumer. It also allowed governments to focus on other priorities.

Africa and South Asia were able to leapfrog over expensive and time-consuming technologies and to achieve a degree of catch up with other parts of the world. Moreover, this mobile network was largely built by the private sector, illustrating the potential of African markets to attract foreign investment under the right conditions. The continuation of these investments would, in time, enable mobile phone and internet access rates in sub-Saharan Africa that would have seemed unthinkable a few decades earlier.

In 2000, fixed telephone lines were still relatively rare in the developing world, with a global access rate of about 16 subscriptions per 100 people. North America led the way with 68 fixed lines per 100 people, followed by Europe at 46 per 100 people. Sub-Saharan Africa meanwhile, had access rates that were significantly lower than other developing regions. People in sub-Saharan Africa were more than 90% less likely to have access to a fixed telephone than people in East Asia or Latin America. That gap continued to widen until about 2005, when there was a clear shift away from fixed phone lines and towards mobile subscriptions.[34]

Sub-Saharan Africa has managed to start closing the gap between itself and the rest of the world in terms of access to telephony since mobile technology became widely available. Young Africans in urban areas are well connected, with about 80% owning their own mobile phone and most using it daily.[35] While more than half of households in Morocco, Mauritius, South Africa and the Seychelles have internet access at home, in Liberia, the DRC, Congo, Guinea-Bissau and Eritrea, that number is less than three percent.[36] Although it still trails the rest of the world in terms of mobile subscriptions, the gap is much narrower now than it was when fixed-line technology dominated the world of personal connectivity, again illustrating how modern technology allows countries to leapfrog.

Although only about half of Africans own a mobile phone, another 15–20% who do not own a mobile phone have access to one, making the mobile phone access rate about 65–70%. A strange paradox arises from this in that

---

[34] Europe and Central Asia was excluded from Fig. 10.1 because their significantly higher access distorts the trends evident in the less developed regions.
[35] Mo Ibrahim Foundation, 2019. *Africa's Youth: Jobs or Migration?* London: Mo Ibrahim Foundation, p. 75.
[36] Ibid.

more Africans have access to mobile phones than to anything else, such as access to financial services, electricity or improved sanitation.[37]

The world has become significantly more connected over the last 15 years. At the height of demand for fixed telephone lines in East Asia there were little less than one per household using the average household size in 2005. In Latin America it was closer to one out of every two households. Today, there are more than 100 mobile subscriptions per 100 people in East Asia, Latin America and in sub-Saharan Africa.

Cellular phone penetration has specific and increasingly well-documented economic advantages. On average, GDP grows between 0.7 and 1.4% for every 10% increase in fixed lines and an additional 10% penetration of mobile phones increases GDP by around 0.8% per annum.[38] Or, as a special report by *The Economist* put it in 2009, 'adding an extra ten mobile phones per 100 people in a typical developing country boosts growth in GDP per person by 0.8 percentage points'.[39]

This is not only about allowing people to speak and text one another. Among the many studies on the relationship between broadband access and economic growth is one done by Nina Czernich and others.[40] This study worked out what the effect of broadband infrastructure, which enables high-speed internet, is on growth in developed Organization for Economic Cooperation and Development (OECD) countries in 1996–2007. 'We find that a 10 percentage point increase in broadband penetration raised annual per capita growth by 0.9–1.5 percentage points', the authors concluded.

Increased cellular phone penetration guarantees further innovation and additional investment. In 2013, Google unveiled Project Loon, to send a fleet of balloons into the stratosphere to beam internet service to people below. In mid-2018 Loon announced its first partnership with Telkom Kenya, Kenya's third largest telecommunications provider. Other tech giants such as SpaceX, Facebook and SoftBank-backed startup Altaeros all have similar plans involving satellites, drones and blimps respectively.[41]

---

[37] Johnson, O., 2019. *United Nations Economic Commission for Africa Conference of Planning, Economic And Finance Ministers Adebayo Adedeji Lecture 2019*. Marrakech: United Nations Economic Commission for Africa.

[38] http://www.economist.com/node/14483872.

[39] Ibid.

[40] Czernich, N., Falck, O., Kretschmer, T., & Woessmann, L., 2011. Broadband Infrastructure and Economic Growth. *The Economic Journal*, 121(552).

[41] Houser, K., 2018. *Alphabet Will Bring Its Balloon Powered Internet to Kenya*. [Online] Available at: https://futurism.com/the-byte/balloon-powered-internet-alphabet-kenya.

M-Pesa and Innovation in Mobile Banking

Not only does cell phone and internet technology rapidly expand communication and information, it also spawns new innovations.

It is notoriously difficult to obtain credit in Africa, even for qualified borrowers, in part because currencies and markets are so vulnerable, but also because many institutions lack the capacity or resources to run large-scale lending operations. An example of one such innovation in banking is M-Pesa (pesa means money in Kiswahili, widely spoken in East Africa).

M-Pesa is a mobile money service that was launched in 2007 by Vodafone for Safaricom (Kenya) and Vodacom (Tanzania), the largest mobile network operators in their respective countries. It allows users to store and exchange money on their mobile phones. Today there are 37 million active users across ten countries and the service processes more than eleven billion individual transactions per annum.[42] Its success has created an entire mobile banking industry.

Even more impressive than these figures, though, has been the impact of the new service on people's livelihoods. A 2016 study by Tavneet Suri and William Jack from the Massachusetts Institute of Technology[43] estimates that M-Pesa has lifted nearly 200,000 households out of poverty since its inception and that number would have increased substantially thereafter. The improvements were more significant for female headed-households and helped about 185,000 move from agriculture to some other business venture. Access to mobile money helped borrowers navigate uncertainties caused by drought, adverse health conditions or other unforeseen events.[44]

The mobile money service also drove an increase in savings rates of more than 20%, because the more secure method of storing money instills confidence in people that the future is worth investing in.[45] Sub-Saharan Africa is responsible for almost half of mobile money activity in the world valued at almost US$30 billion in 2018 and Africa today has more mobile money subscribers than any other region in the world.[46]

---

[42] What is M-Pesa, [Online] https://www.vodafone.com/what-we-do/services/M-Pesa.
[43] Suri, T., & Jack, W., 2016. The Long-run Poverty and Gender Impacts of Mobile Money. *Science*, 354(6317), pp. 1288–1292.
[44] Leke, A., Chironga, M., & Desvaux, G., 2018. *Africa's Business Revolution: How to Succeed in the World's Next Big Growth Market*. Brighton: Harvard Business School Press.
[45] Ibid.
[46] Jalakasi, W., 2019. After Years of Rapid Growth in Africa We're About to Enter the Age of Mobile Money 2.0, Quartz Africa, October 4, 2019. [Online] Available at: https://qz.com/africa/1721818/africa-mobile-money-industry-is-entering-its-next-stage-of-growth/.

Mobile Phones and Social Change

Beyond their direct impact on economic growth and prosperity, internet access and mobile phones have also become tools for social transformation. It allows small-scale farmers to link up with markets, citizens can report and videos of instances of the abuse of state power; election officials and observers can document and report results instantaneously and citizens can identify crime incidents. For example, shoppers in Dubai regularly posted photographs on the internet of the latest luxury purchases by African leaders, including the wife of former President Robert Mugabe of Zimbabwe, Grace. And the alleged money-laundering perpetrated by family relatives and other close associates of Equatorial Guinea's President Teodoro Obiang Nguema Mbasogo has been disseminated to a wide audience.[47]

In today's world it is much more difficult to hide and conceal wrongdoing as the release of thousands of confidential US government and private-sector correspondence by the website Wikileaks proved most dramatically in 2010. In South Africa, whistleblowers released troves of emails that documented the extent to which an Indian family, the Gupta's and their associates, had used former President Jacob Zuma and others in the ruling party to defraud South Africans of hundreds of millions of dollars.

The impact of internet access and mobile phone technology on elections, government accountability and potentially on the spread of democracy has been profound. For example, after no candidate received the required 50% in the first round of presidential elections in Ghana on 7 December 2008, the runoff between former Foreign Minister Nana Akufo-Addo and former Vice President John Atta Mills on 28 December fewer than 31,000 votes separated the winner from the loser (a margin of less than 0.4%, with 73% of registered voters voting). Despite a history of coups and social turbulence in Ghana, the country and the region accepted Mills's victory.

The reason for this was that civil society had been able to harness cellphones and the internet to place 4000 trained election monitors armed with

---

[47]Open Society Justice Initiative, 2010. *Corruption and Its Consequences In Equatorial Guinea.* [Online] Available at: https://www.opensocietyfoundations.org/publications/corruption-and-its-conseq uences-equatorial-guinea. For reports on Mrs Grace Mugabe and her shopping addiction see Martin, G., 2017. Zimbabwe's Grace Mugabe: How Her Addition to Luxury Caused Her Fall From Power. *Forbes* [Online] Available at: https://www.forbes.com/sites/guymartin/2017/11/18/zimbabwes-grace-mugabe-how-her-addiction-to-luxury-caused-her-fall-from-power/#2c7bc0ecd8e2.

mobile phones and an SMS-based coding system to check, report and tabulate results. In this manner a parallel civil society system could verify official tallies and ensure a credible result.[48]

This pattern has been emulated in various forms across the continent, reducing the ability of incumbents and special interest groups to manipulate and distort results to their own advantage—although not always successfully so.

The story of transformation thanks to the internet is likely only starting. The next generation of 5G networks will have almost no delay, be at least a hundred times faster than current networks, allow driverless cars to make decisions through the cloud, allow medical robots to become more common and doctors to perform more complex operations remotely. In Africa 5G is likely to first come to South Africa with a commercial service available in 2020.[49]

At the time of writing the COVID-19 pandemic is giving the digital economy a huge boost globally. It has seen businesses and governments move their operations and services online to limit physical interaction and the spread of the virus, given an extraordinarily impetus to digitisation. Collaboration tools such as Microsoft Teams, Skype for Business and Zoom have seen the demand for their products skyrocket as the virus hit and countries adopted lock-down practices to limit the spread of the virus.

Formalising the Informal Sector

Chapter 9 dealt, at some length, with the relationship between the formal and informal sectors and examined the potential benefits that the more rapid formalisation of the informal sector would have on Africa's economic and developmental prospects, using Ghana as an example. For the ILO the transition to formality is 'a central goal in national employment policies'.[50] All things being equal, reducing the size of the informal sector has distinct advantages as long as it does not detract from economic activism, is carefully managed and serves to incentivise employment and does not stunt growth, although, as we saw, it plays an important role in providing employment and incomes for millions of poor Africans.

---

[48] Dugmore, H. The impact of new media on recent sub-Saharan Africa elections (and African Democracy in general), Powerpoint presentation shared with the author on 26 November 2010.
[49] Gilbert, P., 2018. *Rain Will Launch 5G in Early 2019*. [Online] Available at: https://www.itweb.co.za/content/6GxRKqY8n3LMb3Wj.
[50] International Labour Organization, 2018. *Women and Men in the Informal Economy: A Statistical Picture*. Geneva: International Labour Office, p. 3.

The internet, mobile phones and digitisation all allow African governments to break down the barriers between the formal and the informal sectors and facilitate more rapid development. To steadily and incrementally lower the barriers for access to credit and to also monitor and tax (at very, very low levels) all types of services. In this manner it is possible to draw large informal communities into the formal sector—although it is a process that would need to happen incrementally and carefully.

Using the digital economy and modern technology is an unexplored avenue through which to look at the potential of leapfrogging and increasing government capacity and more rapid economic growth.[51] Normally, as GDP per capita increases, the size of the informal sector decreases, or put differently, the informal sector gradually 'formalises', reflected graphically in Fig. 9.3 in the previous chapter. This is positive because workers in the formal sector in African countries are four to five times more productive than those in the informal sector.[52]

The provision of digital identification, for example, unlocks access to banking, government benefits, education and other critical services. In the words of a recent study on digital ID and payment, digital technology enables 'the precise identification of all parties to an interaction; low-cost communications; and accurate, accountable, and convenient payment processes'.[53] A study of seven focus countries (Brazil, China, Ethiopia, India, Nigeria, the United Kingdom and the USA) by McKinsey found that, extending full digital ID coverage to citizens could unlock economic value equivalent to 3–13% of GDP in 2030—if the digital ID program enables multiple high-value use cases and attains high levels of usage.[54]

In the scenario that follows I include that as a powerful component of leapfrogging.

---

[51] See Gelb, A., Mukherjee, A., & Navis, K., 2020. Citizens and States: How Can Digital ID and Payments Improve State Capacity and Effectiveness? Center for Global Development, 31 March 2020. Available at https://www.cgdev.org/publication/citizens-and-states-how-can-digital-id-and-payments-improve-state-capacity.

[52] International Monetary Fund, 2017. *Chart of the Week: The Potential for Growth and Africa's Informal Economy*. [Online] Available at: https://blogs.imf.org/2017/08/08/chart-of-the-week-the-potential-for-growth-and-africas-informal-economy/.

[53] Gelb, A., Mukherjee, A., & Navis, K., 2020. Citizens and States: How Can Digital ID and Payments Improve State Capacity and Effectiveness? Center for Global Development, 31 March 2020, Executive Summary. Available at https://www.cgdev.org/publication/citizens-and-states-how-can-digital-id-and-payments-improve-state-capacity.

[54] The average potential for improvements for emerging economies is, according to them, roughly 6% of GDP in 2030. McKinsey Global Institute, 2019. *The Value of Digital ID for the Global Economy and Society*. [Online] Available at: https://www.mckinsey.com/featured-insights/innovation-and-growth/the-value-of-digital-id-for-the-global-economy-and-society.

Modelling the Impact of Improved Electricity Access, ICT and Digitisation: The Leapfrogging Scenario

The Leapfrogging scenario presented in this section illustrates the impact of African governments taking maximum benefit from the potential of new technologies and the digital economy to extract the maximum development benefits for their societies.

The first set of interventions emulates a more rapid transition to an energy solution that includes more solar, wind and much better energy storage that is then used in intelligent power systems in decentralised micro, mini and off-grid solutions. To model such a scenario I first reduce the capital cost-to-output ratio for renewables, implying even more rapid technological progress than the forecast within IFs.[55] A second, less impactful intervention, reduces electricity transmission losses because of high-voltage direct current transmission technology.[56]

The second set of interventions is faster rollout of mobile broadband and general improvement in ICT. In spite of rapid uptake, Africa trails significantly behind others in this regard.

In a third set of interventions I emulate the impact that digitisation and modern technology could have on more rapidly formalising the informal sector, building on the example of Ghana in Chapter 9, but doing it a bit slower at the continental level than the scenario used there.[57]

Two final interventions modestly improve the effectiveness of African governments, using the World Bank index of Governance Effectiveness[58] and increase levels of economic freedom, using the Fraser Institute Index of

---

[55]The intervention lowers the capital to output ratio for renewables by 30% between 2020 and 2040.

[56]The intervention lowers electricity transmission loss by 15% from 2020 to 2030. According to *The Economist*, 2017. *China's Embrace of a New Electricity-transmission Technology Holds Lessons for Others*. [Online] Available at: https://www.economist.com/leaders/2017/01/14/chinas-embrace-of-a-new-electricity-transmission-technology-holds-lessons-for-others. China is rolling out ultra-high-voltage direct-current transmission technology on a large scale. Liu, Z., 2015. Ultra-High Voltage AC/DC Grids. Amsterdam: Elsevier Inc. *The Economist*, 2017. Electricity Now Flows Across Continents, Courtesy of Direct Current. [Online] Available at: https://www.economist.com/science-and-technology/2017/01/14/electricity-now-flows-across-continents-courtesy-of-direct-current.

[57]The interventions reduce the size of the informal sector as percent of GDP by 14% and the informal labour share by 14% by 2040.

[58]Government Effectiveness captures perceptions of the quality of public services, the quality of the civil service and the degree of its independence from political pressures, the quality of policy formulation and implementation, and the credibility of the government's commitment to such policies. See https://datacatalog.worldbank.org/government-effectiveness-estimate-0. The intervention improves government effectiveness by 10% by 2040.

Economic Freedom.[59] On the one hand the impact of digitisation would be to improve the ability of African governments to raise taxes, provide services and oversee regulatory implementation, hence improving effectiveness. On the other hand, benefiting from the opportunities of the digital economy requires providing greater space for small business and entrepreneurship, implying that the exploitation of these opportunities would need to go hand in hand with greater economic freedom.

All of these scenarios imply greater investment in the ICT sector including the need to expand broadband and associated infrastructure. As a result the contribution of the ICT sector to African economies increases by roughly US$23 billion in 2040, although, even then, the ICT sector will constitute less than four percent of the African economy. Imagine what a more aggressive investment and determined government implementation could deliver!

The results are that the average growth rate for Africa for the period 2020–2040 improves from 4.7% in the Current Path to 5.1%, resulting in an African economy that is US$560 billion larger in 2040 than would otherwise be the case. Growth among low-income countries is particularly rapid with the average growth rate increasing with 0.6 percentage points above the Current Path average. The result is a strong increase in GDP per capita, reflected in Fig. 10.1 as the difference between the GDP per capita in 2040 between the Current Path forecast and the Leapfrogging scenario. Figure 10.1 reflects the result of an average increase of almost US$400 per person for Africa's 2.1 billion people.

All countries experience an increase in the size of their economies. Figure 10.2 presents the percentage point difference in each African economy in 2040 in the Leapfrogging scenario compared to the Current Path.

Six countries experience an increase in the size of their economy of more than 20 percentage points (Côte d'Ivoire, Uganda, Ghana, Kenya, Tanzania and Angola). Ethiopia, South Africa, Egypt and Nigeria do even better, with the latter forecast to experience an increase of 112 percentage points. Of course, lots of additional work needs to be done to verify these very large increases, but the forecast does indicate the extent to which leapfrogging can unlock potential. Most increases are generally in the range of one to three percentage points. Because the economies being compared are quite different in size, the actual dollar numbers are much more impressive. For

---

[59] The index measures the degree of economic freedom present in five major areas: [1] Size of Government; [2] Legal System and Security of Property Rights; [3] Sound Money; [4] Freedom to Trade Internationally; [5] Regulation. See https://www.fraserinstitute.org/economic-freedom/approach. The intervention improves economic freedom by 10% by 2040.

Fig. 10.1 Difference in GDP per capita in 2040 between the Leapfrogging Scenario and the Current Path (*Source* Forecast in IFs 7.45 initializing from World Development Indicators)

example, the Nigerian economy will, in 2040, be US$125 billion bigger than in the Current Path. The corresponding figures for Egypt and South Africa are US$80 billion and US$49 billion respectively. In the case of Guinea and Malawi the difference is US$3 billion.

Leapfrogging is not only about improving growth, infrastructure and income. The Leapfrogging scenario will also reduce poverty in Africa. Madagascar, a low-income country, will benefit the most, reducing its 2040 poverty headcount (using US$1.90) by 13 percentage points below the Current Path. São Tomé and Príncipe, a lower-middle-income country, will reduce its poverty headcount (using US$3.20) by five percentage points below the Current Path. Africa's eight upper-middle-income countries do not experience large decreases in poverty. Only South Africa, Algeria and Gabon reduce poverty rates by more than one percentage point compared to the Current Path forecast by 2040 (using US$5.50). The Leapfrogging scenario also slightly reduces inequality.

Conclusion: Harnessing Technology for the Future

Technological innovation and the notion of leapfrogging are imperative to Africa's future. It will shape development on the continent in ways that are almost impossible to anticipate.

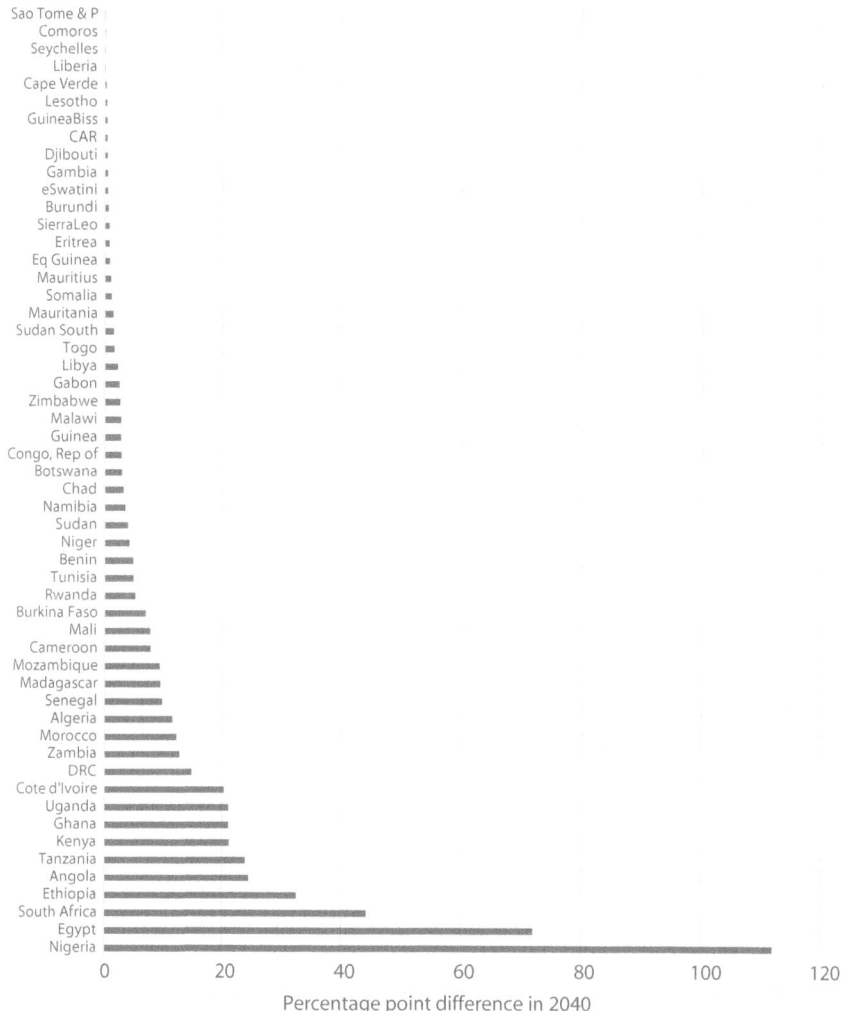

Fig. 10.2 Percentage point difference in size of economy when comparing Leapfrogging Scenario and Current Path in 2040 (*Source* Forecast in IFs 7.45 initializing from the IMF World Economic Outlook 2017)

A wealth of innovation is already available for electricity provision through off-grid solutions using wind and solar that can bring power to remote locations across the continent. Electricity consumption per person in large African countries such as Ethiopia, Kenya and Nigeria is less than one-tenth of that in Brazil or China. In poorer countries like Mali, a typical household uses less electricity in a year than someone in London uses to boil a kettle each day. And nearly 600 million people in sub-Saharan Africa lack access to electricity altogether. Attention is shifting to more intractable solutions such as how to provide water and sanitation services to communities such as those in rural Chad, where 97% of the population—just shy of 5 million people—lacks access to an improved sanitation facility.

Digitisation and the fourth industrial revolution will allow the continent to leapfrog in crucial areas such as energy supply, some aspects of infrastructure and in health among others—but could also leave the continent trailing further behind. Where technological adaptation is inevitable, its impact will be magnified by efficient and open markets, clear and transparent regulatory frameworks and effective governance in the public and private sectors, as well as the ability to bypass or short-circuit established systems.

That is particularly important given the potential environmental impact of the large hydroelectric schemes mentioned earlier that could result in the rerouting of rivers and flooding of valleys and the opportunity cost of developing Africa's biodiversity. Environmental pressure groups have been raising the alarm bell about several proposed hydropower projects in Africa and governments will need to carefully balance environmental sustainability with economic development.

A strong focus on technology can provide leapfrogging opportunities for low and middle-income countries, but governments must not lose sight of 'traditional' developmental issues, such as governance, infrastructure and skills. According to Saadia Zahidi:

> With opportunities for economic leapfrogging, diffusion of innovative ideas across borders and new forms of value creation, the Fourth Industrial Revolution can level the playing field for all economies. But technology is not a silver bullet on its own. Countries must invest in people and institutions to deliver on the promise of technology.[60]

In and of itself technology is, of course, neither good nor bad, and it can be used by criminals, terrorists, governments and the private sector alike to further their interests.

Many areas of leapfrogging are not examined in this chapter, of which health and education are the most important (see Chapters 3 and 6) as well as the potential to use digital technology to enormously increase the ability of states to undertake cash transfers (or provide social grants) to their citizens (see Chapter 7). General improvements in medical science could curb malaria, AIDS, COVID-19, tuberculosis and other diseases that currently ravage large populations in Africa. In the next few decades, the world,

---

[60] von Haldenwang, C., 2018. *T20Argentina: Tax, Investment and Tax Cooperation.* [Online] Available at: https://t20argentina.org/wp-content/uploads/2018/05/GSx-TF-7-Tax_competition-DEF_vf-1.pdf.

including Africa, could move towards dramatic reductions in mortality and morbidity with large implications on population trends.

There is also enormous potential for technology to help fight organised criminal activity on the continent, as game wardens at the Maasai Mara National Park in Kenya and Tanzania have discovered. By using an infrared camera that can detect the body heat of poachers and animals from up to three kilometers away, wardens have been able to significantly deter poaching in the park. In partnership with the World Wildlife Federation (WWF) World Crime Technology Project, the park installed static cameras around the perimeter of the park, along with vehicle mounted roaming cameras to detect activity around the park.

In other parts of Africa, park rangers are using drones to significantly expand their ability to survey parks, at a fraction of the cost of alternative aerial options like airplanes or helicopters. The same technology could eventually be rolled out to monitor remote borders such as those in the Sahel.

Last but not least there are truly globally transformational ideas such as the ambition by Alibaba's Jack Ma from China to establish an Electronic World Trade Platform, or eWTP. What is so interesting is that Ma launched the platform, which is designed to level the playing field for small and medium-sized businesses by allowing them to trade without tariffs and bypass the established systems, in Kigali in Rwanda in October 2018.[61]

Generally, a well-designed digital trade clearance platform could have enormous benefits for regional trade and growth, the topic of the next chapter.

Further Reading

Doug, Vogel, Davison Robert, Harris Roger, and Jones Noel, January 2000. Technology Leapfrogging in Developing Countries-An Inevitable Luxury? TY. https://doi.org/10.1002/j.1681-4835.2000.tb00005.x. Electronic Journal on Information Systems in Developing Countries Jose Goldemberg. Technological Leapfrogging in the Developing World. *Georgetown Journal of International Affairs*, 12(1) (Winter/Spring 2011), pp. 135–141.

United Nations Conference on Trade and Development. December 2018. *Leapfrogging: Look Before You Leap.* Policy Brief No. 71.

---

[61] Grow Global, 2018. *Jack Ma Launches New Global e-trading Platform in Kigali, Rwanda.* [Online] Available at: https://www.growglobal.com/jack-ma-launches-new-global-e-trading-platform-in-kigali-rwanda/.

Open Access This chapter is licensed under the terms of the Creative Commons Attribution 4.0 International License (http://creativecommons.org/licenses/by/4.0/), which permits use, sharing, adaptation, distribution and reproduction in any medium or format, as long as you give appropriate credit to the original author(s) and the source, provide a link to the Creative Commons license and indicate if changes were made.

The images or other third party material in this chapter are included in the chapter's Creative Commons license, unless indicated otherwise in a credit line to the material. If material is not included in the chapter's Creative Commons license and your intended use is not permitted by statutory regulation or exceeds the permitted use, you will need to obtain permission directly from the copyright holder.

11

Trade and Growth

Abstract Cilliers starts by exploring the modern history of international trade and the importance of trade to economic growth and global cooperation. The chapter then provides an overview of Africa's trading partners, the need for greater regional integration in the continent and the challenges to achieving intra-regional cooperation. It examines the need to improve the quality of governance, bridge the infrastructure deficit and eventually focus on a manufacturing-led growth path. Reducing both tariff and non-tariff barriers could facilitate the successful implementation of African Continental Free Trade Area (AfCFTA), induce economic growth, increase per capita incomes and reduce poverty. A penultimate section models the potential impact of the AfCFTA on growth, poverty reduction and increased average incomes.

Keywords Trade · Globalisation · Multilateralism · Tariffs · Regional integration · Preferential access · Economic partnership agreements · Technology · Infrastructure

Learning Objectives

- Understand why countries trade- the benefits and challenges of cooperation in trade.
- Internalise the basic conditions Africa needs to meet to promote trade and greater intra-regional trade in the continent
- Understand why Africa needs to go up the production curve towards high-end manufacturing to promote economic growth.

Trade and globalisation are often associated with neoliberal economics that is generally lambasted in much of Africa in the belief that it is solely aimed at rewarding US-style capitalism and those that sit at the pinnacle of the free-market system. But for all its shortcomings, trade and globalisation have made an immense contribution to humanity's current levels of unprecedented prosperity and human development.

The reasons for the hostility towards neoliberalism if not hard to fathom for the first wave of globalisation and expanding trade in the modern world was substantially fuelled by colonialism and the associated flows of goods from India, Africa and elsewhere to Europe. It peaked in the years immediately before the First World War at level of 11–12% total value of exports as a share of global gross domestic product (GDP) before crashing down during the Great Depression of the 1930s and the Second World War to bottom out at four percent of GDP. The second, much longer wave, started in 1945 during which the world experienced unprecedented improvements in general wealth, health and wellbeing.[1]

The value of exports as a share of GDP rapidly advanced during the intervening years, from below five percent in 1945 to 9% in 1960, 15% in 1990 and to its recent peak, in 2008, at around 26% before subsequent declines to about 21% of global GDP in the wake of the 2007–2008 financial contraction. Another contraction, this time due to the impact of COVID-19, is currently in full swing but its impact, depth and duration is currently unsure. Pre-COVID-19 trade volumes were 40 times larger than at the end of the first wave of globalisation in 1913.[2]

The post-1945 wave of globalisation and the associated growth in trade was enabled by advances in technology such as commercial civil aviation, modern communication and improvements in shipping.[3] There was also no war between the core states that lay at the heart of the bipolar system, such as between the USA and the former Union of Soviet Socialist Republics (USSR), although a number of proxy conflicts were fought in Asia and Africa which is a second reason why many Africans react to negatively at any mention of globalisation. Generally few outside of Africa fully comprehend the intensity of the proxy wars fought in the Horn of Africa and in Angola during this period. In addition, China's rapid integration into the global economy, including its eventual admission into the WTO in 2001, the impact of

---

[1] Ortiz-Ospina, E., Beltekian, E., & Roser, M. Trade and Globalization, 2018, Our World in Data, October 2018. [Online] Available at: https://ourworldindata.org/trade-and-globalization#trade-from-a-historical-perspective.

[2] Ibid. The rates within IFs, calculated from the IMF World Economic Outlook 2017, World Bank and OECD national accounts data, is consistently about five percentage points lower.

[3] Ibid.

the single European market and the opening up of the Russian and Indian economies also boosted trade.

As trade expanded, it had a significant positive impact on growth, although the exact impact on wages, household incomes and poverty necessarily differ from country to country and sector by sector. Generally the growth in trade is driven by trade liberalisation with the result that much of the increase in trade is believed to be the result of the reduction in average tariffs from around 22% of value during the 1940s to below five percent by the time that the WTO was established.[4]

The extent to which globalisation has led to a race to the bottom in terms of the location of factories in locations where labour costs are low, resulting in sweatshop practices in developing countries, is often cited in mainstream media and is a third reason for the general negative views about globalisation in Africa.

But the most important reason for a general hostility towards neoliberalism is undoubtedly the impact of the structural adjustment programmes that the World Bank and International Monetary Fund foisted on Africa during the 1980s and 1990s, as discussed in Chapter 2. Government was bad and the private sector was the answer to all of Africa's manifold challenges, Africans were told in a charge led by the World Bank and the International Monetary Fund.

None of these perceptions substantively question the contribution that more trade has made to improvements in livelihoods, although all point to the extent to which Africa has not benefited. As I examine below, this could change in the future.

From GATT to the Decline of Multilateralism

A significant development to advance trade was the General Agreement on Tariffs and Trade (GATT) that was signed by 23 countries in Geneva in 1947. The international community undertook a series of subsequent negotiations to expand and broaden the impact of trade, but much of that was to the benefit of established trading nations. Eventually, at the conclusion of the so-called Uruguay Round of negotiations in 1994, WTO members agreed that the next round of negotiations, the Doha or development round would look

---

[4] Ortiz-Ospina, E., 2018. *Does Trade Cause Growth?* [Online] Available at: https://ourworldindata.org/trade-and-econ-growth. Also Ortiz-Ospina, E., 2017. *Is Globalization an Engine of Economic Development?* [Online] Available at: https://ourworldindata.org/is-globalization-an-engine-of-economic-development.

towards the needs of poorer, developing countries. That would occur under the auspices of the World Trade Organization (WTO) established to update and institutionalise GATT.[5]

That never materialised, for although the Doha Round commenced in 2001 it has not been concluded and the focus has shifted away from global arrangements. In fact, in the decades since the Uruguay Round of negotiations that established the WTO, its only success was the conclusion of the Trade Facilitation Agreement that entered into force in 2017.[6] Under Donald Trump's presidency the future of the WTO has come under threat as economic nationalism and populist protectionism in the USA ran its course. The WTO's Appellate Body—the final arbiter on trade disputes, was, for example, no longer operational by mid-2020 when the USA has blocked the appointment of new judges to restore its quorum. Without a dispute resolution mechanism the entire global trade regime is at risk but it is probably too early to speculate on the demise of the WTO given the incoming Biden presidency and ongoing behind the scenes discussions and negotiations.

With the rules-based trading system in a mess, the trend in recent years has been towards regional agreements and the emergence of so-called plurilateral negotiating structures that allow some countries to agree on specific issues beyond WTO rules but that are insufficiently inclusive to be called multilateral agreements. Examples include the Comprehensive and Progressive Agreement for Trans-Pacific Partnership (CPTPP) that came into effect in December 2018 and the conclusion of negotiations among Asia-Pacific countries on the Regional Comprehensive Partnership (RCEP) that will, once ratified, be the largest trade agreement globally by value.[7] I also remarked on this trend towards regionalisation in discussing the potential of Africa to industrialise (Chapter 8) since the impact of digitisation and the fourth industrial revolution is to slowly shift considerations about the location of manufacturing towards the consumer, including in Africa.

---

[5] In 1995 when 124 countries agreed to the Marrakesh Agreement. Ibid.

[6] TFA contains provisions for expediting the movement, release and clearance of goods, including goods in transit. It also sets out measures for effective cooperation between customs and other appropriate authorities on trade facilitation and customs compliance issues. It further contains provisions for technical assistance and capacity building in this area. See WTO, Trade facilitation at https://www.wto.org/english/tratop_e/tradfa_e/tradfa_e.htm.

[7] The CPTPP was signed between 11 countries, including Canada, Australia, Vietnam and Japan but excludes the USA and China. The RCEP is an agreement between the ten member states of the Association of Southeast Asian Nations (ASEAN) and the six Asia-Pacific states and would therefore include China, India and Japan.

The Impact of Preferential Access: Everything But Arms and AGOA

Even before the final Doha impasse, a number of efforts have been made to assist the integration of developing countries into the global economy and to unlock the potential inherent in export-driven growth—largely by granting Least Developed Countries 'special and differential treatment'.[8] Typically these agreements provide greater access to the large domestic markets most especially those of the European Union and the USA.

The legal basis for these trade preferences is the Generalized System of Preferences (GSP) that provided for exemption on the basis of a list of criteria such as per capita gross national income and economic vulnerability to external shocks.[9] The two most important ones that relate to Africa are the EU's Everything But Arms initiative and the US's African Growth and Opportunity Act (AGOA).[10]

In the case of the EU cooperation between the Union and the 79 member group of African, Caribbean and Pacific countries dates from the 1975 Lomé Convention. After three revisions the Lomé Convention was replaced in June 2000 by the more expansive Cotonou Agreement, named after Benin's capital city where it was signed. The Cotonou Agreement gives a stronger political foundation to EU-ACP cooperation and includes matters such as good governance, peace and security, arms trade and migration. Most important is that Cotonou replaces the previous system of non-reciprocal trade preferences to ACP countries with reciprocal Economic Partnership Agreements (EPAs). Aid is steadily being replaced with an emphasis on trade.

Today the EU has a comprehensive and progressive trade dispensation consisting of several layers. The first and most important is the Everything But Arms initiative (still from the Lomé Convention) that was introduced in 2001. It grants Least Developed Countries duty and quota-free access to the EU single market for almost all their exports except arms and armaments. It is also the most extensive. Currently 22 of Africa's low and lower-middle-income countries benefit from Everything But Arms. Countries in Northern

---

[8] The Decision on Differential and More Favorable Treatment, Reciprocity and Fuller Participation of Developing Countries—called the Enabling Clause in trade jargon—was adopted under the Tokyo round of the GATT in 1979.

[9] The principle of a GSP was agreed on at the UN World Trade Conference (UNCTAD ll) in 1968 as a non-reciprocal facility that countries such as the European Union and the US bestow on least developed countries. The former European Community first introduced a non-reciprocal scheme for developing countries in 1971 followed by the US in 1976.

[10] Trade under AGOA quadrupled in value from 2002 to 2008, a year when it reached $100bn, but fell back in 2017 to $39bn, according to figures compiled by the US Agency for International Development (USAID).

Africa and South Africa are generally excluded since none have Least Development Country status. The scheme has no expiry date and it includes access for processed agricultural products, as well as textiles.[11]

The next level in the EU layer is the so-called 'Standard GSP' that applies to low and lower-middle-income countries. The Standard GSP reduces EU import duties for about two-thirds of all product tariff lines and currently applies to Kenya and Nigeria. Then Cape Verde is currently the only African country that benefits from GSP Plus which is a special incentive arrangement for sustainable development and good governance that further slashes tariffs when countries implement 27 international conventions related to human rights, labour protection, protection of the environment and good governance.[12]

However, as the EU concluded trade agreements with other developing countries and lowered its tariffs from them, the preferences granted to Africa inevitably eroded, a problem also evident with AGOA.[13]

Different to Everything But Arms, the EPA's are not unilateral concessions by the EU. They also go beyond conventional free-trade agreements to include sustainable development and poverty reduction goals. They are, however, controversial for two reasons. First is that they include explicit language on human rights, democratic principles, the rule of law, and good governance that are, of course, resisted by countries that do not meet these requirements. Second, in addition to the advantages that an EPA member would have in trade with the EU, each EPA provides that countries in the same region (such as West Africa) provide at least the same advantages to each other as they do to the EU as an incentive to grow regional trade. Future trade agreements between ACP countries or with other developing countries will automatically also apply to the EU, granting the latter 'most favoured' nation status.[14]

Progress with EPA's has, however, been slow amidst concerns that the EPAs may actually be detrimental to expanding intra-African trade. The requirement to provide the EU with most favoured nation status as part of EPAs is of particular concern. Moreover, some national governments now baulk at the realisation that the agreements would initially reduce tariff

---

[11] European Commission, *List of GSP Beneficiary Countries (as of 01 January 2019)* [Online] Available at: https://trade.ec.europa.eu/doclib/docs/2019/may/tradoc_157889.pdf.

[12] European Commission, *Generalized Scheme of Preferences (GSP)* [Online]. Available at: http://ec.europa.eu/trade/policy/countries-and-regions/development/generalised-scheme-of-preferences/.

[13] Schmieg, E., *2019. EU and Africa: Investment, Trade, Development*, Berlin: Stiftung Wissenschaft und Politik.

[14] European Commission, 2018. Economic Partnership Agreements (EPAs) September 2018 [Online] Available at: https://trade.ec.europa.eu/doclib/docs/2017/february/tradoc_155300.pdf.

revenues from trade with neighbouring countries—a challenge that will also face these countries under the proposed African Continental Free Trade Area (AfCFTA).[15]

As opposed to Everything But Arms, AGOA is based on progress in meeting criteria such as the establishment of a market-based economy, adherence to the rule of law, elimination of barriers to US trade, and investment and protection of workers' rights.

The US Congress approved the African Growth and Opportunity Act in May 2000 and after its initial 15 years it was extended for ten years to 2025. AGOA provides tariff-free access on 6500 products to 39 countries ranging from oil and agricultural goods to textiles and handicrafts. Congress determines annually which countries qualify for AGOA benefits.

Before the shale revolution discussed in Chapter 10 (as part of Africa's potential to leapfrog), the US/Africa trade surplus was historically in Africa's favour because of oil or petroleum-based exports from countries such as Angola and Nigeria. In the wake of the shale revolution the USA has largely lost economic interest in Africa except as an arena to assist in confronting Islamic terror and to compete with China. As discussed in Chapter 14, the USA remains the largest bilateral provider of aid.

Among others, AGOA allowed duty-free entry of apparel into the US market. As a result, apparel exports from a handful of African countries to the USA increased rapidly but the limits of unilateral arrangements such as AGOA soon became evident when the advantage started eroding from 2005 when quota restrictions on apparel from China and other Asian countries were phased out.[16]

AGOA and Everything But Arms are not trade agreements negotiated between two partners, but a unilateral concession made by one party (the USA or the EU) for the benefit of another (developing countries that meet certain minimum criteria). It implies temporary relief that can be revoked at any point, i.e. goods may be taken off the eligibility list or the entire

---

[15] Mevel, S., Valensisi, G., & Karingi, S., 2015. *The Economic Partnership Agreements and Africa's Integration and Transformation Agenda: The Cases of West Africa and Eastern and Southern Africa regions*. [Online] Available at: https://www.gtap.agecon.purdue.edu/resources/download/7649.pdf.

[16] In terms of the WTO's Agreement on Textiles and Clothing. Fernandes, A. M., Maemir, H., Mattoo, A., & Rojas, A. F., 2018. *Are Trade Preferences a Panacea? AGOA and African Exports*. Kigali, pp. 4, 21–22. Before the agreement took effect a large portion of textiles and clothing exports from developing countries to developed countries was subject to quotas under a special regime outside of normal GATT rules. Under the agreement, WTO Members committed to remove the quotas by 1 January 2005 by integrating the sector fully into GATT rules. See World Trade Organization, n.d. *Textiles Monitoring Body (TMB) The Agreement on Textiles and Clothing*. [Online] Available at: https://www.wto.org/english/tratop_e/texti_e/texintro_e.htm.

arrangement can be cancelled, meaning that the beneficiary countries have no recourse to remedies or dispute resolution.

Although it appears as if preferential access does improve access to say the American or European market, it is much less clear whether these improvements result in lasting improvements in export performance once countries exit from preferential access. Like aid (discussed in Chapter 14), these types of concessions have a limited effect if not accompanied by vigorous domestic reform.

Lasting trade progress requires that preferential access should be complemented by domestic reforms like improved access to imported inputs through reduction of tariffs, a lighter regulatory burden and enhanced access to infrastructure (such as through the creation of effective special economic zones) and flexible exchange rate regimes that lead to competitive exchange rates.[17]

While Europe and the USA have therefore made various efforts to improve trade with Africa, today China is Africa's largest single bilateral trading partner and speed at which this has occurred is truly amazing.

Africa's Shifting Trade Relations with the Rest of the World

In 1970, Europe represented nearly 70% of Africa's total trade with its share declining to about 45% by 2014 as Africa's trade with emerging markets improved. Africa's trade with North America has also declined significantly, falling from a peak of nearly 30% of total trade in the late 1970s to roughly seven percent of total trade in 2014. By 2018 the EU-28 is responsible for 36% of Africa's exports and 33% of imports. Whereas Africa's trade with the USA quadrupled in value from 2002 to US$100 billion in 2008 it fell back to just US$39 billion in 2017.[18] In 2018 only 7% of Africa's exports and 5% of Africa's imports are with the USA. By contrast African trade with countries and regions considered to be in the Global South has steadily increased over the last four decades, particularly with China.[19]

Today China is Africa's largest single country-trading partner in both exports and imports, at 9 and 13% respectively. So considerably less than

---

[17] Fernandes, A. M., Maemir, H., Mattoo, A., & Rojas, A. F., 2018. *Are Trade Preferences a Panacea? AGOA and African Exports.* Kigali, pp. 41–42.

[18] US-African trade lagging despite free access 8 August 2019. https://agoa.info/news/article/15638-us-african-trade-lagging-despite-free-access.html.

[19] Analysis based on COMTRADE data.

Africa's trade with the EU-28.[20] As China and India rise, they are dragging Africa along with them, for the continent has been able to maintain its relative trade position with both, but with an increased commodities content as opposed to higher value goods and services.[21] Soon Africa will be trading the majority of its goods with non-western partners and its political orientation will inevitably follow those shifts in economic power and influence.

China–Africa bilateral trade steadily increased from US$10 billion in 2000 to US$222 billion in 2014 before contracting in 2015 as the Chinese economy rebalanced and became less dependent upon commodity imports for growth. Crude oil, minerals ores, tobacco and wood contribute over 90% of China's imports from Africa, which is in sharp contrast to its more diversified export profile to Africa largely consisting of value-added goods with an ever widening trade imbalance in China's favour.[22]

Then, from 2017 to 2018, trade between Africa and China expanded by 20% from US$170 billion to US$205 billion, Standard Bank forecasts that bilateral trade should surpass US$300 billion in the next three to five years, but the associated widening trade imbalance that started in 2015 could be unsustainable and the impact of COVID-19 is sure to see a sharp reversal of trade flows at least in 2020 and 2021.[23] Before COVID-19 more than forty African countries ran a trade deficit with China. That of Kenya was particularly large. The largest volume of China-Africa trade is with South Africa—also the largest African investor in China—while trade with the DRC, Mozambique and Zambia was growing most rapidly before the virus struck[24] (Fig. 11.1).

Perhaps even more important than total trade is its composition. The share of manufacturing in total African exports was close to 30% two decades ago

---

[20]Prior to Brexit the EU accounted for 38% of Africa's exports and 37% of its imports in 2017. China follows with 14% of exports and 19% of imports. Eurostat, 2018. *Africa-EU—International Trade in Goods Statistics*. [Online] Available at: https://ec.europa.eu/eurostat/statistics-explained/index.php/Africa-EU_-_international_trade_in_goods_statistics#Africa.E2.80.99s_main_trade_in_goods_partner_is_the_EU.

[21]Freemantle, S., & Stevens, J., Placing the BRIC and Africa commercial partnership in a global perspective, Standard Bank, 19 May 2010, pp. 2, 6–7.

[22]Mureverwi, B., July 2016. TRALAC, China-Africa Trading Relationship. https://www.tralac.org/resources/our-resources/9174-china-africa-trading-relationship.html.

[23]Stevens, J., 16 January 2019. China-Africa Trade Expanded by 20% in 2018. *Inside China*, Standard Bank [Online] Available at: https://ws15.standardbank.co.za/ResearchPortal/Report?YYY2162_FISRqWkWXsic7FKgCjGcLn4JFQVBznDhsEVWcAqZhonSBCWKRZHtiYtASPMgyIUm/xoiITm+eZxvGcE6UxHkpQ==&a=-1.

[24]Wenjun, C., 2018. *Twenty Years on, China-SA Relations Embrace a New Chapter*. [Online] Available at: https://www.businesslive.co.za/bd/world/asia/2018-09-25-twenty-years-on-china-sa-relations-embrace-a-new-chapter/.

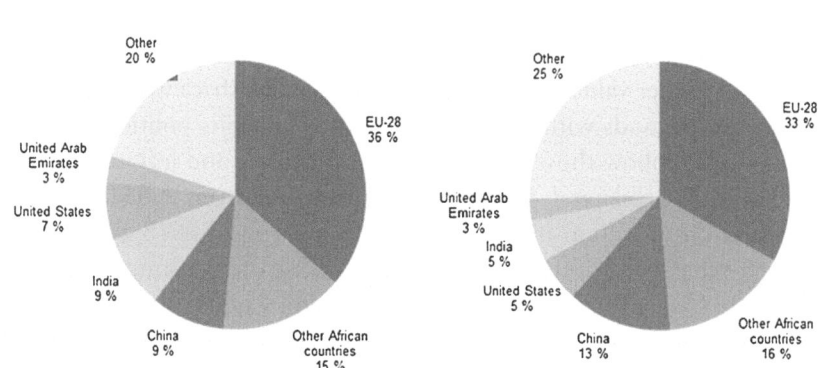

Fig. 11.1 African export and import share with main partners, 2018 (*Source* UNCTAD)

but it has declined for several years before again increasing when the COVID-19 pandemic hit. Generally the value of commodity exports has increased in line with the commodities supercycle that was discussed in Chapter 2.[25] Africa's trade with the EU is, however, more balanced than with other regions but even here the lack of value-add is glaring. The continent 'only' imported 70% manufactured goods from the EU in 2018 while its exports comprised 65% primary goods consisting of food and drink, raw materials and energy.[26]

After recovering from the global financial crisis in 2008, the share of manufacturing as a portion of Africa's trade again increased from 2012 to around 27% by 2016. However, apart from Senegal and Togo, the share that manufacturing represents in total exports has again declined recently, including from countries such as Botswana, South Africa, Madagascar and Namibia that have a relatively high share of manufactured exports.[27]

It is obvious that in spite of African countries benefiting from the various preferential trading agreements such as AGOA and Anything But Arms, preferential market access has not led to a stronger export performance or to more

---

[25] Fernandes, A. M., Maemir, H., Mattoo, A., & Rojas, A. F., 2018. Are Trade Preferences a Panacea? AGOA and African Exports. Kigali, p. 20.

[26] Most European trade is with North Africa, with Spain, France, Italy and Germany being the top four countries trading with Africa. Eurostat, 2018. *Africa-EU—International Trade in Goods Statistics*. [Online] Available at: https://ec.europa.eu/eurostat/statistics-explained/index.php/Africa-EU_-_international_trade_in_goods_statistics.

[27] Fernandes, A. M., Maemir, H., Mattoo, A., & Rojas, A. F., 2018. Are Trade Preferences a Panacea? AGOA and African Exports. Kigali, pp. 17–18.

diversified economies. Rather, other factors such as the demand for commodities from China dominate. Andrew Mold from UN Economic Commission for Africa argues that there are three reasons for this state of affairs:

> The design of those preferential agreements is partly to blame, with strict rules of origin and unnecessarily tough phytosanitary and product standards. In addition, African firms have displayed a lacklustre response to the opportunities. However, the Achilles heel of these agreements has been their impermanence – they are concessional and can therefore be suspended or simply not renewed (requiring as they do a special dispensation through the World Trade Organisation).[28]

The power of geography is particularly strong when it comes to trade. Typically countries trade more with their neighbours rather than with countries that are further away. As a result the natural market of North African countries inevitably lies within the Mediterranean basin given the potential that the sea offers to transport high volume goods and that the Sahara desert forms a substantial barrier to the south. Algeria and Egypt, and to a lesser extent Libya, are already significant exporters of liquefied natural gas to primarily European consumers. In addition, initiatives such as the Mediterranean Solar Plan could eventually help the EU to meet its renewable energy pledge as the pressures of climate change mount globally. The plan, launched in July 2008, envisages generating 50–100 GW of solar power generation in North Africa for potential export to Europe. However, it has come to a standstill since the Arab spring uprisings.[29]

The EU envisions a Euro-Mediterranean free trade area with Algeria, Egypt, Israel, Jordan, Libya (negotiations are currently suspended), Morocco, Syria, Tunisia, the Palestinian Authority and Turkey. In 2016 the region represented 9.4% of total EU external trade but progress is hampered by politics, instability and the very low level of intra-regional trade in North Africa.[30] But at some point stability will return to North Africa and its location next to the EU then offers significant potential but likely only if the region can stop its incessant internal bickering.

---

[28] Mold, A., 2018. *The Case for an Integrated African Market—The Costs of 'non-AfCFTA'*. [Online] Available at: https://www.theeastafrican.co.ke/oped/comment/Integrated-African-market--the-costs-of--non-AfCFTA/434750-4709126-3el6hjz/index.html.

[29] Stoffaës, C., 2016. *The Mediterranean Solar*. [Online] Available at: https://www.plansolairemediterraneen.org/.

[30] The Euro-Mediterranean Partnership (previously the Barcelona Process) was relaunched in 2008 as the Union for the Mediterranean.

Intra-African Trade and Efforts at Advancing Regional Integration

Because agriculture is such a large component of Africa's economy—it has hovered at around 18% of Africa's GDP over several decades, Africans are keen on access to agricultural markets in the developed world, particularly Europe. For decades no meeting on trade in Africa would start without reference to the large subsidies cattle farmers in the EU receive and the extent to which agriculture in the EU benefit from domestic subsidies, as well as the regulatory hurdles in Europe that effectively prohibit most agricultural imports.[31] Then there's the massive subsidies for large commercial farmers in the USA, most of which goes to large producers of corn (maize), soybeans, wheat, cotton and rice.[32]

Actually access to agricultural markets outside of Africa has served as an effective lightning rod to divert attention from other, more important matters relating to trade, namely schemes that would incentivise value-added exports, low-end manufacturing and the beneficiation of its vast mineral exports. And above all, Africa has, until recently, done little to increase intra-regional trade, even as regards foodstuffs.

Ironically, given the lack of real progress, the advantages of trade integration in Africa were recognised even before the establishment of the Organization of African Unity (OAU) in 1963, the predecessor to the African Union. The Southern African Customs Union (SACU) is the oldest customs union in the world, having recently celebrated its centenary. SACU was, of course, not originally established as a vehicle for regional integration but to facilitate commercial integration and tax management by Great Britain, who had various colonial territories in Southern Africa under its control. Then came the Southern Rhodesia (today Zimbabwe) Customs Union, established in 1949, and in 1967, the East African Community (EAC).

---

[31] The EU's Common Agricultural Policy (CAP) provides direct payments to European farmers in the form of a 'basic income support'. It is therefore decoupled from production and payments amount to 72% of the EU farming budget. On average, EU farmers receive €267 per eligible hectare and may be eligible for additional sources of funding. This effectively amounts to a blanket subsidy for farming, even in the absence of targeted subsidies for specific product categories. Furthermore, according to the EU website: 'While the rules governing direct payments are set at EU level, their implementation is managed directly by each member state under the principle known as shared management. This means that national authorities are responsible for the administration and control of direct payments to farmers in their country.' Each country also has a certain level of flexibility in the way they grant these payments to take account of national farming conditions, which vary greatly throughout the EU. European Commission, n.d. *The Basic Payment*. [Online] Available at: https://ec.europa.eu/info/food-farming-fisheries/key-policies/common-agricultural-policy/income-support/basic-payment.

[32] Edwards, C., 2018. *Agricultural Subsidies*. [Online] Available at: https://www.downsizinggovernment.org/agriculture/subsidies.

The latter two arrangements eventually failed and were disbanded, although a new effort is being made with the EAC. The impact of these first regional economic communities was limited, although today SACU accounts for more than 50% of the continent's entire intra-regional trade and SADC[33] for approximately 70%.

Later the 1980 Lagos Plan of Action, which was essentially Africa's response to the World Bank's structural adjustment programs, and the Treaty Establishing the African Economic Community of 1991, generally known as the Abuja Treaty, elaborated on the specific economic, political and institutional mechanisms needed to achieve Africa's economic integration.

Neither made much progress but the tradition of grand schemes continued unabated. The African Union Development Agency-New Partnership for Africa's Development (AUDA-NEPAD) provides an overall integration and development framework for the continent, which again assumes regional integration as one of its core objectives. The most recent grand visions are the Agenda 2063. And then there is the African Continental Free Trade Areas or AfCFTA.

In varying degrees these continental schemes view the various subregional economic groupings such as SADC, the EAC and the Economic Community for West African States (ECOWAS) as building blocks towards greater cooperation.

Generally, levels of trade in all of Africa's regions are significantly below that of other regional blocks like the Asia-Pacific Economic Cooperation (APEC) and the European Union.[34] For example, the comparative data of intra-regional trade for 2017 is as follows:

- Intra-Africa trade at 17%
- Europe 68%

---

[33] Although the launch of a SADC free trade area in 2008 was an important stepping stone towards the SADC common market envisaged by 2015 and a common currency by 2018, both goals have been missed by a large margin. In spite of a well-defined socio-economic roadmap with a harmonised and legally binding protocol on trade liberalisation, intra-regional trade in SADC remains low at about 10%. Overall progress towards more economic integration is slow, although there is some movement via other processes such as a regional power pool, transport corridors and integrated payment systems.

[34] A recent IMF study indicates using micro data that combines various macro datasets and variables, purports to show that integration in sub-Saharan Africa is more extensive than generally believed. Most of the increase in integration is through trade in goods, thus following the standard path to development, the report argues. But increasingly sub-Saharan African countries are also linked together through financial flows—whether through remittances sent home by foreign workers or more formally through the cross-border expansions of banks. There is also evidence of other real-economy linkages, through fiscal policy, foreign direct investment and migration flows. See Arizala, F., Bellon, M., MacDonald, M., Mlachila, M., & Yenice, M, Y., 2018. *Trade and Remittances Within Africa.* [Online] Available at: https://blogs.imf.org/2018/08/01/trade-and-remittances-within-africa/.

- Asia 59%
- Americas at 55%[35]

Trade volumes among African states are low in part because governments depend heavily on the income from tariffs. High tariffs serve as an effective tax on trade and invariably reduce trade volumes. Carlos Lopes, a former head of the UN Economic Commission for Africa estimates that 'the majority of businesses on the continent pay an average of 6.9% tax on cross-border transactions. The cost of the transactions, added to the cost of production, has a huge impact, not only on the competitiveness of the businesses but also on the quality of life of consumers'.[36]

Hefty tariffs invariably inhibit trade flows across borders and often also contribute to smuggling and the growth of the shadow economy if borders are not very well policed. Vast amounts of money can be made smuggling items such as petroleum and cigarettes across borders where prices differ substantially between countries. This is particularly characteristic of economies in West Africa, the Sahel, North and in Central Africa.

In fact, when we recently looked at the future of Tunisia[37] we found that its informal and parallel economic sector is substantially larger than the average for other low-middle-income countries when measured as a portion of the total economy. Many Tunisians are forced to engage in the informal sector in spite of their high levels of education; a situation that contributed to the overwhelming frustration that underpinned the Freedom and Dignity revolution that commenced at the end of 2010 and ignited the brief Arab spring that followed. While democracy has flourished post-2010, Tunisia's new political dispensation has not been able to sufficiently displace the opaque insider/outsider economic system that constrains opportunity and forces many into the informal and parallel economy. As a result Tunisia's large informal and parallel economy is more than survivalist and involves considerable illicit activity—a view borne out by a World Bank estimate that about 25% of the fuel consumed in Tunisia has been smuggled from Algeria, where fuel is cheaper.[38]

---

[35] Based on UNCTADstat (https://unctadstat.unctad.org/EN/).

[36] Institute for Security Studies, 2018. *The African Free Trade Area Could be a Reality by March Next Year*. [Online] Available at: https://issafrica.org/pscreport/psc-insights/the-african-free-trade-area-could-be-a-reality-by-march-next-year.

[37] Kwasi, S., Cilliers, J., & Welborn, L. (2020). The Rebirth: Tunisia's Potential Development Pathways to 2040, Institute for Security Studies. Available at: https://issafrica.org/research/north-africa-report/the-rebirth-tunisias-potential-development-pathways-to-2040.

[38] L. Ayadi et al., 2013. Estimating informal Trade Across Tunisia's Land Borders, World Bank, Policy Research Working Paper WPS 6731. https://documents.worldbank.org/curated/en/856231468173645854/Estimating-informal-trade-across-Tunisias-land-borders. Also Quillen, S., 2017 Informal Economy

Much of the informal sector in Tunisia could therefore more appropriately be described as being part of the shadow economy, consisting of black market transactions such as smuggling and undeclared work—a textbook example of what happens when a ruling elite constrains the economy to its own ends.

In addition to the various structural reasons for Africa's poor growth such as a declining demographic dividend until the late 1980s (see Chapter 5), and its role as a proxy battleground during the Cold War, bad governance, poor policy and lack of implementation of agreements all played an important role. Structurally the continent did not develop regional value chains, does not substantively trade among its members and hence did not form part of the global value chains in goods and services that developed between parts of Asia, North America and Europe since the 1990s.

The results are stark with Africa literally not part of the global discussions on trade. Outside of Africa analysis is no longer fixated only on the growth and structural change in individual economies, but rather use the lens of global value chains—the complex network that ties the flows of goods, services, capital and technology together across national borders—to evaluate the strength of economies.

Global value chains continue to evolve and may do so more rapidly following the trade shocks associated with COVID-19. First, goods-producing value chains are becoming less trade-intensive and trade in cross-border services are growing more rapidly than trade in goods. Second, goods-producing value chains are becoming more regionally concentrated, especially within Asia and Europe. Companies are increasingly locating their production facilities in closer proximity to demand. This could, in time, offer advantages to Africa with its rapidly growing population and growing consumer base.[39]

Presents Tunisia with Thorny Issue. *The Arab Weekly*, 30 June 2017. https://thearabweekly.com/informal-economy-presents-tunisia-thorny-issue.

[39]Lund, S., Manyika, J., Woetzel, J., Bughin, J., Krishnan, M., Seong, J., & Mac Muir. 2019. *Globalization in Transition: The Future of Trade and Value Chains*. New York: McKinsey Global Institute, p. 1.

The Need for Connecting Infrastructure—And the Challenge of Non-Tariff Barriers

Organisations like the World Bank, the African Development Bank and the UN Economic Commission for Africa regularly bring out reports that quantify the extent to which Africa's lack of connecting infrastructure such as road and rail between neighbouring countries increases transport costs and creates delays. Poor infrastructure reduces the competitiveness of business and undermines much-needed investment flows.

In some East African countries, for example, transport costs are estimated at about five times more when compared with countries in Europe and North America.[40] The large number of landlocked states means that many, such as Ethiopia, Uganda, Rwanda, Burundi, Lesotho, Swaziland, Zimbabwe, Malawi, Uganda, Burundi, Rwanda and South Sudan, are dependent on their neighbours for access to the sea.

According to the African Development Bank, Africa has an annual infrastructure funding gap of US$130 billion to US$170 billion, with an annual financing gap of US$68 to US$108 billion.[41] The numbers speak for themselves. Africa has an average of 204 kilometres of roads per 1000 km^2 of which only one quarter is paved. That density lags far behind the world average of 944 kilometres per 1000 km^2, of which more than half are paved. Most of the continent's paved roads can also be found in a single country, South Africa.[42]

Anyone who has had to travel around West and Central Africa can testify to the dire need for better connecting infrastructure. Whether by roads, through ports, buses, planes or trains—but still, significantly better than even a few years ago.

For example, the capital city of Cameroon, Yaoundé, and Nigeria's capital city, Abuja, are about 100 km closer to each other than Madrid is from Paris. Yet the estimated drive time from Yaoundé to Abuja is about five and a half hours longer than from Madrid to Paris.

Before COVID-19 brought air traffic to a standstill the only direct flights from Yaoundé to Abuja were on Tuesdays and Thursdays, which means the

---

[40]African Development Bank Group, 2018. *Eastern Africa Regional Integration Strategy Paper 2018–2022*. Abidjan: African Development Bank Group.

[41]African Economic Outlook 2018, 2018. Available at: https://www.afdb.org/fileadmin/uploads/afdb/Documents/Publications/2018AEO/African_Economic_Outlook_2018_-_EN_Chapter3.pdf, p. 63.

[42]Ashurst, 2016. *Road Infrastructure in Africa.* [Online] Available at: https://www.ashurst.com/en/news-and-insights/insights/road-infrastructure-in-africa/.

weary traveller who wants to avoid multiple stops on any other day needs to fork out US$5000 for a one-stop Air France flight via Charles De Gaulle International Airport in France, or he must fly across the continent to Addis Ababa to get a connecting flight there. It is for these reasons that the various continental development agencies in Africa are promoting a Single African Air Transport Market (SAATM), though progress is painfully slow.

However, there has been recent progress in building and financing infrastructure projects. This is largely spurred by the excess capacity to build infrastructure that became available from China as part of its Belt and Road Initiative that intends to connect China to the rest of Asia, Africa and even Europe.

Modern technology will also offer a way to replace costlier forms of more basic infrastructure. A number of African countries already use drones to transport blood and other vital medicines to rural hospitals bypassing poor, often unpaved, roads. But doctors, nurses and patients are all still dependent on roads and bridges to get to those hospitals and even the advent of mass air transport mentioned in the previous chapter may not sufficiently compensate for the requirement to transport large volumes of heavy cargo over long distances.

Technology is having a further impact in the form of advances in the use of traditional bituminous road construction technologies that translate into reduced cost and construction time. Disruptive change may also be imminent. At the high end of the technological spectrum Dutch engineers have come up with the concept of self-repairing asphalt roads that also serve to charge electric cars as you drive over it.[43] Then there is the promise of self-healing cement created by adding polymers to traditional cement mixes. The resulting cement has re-adhering properties that extend its lifetime. But the most important advance for Africa is likely to be from experiments mixing a chemical polymer with soil that stabilises ground surfaces sufficiently for cheap gravel roads to sufficiently withstand significant traffic volumes and the impact of seasonal rains.[44]

To this end the African Union launched the Programme for Infrastructure Development in Africa and its Priority Action Plan (PIDA-PAP) that is being championed vigorously by AUDA-NEPAD, the AU Commissioner for

---

[43] See Barlow, I. M., 2017. *Self Repairing Roads*. [Online] Available at: https://www.planswift.com/blog/self-repairing-roads/.

[44] See Ashby, S., 2018. *A Sidewalk That Repairs Itself? PNNL Cracks the Code for Self-Healing Cement*. [Online] Available at: https://www.pnnl.gov/news-media/sidewalk-repairs-itself-pnnl-cracks-code-self-healing-cement. Also Vijay, K., Murmu, M., & Deo, S. V., 2017. Bacteria Based Self Healing Concrete—A Review. *Construction and Building Materials,* 152, pp. 1008–1014.

Infrastructure, Energy and Tourism, the African Development Bank and the UN Economic Commission for Africa.

PIDA-PAP is a kind of infrastructure master plan for Africa. Although it regurgitates many previous ambitions, some of which date from colonial times, it has seen some implementation.[45] The PIDA-PAP portfolio from 2012 to 2020 numbered 51 cross-border programmes in transport (235 projects), energy (54 projects), ICT (113 projects) and trans-boundary water resources management (9 projects).

The concept note for a recent (November 2018) PIDA-PAP workshop at Victoria Falls[46] revealed that the capital cost of delivering the plan was estimated at US$68 billion or US$7.5 billion annually—relatively modest ambition compared to the infrastructure funding gap calculated by the African Development Bank that was quoted earlier. Of the more than 400 projects, the conference heard, 26% are moving from concept to pre-feasibility or feasibility phases; 16% are currently being structured for tendering; and 32% are either under construction or are already operational reflecting steady progress. Implementation is slow, however, and, at the end of 2019, PIDA-PAP 2 was being finalised for implementation from 2021 to 2030 now based on an integrated corridor approach including a scoping study for a Continental High Speed Railway Network.[47]

So-called non-tariff barriers are arguably an even larger constraint to trade in Africa and African trade with the rest of the world. Non-tariff barriers refer to onerous regulatory procedures, expensive visa requirements, corruption and inefficiency—including import prohibitions, quotas, export subsidies, export restrictions, technical barriers to trade (such as regulations, standards and assessment procedures), as well as with food safety and animal and plant health standards.[48] Whereas free trade agreements are subject to long and drawn-out processes associated with the negotiations, the removal of non-tariff barriers results from unilateral and bilateral cooperation. Exactly how powerful removing non-tariff barriers are was illustrated with a recent study

---

[45] African Union, 26–28 November 2018. *PIDA Implementation Through Good Governance–Realizing Smart Infrastructure for Africa's Integration.* [Online] Available at: https://www.tralac.org/documents/news/2406-pida-week-2018-concept-note/file.html.

[46] Concept Note for the Second Ordinary Session of the African Union Specialized Committee on Transport, Transcontinental and Interregional Infrastructure, Energy and Tourism, Cairo, Egypt, 14–18th April 2019. Available at: https://au.int/sites/default/files/newsevents/conceptnotes/36272-cn-ie2 4177_e_original-concept_note.pdf.

[47] Statement by Dr. Amani Abou Zeid, AUC Commissioner for Infrastructure and Energy at the Opening Ceremony of the 2019 PIDA Week, 25 November 2019. https://au.int/en/speeches/201 91125/statement-dr-amani-abou-zeid-auc-commissioner-infrastructure-and-energy-opening.

[48] The World Trade Organization tries to address these barriers through the Technical Barriers to Trade Agreement (TBT Agreement) and the separate agreement on food safety and animal and plant health standards (the Sanitary and Phytosanitary Measures Agreement).

done by the Stellenbosch based Trade and Law Centre that found that just reducing by 20% the time it takes to move goods across borders would be more economically advantageous for Africa than removing all import tariffs![49]

The 2018 ease of doing business index still has only seven countries from sub-Saharan Africa in the top 100, namely Mauritius, Rwanda, Kenya, Botswana, South Africa, Seychelles and Zambia, although efforts to remove impediments to improved trade are readily identifiable elsewhere. The COMESA-EAC-SADC Tripartite Free Trade Area website lists examples of 25 non-tariff barriers to trade that range from import bans and product classification to corruption. Progress with eliminating these barriers is, however, slow.[50]

In an effort to regularise such standards, the WTO's Agreement on the Application of Sanitary and Phytosanitary Measures came into force in 1995. The agreement provides uniform rules for all laws, regulations and requirements regarding how a product is produced, processed, stored or transported to ensure that its import does not pose a risk to human, animal or plant health. Sanitary measures are aimed at safeguarding human and animal health, while phytosanitary ones are intended to protect plants.

Imported goods should be from disease-free areas, inspected prior to export and should not exceed maximum levels of pesticide or insecticide use. Health risks posed by fresh foods and agricultural goods include salmonella poisoning, foot and mouth disease and sugar plant pests.

The agreement is also meant to prevent countries from using rules and regulations simply to block trade, stating explicitly that the measures cannot be employed in a manner which would constitute a disguised restriction on international trade. But although importing countries are encouraged to use existing international standards, they are nevertheless allowed to adopt stricter regulations if they can scientifically justify their actions.

---

[49] Grinsted, J., & Sandrey, R., 2015, *The Continental Free Trade Area—A GTAP Assessment*. [Online] Trade Law Centre, Stellenbosch. Available at: https://www.tralac.org/publications/article/7287-the-continental-free-trade-area-a-gtap-assessment.html.

[50] See COMESA, EAC & SADC, *Non-Tariff Barriers to Trade*. [Online] Available at: https://www.tradebarriers.org/ntb/non_tariff_barriers, p. 98.

Perspectives on the Promise of the African Continental Free Trade Area (AfCFTA)

Against this rather concerning background, much hope has been placed in the African Continental Free Trade Area (AfCFTA) as a vehicle to generally boost trade and assist in the transformation of African economies towards the production of higher value-added goods and decline in commodity dependence. The AfCFTA has the potential to unlock significant value-added trade in goods and services. Medium and high technology manufactures account for 25% of intra-African trade but for only 14% of African countries' exports to developed countries.[51] Typical of the situation in other regions it means that intra-African trade has relatively higher industrial content than African countries' trade with the rest of the world and speaks to the advantage of regional trade over international trade. In other words, African countries first need to trade with one another until their products and services are competitive while steadily expanding their participation in regional and global value chains.

Efforts at trade integration have driven repeated attempts at regional integration to the extent that it is possible to count up to 14 overlapping regional economic communities in Africa, ranging from the 21-member Common Market for Eastern and Southern Africa (COMESA) to the three-member Manu River Union. In fact, Africa has a spaghetti-bowl of regional structures although the African Union only recognises eight. In addition to AfCFTA, the Tripartite Free Trade Area that includes COMESA, the East African Community (EAC) and the Southern African Development Community (SADC) is also making progress in its goal towards greater trade integration. Actually, the proliferation of these communities now presents the continent with something of a challenge given the vested interests and bureaucracy that has accompanied each.

The decision to establish the AfCFTA was taken at a summit meeting of the African Union in January 2012 with the intention to create a single market for goods and services as originally envisioned in the 1991 Abuja Treaty. The original target date of 2017 was missed but after a high-level signing ceremony in Kigali on 21 March 2018, momentum has built up rapidly. Following signature, each country has to follow its national legislative processes and then deposit the instruments of ratification or accession

---

[51]African Export-Import Bank. 2018. Africa Trade Report 2018: Boosting Intra-African Trade: Implications of the African Continental Free Trade Area Agreement. Available at https://www.tralac.org/documents/news/2042-african-trade-report-2018-afreximbank/file.html, p. 28.

with the AU Commission.[52] After the treaty crossed the 22 ratification milestone it is scheduled to 'operational' as from 1 July 2020, but exactly what that means is up for debate and has now been delayed due to the impact of COVID-19. The plan is still that by 2034 the full 97% tariff liberalisation will be achieved.[53]

The immediate next step is a conference of state parties, the establishment of an AfCTA secretariat in Accra, Ghana, an African Trade Observatory and the completion of various technicalities. Lots of work still remains, however, since the agreement is essentially a framework, covering trade in goods and services, investment, intellectual property rights and competition policy. Already the establishment of the secretariat has also been delayed due to COVID-19. Once negotiations on trade in goods and trade in services are finalised, rules of origin negotiations have to be concluded as well as negotiations on tariff concessions. Then 'behind the border' trade issues on competition policy, intellectual property rights and investment will follow that will serve to deepen the AfCFTA.[54]

The AfCFTA provides for a single market for goods and services as well as a common market with free movement of capital and business travellers. It does not yet include digital trade and e-commerce. Countries joining AfCFTA must commit to removing tariffs on at least 90% of the products they produce, and can compile a list of sensitive products (amounting to an additional seven percentage points) that are to be temporarily exempted, leaving a three percent exclusion list.[55]

The agreement also provides for a Dispute Settlement Body (DSB) to respond to dumping of foreign products at a lower price than the normal value, allows for Special and Differential Treatment to provide flexibility for states at different levels of economic development and Infant Industry Protection that allows states to impose measures to protect strategic infant industries.[56]

---

[52]Accession is the act whereby a state accepts the offer or the opportunity to become a party to an international agreement after the agreement has entered into force. It has the same legal effect as ratification.

[53]90% of goods will be liberalised over the course of 5–8 years; 7% of goods will be classed as sensitive and liberalised over 10–13 years; and 3% of goods will be exempt from free trade entirely.

[54]ECA, ATPC, AU, UNCTAD & AfDB, 2018. *Concept Note. Assessing Regional Integration in Africa IX Next Steps for the African Continental Free Trade Area*. [Online] Available at: https://www.tralac.org/documents/news/2405-concept-note-assessing-regional-integration-in-africa-ix-report-uneca-2018/file.html.

[55]Ighobor, K., *Africa Set for a Massive Free Trade Area*. [Online] Available at: https://www.un.org/africarenewal/magazine/august-november-2018/africa-set-massive-free-trade-area, p. 3. AU, UNECA & ATPC, 2018. *African Continental Free Trade Area: Questions & Answers*. Addis Ababa.

[56]The dispute resolution mechanism does not, however, provide for private parties.

Trade facilitation will be funded by the AU, member states and external investors, and will address transport infrastructure, customs clearance, technical assistance and capacity building.[57]

Many obstacles remain in moving forward with implementing the AfCFTA. The most obvious is simply the ambition and diversity of its members. The AfCTA includes countries with much bigger levels of income disparity than in blocks such as ASEAN and CARICOM.[58] Agreeing on tariff liberalisation schedules with such large differences is going to require steadfast respect for Special and Differential Treatment by all concerned.

An important feature of the AfCFTA is that it will build on rather than replacing Africa's several existing regional free trade areas. For example in Southern Africa, SACU and SADC free trade areas will continue. The general principle will be that where these regional free trade areas offer better trade terms than the AfCFTA does, the former terms will apply. The same principle will apply to the Tripartite Free Trade Agreement mentioned previously. The result, as with most of these types of arrangements will be complex.

The Potential Impact of AfCFTA?

There have been a number of scenarios on the potential impact of the AfCTA, all very positive. For example, the UN Economic Commission for Africa estimates that it has 'the potential to boost intra-African trade by 52.3% through the elimination of import duties, and by over 100% through the elimination of non-tariff barriers'.[59] Then, in a paper released in February 2018, UNCTAD modelled two scenarios reflecting full and partial elimination of tariffs and concluded that[60]:

> In both long-term scenarios, the largest employment growth rates are found in manufacturing industry followed by some services and agriculture subsectors. All sectors grow, with the exception of a stagnant mining sector. This is in line with the CFTA objective for structural transformation and industrialization.[61]

---

[57] African Union, 2019. *Agreement Establishing the African Continental Free Trade Area*, Addis Ababa, pp. 20, 26 & 52.

[58] Akeyewale, R., 2018. *Who Are the Winners and Losers in Africa's Continental Free Trade Area?* [Online] Available at: https://www.weforum.org/agenda/2018/10/africa-continental-free-trade-afcfta-sme-business/.

[59] AU, UNECA & ATPC, 2018. *African Continental Free Trade Area: Questions & Answers*, Addis Ababa.

[60] Saygili, M., Peters, R., & Knebel, C., 2017. African Continental Free Trade Area: Challenges and Opportunities of Tariff Reductions. *UNCTAD Research Paper No. 15*.

[61] Ibid., p. 4.

According to UNCTAD and the UN Department of Economic and Social Affairs (UNDESA) the short-term revenue losses due to tariff reductions will be wiped out over time as trade increases and countries grow more rapidly. UNCTAD concludes that 'with adequate flanking policies and social safety measures, the AfCTA has an immense potential to promote equitable and inclusive growth'.[62] Under a scenario that emulates the full AfCTA implementation where all tariffs are eliminated, UNCTAD estimates that the net welfare gains could be in the region of US$16 billion and almost one percent more rapid GDP growth than would otherwise be the case. Total employment improves by slightly more than one percent, intra-African trade is forecast to grow by one third and Africa's total trade deficit is cut in half.

During the African Economic Conference 2018 in Kigali, the African Development Bank indicated that it expected the AfCTA to boost intra-African trade by up to US$35 billion per year, reflecting a 52% increase in trade by 2022, and a US$10 billion decrease in imports to Africa.[63] The more recent African Economic Outlook 2019 presented a scenario where, if current bilateral tariffs are eliminated Africa would gain US$2.8 billion in real income and intra-African trade would increase by 15%. Additionally, removing non-tariff barriers could increase total real income gains by US$37 billion; and intra-African trade by 107%.

To reach such a deep level of integration, further progress needs to be made on rules of origin, free movement of persons, financial governance frameworks and regional public goods (infrastructure and regional bodies).

Finally, in its estimate of the impact of the AfCFTA the UNDESA finds that

> Growth in Africa is expected to accelerate by 0.3-0.6 percentage points by 2040 (depending on the liberalization approach or scenario adopted), when compared to the baseline scenario. All African countries would experience an increase in their GDP with the AfCFTA reforms, whatever the scenario. ... However, these forecasts are likely to substantially underestimate the economic benefits of the AfCFTA, as they do not take into account the impact of liberalization in other areas such as services and investment.[64]

---

[62] Ibid. United Nations, 2019. World Economic Situation and Prospects 2019. [Online] Available at: https://www.un.org/development/desa/dpad/publication/world-economic-situation-and-prospects-2019/, p. 124.

[63] Tralac, 2018. AEC2018: Africa Must Focus on Its Big Resource—Its Young People, Experts Urge. [Online] Available at: https://www.tralac.org/news/article/13768-aec2018-africa-must-focus-on-its-big-resource-its-young-people-experts.

[64] United Nations, 2019. *World Economic Situation and Prospects 2019.* [Online] Available at: https://www.un.org/development/desa/dpad/publication/world-economic-situation-and-prospects-2019/, p. 124.

Modelling the Impact of Regional Economic Integration: The Africa Free Trade Area Scenario

The IFs forecasting platform used in this book does not currently include a bilateral trading model. Instead it presently relies on a pooled model for trade, meaning that countries each trade with a pool reflecting the rest of the world. For that reason I have to rely on various proxies to emulate the impact of expanding trade in Africa. The first is a ten percent improvement in the quality of government regulations as a proxy for the impact of the harmonisation of rules of trade within Africa.[65] The second is a ten percent increase in roads as a proxy for a reduction in non-tariff barriers.[66] The third is to boost manufacturing, services and ICT exports through export promotion, since the impact of the AfCTA is to accelerate regional trade.[67] Finally, I use an additive factor to multifactor productivity, a powerful driver of economic growth within IFs as a proxy for the general economic benefits generally associated with trade and globalisation.[68] I calibrate the combined impact in accordance with the lower end of the impact of the AfCFTA scenarios done by UNCTAD, the UN Economic Commission for Africa and UNDESA referred to previously. Collectively these four interventions simulate the impact of the full implementation of the AfCFTA, if imperfectly so.

Timewise the AfCFTA scenario assumes that the implementation of the agreement starts in earnest in 2025, hence allowing for the impact of COVID-19 and other factors, and that tariffs are reduced over the subsequent 10-year period in line with current expectations. The interventions within IFs therefore ramp up from 2025 to 2035 and then levels off to 2040. This is, for sure, an exceptionally optimistic forecast for an agreement as complex and politically fraught as the AfCFTA. That said, if leaders do manage to stick to their commitments and take African citizens, business, labour and other stakeholders along with them, the impact will be very large.

By 2040 Africa's economy should be steaming ahead at more than seven percent growth rate in the AfCFTA scenario compared to 5.9% in the Current Path. Across the entire forecast horizon, from 2020 to 2040, the

---

[65] The intervention improves Africa's average levels of government regulatory quality to slightly above the average for South Asia by 2040, still significantly below the 2040 average for South America.

[66] The intervention marginally reduces the growing gap in roads per capita between Africa and South Asia although Africa continues to trails significantly behind all other regions.

[67] Manufactures imports increase by 1 percentage point of GDP value by 2040. Services exports increase by 0.5 percentage points and ICTechnology exports increase by 0.02 percentage points.

[68] Within IFs the intervention increases the contribution of MFP to GDP growth by 0.24 and 0.82 percentage points above the Current Path in 2030 and 2040 respectively.

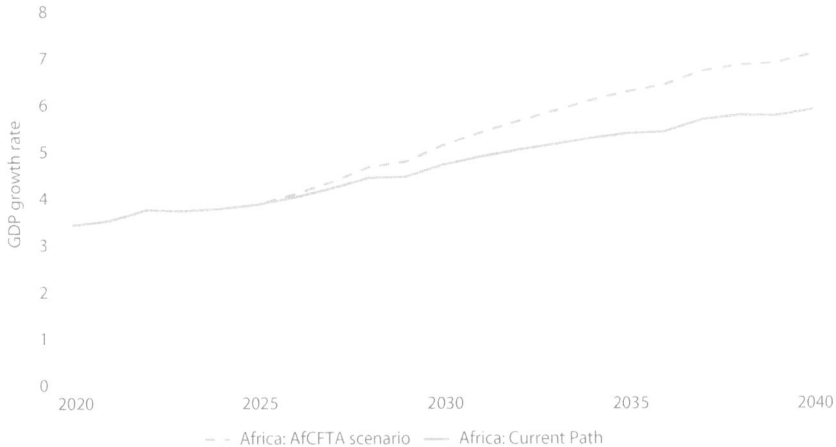

Fig. 11.2 Current Path growth rate vs AfCFTA (*Source* IFs v7.45 initializing from IMF World Economic Outlook)

average economic growth rate for Africa would be 0.5 percentage points above the Current Path.[69] The result is that the African economy is about US$770 billion larger (in market exchange rates) in 2040 than it would be on the Current Path. Even more impressive is that the cumulative increase in the size of the African economy from 2020 to 2040 is a massive US$3.7 trillion. This growth translates into almost 57 million fewer people living in extreme poverty by 2040 (using the US$1.90, US3.20 and US$5.50 extreme poverty lines for low, lower-middle and upper-middle-income countries explained in Chapter 7) or 45 million fewer persons living in extreme poverty using the US$1.90 income level for all 55 African countries. By 2040, GDP per capita in Africa is US$470 on average more for each of Africa's 2.081 billion people (Fig. 11.2).

Since more intra-African trade benefits Africa's manufacturing sector, the services and manufacturing sectors could, on average, be 0.7 and 0.4 percentage points larger in 2040 than in the Current Path scenario. The contribution of the agriculture and energy sectors marginally decline as a portion of the total African economy, but not in absolute values since by 2040 the African economy is significantly larger than it would otherwise be. These sectoral shifts follow the natural and expected evolution of an economy that becomes more productive over time.

---

[69] From 2020 to 2040, the African economy would grow at 5.2 instead of an average of 4.7% per annum.

By 2040 the value of Africa's exports have increased by US$148 billion and imports would have declined by US$124 billion with the greater part of the increase in exports benefitting Africa's 21 lower-middle-income countries.

South Africa, an upper-middle-income country with the continent's most diversified economy gains more than double (US$27 billion) the amount from additional exports in 2040 compared to the next country, Egypt (US$14 billion in 2040). Other countries that gain more than US$5 billion from additional trade in 2040 are Nigeria, Angola, Morocco, Ghana, Algeria and Tanzania. In general the current account improves, government debt reduces (by about 1.5 percentage points) and household saving rates improve.

Conclusion: Advancing Africa's Trade

This chapter has set out the reasons why African countries need to deepen trade agreements with other countries in the region to grow trade, develop and diversify their economies, particularly to facilitate progress up the value-add ladder. Most African economies are simply too small and Africa currently too fragmented to build competitive productive capacity at scale, or indeed to offer sufficiently large markets to attract substantive foreign investment without such agreements.[70]

Since trade potential in goods inevitably diminishes with distance, African countries are best served by first trading with other African countries, although the natural trading relationship for North Africa is with Europe and the Middle East rather than sub-Saharan Africa given the intervening reality of the Sahara desert. In similar vein one could also speculate as to the future orientation of the Horn of Africa as likely more closely linked to the Arabian peninsula and with emerging India rather than with much of the rest of Africa given the facilitation provided through ocean-based transport and the limited rail and road infrastructure in the Horn, although that is changing.

That said, the extent to which Africa will be able to leapfrog to higher-end value in trade will depend on the investments made in selected, well-targeted infrastructure able to support competitive industries and sectors in industrial parks and export-processing zones linked to regional and global markets, invest in appropriate technology and education. But more is required. For

---

[70]Only five African countries have a GDP of more than US$100 billion (Nigeria, South Africa, Egypt, Algeria, Morocco).

example in a recent study on the future of Ethiopia,[71] globally one of the fastest growing economies in the last decade, we found that the average of 2.7 years of education in the adult population over the age of 15 is still one of the lowest in the world. Along with low levels of overall attainment and poor quality outcomes, there is also a very pronounced gender gap in Ethiopia's education system, with males receiving more than twice as much schooling as their female counterparts. Structurally Ethiopia needs to unlock this constraint, the first and most severe blockage in its education pipeline, if it wants to improve its human capital endowment and hence the value of exports.

Digital technologies can help overcome Africa's large infrastructure deficit but will likely dampen trade in goods while further fuelling the growth in trade in services.

Trade integration can help African countries to prioritise investment in sectors where they have a comparative advantage. It could foster the establishment or promotion of industries in which African businesses have the potential to trade regionally and eventually globally. Additionally, regional integration would improve the diversification of goods and the technology content of Africa's exports.[72]

In other words, trade liberalisation works only to the benefit of countries when they actively manage levels of openness to trade.[73] For this reason the policies and support of a national governance that invests in the quality of institutions, and provides policy certainty is important.[74] China is the poster child when it comes to how it has successfully managed access to its large domestic market, protected and nurtured its infant industry and demanded technology transfer from foreign companies. Today it is the world's factory.

Going up the product and services complexity curve requires that national and regional value chains are established where cities, regions and national economies can collaborate on a cost-competitive basis in bringing diverse skills together to produce ever more valuable products and services.

Initiatives like the AfCFTA are therefore crucial for growth and prosperity in Africa. It has the potential to trigger a virtuous cycle of expanded trade

---

[71] Donnnenfeld, Z., Cilliers, J., Kwasi, S., & Welborn, L., 2020, Emerging Giant: Potential Pathways for Ethiopia to 2040, ISS 17 January 2020. Available at: https://issafrica.org/research/east-africa-report/emerging-giant-potential-pathways-for-ethiopia-to-2040, p. 8.

[72] Somé, J., 2018. *African Economic Conference 2018: Industrial Policy, Institutions and Performance of the Manufacturing Sector in Africa.* Kigali: UNDP, ECA & AfDB, p. 5.

[73] Zahonogo, P., 2016. Trade and Economic Growth in Developing Countries: Evidence from sub-Saharan Africa. *Journal of African Trade*, 3(1–2), pp. 41–56.

[74] Somé, J., 2018. *African Economic Conference 2018: Industrial Policy, Institutions and Performance of Manufacturing Sector in Africa.* Kigali: UNDP, ECA & AfDB, p. 5.

on the continent that will, in turn, drive the structural transformation of economies. Detail negotiations are, however, likely to take a long time and a number of uncertainties, for instance about tariff schedules, remain.[75] For this reason the EAC, SADC, ECOWAS and the Tripartite Free Trade Area need to simultaneously press on and pursue trade facilitation reforms and trade integration.

When all is said and done the major obstacles to regional trade in Africa are often political and are shaped by the short-term pain (loss of tariff income) that is required before the long-term gains (higher growth) offsets these losses. Regional integration will eventually grow tax revenues as more rapid growth translates into more government revenues, but in the shorter term governments will have to work hard to get domestic buy-in once the pain from loss in tariff income becomes evident.[76]

Given the political will to overcome the initial tariff losses, structurally the biggest challenge for African integration will be how extremely unequal partners such as South Africa and Botswana, both upper-middle-income countries, can be integrated with surrounding low-income countries like Mozambique, Swaziland and Lesotho.

Expanding trade in Africa requires peace and stability, the topic of the next chapter.

Further Reading

Buyonge, C., and I. Kireeva. January 2008. Trade Facilitation in Africa: Challenges and Possible Solutions. *World Customs Journal*. https://researchgate.net/publication/321300912.

Draper, Peter, Phil Alves, and Nkululeko Khumalo. Africa's Challenges in International Trade and Regional Integration: What Role for Europe? e-cultura.sapo.pt/ieei_pdf/173/11calvesesal.

---

[75] Currently there are 'no tariff schedules, no Annex on rules of origin, nor rules for specific services sectors to regulate such trade. … These are sensitive and technically complicated matters; especially when 55 countries at very different levels of economic development are involved.'; Erasmus, G., 2019. *Where Does the AfCFTA Process Stand and What Happens Next?* [Online] Available at: https://www.tralac.org/blog/article/13855-where-does-the-afcfta-process-stand-and-what-happens-next.html?utm_source=tralac+Newsletter&utm_campaign=6e06277124-Daily_News_23012019&utm_medium=email&utm_term=0_a95cb1d7ad-6e06277124-311097085.

[76] Ogunniyi, A., Mavrotas, G., Olagunju, K., Adedoyin, R., Adewale, A., & Ayodeji, O., 2018. *African Economic Conference 2018: Regional Economic Integration, Governance Quality and Tax Revenue in Sub-Saharan African Countries: Linkages and Pathways*, Kigali: UNDP, ECA & AfDB, p. 12.

Odije, Michael E. December 2018. The Need for Industrial Policy Coordination in the Africa Continental Free Trade Area. *African Affairs*, 118(470), pp. 182–193. https://doi.org/10.1093/afraf/ady054.academia.edu/38542800.

Songwe, Vera. January 2019. *Boosting Trade and Investment. Intra-African Trade: A Path to Economic Diversification and Inclusion.* Brookings Institute.

Open Access This chapter is licensed under the terms of the Creative Commons Attribution 4.0 International License (http://creativecommons.org/licenses/by/4.0/), which permits use, sharing, adaptation, distribution and reproduction in any medium or format, as long as you give appropriate credit to the original author(s) and the source, provide a link to the Creative Commons license and indicate if changes were made.

The images or other third party material in this chapter are included in the chapter's Creative Commons license, unless indicated otherwise in a credit line to the material. If material is not included in the chapter's Creative Commons license and your intended use is not permitted by statutory regulation or exceeds the permitted use, you will need to obtain permission directly from the copyright holder.

12

Prospects for Greater Peace

Abstract In this chapter, Cilliers assesses historical and present conflict dynamics across Africa and how they relate to governance, demographics and socioeconomics. Woven throughout is a discussion on the role of peacekeepers and external involvement more broadly, the surge of terrorism in Africa and how these two phenomena bear upon one another. It assesses the origins, nature and implications of the declining trends in armed conflict and the emergence of urban protests as the key feature of violence and instability in much of Africa. In an alternative future scenario, Cilliers assesses what development outcomes Africa could expect if it were to succeed in reducing levels of instability in a scenario named Silencing the Guns.

Keywords Anocracy · Autocracy · Democracy · Demographic dividend · Fatality rate · Islamist extremism · Non-state conflict · Youth bulge

Learning Objectives

– Understand why conflict patterns are often cyclical in nature
– Be able to explain and interpret key conflict indicators such as the fatality rate and the absolute number of fatalities
– Identify which African countries that have suffered the highest number of fatalities from conflict events and which have suffered the highest fatality rate from conflict events.

There is no magic wand to end armed conflict in Africa by 2020, which is the target year set by the African Union towards its Agenda 2063 vision of 'an integrated, prosperous and peaceful Africa'.[1] Structurally, inclusive economic development coupled with substantive electoral accountability offers the best prospect for greater peace and stability. Generally countries become more peaceful as they become more prosperous and, above certain levels of income and development, democracy is the most stable form of government. Although, at low levels of development democracy may actually hinder development and it may even be that for 'for the poorest countries, development may actually stimulate violence'.[2]

It will take time for Africa to become more peaceful and less violent, in part because of the slow rate at which the structural changes that are needed for stability take place. For example, conflict-affected countries typically have much younger populations than more stable regions and population structure shifts very slowly.

Sustained violence within countries invariably reflects so-called deep drivers of conflict. A history of armed conflict and its social, political and economic legacies, a youthful population, high levels of unemployment and inequality render societies vulnerable to further conflict. And then the causes of violence evolve over time; the political, economic and social dynamics that drove instability a decade ago may no longer do so today. New phenomena in our ever-changing global landscape are sparking conflict. Examples vary, such as efforts by a government to institute a lock-down to manage the spread of the COVID-19 virus when communities live on the margins of survival. Or the deepening of cyclical droughts due to climate change forcing herders to seek new grazing areas and creating conflict with pastoral farming communities. In this context, the threats of climate change loom large as its impact moves from being an accelerator of inequality and deprivation to a direct cause of violent competition over resources such as access to grazing land and water.[3]

Each country is unique, or, to paraphrase Leo Tolstoy in *Anna Karenina*, 'Stable countries are all alike; every unstable country is unstable in its own way'. While broad analysis as contained in this book is important, local

---

[1] See; African Union, n.d. *Agenda 2063: The Africa We Want*. [Online] Available at: https://au.int/agenda2063/overview.

[2] Hegre, H., Ellingsen, T., Gates, S., & Gleditsch, N. P., 2001. Toward a Democratic Civil Peace? Democracy, Political Change, and Civil War, 1816–1992. *The American Political Science Review*, 95(1), pp. 33–48.

[3] See, for example, the discussion in Bowlsby, D., Chenoweth, E., Hendrix, C., & Moyer, J. D., 2019. The Future Is a Moving Target: Predicting Political Instability. *British Journal of Political Science*, Volume Cambridge University Press, pp. 1–13.

history, detail and context is determinant in shaping violent or peaceful outcomes. The reasons why people join armed jihadist groups and become violent, for example, are often *primarily* local, varied and related to personal experiences and circumstances such as abuse at the hands of authorities rather than the import of some type of foreign ideology such as radical Islam. The one, of course, feeds upon the other and eventually a spark or specific event mobilises local leadership that inevitably frame causality within a broader political, ideological or religious context.[4]

Trends in Conflict

Conflict data on Africa is inevitably incomplete and therefore often contentious. But, the quality of data is improving and it is more readily available than ever before.[5]

The two largest publicly available data providers, the Uppsala Conflict Data Program (UCDP) and the Armed Conflict Location and Event Data Project (ACLED) both rely on media sources to collect and categorise events and fatalities, as do others such as the Social Conflict Analysis Database (SCAD). These data providers collect massive amounts of data on specific events and in this manner build a national picture of conflict from the bottom up. Datasets from other organisations such as the Political Instability Task Force (PITF) and Center for Systemic Peace (CSP) follow a different approach. They try to provide an interpretation of the impact of conflict on the economy, politics and social structure of a country using experts and various indices to help calibrate measurements to more readily allow cross-country comparisons. Other organisations, such as the World Bank and the Ibrahim Index on governance (in its subsidiary indices) follow a similar broad approach but use various indicators of risk in an effort to compare and rank countries, and monitor stability over time.

Whichever source one uses, conflict in Africa ebbs and recedes over time, but the general trend when taking population increases into account is an overall decline in volatility. This is most visible in looking at events or fatalities measured per million people (using data from UCDP or ACLED) rather than comparing the number of fatalities in one country with another since

---

[4] See, for example Institute for Security Studies, 2016. Mali's young 'jihadists' Fuelled by Faith or Circumstance? Institute for Security Studies, Policy Brief 89. [Online] Available at: https://issafrica.s3.amazonaws.com/site/uploads/policybrief89-eng-v3.pdf.

[5] See Uppsala Conflict Data Program, n.d. *Department of Peace and Conflict Research.* [Online] Available at: https://ucdp.uu.se/ and ACLED, n.d. And: The Armed Conflict Location & Event Data Project. [Online] Available at: www.acleddata.com/.

it should be self-evident that the likely trend would be for the number of fatalities to increase as population numbers increase.

In this chapter I generally rely on UCDP data given its longer historical datasets and academic rigour.

Since the wave of independence in the late 1950s and early 1960s, the most violent period in Africa coincided with the run-up to the end of the Cold War in 1989. During this period Africa served as a proxy battleground between the former Soviet Union and the USA and its allies. In fact, levels of organised violence in Africa rose much more quickly than the global average during the 1970s and 1980s. Africa was becoming more violent compared to other places.

Instances of organised violence and the burden of fatalities have since steadily declined, with the period from 2004 to 2006 being more peaceful than any other in Africa's recent history.

But, violence accelerated again after 2010 with the Arab Spring and the increase in incidences of violent Islamist terrorism. It seems to have peaked in 2014–2015 before starting to decline, although recent years have again seen an increase in instability, particularly in the Sahel. Today it is the Middle East, not Africa, that has the highest conflict burden of all world regions—that is if one calculates the likelihood of a person being killed in armed conflict.

Figure 12.1 presents the UCDP estimate of the total number of fatalities from organised violence in Africa since 1990 (left-hand y-axis) compared to Africa's increased population size (right-hand y-axis) from 614 million to 1.3 billion in 2018.[6] The periods that saw the highest number of fatalities, excluding the extraordinary peak with the genocide in Rwanda in 1994, were in 1990/1991 (mostly in Ethiopia), 1999/2000 (including the war between Ethiopia and Eritrea) and 2014/2015 (Boko Haram in Nigeria).[7]

The data distinguishes between state-based conflict (involving a government), non-state conflict (no involvement of armed forces from government) and one-sided violence when the government or a formally organised crime uses armed force against civilians. In all instances incidents are only included when fatalities amount to 25 deaths per year and per actor.

When total fatalities are adjusted for Africa's rapid population growth to represent the ratio of fatalities per million people in the population, it is clear

---

[6]UCDP defines such events as 'an incident where armed force was used by an organised actor against another organised actor, or against civilians, resulting in at least one direct death at a specific location and a specific date', Sundberg, R., & Melander, E., 2013. Introducing the UCDP Georeferenced Event Dataset. *Journal of Peace Research*, 50(4), pp. 523–532. And Croicu, M., & Sundberg, R., 2017. *UCDP GED Codebook Version 17.1. Department of Peace and Conflict Research*. Uppsala: Uppsala University.

[7]Egypt was added to the UCP region of Africa for this calculation.

12 Prospects for Greater Peace 283

Fig. 12.1 Total fatalities from all events, Africa, 1990–2018 (*Source* Uppsala Conflict Data Program Georeferenced Event Dataset (GED) Global edition version 19.1, population from United Nations Population Division in IFs v 7.45)

Table 12.1 Most fatalities versus highest fatality rate

Highest number of fatalities	Greatest risk (highest fatality rate per million people)
Nigeria	Central African Republic
DR Congo	Libya
Somalia	Somalia
Sudan	South Sudan
Libya	Sudan
Central African Republic	DR Congo
South Sudan	Mali

Source UCDP version 19.1

that the fatality rate has been steadily, albeit slowly, declining. Today Africans are significantly less exposed to organised armed violence than in the 1980s and 1990s.

Also evident in Fig. 12.1 are four major conflicts: the 1994 genocide in Rwanda, the Eritrean-Ethiopian border war (in and around the town of Badme in 1999 and 2000), the large-scale conflict in the Democratic Republic of Congo (generally known as the Second Congo War or Great War of Africa, that wound down from July 2003 after having involved nine African countries and nearly 20 rebel groups) and the surge in fatalities associated with the activities of Boko Haram in Nigeria in 2014–2015.[8]

With the exception of these four conflicts, the absolute number of fatalities from armed conflict has slowly declined over time and is limited to a handful of countries. The seven countries that experienced the highest number of fatalities due to armed conflict from 2009 to 2018 are Nigeria, the Democratic Republic of Congo, Somalia, Sudan, Libya, the Central African Republic and South Sudan.

Inevitably countries with large populations such as Nigeria, Ethiopia, Egypt and the Democratic Republic of Congo tend to record a corresponding high number of fatalities from armed conflict. However, when taking population size into consideration, i.e. fatalities per thousand or million people, the seven countries where citizens were most at risk for 2009–2018 are Central African Republic, Libya, Somalia, South Sudan, the Democratic Republic of Congo and Mali (Table 12.1).[9]

---

[8] The support of Rwanda and Uganda enabled Congolese rebel Laurent-Désiré Kabila to overthrow Mobutu Sese Seko during the First Congo War. After Kabila was installed as the new president, he broke ties with both countries who retaliated by invading the Democratic Republic of Congo, starting the Second Congo War. Thompsell, A., 2019. *The Second Congo War*. [Online] Available at: www.thoughtco.com/second-congo-war-43698.

The list in the table includes countries with quite small populations (Central African Republic, Libya, Somalia and Sudan) who have an extraordinarily high casualty burden. Also evident is the profound lethality of violent Islamist extremism and the extent to which that is driving the fatality count. Whereas in 2010 only five countries experienced sustained activity from violent Islamist extremism (Algeria, Mali, Niger, Nigeria and Somalia), that number has now increased to 12 countries, with Burkina Faso, Cameroon, Chad, Egypt, Kenya, Libya and Tunisia added to the original list.[10]

Should Africans or the international community manage to bring stability to these countries, it would have a disproportionately positive impact on continental levels of armed conflict, on investor confidence, the ability of governments to invest in development and improved wellbeing.

The link between transnational organised crime and terrorism is also growing, since the latter generally needs resources to conduct their operations, even as the allegiances between Africa's domestic violent radicals and those in the Middle East have shifted away from al-Qaeda towards the Islamic State.[11]

In the Sahel, the African region most affected by terrorism, violent extremism is again driven by deeply domestic matters, particularly poor governance and neglect rather than influences from elsewhere. Two considerations inform this belief: the first is the reduction in the flow of money from Saudi Arabia who, for several decades was the main source of financial support to fundamentalist Islam that eventually spawned its violent offspring. The second relates to the defeat of the Islamic State in Iraq and Syria, where it has lost the territories that once provided it with a relatively safe haven, although the Islamic State is clearly seeking fertile ground in a number of African countries.

However, a relatively recent trend is the emergence of a number of copycat insurgencies that have borrowed the Islamic state nomenclature such as in northern Mozambique and the eastern Democratic Republic of the Congo.

Repeat violence, or recurring historic conflicts, is a huge problem in Africa. 'Globally, cycles of war tend to repeat themselves in the same countries such as in Sudan, Ethiopia and Somalia. Apart from inhibiting development, they

---

[9] While per capita fatality measures can help measure the comparative conflict burden across countries, it obscures subnational discrepancies. For instance, in Nigeria people in the north are significantly more likely to experience violence at the hands of Boko Haram than people living in Lagos.

[10] The Africa Center for Strategic Studies, 2018. *Militant Islamist Groups in Africa Show Resiliency over Past Decade*. [Online] Available at: https://africacenter.org/spotlight/militant-islamist-groups-in-africa-show-resiliency-over-pastdecade/?utm_source=June+2018+Month+in+Review&utm_campaign=June+2018+Newsletter&utm_medium=email.

[11] Alda, E., & Sala, J. L., 2014. Links Between Terrorism, Organized Crime and Crime: The Case of the Sahel Region. *Stability: International Journal of Security and Development*, 3(1).

also spillover into the neighbourhood'.[12] Unaddressed grievances are often the drivers of recurrent violence, suggesting that lasting peace, or at least greater stability, will not be achieved until these grievances are addressed. Indeed, the seeds of the next war are often sown during the preceding war.[13] Doing that takes a long time, often much longer than anyone initially suspects and the result is that efforts at negotiating an end to violence or stabilising a situation through the deployment of peacekeepers, such as in South Sudan or the Central African Republic, often needs to be measured in decades rather than years.

Given that only inclusive economic growth can produce the resources required to alleviate these root causes, conflict-torn countries in Africa are caught in a catch-22 situation. Poor countries are more violent and because of this they cannot grow rapidly enough to alleviate the stresses and grievances that lead to instability.

Moreover, being situated in a conflict-ridden region is a major risk factor for conflict; neighbouring countries are very likely to experience the spillover effect of the instability.[14] This is currently most evident in the Sahel. Briefing the United Nations Security Council, in January 2020, Mohamed Ibn Chambas, UN Special Representative and Head of the UN Office for West Africa and the Sahel (UNOWAS), described a region that has 'experienced a devastating surge in terrorist attacks against civilian and military targets'. Chambas, who serves on the Board of the ISS where I work, proceeded to paint a picture of relentless attacks on civilian and military targets that he said, have 'shaken public confidence'. Casualties in Burkina Faso, Mali and Niger, have leapt five-fold since 2016—with more than 4000 deaths reported in 2019 compared to some 770 three years earlier. 'Most significantly, the geographic focus of terrorist attacks has shifted eastwards from Mali to Burkina Faso and is increasingly threatening West African coastal States.... And displacement has grown ten-fold to about half a million, on top of some 25,000 who have sought refuge in other countries'.[15]

According to the World Development Report 2011, a 'country making development advances, such as Tanzania, loses an estimated 0.7% of gross

---

[12]Gates, S., Nygård, H. M., & Trappeniers, E., 2016. Conflict Recurrence. *PRIO Conflict Trends 02*.
[13]Ibid.
[14]Goldstone, J. A., Bates, R. H., Epstein, D. L., Gurr, T. R., Lustik, M. B., Marshall, M. G., Ulfelder, J., & Woodward, M. 2010. A Global Model for Forecasting Political Instability. *American Journal of Political Science*, 54(1), pp. 190–208 and Hegre, H., Nygård, H. M., Karlsen, J., & Strand, H., 2013. Predicting Armed Conflict, 2010–2050. *International Studies Quarterly*, 57(2), p. 7.
[15]UN News, 'Unprecedented Terrorist Violence' in West Africa, Sahel Region, 8 January 2020. https://news.un.org/en/story/2020/01/1054981?utm_source=Media+Review+for+January+9%2C+2020&utm_campaign=Media+Review+for+January+9%2C2020&utm_medium=email.

domestic product (GDP) every year for each neighbour in conflict'.[16] Furthermore, neighbouring countries that are in turmoil regularly offer safe havens for rebel groups and insurgents that operate across borders.[17]

Africa's Leadership in Conflict Prevention and Management

An important reason for Africa's declining conflict burden is that, over the last two decades, Africans have increasingly taken the lead in making peace through political efforts including mediation, diplomacy and, when these fail, the provision of peacekeeping forces. Clearly, preventing conflict is where the focus should be and is pursued through structures such as the African Union's Peace and Security Council and the various components of the African Peace and Security Architecture (APSA), both at the level of the African Union and in subregions such as in West and East Africa. Once conflict has erupted the introduction of peacekeepers remains the most important and effective means through which to respond to conflict with substantial benefits. Based on extensive research, the Peace Research Institute Oslo (PRIO) holds that the risk of conflict recurrence drops by as much as 75% in countries where United Nations peacekeepers are deployed.[18] It is here that the impact of COVID-19 is likely to have a considerable impact on, for example, the rotation of peacekeepers and on the ability of peacekeepers to undertake their tasks amidst travel restrictions and the need for social distancing and other measures. More broadly COVID-19 is also likely to limit diplomatic and related peacemaking efforts although it will affect peacekeepers, civilians and troublemakers equally.

Côte d'Ivoire is often used as a recent example of successful peacekeeping (there are many previous ones). On 30 June 2017, the UN Operation in Côte d'Ivoire (UNOCI) concluded its mandate, some 13 years after it was established. It was a turbulent ride, for resurgent post-electoral violence in 2011 had led to the deaths of approximately 3000 people. But eventually the contribution the UNOCI made to stability and the country's economic recovery enabled the withdrawal of the peacekeepers.

---

[16] The World Bank, 2011. *World Development Report 2011 Conflict, Security, and Development*, Washington: The International Bank for Reconstruction and Development, p. 5.
[17] Hegre, H., Nygård, H. M., Karlsen, J., & Strand, H., 2013. Predicting Armed Conflict, 2010–2050. *International Studies Quarterly*, 57(2), p. 7.
[18] Gates, S., Nygård, H. M., & Trappeniers, E., 2016. Conflict Recurrence. PRIO Conflict Trends 02.

From 2012 to 2018 Côte d'Ivoire averaged growth in excess of eight percent per year. The government of President Alassane Ouattara placed particular emphasis on making the country attractive to private-sector investment that came at some costs to the fiscus. The measures include various exemptions from value-added tax, reductions in customs duty and tax exemptions on profits as it seeks to increase trade and attract opportunities in agriculture, industry, mining and services. Such measures inevitably imply a degree of short-term pain, but eventually more rapid economic growth, more job opportunities and better wages, if accompanied by appropriate redistributive policies.

In the longer term, fundamental political, social and economic reforms are often required to ensure durable peace. At least some of these measures have been put in place in Côte d'Ivoire. However, even after more than a decade of peacekeeping it will still take several years to decisively break the cycle of violence that prevailed before.

Africa itself has limited ability to fund and sustain expensive peace missions, such as those required in the Democratic Republic of the Congo, the Central African Republic, Mali and Somalia. As such, it often looks towards the United Nations to either undertake or support the efforts by Africans.

In spite of the UN's unwillingness to assume direct responsibility for peacekeeping in Somalia where its previous efforts ended so ignominiously and the ever-present legacy of the failure by the international community to prevent the genocide in Rwanda, the UN remains the most important player in this regard. But there are many number of conflict situations in Africa where the UN is unwilling or unable to deploy, leaving the ball in Africa's court. The result is a clear trend towards peacekeeping in Africa by Africans and a strong desire from the continent to move towards a system whereby peacekeeping missions in Africa are funded through a system of assessed contributions from UN member states instead of the messy and complex system of voluntary contributions currently used.

Changing Characteristics of Organised Violence

Unlike other regions, Africa experiences a high level of conflict between armed groups and factions that are fighting one another instead of the government, with the UCDP referring to this as 'non-state conflict'. This type of violence is mostly due to absent, weak and unconsolidated governance. Simply put, in areas where the government is not able to exert its authority, provide stability, political, economic or social competition between tribes, herders and pastoralists, local militias and traditional groups become more readily violent.

And as the number of conflict actors has increased, conflict in Africa has become more complex. Rebel (and extremist) groups often split into further groupings, which complicates efforts at mediation or reconciliation. Attempts to craft inclusive peace agreements invariably fall short of their stated goal to include all key protagonists, for no sooner do mediators persuade all parties to sign an agreement that a group splits off and a new faction emerges. Additional demands follow while commentators and interest groups readily agitate for the maximum inclusion as part of agreements. Although, actually the problem with most peace agreements is not that they are not inclusive enough, as is frequently claimed, but that they are not implemented![19]

While the level of resources within a country impacts on state capacity, it is generally not the absolute level of resources (or the absence thereof) that fuels discontent, but rather the distribution of the limited resources within and between groupings. Civil wars generally occur more frequently in countries with a large population with one or more dominant ethnic, linguistic or religious grouping compared to countries that may have a more evenly balanced ethnic composition.[20] Recent research on the factors that underlie ethnic strife contends that nearly 80% of the continent's major ethnic groups have never participated in any civil war. The origins of most ethnic conflicts, it found, can generally be traced to the existence of precolonial states and the extent to which insecure postcolonial leaders privileged particular ethnic groups above others.[21]

The comprehensive 2018 World Bank/United Nations report *Pathways for Peace* highlights that: 'Exclusion from access to power, opportunity, services, and security creates fertile ground for mobilizing group grievances to violence, especially in areas with weak state capacity or legitimacy or in the context of human rights abuses'.[22] Conflict in Africa is not directly driven by ethnic divergence as is often assumed, but by the old adage of history and

---

[19] Joshi,. M., & Quinn, J. M., 2017. Implementing the Peace: The Aggregate Implementation of Comprehensive Peace Agreements and Peace Duration After Intrastate Armed Conflict. *British Journal of Political Science*, 47(4), pp. 869–892.

[20] Hegre, H., Ellingsen, T., Gates, S., & Gleditsch, N. P., 2001. Toward a Democratic Civil Peace? Democracy, Political Change, and Civil War, 1816–1992. *The American Political Science Review*, 95(1), pp. 33–48.

[21] Paine, J. (n.d.). Ethnic Violence in Africa: Destructive Legacies of Pre-Colonial States. International Organization, 1–39. https://doi.org/10.1017/s0020818319000134.

[22] United Nations and World Bank, 2018. *Pathways for Peace: Inclusive Approaches to Preventing Violent Conflict*, Washington: The International Bank for Reconstruction and Development, p. xviii.

the ongoing mobilisation of identity for political and economic participation and influence.

This discussion takes us to an important trend. In sharp contrast to the declining impact of armed violence, Africa is experiencing an increase in incidents of anti-government social violence, including riots and violent protests.

More Riots

While larger-scale armed conflict is likely to continue its steady long-term decline, it's less clear what the short-term impact of the increase in social instability and protests will be. As is the case elsewhere in the world, democratic African governments are less repressive and tend to use less violence against civilians than their autocratic counterparts. In general, few civilians are killed during protests even if the number of protest events may increase compared to incidents of armed conflict.[23]

According to ACLED, non-violent protests and violent riots in Africa have increased 12-fold since 2001 and accelerated since the start of the Arab Spring in December 2010. The Arab Spring eventually impacted a belt of North African countries from Morocco to Egypt, as well as Somalia, Nigeria and Sudan, but only Tunisia emerged with significantly improved levels of democracy.[24]

Particularly evident from the data on riots and protests are events in Egypt in 2013 with the one-year anniversary of the inauguration of President Mohamed Morsi in June when millions of Egyptians called for his departure. These developments culminated in the coup d'état or Second Egyptian Revolution during which General (now President) Abdel Fattah el-Sisi assumed power. In Libya, the Arab spring loosened Muammar Gaddafi's grip on the nation and eventually prompted the North Atlantic Treaty Organisation (NATO) to abuse a UN Security Council mandate to settle old scores that in turn ignited an active civil war that has devastated the region.

Nigeria also experienced a peak in riot and protest in 2015 during the country's closely contested national elections when the incumbent Goodluck Jonathan lost to General Muhammadu Buhari. Riots and protests have also

---

[23]Cilliers, J., & Hedden, S., 2014. *Africa's Current and Future Stability.* Pretoria: Institute for Security Studies, p. 16.

[24]According to the ACLED codebook a protest is 'a non-violent, group public demonstration, often against a government institution. Rioting is a violent form of demonstration.' Raleigh, C., & Dowd, C., 2015. *Armed Conflict Location and Event Data Project (ACLED) Codebook.* s.l.: The Armed Conflict Location & Event Data Project, p. 9.

been increasing in Ethiopia, Tunisia, Algeria, Kenya and Sudan in recent years. In 2019, large-scale protests erupted in Algeria and in Sudan where thousands of people took to the streets to demand the end of two of Africa's longest ruling presidents, Abdelaziz Bouteflika, who had presided over Algeria since 1999, and Omar al-Bashir, who served as president of Sudan since a coup d'etat in 1993. Public displays of anger and resistance eventually forced both from power.

The extraordinary increase in the number of riots and protests probably reflects the impact of increased levels of education on Africa's young amidst limited job opportunities. It reflects Africa's, urbanising social landscape as well as the impact of social media and internet access, which has fomented a broader shift in power away from the few political elites and towards the public, now armed with information and the ability to communicate in real time with one another.

The nature of violence and instability seems to change as countries transition to democracy. Whereas political change is often associated with large-scale violent rupture, lower intensity riots and protests are more prevalent in democracies, South Africa and Kenya offering two good examples.

By comparative African standards, South Africa is very democratic and protests are the order of the day. Since South Africa has undergone a fairly recent political transition from apartheid to democracy, it is inherently more prone to civil conflict, particularly given its very high levels of inequality and unemployment. In recent years the political crisis associated with slow growth, corruption and patronage under former President Jacob Zuma gathered speed, sparking protests across the country as part of the #ZumaMustFall campaign. The transition to President Cyril Ramaphosa in 2018 has the promise to reverse this trend but the country remains unsettled due to rising unemployment and falling incomes.

However, it is in Ethiopia that has experienced the most riots and protests on a per capita basis, and Somalia where they were most fatal. In 2016 Ethiopia experienced an extraordinary increase in the number of riots and protests as the Oromo and eventually also the Amhara ethnic groups started protesting against the perceived dominance of the minority Tigray ethnic group. Whereas Tigrayans make up only about six percent of Ethiopia's population, they have long been accused of holding inordinate economic, political and security influence. An acute drought and the floods in the highlands, particularly in the Amhara and Oromia regions, deepened this sense of discontent.

The first reaction from the Tigrayan-dominated government was to institute a national state of emergency in 2016 that was accompanied by brutal suppression. But eventually in March 2018, Prime Minister Hailemariam Desalegn stepped down to make way for a much younger replacement, Abiy Ahmed, from the Oromo ethnic group. Abiy has embarked on a raft of reforms, including ending the state of emergency, releasing political prisoners, reforming the security agencies, reaching out to Eritrea (for which he was awarded the Nobel peace prize) and opening up the economy with far-reaching implications for Ethiopia and the region. That this did not go down well with all concerned became apparent in June 2019 when the Army Chief of Staff and others were assassinated during a failed coup attempt in the Amhara region and as this book goes to print, the country may be teetering on the brink of a wider conflagration as Tigray tries to assert greater autonomy from the center.

Generally riots and protests appear to have become less deadly over time, meaning that there are fewer fatalities per event. For example, while Africa experienced an average of eight fatalities per riot/protest event from 2001 to 2003, that average declined to three from 2015 to 2017, although wider access to social media reporting may also have played a role.[25]

The steady rate of urbanisation is clearly associated with the increasing number of riots and protests since these are overwhelmingly urban phenomena. Although estimates of urbanisation conceal vast subnational differences, Africa was on average only 34% urban in 2001, but this increased to 42% by 2018. Being significantly less urbanised than other regions in the world, the inevitable process of more rapid urbanisation in the future could prove to be politically destabilising. It will increase the opportunity for riots and protests since the region is also undergoing changes in regime type and democratising (see Chapter 13).

North Africa, the location of the Arab Spring, is significantly more urban than sub-Saharan Africa. In 2010, the year in which it erupted, 53% of people in North Africa lived in urban areas compared to 35% in sub-Saharan Africa. With a large portion of people in towns and cities, that population density facilitated the kind of crowd and mass dynamics that eventually ejected Zine El Abidine Ben Ali from his presidency in Tunisia, forced a rotation in the governing elite in Egypt and culminated in civil war in Libya.

---

[25] See the analysis in Cilliers, J., 2018. *Violence in Africa: Trends, Drivers and Prospects to 2023*. Pretoria: Institute for Security Studies, p. 10.

Structural Drivers of Violence

The structural drivers of violence in Africa are complex and country specific, although there are a number of common themes that relate to poverty, democratisation, regime type, population age structure, repeat violence, the bad neighbourhood effect and poor governance. Crowd and mass violence typically requires politicisation and triggering event(s), such as the decision by the young Tunisian fruit seller Mohamed Bouazizi to self-immolate on 18 December 2010—the event that is generally accepted as having started the Arab Spring.

For such a spark to have ignited the widespread violence and unrest that followed, societies need to be afflicted by very high levels of social tension and discontent. In this instance, tension was largely the result of limited social, economic and political opportunity in North Africa and the Middle East against a backdrop of relatively high levels of education. In addition, North Africa experienced a downturn in economic growth before the Arab Spring that inevitably increased the sense of relative deprivation.[26]

While the debate about causation is contentious, some things are fairly obvious. In southern Africa the extraordinarily high level of inequality in countries like Namibia, Botswana and South Africa presents a potential threat to stability. An interesting reason for this is the fact that the informal sector in these countries is quite small by comparative standards. The extent of autocratic repression in countries such as Equatorial Guinea and the Kingdom of Eswatini will certainly present a problem in the future if left unattended. Recurrent efforts by leaders such as Obiang Nguema Mbasogo (Equatorial Guinea), Mswati lll (Eswatini), Paul Biya (Cameroon), Yoweri Museveni (Uganda) and Idriss Déby (Chad) to extend their terms in office or effect dynastic succession present obvious challenges as pressure mounts without the prospects for either democratic change or generational succession.

However, so far there is no scholarly consensus on the direct causal link between factors brought about by climate change, such as desertification, and the outbreak of conflict in Sudan (Darfur) and Mali, although it is clear that specific events such as droughts sometimes lead to violence. One example

---

[26]In respect of the latter, Hughes found that 'a 1.0% drop in a moving average of economic growth (carrying 60% of the moving average forward) is associated with a 0.04 point increase on a 0 1 scale for the rate of internal war'. Hughes, B. B., 2019. *International Futures: Building and Using Global Models*. Cambridge: Academic Press, p. 180. Also see Ianchovichina, E., Mottaghi, L., & Devarajan, S., 2015. *Inequality, Uprisings, and Conflict in the Arab World*. New York: The World Bank.

would be the drought in Ethiopia before the 2016 riots and protests.[27] In many countries in the Sahel, a region with a particularly rapidly growing young population, conflict between herders and farmers causes more fatalities than terrorism and the role that climate change plays in accelerating a trend towards armed conflict is increasingly evident.

As climate change alters the nature of resource dependence, it will impact states with large natural resource benefits. A report by Cullen Hendrix and Idean Salehyan found that

> Water shocks may lead to social conflict via their effects on resource competition, poor macroeconomic outcomes, and reduced state capacity … deviations from normal rainfall patterns have a significant effect on both large-scale and smaller-scale instances of political conflict… wetter years are more likely to suffer from violent events. Extreme deviations in rainfall – particularly dry and wet years – are associated with all types of social conflict (violent and nonviolent, government-targeted and non/government-targeted), although the relationship is strongest with respect to violent events, which are more responsive to abundant rather than scarce rainfall.[28]

African countries will experience widely different effects from climate change in the coming decades (see Chapter 15), which will strain the ability of large regions to support local populations under current developmental conditions. Some areas of the continent are likely to become warmer and drier and experience more frequent and severe droughts close to major population centres, particularly in the Sahel.[29] Other parts of the continent may experience widespread drought and potentially famine without proper government intervention, while the Eastern swathes of the continent will likely experience heavier rainfall, which could also adversely affect crops and food security.

Current evidence on the impact of climate change and conflict is country- and region-specific. For example, while the evidence from East Africa is that socio-political factors are more robust drivers of conflict than climate

---

[27] See, for example, Buhaug, H., Gleditsch, N. P., & Theisen, O. M., 2008. *Implications of Climate Change for Armed Conflict*, Washington: Social Development, The World Bank. Also see Andrews-Speed, P., Bleischwitz, R., Boersma, T., Johnson, C., & Kemp, G., 2012. *The Global Resource Nexus The Struggles for Land, Energy, Food, Water, and Minerals*, Washington: Transatlantic Academy, pp. 3–4.
[28] Hendrix, C. S., & Salehyan, I., 2012. Climate Change, Rainfall, and Social Conflict in Africa. *Journal of Peace Research*, 49(1), p. 36.
[29] Kwasi, S., Cilliers, J., Donnefeld, Z, Welborn, L and Maiga, I. 2019. Prospects for the G5 Sahel Countries to 2040, Institute for Security Studies, 4 December 2019 [Online]. Available at: https://issafrica.org/research/west-africa-report-for-the-g5-sahel-countries-to-2020.

change,[30] our work on the future of the five Sahel countries points to a more direct link between climate change and conflict as herders are being forced to move earlier and further south in search of grazing, intensifying competition within pastoral communities.

Regime Capacity, Type and Regime Dissonance

The capacity and nature of the governmental system of a country has an important impact on the probability of violence.

The changes in Africa's growth prospects during the last two decades signify a structural transformation in the continent's fortunes. Improvements in general living conditions are very likely to translate into stability. The reason for this is actually not that people are more content with improved standards of living, but because the capacity of governments to provide or enforce security increases as countries develop.

Stability not only depends on the nature of the government (i.e. democratic or autocratic) or inequality and unemployment but also on whether the government has the means to provide or enforce security. Poor countries have limited capacity which constrains the state's ability to govern and enforce security. In that sense, Africa was trapped in a vicious circle—many countries are unstable because they were poor, and because they are poor they were unstable.

Furthermore, and contrary to popular belief, government spending on security in Africa tends to be quite low when compared to the level of insecurity on the continent and to other regions such as the Middle East. Spending is also skewed towards providing security for the president or governing elite rather than on responding to real security needs. Given the continent's long history of coup d'etats and interference by the military in government, security spending is often also divided between a number of competing and overlapping security services as leaders try to ensure that no single agency could pose a threat to them. At the same time many areas in Africa are unpoliced and national and local government representation is thin or non-existent. Institutions are weak and because of high levels of poverty, rent-seeking is high.

Because military rule and one-party governments have generally been an unmitigated disaster, there is strong support for democracy, discussed in more

---

[30] Maslin, M., 2018. *Politics and Poverty Caused Past Conflicts in East Africa—Not Climate Change*. [Online] Available at: https://theconversation.com/politics-and-poverty-caused-past-conflicts-in-east-africa-not-climate-change-96372.

detail in Chapter 13. The problem, however, is that when leaders eventually are pushed in this direction they allow for nominal not substantive democracy. Nominal democracy can be found in Zimbabwe, the Democratic Republic of Congo, Uganda, Ethiopia, Rwanda and Algeria where the theatrics of regular elections regularly proceed but there is no real choice or true debate.

A significant amount of research underpins the finding that only when there are truly free and fair elections that offer prospects for change in leadership, can democracy lead to improved human development. This is because electoral competition incentivises politicians to provide public goods and services. Improved government effectiveness (and hence better service delivery) can therefore be associated with substantive democracy but generally not with nominal electoral democracies.[31]

At this point in time most African countries are so-called anocracies[32]—countries that have elements of both autocracy and democracy. Examples of anocracies include Côte d'Ivoire, Zimbabwe, Tanzania, Algeria, Burundi and The Gambia. In these mixed or intermediate regimes regular competitive elections take place, but the legislature has little effective control over the executive branch of government. Thus anocracies are

> characterized by institutions and political elites that are far less capable of performing fundamental tasks and ensuring their own continuity. Anocratic regimes very often reflect inherent qualities of instability or ineffectiveness and are especially vulnerable to the onset of new political instability events, such as outbreaks of armed conflict, unexpected changes in leadership, or adverse regime changes (e.g. a seizure of power by a personalistic or military leader in a coup). Anocracies are a middling category rather than a distinct form of governance.[33]

Anocracies are less stable than full autocracies, which are in turn less stable than consolidated democracies. The relationship takes the form of an inverted U with intermediate regime types six times more likely than democracies and 2.5 times more likely than an autocracy to experience new outbreaks of

---

[31] Ibid., p. 6.
[32] On the Polity score a mixed/intermediate regime type (s) has a score from +5 to -5 in an index that ranges from + 10 to − 10. V-Dem distinguishes between different types of democracy each with its own index. Its electoral democracy index is closest to the Polity IV index.
[33] Marshall, M. G., & Elzinga-Marshall, G. C., 2017. *Global Report 2017 Conflict, Governance, and State Fragility.* Vienna: Center for Systemic Peace, p. 30.

civil conflict. More than half of anocracies experience a major regime change within five years and 70% within ten years.[34]

Anocracies with factionalised party systems, where one ethnic grouping is advantaged, are particularly vulnerable to political instability since political mobilisation generally transforms diversity into violence.

Finally, research at the Institute for Security Studies points to two important albeit tentative outcomes in terms of violence as it relates to regime type. First, if a country is significantly more democratic than other countries at similar levels of income and education, such an imbalance increases opportunities for corruption and the risk of acute episodes of violent protests and demonstrations. Examples include Mozambique (low income), Kenya (lower-middle income) and South Africa (upper-middle income). Second, if a country is significantly less democratic than could be expected given its levels of income and education, the pressure for political participation and accountability is likely to grow, with Equatorial Guinea and the Kingdom of Eswatini serving as textbook examples to watch. Such pressure could lead to instability and even a violent rupture, particularly around leadership renewal. Other examples include North Africa before the Arab Spring but also possibly Ethiopia (low income), the Republic of the Congo (lower-middle income) and Libya (upper-middle income).

Youth and Unemployment

Given its current median age of 19 years (18 for sub-Saharan Africa), Africa has an exceptionally youthful population although fertility rates differ significantly across regions and within countries. Large youth bulges, defined as the presence of a large population between 15 and 29 years of age relative to the total adult population, are robustly associated with an increased risk of conflict and high rates of criminal violence. This is particularly true when young people lack opportunities in terms of education, training and employment and feel they have no voice.[35]

---

[34] Ibid. p. 12; Goldstone, J. A., Bates, R. H., Epstein, D. L., Gurr, T. R., Lustik, M. B., Marshall, M. G., Ulfelder, J., & Woodward, M. (2010). A Global Model for Forecasting Political Instability. *American Journal of Political Science*, 54: 190–208, p. 195; Knutsen, C. H., & Nygård, H. M., 2015. Institutional Characteristics and Regime Survival: Why Are Semi-Democracies Less Durable Than Autocracies and Democracies? *American Journal of Political Science*, 59(3), pp. 656–670; Hegre, H., Ellingsen, T., Gates, S., & Gleditsch, N. P., 2001. Toward a Democratic Civil Peace? Democracy, Political Change, and Civil War, 1816–1992. *The American Political Science Review*, 95(1), pp. 33–48.

[35] Urda, H. 2011. Demography and Armed Conflict: Assessing the Role of Population Growth and Youth Bulges, Centre for Research on Peace and Development, Working Paper No. 2; World Bank, World Development Report 2011, p. 6.

However youth bulges appear to be more closely related to low-intensity conflict than to civil war.[36] Figure 12.2 shows the size of the youth bulge in 2018 and 2040 for different global regions. Sub-Saharan Africa is the youngest region globally with almost half of its adult population currently between 15 and 29 years, declining modestly to 43% by 2040.

Generally, higher education levels are associated with lower conflict vulnerability, but this depends on the size of the youth bulge, levels of employment and degree of urbanisation.[37]

Many of these correlations were evident in North Africa at the time of the Arab Spring and again now in Algeria and Sudan.[38] In the next five years, Somalia, Niger, Central African Republic, Chad, South Sudan, Uganda, Mali, Zambia and Uganda and Angola, Malawi, Zambia, Mozambique and Burkina Faso all have more than half of their adult population in the age bracket from 15 to 29 and therefore be particularly at risk of violence and conflict, given that they also have high levels of unemployment.[39] The only African countries with less than a third of their adult population in the youth bulge are Libya, Morocco, Algeria, Tunisia, Mauritius and the Seychelles. The fact that the youth bulge is coming down rapidly in a number of North African countries is particularly important in reducing this important structural driver of violence, but is only likely to have an impact if accompanied by substantive economic freedom that provides economic opportunity to a much larger swathe of citizens.

---

[36] Hegre, H. Karlsen, J., Mokleiv, H., Strand, H., & Urdal, H. 2013. Predicting Armed Conflict, 2010–2050. *International Studies Quarterly*, 57(2), pp. 250–270, p. 6.

[37] Ibid., p. 5.

[38] Although the size of the youth bulge is often considered as an important factor in the Arab Spring, the size of the bulge in North Africa is considerably lower than in the rest of Africa, pointing to the role played by other factors, most likely the low levels of political, economic and social inclusion in the region compared to other countries at similar levels of income and education. Tunisia had the lowest poverty rates among these countries but inequality is significantly lower in Egypt. The average income levels of Libya and Algeria are substantially higher than that of Tunisia and Egypt. Mobile phone subscriptions were highest in Libya. Country level differences are important. For example the youth bulge in Tunisia (where the Arab Spring started) was 8 percentage points below the average in Algeria, Egypt and Libya (all at roughly 42/42% in 2010). Yet Tunisia, a much smaller and more homogeneous country, is the only one to have seen a successful transition from autocracy to democracy. Some reasons for the heterogeneous outcomes are self-evident, for example Egypt and Algeria both have strong central governments and large security structures while Libya was a dysfunctional state that descended into civil war even before the NATO military intervention that tipped the country into widespread instability and chaos. Brown, C., 2014. *The Tunisian Exception*. [Online] Available at: www.juancole.com/2014/10/the-tunisian-exception.html.

[39] Ethiopia's youth bulge is coming down more rapidly than most other low-income countries in Africa due to the successful implementation of the provision of water, sanitation, basic health care and availability of contraceptives that have, in combination, resulted in a rapid decline in total fertility rates in recent years. Ethiopia is expected to experience a decline in fertility rates from 4.6 currently to 3.7 children by 2030. See Donnenfeld, Z., Porter, A., Cilliers, J., Moyer, J., Scott, A., Maweni, J., & Aucoin, C., 2017. Ethiopia Development Trends Report, Institute for Security Studies, pp 16–17.

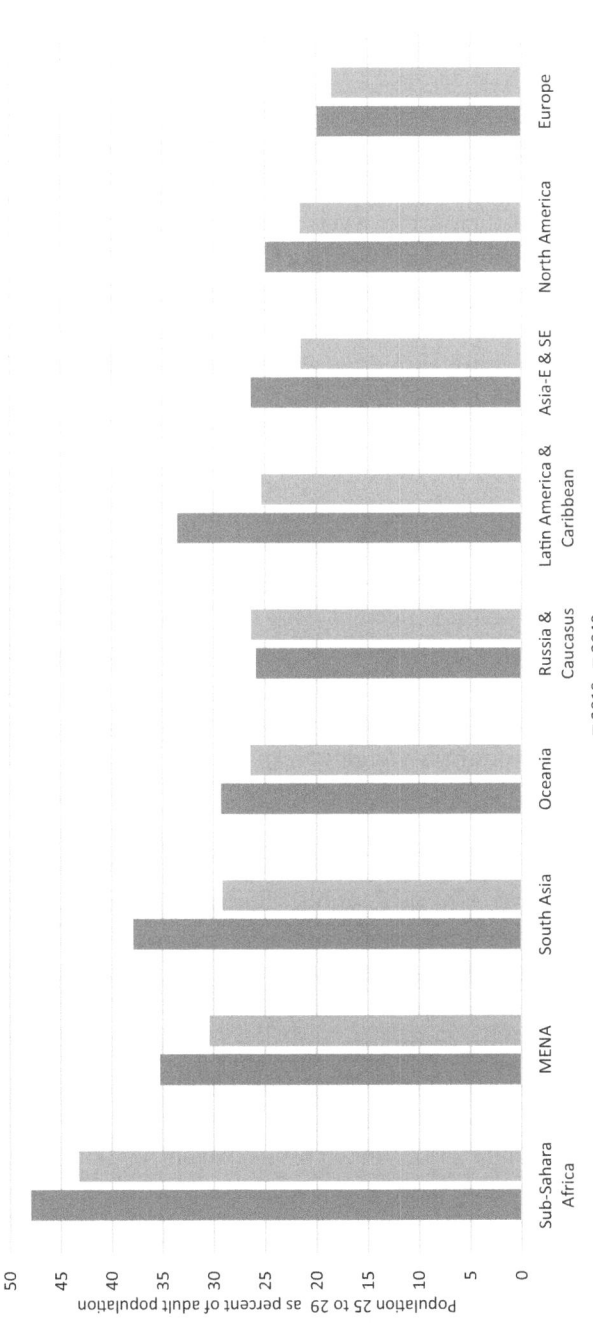

Fig. 12.2 Ratio of youth (15–29) to adults (+15), selected regions in 2018 and 2040 (*Source* IFs version 7.45 initialising from United Nations Population Division medium variant life-expectancy the 2017 revision)

A causal link between youth unemployment and violence in developing countries is widely assumed, particularly crime, gang violence and domestic violence, but solid evidence remains insufficient.[40]

Poor Governance and High Levels of Inequality

In Chapter 13, I contend that at low levels of income and development, the nature of the governing elite is more important for economic growth and for positive development outcomes than the extent to which countries are democratic or authoritarian. Countries fortunate enough to have a developmentally oriented governing elite grow much more rapidly, particularly if there is a cohesive governing party or coterie of leadership with a clear focus on development.

The difference between stable and unstable poor countries is often a political elite that effectively distributes services (particularly among different ethnic groups), develops sustainable institutions, minimises corruption and encourages the development of the private sector while focusing on equitable growth. To this end the Ibrahim Index of African Governance defines governance as 'the provision of the political, social and economic public goods and services that every citizen has a right to expect from their state, and that a state has the responsibility to deliver to its citizens'.[41]

The index measures a country's overall governance performance across four sub-components, namely safety and rule of law, participation and human rights, sustainable economic opportunity and human development. Countries that score the worst in the overall governance index are Somalia, South Sudan, Eritrea, the Central African Republic, Sudan, Libya, the Democratic Republic of Congo, Chad, Equatorial Guinea, Angola and Burundi. All of these countries were allocated a score below 40 out of a possible 100.

High levels of inequality often point to a government that largely looks after the interests of specific sectors or elites or is unwilling to undertake the necessary measures to address inequality. This is reflected in the high inequality scores of South Africa, Botswana, Namibia, Equatorial Guinea, Lesotho, Comoros, Zambia and the Central African Republic.[42] Today former liberation parties that have grown complacent in power dominate

---

[40] See for example Idris, I., 2016. Youth Unemployment and Violence. Rapid Literature Review. *GSDRC University of Birmingham*, November.

[41] Ibrahim, Mo, 2018. *Ibrahim Index of African Governance (IIAG)*. [Online] Available at: http://mo.ibrahim.foundation/iiag/.

[42] Rates of infant mortality are widely used as an indicator of poor service delivery and even as a short-term indicator of impending problems including a violent rupture.

governments in southern Africa. Their inability to grow their economies means they have also been unable to change the patterns of inequality inherited from colonialism, white settler dominance and apartheid. Instead of growth, they turn their attention to (re)distribution which has much more limited potential. With no prospects for political, generational and policy renewal that could impact on these structural imbalances, the promise that is inherent to regular free and fair elections is now also being frustrated. This is perhaps best reflected in the recent change in the top leadership in Zimbabwe (octogenarian Robert Mugabe was replaced by the slightly younger Emmerson Mnangagwa) that has brought little substantive change to a country that has levels of income much lower than when its white minority government declared unilateral independence from Britain several decades ago.

In South Africa, only its relatively high scores of governance (and democracy) outcomes have been able to constrain violence, given its high levels of inequality and unemployment. And in Gabon, Ali Bongo Ondimba assumed power from his father in 2009 who had controlled the country since the 1960s. Eventually, without leadership and political renewal, countries inevitably grow below their potential and consequently social problems fester.

Perceptions about the distribution of wealth between groups and levels of equity in a society play an important role and fuel discontent. But as discussed in Chapter 7, inequality changes very slowly.

In Central Africa the recent downturn in global commodity prices has exacerbated an already fragile situation. There, as elsewhere, the government is unable to deliver the most basic services yet the political elite have been exceptionally creative in designing strategies to retain their hold on power through 'personalised presidential systems supported by patronage networks sustained mainly through elite bargaining and collusion with traditional rulers'.[43]

Besides a history of conflict and chronic underdevelopment, those countries in sub-Saharan Africa that suffer severe inequality, rely heavily on primary commodities, have a large youth bulge and an oppressive regime are virtually assured of future instability and even a violent rupture.

Even then growth in itself could be insufficient to forestall instability. This was demonstrated in Ethiopia where the government instituted a national state of emergency in October 2016 after a decade of remarkable economic

---

[43] Donnenfeld, Z., & Akum, F., 2017. *Gathering storm Clouds: Political and Economic Uncertainty in Central Africa*. Pretoria: Institute for Security Studies, p. 11.

growth. Growth had, in fact, widened discontent in a country that many felt was being controlled by a small ethnic elite from Tigray.

Modelling the Prospects for Greater Peace: The Silencing the Guns Scenario

The IFs forecasting platform uses historical data from the Center for Systemic Peace to initialise its forecasts on stability. Different from the datasets from UCPD and ACLED, the dataset interprets the impact of instability on each country since smaller and poorer countries (for example) have different conflict absorptive capacities to richer countries. The algorithms that drive the forecast on instability in turn relies on many of the conflict drivers and correlations discussed in this chapter.[44]

In the Silencing the Guns scenario, I reduce the general governance risk in the fourteen countries that have repeatedly featured in this chapter, namely Burkina Faso, the Central African Republic, Chad, the Democratic Republic of the Congo, Egypt, Ethiopia, Libya, Mali, Niger, Nigeria, Somalia, South Sudan, South Africa and Sudan.[45] The impact is to improve the contribution that social capital makes to multifactor productivity within the IFs forecasting platform. Improved multifactor productivity (or technology) is, in turn, one of the three components of economic growth, the other two being labour and capital.

Stability translates into lower levels of corruption and more effective and capable governance—all of which will improve the investment climate on the continent. By 2040 these 14 countries should, according to the IFs forecast, have increased their exports by US$26 billion and increased their stock of foreign direct investment by more than US$70 billion. While more stability translates into bigger inflows of foreign direct investment it is likely to reduce development assistance as funds are diverted to countries in greater need.

---

[44] The Center scores and categorises all major episodes of political violence in countries with a population larger than 500,000. Each Major Episode of Political Violence, or MEPV, is allocated a score to reflect the magnitude or national impact of that event per year from 1 (sporadic or expressive political violence) to 10 (extermination and annihilation) and allows for comparisons across categories and cases. To date the highest value allocated to an event is a 7 (pervasive warfare). As opposed to the datasets from UCDP and ACLED that try and gather much more granular data (such as all riots and battles that resulted in fatalities), the threshold for inclusion in the dataset is a minimum of 100 'directly-related fatalities' per year and at least 500 over the event duration. See Center for Systemic Peace, 2017. *Global Conflict Trends: Assessing the Qualities of Systemic Peace*. [Online] Available at: www.systemicpeace.org/conflicttrends.html.

[45] Normally such a scenario would imply an increase in general defence and security expenditure that would offset some of the improvements in growth. This is not included in the scenario.

Governments in these countries would be able to roll out more electrification schemes (according to IFs a million more persons would be connected), allow more people to be connected to safe water and sanitation, education and offer more health care services for more citizens, and tourism can also flourish. The results are improvements across various dimensions such as a small reduction in infant mortality rates and, as conditions improve, fertility rates will decline. For example by 2040, Africa will have almost 140,000 fewer births than in the Current Path. More stability in these fourteen countries will have a regional impact, indeed on the prospects of the entire continent. Fewer children would suffer from malnutrition compared to the Current Path forecast. Furthermore, fewer Africans will seek to flee their home countries, resulting in lower levels of refugees and reduced migration.

More stability and foreign investment translate into a bigger economy and improved economic growth. In the Silencing the Guns scenario, the African economy is US$182 billion larger than in the Current Path forecast in 2040 (in market exchange rates). The cumulative gains from 2020 to 2040 are impressive, amounting to an increase of US$979 billion. By 2040 the average GDP per capita in the fourteen countries will have increased by US$230, and nearly 18 million fewer Africans would be living under the international extreme poverty line of US$1.90 per day. In addition, levels of democracy are likely to increase and governance will improve.

Conclusion: Focusing on Conflict Prevention

The complex and country-specific structural drivers of conflict in Africa are interlinked with external factors like the impact of radical ideology, currently in the form of fundamentalist Islamism, and geopolitical competition. Yet we are likely to see further reductions in instability in the twenty-first century since levels of education and literacy are increasing, as are levels of substantive democratic accountability, while trade and travel all connect us more closely than before. The COVID-19 pandemic will slow and may disrupt these trends but is unlikely to disrupt globalisation in a fundamental way.

Poor governance and lack of inclusive economic development lie at the heart of Africa's instability challenge. For instance, in West Africa and the Sahel political violence is being driven by a sense of marginalisation and exclusion from the political centre. Africans need to confront this reality instead of succumbing to the militarised approaches to combating terror that, with much more resources, have failed in Afghanistan and in the Middle East.

Generally, states in sub-Saharan Africa are younger and poorer (in terms of income) than most of their international peers. Colonialism and its legacies have severely disrupted their natural evolution, and political violence has been a central feature of the region's colonial and postcolonial history.

While armed conflict is often more prevalent in rural areas, riots and protests are becoming an overwhelmingly urban phenomena, particularly since the share of Africa's urban population living in slums is steadily rising. Political violence in Africa is already largely urban-based, and instability in Africa is likely to affect cities and the unpoliced and unplanned urban sprawls rather than rural areas going forward.[46] Clearly conflicts over land, property rights and services for urban residents need to be addressed by integrated urban development strategies.[47]

Against that backdrop, the gains in peace and stability over the past two decades are impressive. These include significant multilateral, regional and bilateral efforts and investments in conflict prevention, peacemaking, peacekeeping[48] and peacebuilding. Much remains to be done, however, such as ending the extent to which conflict in one country, such as Libya, is instigated and fuelled by neighbouring countries.

Africans have to further expand and capacitate the structures that form part of the African Union's African Peace and Security Architecture. To be effective, however, these institutions need to adopt different practices from those of the recent past where the organisation looked the other way when elections were being stolen in Zimbabwe, the Democratic Republic of the Congo and elsewhere. An approach premised on longer-term stability requires clear standards for governance, accountability and the provision of security. Africa needs to move from its focus on conflict management to substantive conflict prevention and a focus on the structural drivers of violence such as poor governance. Few investments can compete with the provision of education, for example, as a means to drain the swamp of ignorance that allows radical ideologies to flourish.

Clearly violence, instability and armed conflict in Africa will remain a major concern that requires an ongoing and dedicated response from the African Union, its member states and the international community for the provision of continued aid and humanitarian assistance to poor countries,

---

[46] See for example, Commins, S., 2018. *From Urban Fragility to Urban Stability*, Washington: The Africa Center for Strategic Studies.

[47] Bello-Schünemann, J., & Aucoin, C., 2016. *African Urban Futures*. Pretoria: Institute for Security Studies.

[48] Of the 15 current United Nations peacekeeping missions, five are in sub-Saharan Africa.

in peacekeeping in fragile ones and towards the promise of the Sustainable Development Goals.

Africa is set to remain turbulent because it is poor and young and because African governments have limited capacity to provide security. Perhaps more importantly, Africa can expect instability because it is growing and dynamic. Many African countries are experiencing a political awakening that is uncharacteristic of a continent that has long suffered at the hands of foreign intervention and autocratic exploitation by their own elites. The challenge is to productively channel that energy.

Protest has become a more acceptable public behaviour in many countries since there is an increased number of electoral democracies, although the quality of democracy is thin. This is reflected in the changing nature of violence whereby the ballot, not the gun, is slowly becoming the main source of political contestation. This is the theme of the next chapter.

Further Reading

Hendrix, Cullen, and Henk-Jan Brinkman. 2013. Food Insecurity and Conflict Dynamics: Causal Linkages and Complex Feedbacks. *Stability: International Journal of Security and Development*, 2(2). http://doi.org/10.5334/sta.bm.

Stapleton, Timothy. 2018. *Africa: War and Conflict in the Twentieth Century*. Routledge.

Williams, Paul D. 2016. *War and Conflict in Africa*. John Wiley & Sons.

Open Access This chapter is licensed under the terms of the Creative Commons Attribution 4.0 International License (http://creativecommons.org/licenses/by/4.0/), which permits use, sharing, adaptation, distribution and reproduction in any medium or format, as long as you give appropriate credit to the original author(s) and the source, provide a link to the Creative Commons license and indicate if changes were made.

The images or other third party material in this chapter are included in the chapter's Creative Commons license, unless indicated otherwise in a credit line to the material. If material is not included in the chapter's Creative Commons license and your intended use is not permitted by statutory regulation or exceeds the permitted use, you will need to obtain permission directly from the copyright holder.

13

Good Governance, Democracy and Development

Abstract In this chapter, Cilliers explores how democracy has swept across the globe to become the dominant form of governance. Africa, too, has become increasingly democratic, but often in name only: regular elections are often façades for corrupt, autocratic regimes. Cilliers explains how, in fact, competitive politics in poorly developed countries with weak political institutions may actually hinder development. However, public support for democracy has surged in Africa and it is critical that African countries protect and advance the strides they have made towards substantive democratic governance. The Fourth Wave scenario laid out in this chapter demonstrates how a more democratic Africa would impact on development.

Keywords Afrobarometer · Crests and troughs · Democracy · Neopatrimonialism · Polity IV Project · Varieties of Democracy (V-Dem)

Learning Objectives

- Explain the historical cycles of democracy from a global perspective and its manifestations on the African continent;
- Identify the core challenges democratisation has faced in Africa and their causes
- Understand how different regime types bear upon development
- Understand the Varieties of Democracy and Polity IV Projects and how each categorise and measures democracy and regime types.

Over the last two centuries, democracy has advanced in three global waves. With each wave, its quality, depth and reach has peaked and ebbed in crests and troughs that have come to define the evolution of governance—and what it means to be governed. Each crest has raised the high-water mark left by its predecessor, granting momentum to the tide of democracy as it envelops increasingly larger shares of the world's population.[1]

The first wave surged in the early nineteenth century particularly when the vote was granted to the white, male population of the USA, and ebbed in the turbulent years leading up to the Second World War. At the crest of this wave, democracies governed 29 states; at its trough at the height of the war in 1942, only 12 democracies remained.[2]

The end of the Second World War precipitated the second wave of democracy. As the number of independent states grew, so too did the number of democracies, rising to 36 internationally recognised democratic regimes in 1962 before falling modestly to 30 by the mid-1970s. During this wave, rapid decolonisation swept first across North Africa (following the defeat of Italy during the Second World War), affecting Eritrea, Ethiopia and Libya. Sudan gained independence from the United Kingdom and Egypt in 1956, followed by Tunisia and Morocco from France later that year. In Sub-Saharan Africa, Ghana was first becoming independent in 1957, followed by numerous Anglophone, Francophone and Belgium colonies.

Burdened by its vast colonial empire, a stagnant economy and 48 years of authoritarian rule it was perhaps no surprise that the third wave of democracy began in Portugal in 1974, with the Carnation Revolution. The following year all of Portugal's colonies achieved independence, a hasty and chaotic affair that swept from Cape Verde, Guinea-Bissau and Mozambique, Angola to São Tomé and Príncipe.

The end of Portuguese colonial rule set off a train of events that would eventually result in a series of liberation wars and the end of colonial rule in Rhodesia (now Zimbabwe) in 1980 and South West Africa (now Namibia) in 1990.

However, the key event that would eventually trigger large changes in the levels of democracy in Africa was the collapse of the Soviet Union in 1989. It ended a series of proxy wars in Africa and, as a result, also Western support for a number of unsavoury regimes that the West had instrumentalised to counter Soviet expansion. In 1990 it would also allow the start of a negotiated settlement process that witnessed Nelson Mandela elected as president

---

[1] Waves don't mean that all countries become more democratic, simply that there is a generalised, sustained and significant increase.
[2] https://en.wikipedia.org/wiki/List_of_sovereign_states_in_1939.

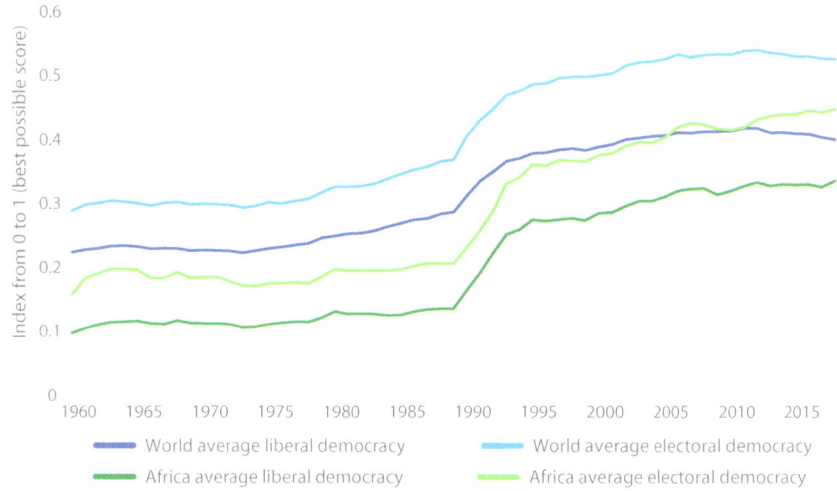

Fig. 13.1 Average levels of electoral and liberal democracy in the world and in Africa according to V-Dem: 1960–2018 (*Source* V-Dem v8)

of South Africa, then Africa's largest economy and with the most powerful military, four years later.

Also part of the third wave was a rash of democratic transitions in Latin America in the 1980s and shortly thereafter in several Asia-Pacific countries. The dissolution of the former Soviet Union further allowed a number of countries in eastern and central Europe to break away and establish representative systems of government.

These events all need to be borne in mind when considering Fig. 13.1, a line graph that uses data from the Varieties of Democracy project (V-Dem) to present average levels of liberal and electoral democracy in Africa and the world from 1960 to 2018.[3] V-Dem is a large and complex effort to conceptualise and measure democracy over time. It distinguishes between five types of democracy. In addition to liberal and electoral democracy, the two indices used in this chapter, it also measures participatory, deliberative and egalitarian democracy. It does so by providing a score, based on extensive subsidiary measures and expert opinion, of the extent to which each country in the dataset meets the ideal of the different types of democracy. Of the five types, liberal democracy is the most mature and developed where individual and

---

[3] See University of Gothenburg, 2019. *Varieties of Democracy*. [Online] Available at: https://www.v-dem.net/en/.

minority rights are protected against the tyranny of the majority[4] while electoral democracy is the least substantive. The index on the left-hand y-axis in Fig. 13.1 ranges from 0 (complete absence of democracy) to 1 (full liberal or electoral democracy in all countries).

According to the V-Dem data presented in Fig. 13.1 neither average levels of electoral democracy nor levels of substantive democracy changed significantly in Africa until 1989. By contrast, global averages steadily improved. Then, in the five years from 1989 to 1993, levels of democracy in Africa and globally increased sharply, although the increase in electoral democracy is more pronounced than for liberal democracy.

This is to be expected, as governments can easily adopt the trappings of electoral democracy such as going through the motions of regular elections but without substantive accountability and protection of individual rights. Liberal democracy requires much greater effort and time to establish—to separate the powers of the executive, judiciary and legislature, a truly competitive political environment, a free media and independent oversight mechanisms that have some teeth.

In the years that followed 1993, the gap between levels of electoral and substantive democracy in Africa has widened. More African countries hold regular elections and provide varying degrees of civil liberties, but these changes are not always substantive.

The V-Dem data presented in Fig. 13.1 coincides with data from other sources, such as from Freedom House, which contends that while only 17 of the 50 African countries on which it reported could be classified as 'free' or 'partly free' in 1988, 32 of 54 African countries were either 'free' or 'partly free' in 2018.

Many analysts hailed the so-called Arab Spring of 2010 as either the start of a fourth wave of democratisation—since it originated in the region with the lowest levels of political and economic inclusion globally—or proof that the third wave had not yet fully run its course. Sadly, Libya, Egypt and a number of countries in the Middle East and North Africa have suffered devastating blows to peace and stability. To date, only Tunisia has emerged from this turmoil with substantially higher scores on the various measures of democracy.

In 2018 and 2019, a new wave of popular protests swept first across Ethiopia, followed by Sudan and Algeria as citizens challenged long-standing parties and rulers. These events indicate that democratisation in Africa is

---

[4] As used by V-Dem in their codebook v8, April 2018, pp. 38–39. Available at University of Gothenburg, 2018. *Varieties of Democracy Codebook v8*. [Online] Available at: www.v-dem.net/media/filer_public/e0/7f/e07f672b-b91e-4e98-b9a3-78f8cd4de696/v-dem_codebook_v8.pdf.

indeed still on an upward trajectory. I pursue this line of reasoning in devising a subsequent scenario.

These trends in Africa stand in sharp contrast to developments elsewhere. Outside of Africa, democratic setbacks have affected countries as diverse as Brazil, Burundi, Hungary, Russia, Serbia and Turkey, a phenomenon evident in the decline in the average levels of liberal democracy globally from 2012 as can be seen in Fig. 13.1.

From a global perspective, the rise of terrorism, populism and the influence of an authoritarian China has turned the early optimism about a rising tide of democracy into a degree of democratic pessimism. In fact, a recent report by the global survey company Pew Research Centre[5] refers to global dissatisfaction with democracy as anti-establishment leaders, parties and movements have emerged on both sides of the political spectrum.

The future of democracy in the developed world is apparently fragile. The 2016 democracy index by the Economist Intelligence Unit, another well-known index, described the rise of populism in the West (and elsewhere) and the extent to which democracy in the West has retreated. 'An increased sense of personal and societal anxiety and insecurity in the face of diverse perceived risks and threats – economic, political, social and security – is undermining democracy, which depends on a steadfast commitment to upholding enlightenment values (liberty, equality, fraternity, reason, tolerance and free expression) …'.[6]

Roberto Foa and Yascha Mounk go so far as to question the durability of the world's affluent, consolidated democracies. Writing in the *Journal of Democracy*[7] they note that 'trust in political institutions such as parliaments or the courts have precipitously declined … as has voter turnout, party identification has weakened and party membership has declined'. In these societies today 'voters increasingly endorse single-issue movements, vote for populist candidates, or support "anti system" parties … Even in some of the richest and most politically stable regions in the world, it seems as though democracy is in a state of serious disrepair'.

---

[5] Wike, R., Laura, S., and Alexandra, C., 2019. *Many Across the Globe Are Dissatisfied With How Democracy Is Working*. [Online] Available at: https://www.pewglobal.org/2019/04/29/many-across-the-globe-are-dissatisfied-with-how-democracy-is-working/?utm_source=Pew+Research+Center&utm_campaign=089cb932c8-Global_2019_05_06&utm_medium=email&utm_term=0_3e953b9b70-089cb932c8-399996073.

[6] The Economist Intelligence Unit, 2015. *Democracy Index 2015: Democracy in an Age of Anxiety*. [Online] Available at: https://www.eiu.com/public/topical_report.aspx?campaignid=DemocracyIndex2015.

[7] Ibid. Foa, R. S., and Mounk, Y., 2016. The Danger of Deconsolidation: The Democratic Disconnect. *Journal of Democracy*, 27(3), pp. 5–17.

Foa and Mounk refer to the 'structural problems in the functioning of liberal democracy'.[8] Having no experience of life without democracy and no memory of the struggle to secure and sustain it, young voters in the industrial democracies of the West are not engaged in traditional party politics. Voter turnout is falling, political party membership has plummeted and support for unapologetically undemocratic regime types is on the rise. Instead of consolidating, the authors believe that democracy in the rich West may be under threat of 'deconsolidating'.[9]

Today the relative decline of the West has led to a commensurate weakening of the global impetus towards democratisation outside of Africa. As the leadership vacuum in established liberal democracies becomes evident, the USA in particular, in the face of challenges such as migration and globalisation, the example and influence of successful authoritarian development models such as China increases, backed by its rising economic muscle. In addition, Western influence within institutions such as the UN Security Council, the International Criminal Court and support for civil society and pro-democracy advocacy groups is declining in line with the reduction in Western economic dominance. Overt discord among previously unified Western nations is accelerating this trend.

On a positive note, by 2019 the Economist Intelligence Unit noted that 'for the first time in three years, the global score for democracy remained stable'.[10] The Unit's 2019 report points to improvements in voter turnout and membership of political parties, but warns that 'the rise of engagement combined with a continued crackdown on civil liberties is a potentially volatile mix, and could be a recipe for instability and social unrest in 2019'.[11]

The State of Democracy in Africa

The steady improvements in the levels of electoral and liberal democracy in Africa, particularly since 1989, means that democracy is now the dominant form of government on the continent. However, the quality of democracy

---

[8] Ibid., p. 6.

[9] They base their findings on survey data from the World Values Survey (conducted from 1995–2014) that finds a crisis of democratic legitimacy among younger generations of voters in North America and Europe that they argue, is much wider than previously appreciated.

[10] The Economist Intelligence Unit, 2018. *Democracy Index 2018: Me Too? Political Participation, Protest and Democracy*. [Online] Available at: https://www.eiu.com/public/topical_report.aspx?campaignid=Democracy2018, p. 4.

[11] Ibid. pp. 3, 6.

is often weak and the associated procedures are regularly flaunted as incumbents cook the books to stay in power and use any of a host of legal tricks to undermine competitive politics.

Benin is an example of an African country where democracy has deteriorated significantly in recent years. When the country voted for a new parliament in April 2019 not a single opposition candidate could take part after electoral authorities ruled that only two parties, both loyal to President Patrice Talon, met the requirement to participate—and a new electoral law required that parties pay US$424,000 to field a list for the 83-member parliament.[12]

Another way to measure democracy in Africa would be to classify countries as either (1) authoritarian (or non-democratic), (2) as electoral (or thin) democracies, or (3) as liberal (or substantive) democracies. Freedom House[13] adopted this approach when it classified ten African states as 'free' (roughly equating to liberal democracy), 22 as 'party free' (roughly equating to electoral democracy) and the remaining 22 as 'not free' in its most recent data release for 2018.

The ten free countries are Benin, Botswana, Cape Verde, Ghana, Mauritius, Namibia, São Tomé and Príncipe, Senegal, South Africa and Tunisia, in total home to only 133 million people, or ten percent of Africa's population. The 22 'partly free' countries that meet the minimum criteria to be classified as electoral democracies represent an additional 47% of Africa's population. The remainder, roughly 42%, of Africa's total population live in countries that Freedom House consider to be 'not free'.

Based on this analysis, 58% of Africans live in countries that could be considered democratic, even if the quality of that democracy is uneven. This finding is the basis of the introductory statement that democracy today is the dominant form of government in Africa, both in terms of the number of countries (32 out of 54) and the portion of total population (58%). Should Nigeria, with its 195 million people, move from being 'partly free' to 'free', the scales would tilt even more decisively in favour of democracy in Africa.

---

[12]Okello, C., 2019. *No Opposition, No Internet: Benin Election Raises Fears of Authoritarianism.* [Online] Available at: http://en.rfi.fr/africa/20190429-benin-parliamentary-election-no-opposition-no-internet-raises-fears-authoritarianism.

[13]Freedom House uses 25 indicators, where each country and territory is assigned a score from zero to four, for an aggregate score of up to 100. These scores are used to determine two numerical ratings, for political rights and civil liberties, with a rating of one representing the most free conditions and seven the least free. It assigns the designation 'electoral democracy' to countries that score seven or better in the 'electoral process' subcategory (one of four subcategories that form part of the political rights indicators) and an overall political rights score of 20 or better. Source: Freedom House, Freedom in the world 2016, and Freedom House, Methodology: Freedom in the world 2016.

These two measurements, by V-Dem and Freedom House, are imperfect, but nonetheless offer a useful way to understand the challenge of quantifying the depth and extent of democracy in Africa and how it has evolved over time.

A number of additional insights are also evident from the data presented in Fig. 13.1. The first is that the average levels of electoral democracy in Africa are slowly approaching (and even exceeding) the global mean. This convergence is occurring despite the fact that the average GDP per capita in Africa is much lower than and growing more slowly than the global average. In short, African nations are now transitioning to democracy at steadily lower levels of income than before.

Historically, the reason for this trend towards earlier democratisation is likely because of the dominance, until recently, of the liberal democratic West who provided significant amounts of development assistance to Africa (see Chapter 14). Furthermore, in an interconnected world citizens can compare their domestic conditions with other countries. The impact is to firmly establish democracy as the most desirable governance model. Proof of this support can be found in the data collected by the research organisation Afrobarometer, which has completed extensive and repeated surveys on attitudes to democracy in Africa over many years.[14]

The findings from Afrobarometer show that the demand for and support of democracy in Africa is strong and continues to expand. The push for greater democratisation in Africa comes from a citizenry who has endured decades of authoritarianism. Although electoral democracy has hardly delivered better developmental results, the process of being consulted and having the power to affect changes in leadership reshape the dynamics of power and the perception of accountability. Africans are tired of autocrats and big men.[15]

Finally, as mentioned in Chapter 12, most African regimes are of a mixed (and hence unstable) nature. They are neither fully autocratic nor fully democratic, but rather include some democratic systems and practices that coexist with undemocratic systems and practices. These mixed regime types (or anocracies) are more susceptible to abrupt regime change and governance setbacks than countries that are either fully autocratic or consolidated liberal democracies.[16]

---

[14]Afrobarometer, n.d. [Online]. Available at: http://afrobarometer.org/online-data-analysis.
[15]Ibid.
[16]This analysis is largely taken from the Polity IV project. See Center for Systemic Peace, 2018. *The Polity Project*. [Online] Available at: http://www.systemicpeace.org/polityproject.html.

While regular elections in Africa are becoming increasingly frequent, the number of incumbents who cling to power and block executive rotation or replacement presents a worrying trend. President Dennis Sassou Nguesso of the Republic of Congo, Yoweri Museveni of Uganda and Paul Kagame of Rwanda all recently amended their constitutions to allow for unlimited presidential incumbency. In the Democratic Republic of the Congo, outgoing president Joseph Kabila and his party simply ignored the actual results of the December 2018 elections, which Martin Fayulu of the Lamuka coalition had clearly won. Kabila instead installed his own choice in the form of Felix Tshisekedi who was duly inaugurated as president on 24 January 2019.[17] As in other regions, democratisation in Africa is turbulent and progress seldom linear.

Levels of democracy in Africa have however improved over time, despite the absence of many of the supposed preconditions for democratic consolidation. Nic Cheeseman understands these preconditions as 'a coherent national identity, strong and autonomous political institutions, a developed and autonomous civil society, the rule of law, and a strong and well performing economy'.[18]

Taking a decidedly pessimistic view of democratisation in Africa, Cheeseman argues that since 1990, democratisation has taken place against the odds in a number of poor and unstable countries that have lacked these preconditions for democracy. According to him, democratisation in Africa essentially rests on weak foundations, opening the possibility of a regression to lower or more 'appropriate' levels, while a façade of regular elections hides the reality of no or little change in the balance of political and social power.[19]

Indeed, democracies generally operate better above certain minimum levels of income and education, when the web of institutions and the rule of law are able to constrain the misuse and abuse of state institutions.[20]

Whatever the exact relationship between democracy, income and education, the indices tell an optimistic story of increased levels of democracy in

---

[17] To date CENI, the Commission Electorale Nationale Independante, has yet to release the results per polling station as required by law. The results announced by CENI was, among others, vastly at odds with the findings from the 40,000 observers deployed by the Catholic Church that established a large and comprehensive parallel compilation process.

[18] Cheeseman, N., 2015. *Democracy in Africa: Successes, Failures, and the Struggle for Political Reform.* Cambridge: Cambridge University Press. Also Cheeseman, N., 2015. *The State of Democracy in Africa.* [Online] Available at: http://democracyinafrica.org/the-state-of-democracy-in-africa/.

[19] Ibid.

[20] The American social scientist Barrington Moore popularised the notion of 'no bourgeois, no democracy', meaning minimum levels of economic development were required for democracy. See Moore, B., 1966. *Social Origins of Dictatorship and Democracy: Lord and Peasant in the Making of the Modern World.* Boston: Beacon Press. For more recent work see Przeworski, A., and Limongi, F., 1993. Political Regimes and Economic Growth. *The Journal of Economic Perspectives,* 7(3), pp. 51–69.

Africa over time. This is certainly good news in Africa for, once established and in conjunction with minimum income levels and education, democracy is the most stable form of governance. Thus Glaeser, Ponzetto and Shleifer find that:

> Averaging across the starting years 1960, 1970 and 1980, the probability of a well-educated democracy remaining a democracy twenty years later is 95 percent. The probability of a well-educated dictatorship becoming a democracy within 20 years is 87 percent.[21]

But the essential question for this book is: is democracy improving the living conditions of Africans?

Is Democracy Making a Difference to Development Prospects in Africa?

Over the long term—that is, over several successive decades—the response to that question is positive, democracy improves livelihoods. Through elections, democracy provides a mechanism to hold the power of the elite or special interest groups in check, it ensures the separation of state powers into discrete branches of government and protects human rights and the rule of law. In turn, democracies engender confidence for the pursuit of long-term investments. In this line of reasoning democracy is often conflated with good governance as a force multiplier on all development aspects: African countries with stronger institutions and better governance indicators, particularly in terms of government effectiveness and regulatory quality, generally fare better. However, such substantive democracies (that V-Dem would term liberal democracies) require significant time and resources to mature.

But, democracy is not the answer to economic stagnation, inequality or corruption in poor countries. In fact, at low levels of development democracy may have a negligible impact or actually constrain economic growth. This is because democracy generally only contributes to growth at more advanced levels of development where a more competitive political system reinforces a competitive economic system. Instead, at low levels of development, the nature of the governing elite is much more important for economic growth than the institutional setting (democratic or not).

---

[21] Glaeser, E. L., Ponzetto, G., and Shleifer, A., 2006. Why Does Democracy Need Education? *NBER Working Paper No. 12128*. Tunisia would be a good example of the impetus that high levels of education provide to democratisation.

In fact, a number of countries have achieved remarkable development under an autocratic system where the governing elite displayed a strong commitment to development. In the 1960s, the initial conditions in the Southeast Asian countries (such as China, Indonesia, Malaysia and Vietnam) and African countries were similar in many respects—the population suffered from widespread poverty, hunger, poor infrastructure, bad health and poor quality of education. Despite having strong neopatrimonial political systems (i.e. politically corrupt patron–client relations), as was the case in many African countries, the Southeast Asian economies grew rapidly and achieved massive reductions in levels of extreme poverty. That was not the case in Africa.

At a global level, China's authoritarian post-1978 developmental model is often quoted as proof of a positive relationship between autocracy and development at low levels of income. Its track record is sometimes compared to the much poorer progress of India, the world's largest democracy, which has struggled to gain economic momentum. Meanwhile, the Asian Tiger economies (Hong Kong, South Korea, Singapore and Taiwan) all experienced rapid progress without democracy—they only democratised after achieving middle-income status, further supporting the Chinese model.

In Africa, the most commonly quoted examples of successful authoritarian regimes are Rwanda and Ethiopia. In recent years, both countries have made more developmental progress than virtually any other African country. They benefited from very rapid growth in the size of their working-age population relative to dependants, improvements matched by solid, if unspectacular, advances in primary school education and literacy.

On both these measurements Rwanda comes off a higher base than Ethiopia, making the improvements in average levels of income of Ethiopians even more impressive. As discussed in Chapter 4, economic growth generally follows rapidly declining fertility rates and subsequent improvements in the portion of working age persons to dependants. In addition, the advancement of primary school and general literacy levels are important preconditions for turning this larger working force into productive human capital—areas where Ethiopia still faces many challenges.

These two countries are, however, exceptions in a sea of many poor-performing authoritarian countries. Their positive outcomes have been highly contingent on the nature of the governing elite and the personality of the president. In both countries, a national trauma has driven the burning desire to develop—the genocide of the Red Terror in Ethiopia under Mengistu Haile Mariam, which lasted until 1978, and the Rwandan genocide of 1994.

In the wake of these trauma, governing elites in the two countries intervened decisively in the economy in favour of productivity, often exerting considerable short-term pain for the sake of achieving long-term gain—policy choices that are much easier to implement in an autocratic than in a democratic setting. All have clear pro-growth policies and stick to them. In each of these countries a determined pro-development governing elite is united in their vision to escape debilitating poverty and underdevelopment.

At an average rate of nearly 10% per year over a recent decade, Ethiopia has achieved the most robust GDP growth of any country globally, surpassing countries like China, Qatar and Rwanda. Over that same period, average incomes in the country nearly tripled, and the proportion of the population who have access to electricity, for example, has doubled.[22] But, the wheels eventually began to come off.

In 2015 Ethiopia held parliamentary elections, as well as elections for its regional assemblies. The ruling Ethiopian People's Revolutionary Democratic Front (EPRDF) gained 500 of the available 547 seats, but the process and the political environment fell short of being considered substantively free and fair. Shortly afterwards, the government announced its intention to expand the city limits of Addis Ababa into the surrounding Oromia province.

The plan triggered widespread resentment and suspicion that the EPRDF was aiming to enhance federal authority at the expense of the nation's largest ethnic group, the Oromo, who were poorly represented in government. Protests began in November 2015 in Ginchi, a small town in Oromia about 80 kilometres southwest of Addis Ababa. Although the government formally abandoned the plan to expand the capital in January 2016, tensions continued to simmer.

By October 2016 the crisis reached a tipping point. A heavy-handed response by the security forces during an annual cultural festival in Oromia on 2 October triggered a stampede that killed dozens, possibly hundreds, of people. Three days later, the government blocked mobile phone access to popular social media websites like Facebook and WhatsApp. On 9 October 2016, the government declared a nationwide state of emergency that restricted freedom of movement and assembly and access to social media and suspended due process for arrest and detention.[23]

---

[22] The World Bank, 2016. *Access to Electricity (% of Population)*. [Online] Available at: https://data.worldbank.org/indicator/EG.ELC.ACCS.ZS?locations=ET.

[23] Human Rights Watch, n.d. *Ethiopian Protests*. [Online] Available at: https://www.hrw.org/tag/ethiopian-protests. Human Rights Watch, 2016. *Ethiopia Events of 2016*. [Online] Available at: https://www.hrw.org/world-report/2017/country-chapters/ethiopia.

In the weeks and months that followed, Ethiopia's formidable security apparatus detained more than 10,000 opposition members, the majority of whom came from the Amhara and Oromia regions.[24] Tensions simmered throughout 2017, with armed clashes between ethnic groups becoming commonplace in several regions. By the end of 2017, Public Radio International reported that there were as many as 400,000 internally displaced persons in Ethiopia's Oromia and Somali regions.[25] In February 2018 Prime Minister Hailemariam Desalegn resigned in response to the escalating unrest.

This unrest continued until, in April 2018, Abiy Ahmed Ali, the chairman of the Oromo Democratic Party, was elected as chairman of the EPRDF and as prime minister. He launched a sweeping political, economic, social and foreign policy reform programme in an effort to undercut the discontent that had led to the violence, even changing the name and character of his party.

The experience of Ethiopia helps provide a possible answer to the democracy-development quandary. On the one hand Ethiopia ran into trouble due to the extent that a small group, the Tigrayans, were perceived to benefit from economic growth, pointing to the dangers of ethnic favouritism and the importance of balancing economic and political progress. Eventually rapid development required that Ethiopia expand the extent to which its political system too had to evolve but the sense of victimization by the Tigrayans would see the country under threat of civil war as this book went to print.

Today, liberal democracy is a prerequisite for growth in high-income countries. Since democracy in low-income countries is invariably of a low, procedural type (i.e. electoral, not liberal) it makes little contribution to improvements in well-being or even to the way in which the country is governed.

The challenge with many of Africa's democracies is their reliance on a single mechanism, elections, as a means to determine the 'will of the people', while the institutions required to translate that mechanism into practice are immature or missing. The result is a choice between violent and disruptive elections that are often a sham, or the continuation of the status quo that had given rise to the governance crisis in the first instance. No country demonstrates this challenge better than Somalia—Africa's pre-eminent failed state, and recently South Sudan.

---

[24] Al Jazeera and Agencies, 2016. *Ethiopia State of Emergency Arrests Top 11,000*. [Online] Available at: https://www.aljazeera.com/news/2016/11/ethiopia-state-emergency-arrests-top-11000-161112 191919319.html.

[25] Jeffrey, J., 2017. *Hundreds of Thousands of Displaced Ethiopians Are Caught Between Ethnic Violence and Shadowy Politics*. [Online] Available at: https://www.pri.org/stories/2017-12-15/hundreds-thousands-displaced-ethiopians-are-caught-between-ethnic-violence-and.

In their study on the relationship between democracy and human development, Gerring et al. find that the electoral democracy–human development relationship is maximised when '(a) elections are clean and not marred by fraud or systemic irregularities, (b) the chief executive of a country is selected (directly or indirectly) through elections, (c) suffrage is extensive, (d) political and civil society organizations operate freely, and (e) there is freedom of expression, including access to alternative information'.[26] These five components interact with one another and the absence of any one of them severely mitigates impact on development prospects, although clean elections have the strongest correlation with positive outcomes on human development.[27] These five components lie at the heart of substantive, or liberal democracy.

The same sequence holds for so-called good governance, a general term that is difficult to operationalise objectively, but is often indistinguishable in much writing from broad notions of democracy. Many books have been written about exactly what is meant by good governance, but suffice to say that these definitions often share many of the characteristics of democracy and include reference to participation, the rule of law, equity and inclusiveness, accountability, transparency and responsiveness.[28]

Good governance, like democracy, accompanies and generally follows, rather than precedes, development. Therefore, 'the full set of institutional improvements associated with the idea of good governance becomes feasible for countries only *after* substantial economic transformation has occurred'.[29] Yet, in the eyes of many donors, policymakers and often the general public in Africa and the West, democracy, good governance and development all go together and should be pursued in that order, despite the fact that this reverses the historical developmental sequence.

Moreover, there is considerable evidence that the introduction of competitive politics and economic liberalisation in fragile settings can be costly in terms of violence and loss of human life.[30] This has been most evident in so-called post-conflict fragile states such as South Sudan, Somalia, the Central African Republic, Chad, Côte d'Ivoire, the Democratic Republic of Congo and others. In the absence of other mechanisms to make the government

---

[26] Glaeser, E. L., Ponzetto, G., and Shleifer, A., 2006. Why Does Democracy Need Education? *NBER Working Paper No. 12128.* p. 16.

[27] Ibid., p. 23. In line with standard democracy theory, the authors argue that public policies serve as the key causal mechanism that binds the elected to their electorate.

[28] These are actually the eight principles listed by the UN. See, United Nations, n.d. *What Is Good Governance?* Bangkok: UNESCAP.

[29] Booth, D., 2012. *Development as a Collective Action Problem: Addressing the Real Challenges of African Governance.* London: Africa Power and Politics Programme.

[30] Ibid.

accountable to its citizens in the aftermath of conflict, civil society, regional organisations and the international community generally insisted on creating governments of national unity as part of every post-conflict process, and, shortly thereafter, scheduled competitive elections. The result is generally to undo much of the progress previously made in ending the conflict.

The problem is that we don't know how else to legitimise a government.

The Realities of Neopatrimonialism in Africa

Many academics have commented on the apparent resilience of neopatrimonialism as part of Africa's democratisation processes. The term is widely used to describe a system of politically corrupt patron–client relations that has dominated politics in Africa, particularly in 'not free' and 'partly free' countries. Neopatrimonialism can exist at the highest national level down to community level in small villages.

Pierre Englebert and Kevin Dunn find that the degree to which authoritarian neopatrimonial regimes have been able to adapt to the formal trappings of electoral democracy is one of the most remarkable characteristics of contemporary African politics. 'Thus, to a large extent, neopatrimonialism has proved compatible with democracy rather than having dissolved in it. It has endured and reproduced despite a generalized change in the formal rules of politics'.[31]

Cheeseman is one of many academics to accept the resilience and widespread occurrence of corruption and inappropriate patron–client relationships. He argues that 'patrimonialism itself is not the problem: what matters, is the type of patrimonialism that emerges'.[32]

One approach is to distinguish between centrally managed patrimonial relations, so-called 'developmental patrimonialism',[33] and decentralised, competitive patrimonial systems. The former is evident in countries like Ethiopia and Rwanda. Here, elites provide coherence and order in the political system, take a longer, developmental view on public provision and generally provide better outcomes over the medium and long term.

---

[31] Englebert, P., and Dunn, K. C., 2013. *Inside African Politics.* Cape Town: UCT Press, p. 191.

[32] Cheeseman, N., 2015. *Democracy in Africa: Successes, Failures, and the Struggle for Political Reform.* Cambridge: Cambridge University Press. p. 200.

[33] Thus: 'Rent centralisation permitted the leadership in these countries to put some limits on rent seeking and to play a coordinating role, steering rent creation into areas with high economic potential, or to areas that must be resourced in the interests of political stability'. Booth, D., 2012. *Development as a collective action problem: Addressing the real challenges of African governance,* London: Africa Power and Politics Programme.

More decentralised or competitive neopatrimonial systems, such as Kenya and Nigeria, show the opposite outcomes. Here competition is about personal benefit, and politics is about who governs and not about policy or improved livelihoods. Issues around personality, affiliation and identity dominate. It is particularly damaging if the national constitutional dispensation is of the winner-takes-all variant, which gives the electoral victor wide discretionary powers to appoint, approve and reward.

While politics are exceptionally competitive and robust in Kenya and Nigeria, electoral democracy alone does not really deliver improved livelihoods. However the two countries may in due course reveal the potential of political experimentations to disperse power. Nigeria has a steadily expanding federal system while Kenya recently introduced a county system that provides for a significant devolution of power—an example now being copied in many African countries such as Mozambique, Angola and South Africa.

We do not yet have firm evidence of whether decentralised systems advance accountability or merely increase the opportunity for corruption, although recent findings from Ethiopia are promising,[34] but what is clear is much greater community activism is required to accompany such efforts. And it is crucial that the delimitation of municipalities or counties be primarily based on their potential towards financial viability and their capacity to manage those matters for which they are responsible. In Angola, for example, the government is embarking upon an ambitious decentralisation programme from the central government to its 164 municipalities (autarquia), largely bypassing its 18 provinces. The project is staggered with the first 70 municipalities to receive legal personality and considerable autonomy in 2020. The entire process is to be completed by 2035 but without significant efforts to build the technical capacity of these authorities it will struggle.

In the absence of civil war or some other calamity, it is almost inevitable that both Nigeria and Kenya will grow given the expansion of the working age population, rising levels of education and rapid rates of urbanisation. However, this growth is unlikely to promote sustainable, broad-based human development outcomes without a change in political culture or the emergence of decisive, forward-looking leadership.

The problem with the twofold distinction between centralised and decentralised patrimonialism systems is that countries with centralised patrimonial systems do not necessarily produce better outcomes. Other factors may come

---

[34]See, for example, Faguet, J-P., Qaiser Khan, Q., and Kanth, D.P., 2019. Decentralization's Effects on Education and Health: Evidence from Ethiopia, Social Protection and Jobs. *Discussion Paper No. 1934*, World Bank Group, September 2019, http://documents.worldbank.org/curated/en/128791568874876991/pdf/Decentralization-s-Effects-on-Education-and-Health-Evidence-from-Ethiopia.pdf.

into play. In fact, a number of relatively recently liberated countries in Southern Africa, such as Namibia, Angola, Zimbabwe, Mozambique and South Africa, would probably fit into the category of a centralised patrimonial system, since former liberation parties still dominate politics, but generally with disappointing results. In South Africa, where the governing African National Congress (ANC) did not come to power through the extensive political indoctrination and associated broad-based people's war that took place in countries like Namibia, Mozambique and Zimbabwe, a liberal constitution, active civil society, entrenched Bill of Rights and independent judiciary have barely been able to constrain the ANC's neopatrimonial inclinations.

Eventually, the degree to which centralised patrimonial systems can advance development depends heavily on the quality of the top leadership. A strong, visionary leader such as Paul Kagame (Rwanda), Thabo Mbeki (South Africa) or Meles Zenawi (Ethiopia) can have a significant impact on development outcomes while they are in power. But there is no guarantee that he or she will not succumb to the attractions of office—as was the case with Yoweri Museveni in Uganda and eventually also Kagame. Both Museveni and Kagame are now seeking to extend their terms in the belief that their leadership is indispensable for their country's future. And in South Africa Thabo Mbeki tried to extend his leadership of the ruling party as a way to maintain his power beyond the two-term constitutional limit as president of the country.

Booth's view is that the centralised or developmental patrimonial states are the result of very specific conditions—and never of peaceful multi-party elections. He presents two examples of such conditions, namely (a) where the leadership consists of national liberation forces after war as still evident in many countries in Southern Africa; and (b) in the aftermath of a severe crisis or shock to the system involving large-scale violence such as experienced in Rwanda and Ethiopia.[35]

Cheeseman comes to these issues from a slightly different perspective, namely the extent to which democracy in Africa is inclusive or competitive. He uses the examples of Côte d'Ivoire and Kenya to argue for the need for greater inclusion and cites Ghana and Senegal as two examples where political competition has driven progress.

Cheeseman notes that 'while elements of competition and inclusion strengthen multiparty systems, too much of either can be fatal to the process of democratization'.[36] The most notable examples of 'excessive inclusion' are

---

[35] Ibid., p. 48. At a global level China is the most enduring example.
[36] Cheeseman, N., 2015. *The State of Democracy in Africa*. [Online] Available at: http://democracyinafrica.org/the-state-of-democracy-in-africa/.

governments of national unity or where there are power-sharing arrangements. Since such governments are largely premised on the need for the political compromises associated with conflict management they are often unable to sustain or promote economic growth.

Following instances of electoral violence in Kenya and Zimbabwe in the mid-2000s, regional actors helped craft governments of national unity. While it produced a measure of political stability, it also engendered paralysis in governance and economic performance.[37] Lack of development in turn leads to social instability and in these circumstances a government of national unity sometimes unwittingly plants the seeds for the next crisis.

Cheeseman therefore argues that 'excessive inclusion is therefore just as bad for democracy and development as excessive competition'.[38] But, the point at which inclusion becomes excessive remains unclear and highly subjective.

The Role of Leadership in Development

Our understanding of the relationship between democracy, development and governance is clearly still incomplete. As is the case with violence, specific national conditions determine actual outcomes.

What is clear, however, is that leadership, government capacity and intent are particularly important. It's possible to argue that the winner of the August 2016 elections in Zambia or Gabon made little short or medium-term difference, since neither government has the capacity to deliver improved development outcomes due to an incapable civil service and a lack of policy space because of their dependence on single commodities—a function of the choices made by previous elites as well as the dictates of the global economy. Therefore, given Zambia and Gabon's lack of government capacity, poor leadership and absence of a clear development goal, these two countries will likely bumble along. Burgeoning populations will push up the countries' economic growth rates and the trickle-down of the wealth that accrues to a small political elite at the high table of patronage will improve living standards—but among a very small middle class.

---

[37] Miguna, M., 2012. *Peeling Back the Mask: A Quest for Justice in Kenya*. Nairobi: Arrow Press. On Zimbabwe see Thys Hoekman, 2013. Testing Ties: Opposition and Power-Sharing Negotiations in Zimbabwe. *Journal of Southern African Studies*, 39(4), 903–920; Raftapoulos, B., 2012. Towards Another Stalemate in Zimbabwe, Norwegian Peacebuilding Resource Centre (NOREF), Report, October 2012.
[38] Ibid.

Intent and leadership can make a major difference, both negatively and positively. A good example is President John Magufuli of Tanzania—nicknamed 'The Bulldozer'—for his apparent no-nonsense' approach to corruption and waste. However, the impact of his 'government by gesture', as *The Economist* magazine coined it, remains unimpressive.[39] 'Mr Magufuli's zeal may be admired, but his party, which has ruled Tanzania since independence, is thuggish and undemocratic: it suppressed dissent during the elections last year and then cancelled a vote held in Zanzibar after the opposition probably won it', the magazine writes.[40]

Recently, in a remarkable display of ignorance, Magafuli stated that Tanzania's women should 'give up contraceptive methods' and that he sees 'no reason to control births in Tanzania'.[41] Actually, with a total fertility rate of almost five children per woman, Tanzania's very high fertility rates preclude reasonable income growth.

This is a discussion that reverts to leadership, the unity and capacity of the ruling party and governments to deliver, rather than the extent to which they are inclusive or exclusive, elected or non-elected. Of course, as countries advance along the development trajectory the need for greater inclusion becomes a more important driver of future development. Diversified economies require innovation and knowledge production to sustain growth, which is quite different to the requirements of an undiversified, single-commodity-based economy largely dominated by informal activity.

Strong authoritarian leaders, as one finds in Rwanda and previously Ethiopia and who are at the helm of an organised party that has a firm grip on the country, politics and development (i.e. centralised patrimonial systems), are likely to deliver more rapid results in low-income countries. But most often the dependence on a single key figure more readily undoes progress once that leadership clings to power or is replaced by a flawed successor, as it has in Uganda, Angola, Zimbabwe, Egypt, Sudan, South Sudan, Equatorial Guinea, Eswatini, Libya and Algeria.

It is easy to underestimate the challenges of governance in Africa and the time horizon required to improve development outcomes. It is also easy to overestimate the ability of political leaders or a particular system such as democracy to deliver improved livelihoods and poverty reduction.

---

[39] *The Economist*, 2016. Government by Gesture: A President Who Looks Good But Governs Impulsively. [Online] Available at: https://www.economist.com/middle-east-and-africa/2016/05/26/government-by-gesture.

[40] Ibid.

[41] AFP, 2018. *Tanzanian President Seeks End to Contraception*. [Online] Available at: https://www.news24.com/Africa/News/tanzanian-president-seeks-end-to-contraception-20180910-2.

Modelling the Impact of More Democracy: The Fourth Wave of Democracy Scenario

Whereas Western donor countries have historically pushed for democracy in Africa and beyond, Africans are now at the helm. Afrobarometer's findings on the strong support for democratisation on the continent reflect this trend. As we explored in Chapter 12, the trend is however, increasingly associated with more protests and violence as expectations steadily rise. 'Over the past decade, mass uprisings in Africa have accounted for one in three of the nonviolent campaigns to topple dictatorships around the world', write Zoe Marks, Erica Chenoweth and Jide Okeke in *Foreign Affairs*.[42] These mass uprisings are more successful in Africa than anywhere else, having effectively toppled autocratic leaders in countries as diverse as Burkina Faso, Côte d'Ivoire, Madagascar, Mali, South Africa, Tunisia, Zambia, and, most recently, Algeria and Sudan.

The likely development is that the next global waves of democratisation will be less pronounced than the previous three waves, although a regional wave in the Middle East, which is clearly headed for massive governance changes, seems inevitable. That reflects a trend where national and regional dynamics play a more important role than the previous stark East/West division did until 1990.

I model the continuation of a positive trend towards more democracy that I refer to as the Fourth Wave scenario, within the IFs forecasting platform using a measure of regime type originally developed by the Polity IV Project on regime types. The Polity measure roughly equates to the concept of 'thin' or electoral democracy also used by V-Dem.[43]

The Fourth Wave, starts in 2010 with the Arab Spring and in the scenario lasts 10 years to 2020 before levelling off. In this scenario, a slow democratic regression will set in by 2030, and will endure until mid-century before the onset of the next (or fifth) wave of democracy, that, in turn, will last for a decade before plateauing.

---

[42] Marks, Z., Chenoweth, E., and Okeke, J., 2019. *People Power Is Rising in Africa*. [Online] Available at: https://www.foreignaffairs.com/articles/africa/2019-04-25/people-power-rising-africa?utm_medium=newsletters&utm_source=twofa&utm_content=20190426&utm_campaign=TWOFA%200 42619%20Hard%20Truths%20in%20Syria&utm_term=FA%20This%20Week%20-%201120177.

[43] In 2014 the Pardee Center published a forecast on governance that includes additional detail on many of these aspects. See Hughes, B. B., Joshi, D. K., Moyer, J. D., Sisk, T. D., and Solórzano, J, R., 2014. *Strengthening Governance Globally: Forecasting the Next 50 Years*. 5 vol. New York: Routledge, Frederick S. Pardee, Center for International Futures, University of Denver. For additional information see International Futures at the Pardee Center, 2019. *International Futures Help System*. [Online] Available at: https://www.du.edu/ifs/help/.

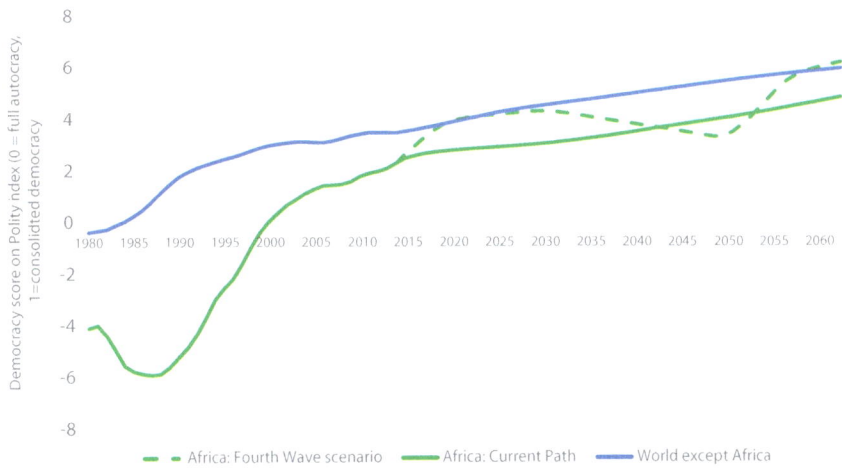

Fig. 13.2 Fourth Wave of electoral democracy scenario using Polity IV data (*Source* IFs version 7.45 initialising from Polity IV data using a 5-year moving average)

Figure 13.2 presents this forecast using data from the Polity IV Project, making a distinction between average levels of electoral democracy in Africa and in the rest of the world. From 2015 onward, the dashed green line represents the Fourth Wave scenario, while the solid green line represents the Current Path forecast. The forecast is to 2063, the final year of the African Union's Agenda 2063. Note that in spite of the fluctuating levels (or waves) the general trend towards steadily higher levels of average democratisation continues across the forecast horizon in line with the historical trend that has been consistent for more than a century.

The big outlier on democratisation is clearly China and for me the question is when—not if—China will adopt or succumb to greater political liberalisation to match the substantive economic liberalisation of the last four decades. Eventually a competitive economic system requires a more competitive political system particularly once a country gets to upper-middle-income status and it is unlikely that China will be able to defy gravity and escape its large democratic deficit forever. In the meanwhile the impact of China on Africa is likely to exert downward pressure on increased democracy, but since I believe domestic politics will triumph, will not be able to effectively counter steady democratisation.

As expected, the impact of a democratic regression from 2030 to mid-century is more pronounced and visible in Africa than in the rest of the world. Democratic backsliding is, however, more likely among low- and lower-middle-income countries and is unlikely to affect upper-middle-income countries that have more entrenched institutions and norms.

Because democracy advances accountability and transparency, low, lower-middle and upper-middle Africa countries all experience associated reductions in corruption, although modestly so. Coming off a low base, the modest improvement is most pronounced in low-income countries

The impact of democratisation on economic growth is small. By 2040, Africa's GDP would be about US$85 billion larger (an increase of about one percent), translating into an increase in GDP per capita of about US$50. In economic terms low-middle-income countries gain most from democratisation within the IFs forecasting platform.

Conclusion: Promoting Democracy, State Capacity and Human Development

Africa faces a unique challenge. It is generally more democratic when compared to the average for countries at similar levels of education and income and is democratising rapidly. The continent therefore faces the double challenge of development and democratisation.

Technically, what poor African countries need is not necessarily a democratic state, although that is highly desirable for many reasons, but a developmental state where the 'political and bureaucratic elite has the genuine developmental determination and autonomous capacity to define, pursue and implement developmental goals'.[44] The challenge is that this requires either a developmentally oriented governing elite or substantive democracy—ideally both. While the latter is a more desirable path than the former, it takes longer to achieve and is fragile at low levels of development.

The problem is the extent to which neopatrimonialism has been able to coexist with the processes of democratisation in Africa and to which incumbents have undermined the core notions of electoral democracy, such as clean elections and freedom of speech. It's not that Africans are more corrupt or self-serving than leadership elsewhere. The Trump presidency in the USA presents many of the features often associated with the negative characterisation associated with Africa rather than of an established, liberal democracy. Rather, the institutions that should serve as a check on the abuse of power in Africa are much weaker than in say, the USA. In some instances, traditions that place particular emphasis on respect for elders and traditional structures accentuate these negative trends in Africa. Only real progress towards substantive democracy is likely to undo this and even then the election of a flawed

---

[44]Leftwich, A., 1993. Governance, Democracy and Development in the Third World. *Third World Quarterly,* 14(3), p. 620.

character to the highest office can do incalculable damage even to a mature and established polity such as in the USA.

Here modern technology is playing an important role in allowing for the establishment of parallel monitoring systems during elections. It is clear that civil society in Africa is better able to hold governments accountable, to monitor elections and guard against abuse with each passing year. In that way, illustrated recently by Sudan, Algeria and Ethiopia, Africans are taking it upon themselves to hold their leadership to account. In the meanwhile every effort needs to be made to hold on to the gains that have been achieved such as regular elections, ongoing electoral reform, establishing a tradition of robust election monitoring by locals and foreigners, and rigorous adherence to term limits.

In the absence of developmentally oriented elites, greater accountability can be facilitated using modern technology.

By itself democratisation in Africa has clearly not altered the conditions of most Africans. Many Africans still endure high poverty levels and social marginalisation. In addition, in key countries nominal democratisation has not resolved deep-seated divisions based on ethnicity, regionalism and class. These divisions will only be bridged with progress towards substantive democracy. Fortunately regular elections and the growing depth of civil society in Africa mean that progress towards substantive democracy is more probable than the reverse.

That said, democracy should be pursued as a common good in itself—for the contribution that it makes to individual and collective self-actualisation. It is the only regime type that allows for greater self and collective fulfilment for the citizens of states, irrespective of geography, religion or culture. According to the World Values Survey, the desire for free choice and autonomy 'is a universal human aspiration'.[45]

As much as democracy, good governance and civic rights contribute to human well-being, the African continent does not exist in isolation. In fact, the continent has been buffeted by global shifts in power and influence, most recently by a sense of competition between the West and China. The way in which that contestation plays out may have important ramifications globally and the next chapter therefore looks at Africa's external relations.

---

[45]WVSA, n.d. *The World Values Survey*. [Online] Available at: http://www.worldvaluessurvey.org/wvs.jsp.

Further Reading

BenYishay, A., and Betancourt, R. 2014. Unbundling Democracy: Political Rights and Civil Liberties. *Journal of Comparative Economics*, 42(3): 552–568.

Brown, Wendy. 2009. We Are All Democrats Now.... Theory & Event 13, no. 2. Project MUSE. https://doi.org/10.1353/tae.0.0133.

Green, Alan. 2018. Democracy and Institutions in Postcolonial Africa. *Journal of Institutional Economics*, 14(2), pp. 207–231. https://doi.org/10.1017/s1744137416000278.

Wrong, Michela. 2009. It's Our Turn to Eat: The Story of a Kenyan Whistle-Blower Paperback. Harper Perennial. 10 East 53rd Street, New York, NY, 10022.

Open Access This chapter is licensed under the terms of the Creative Commons Attribution 4.0 International License (http://creativecommons.org/licenses/by/4.0/), which permits use, sharing, adaptation, distribution and reproduction in any medium or format, as long as you give appropriate credit to the original author(s) and the source, provide a link to the Creative Commons license and indicate if changes were made.

The images or other third party material in this chapter are included in the chapter's Creative Commons license, unless indicated otherwise in a credit line to the material. If material is not included in the chapter's Creative Commons license and your intended use is not permitted by statutory regulation or exceeds the permitted use, you will need to obtain permission directly from the copyright holder.

14

Aid, Remittances and Foreign Direct Investment

Abstract Cilliers sheds light on the evolving global aid, investment and remittance landscape and what it means for Africa, with special attention to China's growing presence on the continent, and compares that with others. Collectively the EU and its member states provide most aid although the USA is Africa's largest single aid provider. Aid will remain important for low-income countries but its importance is declining in favour of a focus on the need to attract larger volumes of foreign direct investment (FDI). An External Support scenario explores the impact of heightened aid, remittances and FDI on Africa's development trajectory.

Keywords Aid · Bilateral aid · China · The USA · EU · Concessional loans · Foreign direct investment (FDI) · Remittances · Trade · World Bank

Learning Objectives

– Understand China's involvement in African development, how and why it has evolved, comparing that with EU members and the USA
– Critically evaluate and compare the advantages and drawbacks of aid and foreign direct investment as development strategies
– Discuss the contribution and role of remittances.

Africa and its people have received more aid than any other region in the world. From 1960 to 2018 the international community provided a cumulative amount of more than US$2.4 trillion in aid to Africa.[1] Asia and the Middle East, the other two regions that have historically received large amounts of aid, trail significantly behind Africa in total aid receipts. Today Africa gets about 32% (US$59.7 billion in 2017) of total global aid (US$190 billion), slightly more than the amount that goes to Asia. But since Asia has almost four times the population of Africa, Africans receive much more aid per person than Asians, although the ratio is shifting towards Asian countries.[2]

There are, however, a number of important problems with aid data. First, aid data often excludes China and sources differ widely in their calculations of the amount of Chinese money that qualifies as aid as opposed to loans. The China Africa Research Initiative estimates that China provided US$3 billion globally in 2015 followed by a significant reduction to US$2.3 billion in 2016. It is likely that the bigger portion of this amount went to Africa, but there is disagreement about how much of this would really qualify as aid rather than commercial loans.[3]

Second, until recently calculations of aid flows also excluded contributions from private sources like the Open Society Foundations of billionaire George Soros and the Bill & Melinda Gates Foundation. The OECD's own large-scale survey on global private philanthropy estimates flows of US$7.96 billion per annum, which is equivalent to around five percent of government aid flows. Slightly less than a third of private donations goes to Africa.[4]

Actually, according to these estimates, China provides roughly the same amount of aid to Africa as the total from private aid sources.

---

[1] Calculated in IFs v7.465 and converted to constant 2018 dollars.

[2] As opposed to official aid, most private money flows to Africa (and elsewhere) goes to health and reproductive health in middle-income countries such as Nigeria and South Africa. OECD, 2018. *Private Philanthropy Funding for Development Modest Compared to Public Aid, But Its Potential Impact Is High, Says OECD.* [Online] Available at: http://www.oecd.org/dev/private-philanthropy-funding-for-development-modest-compared-to-public-aid-but-its-potential-impact-is-high.htm. Aid data taken from UNECA and WTO. 2019. An Inclusive African Continental Free Trade Area: Aid for Trade and the Empowerment of Women and Young People, Available at: www.tralac.org/documents/resources/cfta/2892-an-inclusive-afcfta-aid-for-trade-and-the-empowerment-of-women-and-young-people-eca-wto-july-2019/file.html, p. 6.

[3] Kitano, N., 2017. *A Note on Estimating China's Foreign Aid Using New Data: 2015 Preliminary Figures.* Tokyo: JICA. Also see OECD, 2017. *Development Co-Operation Report 2017: Data for Development.* Paris: OECD, and China Africa Research Initiative, 2019. *Data: Chinese Foreign Aid.* [Online] Available at: http://www.sais-cari.org/data-chinese-foreign-aid-to-africa.

[4] OECD, 2018. *Private Philanthropy Funding for Development Modest Compared to Public Aid, But Its Potential Impact Is High, Says OECD.* [Online] Available at: http://www.oecd.org/dev/private-philanthropy-funding-for-development-modest-compared-to-public-aid-but-its-potential-impact-is-high.htm.

These data issues aside, how intergovernmental financial institutions approach aid has undergone significant changes since the turn of the century.

Key milestones include the 2000 United Nations Millennium Summit in New York, which put aid to Africa in the spotlight after it had gone out of favour in previous years; the Report of the Commission for Africa released in 2005 that was spearheaded by then UK Prime Minister Tony Blair; as well as the European Consensus on Development—an EU policy declaration on aid—also issued in that year. Collectively these efforts paved the way to the 2005 World Summit in New York, which called for increased aid transfers in order to reach the eight Millennium Development Goals set in 2000. Key among its goals was to halve poverty and hunger by 2015.

Actually the push to halve poverty by 2015 was met five years ahead of the deadline largely on the back of rapid economic growth and pro-poor policies in China, which had little to do with aid.[5] Rapid economic growth in China saw the number of people living in extreme poverty fall from 1.9 billion in 1990 to 836 million in 2015. The target to halve the portion of people suffering from hunger was narrowly missed, however, as were a number of other Millennium Development Goals.[6]

A key development on the road to the final year of the 2015 MDG goal was the 2011 Busan Partnership for Effective Development Cooperation (named after the city in South Korea that hosted the final meeting), which established, for the first time, an internationally agreed-upon framework for development cooperation that included traditional and new donors from the South, civil society organisations and private philanthropy. Under the Busan commitments, donors agreed to untie aid to allow recipients to use their aid dollars to procure from the cheapest suppliers and not those prescribed by donors—an issue that aid advocates had been lobbying for decades—as well as various other measures that harmonised aid modalities among donor countries.

These reforms, among others, precipitated more effective aid that was, henceforth, increasingly being channeled towards low- and lower-middle-income countries, where the majority of poor people are to be found, rather than towards upper-middle-income countries. Whereas, if aid were distributed equally among African countries, it would equate to about 2.5% of GDP, these reforms would see aid to low-income countries increase to ten percent of GDP—equating to more than 50% of government revenue.

---

[5] Aid has a modestly positive effect on growth with an average internal rate of return of around 10%.
[6] Ritchie, H., and Roser, M., 2018. Now It Is Possible to Take Stock—Did the World Achieve the Millennium Development Goals? 20 September 2018. [Online] Available at: https://ourworldindata.org/millennium-development-goals.

In contrast, aid as a percent of government revenue in lower-middle-income African countries dropped to below ten percent and below one percent in upper-middle-income countries, illustrating the progress that has been made in shifting aid to where the need is greatest.

Since North African countries have long since graduated to middle-income status, by 2017 more than 90% of the aid to Africa went to Sub-Saharan Africa.[7]

On average, approximately 70% of aid is provided bilaterally and the balance through multilateral channels. Bilateral aid is provided directly from a national agency such as the US Agency for International Development (USAID) or the Swedish International Development Cooperation Agency (SIDA) to the country or region concerned. Multilateral aid is provided through organisations such as the UN Development Programme (UNDP), the World Bank and the African Development Bank. The latter are able, through aid, to provide grants as well as concessional loans to African countries at below market rates.

Aid serves as an important avenue through which external partners can augment governments' ability to meet the most pressing needs of their populations, and will remain critical for Africa's low-income countries for at least a next decade. For example, aid boosted government revenues in low-income Africa by an astounding ten percentage points in 2018. In a country such as Ethiopia, donors provided US$600 million in health funding in 2015, accounting for roughly half of the total health spending in the country.[8] Here aid has enabled rapid improvements in maternal and infant mortality rates. These improvements have in turn accelerated Ethiopia's demographic transition and will have a substantive positive impact on the nation's long-term future development prospects.

The Shifting Global Aid Landscape

The USA remains Africa's single largest bilateral aid donor, but provides significantly less aid than the EU and its member states and aid from the USA is declining. The trend is similar to the weakening US trade relations with Africa that were examined in Chapter 11.

---

[7]OECD, 2019. *Development Aid at a Glance: Statistics by Region. 2. Africa 2019 Edition.* [Online] Available at: http://www.oecd.org/dac/financing-sustainable-development/development-finance-data/Africa-Development-Aid-at-a-Glance-2019.pdf, p. 2.

[8]The Federal Democratic Republic of Ethiopia Ministry of Health. 2015. Ethiopia Health Sector Transformation Plan. Available at: www.globalfinancingfacility.org/sites/gff_new/files/documents/HSTP%20Ethiopia.pdf.

The EU and its member states provide about half of all aid to Africa (about €20 billion per annum) and the USA about 24%.[9]

In response to domestic and international affairs alike, the USA' primary interests in the African continent have evolved. After 9/11, its focus shifted to the war on terror, culminating in the disastrous Western interventions in Iraq and Libya that have destabilised the Middle East and North Africa. Then the shale energy revolution has reduced America's dependence on imported oil that previously determined its relationship with oil-producing countries like Nigeria and Angola. Lately it has also started to draw down on its military engagement on the continent but the USA will retain an important role in providing humanitarian support as public support for this role remains stronger than for aid. The USA' escalating competition with China, domestic political divisions and trade disputes with friend and foe alike under the Trump presidency led to an incoherent and distracted policy towards Africa.

Most large donors are redoubling their efforts to push for a larger role for the private sector. For example, after several years of inaction the Better Utilisation of Investments Leading to Development (BUILD) Act (passed in the US Senate in October 2018) supports private investment.[10] In addition, the newly established US International Development Finance Corporation (USIDFC) will be able to invest up to US$60 billion in Africa, focusing on small- and medium-sized enterprises and support to local companies.[11]

BUILD was established as part of the Trump administration's Prosper Africa initiative that, according to former US National Security Advisor John Bolton, 'will support US investment across the continent, grow Africa's middle class, and improve the overall business climate in the region'.[12] Launched on 13 December 2018, Prosper Africa is aimed at helping US companies navigate the US bureaucracy and enable them to benefit from its various programmes and services. Its primary aim is therefore to open markets

---

[9]The Africa-EU Partnership, https://www.africa-eu-partnership.org/en/about-us/financing-partnership.
[10]The BUILD Act replaces the Overseas Private Investment Corporation (OPIC) that was created in 1971.
[11]The USIDFC will be able to take a minority equity stake or financial interests of its own in development projects. USIDFC will also provide insurance or reinsurance services, technical assistance, administer special projects, establish enterprise funds, issue obligations, and charge and collect service fees. 'Through these market-based fees, the USIDFC will operate at no net cost to [US] taxpayers'. Runde, D. F., and Bandura, R., 2018. *The BUILD Act Has Passed: What's Next?* [Online] Available at: www.csis.org/analysis/build-act-has-passed-whats-next.
[12]Airey, J., 2018. *Bolton: New Africa Strategy Is Tough On China, Russia, U.N.* [Online] Available at: www.dailywire.com/news/39347/watch-bolton-new-africa-strategy-tough-china-jacob-airey.

for American businesses, and, in that process, to enable the USA to compete with China in Africa.[13]

It is unlikely that Europe will follow US disengagement with Africa. Europe remains connected with Africa through shared histories, languages and physical proximity. The EU has also been diligent in nurturing a collaborative and consultative relationship with Africa over successive decades. And whereas the USA is cautious if not dismissive of regional organisations such as the African Union and the various regional economic communities, the EU often sees them as its primary point of engagement that reflect its own economic and political architecture. Decades of European investment in building the capacity of the African Union as well as relationships of aid and trade have created a network of friendship and collaboration that remains important for both parties although Brexit and widespread anti-migrant sentiments across Europe are undermining the strength of this relationship.

For instance, without European assistance, the African Union's much-vaunted African Peace and Security Architecture (APSA) would not have been able to establish its three (out of an envisioned five) brigade-size capabilities for conflict prevention and management in South, West and East Africa. Since 2004, the European Union (EU) has spent more than €3.5 billion of its aid commitment to support APSA and various peace support missions in Africa.[14]

The EU's intent to move beyond a donor–recipient relationship towards a more mature engagement was first captured in the comprehensive Joint Africa-EU Strategy (JAES) of 2007 that was adopted by the Heads of State and Government of the African Union and the EU at their second EU-Africa Summit in Lisbon. The most recent (third) JAES plan of action outlines four strategic areas from 2018 onwards: investing in people—education, science, technology and skills development; strengthening resilience, peace, security and governance; migration and mobility; and mobilising investments for sustainable structural transformation. Subsequently, at the 5th African Union-European Union Summit, the partners agreed that economic investment, job creation and trade were common priorities that require a joint commitment.

In line with the latter goal, in 2017 the EU launched its External Investment Plan (EIP) that includes a new guarantee mechanism where aid is used to mobilise private capital flows through 'blended arrangements' and

---

[13]Runde, D. F., and Bandura, R., 2019. *U.S. Economic Engagement in Africa: Making Prosper Africa a Reality*. Washington: Center for Strategic & International Studies.

[14]European Commission, 2020. Questions and Answers: Towards a Comprehensive Strategy with Africa, 9 March 2020, https://ec.europa.eu/commission/presscorner/detail/en/qanda_20_375.

the provision of guarantees to mobilise additional resources for investment in Africa.[15] That was followed, in 2018, with the announcement of a new Africa-Europe Alliance for Sustainable Investment and Jobs. The intention is that the EU-AU Summit originally scheduled for October 2020 but then delayed due to COVID-19, will approve partnerships in five key areas: green transition; digital transformation; sustainable growth and jobs; peace and governance; and migration and mobility.[16]

Considerable attention is being given to efforts such as Aid for Trade and arrangements to mobilise additional financial support to the region in the form of loans or equity.[17] Aid for Trade uses a portion of aid (US$13.3 bn of US$59.7 bn total aid to Africa in 2017)[18] to build trade capacity in poor countries and on improving trade diversification and helping economically marginalised groups.

On the Current Path forecast, Africa will receive US$102 billion net aid in 2030 and US$124 billion in 2040. Most of the increase will (and should) go to low-income countries that are expected to experience a doubling of aid to US$85 billion by 2040, although, as a portion of GDP the contribution of aid to these countries will decrease from its current 10% to 5.7%. The reason for the decline in aid as a portion of GDP is, of course, due to the rapid economic growth that most of these countries will experience, in part because they all have young and fast-growing populations.

The expected near doubling of aid in constant dollar amounts would be significantly larger if developed countries met the 0.7% of gross national income (GNI) target for aid contributions as set out in the SDG ambition.[19]

---

[15] Its thematic objectives are (i) local private sector development, (ii) social and economic infrastructure development, (iii) climate change mitigation and (iv) root causes of migration and, in addition to financial support, it provides technical assistance and offers a policy dialogue. Gavas, M., and Timmis, H., 2019. The EU's Financial Architecture for External Investment: Progress, Challenges, and Options.*CGD Policy Paper 136*, pp. 1–2. Also European Commission, n.d. *Joint Africa—EU Strategy*. [Online] Available at: https://ec.europa.eu/europeaid/regions/africa/continental-cooperation/joint-africa-eu-strategy_en.

[16] EU Press Release, 2020. EU Paves the Way for a Stronger, More Ambitious Partnership with Africa, 9 March 2020 [Online]. Available at: https://ec.europa.eu/commission/presscorner/detail/en/IP_20_373.

[17] The Aid for Trade Initiative was formally launched at the Sixth WTO Ministerial Conference in Hong Kong in 2005. See World Trade Organization, 2019. *Aid for Trade*. [Online] Available at: www.wto.org/english/tratop_e/devel_e/a4t_e/aid4trade_e.htm.

[18] Calculated from UNECA and WTO. 2019. An Inclusive African Continental Free Trade Area: Aid for Trade and the Empowerment of Women and Young People. Available at: www.tralac.org/documents/resources/cfta/2892-an-inclusive-afcfta-aid-for-trade-and-the-empowerment-of-women-and-young-people-eca-wto-july-2019/file.html, p. 6.

[19] United Nations, n.d. *Goal 17: Revitalize the Global Partnership for Sustainable Development*. [Online] Available at: www.un.org/sustainabledevelopment/globalpartnerships/.

That is unlikely and the increase in the amount of aid within the International Futures forecasting platform (IFs) is driven by the rapid growth in the economies of donor countries rather than any increases in the aid as a percent of GDP by donors. Much more realistic is to expect that aid, as a portion of the GDP of rich countries will remain stable or, more likely, moderately decline. As countries become wealthier they tend to also become more stingy.

The COVID-19 crisis will also impact upon aid. The initial reaction may be to shift all resources closer to home and to reduce aid or spend it on housing or deterring migrants as was the case recently. The longer-term impact of COVID-19 will be to increase poverty and hence migrant flows to Europe in particular. Inevitably partners will be forced to consider how best to improve the ability of African governments to constrain migration and that may, in time, modestly increase rather than decrease aid flows.

Leveraging Foreign Direct Investment for Africa

As countries develop, aid inevitably diminishes in importance and aid-providers inevitably focus on increasing the role of the private sector, in line with the adage that trade follows aid. In the process, foreign direct investment (FDI) becomes an important tool through which governments can unlock additional private-sector capacity and grow the economy of the recipient country more rapidly. The intention is that aid recipients steadily be weaned off aid.

FDI is essentially a long-term investment made by a company in one economy or country in another—a definition that distinguishes it from more volatile foreign portfolio investments. It is typically discussed as consisting of a *stock* of investment that has been built up (or that is depleted) through annual in- or out*flows*. FDI has many advantages, some of which were examined in Chapter 11 that dealt with trade. Because FDI typically involves the transfer of technology, capacity and skills from a multinational (or mother) corporation to an affiliate in the host country, FDI is broadly viewed as the best way to stimulate economic development and the private sector as the best vehicle to implement the associated projects and services.[20]

Domestic factors, generally discussed as the absorptive capacity of recipient countries, are often a determining factor in translating FDI inflows into growth and development. And generally it seems that 'the growth gains from

---

[20]See, for example: Bjorvatn, K., Kind. H. J., and Nordas. H. K., 2002. The Role of FDI in Economic Development. *Nordic Journal of Political Economy*, pp. 109–126. http://www.nopecjournal.org.

FDI are unlocked only when the host country has reached a certain optimal level of financial development ... and in countries with a minimum threshold level of human capital stock'.[21]

The advantages of seeking to attract larger portions of FDI appear self-evident when one considers the large potential pool: globally insurance companies, pension funds and sovereign wealth funds have more than US$100 trillion in assets under management.[22] Africa needs a very small fraction of these amounts to plug its large infrastructure financing gap, for example.

Private-sector investment is, however, not a substitute for efforts by national governments or contributions from the public sector or multilateral development banks, which are critical to the development of large, basic infrastructure, such as water and sanitation systems. Historically most private financing in Africa has occurred in the information and communications, renewable energy and transport sectors, but not in these core infrastructure. The reason is self-evident—returns on large infrastructure development often take decades to materialise and may even require ongoing subsidies.

Most research and efforts to encourage private-sector investment to build basic infrastructure gloss over its shortcomings that include much higher interest rates than those of public or multilateral creditors (such as the World Bank and International Monetary Fund) while maturities (lending periods) are typically also significantly shorter. Most private financiers also lack a development mandate, looking instead to maximise profit, and are reluctant to invest in the early stages of infrastructure development where the need is most severe. They inevitably tend to cherry-pick the projects that they are prepared to fund and are generally risk-averse. Meanwhile, concessional financing available to Africa has declined. The result is that, in 2017, only 2.8% of infrastructure commitments in Africa came from the private sector.[23]

In addition to national governments that provided roughly 42% of funds for infrastructure, Africa generally has to look to financial institutions such as the World Bank and the African Development Bank or state-backed lending

---

[21] Yeboua, K., 2019. Foreign Direct Investment, Financial Development and Economic Growth in Africa: Evidence from Threshold Modeling, Transnational Corporations Review, https://doi.org/10.1080/19186444.2019.1640014, pp. 2–3.

[22] Rabah, A., Bolton, P., Peters, S., Sanama, F., and Stiglitz, J. 2017. From Global Savings Glut to Financing Infrastructure. *Economic Policy* 32, pp. 221–261.

[23] Prinsloo, C., 2019. The Pitfalls of Private Sector Investment in Infrastructure Financing. SAIIA Policy Briefing No. 187, June 2019. Available at: https://saiia.org.za/research/the-pitfalls-of-private-sector-investment-in-infrastructure-financing/; Alley, I., 2017. Capital Flow Surges and Economic Growth in Sub-Saharan Africa: Any Role for Capital Controls? African Development Bank Group Working Paper Series 252, March 2017.

from a country with deep pockets such as China to fund its infrastructure deficit.[24] China has a number of additional advantages when it comes to building large infrastructure projects in Africa: it largely operates on a government-to-government basis instead of private sector to private sector approach; boasts significant finances to invest since it has consistently had a positive balance of trade since 1990' and has massive overcapacity and significant domestic experience in building infrastructure such as roads and railways. None of these advantages are readily available from the USA or Europe.

This does not mean that private investment in infrastructure from these other sources does not occur. Rather, the associated return on investment needs to be high enough to attract the private sector. That typically only happens in the case of oil, gas and other commodities. For example, in June 2019, the USA energy firm Anadarko Petroleum Corporation[25] gave the go-ahead for the construction of a US$20 billion gas liquefaction and export terminal in Mozambique—the single largest liquid natural gas project in Africa and an amount equivalent to almost half of total FDI to Africa in 2018. By the end of 2019, total investments in Mozambique for the next decade were estimated at US$128 billion—more than the entire amount of aid and FDI to all of Africa in 2018.[26]

Prior to that uptick, FDI flows to Africa peaked at 3.8% of GDP in 2008 at the start of the global financial crisis, and declined thereafter. By 2017, FDI had recovered to three percent of GDP or US$42 billion—a fraction of the US$476 billion that went to developing Asia. But then the African economy is only 14% the size of developing Asia.[27] Historically Africa has received less FDI as a percent of GDP than a region such as South America. For several years China started to buck that trend, but its attention is currently shifting closer to home, particularly regarding the implementation of the Belt and Road Initiative in Asia. The COVID-19 crisis will inevitably see FDI flows to Africa decline sharply in 2020, also possibly for subsequent years.

---

[24] In 2017 China provided 23.8% of Africa's infrastructure commitment. Prinsloo, C., 2019. The Pitfalls of Private Sector Investment in Infrastructure Financing. South African Institute of International Affairs, Policy Briefing No. 197, June 2019 [Online] Available at: https://saiia.org.za/research/the-pitfalls-of-private-sector-investment-in-infrastructure-financing/.

[25] Zawadzki, S., 2019. Anadarko Approves $20 Billion LNG Export Project in Mozambique. Reuters. 18 June 2019. Available at: www.reuters.com/article/us-mozambique-anadarko-lng/anadarko-approves-20-billion-lng-export-project-in-mozambique-idUSKCN1TJ2DI.

[26] Sasha Planting, Gas in Mozambique—A $128bn Opportunity, Business Maverick, 24 September 2019, https://docs.google.com/document/d/1kNSyt_v7NmK2S8W5L7iEogw4Jv1Oi7CwlhZ_yYVnl_o/edit#.

[27] United Nations Conference on Trade and Development, 2018. *Regional Fact Sheets.* [Online] Available at: https://unctad.org/en/Pages/DIAE/World%20Investment%20Report/Regional-Factsheets.aspx.

To access capital markets in the West, countries need a sovereign credit rating by an international rating agency to independently evaluate its creditworthiness. In mid-2019 the only African countries with a sovereign credit rating by all three key international rating agencies (Moody's, Standard & Poor's and Fitch) were Angola, Egypt, South Africa and Morocco and it is perhaps no surprise that the majority of FDI goes to these countries.[28] These considerations are, of course, less significant in the case of state-backed loans from a country such as China—although the latter are seldom offered at concessional rates.

In addition to being the largest national provider of aid to Africa, the USA also leads on the stock of FDI that has built up from any single country although recent inflows have declined. It is followed by the United Kingdom and France. Investments by South Africa in the rest of Africa have also expanded rapidly. However, when comparing the stock of FDI from all EU member states with the USA and China, the former accounts for 40%, the USA for seven percent and China for 5%.[29]

The slow pace of post-2008 rates of growth in FDI globally were temporarily affected when, at the end of 2017, the Trump administration introduced tax reforms that allowed the large-scale repatriation of accumulated foreign earnings by US multinationals. Global foreign direct investment temporarily plummeted—except in Africa, where it remained surprisingly resilient—amounting to US$46 billion in 2018 but is still below the US$50 billion average of the previous ten years.

More broadly, FDI to Africa has slowed in recent years, largely due to the impact of the Arab spring and declining oil prices that have seen economic stagnation in Libya, Algeria, Egypt and Tunisia, and placed the economies of countries such as Angola and Nigeria under tremendous strain. Domestic policies have also played a role in South Africa, traditionally a large recipient of FDI, where a raft of controversial policies on land and investment agreements undermine investment confidence.[30]

---

[28] A further 13 countries were rated by two of the three agencies, namely Botswana, Republic of Congo, Cameroon, Cape Verde, Ghana, Kenya, Namibia, Nigeria, Rwanda, Senegal, Tunisia, Uganda and Zambia. See Country Economy, n.d. *Sovereigns Ratings List*. [Online] Available at: https://countryeconomy.com/%20ratings.

[29] European Commission, 2018. Africa-Europe Alliance. [Online] Available at: https://ec.europa.eu/commission/africaeuropealliance_en. This data would still include the UK as a member of the EU.

[30] UNCTAD, 2018. *World Investment Report: Investment and New Industrial Policies*. New York and Geneva: United Nations Publication. Available at: https://unctad.org/en/PublicationsLibrary/wir2018_en.pdfand; UNCTAD, 2019. World Investment Report: Special Economic Zones. New York and Geneva: United Nations Publication. Available at: https://unctad.org/en/PublicationsLibrary/wir2019_en.pdf, p. x.

China's Growing Footprint in Africa

A recent study indicates that China has pumped more than US$72 billion worth of FDI into Africa between 2014 and 2018, followed by France (US$34.17 billion), the USA (US$30.85 billion), United Arab Emirates (US$25.27 billion) and the United Kingdom (US$17.68 billion). Other key investors on the continent are South Africa (US$10.18 billion), Germany (US$6.88 billion), Switzerland (US$6.43 billion), India (US$5.4 billion) and Spain (US$4.38 billion).[31] Africa is the third largest destination for Chinese investment after Asia and Europe, although investment in Sub-Saharan Africa slightly declined in 2017 following a drop in aggregate Chinese investment.[32]

In a comprehensive study on China in Africa published in June 2017, the Mckinsey Global Institute concludes that 'the Africa-China opportunity is larger than that presented by any other foreign partner - including Brazil, the European Union, India, the United Kingdom, and the United States'.[33]

The authors set out two scenarios. In the first scenario revenues of Chinese firms in Africa grow from US$180 billion to around US$250 billion in 2025. A second scenario sees Chinese firms in Africa expand aggressively in both existing and new sectors, achieving revenues of US$440 billion in 2025. Before COVID-19 FDI flows to Africa was on track to return to increases of around 15–20% per annum.

The IFs Current Path forecast is that inflows from FDI to Africa will increase from its current 3.1% of GDP per annum to around 3.9% by 2040—roughly equivalent to the size of the African economy as a portion of the global economy. This will be a continuation of a trend that has seen FDI flows overwhelmingly go to Asia. Clearly much more needs to be done

---

[31] As reported by James Anyanzwa, 2019. China Injects $72b in Africa as Its Continental Influence Gathers Pace. *The East African*, 9 October 2019, www.theeastafrican.co.ke/business/China-injects-72b-in-Africa-as-its-influence-gathers-pace/2560-5303134-10sv8vf/index.html?utm_source=Media+Review+for+October+9%2C+2019&utm_campaign=Media+Review+for+October+9%2C+2019&utm_medium=email. Accessed 14 October 2019.

[32] American Enterprise Institute, 2019. *China Global Investment Tracker*. [Online] Available at: http://www.aei.org/china-global-investment-tracker/; Jayaram, K., Kassiri, O., and Sun, I. Y., 2017. *The Closest Look Yet at Chinese Economic Engagement in Africa*. [Online]. Available at: www.mckinsey.com/featured-insights/middle-east-and-africa/the-closest-look-yet-at-chinese-economic-engagement-in-africa.

[33] Jayaram, K., Kassiri, O., and Sun, I. Y., 2017. *The Closest Look Yet at Chinese Economic Engagement in Africa*. [Online] Available at: www.mckinsey.com/featured-insights/middle-east-and-africa/the-closest-look-yet-at-chinese-economic-engagement-in-africa.

to increase flows to Africa though the steady increase in tensions between the USA and China may reward Africa.

Africa has already benefited significantly from China's remarkable economic transition over the last two decades, first through its demand for commodities, second from China's positive balance of payments (in other words, it had funds to invest) and finally from China's coordinated effort to export its surplus construction capacity that eventually led to the Belt and Road Initiative. The latter has gone through various name changes since its announcement in 2013. Africa, which was not part of the original scheme, was only included in 2015 as it and other regions clamoured to benefit from potential investments in infrastructure.

Investments inevitably require collateral—pointing to another advantage for China, which has proven more flexible in accepting 'non-traditional' collateral. In fact China's willingness to accept airports, harbours and future commodity exports (or even mines) as security has raised alarm bells in conservative circles in the USA who see this as a ploy through which China can lay its hands on strategic infrastructure with potential security implications. This complaint is, however, seldom a concern in Africa and not borne out by deeper analysis although there have been many number of instances in which African governments have been induced to enter into expensive prestige projects (such as the airport in Lusaka) and overpriced railway lines (such as the Mombasa-Nairobi standard gauge line). And then there is the Chinese habit of trying to tie countries into agreements where it pays for commodities by offering the services of Chinese companies such as with Angola and South Sudan. Today Angola has a debt-to-GDP ratio of 91%, half of which is owed to China and guaranteed by oil.[34]

But there is also clear evidence of rising concerns in Beijing about the ability of key African governments to service their loans from China.

A more serious concern that has often been repeated in mainstream media is that many of the large Chinese construction (and other) projects apparently provide little work for locals. That may have been the situation several years ago but research based on extensive field research in Ethiopia and Angola[35]

---

[34] The Challenges of Reform in Angola (2020) Africa Center for Strategic Studies, 21 January 2020 and Staff writer (2020) Angola negotiates the end of oil-backed debt with China, 23 January 2020, Macauhub, https://macauhub.com.mo/2020/01/23/pt-angola-negoceia-com-china-fim-de-petroleo-como-garantia-para-divida/.

[35] Oya, C., and Wanda, F. 2019. Working Conditions in Angola. Infrastructure Construction and Building Materials Factories. Angola Research Brief, SOAS, University of London. [Online] Available at: www.soas.ac.uk/idcea/publications/reports/file141347.pdf; Schaefer, F., and Oya, C., 2019. Employment Patterns and Conditions in Construction and Manufacturing in Ethiopia: A Comparative Analysis of the Road Building and Light Manufacturing Sectors. IDCEA Research Report,

indicate that national labour participation is substantially higher than generally assumed in Western media, that wages in Chinese firms abroad are largely similar to other firms in the same sector and that Chinese firms contribute as much to training and skills development as other companies in the same sector.

Then there is the issue of the quality of infrastructure, which is often quite poor, and the extent to which China is 'exporting corruption' in the manner in which it uses development assistance to buy influence (and contracts) from African leaders. Nor are these companies able to be held to account domestically in China through shareholder activism or public disclosure.

The problem with the quality argument, borne out by my many travels across Africa, is that Africans generally get what they pay for (low quality at low prices) and that an argument can be made that much is of 'appropriate' quality.

This brings us to the most important difference between Chinese and Western practices: large Chinese loans do not come with a requirement to discuss matters around the rule of law, good governance or human rights as done by the IMF and the World Bank. China does not share the views and approaches of the West in terms of rule of law and transparency and competitive tendering as an antidote to corruption and what has generally become known as 'standards of good governance'. Like US and European practices pf some decades ago, it has little qualms about leaning on African governments and offering inducements such as recently happened in Uganda where long-standing President Museveni intervened in a bidding process for a contract to surface the highway linking Kampala to Jinja by noting that he had identified the appropriate investor, China Railway 17th Bureau Group Company.[36]

China has deep pockets and, 'through its major policy banks, state-owned commercial banks, and government agencies—now represents the largest official external creditor to developing country governments worldwide'.[37] It ran a year-on-year positive trade balance for decades with the result that total overseas lending from China's two main policy banks amounted to US$675

SOAS, University of London. [Online] Available at: www.soas.ac.uk/idcea/publications/reports/file14 1205.pdf.

[36] Muhumuza, R. 2019. As China Builds Up Africa, Some in Uganda Warn of Trouble, AP News, 24 October 2019, https://apnews.com/62ab13badad04dd7b38a69b69eac61d1?utm_source=Media+Review+for+October+24%2C+2019&utm_campaign=Media+Review+for+October+24%2C+2019&utm_medium=email.

[37] Morris, S., Parks, B., and Gardner, A., 2020 Chinese and World Bank Lending Terms: A Systematic Comparison Across 157 Countries and 15 Years. *Policy Paper 170*, Center for Global Development, 2 April 2020. [Online]. Available at https://www.cgdev.org/publication/chinese-and-world-bank-lending-terms-systematic-comparison.

billion at the end of 2016—already more than twice the size of World Bank loans although a very modest portion of this goes to Africa.[38]

At the time that COVID-19 came to the continent Chinese lending to Africa was already set to decline amid concerns about high debt levels in Africa. In fact, Africa is steadily moving down the Chinese list of priorities as its economy transitions away from infrastructure investment and commodity dependence towards domestic consumption.

The change could have an important impact in Africa since China has become the biggest single country funder and builder of infrastructure projects in Africa, having spent about US$11.5 billion per annum since 2012.[39] China is therefore the largest contributor in helping to fill Africa's gap in infrastructure, which the African Development Bank estimates at anything between US$130 and US$170 billion annually.[40]

In addition to the visible, large, state-led infrastructure companies from China active on the continent, McKinsey estimates that more than 10,000 privately owned small Chinese companies operate in Africa. This number is substantially higher than official data from China's Ministry of Commerce. McKinsey concludes that China's engagement in Africa is 'unparalleled' and that the true picture is understated with total financial flows around 15% higher than official figures convey.[41]

Infrastructure is not the only (Chinese) game in town. To ease the long-running pressure on the naira after it steadily lost value against the US dollar since 2015, Nigeria began selling Chinese renminbi (yuan) to local traders and businesses. The move has made it easier for local businesses in Nigeria to trade and engage with their Chinese counterparts without the need of first converting their local currency to dollars. After the 2015 drop in global oil prices Nigeria faced a major dollar shortage and its foreign reserves dwindled. Setting up the renminbi as an alternative trading currency eases all of this, although China's conditions and requirements to access funding and

---

[38]Neuweg, I., 2018. *What Types of Energy Does China Finance with Its Development Aid?*. [Online] Available at: http://www.lse.ac.uk/GranthamInstitute/news/china-energy-development-aid/.

[39]Partington, R., 2019. *Fears Grow in Africa That the Flood of Funds from China Will Start to Ebb*. [Online] Available at: www.theguardian.com/business/2019/jan/05/africa-fears-grow-flood-funds-china-start-to-ebb?utm_source=Media+Review+for+January+7%2C+2019&utm_campaign=Media+Review+for+January+7%2C+2019&utm_medium=email.

[40]AfDB, 2018. African Economic Outlook 2018. Available at: www.afdb.org/fileadmin/uploads/afdb/Documents/Publications/African_Economic_Outlook_2018_-_EN.pdf, see Chapter 3. [Online], pp. 63–93.

[41]Jayaram, K., Kassiri, O., and Sun, I. Y., 2017. *The Closest Look Yet at Chinese Economic Engagement in Africa*. [Online] Available at: www.mckinsey.com/featured-insights/middle-east-and-africa/the-closest-look-yet-at-chinese-economic-engagement-in-africa.

loans have also hardened of late.⁴² A number of other African countries have subsequently followed suit in allowing the renminbi as a trading currency.

To safeguard its growing investments in Africa, China has also expanded its direct and indirect role in peace and security in Africa, similar to Europe and the USA some decades previously. In addition to a naval base in Djibouti, the inaugural China–Africa Defence and Security Forum held in June/July 2018 established the overarching framework for China's security programs in Africa. In February 2019 China announced that it had provided the US$180 million to fund peace and security efforts in Africa and it is already the largest supplier of weapons to Sub-Saharan Africa. China's role in support of the African Union and numerous African armed forces is therefore steadily expanding as does its efforts at mediation.⁴³

Although there is a dearth of data about the precise nature and scale of China's investments and overseas lendings, including in Africa,⁴⁴ there is a clear danger that through the combined impact of China and others, a number of African countries could again find themselves in a debt trap as discussed in Chapter 2. Already, in January 2019, the International Monetary Fund assessed that about 17 low-income African countries were either in or at risk of debt distress or close to one and, in April 2020, the G20 countries, the IMF and the World Bank announced a first COVID-19 related debt standstill for low-income countries.⁴⁵

The third, and much smaller flow of external funds to Africa is through remittances.

---

⁴²Kazeem, Y., 2018. *Nigeria Has Taken Its First Steps in Adopting China's Yuan as a Reserve Currency.* [Online] Available at: https://qz.com/africa/1346766/chinas-yuan-trades-in-nigeria-africa-top-economy/.

⁴³Nantulya, P., 2019. *Chinese Hard Power Supports Its Growing Strategic Interests in Africa.* [Online] Available at: https://africacenter.org/spotlight/chinese-hard-power-supports-its-growing-strategic-int erests-in-africa/?utm_source=Media+Review+for+January+22%2C+2019&utm_campaign=Media+Rev iew+for+January+22%2C+2019&utm_medium=email.

⁴⁴Reinhart, C. H., 2018. *Exposing China's Overseas Lending.* [Online] Available at: www.project-syn dicate.org/commentary/china-opaque-foreign-development-loans-by-carmen-reinhart-2018-10?barrier= accesspaylog. Large portions of Chinese (and other) grants and investment in Africa is opaque while many African countries abet this unhealthy situation through lack of open, competitive tendering processes and lack of legislative oversight of public spending, amongst others.

⁴⁵International Monetary Fund, 2018. Regional Economic Outlook. Sub-Saharan Africa, Washington: Monetary Fund.

Remittance Flows to Africa

Data on remittances needs to be treated with care: such flows mostly occur through informal channels and are driven by the size of the migrant population for which data is equally unreliable. Different from aid and FDI, remittance flows do not affect government revenues since they generally consist of money sent home by migrants, and serve to support the livelihoods of poor families.[46]

Generally migrants have a positive economic impact in hosting countries and are often less likely to be involved in crime. According to the IMF, each one percent increase in the share of migrants in the adult population of advanced economies can increase the GDP per capita by up to two percent in the long term. But anti-migrant sentiments have become an important domestic policy issue in most Western countries as well as in countries like South Africa.[47]

The average annual growth figure for remittances is at around five percent. Nigeria (at US$22.3 billion in 2017), with its large diaspora, is the largest recipient of remittances in Africa.[48] As a percentage of GDP Liberia is the biggest recipient of remittances (at 26%).[49]

The IFs Current Path forecast is that remittance flows to Africa will remain constant at around US$50 billion per annum to 2040.

Remittances have benefited from new technologies that have lowered the costs of sending small amounts of money privately from one country to another, but the impact of the war on terror and concerns about money flows to groups and individuals associated with terrorists have created numerous obstacles for Africans to send money home. Furthermore, it still costs more

---

[46] African migrants (including refugees, regular and illegal migrants, short and long-term migrants, etc.) represent about 14.1% (or 36.3 million) of the global migrant population. An estimated nine-tenths of African migrants stay within the continent, moving to neighbouring countries or elsewhere within their region. Most are in Côte d'Ivoire, Uganda, South Africa, South Sudan and Burkina Faso. The EU hosts nine million African migrants, consisting of an estimated five million from North Africa (most from Algeria and Morocco in France, and Moroccans in Spain) and four million from Sub-Saharan Africa. In the Middle East, most African migrants are from Egypt and to be found in Saudi Arabia and the United Arab Emirates. Mo Ibrahim Foundation, 2019. *Africa's Youth: Jobs or Migration?*, London: Mo Ibrahim Foundation, pp. 13–15.
[47] World Bank Group, 2017. Migrations and Remittances: Recent Developments and Outlook. Special Topic. Return Migration. *Migration and Development Brief 28*, October 2017, p. 10.
[48] Remittance flows in North Africa mostly go to Egypt (at US$18.2 billion). Other large recipients are Morocco (at US$7.1 billion) and Senegal (US$2.3 billion) followed, in declining order of importance, by Algeria, Ghana, Tunisia, Kenya, Uganda, Mali, Ethiopia, South Africa, Liberia and Burkina Faso (at US$0.5 billion). Ibid. Box on pp. 25 and 28.
[49] Followed by Comoros, The Gambia, Senegal, Cape Verde, Togo, Mali, Morocco, Nigeria, São Tomé and Príncipe, Tunisia, Egypt (5%), Djibouti and Algeria (1.1%) Ibid. Box on pp. 25 and 28.

to remit money to Sub-Saharan Africa than any other region globally. Moving money between neighbouring African countries is even more expensive.[50]

Modelling Increased FDI, Aid and Remittances: The External Support Scenario

In this section I model the impact of an External Support scenario on the continent's medium to long-term development trajectory consisting of modest increases in aid, FDI and an increase in remittances.

Against the backdrop of a global focus on the achievement of the SDG's by 2030, and the impact of COVID-19, the aid component of the External Support scenario envisions an increase in the amount of development aid to Africa in the run-up to the 2030 target year that then modestly tapers down by 2040. In the External Support scenario Africa would receive a total of US$137 billion more aid (cumulatively over the forecast horizon) than in the Current Path forecast.[51] Instead of US$102 billion aid in 2030, the final year of the SDGs, Africa would get US$115 billion. Most of the additional funds would go to low-income countries.

The intervention in the External Support scenario increases the levels of FDI inflows to 4.6% of GDP by 2040 (instead of 3.9% in the Current Path).

Such inflows would only be possible with improved levels of stability and policy certainty, but would still constitute a relatively small portion of global FDI flows.

The final intervention is on remittances.

The IFs Current Path forecast is that remittances will drop from 1.6% of GDP in 2020 to 0.6% by 2040 as the size of African economies increases. This translates into an increase from the current estimate of US$49 billion in the Current Path forecast to US$75 billion by 2040 in the External Support scenario. The largest portion of the increase in remittances goes to Nigeria, followed by Egypt, Morocco, Ghana, Senegal, Tunisia, Somalia, Libya and Lesotho.

Figure 14.1 presents the contribution from remittances, aid and FDI in the Current Path compared to the External Support scenario for 2020, 2030 and 2040. It shows the extent to which remittances generally remain flat in absolute terms. Aid amounts increase but the bulk of increases comes from FDI. Whereas the three sources of funds contribute roughly equal amounts in

---

[50] Ibid., p. 5.
[51] At its peak in 2030 Africa would receive US$113.3 billion instead of US$100.1 billion.

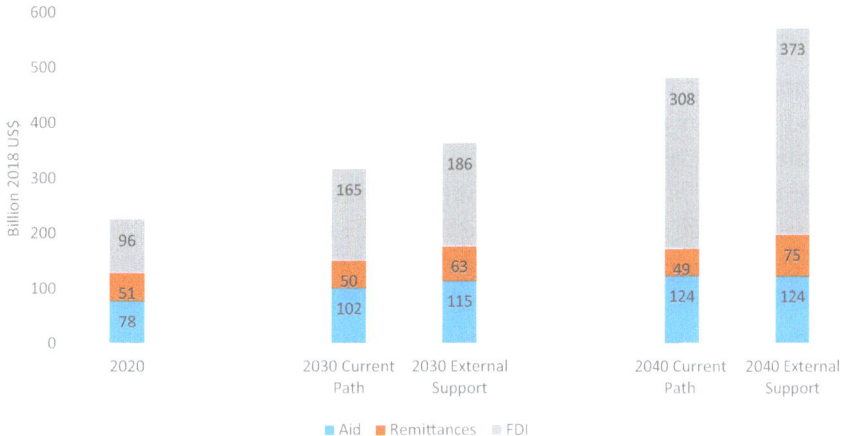

Fig. 14.1 Contribution of remittances, aid and FDI in 2020, 2030 and 2040: Current Path vs External Support scenario (*Source* IFs version 7.45 initialising from IMF World Economic Outlook 2017 and other sources)

2020, by 2040 FDI contributes nearly twice as much as aid and remittances combined in the External Support scenario. In the External Support scenario the increase in aid to 2030 reverts to the Current Path forecast by 2040.

The financial pool from which FDI is able to draw is so large that it necessarily needs to be prioritised as a source of growth and development for Africa. Hence the importance of measures such as trade facilitation (through Aid for Trade and other measures), ease of doing business and efforts to establish Special Economic Zones as vehicles to attract FDI, all of which were discussed in Chapter 8.

The Impact of the Combined External Support Scenario

By 2040, Africa benefits from a total additional inflow of almost US$90 billion in the External Support scenario compared to the Current Path forecast for that year—the difference in the columns' height for the Current Path and External Support in Fig. 14.1. The majority of aid goes to low-income countries (where most poor people are), remittances are spread across countries in line with historical levels and most FDI goes to upper-middle-income countries.

The combined impact of the External Support scenario is to increase total government revenues in Africa by US$47 billion in 2040. The cumulative increase in government revenues from 2020 to 2040 is much more impressive, amounting to US$463 billion. Although the interventions in all three areas are aggressive, the impact of FDI is significantly larger than that from aid and remittances as its contribution grows much more rapidly than that of the others, as is reflected in Fig. 14.1.

The increase in government revenues translates into tangible outcomes, although generally only towards the end of the forecast horizon. For example, in 2040 African governments consumption on education would increase by US$9 billion and by US$5 billion above the Current Path forecast.

Increased external support means that the total Africa economy is US$174 billion larger in 2040 than it otherwise would have been and that GDP per capita increases by US$112.

Beyond these findings the External Support scenario reminds that more aid, although important, would only modestly reduce extreme poverty in Africa. By 2030 the External Support scenario reduces the number of Africans living in extreme poverty (using US$1.90) by only two million. By 2040 the number has increased to 16 million, of which two-thirds are in low-income countries. That is in spite of the fact that the bulk of additional aid goes to low-income countries, where most extremely poor people are to be found.

Conclusion: Unlocking Foreign Assistance

China's footprint in Africa has grown enormously in recent years, but Europe and the EU in particular remain Africa's most important partner in trade, stock of FDI and aid. For the 2017–2020 External Investment Plan the EU budgeted €32.5 billion in grants to Africa and, in its 2021–2027 budget, it provides for €40 billion. In addition, the EU budgeted for €3.7 billion in grants for blending and guarantees in its current plan. These amounts exclude bilateral aid from individual EU member states.[52]

Looking eastward, the Belt and Road Initiative will connect China with the resources for growth and development with a large potential future market while Chinese peacekeepers and arms help to secure its investments. At the same time Africa needs to realise that the focus of the Belt and Road Initiative is largely on connecting China to its immediate neighbourhood in Asia and its impact in Africa is likely to be limited. In fact, Africa may already have experienced peak Chinese interest and may increasingly have to look elsewhere for future investment growth.

---

[52] European Commission, 2018. Africa-Europe Alliance. [Online] Available at: https://ec.europa.eu/commission/africaeuropealliance_en.

The claim of the demise of aid is still premature and, together with remittances, aid will remain important for many poor African countries into the future. The growth of private capital flows from outside Africa has benefited only a few countries although it will grow in importance. African countries will have to learn to manage the associated volatility. Generally FDI is conservative and follows rather than leads other sources of investment. FDI generally tracks investment decisions by locals and requires policy stability.

Remittances have become significantly more important for some countries but its impact is limited. Eventually infrastructure development in Africa will largely depend upon investment decisions from its own governments that need to focus on sectors and segments (such as water and sanitation infrastructure) for which other financiers have little appetite.

That said, the continent needs to work much harder to unlock investment from the wall of money searching for returns in Europe, North America, China and eventually India, although short-term prospects in the light of COVID-19 is necessarily poor. FDI boosts economic growth and is key in contributing to knowledge transfer and hence to Africa's economic transformation. But the inadequate technical, governance and implementation capacity in African countries requires a dedicated effort to strengthen domestic legislation, institutions and policies governing investment as well as its ability to negotiate and oversee the associated agreements. If the international community wants to help Africa it needs to incentivise private investment in Africa through tax benefits, de-risking foreign investment and building African capacity to negotiate, manage and evaluate projects.

The rise of China is certainly the most noteworthy feature of the twenty-first century and its demand for natural resources played a big part in the story of Africa's growth for several decades from the mid-1990s. This is also evident from the extent to which commodity exports from Africa increased more rapidly than the global average (see Fig. 11.1 in Chapter 11). As a result Africa's broad pattern of increased dependence on commodity exports to earn foreign exchange and continued deindustrialisation from already low levels has continued unabated. In the meanwhile the Chinese economy is rebalancing and its once insatiable appetite for commodities has tempered. As the hubris around the Belt and Road Initiative calms down China has limited interest to maintain the breakneck speed of investment growth in Africa that has been evident over the last two decades.

Africa should therefore not rely only on China's hunger for raw materials, its loans and future investment in infrastructure projects. In fact, China is itself concerned about the viability of African governments to service loans and, at the 2018 Forum on China–Africa Cooperation meeting in Beijing, scaled back its forecast of future partnership with Africa, expressed its concern about rising debt levels, noted that projects need to be subject to cost-benefit analysis and warned that it intends to pull back on vanity projects.[53]

If China stumbles, it would have a massive impact on Africa. According to Bloomberg, China's credit boom has been 'the largest factor driving global growth' in the decade from 2010, and debt is rising fast.[54] Over the same period, China's debt-to-GDP ratio has risen from about 140% to more than 250%. China has defied expectations before, but it is unlikely to do so indefinitely. In an important recent book Nicholas Lardy recently argues that China's growth prospects are now being shadowed by the spectre of resurgent state domination.[55] Whereas China's private sector is responsible for much of its economic growth, the attention has shifted to ailing, underperforming and indebted state-owned companies. Inefficiencies are therefore mounting. Additionally, the country has a debt problem that was accelerated by the large stimulus project that Beijing launched in response to the global financial crisis in 2008. Normally countries experience growth problems when the GDP to debt ratio is in excess of 60%. Chinese debt, now at more than 250% of GDP, may already be responsible for a loss of up to two percentage points of economic growth, opines Lardy.

Looking to the future, Africa has significant scope to improve matters by investing in the capacity of its institutions to oversee and manage trade, FDI, aid and develop formal remittance processes. The source of aid and investment support is eventually less important except to ensure that African countries are not forced to choose particular alliances as happened during the Cold War but rather encourage collaboration and mix-and-match. In this vein the recent trend in funding large projects is towards so-called basket funding that may include various partners such as from the World Bank, the African Development Bank, the European Investment Bank and the Bank of China—and where project implementation is a collaborative venture that may involve a German engineering company to oversees technical compliance, American project management and Chinese construction capacity to do the heavy lifting.

---

[53] Staff Reporter, 2019. China's Xi Offers Another $60 Billion to Africa, But Says No to 'Vanity' Projects. Reuters [Online], 3 September 2018. Available at: www.reuters.com/article/us-china-africa/chinas-xi-offers-another-60-billion-to-africa-but-says-no-to-vanity-projects-idUSKCN1LJ0C4.

[54] Orlik, T., Chen, F., Wan, Q., and Jimenez, J., 2018. *Sizing Up China's Debt Bubble: Bloomberg Economics*. [Online] Available at: www.bloomberg.com/news/articles/2018-02-08/sizing-up-china-s-debt-bubble-bloomberg-economics.

[55] Lardy, N. R., 2019. The State Strikes Back the End of Economic Reform in China? Washington: Peterson Institute for International Economics.

Eventually there is little difference between Africa's old and new partners. Each inevitably put their own interests first, as should Africa. But this time around Africans should work more diligently in setting the terms for how best it can benefit from aid, FDI and the flow of remittances. Africa needs to become a rule-maker and assume a larger role in its own destiny, particularly in the mode of development that it pursues.

The West and China have developed and industrialised at the cost of others in terms of the impact on the global climate. Africa, the region that will be the development latecomer has little option but to pursue a different pathway, namely that of sustainable and green development, the topic of the next chapter.

Further Reading

Addison, Tony, Morrisey, Olver, and Tarp, Finn. 2017. The Macroeconomics of Aid: Overview. *The Journal of Development Studies,* 53(7), pp. 987–997. https://doi.org/10.1080/00220388.2017.1303669.

Duggan, William, and Hubbard, Glenn. 2009. The Aid Trap: Hard Truths About Ending Poverty. Columbia University Press.

Moyo, Dambisa. "Dead Aid: Why Aid Is Not Working and How There Is a Better Way for Africa."

Watkins, Kevin. 2009. Why Dead Aid Is Dead Wrong. *Huffington Post.* www.huffpost.com/entry/why-idead-aidi-is-dead-wr_b_191193.

Open Access This chapter is licensed under the terms of the Creative Commons Attribution 4.0 International License (http://creativecommons.org/licenses/by/4.0/), which permits use, sharing, adaptation, distribution and reproduction in any medium or format, as long as you give appropriate credit to the original author(s) and the source, provide a link to the Creative Commons license and indicate if changes were made.

The images or other third party material in this chapter are included in the chapter's Creative Commons license, unless indicated otherwise in a credit line to the material. If material is not included in the chapter's Creative Commons license and your intended use is not permitted by statutory regulation or exceeds the permitted use, you will need to obtain permission directly from the copyright holder.

15

Climate Change

Abstract On its current development trajectory the world is headed for serious climate change trouble. More carbon emissions will affect all of humanity and with its low adaptation capacity, arid climates and rainfall-dependent agriculture, Africa is particularly at risk. Cillliers offers an in-depth assessment of the implications of climate change for Africans. In addition to reviewing the scientific consensus on the threats climate change is likely to pose in the coming decades, he sheds light on how Africa's future trends in energy, population and lifestyle will affect carbon emissions. The chapter concludes by comparing Africa's carbon emissions in four scenarios with the Current Path forecast, namely Made in Africa and Free Trade (highest carbon emissions) and Leapfrogging and Demographic Dividend (lowest carbon emissions).

Keywords Climate change · Anthropocene · Emissions · Adaptation · Mitigation · Desertification · Energy · Oil · Coal · Renewables

Learning Objectives

- Understand how and why Africa is especially vulnerable to the impacts of climate change
- Explain and critically evaluate the difference between climate change mitigation and adaptation
- Understand key climate change projections and their potential implications for Africa.

The 1997 blockbuster series *The Matrix* describes a world within a world where the earth has effectively been rendered uninhabitable and is run by artificial intelligent systems. The villain, Agent Smith, captures the leader of the human resistance movement, Morpheus, and in the subsequent interrogation talks about the impact that humanity has on the environment:

> Every mammal on this planet instinctively develops a natural equilibrium with the surrounding environment. But you humans do not. You move to an area and you multiply and multiply until every natural resource is consumed and the only way you can survive is to spread to another area. There is another organism on this planet that follows the same pattern. Do you know what it is? A virus. ... Human beings are a disease, a cancer of this planet. You are a plague.[1]

The Matrix trilogy were for entertainment and do not purport to present reality, but many scientists believe that the world is in the midst of its sixth mass extinction event, known as either the Holocene or Anthropocene.

Human activity may not be causing the extinction but humanity has clearly accelerated the onset. That message is set out starkly in a statement released in November 2017 titled *World Scientists' Warning to Humanity: A Second Notice* by several thousand scientists from 184 countries who warned: '... we have unleashed a mass extinction event, the sixth in roughly 540 million years, wherein many current life forms could be annihilated or at least committed to extinction by the end of this century'.[2]

The statement went on to include twelve 'examples of diverse and effective steps humanity can take to transition to sustainability', none of which have been implemented.

Six months later, in May 2019, the United Nations released the summary findings of sweeping a 1 500-page assessment compiled by hundreds of international experts that provides the most exhaustive look yet at the decline in biodiversity on earth. Among various depressing findings was that the average abundance of native plant and animal life has fallen by 20% or more over the last century and that many species are being pushed closer to extinction.[3]

---

[1] *The Matrix*. 1999. [Film] Directed by Lana and Lilly Wachowski. US: Warner Bros.
[2] Ripple, W. J., Wolf, C., Galetti, M., Newsome, M. T., Alamgir, M., Mahmoud, E. C., Mahmoud, M. I., and Laurance, W. F. 2017. World Scientists' Warning to Humanity: A Second Notice. *Bioscience*, 67(12), pp. 1026–1028, p. 1.
[3] Díaz, S., Settele, J., and Brondízio, E., 2019. *Summary for Policymakers of the Global Assessment Report on Biodiversity and Ecosystem Services of the Intergovernmental Science-Policy Platform on Biodiversity and Ecosystem Services.* Bonn: Intergovernmental Science Policy Platform on Biodiversity and Ecosystem Services.

This chapter presents the challenge of climate change and Africa's role within the global context. Rather than explore an alternative scenario, it reviews the impact of four scenarios from previous chapters that have the greatest impact on carbon emissions, namely demographics, manufacturing, leapfrogging and trade, and compares these with the Current Path forecast. The combined impact of all eleven scenarios, the Closing the Gap scenario, is presented in the concluding chapter.

Before proceeding, it is important to underline that IFs is not a climate model. It uses data from the Intergovernmental Panel on Climate Change (IPCC), the Carbon Dioxide Information Analysis Centre and other sources to initialise its forecasts and bases these on relationships from the academic literature reflected in various algorithms for the associated forecasts.

Africa as a Climate Change Taker

Africa is a climate change taker, even if it was not a climate change maker. Despite having very little to do with creating the problem, Africa is disproportionately vulnerable to the impacts of climate change—the most severe challenge facing human life on earth today.

Although natural climatic variability is undoubtedly at play (El Niño was clearly a factor in Cape Town when it almost ran out of water in 2018, for example), the scientific consensus is that human activity, primarily the release of CO_2 and other greenhouse gases, has caused all global warming since 1970.[4]

The 2018 water crisis in Cape Town is a textbook example of the dangerous confluence of long-term anthropogenic climate change, natural variation in weather and poor planning. Cape Town has long been a water-stressed area, but has been able to cope. That is, until temperatures got a little warmer, El Niño got a little worse and the national government failed to upgrade and maintain the necessary water infrastructure and invest in alternative water purifying and treatment systems.

A three-year drought started in the Cape metropole in 2015 and peaked in mid-2017 to mid-2018 when dam water levels hovered between 15 and 30% of total dam capacity. By late 2017 authorities were talking about 'Day Zero', when municipal water supplies would largely be switched off and residents would have to queue for a daily ration of water, much of which would

---

[4]IPCC, 2014. *Climate Change Synthesis Report Summary for Policymakers*. Geneva: s.n.

have to be trucked in. Eventually the City of Cape Town was able to implement significant water restrictions and, after good rains in June 2018, water restrictions were eased.[5]

The line between barely getting by and a national emergency can be very thin indeed.

Cape Town managed to forestall a water crisis by the skin of its teeth, but going forward this 'new normal' will leave the city and surrounding area increasingly vulnerable, particularly because it serves as a destination for many poor South Africans who move there from the Eastern Cape and because it is a global tourist destination. The result is extremely rapid urbanisation and intense pressure on infrastructure.[6]

The amount of CO_2 and other greenhouse gases that human activities have already released into the atmosphere has locked the world into a temperature increase of at least 1.2°C above pre-industrial levels.[7] The United Nations Environment Programme (UNEP) warns that on the current trajectory it is realistic to prepare for a 3°C increase. However, should greenhouse gas emissions continue unmitigated, warming of 3.4°C above pre-industrial levels will occur by the end of the century.[8] In this world 'the limits for human adaptation are likely to be exceeded in many parts of the world, while the limits for adaptation for natural systems would largely be exceeded throughout the world'.[9] As a result large portions of the Sahel and West Africa are likely to be unsuited for human habitation.

This is a world that has moved beyond a tipping point and large parts of Africa could consist of desert.

The IPCC expects that the 'current cropping areas of crops such as maize, millet and sorghum across Africa could become unviable'.[10] In a report on a 4°C warmer world the World Bank noted some of the better known foreseen consequences, such as 'the inundation of coastal cities; increasing risks for food production potentially leading to higher malnutrition rates; many dry regions becoming dryer, and wet regions wetter; unprecedented heat waves in many regions, especially in the tropics; substantially exacerbated

---

[5] City of Cape Town, 2018. *Water Outlook Report*. Cape Town: Department of Water and Sanitation.
[6] Department of Water and Sanitation, 2019. *National Integrated Water Information System*. [Online] Available at: http://niwis.dws.gov.za/niwis2/SurfaceWaterStorage.
[7] Pre-industrial is defined as the average for the period 1850–1900.
[8] United Nations Environment Programme, https://www.unenvironment.org/explore-topics/climate-change.
[9] Warren, R., 2011. The Role of Interactions in a World Implementing Adaptation and Mitigation Solutions to Climate Change. *The Royal Society*, 369(1934).
[10] IPCC, 2014. *The IPCC's Fifth Assessment Report: What's in It for Africa?* s.l.: Climate & Development Knowledge Network.

water scarcity in many regions; increased frequency of high-intensity tropical cyclones; and irreversible loss of biodiversity, including coral reef systems'.[11]

Meanwhile, a 2018 special report from the IPCC found that an increase to 1.5°C is essentially inevitable and may be reached as early as 2030.[12] According to the report, limiting warming to this 1.5°C marker as reflected in the Paris Agreement, would require the entire world to cut greenhouse gas emissions by nearly half of 2010 levels by 2030 *and* make an aggressive push to reach net-zero emissions by 2050.

Instead, the Current Path forecast is that annual global emissions will *increase* by 600 million tonnes by 2037. World annual emissions would only plateau between 2035 and 2040 before starting to decline, as is reflected in Fig. 15.1. Even though developed countries are weaning themselves off fossil fuels and moving towards renewable energy—albeit with varying degrees of urgency—the pace of global emissions is increasing, with the digital world requiring increased amounts of electricity to power its electric cars, artificial intelligence and higher levels of automation.

Drawing on data provided by the Carbon Dioxide Information Analysis Centre, the Current Path forecast is that global CO_2 in the atmosphere will increase from the current levels of just above 415 parts per million to 460 parts per million by 2040 and to 520 parts per million by 2100, translating to a 2.1°C warming over 1990 levels by 2100.

Carbon can be released in many ways, but the three most important contributors to greenhouse gasses are carbon dioxide (CO_2), carbon monoxide (C0) and methane (CH_4) with the latter having the biggest negative impact. Since each gas has a different molecular mass, i.e. they have different weights (carbon dioxide/CO_2 weighs about four times more than CH_4/methane), the unit of measure that is used when calculating carbon emissions is known as the carbon contribution, i.e. just the mass of the carbon component of each of the various greenhouse gasses.[13]

Globally, carbon emissions are projected to increase from a current 9.6 billion tonnes per annum, peak at 10.22 billion tonnes in 2037 and decline to 5.8 billion tonnes per annum by 2100, as reflected in Fig. 15.1, which

---

[11] As summarized by The GreenFacts initiative, n.d. *Impacts of a 4°C Global Warming*. [Online] Available at: https://www.greenfacts.org/en/impacts-global-warming/l-2/index.htm.

[12] Intergovernmental Panel on Climate Change, October 2018, An IPCC Special Report on the impacts of global warming of 1.5°C above pre-industrial levels and related global greenhouse gas emission pathways, in the context of strengthening the global response to climate change, sustainable development and efforts to eradicate poverty: IPCC, 2018. *Global Warming of* 1.5°C. Geneva: Intergovernmental Panel on Climate Change.

[13] What this means is that the mass of CO_2 is 44.01 grams per 22.4 L at 25^0 Â°C and at sea level. CO weighs 28.01 grams per 22.4 L and CH_4 weighs 16.04 grams per 22.4 L. However, the carbon contribution for each is 12.01 grams per 22.4 litres.

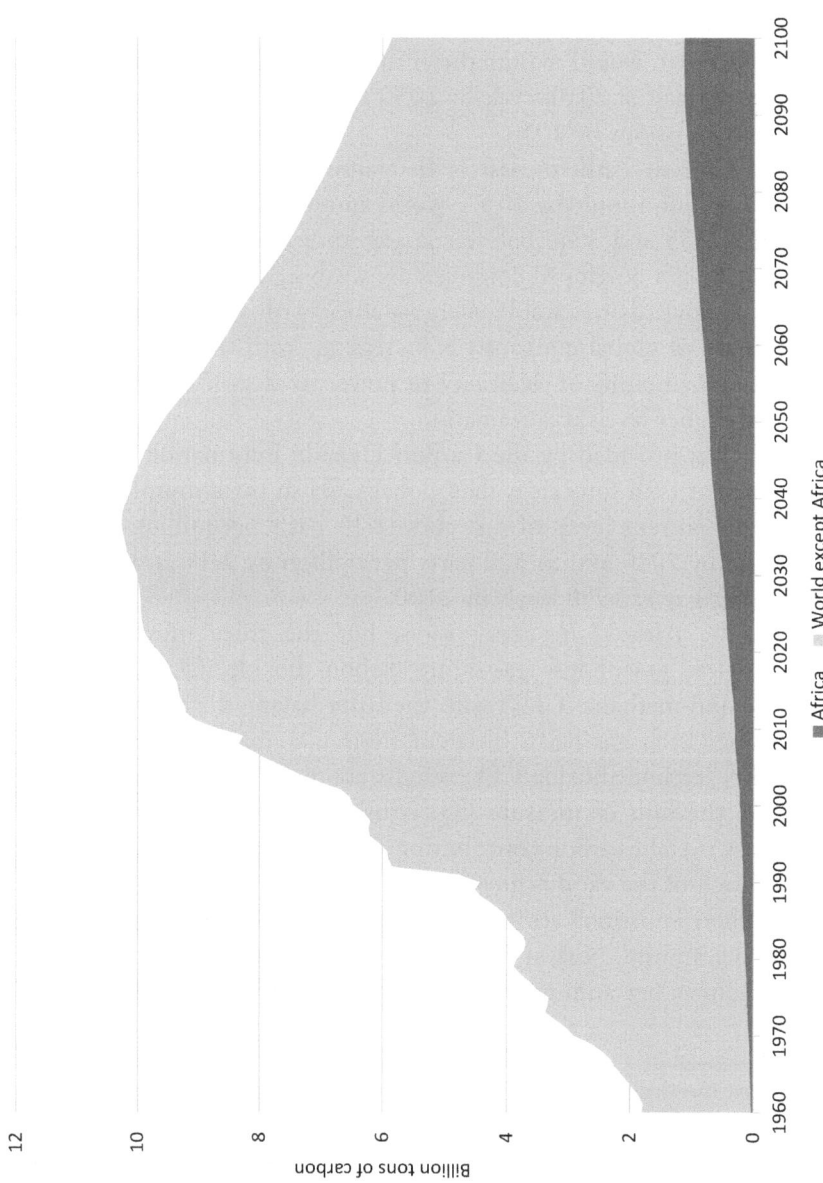

Fig. 15.1 History and Current Path forecast of carbon emissions from Africa and the world: 1960 to 2100 (*Source* IFs version 7.45 initialising from Intergovernmental Panel on Climate Change and Carbon Dioxide Information Analysis Centre)

also highlights the Current Path emissions from Africa. To be sure, this is a cataclysmic forecast.

Most emissions are essentially locked into an expensive energy infrastructure. In Asia the average coal plant is just 11 years old and has decades left of its operational life. Coal plants in the USA and Europe, meanwhile, are roughly 40 years old, on average.[14] Countries like China and India would have to be willing to prematurely decommission a very large number of recently built coal plants for the world to make progress towards global sustainability. In the absence of an extraordinary technological breakthrough, there is no other pathway for reducing emissions. All regions, including Africa, will have to contribute to the necessary shift towards renewable energy to the best of their ability, although the largest contributions inevitably have to come from the biggest polluters.

Climate change might be taking place at a slow pace, but it has lots of momentum. Even if we were to magically cease adding more greenhouse gases to the atmosphere today, the climate would still warm for a few hundred years before slowly returning to pre-industrial levels of atmospheric carbon concentrations.[15]

On our current trajectory extended droughts, heat waves, and other extreme weather events will become the norm; the sea will continue to rise and acidify, killing off vast swathes of marine species; and biodiversity is increasingly threatened. Already research done by the University of Melbourne has found that extreme winds in the Antarctic Ocean have increased by 1.5 metres per second over the past 30 years and that extreme waves have increased by 30 centimetres.[16]

In the short term, these impacts pose grave threats to 'health, livelihoods, food security, water supply, human security, and economic growth'.[17] And the IPCC has acknowledged that their previous risk assessments likely understated the risks of a 1.5°C–2°C temperature increase. In addition, extreme weather events and increased threats to biodiversity all become more acute and pervasive with warmer temperatures.

---

[14]International Energy Agency, 2018. *World Energy Outlook*. [Online] Available at: https://www.iea.org/weo2018/.
[15]https://www.atmos.washington.edu/academics/classes/2011Q1/101/Climate_Change_2011_part2.pdf.
[16]Young, I. R., and Ribal, A., 2019. Multiplatform Evaluation of Global Trends in Wind Speed and Wave Height. *Science*, 364(6440), pp. 548–552.
[17]Intergovernmental Panel on Climate Change, October 2018, An IPCC Special Report on the impacts of global warming of 1.5°C above pre-industrial levels and related global greenhouse gas emission pathways, in the context of strengthening the global response to climate change, sustainable development and efforts to eradicate poverty: IPCC, 2018. *Summary for Policymakers: Global Warming of 1.5*. Geneva: Intergovernmental Panel on Climate Change.

Even limiting warming to 2°C would require dramatic action. Meeting that target would involve a 25% reduction in global greenhouse emissions by 2030 and a net-zero world by 2070. That seems highly unlikely when one looks at the Current Path global forecast of emissions to 2100 in Fig. 15.1.

The Global Energy Transition

Like fossil fuels shaped the geopolitical map over the last two centuries, so 'the energy transformation will alter the global distribution of power, relations between states, the risk of conflict, and the social, economic and environmental drivers of geopolitical instability'.[18] Whereas fossil fuels are concentrated in specific geographic locations and vulnerable to disruption, renewable energy resources are distributed in one form or another in most countries. This means that renewables are better suited to decentralised forms of energy production and consumption.

Countries like the USA are already close to being self-sufficient in terms of energy, largely due to the shale oil and gas revolution. Energy self-sufficiency is accelerating the international withdrawal and isolation of the USA, while China's determined investment in connecting Asia through the Belt and Road Initiative, its leadership in research and development and investments in renewables is likely to improve its geopolitical standing.[19]

Once the energy storage problem is resolved, countries and populations across Africa will benefit greatly from the dispersed nature of renewables, particularly through reduced fossil fuel imports. Actually most African countries have a unique opportunity to leapfrog the fossil-fuel centred development model to renewables. Some, such as Libya, the Republic of Congo, Angola, Equatorial Guinea, South Sudan and Gabon will suffer since they are extraordinarily dependent on the foreign exchange earnings from their fossil fuel exports. Others with large fossil fuel import bills, such as Tanzania, Côte d'Ivoire, Guinea and Senegal, will benefit.

High energy bills transfer large amounts of wealth abroad and make countries vulnerable to price swings. Renewables have none of these risks. Some countries, such as Ethiopia and Lesotho, could obtain all or most of their electricity from hydropower. Others, like Kenya, can achieve similar results

---

[18]Global Commission on the Geopolitics of Energy Transformation, 2019. *A New World: The Geopolitics of the Energy Transformation*. Abu Dhabi: s.n., p. 12.

[19]This analysis is based on Global Commission on the Geopolitics of Energy Transformation, 2019. *A New World: The Geopolitics of the Energy Transformation*. Abu Dhabi: s.n.

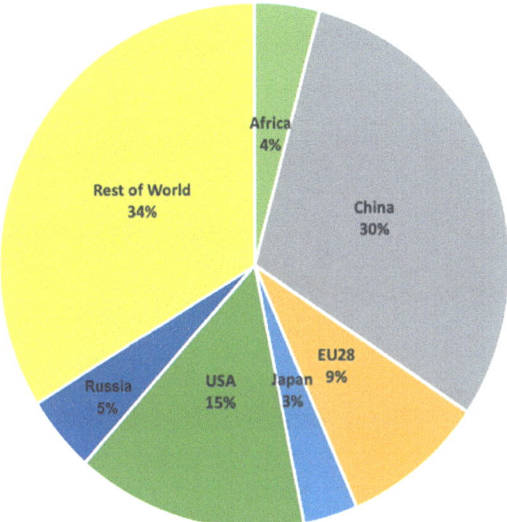

Fig. 15.2 Carbon Emissions by countries or region as a percent of the total (2018) (*Source* United States Environmental Agency, Global Greenhouse Gas Emissions Data)

using a mix of renewables, such as hydro, geothermal, wind, biomass and solar power.[20]

Most carbon dioxide (CO_2) is emitted from the energy sector, followed by transport, agriculture land and forestry, residential and commercial and industry. Most methane (CH_4) comes from agriculture and energy production and most nitrous oxide (N_2O) emissions are from agriculture.[21]

Data on emissions is often, and quite misleadingly, presented on the basis of emissions per country. That is presented for key countries in Fig. 15.2, with all of Africa responsible for about four percent of global emissions in 2018. A much more appropriate comparison would be to calculate emissions per person. On average Africans produce around 1.2 tonnes of CO_2 per annum compared to more than 16 tonnes by Americans, almost 12 tonnes by Russians, more than nine tonnes by Japanese and around seven tonnes by Chinese. The global average is about 4.8 tonnes. In other words, the average

---

[20] Ibid. Yet Kenya is ironically building a coal-fired plant near the Lamu Port South Sudan Ethiopia Transport corridor project that may even be dependent on coal imports. Leithead, A. 2019. Row over Chinese Coal Plant Near Kenya World Heritage Site of Lamu. [Online] Available at: https://www.bbc.com/news/uk-48503020.

[21] Ritchie, H., and Roser, M., 2017. *CO_2 and Greenhouse Gas Emissions*. Our World in Data. [Online]. Available at: https://ourworldindata.org/co2-and-other-greenhouse-gas-emissions Also see United States Environmental Protection Agency, n.d. *Global Greenhouse Gas Emissions Data*. [Online] Available at: https://www.epa.gov/ghgemissions/global-greenhouse-gas-emissions-data (Fig. 15.2).

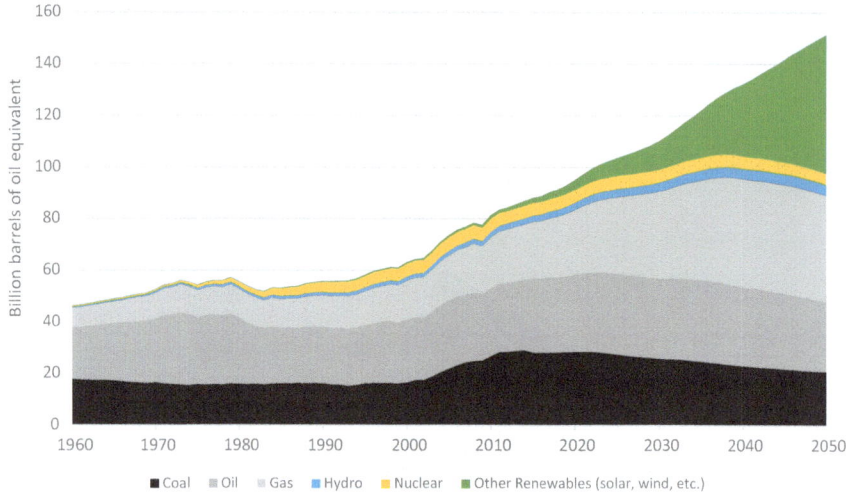

Fig. 15.3 Current Path forecast of world energy production by type: 1980 to 2050 (*Source* IFs version 7.45 initialising from International Energy Agency World Energy Outlook)

African produces less than eight percent of the emissions of the average American. Few numbers better illustrate the stark differences in responsibility for global emissions—and these numbers do not account for the stock of carbon emitted by the populations of these different countries over time.[22]

The Current Path forecast for world energy production is presented in Fig. 15.3 in billion barrels of oil equivalent from coal, oil, gas, nuclear, hydro and other renewables.[23] In this forecast the production of coal oil and gas dominates out to 2060, although renewables start growing strongly beyond 2030. The forecast is that the contribution made by renewables will be larger than that from coal in 2038, bigger than that from oil in 2040 and will surpass natural gas in 2046. Clearly this Current Path forecast is nowhere near the target of keeping global warming to 1.5 or even 2 degrees Celsius by the end of the century.

---

[22]Calculated from data available from the csv file on the chart CO_2 emissions per capita: Ritchie, H., and Roser, M., 2017. *CO_2 and Greenhouse Gas Emissions*. Our World in Data. [Online]. Available at: https://ourworldindata.org/co2-and-other-greenhouse-gas-emissions.

[23]The forecasts from the International Energy Agency (IEA) in its World Energy Outlook 2018 is that almost two-thirds of global capacity additions to 2040 will come from renewables, thanks to falling costs and supportive government policies. In the most recent forecast from the IEA, natural gas overtakes coal in 2030 to become the second largest fuel in the global energy mix. By 2040, the most likely IEA scenario is that the share of renewables in generation would have increased from its current 25% to more than 40%, but that coal is likely to remain the largest source of energy globally and gas the second largest.

Globally the energy transition path in high-income countries is typically from coal to oil and then to natural gas, which emits 50–60% less greenhouse gases than coal, and, finally, to renewables.

Carbon Emissions and Energy in Africa

Next to the uninhabited Antarctic, Africa and Australia are probably the continents that are most vulnerable to the impact of climate change. Yet Africa contributes very little to global carbon emissions, as can be seen from Fig. 15.1. In 2018 Russia's net emissions were higher than that of the entire African continent.

The Current Path forecast is that, by 2040, Africa will be responsible for 6.6% of carbon emissions. Its relative contribution would modestly increase thereafter as emissions in the rest of the world decreases. Emissions from Africa will increase for several subsequent decades in the Current Path forecast given increased populations and industrialisation.

On the Current Path, most African countries will, by 2040, be releasing more than one million tonnes of carbon each year. Figure 15.4 presents the African countries that will release more than 10 million tonnes of carbon per year in 2018 and 2040. As expected, Nigeria is projected to experience the largest increase in carbon emissions levels by 2040. In South Africa, total emissions will decline as older coal-fired electricity plants are retired and the country experiences modest economic growth. Egypt and Algeria, Nigeria and South Africa consistently release the most carbon in Africa.

The Current Path forecast for Africa for energy production is presented in Fig. 15.5. Gas production will be greater than oil in 2026. Coming from a very low base, renewables overtake coal in 2034 and gas in 2050. From this graph it should be evident that Africa is well-positioned for a much earlier transition to renewables than other regions. It also has some of the most valuable solar, hydro and wind real estate on the planet. Wind and solar are both becoming increasingly price-competitive and electricity storage and efficiency are also improving.

Although gas features prominently in Fig. 15.5, it is important to note that this is a graph of *production* by type, often for export, not in-country use by type. African countries with big proven natural gas reserves are Nigeria, Algeria, Mozambique, Egypt, Tanzania and Libya. However, even in these countries there is very little installed gas infrastructure that would allow for domestic use. Instead, since demand for gas is expanding particularly rapidly

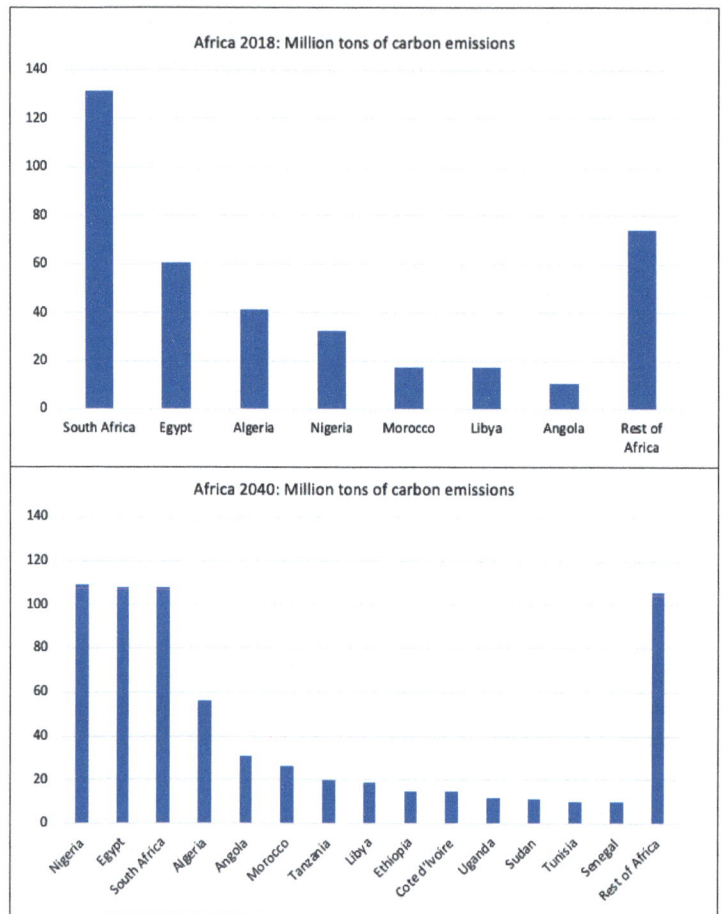

Fig. 15.4 Current Path carbon emissions: African countries that release more than 10 million tonnes in 2018 and 2040 vs Rest of Africa (*Source* IFs version 7.45 initialising from Carbon Dioxide Information Analysis Centre)

in Asia it is very likely that the vast majority of Africa's natural gas production (like its oil) will end up as exports to feed demand in China, India and elsewhere.

Oil is currently the largest source of energy produced in Africa and is likely to remain central to oil-producing Nigeria, Angola, Algeria, Libya, Egypt, the Republic of Congo, Equatorial Guinea, Gabon, Chad, Ghana and Cameroon. Most of that oil is exported rather than refined and then the refined product is imported again although various plans are afoot to build refineries. Libya and Nigeria have globally significant proven oil reserves, while Nigeria and Algeria hold Africa's largest proven gas reserves. In general,

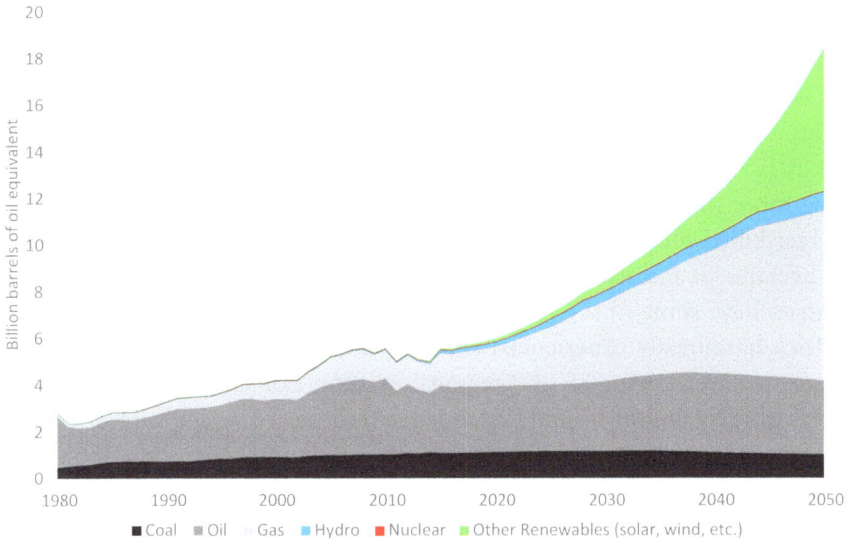

Fig. 15.5 Current Path forecast of Africa's energy production by type: 1980 to 2050 (*Source* IFs version 7.45 initializing from International Energy Agency World Energy Outlook)

though, Africa remains quite unexplored and the potential for additional oil and gas finds is therefore quite good.

The Impact of Climate Change

Chapter 6 showed that agricultural yields in Africa are low by comparative regional standards, but that production can be improved considerably by increasing the amount of land under irrigation, using more fertilisers and genetically modified seeds, and by improving farming practices. However, climate change poses a major threat and will constrain such improvements, particularly in North and West Africa as higher temperatures and shifting rainfall takes its toll.

In 2006, three major flood events (normally a once in every 10–20-year phenomenon) occurred within the space of two months in East Africa, displacing almost 200,000 people in Ethiopia, Somalia and Kenya and destroying thousands of hectares of cropland.[24]

---

[24] Swarup, A., 2007. *Eastern Africa: Worst Floods in Decades*. [Online] Available at: https://www.ifrc.org/en/nouvelles/nouvelles/common/eastern-africa-worst-floods-in-decades/.

Maize and wheat production have already been affected in many countries, including fisheries in the Great Lakes Region and fruit trees in the Sahel.[25] Droughts and floods are likely to become more frequent and more difficult to predict and could exacerbate food security issues and migratory push factors.

In 2017, weeks of heavy rain led to catastrophic mudslides in Sierra Leone, killing more than 600 people outside Freetown.[26] In 2018 extreme flooding in Niger killed more than 80 people, displaced 50,000 more and wiped out 400 hectares of farmland and 26 000 head of livestock. Meanwhile, these countries have some of the fastest growing populations in the world.[27]

Africa has already experienced some of the most severe effects of climate change to date. Owing to the regions' existing hot and dry climate, high rates of poverty and profound dependence on rain-fed agriculture, the IPCC has identified the Sahel and West Africa as climate change 'hot spots' that are projected to experience unprecedented effects of climate change before anywhere else in the world. In typically antiseptic language the IPCC notes that during the 1970s and 1980s, the Sahel region 'experienced the most substantial and sustained decline in rainfall recorded anywhere in the world within the period of instrumental measurements'.[28]

It was initially thought that this drought was caused mainly by human modification of the surrounding landscape, i.e. desertification. However, it has subsequently become clear that rising sea temperatures was the primary driver, reflecting the extent to which climate change is a truly global problem.[29]

West Africa has recently also been exposed to massive flooding, illustrating the complexity of the challenges. For example, in Nigeria nearly 200 people lost their lives and more than 150 000 were displaced in the 2018 floods which also led to a spike in cholera cases.[30]

---

[25] IPCC, 2014. *The IPCC's fifth assessment Report: What's in it for Africa?* s.l.: Climate & Development Knowledge Network.

[26] UNOCHA, 2017. *West and Central Africa: 2017 Flood Impact.* [Online] Available at: https://reliefweb.int/sites/reliefweb.int/files/resources/OCHA-ROWCA%20West%20and%20Central%20Africa%202017%20Flood%20Impact_18%20Oct%202017.pdf.

[27] Countries are listed in order of fastest growing populations. All in all, 18 of 25 the fastest growing populations are in Africa, interestingly the rest are all in the Middle East.

[28] The Sahel is a poorly defined area but is generally considered to consist of the area underlying the Sahara desert—stretching from Mauritania in the west to Ethiopia or Eritrea or Djibouti or Somalia in the east. IPCC, 2001. *Climate Change 2001: Impacts, Adaptation, and Vulnerability.* New York: Cambridge University Press, p. 518.

[29] Giannini, A., Saravanan, R., and Chang, P., 2003. Oceanic Forcing of Sahel Rainfall on Interannual to Interdecadal Time Scales. *Science*, 302(5647), pp. 1027–1030.

[30] UN OCHA, 2018. *West and Central Africa: Weekly Regional Humanitarian Snapshot.* [Online] Available at: https://reliefweb.int/sites/reliefweb.int/files/resources/External%20weekly%2025%20sep%201%20oct.pdf.

While vulnerable populations are the most susceptible to the direct effects of climate change like flooding and drought, there are also other impacts such as the incidence and distribution of infectious diseases like malaria. Increased temperatures will enable malaria to develop in regions where it was previously absent, such as in the African highlands of Ethiopia, Uganda and Kenya.[31] Heavy rainfall in parts of Central Africa, particularly in areas with limited access to improved sanitation and proper waste management, is again likely to drive an increase in the transmission of water and vector-borne diseases.[32]

The increased desiccation of arid climates like the Sahel and parts of Southern Africa will also affect groundwater recharge rates. Combined with cyclical weather phenomena like droughts or El Niño, it will further exacerbate water security issues. In more affluent communities, this could mean higher prices or even restrictions on the use of basic services, but in poor communities this could lead to an inability to access these fundamental rights, with dire consequences. These trends threaten to negate the progress Africa has made on reducing the burden of communicable diseases and the associated maladies of undernutrition and chronic hunger.

In March 2019 Cyclone Idai smashed into Mozambique, unleashing hurricane-force winds and rain that flooded swathes of this poor country before battering eastern Zimbabwe. More than 700 people died in the two countries, leaving some 1.85 million people in need of assistance in a catastrophe that United Nations Secretary-General Antonio Guterres said rang 'yet another alarm bell about the dangers of climate change'.[33] As if to emphasise the point, Cyclone Kenneth arrived a few days later, first smashing its way across the Comoros islands before making landfall in northern Mozambique. Kenneth was reportedly the strongest cyclone to ever hit Africa.

Climate change makes things worse in areas that are already struggling with high levels of poverty and poor governance. In the first half of 2018 in Nigeria, farmer–herder conflict resulted in more than six times as many fatalities than has been attributed to terrorist group Boko Haram.[34] With climate changes, grazing lands have shifted, which has forced herders to move southward. This has led to competition and violence between farmers and

---

[31] IPCC, 2014. *The IPCC's fifth assessment Report: What's in It for Africa?* s.l.: Climate & Development Knowledge Network, p. 14.
[32] Field, C. B., and Barros, V. R., 2014. *Climate Change 2014 Impacts, Adaptation and Vulnerability: Part A Global and Sectoral Aspects.* New York: Cambridge University Press.
[33] Rumney, E., and Eisenhammer, S., 2019. *Destructive Cyclone Idai Rings 'Alarm Bell' on Climate Change: U.N. Chief.* [Online] Available at: https://af.reuters.com/article/topNews/idAFKCN1R80JJ-OZATP.
[34] Crisis Group, 2018. Stopping Nigeria's Spiralling Farmer-Herder Violence. *Report 262*, 26 July.

herders. In Mali, the situation has escalated to the point where, '[m]ass repression based on faulty generalisations, and ethnic tensions between farmers and pastoralists are at the core of the ongoing insecurity'.[35]

Western Africa is home to diverse climates that range from rainforests to hyper-arid deserts and is, in a sense, a microcosm of the continent. Its arid regions are likely to get significantly warmer and drier, with droughts becoming more severe and frequent. This will harm agricultural production and could in turn drive large internal and international displacement.

Rising temperatures are likely to have the greatest negative effect on agricultural production with many crops already at their tolerance limits. This problem will be exacerbated by the increasing variability of rainfall that is most pronounced in Eastern and Southern Africa. These regions experience year-to-year variations exceeding 30% around the mean, a rate much greater than the temperate climates in Europe and North America. High seasonal variability compounds these effects, causing droughts and floods.[36] High inter- and intra-annual rainfall variability explains the unpredictable, and relatively low, seasonal and annual flows in many African rivers.

The IPCC expects that agricultural production could decline by more than 20% across Sub-Saharan Africa by 2050, with South Africa and Zimbabwe experiencing reductions of around 30% or more.[37]

These negative effects are likely to be most severe in semi-arid regions, much of which is in North and West Africa. In the Current Path forecast the countries that would be most affected by 2050 would be Mauritania (at 7.5% loss in agricultural yields compared to 2015), Mali, Eritrea, Sudan, South Sudan, Senegal, Burkina Faso and Djibouti (at six percent loss). Countries that will suffer a yield loss of between five and six percent are Egypt, Niger, Gambia, Namibia, Chad, Botswana, Algeria, Benin, Guinea and Morocco.

Although Africa's climates will generally become more arid, Central and Eastern Africa will experience heavier rainfall, especially after mid-century. These changes will likely increase the incidence and spread of water- and vector-borne diseases.[38]

---

[35] Diallo, O. A., 2017. Ethnic Clashes, Jihad, and Insecurity in Central Mali. *Journal of Social Justice*, 29(3), pp. 299–306.

[36] Foster, V., and Briceno-Garmendia, C., 2010. Africa's Infrastructure: A Time for Transformation. *Africa Development Forum Series World Bank*.

[37] IPCC, 2014. *The IPCC's Fifth Assessment Report: What's in It for Africa?* s.l.: Climate & Development Knowledge Network.

[38] Field, C. B., and Barros, V. R., 2014. *Climate Change 2014 Impacts, Adaptation and Vulnerability: Part a Global and Sectoral Aspects*. New York: Cambridge University Press, p. 762.

Comparing Carbon Emissions in Different Scenarios

In this section, I compare the results of the Current Path with the four scenarios in this book that have the greatest positive and negative impact on carbon emissions. These are Africa achieving a Demographic Dividend (Chapter 4), Made in Africa on industrialisation (Chapter 8), and the implementation of the African Continental Free Trade Agreement (Chapter 11).

Africa has roughly the same population size in 2040 (at about 2.1 billion people) in all scenarios, except for the Demographic Dividend scenario that results in 100 million fewer people than in the other scenarios.

Just as development elsewhere in the world has increased carbon emissions, Africa, with its burgeoning population and huge demands for improved livelihoods, will also increase its carbon contribution, even if relatively marginally compared with the development path of other regions. Consequently, even the Current Path forecast of solid but unspectacular economic growth would see Africa's annual carbon emissions increase from the current level of roughly 410 million tonnes per year to 660 by 2040 and 750 million tonnes by 2050. The Current Path forecast is indicated with a dashed line in Fig. 15.6.

Generally one would expect that carbon emissions would follow rates of economic growth, i.e. that the scenario where the size of the African economy increases the most would also have the largest emissions, but this is not evident in Fig. 15.6. Each of the five scenarios depicted in Fig. 15.6 presents an aggressive but reasonable positive development pathway on which economic growth rates are above those of the Current Path. However, in two scenarios, the Demographic Dividend and Leapfrogging, CO_2 emissions are actually *below* the Current Path forecast.

In the case of the Demographic Dividend, a smaller population translates into less carbon emissions. In the Leapfrogging scenario growth rates increase but because of the impact of digitisation that is less resource-intensive, and the more rapid transition to renewable energy, carbon emissions is below the Current Path forecast.

The implementation of the African Continental Free Trade Area (Chapter 11), Made in Africa (Chapter 8) and the Agricultural Revolution (Chapter 3) release more carbon emissions over the time horizon 2020–2050 than in the Current Path. Previously I noted that globally the agricultural sector is responsible for almost a quarter of global emissions so it comes as no surprise that a larger agricultural sector increases emissions above the Current Path. Manufacturing is by nature more energy-intensive than other sectors

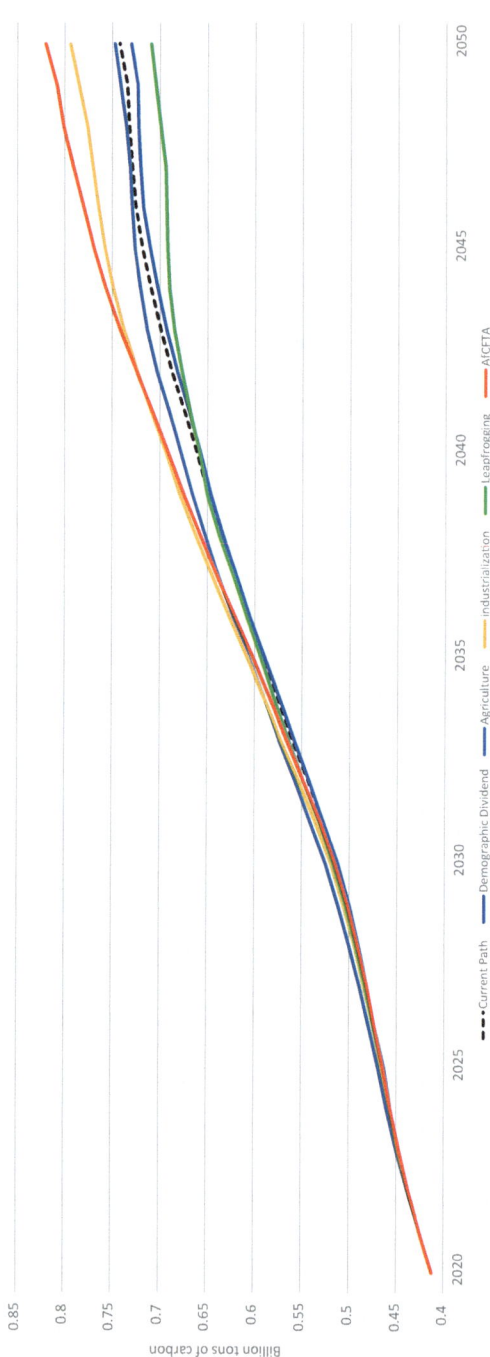

Fig. 15.6 Africa's carbon emissions under different scenarios: 2020–2050 (*Source* IFs version 7.45 initialising from Intergovernmental Panel on Climate Change and Carbon Dioxide Information Analysis Centre)

and hence, in the Made in Africa scenario, carbon emissions increase above the Current Path.

A different and perhaps more useful measure is to see which scenario provides the highest GDP per capita for the lowest carbon emissions. Social Grants (Chapter 7) shows the least improvement in GDP per capita (since it results in slow economic growth) while Leapfrogging (Chapter 10) again gives the best results. In the case of the Social Grants scenario the lower levels of emissions likely follows the transfer of resources to poorer families that are responsible for less emissions.

Responding to Climate Change

The previous comparisons demonstrate how the nature of economic growth and the associated policy decisions impacted Africa's carbon emissions. In responding to this environmental challenge one can either adapt your way of life to the inevitable impacts of climate change, resort to mitigative actions, or both. Mitigative efforts focus on reducing emissions and stabilising the levels of greenhouse gases in the atmosphere. In this way, mitigation is a long-term climate change response as its benefits will only emerge during the second half of the century.

The Paris Agreement represents a global effort to mitigate the future impacts of climate change by trying to reduce greenhouse gas emissions now. And under the Kigali Amendment to the Montreal Protocol (the 1987 agreement to protect the stratospheric ozone layer) that came into force in January 2019, all countries will gradually phase down production and consumption of hydrofluorocarbons (HFCs) and replace it with more environmentally friendly alternatives. Indeed, the global regime to protect the ozone layer remains one of the most successful coordinated international environmental efforts to date.

A second possible reaction is to adapt to life in a changing climate, therefore to the change that is already locked into the climate system. For example, in June 2018 Tanzania completed 2.4 kilometres of sea walls at a cost of US$8.34 million in an effort to protect Dar es Salaam and surrounding areas from rising sea levels. According to USAID, the country could suffer about US$200 million per year in lost land and infrastructure damage due to sea-level rise.[39]

---

[39]Cusick, D., 2018. *New Walls Aim to Hold Back Rising Seas off Tanzania.* [Online] Available at: https://www.scientificamerican.com/article/new-walls-aim-to-hold-back-rising-seas-off-tanzania/?redirect=1.

On the other side of the continent Lagos is one of the largest and fastest growing cities in the world, but much of the city is less than one meter above sea level.[40] Lagos is, and has always been, a city-oriented towards the sea. In fact, it is expanding into the Atlantic through expensive developments on newly reclaimed land on the one hand and overpopulation in slum settlements on the other. With many of its slum communities literally built in the sea, vulnerable communities in Lagos are already highly exposed to rising sea levels and more severe storm activity caused by climate change.

Seventy percent of Lagos' population live in slums and, with a population density 10 times that of New York City, a powerful storm would affect millions. Furthermore, average sea-level rise is projected to reach approximately 30 cm by 2050 and between 30 cm and 1.8 m by 2100 (then rising an additional 30 cm or more after each decade).[41]

Against this backdrop the 'Great Wall of Lagos' promises to offer protection from climate change, but only for those Nigerians who can afford to live in Eko Atlantic—a massive Dubai-style city under construction. The 8.5 km seawall will protect the shoreline of Victoria Island[42] and early phases of Lekki (a city on a peninsula to the east of Lagos) from coastal erosion.[43] What will happen to the people of Makoko and other slum areas is, of course, an entirely different matter.

And then there is the Great Green Wall. For more than a decade affected countries in the Sahel and others have advanced and promoted the Great Green Wall of the Sahara and the Sahel Initiative (*Grande Muraille Verte pour le Sahara et le Sahel*) that aims to halt the southward spread of the Sahara desert and to constrain the impact of climate change. The original concept, that dates from colonial times, is for a front-line of trees 50 km deep (now reduced to 15 km) to be planted to help contain the desert.

The project has subsequently evolved into an integrated rural development effort to respond to the detrimental social, economic and environmental impacts of land degradation and desertification straddling eleven countries and 8000 km from Senegal in the west to Djibouti in the east.[44] In 2017 it was adopted as a flagship project by the UN Conference on Sustainable

---

[40]The UN Population Division uses data from the state of Lagos that is then standardized.
[41]Romm, J. J., 2015. *Climate Change: What Everyone Needs to Know.* Oxford: Oxford University Press.
[42]Victoria Island is the financial heart of Lagos and historically one of the city's more affluent areas.
[43]Eko Atlantic's website boasts the 'best prime real estate in West Africa' and features a video starring the 42nd President of the United States Bill Clinton. Eko Atlantic, n.d. *Prime Real Estate in West Africa.* [Online] Available at: https://www.ekoatlantic.com/.
[44]The width of the wall has been scaled back to 15 km and it is estimated to cost US$8 billion. See BBC News, 2017. *YouTube. Why Is Africa Building a Great Green Wall?.* [Online] Available at: https://www.youtube.com/watch?v=4xls7K_xFBQ; BBC Newsnight, 2017. *The Great Green Wall of*

Development and 20 countries have pledged support to it but according to the United Nations, the initiative has only reached 15% of its targets over a decade.

Apart from a minimum effort in Burkina Faso and Senegal, little progress has been made. Recently (on 30 July 2019) Ethiopia claimed to have planted more than 353 million trees in just twelve hours as part of a wider reforestation campaign that is being spearheaded by Prime Minister Abiy Ahmed as part of 'Green Legacy'—an example of what could be possible.[45] The slow progress with the rest of the Great Green Wall notwithstanding, this is the kind of effort that will be required in all countries that form part of the Wall as well as moving away from the idea of a narrow band of trees along the southern edge of the Sahara.

Africa's forests could actually be a game changer in terms of tackling climate change. Approximately 2.6 billion tonnes of carbon dioxide, one-third of the CO_2 released from burning fossil fuels, is absorbed by forests each year. 'Halting the loss and degradation of forest ecosystems and promoting their restoration', according to the International Union for Conservation of Nature 'have the potential to contribute over one-third of the total climate change required by 2030 to meet the objectives of the Paris Agreement'.[46] According to the Global Forest Watch, tree-cover loss peaked in 2016 but the overall trend is still negative. The Democratic Republic of the Congo is now the country with the second largest losses by area and Madagascar lost two percent of its entire primary forest in 2018. Ghana and Côte d'Ivoire showed the highest rise in percentage terms in losses of primary forest.[47]

Most of this increase, particularly in Ghana, is likely to be due to small-scale gold mining. There has also been an expansion of cocoa farming that has led to forest loss.

Africa does have some ability to mitigate climate change—massive tree planting is just one example—but needs to direct significant effort at adaptation. The African Union has acknowledged as much in the Agenda 2063 planning document, which states that 'Africa shall address the global challenge of climate change by prioritizing adaptation in all our actions…

Africa: Will It Help Fight Climate Change? [Online] Available at: https://www.youtube.com/watch?v=HVOYN70scS8.

[45] Karasz, P., 2019. Ethiopia Says It Planted Over 350 Million Trees in a Day, a Record. *New York Times*. 30 July 2019 [Online] Available at: https://www.nytimes.com/2019/07/30/world/africa/ethiopia-tree-planting-deforestation.html.

[46] Rizvi, A. R., Baig, S., and Kumar, C., 2016. *Forests and Climate Change*, Gland: IUCN.

[47] World Resources Institute, n.d. *Global Forest Watch*. [Online] Available at: https://www.globalforestwatch.org/.

for the survival of the most vulnerable populations… and for sustainable development and shared prosperity'.[48]

Development as a Coping and Planning Mechanism

Developed countries which often have carbon-intensive economies, have, by definition, more capacity to adapt to climate change and are also more responsible for mitigating it.

A good proxy with which to measure the mitigation capacity of a country is average income levels or GDP per capita—a well-known yardstick for measuring and comparing technological sophistication and well-being across countries. Generally the higher a country's GDP per capita the more developed its infrastructure, the larger its carbon emissions and the greater its ability to adapt to and mitigate climate change. Countries with developed water-borne sewerage systems and that provide safe drinking water to the majority of its citizens through appropriate piped systems have more capacity to absorb the impact of climate change including responding to severe weather events. Only 3.5% of Africa's agricultural land that is equipped for irrigation, some seven million hectares concentrated in a handful of countries. Expanding land under irrigation means that countries are less susceptible to the impact of climate change.[49]

Conversely, countries with large poor communities, who often lack basic infrastructure and agricultural technology, have much more limited adaptation capacity.

The provision of improved water is particularly critical in the context of climate change. In Central Africa, for example, only around 60% of the population is estimated to have access to an improved water source (piped supplies, boreholes, protected wells and springs and collected rainwater)—the lowest regional access rate on the continent. Across all of Africa, an estimated 290 million people are living without access to improved water owing to poor physical water infrastructure.

On the Current Path, the number of people without access to improved water is projected to grow for the next five to 10 years in all African regions

---

[48]African Union Commission, 2015. *Agenda 2063: The Africa We Want*, Addis Ababa: African Union.
[49]Foster, V., and Cecilia Briceño-Garmendia, C. (eds.), 2010. Africa's Infrastructure: A Time for Transformation, Africa Development Forum Series, Agence Française de Développement and the World Bank. n.d. [Online] Available at: https://openknowledge.worldbank.org/handle/10986/2692, pp. 1–14, 272 and 287.

except Northern Africa, although the region will face increasing water scarcity and likely deteriorating water quality.[50] More rapid development will therefore mitigate some of these effects. The scenarios with the largest impact on improving access to safe water are the Improved Health scenario (Chapter 3) and Leapfrogging (Chapter 10).

Conclusion: Finding an Environmentally Sustainable Pathway

On its current development trajectory, the world is headed for serious climate change trouble. More carbon emissions will affect all of humanity and with its low adaptation capacity, arid climates and rainfall-dependent agriculture, Africa is particularly at risk.

In recognising the role of humanity in accelerating climate change, leaders have to make difficult choices that would impact upon their election prospects. There are some leaders, such as former US President Donald Trump, who are unwilling to make these choices, instead arguing that humans have not contributed to climate change and that what we are seeing is a natural change in the global system. Their denialism is based on short-term, self-serving political considerations. Politics is supposed to be about leadership, not only about attaining and retaining power. Many of today's young children will be alive by 2100. Theirs may be a world of technological wonders but could also be one of environmental disasters.

Africa is a small player in this unfolding drama. However, it can play an important role in combating deforestation and forest degradation. The impact of climate change upon the continent will be huge and its leaders should therefore seize every opportunity to prepare and to make their voice heard. With a large, vulnerable population it has more to lose than almost any other world region. Climate change is also a potential long-term accelerator of violent resource competition. Shifts in precipitation patterns are likely to have negative impacts on regions that are already water stressed. Together with a growing population this is becoming a lethal combination. Decreases in agricultural yields may impact both human development and governmental legitimacy.

Increases in carbon in the atmosphere are driving more intense weather patterns that lead to more and greater threats from famines, droughts

---

[50] Niang, I., and Ruppel, O. C., 2014. Africa. In: IPCC, ed. *Impacts, Adaptation, and Vulnerability: The Assessment of Impacts, Adaptation, and Vulnerability in the Working Group II Contribution to the IPCC's Fifth Assessment Report (WGII AR5)*. Cambridge: Cambridge University Press.

and plagues. These disruptive climate and weather conditions will change migration patterns with possibly significant impacts.

Africa needs faster demographic change, higher productivity but at lower levels of emissions, better education, a functioning health system, investment in basic infrastructure such as the provision of potable water, needs to extend agricultural land under irrigation and good governance to drive development and to provide improved living conditions and security.

However, these development gains will need to be weighed against the long-term goal of mitigating and adapting to climate change. Good governance and long-term planning in Africa is now more important than ever. Mitigation and adaptation to climate change should be an intrinsic part of the African development agenda, such as the purposeful choice to transition to renewable energies and away from fossil fuels.

Africa's leadership is fully aware of the challenges that the continent faces in respect of climate change but action is limited. A purposeful response is required if Africa is to embark upon a sustainable development pathway. This includes the insistence that its development projects and those of its partners, China in particular, are based on the requirements of an environmentally sustainable development pathway.

Hence, when looking in the final chapter at the combined impact of the scenarios that have been modelled in each of the chapters, it is important to weigh the costs associated with an environmentally unsustainable development pathway.

Further Reading

Daly, Herman E., and Farley, Joshua. 2004. *Ecological Economics: Principles and Applications*. Island Press.

Kamkwamba, William, and Mealer, Bryan. 2009. *The Boy Who Harnessed the Wind*. HarperCollins.

Romm, Joe. 2018. Climate Change: What Everyone Needs to Know. New York: Oxford University Press.

UNESCO. 2019. *Co-Designing Science in Africa: First Steps in Assessing the Sustainability Science Approach on the Ground*, ed. C. Aguirre-Bastos, J. Chaves-Chaparro and S. Aricò. Paris: UNESCO.

Open Access This chapter is licensed under the terms of the Creative Commons Attribution 4.0 International License (http://creativecommons.org/licenses/by/4.0/), which permits use, sharing, adaptation, distribution and reproduction in any medium or format, as long as you give appropriate credit to the original author(s) and the source, provide a link to the Creative Commons license and indicate if changes were made.

The images or other third party material in this chapter are included in the chapter's Creative Commons license, unless indicated otherwise in a credit line to the material. If material is not included in the chapter's Creative Commons license and your intended use is not permitted by statutory regulation or exceeds the permitted use, you will need to obtain permission directly from the copyright holder.

16

Closing the Gap

Abstract In this concluding chapter Cilliers presents a combined Close the Gap scenario that integrates the eleven scenarios that were modelled in the previous chapters and compares the impact with the Current Path prospects on dimensions such as income growth, economic size, impact on extreme poverty and carbon emissions. The chapter then moves on to compare the impact of the scenarios with one another. The results differ for low, lower-middle and upper-income countries as well as over time. The differences are illustrated with reference to improvements for each income group in 2030, 2040 and 2050. The chapter then sketches out a broad description of a 'standard economic growth model' that emerges from the preceding analysis. It concludes by pointing to the similarities and differences compared to China's recent history.

Keywords Economic growth · Africa · Health · Demographics · Demographic dividend · Basic infrastructure · Industrialisation · Manufacturing · Trade · African Continental Free Trade Area · Leapfrogging · Governance · External support · Trade · Remittances · Foreign direct investment · Peace · Good governance · Democracy · Trade integration · Jobs · Work · Social capital · Human capital · Multifactor productivity · Knowledge capital · Physical capital · Agriculture · Services · Scenarios · Forecasts · Poverty · Inequality · Income · Population · Carbon emissions · Climate change · Low-income countries · Lower-middle-income countries · Upper-middle-income countries · Value-add · Economic composition · Social grants · Inequality · Education · China · Innovation · Regional integration · Urbanisation

Learning Objectives

- Understanding the contribution that improvements in basic infrastructure, demographics, agriculture, education, health, industrialisation, leapfrogging, increased trade, stability, democracy and external support could make to reductions in poverty, increases in income and inequality for low-, lower-middle and upper-middle-income countries in Africa

In this book, I have taken the reader on a journey across the improvements that are required to help close the growing income gap between Africa and the rest of the world. Figure 1.1 in Chapter 1 shows the extent to which the gap has grown incrementally with each passing decade since independence in the 1960s. The Current Path forecast is for that gap to continue to widen to 2040 and beyond.

Things are improving in Africa but it is happening at a slower pace than elsewhere. As a result, Africa is falling further and further behind on most averages of well-being compared to the rest of the world.

The 55 countries that collectively constitute Africa are expected to experience an average economic growth rate of 4.7% from 2020 to 2040 and the continent's economy will increase by more than 150% in size. But because Africa's population will have increased by almost 60% by then, Gross Domestic Product (GDP) per person (in purchasing power parity or PPP) will only increase by 35%. Contrast that with the expected increase of more than 150% in the rest of the world! While it is still too early to factor in the impact that the COVID-19 pandemic will have on Africa and the global economy, it will inevitably be negative and likely further increase the challenge of catching up since Africa has less ability to cope with the associated effects.

To this end, the preceding chapters have looked at the impact of successive interventions that could reverse the trend of growing divergence, namely: Improved Health, achieving a Demographic Dividend; an African Agricultural Revolution; a Rejuvenation in Education; rolling out Social Grants for Africa; a manufacturing transition through the Made in Africa scenario; Leapfrogging through various technologies; trade integration through the implementation of the African Continental Free Trade Area; a rapid decline in violence and insecurity by Silencing the Guns; continuing progress as part of a Fourth Wave of Democracy; and gaining from External Support.

I have taken care to benchmark the interventions used in each scenario to ensure the impact is aspirational but realistic. That benchmarking is available at www.jakkiecilliers.org and provides a degree of confidence that the scenarios represent levels of progress comparable to what has been historically achieved by countries at similar levels of development and that have done particularly well in a particular area.

In addition, two chapters reviewed the future of work in Africa and provided an overview of the effects of climate change. These two chapters compared the impact of some of the scenarios listed above with one another.

Forecasts and scenarios are not predictions and it is certain that the future will unfold quite differently to what is set out in this book. So-called Black Swan or unexpected, high-impact events, such as the COVID-19 pandemic, could temporarily derail trends but since the IFs system does its forecasts based on longitudinal trends, it bakes in some of the impact of unforeseen events. Eventually informed analysis of the future is simply much better than bumbling along blindly.

Although it is unlikely that all of Africa will be able to simultaneously advance on all eleven of these transitions in the section below I first present the impact of the Close the Gap scenario that includes a combined forecast of the impact of all eleven scenarios.

Prospects in the Close the Gap Scenario

When discussing the combined Close the Gap scenario, it is important to re-emphasise that the IFs forecasting platform is highly integrated, meaning that improvements in education, for example, would positively impact on social capital (and hence economic growth) and therefore improve productivity in the Made in Africa scenario on manufacturing.

This holds true across various dimensions. It means that some improvements could have an unexpected or greater than foreseen impact, although it is equally true that some interventions also compete with each other. For example, while more social grants reduce poverty it eventually starts to detract from economic growth prospects although the relationship is complex.[1] But generally speaking, all good things come together in the Close the Gap scenario and the combined impact of the eleven positive scenarios present a step change in Africa's development prospects.

---

[1] On the other hand, over longer time horizons reductions in poverty would improve human capital and eventually have a positive impact upon economic growth.

GDP Per Capita in the Close the Gap Scenario

Figure 16.1 presents the same information as presented in Fig. 1.1 in Chapter 1, and now includes the results from the combined Close the Gap scenario and extends the forecast to 2063.

It presents in a single graph the dramatic change in fortunes that could follow from the combined effect of the various scenarios. Such long-range forecasts are highly speculative but illustrate that from the middle of this century, Africa could actually start to catch up with the rest of the world. Although, even then Africa would have to maintain its positive trajectory for several decades to start achieving true convergence and, given the impact of technology and climate change, it will occur in a different world than the one we currently know.

If we were to consider progress in GDP per capita in each of Africa's five regions to a more reasonable 2040 time horizon, Central Africa performs the worst and Northern Africa the best. The most important reason for this divergence is the very rapid population growth in Central Africa compared to Northern Africa which also comes off a much higher income, education and health base. The Current Path forecast of economic growth will simply be insufficient to substantially improve the incomes of the rapidly growing populations in Central African countries.

There are many other considerations, too. Central Africa differs from other regions in that it does not have locomotive states (such as Nigeria in West Africa and South Africa in Southern Africa) where the size of a single national

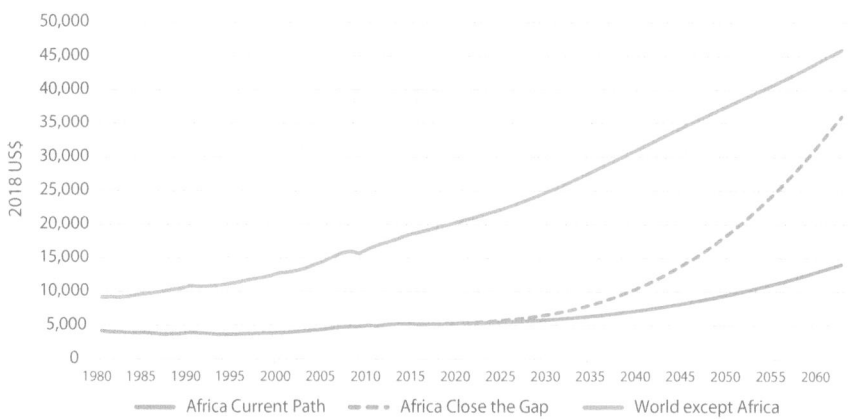

Fig. 16.1 GDP per capita: Africa vs World except Africa (*Source* IFs v7.45 initialising from World Bank World Development Indicators 2018)

economy provides a sufficiently large market that could boost the region as a whole.

I have generally used the three standard World Bank country income classifications in this book as a kind of shorthand to present general trends among low, lower-middle and upper-middle-income countries. Figure 16.2 presents the average GDP per capita of the 24 low, 21 lower-middle and eight upper-middle-income countries in Africa in 2018 and in 2040 in the Current Path forecast and then the 2040 forecast in the Closing the Gap scenario. The increase in column height reflects the improvement in GDP per capita from 2018 to 2040, first for the Current Path forecast and then for the Closing the Gap scenario.

In the Close the Gap scenario the average GDP per capita in 2040 in low-income Africa would be US$5290 instead of US$3340. In lower-middle income Africa it would be US$13,300 instead of US$9210, and in upper-middle-income countries it would be US$22,260 instead of US$18,120.

The five countries that would gain the most in increases in average income levels when comparing the Current Path forecast with the Closing the Gap scenario are Mauritius, Botswana, Seychelles, Namibia and Gabon. The countries that gain the least are Niger, Central African Republic, Somali, Liberia and Burundi. All are low-income countries with high levels of conflict and instability.

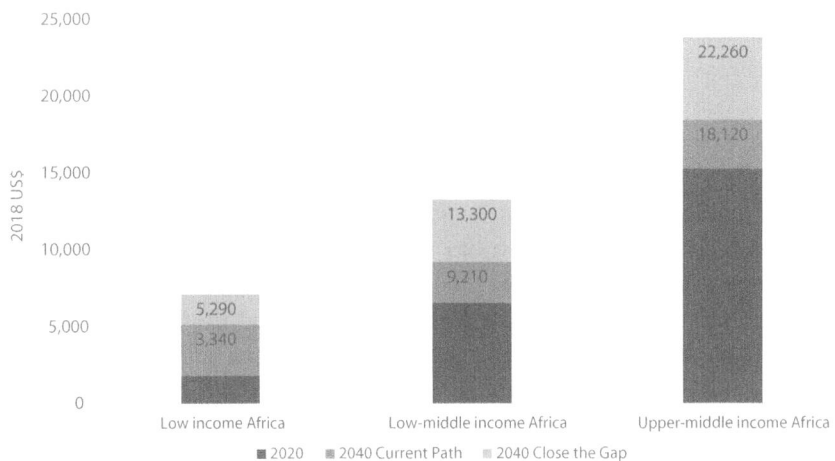

Fig. 16.2 GDP per capita in Current Path and Close the Gap in 2018 and 2040 (*Source* IFs v7.45 initialising from World Bank World Development Indicators 2018)

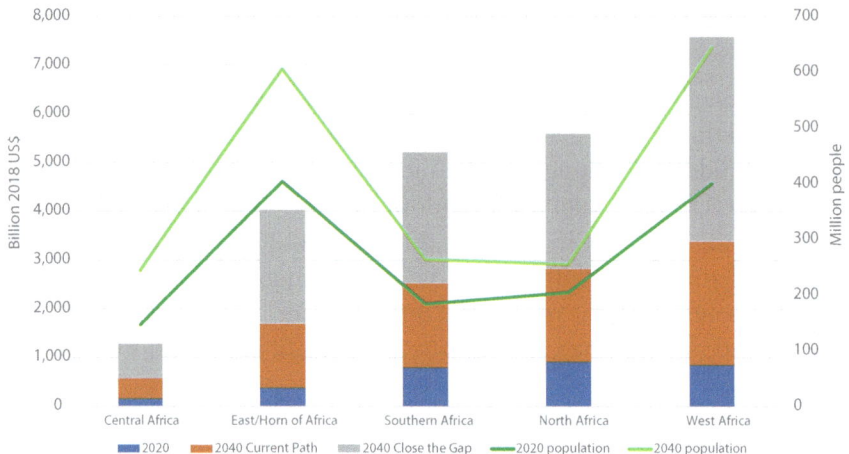

Fig. 16.3 Size of the regional economy in MER in Current Path vs Close the Gap scenario compared to population size (*Source* IFs v7.45 initialising from IMF World Economic Outlook 2017)

Size of Economies in the Close the Gap Scenario

Figure 16.3 is a bit more complicated. Using the left-hand scale it presents a stacked column that compares the size of the regional economies (Central, East/Horn, Southern, Northern and West Africa) in 2020 and then adds the increase from the Current Path and the Close the Gap scenario by 2040. That is similar to the presentation in Fig. 16.2. The line graph refers to the right-hand scale and presents the population in 2020 and 2040 for in the Closing the Gap scenario. Because of the impact of the demographic dividend scenario as well as improved education and health, the population numbers are lower than those for the Current Path forecast, which is not shown.[2]

By one measure, total population size, it's no wonder that West Africa has the largest economy since it also has the largest and most rapid population growth from 2020 to 2040. East Africa (including the Horn of Africa) has almost a comparably large population, but it's Closing the Gap economy is much smaller meaning the average citizen is much poorer. Central Africa has a relatively small economy compared to its population size and the economy experiences a very modest increase in size. Southern and North Africa do the best in terms of improvements in incomes given their more modest population growth.

---

[2]The population of Central Africa is 13 million smaller in Close the Gap in 2040 compared to the Current Path, 42 million in East/Horn of Africa, one million in North Africa, 12 million in Southern Africa and 28 million in West Africa.

An important dynamic is the way in which the Demographic Dividend combines with the Rejuvenation in Education scenario to reduce total fertility rates quite rapidly. As a result, Africa's total economy could be US$12.6 trillion in size in 2040 in the Close the Gap scenario instead of US$7.9 trillion in the Current Path, despite (or because) of a population that is almost 100 million people smaller.

The impact accelerates over time. In 2063 in the Close the Gap scenario, Africa would have a population of 410 million *fewer* people, but its economy will be 2.5 times *larger* than in the Current Path forecast (US$77 trillion instead of US$30 trillion). If this were to occur, it would ensure a truly remarkable change in various other indices but then forecasts of such a long time horizon are quite shaky.

Extreme Poverty in the Close the Gap Scenario

The Close the Gap scenario has an even more impressive impact on poverty than on economic size and GDP per capita. Figure 16.4 provides a forecast of the number of extremely poor people in Africa using two income measures. The first uses US$1.90 for all of Africa and the second uses a combination of US$1.90 for low-income, US$3.20 for lower-middle and US$5.50 for upper-middle-income countries. The reason and thinking behind these different measures are discussed in Chapter 7. The general trend is the same with both forecasts. The number of extremely poor people will expectedly remain

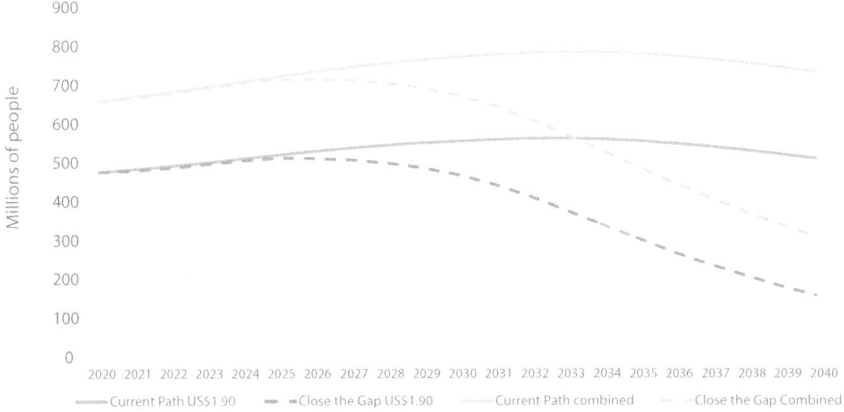

Fig. 16.4 Extremely poor people: 2020 to 2040 using US$1.90 and other extreme poverty lines (*Note* that the combined scenario uses US$1.90, US$3.20 and US$5.50 for low, lower-middle and upper-middle-income countries. *Source* IFs 7.45 initialising from World Bank, PovCalNet)

constant out to 2040 in the Current Path forecast, but, whereas Africa either has 480 or 660 million extremely poor people in 2020 (depending upon the income definitions used), in 2040 this number could be reduced to 160 or 315 million people in the Close the Gap scenario, again depending upon the income definitions used.

It is clear that even in the Close the Gap scenario, Africa will miss the SDG target of eliminating extreme poverty by 2030 by a very large margin. Using the US$1.90 extreme poverty line that is used to measure progress towards the SDG target, 475 million Africans will still be extremely poor. Or if presented as a portion of the total population, extreme poverty will decline from about 35 to 33% by 2030 and to 24% by 2040. In the Closing the Gap scenario the numbers are 28% by 2030 and eight percent by 2040.

Again a caveat: COVID-19 will negatively impact upon these forecasts since it seems inevitable that the global economy will contract sharply in 2020, perhaps longer as our understanding of the medium and long-term impacts are still unfolding.

Nevertheless, the scenario demonstrates that change is possible, and these changes represent a potential seismic shift in Africa's fortunes, as poverty is perhaps the single most important measure of improved well-being.

Table 16.1 presents the difference in millions of extremely poor people between the Current Path and Close the Gap in 2040 for four low-income, three lower-middle-income and two upper-middle-income countries. Again, these forecasts do not yet factor in the impact of COVID-19.

In Nigeria, the absolute number of extremely poor people will inevitably increase due to its rapid population growth and relatively slow economic growth rates, and the modelling used here suggests that trend cannot be reversed within the next two decades. Instead of 225 million extremely poor

Table 16.1 Impact on selected countries: millions fewer extremely poor people in 2040: difference between Current Path and Close the Gap scenarios

Country and relevant poverty line	Difference
Ethiopia ($1.90)	−9 million
Democratic Republic of Congo ($1.90)	− 68 million
Tanzania ($1.90)	−14 million
Nigeria ($3.20)	−59 million
Côte d'Ivoire ($3.20)	−5 million
Zambia ($3.20)	−10 million
Algeria ($5.50)	−9 million
South Africa ($5.50)	−11 million

Source IFs 7.45 initialising from World Bank, PovCalNet

people in 2040 (Current Path), it would only have about 166 million (Close the Gap), which is about seven million more than currently.

Nigeria currently has around 210 million people. By 2040 Nigeria's population is forecast to be 360 million people on the Current Path but less than 350 million in the Close the Gap scenario as fertility rates decline, largely due to the impact of the Demographic Dividend scenario and better education. The percent of its population living in extreme poverty will therefore decrease from 76% in 2020 to 65% in the Current Path by 2040, or only 48% in the Close the Gap scenario.

Carbon Emissions in the Close the Gap Scenario

The improvements in Africa's development prospects in the Close the Gap scenario come at a cost, even if it is a low cost by comparison to trends in the rest of the world. In the Close the Gap scenario, Africa would release about 120 million tonnes more carbon into the atmosphere by 2040 than in the Current Path. This may sound like a lot, but by 2040 annual global emissions would be about 10 billion tonnes, meaning that the additional emissions from Africa are quite modest. Had it not been for the reduction in Africa's total population as it progresses more swiftly through its demographic transition, the increase in annual carbon emissions would be larger. Noted in Chapter 15, most African countries have a unique opportunity to leapfrog a fossil-fuelled development model towards renewables.

Therefore in the Close the Gap scenario Africa would by 2040 contribute closer to seven instead of six percent to global carbon emissions. This means that the continent would have added around 900 million tonnes of additional carbon to the atmosphere (i.e. more than in the Current Path) over the preceding 20 years.

Still, the increased emissions in Africa occur at a time when the world needs to urgently reduce carbon emissions if it is to constrain global warming to below two degrees by the end of the century. Climate change is real and these forecasts indicate that even greater efforts are needed to transition to a greener economy and a sustainable planet, including in Africa. There are prospects for rapid improvements. For example a 2019 report by the International Energy Agency calculates that Africa could, using renewables, meet the 2040 energy demands of an economy four times larger than today's with only 50% more energy than today.[3]

---

[3] IEA, Africa's Energy Outlook 2019, Special Report. [Online] Available at www.iea.org/reports/africa-energy-outlook-2019.

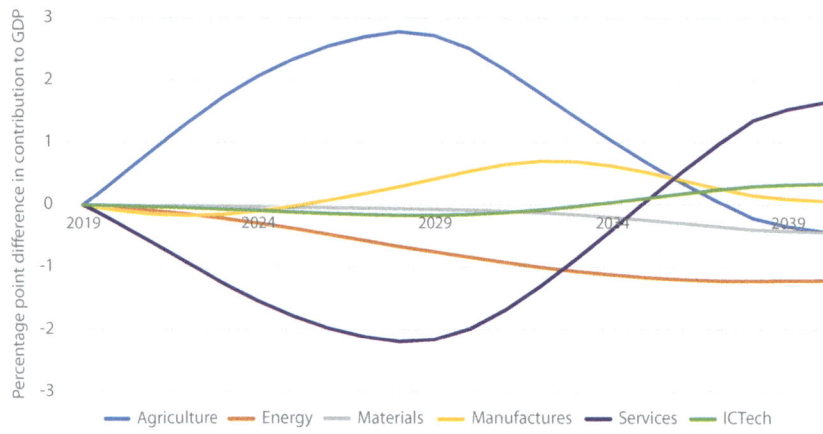

Fig. 16.5 Changes in value added to the economy in percent of GDP: Close the Gap vs Current Path for lower-middle-income Africa: 2019 to 2040 (*Source* IFs 7.45 initialising from IMF World Economic Outlook 2017 Note that his graph uses a five-year moving average)

Structural Change of Economies in the Close the Gap Scenario

The transitions modelled in this book are intended to emulate a process where Africa is able to reverse its growing commodities dependency and proceed on a pathway towards economic diversification. Many studies have sought to point to the potential, including that by African Growth Initiative at the Brookings Institution that have popularised the potential of 'industries without smokestacks'.[4]

To this end Fig. 16.5 presents the *difference* in the growth of the six economic sectors modelled in IFs, namely agriculture, energy, materials, manufactures, services and ICTech for Africa's 18 lower-middle-income countries when comparing the Close the Gap scenario with the Current Path. The comparison is presented as a percent change to GDP from 2020 to 2040. A similar graph could be drawn for low- and upper-middle-income country groups.

The scale on the left hand or y-axis of Fig. 16.5 indicates that the shifts are modest, at a maximum amplitude of below two and a half percent in either direction, but the impact of compound interest is such that these small changes have a large impact over time.

---

[4]Newfarmer, R., Page, J., and Tarp, F., 2018. *Industries Without Smokestacks: Industrialization in Africa Reconsidered*. WIDER Studies in Development Economics. Oxford University Press. [Online] Available at: https://www.wider.unu.edu/publication/industries-without-smokestacks-2.

In fact, all sectors in Africa's 2040 economy will be bigger in the Close the Gap scenario than in the Current Path scenario. Whereas Fig. 16.5 presents the *change in the composition* of the economic structure of lower-middle-income African countries over time when comparing the Close the Gap with the Current Path scenario, Fig. 16.6 presents the *size* of each sector in 2018 with the Current Path and Close the Gap scenarios in 2040.

In this figure the changes to the size of each sector become evident. Note that whereas Fig. 16.5 is for lower-middle-income African countries, Fig. 16.6 is for Africa as a whole.

At a continental level, the Close the Gap scenario modestly constrains the growth of the services sector in favour of growth in the size of the agricultural sector until 2030. The Close the Gap scenario incentivises more growth in the manufacturing sector across the forecast horizon compared to the Current Path, while the contribution of the energy sector declines in the Close the Gap scenario compared to the Current Path.

Figures 16.5 and 16.6 reflect the structural transition of African economies to become more productive (the key contribution that flows from a larger manufacturing sector). In line with global trends the services sector will grow exponentially. It already constitutes the single largest share of the African economy although as I pointed out in Chapter 8 the traditional distinction between services, manufacturing and the like is really of limited value in the modern world.

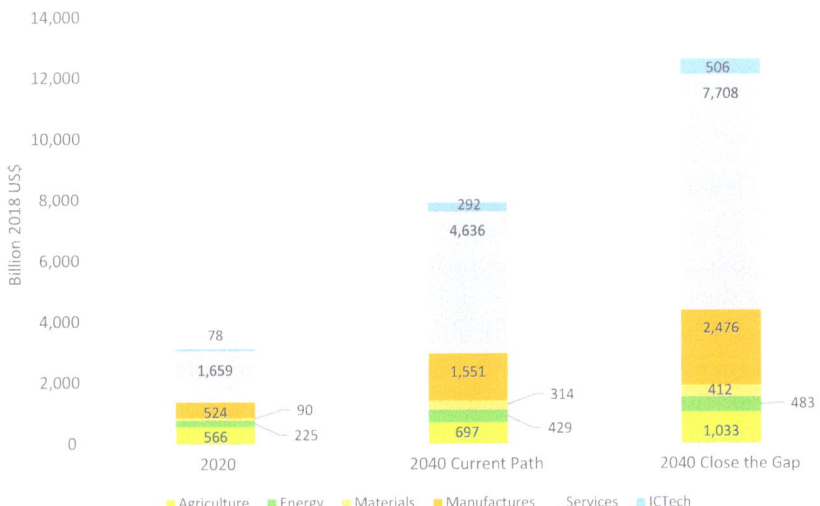

Fig. 16.6 Africa: value added by sector in billion US$: 2020 vs 2040 for Current Path and Close the Gap scenario (*Source* IFs 7.45 initialising from IMF World Economic Outlook 2017)

Even with the best will and good fortune it is unlikely that all countries in Africa would be able to achieve similar success in advancing across all dimensions. In addition, the type of reforms required to advance from low levels of development is quite different from that required at middle-income level. Eventually only individual country studies can provide an indication of the potential growth that a determined and far-sighted leadership can achieve.

Comparing the Impact of Individual Scenarios Over Time

The preceding sections presented the remarkable impact of the Close the Gap scenario on key indicators. In this section I compare the individual impact of the eleven scenarios on GDP per capita with one another.

My goal with this section is to illustrate the impact that different priorities could have, although much more detailed additional work is necessarily required at the national level. The analysis builds on the premise in Chapter 13 on governance that one of the greatest challenges is to ensure that governing elites will pursue national development, not personal or factional interests.

Scenario Comparison Using Income Per Person as Key Indicator

In addition to the fact that the impact of the various scenarios differs between low, lower-middle and upper-middle country groups, the impact also changes over time. So what contributes most to income growth for first decade (to 2030) for low-income countries may change during a second and third decade.

For example, in low-income countries agriculture and leapfrogging initially contributes the most to GDP per capita income growth. Actually the contribution from a Revolution in Agriculture is substantially higher than others. By 2040 agriculture still makes the largest contribution but starts to level off after that. By 2050, the implementation of the African Continental Free Trade Area is significantly larger than any other, followed by Leapfrogging, Made in Africa and Boosting Education. The increase in income from a Revolution in Agriculture is in a distant fifth place and waning.

A similar story holds for the group of lower-middle-income countries. Initially agriculture contributes most to income growth but loses momentum such that, by 2040, Made in Africa, the implementation of the African

Continental Free Trade Area and Leapfrogging have overtaken agriculture in increasing incomes. Beyond 2040 the implementation of the African Continental Free Trade Area outpaces all others and continues to accelerate. By 2050 agriculture has fallen even further back in contributing to income growth. By mid-century the top five contributors are the African Continental Free Trade Area, Made in Africa, Leapfrogging, Boosting Education and Health (in that order).

The average differences between the impacts of the various scenarios across Africa's group of upper-middle-income countries are less pronounced, simply reflecting that as countries become wealthier, it becomes more difficult to achieve more rapid income growth from any set of interventions. That said, until around 2036 this group of countries gains most from the Leapfrogging scenario but thereafter the implementation of the African Continental Free Trade Area is most impactful.

So, because intra-African trade comes off such a low base, by 2050 the African Continental Free Trade Area scenario generally outpaced all other scenarios across all country income categories by a significant margin. It is for this reason that the African Development Bank, the UN Economic Commission for Africa, the World Bank and development economists are so excited about the progress being achieved with the implementation of the African Continental Free Trade Area and the potential that it holds for the future although events such as COVID-19 is sure to delay progress.

The contribution of the Demographic Dividend remains constant as the fourth or fifth most powerful scenario to 2050 and beyond. It serves as a timely reminder of the importance of the need for Africa to rapidly move through its demographic transition. Even then its impact is underplayed as the Demographic Dividend scenario is a kind of force multiplier on all other scenarios. It reduces the number of children that need to be educated (and increases the money available for those children already in school) and reduces the demand for basic infrastructure such as water and sanitation, for example.

The Social Grants scenario contributes the least to average income growth in all scenarios. That is not surprising as it largely deals with the symptoms of low growth and high inequality. Social protection against livelihood risks and to reduce the economic and social vulnerability of poor and marginalised groups is extremely important on a continent where the vast majority of the labour force does not have social insurance or related protection. However, it increases spending on recurring items rather than on investments for long-term growth. This is an important lesson for a country such as South Africa that has, since the end of apartheid, generally focussed on redistribution rather than on investing for growth. Although social protection is important, it should generally be seen as a short- to medium-term transitory programme while investing in appropriate education and hard infrastructure that would eventually unlock more rapid growth.

In the medium term, the provision of jobs in the formal sector can structurally shift inequality and reduce poverty at a much greater rate than education. But in the long term, improvements in relevant education are an indispensable requirement if countries are to go up the productivity curve. But it takes a very long time. By 2050 Boosting Education makes only the sixth largest contribution to income growth in low-income countries, fourth largest in lower-middle-income countries and third largest in upper-middle-income countries. In the very, very long-term education is the great leveller in providing improved opportunities to poor people and the relationship between better education and improved levels of income is strong. A rapidly growing low-income country such as Ethiopia cannot progress into low-end manufacturing (its stated goal) in spite of the large amounts of money that it spends in this sector since the language policies that it pursues in schools mean that kids do not understand what they are being taught by teachers who barely speak English themselves. Ethiopian children are currently taught in their mother tongue in grades 1–4, then in Amharic until, in grade 8, education switches to English.[5] Tunisia and Algeria face similar challenges in trying to undo the damages that colonialism wreaked on their Arabic educational systems.

As I discuss in Chapter 6, the continent needs to change the way in which it rolls out education. The traditional methods of rote learning will not keep pace with the demand, never mind reducing the backlog in education and bold innovation and hard work is required in this domain. Governments need to fix education from the bottom upward, starting with ensuring literacy and investing in primary school enrollment and completion. Once progress is achieved in primary, the priority should shift to improving enrollment and completion in lower secondary schools; where after investment needs to shift to fixing, upper secondary and, eventually, tertiary education. Not all countries do this and some, such as Malawi, spend inordinate portions of their budget on tertiary education while neglecting primary and secondary education.

Generally quality is more important than quantity when it comes to education. Simply pushing children through school is not a solution if the education that is provided does not comprehensively and fundamentally

---

[5]Donnenfeld, Z., Cilliers, J., Kwasi, S., and Welborn, L., 2019. Emerging Giant Potential Pathways for Ethiopia to 2040. Institute for Security Studies. [Online] Available at: https://issafrica.org/research/east-africa-report/emerging-giant-potential-pathways-for-ethiopia-to-2040.

address the basics of reading, writing and arithmetic, never mind the skills required for the fourth industrial revolution. And then much greater attention needs to be paid to vocational and technical training as opposed to the singular focus on academic teaching so evident across many African countries.

As with education, improvements in general indices of health take time and only translate very slowly into improved human capital where school pupils, students at technical colleges and universities, as well as workers, are better nourished and healthier, and therefore more productive.

The apparent limited impact of democracy also needs to be placed in context. In Chapter 13, I noted that democracy is not a prerequisite for economic growth at lower levels of development and that it should rather be viewed as a general or inherent good in its own right. Yet democracy is clearly the most desirable system of government. And eventually it does pay off. For example, countries with high levels of substantive (or liberal) democracy are generally richer than others and they are also healthier, particularly when using a key indicator such as rates of child mortality. Furthermore, citizens of democracies are generally happier. Without exception, people across the world aspire to have a say in who governs them, particularly in Africa where the alternatives have generally proven disastrous.

Scenario Comparison Using Progress with the Human Development Index, Inequality and Extreme Poverty

Using the Human Development Index as an alternative measure of progress, the Rejuvenation in Education scenario consistently performs better than any other scenario. It raises Human Development Index scores across the forecast horizon to 2040 and even beyond. Since the Human Development Index includes a substantial education weighting in its basket of indicators, this is an expected impact.

At the continental level the intervention on social grants (Chapter 7) and the scenario on a Revolution in Agriculture compete for the largest impact in reducing inequality across the forecast horizon, using the Gini index to 2040 for low- and lower-middle-income Africa. Upper-middle-income African countries do not experience the same reductions in extreme poverty from agriculture since it generally constitutes a much smaller component of their economies.

Another useful measure of progress that is used extensively in almost all chapters is rates of extreme poverty. The average results for low-income Africa are presented in Fig. 16.7, which compares the increase or decrease in poverty rates for selected scenarios with the forecast in the Current Path for

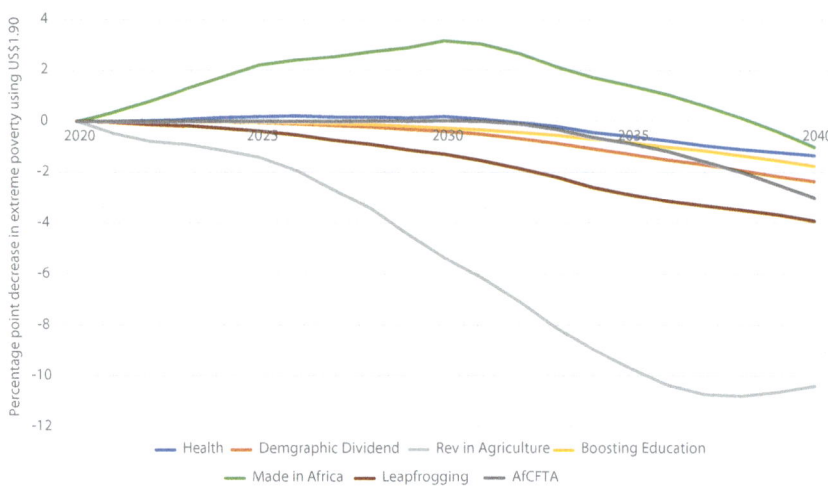

Fig. 16.7 Comparing the results of selected scenarios for lower-income Africa: percentage point reduction in people living below US$1.90 per person per day (*Source* IFs 7.45 initialising from World Bank, PovCalNet)

Africa's current group of 24 low-income countries. The y-axis scale is therefore the percentage point difference between the scenario and the Current Path. Most visible is that the portion of Africans in extreme poverty initially increases by about three percentage points in the Made in Africa scenario. A manufacturing development pathway implies the use of scarce resources for more capital-intensive activities. The result is that poverty and inequality initially in low-income countries increase before quicker economic growth starts reducing both.

On the other hand, the Revolution in Agriculture scenario is significantly more powerful in reducing the percent of extremely poor Africans in low-income countries than any other, in part because agriculture constitutes a significantly larger portion of the economy (on average about a third of GDP by value) than in lower-middle and upper-middle-income countries where it constitutes a quarter or less than eight percent.

Chapter 7 dealt with poverty and inequality and modelled the impact of social grants which has proven a particularly effective short to medium-term strategy to reduce poverty and inequality. The provision of social grants is, however, a strategy that is more impactful for lower-middle and upper-middle-income countries that cannot lever off a large agricultural sector as a means towards poverty reduction. The general tendency in these countries has, however, been to try and subsidise fuel and foodstuffs that have often locked governments into expensive programmes that they then find impossible to retreat from. It is for this reason that the World Bank and the

IMF generally target the reduction of subsidies as a key component in their assistance strategies.

Poor countries generally have limited financial means to effect substantive transfers to the poor through social grant programs but it remains a strategy that is particularly well suited to poor countries that discover new mineral resources, such as the gas potential of Tanzania and Mozambique. In these countries the idea of ring-fencing natural resource income for distribution as cash grants rather than through subsidies on fuel and food that are more prone to wastage would have a salutary impact on levels of extreme poverty.

Figure 16.7 reinforces the traditional sequencing of development first discussed in Chapter 14, namely a governing elite that was strongly committed to economic growth that starts the developmental transformation process with a focus first on agriculture (that provides sufficient nutrition and food security), basic education and literacy (to improve human capital), and ensures a rapid demographic transition (through more rapid urbanisation and the provision of basic health care and modern contraceptives) while embarking on low-end manufacturing, even as the educational focus now shifts to secondary, vocational and tertiary education. Entry into manufacturing requires participation in regional value chains, the need to attract foreign direct investment and foreign companies with clear incentives for them to build local capacity and ensure technology transfer.

Africa needs to look at modern manufacturing and seek competitive advantages in areas such as ICT, food processing and horticulture that can play a role analogous to that played by manufacturing in East Asia.[6] Much as economists struggle to explain the origins of economic growth, these broad outlines serve to frame a kind-of 'standard model' of development.

Given country differences, that model can only be described in the most general terms.

The role of government is crucial at low and middle levels of development. Then, as countries go up the income ladder economic growth in the twenty-first century becomes increasingly dependent on the role of the private sector as much in China and India as in Africa. Even then the role played by government remains crucial, although it now should shift to a predominantly regulatory and compliance function while ensuring inclusive growth by progressive tax policies and other measures of redistribution.

---

[6] This is the notion of 'industries without smokestacks' advanced by the Brookings Institution arguing in favour of sectors that are tradable, employing low and moderately skilled labor, having higher-than-average value added per worker, exhibiting capacity for technological change and productivity growth, and displaying evidence of agglomeration economies. See Newfarmer, R., Page, J., and Tarp, F., 2018. *Industries Without Smokestacks: Industrialisation in Africa Reconsidered*. WIDER Studies in Development Economics. Oxford University Press.

Few facts illustrate the key role of private capital in Africa's development than the contribution that it could make to help fill Africa's energy shortfall. A 2019 report by the International Energy Agency calculates that cumulative investments of US$120 billion per annum (or 2.4% of gross domestic product [GDP]), will be needed between 2019 and 2040 to meet growing demand and improve access to modern energy services in Africa including electricity.[7] That investment is clearly significantly beyond the ability of African governments without significant assistance from elsewhere.

As countries go up the manufacturing value chain, the spill overs from manufacturing facilitate and incentivise a more productive agricultural sector and the development of higher-end services like finance until, in some instances, services start to serve as the main engine of growth.

What Is Possible? A Comparison with China

Africa is young, rapidly urbanising and its population and economy will grow quite quickly. The levels of energy that are available on the continent remind one of China 25 years ago, but with important differences.

First, technology can allow Africa to leapfrog faster than even China, but the quality and nature of governance is likely to inhibit this potential. Compared to Africa China has an extraordinarily effective government. To date politics in Africa have often served as a constraint on development, and we have to find ways to make democratic accountability on the continent real.

While China is a single country with a centralised, authoritarian government, the African continent consists of 55 countries, each jealously guarding its sovereignty, and with large disparities in governance systems and traditions. Continental ambitions for regional economic integration are therefore likely to progress slowly, so regions such as Southern, West and East Africa should simultaneously move ahead with trade integration in their neighbourhood. As we saw in previous sections, the contribution from the African Continental Free Trade Area to growth, income and poverty alleviation is the biggest over longer time horizons and the same results will hold at sub-regional levels.

Second: Africa needs to take a leaf out of the Chinese textbook on empowering small-scale farming. Indeed, development is about empowering

---

[7] IEA, Africa Energy Outlook 2019.

communities to become self-sufficient and independent from the helping hand of government and foreign donors alike.

Third, while the fast development of China was hugely aided by the country's very rapid (and politically driven) demographic transition, including its high peak demographic dividend, growth in Africa will be constrained by the slow pace of its demographic transition and the low levels of its peak demographic dividend.

The continent needs to engage in constructive debate about the extent to which its very youthful population serves as a drag on development and how it could encourage appropriate measures to reduce fertility rates in a responsible manner.

An important step would be to invest in improving the education levels of Africa's expanding labour pool, as well as to close the gender gap in education. And then some African countries such as Tunisia, Mauritius and Libya actually have to invest in maintaining their total fertility rate above the replacement level of 2.1 children per woman if they want to extend the time they will be lingering in the demographic sweet spot, or allow for inward migration. That is a challenge that China is currently grappling with.

Unlike Asia, where industrialisation and democratisation generally occurred *sequentially*, Africa has to balance the *simultaneous* challenges of democratisation and development on top of many others. This requires a fine balancing act and consummate political leadership.

A Passion for Knowledge and Development

On a structural level, many of Africa's challenges are rooted in the process of imposed state-formation that started with imperialism and lasted through the colonial period. Only very recently did the end of the Cold War release Africa into an international state-based system, when its own constituent states had not yet been consolidated. That is very different from the process of war against external forces through which the Westphalian state was established in Europe and from which we often draw our examples.[8]

Subsequently, Africa and its amalgamation of unconsolidated 'states in name' has been poorly served by elites who often appear to place politics and not evidence-based policy ahead of the continent's development. Eventually, neither Western donors nor China or India will develop Africa—only Africans can. To do this we need to understand where we come from but then

---

[8]The Peace of Westphalia signed in 1648 concluded the Thirty Year 'wars of religion' and is generally accepted as the start of the modern state system.

also accept responsibility for shaping our future, manage our debt levels and invest responsibly.

Africa needs strong, developmentally minded governments that regulate, empower and support small and medium-sized businesses in the private sector, which is the primary wealth and employment creator in the twenty-first century. In fact, experience from around the world highlights the need for growth policy to place particular emphasis on institutions and policies that promote strategic collaboration between the government and the private sector.[9]

The private sector in Africa is showing steady growth and doing so from the smallest informal trader to large multinationals. A recent study by McKinsey[10] reveals that some 400 companies in Africa earn revenues of US$1 billion or more and that nearly 700 companies have revenues greater than US$500 million. Most have grown faster than their peers in the rest of the world in local currency terms, and most are more profitable than their global peers. Just over half are owned by Africa-based private shareholders, 27% are foreign-based multinationals and 17% are state-owned enterprises.

The continent also needs governments that consistently invest in knowledge creation.

In his epic study of economic history, the Norwegian scholar and economic philosopher Erik Reinert captures what lies at the heart of development. 'The global economy', he writes, 'can in many ways be seen as a pyramid scheme of sorts – a hierarchy of knowledge – where those who continually invest in innovation remain at the apex of welfare'.[11] Reinert points to the importance of 'going up the productivity and technology curve' generally a function of investments in research, development and expanding the manufacturing sector.

In a different context, the McKinsey Global Institute makes the same argument in concluding that 'all global value-chains are becoming more knowledge-intensive'.[12] The associated response could take many forms like

---

[9]United Nations Economic Commission for Africa, 2013. *Making the Most of Africa's Commodities: Industrializing for Growth, Jobs and Economic Transformation.* Addis Ababa: Economic Commission for Africa; UNECA, 2013. *Making the Most of Africa's Commodities: Industrialising for Growth, Jobs and Economic Transformation.* Addis Ababa: United Nations. Economic Commission for Africa.

[10]Jayaram, K, Kassiri, O., and Sun, I. Y., 2017. The Closest Look Yet at Chinese Economic Engagement in Africa. McKinsey & Company Report, June 2017. Available at: www.mckinsey.com/featured-insights/middle-east-and-africa/the-closest-look-yet-at-chinese-economic-engagement-in-africa.

[11]Reinert, E. S., 2007. *How Rich Countries Got Rich and Why Poor Countries Stay Poor.* London: Constable, p 148.

[12]Lund, S., Manyika, J., Woetzel, J., Bughin, J., Krishnan, M., Seong, J., and Muir, Mac., 2019. *Globalization in Transition: The Future of Trade and Value Chains.* New York: McKinsey Global Institute, p. 1.

developing modern industrial policies, but only deliberate efforts to unlock the promise of digitisation and the fourth industrial revolution will achieve this in the twenty-first century.

In the aftermath of the great global recession of 2008/2009, globalisation is again deepening, but growth and trade within regional trading blocs (as opposed to between these blocs) has become more important.[13] Global value chains now appear to be shortening as production moves closer to consumers. This seems to be partly the result of efforts to improve the speed of getting goods to market, but is also a reaction to global tensions caused by a growing sense of nationalism like the very visible efforts by Europe and the USA to constrain technology transfer and competition from China. The impact of COVID-19 is likely to further accelerate this trend. Previously the costs of labour had been a deciding factor in the location of manufacturing, but in the last two to three decades non-labour costs—including the costs of managing complex global value chains—have increased in importance.

Regional value chains and localised production that is closer to the end-market have become more attractive in advanced and emerging economies alike, with some even talking about doing manufacturing on demand based on technologies such as 3D printing.[14] This is the emergence of the Alibaba model of decentralised, cottage-industry model of industrialisation referred to in Chapter 8.

Africa needs to integrate itself regionally and into the global economy to facilitate knowledge transfer, as China has done so successfully. It can do so by embarking on a digital and urban transition that has the combined potential to unlock other transitions in, for instance, education and the provision of basic infrastructure. Africans need to actively encourage foreign companies to invest and locate on the continent, as well as by attracting skilled foreigners. Technological knowledge transfer is crucial in addition to steadily expanding local content requirements to make sure that these companies are embedded in city and national value chains. Too narrow (or high) an area of specialisation often means that knowledge transfers do not occur. Over time, local value chains will allow African companies to also participate in and become part of international value chains.

Instead many African countries, Nigeria, Kenya and Zambia are three examples, specialise in what I refer to as the 'foreign ambush'. Their primary orientation is not to attract and nurture foreign business, but to trap them.

---

[13] McKinsey Global Institute, 2016. *Digital Globalization: The New Era of Global Flows*. New York: McKinsey & Company, p. 3.
[14] De Backer, K., & Flaig, D. 2017. The Future of Global Value Chains: Business as Usual or "a New Normal"? *OECD Science, Technology and Industry Policy Papers, No. 41*, pp. 8–9.

Once a foreign company has been attracted by a liberal legal framework and fiscal incentives to invest, the rules are changed in an effort to extract greater profits and possibly even to benefit particular nationals or families. Nothing scares private investment more than uncertainty, and the threat of changes to their legal status or tax status is often a very large disincentive. The result is that those companies that do invest eventually capitulate and leave, as many South African (and other) companies have done in Nigeria, Kenya and Zambia. Then, to compound its general shoot-itself-in-the-foot policies, South Africa has been working hard since the end of apartheid to keep skilled foreigners at bay, making it as difficult as possible for them to obtain work permits and to invest.

In this regard, there is much that Africa can learn from China, which has perfected the art of setting up a subtler 'ambush' by requiring foreign companies to partner and transfer technology to local partners. In the process China, not the West, has emerged as the global manufacturing hub. It achieved these goals by making technology transfer and skills requirements law, including them in every agreement and then negotiating hard. China has set its intentions clearly to rival the USA as technology leader in a number of key areas including artificial intelligence and has been so successful that the West now scrambles to constrain its growth.

Many of Africa's post-independence efforts at industrialisation failed because of efforts to effectively create islands of technological sophistication and prestige projects in a sea of low-technology, informal economies. Without forward and backward linkages to the domestic economy, these projects were dependent on government subsidies and handouts in terms of access to foreign markets, for instance through the African Growth and Opportunity Act. Some of the recent investments in heavy-duty infrastructure (as opposed to basic infrastructure) threaten to replicate these mistakes.

When these agreements came to an end, the investments proved unsustainable and the company inevitably folded or left. It is for the same reason that highly capital intensive projects like gas and petroleum extraction projects provide little spillover effect to the wider economy in northern Mozambique, in Angola, Nigeria, Equatorial Guinea and Gabon. All provide a stream of money to state coffers and the fight for control of that money often determines who governs. But oil or gas income on its own does not develop a country. Above all, it needs appropriate government policy, ethical leadership and oversight that unlocks the one thing we have in abundance, our human capital.

Eventually the transformation of Africa is less about grand schemes and ambitions (of which there have been many) and more about the mundane functions of improving food security through land reform and support of small-scale farming; ensuring a hassle-free and facilitative investment environment; holding one another to account; and facilitating foreign investment in clear terms. It requires a technical and bureaucratic process, where governments have to meticulously go through every single impediment that deters or inhibits innovation, entrepreneurship and doing business. This is about a government that gets behind success, offering support and helping to facilitate a potential growth sector that is already showing potential and doesn't merely shovel money in that direction.

Planning long-term requires policy certainty, and there are many challenges in this domain as civil resistance campaigns against dictators and lifetime presidents mount. For investment, as opposed to war profiteering, policy predictability is a prerequisite. Stability is also important, and, as I explored in Chapter 13, instability has become characteristic of an increasingly small number of countries.

In Conclusion

Development is about countries empowering themselves and learning how to help themselves. It is not about handouts and there is no magic wand. The absence of a sense of nationhood is a major distraction in many African countries, and it is a sad reality that many nations that have done well in recent times (Korea, Ethiopia, Rwanda, South Korea, Taiwan and China) did so only after suffering a national trauma like war or genocide.

This book presented a host of policy recommendations that seek to advance the development of Africa. The general result that emerges from the analysis is to work from the bottom upward—to fix the basics. For example the need to invest in basic infrastructure such as electricity, sanitation, water and roads and literacy and primary education, and to invest in empowering and helping small-scale farmers and businesses to improve productivity. Leapfrogging should be seen within this context—how can Africa benefit from new technologies to do things more rapidly and cheaply, such as using digital ID systems and electronic payments systems to improve the capacity of governments to deliver more effective programs, and to provide electricity to their citizens through decentralised mini-grids using renewables. Access to electricity and the global village (through access to the internet) offers huge potential to embark on a rapid digitisation process and its potential as a key enabler was explored in the Leapfrogging scenario.[15] Large infrastructure projects are important, but the trade-off is really to make sure that there are, first, enough paved roads before investing in hugely expensive railway lines unless these are to service specific heavy-duty exports such as iron ore.

Underlying much of this is the need for Africa to progress more swiftly through its demographic transition by reducing fertility rates and more rapid but planned and deliberate urbanisation. Although Africa is urbanising it is generally not planned or maximised. Some countries are already largely urban but the East/Horn of Africa is probably the most rural region in the world.

The solutions to Africa's urbanisation trap are well documented. The first is urban land rights. Without clear legal rights and a formal property market that allows for the secure transfer of property rights, land cannot serve as a tradeable asset and investments are limited to those done by the state. Digitisation and modern technology allows Africa to do much of this more rapidly than is the case historically anywhere else.

The second is the early installation of infrastructure like roads, water, sewage and electricity connections at low levels of density as was done in China. And it serves as an opportunity to build climate-resilience and to manage the spread of infectious diseases such as COVID-19. Thirdly, cities develop if they are able to formalise business practices, hence increase the tax base and improve efficiencies and productivity. Cities that are overcrowded and congested also have higher costs of production and are generally unable to produce internationally traded goods.[16]

Basic infrastructure must largely be put in place *before* people arrive. Once an informal settlement has reached the size of Khayelitsha in Cape Town or Kibera in Nairobi, it is very difficult to uproot populations to install plumbing or build proper roads. Providing water and sewer connection for half a million people is a challenging enough task. However, if all these people must be relocated to provide that infrastructure, it is not only significantly more expensive, but also more difficult on a political level. In the absence of clean water and adequate sanitation facilities, it remains to be seen to what extent modern medicine can continue to offset the absence of basic

---

[15] United Nations Economic Commission for Africa, 2019. *Fiscal Policy for Financing Sustainable Development in Africa*. Addis Ababa: Economic Commission for Africa, p. xiii.

[16] Collier, P., 2016. *African Urbanisation: An Analytic Policy Guide*. London: International Growth Centre, pp. 23–25. On p. 26 he writes as follows on the issue of 'active city government': 'Five types of government action are required: land registration; provision of public infrastructure and services for transport; provision of public social goods and services for decent quality of life; enforcement of those private behaviours which are socially beneficial but not individually advantageous; coordination of those private decisions which are interdependent; and revenue generation through taxation and debt to finance these activities'.

infrastructure that traditionally provided for a reasonable standard of healthy living.

Urbanisation, digital transformation and electrification should be adopted as deliberate strategies towards providing basic services, better education, improved health care, educational opportunities, economic growth and mitigating the impact of climate change. The digital transformation of Africa will require huge investment to make the internet and the web-accessible but there is really potential in initiatives such as that from SpaceX or OneWeb that promise global, satellite internet coverage within the next few years.[17]

Current forecasts would indicate that the rise of India could again see a global resources boom starting within the next decade. Much as African economies need to diversify, it is unlikely that this will be possible by then. Nor is it a given that Africa will be the region to benefit most from this boom for, according to the Fraser Institute, much of Africa ranks near the bottom in their annual survey of mining and exploration attractiveness with Kenya and Mozambique the least attractive and Ghana and Mali the most attractive.[18]

Resource extraction can provide an opportunity to invest in the efforts required to transform Africa's economies and education systems for greater productivity. However, this is only possible if Africa uses that income and opportunity as a foundation and opportunity for structural economic transformation—going up the productivity value chain.

For countries to develop and grow they need to gain and invest in knowledge creation, which must be done by investing in education through knowledge transfers and by a focus on spurring innovation and entrepreneurship, as well as domestic research and development.

Apart from everything else, African countries need a modern leadership that is able to connect with the aspirations of its youthful population; one that is prepared to move on after a set term and to look to the future, not the past. They need a leadership attuned to tomorrow, not fixated on yesterday, and that rely on evidence-based policymaking, not ideology. That is the essence of the call by Nelson Mandela[19] to no longer 'seek to place

---

[17]Moya, A., 2019. How Africa Can Tap into SpaceX's Starlink Satellites. itWeb. [Online] Available at: https://www.itweb.co.za/content/KWEBbvyaw43vmRjO.

[18]Investment decisions are not only based on pure mineral potential but on policy certainty and confidence in a policy regime that will remain stable. Policy factors account for approximately 40% of investment decisions. Regionally only Latin America and the Caribbean fares worse than Africa. Stedman, A., & Green, K. P., 2018. *Annual Survey of Mining Companies: 2017*. [Online] Available at: https://www.fraserinstitute.org/studies/annual-survey-of-mining-companies-2017.

[19]Mandela, N. R., 2002. Address by Nelson Mandela at Gala Banquet Celebrating Africa's 100 Best Books of the 20th Century, 23 July. Available at: www.mandela.gov.za/mandela_speeches/2002/020723_books.htm.

blame for our condition elsewhere or to look to others to take responsibility for our development', but to become the masters of our own fate.

These then, are the challenges and opportunities that confront Africa today, as it aims to Close the Gap with the rest of the world.

Further Reading

Africa Growth Initiative, Brookings, online resource. https://www.brookings.edu/project/africa-growth-initiative/.

Banerjee, A.V., and Duflo, E. 2020. How Poverty Ends: The Many Paths to Progress—and Why They Might Not Continue. *Foreign Affairs*, January/February.

Institute for Security Studies, African Futures & Innovation, online resource. https://issafrica.org/topics-regions/search?topics=218&regions.

OECD, Shaping Africa's Urban Future Together, online resource. http://www.oecd.org/africa-urbanisation/?utm_source=Adestra&utm_medium=email&utm_content=Digital%20Report%3A%20Africa%20Urbanisation&utm_campaign=What%27s%20New%20-%2014%20February%202020&utm_term=demo.

Open Access This chapter is licensed under the terms of the Creative Commons Attribution 4.0 International License (http://creativecommons.org/licenses/by/4.0/), which permits use, sharing, adaptation, distribution and reproduction in any medium or format, as long as you give appropriate credit to the original author(s) and the source, provide a link to the Creative Commons license and indicate if changes were made.

The images or other third party material in this chapter are included in the chapter's Creative Commons license, unless indicated otherwise in a credit line to the material. If material is not included in the chapter's Creative Commons license and your intended use is not permitted by statutory regulation or exceeds the permitted use, you will need to obtain permission directly from the copyright holder.

Index

Aadhaar 160
Abdel Fattah el-Sisi 290
Abuja Treaty 261, 268
activist government 170, 172, 174, 192
Addis Ababa 1, 2, 43, 72, 82, 265, 318
Afghanistan 14, 150, 303
Africa Cashew Alliance 108
Africa Cocoa Initiative 107
Africa-Europe Alliance for Sustainable Investment and Jobs 337
African Agriculture Revolution scenario 112–114
African brain drain 126
African Center for Economic Transformation 116, 135, 205
African Continental Free Trade Area (AfCFTA) 255, 261, 268, 371, 382, 392, 393, 398
African Development Bank 28, 106, 135, 174, 183, 199, 207, 264, 266, 271, 334, 339, 345, 352, 393
African Economic Conference 271
African Economic Outlook 42, 271
African Growth and Opportunity Act (AGOA) 253, 255, 402
African leadership 13, 42, 143
African National Congress 131, 323
African Peace and Security Architecture (APSA) 287, 304, 336
African slavery 53
African Trade Observatory 269
African Union 1, 3, 21, 72, 260, 265, 268, 280, 287, 304, 336, 346, 375
African Union Development Agency 229, 261
5th African Union-European Union Summit 336
African welfare state 163, 168
African workers 13
African Youth Charter 72
Afrobarometer 39, 126, 314, 326
age-appropriate children 138

ageing 9, 80
Agenda 2063 3, 4, 261, 280, 327, 375
Agenda for Sustainable Development 4, 46
Agent Smith 356
Agreement on the Application of Sanitary and Phytosanitary Measures 267
agricultural potential 9, 105, 114
agricultural products 31, 34, 108, 121, 172, 254
agricultural yields 10, 19, 102, 103, 111, 367, 377
AgroCenta 118
agro-processing sector 116
Agulhas current 224
Ahmed, Abiy 163, 292, 375
airports 2, 212, 343
Akufo-Addo, Nana 238
Aliko Dangote 185
Alliance for a Green Revolution in Africa (AGRA) 105, 118
Al-Qaeda 124
Altaeros 236
Amhara region 291, 292, 319
Anadarko Petroleum Corporation 340
annual global emissions 359, 389
anocracies 296, 297, 314
anti-corruption 28
anti-migrant sentiments 336, 347
arable land 9, 104, 105
Arab Spring 24, 30, 132, 153, 259, 262, 282, 290, 292, 293, 297, 298, 310, 326, 341
Argentina 112
arid climates 369, 377
Armed Conflict Location and Event Data Project (ACLED) 281, 290, 302
artificial intelligence (AI) 11, 12, 142, 143, 177, 192, 206, 207, 214, 359, 402

Asia 8, 14, 15, 30, 50–52, 56, 125, 150, 173, 174, 176, 177, 179, 187, 204, 250, 263, 265, 332, 340, 342, 350, 361, 362, 366, 399
Asian Tiger economies 7, 9, 203, 317
Asian Tigers 77, 172, 179
Asia-Pacific Economic Cooperation (APEC) 261
Atlantic slave trade 53
atmospheric water generators 223
AU Commission 72, 269
augmented reality 142
Australia 116, 365
autarquia 322
autocracy 4, 8, 296, 317
automated bulk delivery systems 223
automation 11, 12, 177, 192, 195, 202, 206–208, 210, 211, 216, 359
average growth 13, 24, 64, 153, 189, 242

B

Baldwin, Richard 175
Bangladesh 14, 186, 187, 190, 231, 232
Base Case 20
basic health care 6, 152
Bawumia, Mahamudu 212
Belgium 99, 308
Belt and Road Initiative 15, 36, 40, 265, 340, 343, 350, 351, 362
Berlin conference 99
Better Utilisation of Investments Leading to Development (BUILD) Act 335
Bhutan 14
Bill and Melinda Gates Foundation 65, 332
Biya, Paul 39, 293
Blair, Tony 26, 333

Bob Geldof 26
Boko Haram 124, 284, 369
Bolton, John 335
Bono 26
Boosting Education scenario 138–142
Bouazizi, Mohamed 293
Brazil 111, 112, 159, 173, 240, 244, 311, 342
Breakthrough Energy Ventures 233
Bronze and the Iron Ages 52
Brundtland Commission 25
Brundtland, Gro Harlem 25
bubonic plague, Black Death 52
Buhari, Muhammadu 290
Busan Partnership for Effective Development Cooperation 333
Business as Usual 20
BYD 178, 233

Cairo 42
calories 10, 107, 108, 111, 113
cancer screenings 57
Cape Town 59, 357, 358, 404
capital 8, 9, 30, 61, 74, 77, 79, 83, 91, 94, 95, 105, 117, 126, 140, 170, 172, 174, 179, 188, 202, 206, 208, 209, 222, 233, 241, 263, 266, 269, 275, 302, 317, 318, 336, 339, 341, 351, 383, 395, 396, 398, 402
Capital in the Twenty-First Century 151
capitalism 38, 148, 151, 250
carbon contribution 359, 371
Carbon Dioxide Information Analysis Centre 357, 359
carbon emissions 357, 359, 365, 371, 373, 376, 377, 389
the Caribbean 56, 67, 113, 128, 153
Carnation Revolution 308
cashew nuts 108, 119

Célestine Monga 174
cellular phones 234
Center for Global Development 187, 215
Center for Systemic Peace (CSP) 281
CFA franc 34
Cheeseman, Nic 315
children 56, 61, 62, 64, 72, 73, 76, 78, 81, 82, 85–88, 91, 93, 94, 98, 111, 113, 121, 124, 127, 129, 130, 133, 134, 138, 141, 154–156, 162, 167, 212, 303, 325, 377, 393, 394
China 5, 7–9, 14, 15, 24, 30–32, 35, 36, 40, 52, 75, 77, 83, 110, 111, 116, 124, 143, 148, 150, 152, 157, 161, 172, 173, 178–180, 184, 187, 203, 207, 213, 223, 228, 230, 233, 234, 244, 246, 250, 255–257, 265, 275, 311, 312, 317, 327, 329, 332, 333, 335, 336, 340–346, 350–353, 361, 362, 366, 397, 399, 401, 402, 404
China–Africa Defence and Security Forum 346
China Africa Research Initiative 332
China Railway 17th Bureau Group Company 344
Chinese firms 184, 185, 342, 344
classrooms 129, 134, 141
clean water 42, 58, 60, 63, 64, 66, 68, 94, 231, 404
climate change 4, 5, 10, 11, 20, 22, 41, 83, 89, 102, 106, 115, 119, 120, 218, 227, 259, 280, 293, 294, 357, 361, 365, 367–369, 373–378, 383, 389, 405
Closing the Gap 22, 357, 385, 386, 388
coal plants 361
cocoa 107, 109, 119, 121, 172, 375
cocoa beans 34

cold storage 11, 119, 228
Cold War 2, 25, 26, 28, 55, 263, 282, 352, 399
Collier, Paul 42, 151
colonialism 8, 75, 99, 100, 104, 119, 141, 143, 149, 250, 301, 304, 394
Colonies Francaises d'Afrique 34
Commission on the Future of Work 136
commodity dependent 12, 31
commodity escalator 13
Common Market for Eastern and Southern Africa (COMESA) 268
communicable diseases, burden of 56, 57, 369
competitive patrimonial system 321
completion rates 128, 130, 138
Comprehensive Africa Agriculture Development Programme (CAADP) 109
Comprehensive and Progressive Agreement for Trans-Pacific Partnership (CPTPP) 252
consolidated democracies 296, 311
Continental High Speed Railway Network 266
Cotonou Agreement 253
Creutzfeldt-Jakob's disease 53
crude petroleum 34
cultivated land 102
Current Path forecast 14, 20, 22, 25, 43, 47, 59, 62–67, 77, 83–85, 87, 89, 91, 92, 95, 102, 103, 113, 115, 130, 132, 138–140, 144, 149, 157, 158, 165–167, 172, 189, 190, 193, 200, 205, 214, 218, 227, 242, 243, 303, 327, 337, 342, 347–350, 357, 359, 360, 364, 365, 367, 370, 371, 382, 384–388
Cyclone Idai 369
Cyclone Kenneth 369

Czernich, Nina 236

D

Dar es Salaam 42, 59, 373
Déby, Idriss 293
decentralisation 28
decentralised patrimonial system 321
decent work 154, 197
deindustrialisation 12, 183
democracy 4, 8, 28, 37–39, 151, 191, 238, 262, 280, 291, 295, 296, 305, 309–317, 319, 320, 323–329, 395
  deliberative democracy 309
  egalitarian democracy 309
  electoral democracy 309, 310, 313, 314, 321, 322, 326–328
  liberal democracy 95, 309–312, 319, 320, 328
  participatory democracy 309
demographic dividend 6, 60, 69, 72, 76, 77, 79, 80, 83, 84, 87–89, 91, 94, 95, 141, 263, 371, 382, 387, 393, 399
Demographic Dividend scenario 89, 91, 92, 95, 371, 386, 389, 393
Deng Xiaoping 110
Desalegn, Hailemariam 292, 319
developmental patrimonialism 321
dialysis 57
Diamond, Larry 33
digital economy 80, 206, 210, 215, 239–242
digital ecosystems 12
digital identification 240
Dire Dawa 120
disability adjusted life years (DALYs) 66, 67
diseases 10, 50, 51, 53, 56–58, 61, 64, 66, 67, 69, 79, 87, 98, 164, 245, 369, 404
Dispute Settlement Body (DSB) 269

divergence 4, 13, 24, 95, 127, 289, 382, 384
division of labour 98, 209
Doha Round 252
dos Santos, José Eduardo 39
3D printing 177, 224, 401
Dubai 238
Dunn, Kevin 321
Dutch disease 33

Earth Summit in Rio de Janeiro in Brazil 25
East African Community (EAC) 17, 260, 268
East African Power Pool 229
East Asia 14, 67, 73, 125, 135, 138, 148, 180, 187, 192, 205, 227, 235, 236, 397
Ebola 35, 53, 68
Eco 34
Economic Community of West African States (ECOWAS) 17, 261, 276
economic freedom 188, 241, 242, 298
Economic Partnership Agreements (EPAs) 253
The Economist flail 151
Economist Intelligence Unit 311, 312
Education Policy and Data Center 126
electricity consumption 230, 244
electricity storage 226, 230, 365
electric vehicles 207, 234
El Niño 357, 369
energy infrastructure 361
energy resources 33
energy sector 181, 273, 363, 391
Energy self-sufficiency 362
Englebert, Pierre 321

environmental sustainability 112, 245
epidemiological transition 56–58, 60
Ethiopian People's Revolutionary Democratic Front (EPRDF) 318, 319
ethnic conflicts 289
EU27 15, 73, 74
Euphrates 97
Euro 34
Europe 8, 14, 31, 34, 50–52, 56, 75, 100, 103, 107, 109, 125, 135, 148, 176, 180, 206, 209, 216, 223, 230, 235, 250, 256, 259, 260, 263–265, 274, 309, 336, 338, 340, 342, 346, 350, 351, 361, 370, 399, 401
European Consensus on Development 26, 333
Everything But Arms 253–255
exports 10, 12, 31, 34, 100, 107, 109, 112, 113, 120, 170, 172, 175, 179, 184, 185, 187, 212, 217, 250, 253, 255–258, 260, 268, 272, 274, 275, 302, 343, 351, 362, 366, 404
External Investment Plan (EIP) 336, 350
External Support scenario 348–350
extreme winds 361

Facebook 236, 318
FarmDrive 117, 118
Fayulu, Martin 315
female education 82, 86, 134, 135
female headed-households 237
female unemployment 196
Fertile Crescent 52
fertile farming land 75
2008 financial crisis 3, 4, 11, 31, 32, 37, 149, 150, 173, 258, 340, 352

Finland 128
First World War 124, 250
fixed-line technology 234, 235
floods 10, 291, 368, 370
Foa, Roberto 311
food 6, 7, 10, 11, 50, 55, 56, 78, 97, 98, 100, 102, 103, 105, 106, 108, 110–113, 115, 118–121, 162, 167, 192, 211, 228, 232, 258, 266, 267, 294, 358, 361, 368, 397, 403
food importers 9, 181
food security 100, 119
foot and mouth disease 267
foreign direct investment (FDI) 9, 29, 30, 180, 302, 338, 341, 397
foreign exchange earnings 12, 362
formal jobs 200
formal sector jobs 132, 152, 165, 192, 200, 215, 216
Forum on China–Africa Cooperation 35, 351
fossil fuel 227, 231, 359, 362, 375, 378
fourth industrial revolution 13, 77, 80, 136, 137, 178, 186, 195, 206, 209, 211, 216, 217, 222, 245, 252, 395, 401
Fox, Louise 205
fracking 225, 226
France 34, 79, 99, 144, 163, 265, 308, 341, 342
Francophone members 34
Fraser Institute Index of Economic Freedom 242
Frederick S Pardee Center for International Futures 20
Freedom House 37, 310, 313, 314
Freedom in the World 37
The Future of Work in Africa 116

G

Gaddafi, Muammar 39, 290
game wardens 246
gas producer 225
Gates, Bill 66, 233
GDP per capita 3, 4, 6, 18, 19, 34, 67, 91, 125, 140, 154, 155, 183, 217, 240, 242, 273, 303, 314, 328, 347, 350, 373, 376, 384, 385, 387, 392
Gelb, Alan 186, 187
gender parity 86, 134, 138
General Agreement on Tariffs and Trade (GATT) 251
Generalized System of Preferences (GSP) 253
genocide 282, 284, 288
Germany 99, 137, 149, 163, 178, 207, 209, 342
Ghana Card. *See* national ID system
GhanaPostGPS 213
gig-economy 210, 211
Gini index 62, 152, 153, 395
Glaeser, E.L. 38, 316
global energy transition 362
Global Forest Watch 375
global GDP 14, 32, 172, 250
global population 13, 15, 43, 57, 60, 89, 148
global value chains 173, 176, 185, 186, 263, 268, 401
Google maps 117
governance 2, 5, 20, 22, 28, 37, 40, 134, 154, 163, 203, 212, 230, 245, 253, 254, 263, 271, 275, 281, 288, 300–304, 308, 314, 316, 319, 320, 324–326, 329, 337, 344, 351
Grand Ethiopian Renaissance Dam (GERD) 228
Grand Inga project 229
The Great Convergence 175
Great Depression 250

Great Green Wall of the Sahara and the Sahel Initiative 374
Great Rift Valley 98
Great Wall of Lagos 374
greenhouse gas
    carbon dioxide (CO_2) 359
    carbon monoxide (C0) 359
    methane (CH_4) 359
greenhouse gas emissions 358, 359, 373
Green Revolution 121
gross domestic product (GDP) 3, 28, 114, 124, 125, 154, 171, 197, 223, 250, 287, 382, 398
groundnuts 34
GSP Plus 254
Gupta 238

Haines, Cleary 205
Ha-Joon Chang 171
    Kicking away the ladder 171
Hanushek, Eric 124, 132
Hausmann, Ricardo 144
health 2, 4, 5, 22, 27, 39, 44, 47, 50, 54–60, 62, 63, 65, 68, 69, 87, 94, 95, 108, 123, 152, 154, 167, 170, 172, 202, 215, 245, 250, 267, 317, 361, 378, 384, 386, 395, 397
Heavily Indebted Poor Country (HIPC) Initiative 29
heavy-lift drones 223
Hendrix, Cullen 294
herding 99
high fertility rates 72, 81, 82, 93, 135, 325
high-income countries 11, 16, 124, 149, 151, 183, 319, 365
high-income economies 9, 176, 183
HIV/AIDS 53–57, 63 65, 68, 69
Hobbes, Thomas 148
Holocene, Anthropocene 356

Homo sapiens 9, 50, 51
Human Capital index 202
Human Development Report 155
Human Rights Watch 39
human well-being 2, 329
hunter-gatherer societies 98

Ibn Chambas, Mohamed 286
Ibrahim Index of African Governance 300
identity politics 151
imports 10, 103, 104, 108, 113, 114, 121, 185, 188, 212, 225, 256, 257, 260, 271, 274, 362
Improved Health scenario 63–68, 377
improved sanitation 60, 62, 63, 66, 68, 94, 236, 245, 369
India 5, 14, 15, 31, 32, 83, 84, 150, 152, 159, 160, 174, 175, 177, 230, 250, 257, 274, 317, 342, 351, 361, 366, 397, 399, 405
indoor air pollution 60
Indorama Eleme 120
industrial revolution 75, 148, 178, 206, 207
infant mortality 2, 61, 64, 67, 85, 92, 113, 303, 334
informal sector 13, 21, 159, 161, 196–200, 206, 209, 210, 212, 214, 216, 217, 239–241, 262, 263, 293
information and communications technology (ICT) 11, 175, 209
infrastructure 5, 10, 15, 16, 39, 40, 54, 58–69, 73, 85, 91, 94, 100, 103–105, 116, 121, 152, 167, 170, 175, 179, 180, 184, 186, 192, 198, 199, 209, 211, 217, 222–224, 230, 236, 242, 243, 245, 256, 264–266, 270, 274, 275, 317, 339,

340, 342–345, 351, 357, 358, 365, 373, 376, 378, 393, 394, 401–404
Inga 3 229
Inga Falls 229
innovation 12, 50, 56, 118, 119, 137, 144, 192, 199, 211, 213, 216, 218, 222, 224, 231, 232, 236, 237, 243, 244, 325, 394, 400, 403, 405
InspiraFarms 119
installed capacity 228–230
Institute for Security Studies (ISS) 1, 297
Intergovernmental Panel on Climate Change (IPCC) 10, 357
International Criminal Court 312
International Fund for Agricultural Development (IFAD) 106
International Futures (IFs) 19, 20, 338
International Growth Centre 42
International Labour Organization 110
International Monetary Fund (IMF) 26, 197, 200, 222, 251, 339, 346
international rating agencies 341
intra-African trade 185, 254, 268, 270, 271, 273, 393
Iran 52
Islamic State 124, 285
Italy 99, 198

J

Jack, William 237
Japan 9, 14, 26, 33, 66, 67, 77, 79, 80, 85, 148, 149, 172, 178, 179, 207, 209
Johannesburg 42, 43
Jonathan, Goodluck 290
Josef Korbel School of International Studies 20

Journal of Democracy 311
Juma, Calestous 171

K

Kabila, Laurent 40
Kagame, Paul 315, 323
Kibera 59, 404
Kinshasa 42, 46
Kotoka International Airport 212

L

labour 8, 9, 11–13, 24, 53, 73–75, 77, 79, 81, 83–86, 92, 94, 98–100, 106, 107, 115, 116, 124, 126, 136, 152, 164, 170, 172, 176, 177, 186, 188, 190, 192, 195, 198, 200, 201, 203, 204, 206–208, 211, 215, 216, 241, 251, 254, 272, 302, 344, 393, 399, 401
labour productivity 11, 12, 202
Lagos 2, 42, 59, 207, 374
Lagos Plan of Action for the Economic Development of Africa 3
Lake Turkana Wind Project 230
Latin America 56, 67, 113, 128, 153, 164, 235, 236, 309
Law on Nine-Year Compulsory Education 124
leadership 6, 8, 20, 78, 95, 101, 131, 136, 143, 144, 173, 188, 281, 296, 297, 300, 301, 312, 314, 322–325, 328, 329, 362, 377, 378, 392, 399, 402, 405
leapfrogging 12, 22, 222, 223, 231, 233, 234, 240–243, 245, 357, 371, 373, 382, 392, 393, 403, 404
Least Development Country 254
levels of democracy 37–39, 290, 303, 308, 310, 315

Leviathan 148
Lewis, Arthur 171
life expectancy 2, 54, 55, 57, 64, 66–68, 78, 79, 82
Lions on the move II: Realizing the potential of Africa's economies 190
lithium-ion batteries 233, 234
Lopes, Carlos 262
low-end services 12, 42, 171, 172, 175, 192, 200
lower secondary education 128
low-income countries 16, 17, 25, 29, 36, 37, 82, 103, 124, 133, 157, 174, 179, 181, 183, 191, 197, 205, 242, 276, 319, 325, 334, 337, 346, 348–350, 385, 392, 394, 396
low-intensity conflict 298
low-middle income countries 16, 17, 103, 262, 328
low-productivity services 13
low value commodity exports 12
Luanda 42, 105
Lusaka 2
lymphatic filariasis (elephantiasis) 51

M

Maasai Mara National Park 246
Made in Africa scenario 188–191, 193, 373, 382, 383, 396
Magufuli, John 325
2014 Malabo Declaration on Accelerated Agricultural Growth and Transformation in Africa 109
malaria 51, 57, 63–66, 245, 369
Mandela, Nelson 131, 308, 405
Manu River Union 268
Manyika, James 12, 192
2003 Maputo Declaration 109
Mariam, Mengistu Haile 317
market information 11

Massachusetts Institute of Technology 237
The Matrix 356
Mbasogo, Teodoro Obiang Nguema 39, 238
Mbeki, Thabo 55, 323
McKinsey Institute 12
McNamara, Robert 101, 120
median age 56, 72, 76, 78, 79, 95, 297
medical technology 63
Mediterranean Solar Plan 259
Megapack 233
Microsoft 142, 239
Middle East and North Africa (MENA) 86, 128, 134, 310, 335
middle-income 9, 30, 35, 46, 62, 73, 86, 94, 124, 125, 127, 141, 150, 166, 181, 183, 186, 190, 191, 203, 205, 211, 222, 274, 276, 327, 333, 334, 349, 388, 390–392
migrant population 126, 347
Millennium Development Goals 25, 26, 149, 333
Mills, John Atta 238
mini-grids 227, 231, 233, 403
Miracle on the Han River 126
mixed or intermediate regimes 296
Mnangagwa, Emmerson 301
mobile subscriptions 235, 236
modern medicine 53, 57, 59, 68, 404
Mojo Vision 142
Mold, Andrew 259
Morpheus 356
Morsi, Mohamed 290
Mosbacher, Jack 33
Mosquirix 64
mosquitoes 51, 98
mosquito nets 57
Mounk, Yascha 311
Moyo, Dambisa 151

mPedigree 178
M-Pesa 237
Mpumalanga 207
Mswati lll, King 39
Mugabe, Robert 39, 112, 238, 301
Multidimensional Poverty Index (MPI) 44, 155
multifactor productivity 8, 188, 272, 302
Multilateral Debt Relief Initiative 29
multi-party elections 28, 323
Museveni, Yoweri 39
Muslim slave traders 53

N

Nairobi 2, 59, 101, 120, 404
national ID system 161, 212
nature of the governing elite 300, 316, 317
Neanderthals 50
NEETS 217
Neolithic revolution 98
neopatrimonialism 321, 328
net-zero world 362
Newman, Carol 171, 178
New Partnership for Africa's Development (NEPAD) 3, 109, 229, 261
New Village Movement 7
Nile Valley 52
Nkrumah, Kwame 8
non-communicable diseases, incidence of 56, 63
non-state conflict 282, 288
non-tariff barriers 266, 267, 270–272
non-violent protests 290
Nordic countries 77, 163, 164

O

"Occupy Wall Street" movement 150
OCP Group 120

off-grid renewables 231
oil and debt crises 27
Okeke, Jide 326
Omar Al-Bashir 39, 291
Omar Bongo Ondimba 39
one-sided violence 282
Organization of African Unity 1, 260
Organization of Economic Development (OECD) 197
Organization of Petroleum Exporting Countries (OPEC) 31, 225
Oromo 291, 292, 318
Oromo Democratic Party 319
Our Common Future 25
Oxfam 151

P

the Pacific 13, 67, 138, 150
Page, John 28
Papua New Guinea 14
paradigm shifts 20
Paris Agreement 359, 373, 375
Pathways for Peace 289
Peace and Security Council 287
peacekeeping 2, 105, 287, 288, 304, 305
Peace Research Institute Oslo (PRIO) 287
penicillin 53, 58
Piketty, Thomas 151
PIN 212
Plan of Action 72
plurilateral negotiating structures 252
Political Instability Task Force (PITF) 281
Polity IV Project 326, 327
pollution 57
Ponzetto, G. 316
poor governance 32, 229, 285, 293, 303, 304, 369

population densities 50–53
population pyramid 71, 73, 76, 92
poverty 22, 24–28, 41–44, 46, 47, 55, 61, 66, 72, 80, 81, 91, 100, 101, 103, 107, 109, 110, 119, 121, 141, 147–150, 152–155, 157, 160, 162, 165–167, 190, 196, 251, 254, 317, 333, 338, 350, 368, 369, 383, 388, 394–398
Poverty Reduction Growth Facility 28
Power Africa 226
Powerpack 2 233
power-to-X 232
Pretoria 2
price shocks 106
primary school 86, 125, 126, 128, 129, 132, 133, 135, 138, 139, 141, 317, 394
private agricultural sector 10
productivity 3, 8, 9, 11–13, 24, 28, 41, 54, 59, 61, 63, 64, 75, 77–79, 83, 86, 91, 92, 99–101, 103, 106, 108, 110, 111, 116, 117, 124, 126, 162, 164, 170, 171, 173, 174, 181, 187, 191–193, 198, 201–204, 206, 217, 223, 234, 318, 378, 383, 394, 400, 403–405
productivity gap 198
Programme for Infrastructure Development in Africa 265
Prosper Africa initiative 335
proxy wars 2, 250, 308

quality of education 78, 127, 132, 137, 138, 141, 317

rainfall 10, 102, 118, 294, 367–370, 377
Ramaphosa, Cyril 291
Red Terror 317
Regional Comprehensive Partnership (RCEP) 252
Regional Economic Communities (RECs) 17, 261, 268, 336
Reinert, Erik 171
Reinvent the Toilet. *See* Bill and Melinda Gates Foundation
relative deprivation 150, 151, 293
remittances 9, 30, 346–351, 353
renewable energy 13, 230, 231, 233, 234, 259, 339, 359, 361, 362, 371
renminbi 345
Report of the Commission for Africa 26, 333
rest of the world 2–5, 13–16, 41, 46, 52, 55, 57, 60, 67, 74, 75, 85, 92, 95, 103, 127, 144, 149, 150, 183, 200, 207, 217, 235, 266, 268, 272, 327, 365, 382, 384, 389, 400
retirement age 79
Rhodesia 308
robot-based automation 207
robotics 116, 143, 177, 192, 206, 207
Rodrik, Dani 171
ruling elite 8, 39, 171, 263
rural areas 34, 42, 58, 60, 110, 119, 142, 170, 200, 227, 231, 304
Rwanda 282, 284, 288

Saemaul Undong 7
Sahel 10, 24, 98, 246, 262, 282, 285, 286, 294, 295, 303, 358, 368, 369, 374
Salehyan, Idean 294

salmonella poisoning 267
Sassou Nguesso, Denis 315
science and engineering students 139
SDG Target 8.1 154
Second Congo War, Great War of Africa 284
Second World War 124, 250, 308
seed varieties 121
Selassie, Haile 39
semi-democracies 204
services sector 11, 34, 167, 170–172, 174, 181, 188, 192, 200, 201, 203, 205, 391
sewerage 53, 199, 376
Seychelles 16, 17, 81, 85, 92, 130, 157, 181, 235, 267, 298, 385
shale gas revolution 226
Sharma, Ruchir 11
Shleifer, A. 316
Silencing the Guns scenario 302, 303
simian immunodeficiency virus (SIV) 53
Simons, Bright 178
sleeping sickness 50, 51, 53
smallholder farmers 117, 118, 218
Social Conflict Analysis Database (SCAD) 281
social grants 159–162, 165, 383, 395, 396
Social Grants for Africa scenario 165, 166
social protection 162, 167, 197, 216, 393
SoftBank 236
soil conditions 11
soil quality 98, 117
Soros, George 332
South America 4, 19, 63, 87, 88, 102, 121, 131, 135, 138, 139, 183, 340
South Asia 4, 19, 26, 54–56, 60, 61, 63, 67, 87, 88, 102, 121, 127, 128, 132, 135, 138, 139, 183, 184, 227, 228, 235
Southeast Asia 13
Southern African Customs Union (SACU) 260, 261, 270
Southern African Development Community (SADC) 17, 229, 268
South Korea 6–9, 14, 33, 34, 126, 143, 173, 178, 207
South West Africa 308
Soviet Union 26, 37, 282, 308, 309
soybeans 34, 260
SpaceX 236, 405
Spain 100, 342
special and differential treatment 253, 269, 270
special economic zones (SEZs) 161, 179
stability 1, 5, 27, 34, 154, 170, 231, 259, 276, 280, 285–287, 289, 293, 295, 302–304, 310, 324, 348, 351, 403
Standard Bank 257
Standard GSP 254
state-based conflict 282
The State of Commodity Dependence 31
Strategy for the Harmonization of Statistics in Africa (SHaSA) 21
structural transformation 13, 165, 171, 192, 193, 203, 276, 295, 336
structure of the global economy 11
sub-Saharan Africa 27, 30, 35–37, 51, 52, 54–60, 62, 67, 73, 81–87, 89, 91, 94, 99, 102, 118, 127–130, 132–135, 137, 143, 150, 155, 170, 197, 200, 202, 205, 211, 212, 231, 235–237, 244, 267, 274, 292, 298, 301, 304, 308, 334, 342, 346, 348, 370
sugar plant pests 267

supercycle 30–32, 258
Suri, Tavneet 237
Sustainable Development Goals (SDGs) 25, 132, 149, 154, 197, 305
Swedish International Development Cooperation Agency (SIDA) 334

T

Taiwan 33, 173, 179, 317, 403
Takaful and Karama (Solidarity and Dignity) 162
Talon, Patrice 313
taps 68
Target 8.5 154
Target 10.1 154
tariff protection 8
taxpayers 160
tax revenues 170, 276
Technical and Vocational Training (TVET) 136
technological change 5, 68
technology 5, 8–12, 20, 66, 74, 77–80, 83, 91, 103, 106, 109, 111, 117–119, 126, 135, 141–144, 154, 162, 167, 173–175, 177, 193, 200, 202–204, 206, 208, 213, 215, 217, 218, 222, 224–226, 232–235, 237, 238, 240, 241, 245, 246, 250, 263, 265, 268, 274, 275, 329, 336, 338, 376, 397, 398, 400–402, 404
Teodoro Nguema Obiang 39
3TG
  cassiterite (tin) 229
  coltan (tantalum) 229
  wolfram (tungsten) 229
Thomas, Alun 205
ticks 51
Tigray 291, 302
tobacco 57, 257

toilets 68
Tolstoy, Leo 280
total factor productivity 8
tourism 203, 204, 209, 217, 303
Trade and Law Centre 267
trade deficit 10, 103, 257, 271
trade integration 5, 192, 260, 268, 275, 276, 382, 398
trade shocks 28, 263
transition rates 138
Treaty Establishing the African Economic Community 261
tsetse flies 51
Tshisekedi, Félix 40
tuberculosis 51, 55, 98, 245

U

UN Conference on Trade and Development (UNCTAD) 172
undemocratic government 33
UN Department of Economic and Social Affairs (UNDESA) 271
UN Economic Commission for Africa 68, 259, 262, 264, 266, 270, 272, 393
unemployment 163, 191, 195, 196, 199, 211, 217, 280, 291, 298, 300, 301
UN Food and Agriculture Organization (FAO) 101
Unique Identification Authority of India 161
United Kingdom 14, 124, 126, 240, 308, 342
United Nations Conference on Trade and Development (UNCTAD) 31
United Nations Development Programme (UNDP) 24, 155
United Nations Environment Programme (UNEP) 358
United Nations Millennium Summit 25, 333

United Nations Secretary-General Javier Pérez de Cuéllar 25
United Nations Security Council 286
United Nations University World Institute for Development Economics Research (UNU-WIDER) 171
United States-Mexico-Canada Agreement (USMCA) 176
Universal Basic Share 161, 167
University of Denver 20
University of Melbourne 361
UN Millennium Summit 26
UN Operation in Côte d'Ivoire (UNOCI) 287
UN Population Division (UNPD) 59, 79, 86
unsustainable cultivation practices 105
upper-secondary education 138
Uppsala Conflict Data Program (UCDP) 281, 282
US Agency for International Development (USAID) 334
US International Development Finance Corporation (USIDFC) 335
US National Security Advisor 335
US shale and oil gas revolution 224

V

Varieties of Democracy project (V-Dem) 309
vector-borne diseases 51, 68, 369, 370
violent riots 290
Vodafone for Safaricom 237

W

WASH 60–63, 66, 68, 69, 108
Washington consensus 27, 30
waste-to-biomass conversion 226
wave of democracy 37, 308, 326
weather forecasts 11, 118
weather shocks 106
West Africa 10, 17, 18, 24, 41, 59, 98, 103, 114, 131, 262, 303, 358, 367, 368, 370, 386
West African Economic and Monetary Union 34
Western Europe 58, 133
WhatsApp 318
wireless power 223
working age population 11, 24, 73, 74, 76–80, 89, 92, 175, 317
World Bank 3, 16, 21, 26–29, 36, 37, 46, 73, 94, 101, 104, 106, 108, 117, 120, 132–134, 136, 137, 143, 156, 181, 191, 202, 213, 229, 241, 251, 261, 262, 264, 281, 334, 339, 344–346, 352, 358, 385, 393, 396
World Bank's Logistics Performance Index 105
World Commission on Environment and Development 25
World Crime Technology Project 246
World Development Report 136, 286
World Economic Forum (WEF) 186
World Food Programme Rural Resilience Initiative (R4) 118
World Health Organization (WHO) 61, 67
2005 World Summit in New York 26, 333
World Trade Organization (WTO) 250–252
World Wildlife Federation (WWF) 246
Wössmann, Ludger 124, 132

Y

Yangtze 97
yellow fever 51, 53
yields per hectare 10, 101–103, 113
youth bulges 297

Z

Zahidi, Saadia 245
Zanu(PF) party 43
Zenawi, Meles 163, 323
Zenvus 118
Zine El Abidine Ben Ali 292
Zuma, Jacob 55, 238, 291
#ZumaMustFall 291

The manufacturer's authorised representative in the EU is Springer Nature Customer Service Centre GmbH, Europaplatz 3, 69115 Heidelberg, Germany. If you have any concerns regarding our products, please contact ProductSafety@springernature.com

Printed and bound by CPI Group (UK) Ltd, Croydon, CR0 4YY

23/03/2026

02076664-0011